24591

KF
4757
.R4

Read, Frank T. 1938-

Let them be judged

DATE		
WITHDRAWN		

For
John, Richard, Tomasin, Jefferson and David

and for
Fairchild, Blaine and Allison, our children,

and for all children, black and white,
who were the subjects of the Grand Experiment
and, we hope, its beneficiaries.

While it is proper that people should find fault when their judges fail ... perhaps it is also fair to ask that before the judges are blamed they shall be given the credit of having tried to do their best. Let them be severely brought to book, when they go wrong, but let them be judged by those who will take the trouble to understand.

--Judge Learned Hand

TABLE OF CONTENTS

Preface and Acknowledgments   xi

Prologue, 1896-1955   1

PART I

THE THIN BLACK LINE:
THE HUTCHESON-RIVES YEARS, 1954-1960   21

1. The Great and the Near Great   23
   The Establishment of the Fifth Circuit   23
   Chief Judge Hutcheson and the Changing Guard   27
   The Eisenhower Appointees: Tuttle, Cameron,
   Jones, Brown and Wisdom   38

2. The Early Returns: The Progress of Public School
   Desegregation: 1954-1962   61
   The Texas Example: Peaceful Compliance and
   Violent Resistance   64
   The Texas Example: Judicial Intervention and
   Resistance   71
       Avery v. Wichita Falls: The Enigma of Integra-
       tion vs Desegregation   71
       Dallas: Two Outspoken Octogenarians   76
       Houston: The Dividends of Local Action   91

3. The Second Battle of New Orleans   111
   The Skirmishing: 1950-59   112
   The Battle: 1960-61   131
   The Mop-Up: 1962   158
   Contrasts and Conclusions   162

PART II

COMING OF AGE:
THE TUTTLE YEARS, 1960-1967   169

4. A Different Drum   171
   Ten New Men   171
   The Quickening Pace   182

5. The Matriculation of James Meredith: Crucible for
   the Fifth Circuit   195
       The Desegregation of Higher Education: Preamble to
           Meredith   195
       Meredith v. Fair   207
               "A Man with a Mission and with a Nervous
                   Stomach"   208
               The Battleground Shifts to the Fifth Circuit   222
               Armageddon   237
       Higher Education: Capitulation   248

6. Schism   254
       "The Man in High Office Who Defied the Nation"   254
       The Judge Who Indicted His Court   266
       The Senator Who Threatened the Court   276

7. In Quest of the Vote   281
       The Legacy of Reconstruction   281
       Judicial Intervention and Congressional Response   285
       Progress at a Snail's Pace: Judge Cox and Mr. Lynd   293
       Pettus Bridge and the Voting Rights Act of 1965   303
       The Last Frontier   309

8. Jury Selection: The Right to Sit in Judgment   322
       The "Impartial Jury": A Paper Right   324
       The Paper Right Becomes Absolute   328
       Jury Selection and the Theory of Probabilities:
           Breaking New Ground   332
       Portents of Change   344

9. Public Accommodations: Stonewall Resistance in
   Jackson   353

10. The Search for Standards   373
       Shifting from "Deliberate" to "Speed"   374
               Georgia   377
               Alabama   388
               Mississippi   408
               Florida   418
       The Movement Toward Uniform Standards   424

11. The Zenith of Federal Coordination   431

PART III

THE BLOODLESS REVOLUTION:
THE BROWN YEARS, 1967-1973   447

12. The Era of the Super Court   449
       The Carswell Fiasco   455
       Court Congestion and the Conservation of Judicial
           Energy: Summary Disposition and Standing Panels   464

13. Do It Now!   472
     The Green Case: Freedom of Choice's Death Sentence   472
     Alexander v. Holmes County Board of Education: A
         Political Sellout Boomerangs   479
     Carter v. West Feliciana Parish School Board: The
         Second Slap   492

14. 1970: Upheaval   495
     The Fifth Circuit's Implementation of Carter   495
     Massive Integration in Iberia, Evangeline, and St.
         Landry Parishes   501
     Massive Integration in Jacksonville   510

15. The Word from Mount Olympus   523
     Swann v. Charlotte-Mecklenburg Board of Education   523
     Reactions to Swann   528
     Post-Swann Massive Integration in Savannah and
         Augusta   531
     Letters from Savannah and Augusta, 1971   541

16. The Uncertain Future of Integration and the Uncertain
     Fate of the Fifth Circuit   564
     Five Cases in Five Cities   565
     Division in Doctrine: Three Issues in Synthesis   573
         The De Facto/De Jure Distinction   573
         The Breadth of the Remedy   578
         Busing   584
     The End of the Super Court   587

Epilogue   599

Appendixes   605

Index   641

APPENDICES

A. Members of the Fifth Circuit of Appeals, by Year and Status, 1955-1973

B. Statistical Developments in School Desegregation from 1954

C. School Desegregation Cases in the Fifth Circuit, by State, 1955-1973

D. United States Department of Justice Complaints Filed in the Fifth Circuit Pursuant to School Desegregation, 1954-1973

E. Case Statistics of Judges of the Fifth Circuit Court of Appeals in School Desegregation

F. Status of Segregation--May 1954

G. School Desegregation Cases in the Fifth Circuit by Issues Decided, 1955-1973

H. En Banc Decisions by the Fifth Circuit Court of Appeals in School Desegregation, 1955-1973

PREFACE AND ACKNOWLEDGMENTS

The frenetic pace and extent of change in race relations in the past twenty years has dimmed the memory of what it was to be a Negro citizen in the South in 1954. All public schools were segregated; public accommodations were segregated; only a minute percentage of registered voters was black; and black public office holders were virtually nonexistent. Black families had less than one half the median incomes of white families, and illiteracy rates were appallingly high. The black American in the South was a second-class citizen, an exile in his own country. It appeared that he was destined to remain locked in that status by a myriad of state-imposed Jim Crow laws deliberately designed to perpetuate the segregation of the races and guarantee the disparity between black and white citizens.

Then, on May 17, 1954--"Black Monday" to segregationists-- the United States Supreme Court decided Brown v. Board of Education, unanimously holding that segregation of white and black children in state public schools, solely on the basis of race and pursuant to statutes permitting or requiring such segregation, denied to black children the equal protection of the laws guaranteed by the fourteenth amendment. The Brown decision rocked the South, secured the fame (or infamy, in the opinion of some) of the Warren Court, and propelled the nation into the modern era of its on-going revolution in race relations.

Of course, in a very real sense, any narrative of the development in American race relations law is never complete, posing considerable problems for any chronicler. Every day brings new significant judicial opinions and every year seems to present new problems in the desegregation process, even in areas of the country long since thought to be stabilized in community commitment to interracial harmony. For example, while this manuscript was in final preparation, Boston erupted as a desegregation trouble-spot, boiling over with mass picketing, public demonstrations, and even violent protests over busing and the integration plan ordered by the federal district court. Such a display of public resistance to desegregation is ironic not only because it occurred in the North (particularly in the cradle of the abolition movement) after a century of national castigation of southern resistance, but also because the first public school desegregation suit was filed in Boston in 1848 and thereafter Massachusetts became one of the first states to outlaw segregated schools.

In writing this study, it has been tempting to revise to include the significant, intriguing developments which are even now unfolding. Reluctantly, but of necessity, we have decided to focus upon the two decades immediately following the Brown decision, the most critical and formative years of judicial work toward implementing racial equality under the law.

The purpose of this work is to examine the role of the inferior federal courts of the Deep South which implemented the desegregation mandate of Brown. The work of the United States Court of Appeals for the Fifth Circuit provides the focal point. Supervising all federal judicial activity in Alabama, Florida, Georgia, Louisiana, Mississippi and Texas, the Fifth Circuit shepherded independent federal district judges of widely varying abilities and persuasions through the nation's Second Reconstruction. After handing down its Brown decision, the Supreme Court--contrary to the belief of many citizens--played only a minimal role in the supervision and guidance of its lower federal courts. Left to its Court of Appeals was the task of translating a vague but revolutionary constitutional command into concrete orders for school boards and federal district courts. In that process the Fifth Circuit was the trail blazer, becoming the nation's greatest civil rights tribunal. The story of the evolution of desegregation and race relations law in the twenty years since Brown is, then, also the story of one pre-eminent federal Appeals Court.

There are many possible criteria for judging the performance of judges and courts: reversal rates by a higher court, volume of cases docketed and processed to final judgment, style of opinion writing, repute of colleagues, adherence to precedent, contributions to the development of decisional law, ability to negotiate an attitude of compromise among litigants, community leadership and minimization of state-federal tensions. By all of those standards, the twenty-year odyssey of the Fifth Circuit since Brown has been remarkable. However, by one overriding benchmark the Fifth Circuit has excelled beyond any reasonable expectation: adherence to constitutional duty in the face of a hostile local environment.

While this work focuses on the Fifth Circuit, and evaluates the performance of the Deep South's federal judiciary, some treatment has necessarily been given to the varied roles played by lawyers, legislators, governors, school board members, community leaders, activists and advocates of all stripes, and the black and white citizens of the South. Let them all be judged.

* * *

This work would not have been possible without the generous financial support provided by the Ford Foundation under a grant to Duke University. The Ford grant enabled the writers to interview scores of citizens, attorneys, federal and state officials, school board members and litigants who had firsthand knowledge of many of the events discussed herein.

Chief Judge John R. Brown of the United States Court of Appeals for the Fifth Circuit generously provided introductions to key circuit and district judges and enlisted the help of his Court's record keepers. Because of his splendid cooperation, important information was gathered that might otherwise never have been made known. Those judges, officials and citizens who talked with us and provided us with information and leads to other sources are too numerous to acknowledge individually. Collectively, without their cooperation this work would never have become more than an idea.

In a work of this length--covering a six-state region over a twenty-year time span and involving over one thousand reported judicial decisions rendered for the most part in an atmosphere of social revolution--errors of emphasis, quotation and attribution are inevitable. While the writers have attempted to minimize such mistakes, we accept full responsibility for all material recounted in this chronology.

While not everyone who has helped make this work possible can be individually mentioned, there are many whose contributions cannot pass unnoted. Duke Law School Deans Joseph T. Sneed and A. Kenneth Pye and Emory Law School Dean Ray Patterson encouraged the work in its early stages and cheerfully supplied vital logistical support. Mr. Howard Westwood, of Washington, D.C., was the mentor of this project at its inception; his help and inspiration are deeply appreciated. Of all our colleagues who lent support to our efforts, Professors Robert S. Stubbs, II and William H. Agnor of Emory and Rennard Strickland of the University of Tulsa deserve special mention, as does Elizabeth Peterson, a Durham, North Carolina attorney, who volunteered long hours of valuable counsel. A faithful group of student research assistants and secretaries gave countless hours of careful work for which we are grateful; in alphabetical order, they are Tony Axam, John Bailly, Greg Brown, Elizabeth Buchanan, Betty Gooch, Robbie Deaton, Tim Dowd, Jane DiFolco, Jim Eller, Fred Fulton, Susan Getty, Nathan Goldman, Delores Henley, Kim Kartman, Jim Kizziar, Steve Leckar, Kay Martin, Patricia Nance, Scott Ramey, Tom Sear, Debbie Sheehan, Michele Simon, Charlotte Smith, Norman Smith, Diane Stubbins, Lorraine Traynor and Raymond Yasser. The work of three former law students, Tim Cappell, John Holmquist and Will Sparks, deserves special mention for diligence and loyalty far beyond that any law professor has any right to expect.

Finally, one person, more than any other, kept this project alive. She alone never doubted that it would and should be completed. She refused to let any line of inquiry be foreclosed without complete investigation and kept our team effort organized and as efficient as possible in view of our working separately at our respective law schools. To Mrs. Peggy House, Administrative Secretary at Duke Law School, we are deeply indebted.

* * *

In editing the original manuscript, a decision was made to

eliminate most of the detailed footnoting of sources. Instead, a general summary of the major sources for the material contained in each chapter is listed at the conclusion of the chapter. For the scholar interested in the precise authority for the factual materials covered in the text, copies of the original manuscript, containing exhaustive footnoting of original sources, are available at the Duke University School of Law Library and the Emory University School of Law Library, or by inquiry directed to the writers.

PROLOGUE, 1896-1955:

Segregation and the Supreme Court

> I am not convinced that the Negro wants
> integration in the sense that some of us claim
> to fear that he does. I believe he is American
> enough to repudiate and deny by simple American
> instinct any stricture or regulation forbidding us
> to do something which in our opinion would be
> harmless if we did it, and which we probably
> would not want to do anyway. I think that what
> he wants is equality, and I believe that he too
> knows there is no such thing as equality per se,
> but only equality to: equal right and opportunity
> to make the best one can of one's life within one's
> capacity and capability, without fear of injustice
> or oppression or threat of violence. If we had
> given him this equal right to opportunity ninety
> or fifty or even ten years ago, there would have
> been no Supreme Court decision about how we
> run our schools.
>
> --William Faulkner, "American Segregation
> and the World Crisis," a paper delivered at
> the 21st Annual Meeting of the Southern His-
> torical Association in Memphis, Tennessee,
> Nov. 10, 1955.

In 1848, at the peak of his fame as an ardent abolitionist,
Charles Sumner filed suit on behalf of a five-year-old Negro girl
who had been refused admission to a white Boston public school.
He argued that requiring Negro children to attend separate public
schools was a violation of their right to equal treatment before the
law. Sumner eloquently contended that the mere fact of separate-
ness was the mark of a social system of caste and, when imposed
upon the public school system, served to perpetuate racial prejudice
in a new generation of citizens. Chief Justice Lemuel Shaw, perhaps the most eminent state jurist of his time, wrote the opinion
for the Supreme Judicial Court of Massachusetts that denied Sumner's
claim. Turning his attention first to the argument that segregation
was an invidious social policy which should not be tolerated by the
law, Chief Justice Shaw was not only pessimistic that the law could

1

eradicate prejudice but also, even assuming it could, he questioned whether forced association in the public schools was a progressive step. More important for the tortured development of American law in the next century was Chief Justice Shaw's interpretation of the concept of equal treatment before the law--a legacy of the Magna Carta cherished by the colonists and preserved from the earliest times of their self-government. According to Chief Justice Shaw,

> [W]hen this great principle [of equality] comes to be applied to the actual and various conditions of persons in society, it will not warrant the assertion, that men and women are legally clothed with the same civil and political powers, and that children and adults are legally to have the same functions and be subject to the same treatment; but only that the rights of all, as they are settled and regulated by law, are equally entitled to the paternal consideration and protection of the law, for their maintenance and security.

In short, citizens were entitled only to equal treatment; different or separate treatment was neither forbidden nor mandated.

Segregation in the public schools was abolished by statute in Massachusetts seven years later. Even so, Chief Justice Shaw's view of the limited role of the law in the social affairs of men ultimately would be embraced by the Supreme Court and would dominate the course of American race relations law for the next century. In the mid-nineteenth century Massachusetts granted citizenship to its Negro populace and Chief Justice Shaw grappled with relatively sophisticated questions concerning the meaning and application of the legal grant of equality in such social institutions as the public schools. However, the nation as a whole had not yet resolved the more fundamental question of the status of the Negro.

* * *

The slavery issue reached the Supreme Court in 1857 when Dred Scott, a slave purchased by an Army doctor, sued in federal court for recognition of his emancipation. Scott had been purchased in the slave state of Missouri, had moved with his "owner" to the free state of Illinois and thence to Wisconsin, where slavery was forbidden, and had finally returned to Missouri where the "owner" died. The Supreme Court was bitterly divided: after the case had been argued and then reargued, the Court issued nine separate opinions. The opinion written by Chief Justice Taney, in which a majority of the Justices concurred, held that Scott could not sue because, as an African Negro, he could not be a citizen of any state --regardless of whether he was slave or free. The Taney opinion bluntly denied any claim by Negroes to the right of citizenship:

> ... [African Negroes] are not included, and were not intended to be included, under the word 'citizens' in the Constitution, and can therefore claim none of the rights

and privileges which that instrument provides for and se-
cures to citizens of the United States. On the contrary,
they were at that time considered as a subordinate and inferior class of beings, who had been subjugated by the
dominant race, and, whether emancipated or not, yet remained subject to their authority, and had no rights or
privileges but such as those who held the power and the
Government might choose to grant them.... They had
for more than a century before been regarded as of an inferior order, and altogether unfit to associate with the
white race either in social or political relations; and so
far inferior that they had no rights which the white man
was bound to respect.

Moreover, the Taney opinion concluded that Congress could not interfere with the property rights of slaveowners by forbidding slavery
in the territories.

The Dred Scott decision ignited a fire storm of new controversy over the slavery issue. The fragmentation of the federal
union, barely held together by the uneasy Kansas-Nebraska Act compromise, began to appear inevitable. The reaction of the Northern
press to Dred Scott was unrestrained; editors charged that the Supreme Court had succumbed to political influence and had capitulated
to expediency in reaching its decision. Horace Greeley's Tribune
taunted President Buchanan:

You may 'cheerfully submit,' of course you will, to whatever five slaveholders and two or three doughfaces on the
bench of the Supreme Court may be ready to utter on this
subject. But not one man who really desires the triumph
of freedom over slavery in the territories will do so.

*   *   *

It took a civil war and the ratification of a series of critical
amendments to the Constitution to overrule the noncitizenship doctrine of Dred Scott. Finally, upon the heels of President Lincoln's
Emancipation Proclamation, came the thirteenth amendment which,
when ratified in 1865, abolished slavery.

In interpreting the reach of the thirteenth amendment the
Supreme Court took a consistently narrow, literal view: slavery
meant only economic slavery--the ownership of mankind as a chattel
or the control of his labor and services with no legal right in the
slave to dispose of or control his own person, property and services.
However, the fourteenth amendment, ratified three years later, provided more support for early protagonists of Negro rights. The
Supreme Court later observed that the fourteenth amendment had
been prompted due to the slave states' harsh reaction to abolition:

Among the first acts of legislation adopted by several of
the states ... were laws which imposed upon the colored

race onerous disabilities and burdens, and curtailed their
rights in the pursuit of life, liberty, and property to such
an extent that their freedom was of little value, while they
had lost the protection which they had received from their
former owners from motives both of interest and humanity.
They were in some States forbidden to appear in
the towns in any other character than menial servants.
They were required to reside on and cultivate the soil without the right to purchase or own it.   They were excluded
from many occupations of gain, and were not permitted to
give testimony in the courts in any case where a white
man was a party.   It was said that their lives were at
the mercy of bad men, either because the laws for their
protection were insufficient or were not enforced.

The fourteenth amendment sought to protect the Negro against actions by states which abridged the privileges and immunities of his
citizenship or deprived him of life, liberty, or property without due
process of law and equal protection of the laws.

In 1879, relying upon the clear intent of the new amendment,
the Supreme Court struck down a West Virginia law which limited
the right to serve on juries to white male adults.   The Court noted
that such a law was a discrimination which implied a legal inferiority in civil society, lessened the security of the rights guaranteed
the Negro race by their recognition as freedmen and citizens, and
constituted a step toward reducing the race once more to a condition
of servility.

Riding the last high crest of Reconstruction, Congress enacted the Civil Rights Act of 1875, a pervasive statute aimed at
prohibiting discrimination against Negroes in both the political and
social aspects of citizenship.   The 1875 act reaffirmed the Supreme
Court's West Virginia decision by enacting a positive proscription
against such state laws.   But in a controversial public accommodations section, Congress also sought to prohibit discrimination against
Negroes by innkeepers, public carriers and theatre owners.   The
Supreme Court in the Civil Rights Cases subsequently declared the
public accommodations section unconstitutional, holding that Congress
had exceeded its authority.   As a matter of federal law, Congress
had attempted to guarantee rights to public accommodation in private
contracts between individuals, as opposed to simply forbidding states
from enacting discriminatory laws.

*   *   *

Ten years later, the issue of the constitutionality of a state's
affirmative action in approving or requiring social discrimination,
which had been reserved by the Supreme Court in the Civil Rights
cases, was answered in the celebrated case of Plessy v. Ferguson.

Homer Adolph Plessy was a citizen of Louisiana of mixed
descent.   On June 7, 1892, he bought a first-class railway passage

out of New Orleans and took a seat in a coach reserved for whites.
He refused to leave upon command of the conductor, was forcibly
ejected and imprisoned in the New Orleans parish jail. He was
charged with violating a Louisiana statute which authorized a fine of
$25.00 or imprisonment of up to twenty days for any passenger's
"insisting on going into a coach or compartment to which by race
he does not belong." Under the state statute, railroad companies
were required to provide "equal but separate accommodations for
the white and colored races, by providing two or more passenger
coaches for each passenger train or by dividing the passenger
coaches by a partition so as to secure separate accommodations."
Plessy attacked the constitutionality of the statute as violative of the
fourteenth amendment, relying in part upon the assertion that because he was only one-eighth African and not discernibly "colored,"
he was entitled to every privilege secured to white citizens.   Ironically, it was a man who shrank from admitting that he was a
Negro who forced a constitutional decision which was to have the
most serious and durable impact upon the rights of Negroes of any
case in the history of the republic.

Plessy argued that the guarantees of the fourteenth amendment should be construed to prevent the imposition of any discriminatory treatment which cast onerous disabilities upon a Negro citizen.   However, in the Plessy decision, the Supreme Court explicitly
adopted the distinction first enunciated by Chief Justice Shaw in that
early Massachusetts school case brought by Charles Sumner.   The
Court concluded that there was indeed a difference, inherent in the
command of the fourteenth amendment, between political or civil
disabilities and social disabilities.   Mr. Justice Brown stated for
the majority:

> The object of the [fourteenth] amendment was un-
> doubtedly to enforce the absolute equality of the two races
> before the law, but in the nature of things it could not
> have been intended to abolish distinctions based upon color,
> or to enforce social, as distinguished from political equal-
> ity, or a comingling of the two races upon terms unsatis-
> factory to either.   Laws permitting, and even requiring,
> their separation in places where they are liable to be
> brought into contact do not necessarily imply the inferi-
> ority of either race to the other, and have been generally,
> if not universally, recognized as within the competency of
> the state legislatures in the exercise of their police power.

Furthermore, in deciding Plessy the Supreme Court reached out to
settle by dicta the question of school segregation, sanctioning it at
the same time it approved separation of the races in public transportation:

> The most common instance of this [enforced separation]
> is connected with the establishment of separate schools for
> white and colored children, which have been held to be a
> valid exercise in the legislative power even by courts of

states where the political rights of the colored race have been longest and most earnestly enforced.

The judicial opinion by Chief Justice Shaw in the Boston segregation case was quoted with approval.

At the heart of the Plessy decision was the Court's acceptance of the concept that the United States Constitution was and should be powerless to rectify all social ills, even social prejudice:

> If the two races are to meet upon terms of social equality, it must be the result of natural affinities, a mutual appreciation of each other's merits and a voluntary consent of individuals.... '[T]his end can neither be accomplished nor promoted by laws which conflict with the general sentiment of the community upon whom they are designed to operate. When the government, therefore, has secured to each of its citizens equal rights before the law and equal opportunities for improvement and progress, it has accomplished the end for which it was organized and performed all of the functions respecting social advantages with which it is endowed.' Legislation is powerless to eradicate racial instincts or to abolish distinctions based upon physical differences, and the attempt to do so can only result in accentuating the difficulties of the present situation.

The lone dissenter in Plessy v. Ferguson was the first Mr. Justice Harlan, who had also dissented from the invalidation of the public accommodations section of the Civil Rights Act of 1875. He warned that the decision in Plessy would "prove to be quite as pernicious as the decision made by this tribunal in the Dred Scott case," and counseled further:

> Sixty millions of whites are in no danger from the presence here of eight millions of blacks. The destinies of the two races, in this country, are indissolubly linked together, and the interests of both require that the common government of all shall not permit the seeds of race hate to be planted under the sanction of law.... We boast of the freedom enjoyed by our people above all other peoples. But it is difficult to reconcile that boast with a state of the law which, practically, puts the brand of servitude and degradation upon a large class of our fellow citizens, our equals before the law. The thin disguise of 'equal' accommodations for passengers in railroad coaches will not mislead any one, nor atone for the wrong this day done.

The "separate but equal" brand of segregation had survived constitutional scrutiny and would persist for the next half-century. Plessy v. Ferguson was cited as ruling authority, without qualification, for the last time in 1927 when the Supreme Court agreed that a Chinese-American child was not entitled to attend a "white" school in Mississippi. Thereafter, a slow process of erosion occurred which ultimately resulted in the doctrine's obliteration by the Supreme Court in 1954.

* * *

On October 26, 1934, a conference was held in New York City which would have great significance for the yet unborn civil rights movement and, specifically, for the future of segregated public schools. Representatives of the National Association for the Advancement of Colored People and the American Fund for Public Service met with a man named Charles H. Houston to map out the first coordinated strategy for a legal challenge to educational inequalities faced by twentieth century blacks.

Houston, then the Vice-Dean of Howard University Law School, was retained to direct a campaign of litigation, beginning full-time the following July. This initial alliance of organizations committed to assaulting racial barriers was the genesis of the NAACP Legal Defense and Education Fund (thereafter known as the "Inc. Fund"), which was officially incorporated in 1939 to spearhead litigation in the civil rights field.

According to Jack Greenberg, current Director of the Inc. Fund, there were three basic reasons for an early strategy calling for concentration of resources upon suits challenging exclusionary policies of graduate and professional schools. First, opening these schools to Negroes would augment the supply of highly educated Negro leaders who could be called upon to assist in the more expansive struggle to desegregate all social institutions. Second, the possibility of a state's erecting a separate, parallel set of professional schools exclusively for Negroes seemed foreclosed as a resistance tactic by financial considerations. There were virtually no public Negro graduate and professional schools in the South; and, desegregation of existing facilities seemed the only feasible way for the states to fulfill their constitutional obligations under the Plessy doctrine. Finally, it was reasoned that the absorption of a small number of Negro students into an older, more mature student body of white students would minimize, if not altogether avoid, a violent public reaction.

While wrong in their estimates of public reaction, strategists working for Negro advancement were correct in their projection that it would be impossible, as a practical matter, for states to carry the constitutional burden of establishing separate, substantially equal, state-financed graduate and professional schools for Negroes. As one University President wryly observed, "You can't build a cyclotron for one student."

Beginning in 1938, the Supreme Court moved in a series of cases to check various ploys adopted by states in an effort to avoid wholesale desegregation of their graduate schools. In all outward

apperances, the first higher education challenge seemed to be a
rather routine appeal to the Supreme Court, attracting little notice:
one attorney represented the student and a single reply brief had
been filed on behalf of the state.   Slightly more than a decade later,
however, the gathering momentum of the civil rights movement was
quite evident.   The forces associated with the NAACP gathered new
strength for the final assault on the separate but equal doctrine in
two appeals from Oklahoma and Texas.   In turn, the forces opposed
to any desegregation, even in higher education, organized for the
first time in a collective defensive effort.

In the Texas case, five groups requested permission from the
Supreme Court to file briefs as amicus curiae ("friend of the court")
on behalf of the Negro plaintiff: the United States government, the
American Federation of Teachers, the Committee of Law Teachers
Against Segregation in Legal Education, the American Veterans Committee, Inc. and the American Jewish Committee.   Fearing the impact upon their own statutes and policies of segregation, eleven
states rejoined by filing amicus curiae briefs on behalf of their sister state of Texas: Arkansas, Florida, Georgia, Kentucky, Louisiana, Mississippi, North Carolina, Oklahoma, South Carolina, Tennessee and Virginia.   Never before had the Supreme Court had such
a cross section of viewpoints in a school desegregation case.   If
any informed citizens were still unaware of the existence of the concerted campaign against the separate but equal doctrine, the forces
arrayed to argue the pair of cases decided in 1950 should have
served as an unmistakable alert.

A young Negro named G. W. McLaurin, who was seeking a
doctorate in education, came forward to protest the conditions at
the University of Oklahoma under which he had been forced to study.
University officials subsequently conceded that McLaurin had been
required to sit in a section of a classroom surrounded by a rail on
which there was a sign reading "Reserved for Colored" or, alternatively, to sit apart at a designated desk on the mezzanine floor but
not to use the desks in the regular reading room; and, to sit at a
designated table and to eat at a different time from the other students
in the school cafeteria.   After suit was filed, the dining policy was
amended by the University to permit a Negro to talk with fellow students while waiting in the cafeteria line.   After obtaining his food
and while he ate, he was to remain apart at a special table.

In reviewing the record in McLaurin's case, the Supreme
Court in June, 1950, held that the fourteenth amendment precluded
state-compelled isolation of the races at least in the microcosm of
a state graduate-level institution.   With no citations either to legal
decision or social science opinion, the Court seemed to have taken
judicial notice that learning in isolation from members of another
race constituted "unequal" education.   As the Court observed, "The
result is that appellant is handicapped in his pursuit of effective
graduate instruction.   Such restrictions impair and inhibit his ability to study, to engage in discussions and exchange views with other
students, and, in general, to learn his profession."

Unlike the tack taken by Oklahoma, the Texas Legislature had created law schools with symmetrical policies of exclusivity: no Negro could attend the University of Texas and no white would be admitted to Texas Southern. Despite this statutory facade of equal treatment, the Supreme Court held that members of the minority race were inherently disadvantaged by forced disassociation from whites who constituted "such a substantial and significant segment of society."

Thus, on June 5, 1950, in the area of higher education, the doctrinal victory over Plessy was complete. By setting what one Negro educator later termed "an impossible standard" for assessing the adequacy of segregated or dual collegiate systems, "separate but equal" became a constitutionally impermissible contradiction in terms. The death knell had been sounded for state imposed segregation wherever found. In another case decided in 1950, the Vinson Court further undercut the pinnings upon which Plessy was anchored, by ruling that segregation of whites and Negroes on railroads and buses traveling in interstate commerce was as unlawful as segregation in universities and professional schools. Everything pointed to an imminent decision concerning the continued vitality of segregation in public elementary and secondary schools. In 1953, the first step was taken. Shortly before Chief Justice Vinson died, the Supreme Court agreed to review five cases which collectively depicted the predicament of Negro children seeking an education in segregated school systems.

*   *   *

Brown v. Board of Education of Topeka became the most famous of the quintet because it was docketed first and thus headed the list of cases consolidated for decision. The Brown case challenged the constitutionality of a Kansas law which permitted but did not require segregation. A three-judge federal court had found as a fact that segregation in itself "has a tendency to retard the education and mental development of Negro children." However, since it had also found that the Negro and white schools in question were substantially equal with respect to buildings, transportation, curricula and educational qualifications of teachers, it declined relief, citing Plessy v. Ferguson.

Unlike Brown, the other four cases challenged laws requiring segregation which were in force in Virginia, South Carolina, Delaware and the District of Columbia. The striking common feature of these four cases was evidence that the theory that the states could and would provide "separate but equal" schools for Negro children had been perverted in practice. The dual systems of these four states were indeed separate, but far from equal. For example, in the Delaware case, Gebhart v. Belton, the trial court had found that Negro schools were inferior with respect to teacher training, pupil-teacher ratio, extracurricular activities, physical plant, and time and distance involved in travel between home and school.

John W. Davis, former Democratic Presidential nominee in 1924 and then in private practice in New York City, was selected to coordinate strategy among counsel for the various school boards and state attorneys general who opposed desegregation. Thurgood Marshall, then general counsel for the NAACP and later the first Negro Justice on the United States Supreme Court, was the leading counsel for the Negro plaintiffs. The cases were argued December 8-11, 1952, and again on June 8, 1953. In October, 1953, Earl Warren took the oath of office as the new Chief Justice and the cases were docketed for yet a third round of argument on December 7-9, 1953. During argument, the Supreme Court requested opposing counsel to document their positions concerning the historical intent of the framers of the fourteenth amendment.

Counsel for the NAACP had urged that the Supreme Court had inherent power to reinterpret the commands of the Constitution and to review the validity of Plessy v. Ferguson in light of advances which had occurred in the fields of social science, particularly the findings of child psychologists regarding the inferiority perceptions which forced racial separation produced in Negro children. In contrast, the state attorneys general argued that the Plessy decision and the six subsequent Supreme Court decisions explicitly applying its doctrine to public education were the Court's own precedent upon which the states were entitled to rely, social scientists notwithstanding. As one participant who was then an Assistant Attorney General of Kansas later recalled:

> The arguments advanced by all states were similar, that segregation in the public schools had been regarded as a state policy and that court decisions seemed to approve of classifications of people according to race for purposes of the public schools.... We were not defending segregation. We were upholding the right of the state of Kansas to direct its school boards.

The Supreme Court was obviously troubled by the enormous potential impact of this particular case. Even aside from the social revolution which undoubtedly would occur should it declare segregation unconstitutional, the Court would be assuming the uncommon role of establishing public policy, a responsibility which under the separation of powers doctrine was cast upon the legislative branch. Moreover, the fourteenth amendment explicitly called for congressional action to implement the broad protections it had guaranteed to the newly emancipated Negro race. However, with the exception of the abortive attempt to proscribe segregation in public accommodations in the Civil Rights Act of 1875, Congress had avoided the politically sensitive issue of segregation and had not spoken again in the subsequent seventy-five years. Mr. Justice Jackson pointedly asked Thurgood Marshall as principal counsel for the NAACP about "the propriety of exercising judicial power to reach this result [that segregation was intolerable] ... in the absence of any [congressional] legislation." Later, Mr. Justice Jackson summed up by noting, "I suppose that realistically the reason this case is here is that action couldn't be obtained from Congress."

The Court, in pondering the five segregation cases before it, had to confront the issue--certain to be a point of later criticism-- that, in proscribing segregation, not only was it repudiating its own former precedent but also it was taking on a policy-making function reserved to a Congress which had consistently failed to act.

* * *

Finally, after nearly six months, the long awaited decision was announced. As one on-looker described this historical event:

> On the morning of May 17, 1954, while the Army-McCarthy hearings were shambling into their eighteenth day, the reporters who normally cover the Supreme Court were dawdling over coffee in the pressroom, looking forward to a light day. It was Monday, decision day, but no rulings of stop-the-presses significance were expected. Shortly after noon, however, Banning E. Whittington, the Court's friendly, low-key press officer, suggested they had better get upstairs. They darted up the marble steps and took their places on the old-fashioned ice-cream-parlor chairs set aside for the working press. The Chief Justice had begun to read the Court's ruling in Brown et al. v. Board of Topeka et al.... The new Chief Justice spoke simply, bluntly and briefly (twenty-eight minutes) for a unanimous Court, echoing the sentiments expressed by Justice Harlan in his Plessy dissent.

In the Court's opinion, the historical evidence of the intent of the framers of the fourteenth amendment was "at best inconclusive." But the very ambiguity of intent seemed at least to permit review of the conclusion reached in Plessy that segregation had not been prohibited by the amendment. The opinion noted that education had changed drastically since the turn of the century. No longer the pursuit exclusively of the landed or wealthy, through public finance education had become universally required and what the Court termed "the very foundation of good citizenship." Stressing the impact of schooling upon human development, the Court concluded in the opinion's most famous passage:

> Today [education] is a principal instrument in awakening the child to cultural values, in preparing him for later professional training, and in helping him to adjust normally to his environment.... To separate [Negro children] from others of similar age and qualifications solely because of their race generates a feeling of inferiority as to their status in the community that may affect their hearts and minds in a way unlikely ever to be undone.... Whatever may have been the extent of psychological knowledge at the time of Plessy v. Ferguson, this finding is amply supported by modern authority. Any language in Plessy v. Ferguson contrary to this finding is rejected.
> We conclude that in the field of public education the

doctrine of 'separate but equal' has no place. Separate educational facilities are inherently unequal.

In its now famous footnote eleven, Chief Justice Warren's opinion in Brown v. Board of Education cited the findings of several prominent social scientists, such as Dr. Kenneth B. Clark and Gunnar Myrdal, as "modern authority" which "amply supported" the finding that segregation was damaging to black children. That footnote constituted a source of irritation for many jurists and fueled the segregationists' fires ignited by the Supreme Court's new ruling: it was misconstrued as an essential underpinning to the Court's holding. In fact, the opinion in Brown v. Board of Education is a straightforward legal interpretation of the fourteenth amendment's equal protection clause, recognizing that state-required segregation by race is an invidious classification and for that reason alone is unconstitutional. The Brown holding is thus justifiable without citation to the works of social scientists.

The agony of indecision was over. The Court was now committed to the course of dismantling segregation. The Court postponed the pragmatics of how much a social transition was to be accomplished and sought additional briefs and argument from counsel on the following alternative procedures:

(a) would a decree necessarily follow providing that, within the limits set by normal geographic school districting, Negro children should forthwith be admitted to schools of their own choice, or

(b) may this Court, in the exercise of its equity powers, permit an effective gradual adjustment to be brought about from existing segregated systems to a system not based on color distinctions?

Hinting at a preference for gradual desegregation, the Court asked further for consideration of the type of decree which the Court should elect on the assumption that the second alternative was chosen:

(a) should this Court formulate detailed decrees in these cases;

(b) if so, what special issues should the decrees reach;

(c) should this Court appoint a special master to hear evidence with a view to recommending specific terms for such decrees;

(d) should this Court remand to the courts of first instance with directions to frame decrees in these cases, and if so what general directions should the decrees of this Court include and what procedures should the courts of first instance follow in arriving at the specific terms of more detailed decrees?

New hearings were scheduled for April, 1955 on these implementation questions. Seventy-one lawyers filed briefs representing plaintiffs, ten states, the District of Columbia, the United States Department of Justice and other interested groups as amicus curiae. Not one of the principal parties seriously urged immediate wholesale desegregation, although in retrospect both the Chief Justice and Mr. Justice Black indicated that it might have been the better course of action. Similarly, all parties were in apparent agreement that the Court should rely upon the federal district courts to supervise desegregation. Still, counsel disagreed over whether or not a time-limit for compliance should be included in the Court's mandate to the lower federal courts.

Thurgood Marshall for the NAACP urged the Court to "arm the district judges and appellate judges with authority. If no time limit is set, [the defendants] are going to argue in any event the same way they have argued here, which is nothing." At the opposite pole was the position exemplified in the brief of the Attorney General of Florida; he argued for a "wide-open mandate" giving the district court the complete authority to determine when a community should integrate and to tailor the terms of implementation to the idiosyncrasies of each community. Taking what he termed "a middle-of-the-road concept of moderation with a degree of firmness," United States Solicitor General Sobeloff suggested that the Court instruct its district courts to require school authorities to submit integration plans within ninety days; these plans did not need to call for immediate and complete integration, but they should satisfy the judge that local officials were making an attempt to integrate as soon as feasible. Thus, while complete integration might not occur immediately everywhere, within a year, all would be making a start.

* * *

On May 31, 1955, scarcely a month after argument and a year after the first Brown decision [Brown I], the Supreme Court handed down its second decision. Again it was Chief Justice Warren who was credited with the opinion and who was the Court's spokesman, but like Brown I, the second opinion [Brown II] was generally conceded to be a product of consensus--with each justice contributing in some measure to both its conceptualization and even its phraseology. Mr. Justice Frankfurter, in particular, was most influential. In the oral arguments Justice Frankfurter had been extremely concerned about implementation, even at one point commenting, "nothing could be worse from my point of view than for this Court to make an abstract declaration that segregation is bad and then have it evaded by tricks." In the brief opinion read to the assemblage on May 17, 1955, Chief Justice Warren underlined what had been Justice Frankfurter's principal concern. He warned that the Court would expect "good faith" compliance from local school administrators: "School authorities have the primary responsibility for elucidating, assessing, and solving these problems; courts will have to consider whether the action of school authorities constitutes good faith implementation of the governing constitutional principles." Justice Frankfurter's hand can also be discerned in the terminology of the pace of transition set by the Court: the re-

mand order to the district courts called upon them to enter "such
orders and decrees consistent with this opinion as are necessary
and proper to admit to public schools on a racially nondiscriminatory
basis with all deliberate speed the parties to these cases." Although
the phrase "all deliberate speed" thereafter was forever associated
with the Brown decision, fervently repeated like a liturgy by school
boards and Negro plaintiffs alike, it was originally the coinage of
Mr. Justice Frankfurter in a non-civil rights opinion written in
1944.

In only slight illumination of the touchstone phrase "all deliberate speed," the Court issued a rather cryptic set of instructions
to its district courts. The following passage ultimately became the
most parsed and re-read paragraph of all Supreme Court desegregation opinions:

> In fashioning and effectuating the decrees, the
> courts will be guided by equitable principles. Traditional-
> ly, equity has been characterized by a practical flexibility
> in shaping its remedies and by a facility for adjusting and
> reconciling public and private needs. These cases call
> for the exercise of these traditional attributes of equity
> power. At stake is the personal interest of the plaintiffs
> in admission to public schools as soon as practicable on
> a nondiscriminatory basis. To effectuate this interest
> may call for elimination of a variety of obstacles in mak-
> ing the transition to school systems operated in accordance
> with the constitutional principles set forth in our May 17,
> 1954, decision. Courts of equity may properly take into
> account the public interest in the elimination of such ob-
> stacles in a systematic and effective manner. But it
> should go without saying that the vitality of these consti-
> tutional principles cannot be allowed to yield simply be-
> cause of disagreement with them.

*   *   *

Since the beginning of the seventeenth century, equity had
been a system of positive jurisprudence in Anglo-American law, a
tradition of case decisions written and preserved for future guidance.
Like the rules of the common law, equity developed through a process of accretion, expanding and extending existing doctrine. Yet
its original purpose was to mitigate the rigid, often harsh results
of a legal rule in a particular fact situation. Equity power has
been a controversial development in the law from its inception, dividing legal scholars on the question of its wisdom.

The nineteenth century American legal scholar, John Norton
Pomeroy, spoke in high praise of the ameliorative effects of equity:
"There is no limit to the various forms and kinds of specific remedy
which [a court of equity] may grant, adapted to novel conditions of
right and obligation, which are constantly arising from the move-
ments of society." Less impressed with the necessity, much less

the desirability of such flexibility in decision making was John Selden, the eminent sixteenth century British barrister and father of
legal history, who had warned:

> Equity is a roguish thing. For law we have a measure,
> and know what we trust to. Equity is according to the
> conscience of him that is Chancellor; and as that is larger
> or narrower, so is equity. 'Tis all one as if they should
> make his foot the standard for the measure we call a
> Chancellor's foot. What an uncertain measure would
> this be! One Chancellor has a long foot, another a short
> foot, a third an indifferent foot. 'Tis the same thing in
> the Chancellor's conscience.

Thus, inherent in the use of equity was a tension between certainty,
stability, and uniformity in judicial decision-making, and individu-
alized justice under the particular circumstances of a case.

The federal courts had always possessed powers to grant
equitable relief; the Supreme Court alone had reviewed hundreds of
cases involving questions of the proper scope of federal equitable
jurisdiction. But, because in its directions to the district courts
in Brown II the Supreme Court had specifically cited two cases as
precedents for guidance in fashioning desegregation decrees, those
two cases take on extraordinary significance.

In a footnote the Brown II opinion cited the case of Alexander
v. Hillman as an example of what it meant by the phrase "practical
flexibility" in devising an appropriate remedy. Perhaps anticipating
procedural manipulation and protracted litigation by recalcitrant
school districts, the Supreme Court cited Alexander as an encouragement to the lower courts to disregard formal technicalities in favor
of reaching the merits of the desegregation controversies. As the
Court had noted in Alexander, "Treating their established forms as
flexible, courts of equity may suit proceedings and remedies to the
circumstances of cases and formulate them appropriately to safe-
guard, conveniently to adjudge and promptly to enforce substantial
rights of all the parties before them." In commending the Alexander case for consideration, the Supreme Court was emphasizing
that individual black students have a right to have their complaints
liberally construed and fairly considered. Alexander v. Hillman
was definitely a case calling for extension in the exercise of equitable powers by the district courts in order to dispense full and complete relief in the process of desegregation.

The second case cited by the Supreme Court, Hecht v.
Bowles, seemed to point in the opposite direction. Hecht was apparently cited for the proposition that the district courts should also
consider the public interest in any systematic and effective transition to desegregation. It was a precedent that encouraged restraint
in the exercise of equitable powers. The public interest at stake
in the Hecht case was protection against inflated wartime prices under
the Emergency Price Control Act of 1942. After a spot check fed-

eral audit of the defendant's department store disclosed some 3,700 overcharges to consumers equaling almost $5,000 during a single five-month accounting period, the federal administrator sought an injunction in federal court. In defense, the department store urged the press of an enormous business in which some errors mught be expected, citing the fact that during the audit period over 2,000 company employees had sold over a million articles of merchandise at a total value of twenty million dollars. In short, not unlike the later pleas of metropolitan area school boards, the company spread before the court the enormous administrative problems which compliance with the Price Control Act had created for its high-volume operations. Even more persuasive was the company's open admission that its previous procedures had not produced adequate compliance with the law. Yet the company pointed out that, since the audit, it had quadrupled its internal price control manpower, had made repayment of all overcharges owed to identified customers, and further proposed to donate the remaining unlawful profit to a local charity.

The district court hearing the Hecht case was in a quandary. The price control administrator had proved his case; the past violations were undisputed and, under the explicit terms of the statute, upon such a showing, "a permanent or temporary injunction, restraining order, or other order shall be granted without bond." But, on the other hand, here was a giant department store making a reasonable showing that the instances of overpricing had not been willful and that it had taken substantial steps toward future compliance, as well as having made amends to the public for its mistakes. The district court decided to dismiss the complaint on the basis that any other order would have "no effect by way of insuring better compliance in the future," would be "unjust" and "not in the public interest." The Court of Appeals reversed, taking the rigid view that the price control statute demanded that an affirmative order be issued against the company, regardless of what the company had done in mitigation or to insure no repetition of the violations.

The United States Supreme Court agreed with the district court that federal equitable powers enabled it to deny entry of an affirmative order against the company, noting that factors such as whether an order would "insure better compliance in the future" or would be "just" were indeed appropriate considerations. In essence, the majority of the Court attempted to afford some relief to all parties. Agreeing with the Price Control Administrator, the Court reversed the district court's decision to dismiss the action. However, approving the apparent good faith of the department store owners and, more particularly, encouraging their continued compliance in the future, the Court instructed the trial court to retain the case on its docket of pending cases with the right of the Administrator, upon notice, to renew his application for injunctive relief if there were repeated violations.

Both the expansive Alexander and the restrictive Hecht cases illuminate the hand-tailoring process which was to be expected of the district court judges in hearing desegregation cases. Despite criticism to the contrary, it is doubtful if the Supreme Court could have spoken with any greater precision about the role to be assumed by its lower trial courts. The salient characteristic of equity is its suppleness, its adaptability to the circumstances of each particular case. Yet it is clear from Brown II that adaptability and flexibility in a desegregation case were not to be considered synonymous with untrammeled discretion. Each district court was to focus upon substance rather than form or rigid procedural niceties, balancing private needs and the public interest. Free, at least initially, to withhold entry of injunctive relief, Brown II required that federal district courts retain jurisdiction to supervise the entire transitional process from dual systems to desegregated systems.

* * *

The federal courts were experienced in the application of the principles and precedents of equity; nevertheless, the dismantling of segregated education proved to be without parallel or analogue in legal history. In view of the unique nature of this social revolution, it was not surprising that early desegregation cases presented many problems which even two centuries of evolution of equitable remedies had not resolved. The federal courts were thrown back upon resourcefulness and experimentation, straining their traditional equitable powers and expanding available remedies. Nevertheless, despite the efforts of the federal courts, the transition from segregated to integrated public education took far longer than anyone would have predicted in 1955. Indeed, the process is still going on over twenty years later.

Of the five Negro students--the "test plaintiffs" in the cases consolidated for argument in Brown I--only one, the Kansas plaintiff Linda Carol Brown, ever attended a desegregated school. Shortly after the decision, her family moved from Topeka to Springfield, Missouri, where she became an honor student at its integrated Central High School. After graduation she took a secretarial training course, married and became a homemaker. Dorothy Davis graduated in 1956 from Moton High School, still part of the Negro school system in Prince Edward County, Virginia, and took a nurse's training course at Virginia State College, a predominantly Negro institution. She became a nurse and homemaker, finally leaving her home state for New York. Ethel Louise Belton proceeded to graduate from Howard High School in Wilmington, Delaware, and married shortly thereafter. Subsequently, she took secretarial training from a predominantly Negro college in Delaware, becoming a dental assistant and secretary as well as a homemaker. Spottswood T. Bolling, Jr. transferred to Spingarm Senior High School in Washington, D.C., where there was one white student in that school of 1,600. He later attended a predominantly Negro college in North Carolina where he was active in civil rights demonstrations. Harry Briggs, Jr. was a thirteen-year-old seventh grader at the time of the historic decision and might have entertained every hope that he would yet have a desegregated education in the Clarendon County, South Carolina public school system. However, he never attended a desegregated public school and after graduation did not go on to college. In 1959 he moved to New York and has since worked at a number of jobs from short-order cook to garage attendant.

Though there were few personal benefits for the five who sued and prompted the historic Brown decisions, there were others of their race who followed. Among other things, this book is an account of their progress toward the realization of the ideal held out by one lonely dissenter on the Supreme Court a half-century before:

> [I]n view of the Constitution, in the eye of the law, there is in this country no superior, dominant, ruling class of citizens. There is no caste here. Our Constitution is color-blind, and neither knows nor tolerates classes among citizens. In respect of civil rights, all citizens are equal before the law. The humblest is the peer of the most powerful. The law regards man as man, and takes no account of his surroundings or of his color when his civil rights as guaranteed by the supreme law of the land are involved.

NOTES AND PRIMARY AUTHORITY

The primary sources for the material contained in this Prologue were the early race relations decisions of the United States Supreme Court: State v. Sandford, 19 How. (60 U.S.) 393 (1857); The Slaughter House Cases, 16 Wall (83 U.S.) 36 (1873); Strauder v. West Virginia, 100 U.S. 303 (1879); The Civil Rights Cases, 109 U.S. 3 (1883); Plessy v. Ferguson, 163 U.S. 537 (1896); and Gong Lum v. Rice, 275 U.S. 78 (1927). The Supreme Court cases which involved the desegregation of higher education were Missouri ex rel. Gaines v. Canada, 305 U.S. 337 (1938); Sipuel v. Bd. of Regents, 332 U.S. 631 (1948); McLaurin v. Oklahoma State Regents, 339 U.S. 637 (1950); and Sweatt v. Painter, 339 U.S. 629 (1950).

The five appeals known collectively as the "School Segregation Cases" were Brown v. Bd. of Educ., 98 F. Supp. 797 (D. Kans. 1951); Davis v. County School Bd., 103 F. Supp. 337 (E.D. Va. 1952); Briggs v. Elliot, 103 F. Supp. 920 (E.D. S.C. 1952); Belton v. Gebhart, 87 A.2d 862 (Del. Ch. Ct. 1952), aff'd, 91 A.2d 137 (1952); and Bolling v. Sharpe, (1952). The account of the oral argument of these cases before the Supreme Court can be found in 21 U.S.L.W. 3164 (1952), 22 U.S.L.W. 3158 (1953) and 23 U.S.L.W. 3253 (1954). The two Supreme Court decisions in Brown I and II are found in 347 U.S. 483 (1954) and 349 U.S. 294 (1955).

Secondary sources helpful as a general background for the civil rights movement culminating in the Brown decisions were Pfeffer, This Honorable Court (1965); Greenberg, Race Relations and

American Law (1959); Kelly, "The School Desegregation Cases,"
Quarrels That Have Shaped the Constitution (ed. Garraty) (1964);
Jenkins, "Judicial Discretion in Desegregation: The Hawkins Case,"
4 Howard L. J. 193 (1958); Weaver, Warren: The Man, The Court,
The Era (1967); and contemporary news accounts, such as those
contained in the Kansas City Star, May 17, 1954, and "The Five
Who Sued," 47 Saturday Review 21, May 16, 1964. A more complete manuscript, with detailed documentation of all sources, is
available as indicated in the Preface.

PART I

THE THIN BLACK LINE:
THE HUTCHESON-RIVES YEARS, 1956-1960

21

Chapter 1

THE GREAT AND THE NEAR GREAT

> [T]he felt necessities of the time, the prevalent
> moral and political theories, institutions of pub-
> lic policy, avowed or unconscious, even the pre-
> judices which judges share with their fellow-men,
> have had a good deal more to do than the syl-
> logism in determining the rules by which men
> should be governed.
> --Hon. Oliver Wendell Holmes, Jr., 1881

The Establishment of the Fifth Circuit

In 1789, at its first regular session, Congress enacted the
Federal Judiciary Act, thereby implementing its constitutional authority to establish inferior federal courts. That statute divided the
then eleven states of the union into three judicial circuits and created two tiers of courts. In retrospect, the new federal judicial
system was a strange conceit. The thirteen district courts that had
been established were given trial jurisdiction over federal matters,
with one federal judge authorized for each district. However, the
Federal Judiciary Act also created circuit courts with trial jurisdiction over certain special classes of cases: where an alien was
a party, where the United States sued claiming damages exceeding
five hundred dollars, and in all major federal criminal prosecutions.

In addition, these circuit courts were given responsibility
for deciding appeals from final decisions of the district courts within their respective territories. Unfortunately, Congress did not authorize the appointment of judges to serve exclusively on the circuit
courts; instead, when these courts convened twice each year, the
three-judge panel making up the court was composed of a district
court judge and two justices of the Supreme Court, "riding the circuit."

Despite the increasing administrative problems of such an

Opposite, the 1956 Court with seven judges: standing (l. to r.),
Warren L. Jones, Ben F. Cameron, John R. Brown, John Minor
Wisdom; seated, Richard T. Rives, J. C. Hutcheson, Jr., and El-
bert P. Tuttle.

unwieldy system, the burdens of circuit riding and the anomaly of
district court judges reviewing their own decisions as circuit court
judges, Congress reacted with only piecemeal revisions of the federal court structure during the next century.   In the meantime,
Congress had greatly enlarged federal jurisdiction over various controversies.   By 1890, the pending caseloads on federal court calendars had reached staggering proportions.   In the twenty years preceding 1890, the district court case docket had nearly doubled while
the Supreme Court's appellate burden had tripled.

Finally, in 1891, Congress undertook a major revision of the
federal judicial system.   Circuit Courts of Appeals, the immediate
predecessors of the present eleven United States Courts of Appeals,
were established and vested with exclusive appellate jurisdiction over
decisions of the federal district courts.   Congress also created additional judgeships, providing for three judges to staff each of the
nine newly created judicial circuits.   This landmark statute, the
Circuit Court of Appeals Act of 1891, fixed the basic outline of
modern federal appellate jurisdiction.   The right of direct review
of district court decisions by the Supreme Court was drastically reduced.   Instead, the decisions of the new intermediate federal
courts were to be considered final unless a Court of Appeals certified propositions of law to the Supreme Court for its decision or
unless the Supreme Court elected to exercise discretionary review
by granting a petition for a writ of certiorari.

*   *   *

In 1892 the Court of Appeals for the Fifth Judicial Circuit
was invested with appellate responsibility for federal actions taken
in six states of the Deep South: Alabama, Florida, Georgia, Louisiana, mississippi and Texas.   By 1899, judicial appointments for the
first full Court of Appeals for the Fifth Circuit had been completed.
Guiding the new court through its formative years were two former
Confederate soldiers and a former Major in the Union Army.

The first appointee, Don A. Pardee, had led the 42nd Regi-
ment of Ohio in the Civil War.   He had been introduced to the
South under the worst of conditions as the Provost Marshal of Baton
Rouge in 1863.   However, at the close of the war, he returned to
New Orleans to practice law and was shortly thereafter elected a
state judge.   He was elevated to the federal judicial system when
his comrade in arms of the 42nd Division, James A. Garfield, became President.   According to Garfield's biographer, "It was a
clear case of giving a position to his old war friend and fellow officer."   Yet, despite the apparent cronyism that motivated his appointment, Judge Pardee served with distinction for thirty-eight
years as a circuit judge.

The second member of the first Fifth Circuit Court of Appeals was Andrew P. McCormick from Texas.   Judge McCormick
was a rarity among nineteenth century Southerners.   He was not
only college educated but also a scholar, having graduated with first

honors. He served in the Confederate forces and returned to establish a law practice, serving the public both as a state judge and United States Attorney prior to his appointment to the federal district court, and ultimately to the Court of Appeals.

The third member of the court was David D. Shelby from Alabama. While still in his adolescence, Judge Shelby became a member of the Confederate Cavalry. After the war he studied law and, thereafter, entered into partnership with Leroy Pope Walker, who had been a General in the Confederate Army and a member of the Confederate cabinet. Prior to his appointment to the federal bench, Judge Shelby had pursued a political career, serving in the Alabama Senate.

The first regularly constituted Court of Appeals was a microcosm of contrasting personal characteristics, a situation that was to be mirrored time and again throughout the subsequent history of the Court. There would be differences of political persuasion and differences in experience. Some judges would be purely political appointees and others highly skilled attorneys in private practice or for the government, some even with prior judicial experience. The only common denominators among the men who came to the Fifth Circuit were that all were legally trained and, perhaps more important in the Court's critical times during the Civil Rights Movement, all were Southerners either by birth or by choice. Because of the statutory qualification that they be residents of the particular Circuit in which they were considered for appointment, a certain basic credibility attached to the more controversial decisions of the new Court of Appeals. Under the provisions of the Circuit Court of Appeals Act, the federal judges were appointed for life, a tenure insulating them from pressure by their regional constituents or from shifts in the winds of public opinion. Hamilton earlier had expressed his concern for an independent federal judiciary:

> The most discerning cannot foresee how far the prevalency of a local spirit may be found to disqualify the local tribunals for the jurisdiction of national causes; whilst every man may discover that courts constituted like those of some of the states would be improper channels of the judicial authority of the nation. State judges, holding their offices during pleasure, or from year to year, will be too little independent to be relied upon for an inflexible execution of the national laws.

In retrospect, the provision for life tenure for federal judges is considered the genius of the federal system in the opinion of legal scholars. It more than any other single factor accounts for the resilience of the judicial system during the last century.

The future of the Fifth Circuit Court of Appeals* was in-

---

*The official name of the Court is The United States Court of Appeals for the Fifth Circuit.

evitably to be affected by the region for which it had been given responsibility. As the South entered into a period of enormous development in the twentieth century, the Fifth Circuit as an institution was transformed from the drowsiest of the federal circuits to the busiest. In 1891, the six states of the Circuit had a total population of 8,385,891, with only one major metropolis, New Orleans. By 1950, the population had almost tripled and every state but Mississippi had at least one city of over 300,000. The first Court was required to hold regular terms in New Orleans and Atlanta; by 1950, the Court of Appeals was required to hold terms annually in those two cities as well as in Fort Worth, Jacksonville and Montgomery. No other Circuit Court reigns over such a sprawling territory: a diverse region requiring judicial eclecticism of its judges and extensive modern-day circuit riding.

The Fifth Circuit Court's published opinions are replete with examples of the breadth of its federal controversies. The growth of industry and the great influx of population in the Circuit have brought increased labor disputes. Bounded on two sides by water and threaded throughout with navigable waterways, the United States Court of Appeals for the Fifth Circuit hears cases involving maintenance and cure, Jones Act violations and various other aspects of maritime law--a legal specialty to which a lifetime of study could be devoted. The increased availability of federal writs of habeas corpus produces vast numbers of inmates' petitions from the Atlanta Penitentiary, the largest federal penal institution in the nation, and from two smaller federal prisons in Florida. From Texas come exotic cases of border smuggling and oil and gas law; from Louisiana come cases involving interpretation of the civil law traceable to the early French settlement of the territory; from Florida come cases stemming from the boom in land speculation and fleeing immigrants from Cuba. The Court hears cases of barge collisions on the Mississippi, violations of acreage allotments in Alabama and prosecutions for bootlegging activities in the hills of North Georgia. "We would be busy," said one of the Court's modern day members, "if we never had a civil rights case."

The statistics bear this out. Within the first twelve years of the Court's existence only 1,207 cases were filed. In comparison, during the single fiscal year 1953-54, 510 cases were filed; moreover, the Fifth Circuit disposed of almost one-sixth of the total number of cases concluded in all eleven federal circuits combined. At the close of the fiscal year 1953-54, on the eve of the civil rights explosion, the Fifth Circuit was only seven cases shy of being the busiest circuit court in the nation. Thereafter, this Court consistently has had the dubious distinction of being the most overworked and constantly strained of all the circuits.

One long-time employee who knew the court as it was at the turn of the century remembered with nostalgia that quite commonly Judge Pardee and Judge Shelby would ride their stallions down St. Charles Avenue in the cool twilight of New Orleans evenings. Sixty-five years later the Court more commonly spent the evenings in

New Orleans sitting in extraordinary session hearing heated argument from counsel, tense about the repercussions of their decisions and awaiting news of the latest segregationist bills turned out as easily as counterfeit money by the Louisiana Legislature.

Perhaps the true measure of the resilience of any social institution can only be tested in times of critical stress. That the federal judicial system, its district and appellate courts survived in the South through the sixties and seventies attests to the wisdom of its founders and the abilities of the judges who guided its course. Chief Judge Hutcheson once remarked, "[I]f we select for our judges men of high character and proven ability as lawyers and keep them long enough on the bench, we are bound in time to have a court of first-class judges, with maybe one or two of them great or near great." As fortune would have it, never in the history of the Fifth Circuit had such a gathering of the great and near great sat together as judges than during what was to be the court's most trying period, the two decades of the civil rights explosion.

Chief Judge Hutcheson and the Changing Guard

> But judges, as we are, of a court the Constitution
> calls 'inferior,' we may not turn thus lightly from
> the way of stare decisis. We must, though blown
> about by every wind of changing dichotomy, find,
> if we can, and, if we can, follow the path the Su-
> preme Court has taken, though the way be dark and
> tortuous, its destination uncertain and obscure."--
> Chief Judge Joseph C. Hutcheson in Addison v.
> Commercial National Bank in Shreveport.

In 1954, there were six judges on the Fifth Circuit Court of Appeals then in active service: Chief Judge Joseph C. Hutcheson, Jr., and Judges Louie W. Strum, Robert L. Russell, Edwin R. Holmes, Wayne G. Borah and Richard T. Rives. In shortly more than a year, Judges Strum and Russell died and Judge Holmes retired to senior status. Thus, during his first term of office, President Eisenhower was to make three significant nominations to the Court's membership, nominations which would alter the direction of the Court's work.

Joseph C. Hutcheson had been a member of the Circuit Court since 1931, and since 1949 had been Chief Judge, a position achieved by seniority in judicial commission. He was born in Houston in 1879 and from the age of two, when his mother died, was reared by his father, a former Captain in the Confederate Army, with whom he later practiced law for seventeen years. He attended Bethel Military Academy and college at the University of Virginia but returned to the University of Texas for a home state legal education. He graduated from law school as the class valedictorian, was elected to the Order of the Coif, and remained interested in legal research and writing all his life, publishing two books and many articles in addition to his judicial opinions.

After a brief stint as Chief Legal Advisor to the City of Houston, Hutcheson was elected Mayor of Houston in 1917. He resigned the following year and was appointed to the federal district court bench by President Wilson. Perhaps because he had spent thirteen years as a federal trial judge, when it became necessary to reverse the decision of a district court judge, Chief Judge Hutcheson was deferential and even courtly. He spoke in one of his articles about this delicate task: "As between district and appellate courts, it is the duty of appellate courts, since what they are doing is trying the district judge for error, to give him every courtesy and consideration and not to look down their appellate noses at the trial judges, with little reason, as the wise ones know."

But if he could be sensitive in dealing with his subordinates on the federal bench, Chief Judge Hutcheson was nevertheless considered "temperamental," often flashing anger and displeasure when crossed. As one newspaperman assigned for years to cover the Court wrote:

> The Hutch is an old-time Southern hot-head, and a real overstepping of his ideas of right and wrong, and particularly his ideas of fairness and justice, was like monkeying with a naked bolt of lightning. He could and did 'dress down' offenders--criminals who had swindled poor people, officers who had taken bribes or had taken undue advantage of their authority, lawyers who didn't play by the rules-- with a cold fury that made your skin crawl.

He was a vigorous, vital man and apparently a stern taskmaster.

The Court of Appeals during Judge Hutcheson's tenure as Chief Judge was a formal institution, with the decorum of the courtroom clinging to the judges in their relationships with one another off the bench. Because he had sat as a federal judge for thirty-seven years by 1954, the courtroom, the chambers, the job of judging were by then as natural to Chief Judge Hutcheson as breathing. Perhaps, as a consequence, the Court under his leadership expended little effort to welcome new appointees or to tutor those less experienced in their new responsibilities. Judge Tuttle later recalled his experience as a fledgling member of the Court:

> [When] the court came in to sit the first week, Judges Hutcheson, Holmes and Borah, I think, I had never heard a word from a single member of the court saying, 'Welcome to our court. We hope to see you when we come to Atlanta.' I hadn't heard a word from a soul. All I had was a bunch of records and briefs that the clerk sent up to me. I had hired a law clerk and I knew what the job was--to get ready to hear oral arguments on the second Monday morning in October [1954]. Well, these visit-

ing judges came in here and made themselves at home and
used the courtroom and introduced themselves to me or I
introduced myself to them.   And that was it for the first
week.   The second week, Judge Hutcheson was still here
and he was presiding.   We met at 10:00 a.m. then.   I
put on my robe at five minutes to ten and went in the
robing room there, and Judge Hutcheson walked in, and
we shook hands....   [That week] I sat with Judge Hutcheson,
we'd go to lunch together.   I was then 57 years old, and
he was 70.   I said, "Judge Hutcheson, lots of youngsters
around here call me by my first name, and I get accustomed to it.   I'd be glad if you just called me 'Elbert' or
'Tut' or anything."   "I wouldn't think of it," he said.
"First thing I know, you'll be calling me 'Joe.'"

Politically, Chief Judge Hutcheson described himself as a
Jeffersonian Democrat and accepted as his cardinal principle Jefferson's epigram that no man was ever "born with a saddle on his
back, nor any born booted and spurred to ride him."   He was one
of the first advocates in Texas of women's suffrage and he championed the rights of the individual against pressure or intrusion.
As one colleague on the American Law Institute Council, noted:

> He has always been a stout defender in the Council and
> in the general meetings of the rights of the rugged indi-
> vidual; and the Judge has always risen to insist at least
> upon elbow room for the citizen.   I don't think he even
> likes lights that flash red and make him stop at street
> corners.

Although he was a Southerner by birth, and undoubtedly influenced
by its mores, his racial attitudes were tempered by his philosophy
of individualism.   George Leslie, the Negro messenger who had
served Chief Judge Hutcheson on the Court, recalled an episode
which occurred while he was traveling the Circuit with the Hutche-
sons:

> Traveling ... up through Georgia, we passed something
> that looked much like a restaurant or resort; it bore a
> sign over the door, projecting out where it could be read-
> ily seen and the sign read, 'No Catholics and No Negroes
> allowed.'   After being a short distance away, the Judge
> cleared his throat and said to Mrs. Hutcheson, 'I had
> thought we might stop here and freshen up a little but I
> noticed that neither you or Leslie were welcome.'

According to his colleagues, he never flinched from issuing
unpopular orders if he concluded that was his duty: he sustained
the validity of the Railway Labor Act in a pre-New Deal "era of
hostility to such radicalism"; similarly, in the ten cent oil crisis
in East Texas during the Depression, he enjoined the Governor's deployment of the Texas militia in defiance of a federal court order.

In terms of judicial philosophy, Chief Judge Hutcheson was a passionate adherent of stability in the law, of following the law's precedents where established, and of refusing to engage in what he termed "the role of crystal gazers." His scorn of "judicial activism" could reach even to the Supreme Court, when necessary; on one such occasion, he drew praise from Westbrook Pegler for an opinion in which he wrote:

> Unskilled as we [members of the Court of Appeals] are in the intricacies and involvements of the higher judicial exegesis, its logomancies, its preciosities, its legal dialectics, as these two cases exhibit it, when by shifts in voting the majority has become the minority, the decisions of yesterday the mere dicta of today, to us the question of statutory construction and application this case presents seems a clear and simple one ... [But] however much we may think it plain that a wrong decision should be downrightly overruled, 'inferior' as we are, we have no function to advise our betters, as the great and wise of old have done. ...

Chief Judge Hutcheson's conservatism and his espousal of stability and certainty in the judicial exposition of the law also colored his administration of the Fifth Circuit during his eleven-year tenure as Chief Judge. His predecessors had treated the office of Chief Judge as primarily that of a figure head. Chief Judge Hutcheson apparently saw no reason to change. Federal statutes have little to say regarding the duties of that office. Perhaps the greatest single opportunity for molding the course of decision-making lies in the Chief Judge's authority to name two of the three members of "three-judge district courts." Congress has required that whenever a litigant challenges the constitutionality of a state law and seeks to have the challenged statute enjoined or overturned, the case cannot be heard by a single district court judge, as normally occurs, but instead by a specially convened three-judge panel sitting as the trier of fact. Theoretically, at least, whatever may be hand-picked may also be "hand-packed." However, until the cases generated by the civil rights movement exploded, requests for the convention of such courts were a rarity; there were few occasions calling for this exercise of the Chief Judge's power.

By statute, the powers and responsibilities of the Chief Judgeship are largely ministerial. Where necessary due to the press of business, the Chief Judge is empowered to appoint retired judges of his circuit to sit on panels or to obtain a temporary assignment of judges from other Circuits to sit on cases by special designation. By tradition in the Fifth Circuit, the Chief Judge works in conjunction with the clerk of the Court in the assignment of cases. The Chief Judge devises a panel of available judges, and the clerk calendars the cases for argument. As Judge Tuttle, later Chief Judge of the Fifth Circuit, characterized the office:

> The Chief Judge is like a Chief Justice [of the Supreme

Court] to the extent that he has just one vote on whatever
court he sits. If there are three of us, the Chief Judge
has one vote. The Chief Judge has only the influence on
the panel that he sits with, whether it be an ordinary
three-judge panel or an en banc court, that the strength of
his personality and his ability as an advocate can carry
with his colleagues.

However, as Judge Tuttle conceded, there are occasionally emergency
matters that come up in which the Chief Judge may act as a single judge
granting extraordinary relief, such as an injunction pending appeal or
a stay of an order. During such emergencies, the Chief Judge "will
act maybe more often than any other judge because some of them
will come to [him] as Chief Judge."

Outside of his explicit congressional authorization and those
powers which had inhered in the office by tradition, Chief Judge
Hutcheson considered himself powerless to expand upon the powers
of his office. In 1948, even when the then-Senator Lyndon Baines
Johnson sought appellate relief from an erroneous district court
order in the political battle of his life, Chief Judge Hutcheson declared himself to be without power to convene the members of the
Court for a consideration of the issues because it was then in summer recess. The office of Chief Judge changed significantly under
Chief Judge Hutcheson's successors. Indeed, the Court as an institution became more responsive to the exigencies produced by the
civil rights movement. Within the span of twenty years, "Chief
Judge Hutcheson's Court" seemed like the last relic of a bygone
era.

* * *

Wayne G. Borah had been on the Court since his appointment by President Truman in 1949 and retired from active service
in 1957 before the real onslaught of civil rights litigation. The
third member of the Court, Richard T. Rives, was to have a far
greater influence than either Chief Judge Hutcheson or Judge Borah
in the Court's weathering of the civil rights crises. Also a Truman
nominee, Judge Rives was appointed to the Fifth Circuit in 1951
and served in active status until 1966; thus, his tenure on the Court
of Appeals was inextricably bound to the critical era of civil rights
litigation.

A native of Montgomery, Alabama, Judge Rives was born in
1895. His grandparents on both sides of the family had been reared
in Alabama and, because of these deep Southern roots, many in the
South were shocked by his later progressive attitudes as a member
of the Fifth Circuit. Unlike his colleagues, he had not had an
"Eastern exposure" during his years of undergraduate education. In
fact, his formal collegiate education consisted of one year (1911-
1912), when he was a student at Tulane in New Orleans; thereafter
he returned to Montgomery to study law in the offices of a family
friend. He was admitted to the Alabama Bar at nineteen and prac-

ticed law for thirty-seven years before being named to the Court of
Appeals. Although he served as President of the Alabama Bar Association, he never held public office nor had any prior judicial experience when he was appointed to the Fifth Circuit.

Richard Rives's career as a trial lawyer had involved him in
cases in which he as an advocate sought to exclude as well as to
protect Negroes. He himself later candidly observed, "So I have
been--I'm not really pure on this question of bigotry that way, but
I think my own experience is some indication that people change
their views as they go along." He had once given advice to the
Montgomery Board of Registrars concerning what they could do about
an early Negro voting drive campaign in Montgomery County. He
later described the consultation:

> Here they were, Negroes all the way around the park,
> lined up to register. They [the Board] said, 'What shall
> we do?' I said, 'Well, the only thing to do is to go on
> and let them come in, take their application, let them
> sign up and you all pass on it after they leave.' Of
> course, I didn't tell them how to pass on it; they didn't
> need any advice on that. They did and they soon got rid
> of the line. They turned them all down later.

Judge Rives also had served as Judge Advocate of the Montgomery
American Legion during a period of time in which Negroes were
seeking to join that group. The Legion did not deny membership
outright; instead, its rules were written to provide that all applicants would be voted upon. None of the Negro applicants was admitted.

But on other occasions in his career, Judge Rives struggled
to protect the Negro against the biases of his fellow Alabamians.
Early in his career, he was approached by a Negro family to bring
a lawsuit on behalf of a young women who had met a gruesome
death from a faultily constructed elevator in a new office building.
He agreed to take the case; later he recounted its development:

> A casualty insurance adjuster came to me and said, 'I'll
> pay you a thousand dollars.' I said, 'Now, that's ridicu-
> lous. I wouldn't think of such a thing.' He said, 'Well,
> you must know that no verdict has been obtained over here
> for a Negro death for more than that.' Damages on death
> cases here in Alabama were purely punitive. The Supreme
> Court [of Alabama] had said that it wouldn't reverse them
> if they were more than a penny. It was entirely up to the
> jury what it would be. I almost ran him out of my office,
> offering me a thousand dollars on it, because the liability
> was perfect. The elevator operators under the law then
> were common carriers and subject to the highest degree
> of care. But to my chagrin, the jury awarded $1,000 when
> I got through the case. $1,000 was all I collected in that
> case. That's just typical of where Negroes stood.

In his legal career, Judge Rives drew a personal moral line at what he considered to be "unfairness" to individuals, Negro or white, and he would not cross that line. By 1948, he had reconsidered his prior position on the rectitude of refusing to permit Negroes to vote by whatever stratagem. The so-called "Boswell Amendment" to the Alabama Constitution had been proposed for ratification by the voters of the state: it was a version of what was known popularly as "an understanding clause" test, which required an applicant to be able to demonstrate to the Registrar's satisfaction the "correct" meaning of any constitutional provision. According to Judge Rives, the campaign to ratify the Boswell Amendment was a turning point in his realization of the legal plight of Negro citizens:

> [The proposed amendment] was of course nothing on earth but to keep Negroes from registering. I had had some cases, I had one against Thurgood Marshall back before then, and I had had some cases on the other side of the fence, a good many of them practicing law.... But that was just too much for me. I thought that was just totally unfair ... and I opposed that, openly, and we organized a debating outfit that went through the state arguing it out with people on the other side.... I was constantly saying that if it were passed, it was going to be held unconstitutional. It was passed, but not by too large a vote, I think, around 10,000 in my recollection; then a three-judge court ... held it unconstitutional.

Richard T. Rives hardly could have been described as a flaming liberal when his name was submitted for consideration as a possible federal judge. But then, in 1951, no southern liberal would have received Senate confirmation nor, indeed, would have been nominated by the President. Senatorial courtesy was and still is a powerful control upon the judicial selection process.

Although there was little in his past career to indicate that Judge Rives would become a stalwart defender--much less an advocate--of Negroes' civil rights, scarcely ten years after his appointment Time magazine had included him in its list of seven southern judges whom it termed "Trail Blazers on the Bench--The South's U.S. Judges Lead a Civil Rights Offensive." In describing Judge Rives, the article noted:

> In his handful of segregation cases, Rives has invariably decided for liberalism, but not always without a twinge of regret: in April [1960], he upheld a ruling ... that Montgomery could not segregate its public parks, but noted that the decision was a Pyrrhic one for the Negro plaintiffs since the city was sure to close the parks rather than obey. It did.

Judge Rives' first controversial decision came in 1956 when, as a member of a three-judge district court panel, he wrote the opinion in the Montgomery bus boycott case. The highly successful

boycott in that case catapulted a young Negro preacher, Martin
Luther King, Jr., to national prominence. Negro plaintiffs sought
to have the state statutes and city ordinances which required segregation in public transportation vehicles held unconstitutional. The
squarely fitting precedent blocking such an action was, of course,
the United States Supreme Court's 1896 decision in Plessy v. Ferguson which had upheld a Louisiana statute requiring segregated "separate but equal" facilities on railroads. Since then, the Supreme
Court had discarded the validity of the "separate but equal" doctrine
in public school education in the Brown cases, but those opinions had
not expressly overruled Plessy's impact on public transportation.
Judge Rives concluded on behalf of himself and District Court Judge
Frank M. Johnson that, in the post-Brown era, the Plessy doctrine
had no remaining vitality in any area of the public law.

     While the language of the opinion was mild, it created a ma-
jor furor in Montgomery. District Judge Seyborn Lynne, an erudite
Southern patrician and the third member of the panel, strongly dissented, arguing that the Court should not move a single step further
in such controversial matters until the Supreme Court had explicitly
mandated the way. After all, slightly less than a year before, a
Fifth Circuit panel composed of Chief Judge Hutcheson, Circuit Judge
Holmes and District Judge Dawkins had refused similar action, declining to extend the dictum of Brown to require the desegregation of
Atlanta's golf courses. Judge Lynne professed shock that his colleagues had taken such a precipitous action, particularly in view of
some previous opinions of Judge Rives, declaring it to be the duty
of Circuit Courts to leave modification of the law to the Supreme
Court. As a consequence of this decision, Judge Rives was castigated in print by segregationist writers. The public reaction in his
hometown of Montgomery took on a more violent, even sadistic note.
In the aftermath of the busing decision, Judge Rives received a deluge of mail which he wryly termed "fan letters," 95 per cent of
which were far from complimentary. Despite his participation in
far more important cases later in his judicial career, the reaction
to the Montgomery bus opinion was, according to Judge Rives, the
"peak of the public outcry." Judge Rives remembered the Summer
of 1955:

> There were talks of the Klan burning crosses. I remem-
> ber when the police called me I said, 'Don't be guarding
> my house. I've got my old shotgun and my old pistol,
> I'll take care of myself out there.' A little bit too much
> braggadocio. 'If anybody starts burning a cross in front
> of my house, I'm going to pepper them up with bird shot.'
> Next I heard they had burned a cross in front of [Judge
> Frank] Johnson's house. The FBI finally traced them
> down; it was a couple of high school boys. They were
> members of an old, old family here.
>   Most of the other personal things that happened to me
> were telephone calls. For a good while Judge Johnson had
> his phone taken out or rather had a private line where they
> couldn't get him. I never did, but they would keep us up

all night answering the phone, usually just hanging up,
once or twice telling my wife that she had better make
the best of her husband while she had him, she wouldn't
have him long, things of that kind.

So there were hate letters, telephone calls, burning crosses
and threats of Klan retaliation, yet there was a final indecency in
Judge Rives's case as a result of this single, temperately-toned
opinion on desegregation of public transportation. The Rives's only
son had been killed in an automobile accident during the spring holiday of his second year of law school. As Judge Rives recalled,

We, of course, my wife and I, went to the cemetery
every day for many, many years, and on one occasion
there, we found his grave desecrated. We found it painted
red and garbage thrown on his grave and that kind of thing.
I asked the sexton--nobody except a crazy, demented man
would do such a thing. I said, 'Let's get it cleaned up
and have as little to say about it as we can.' He said,
'Well, I'm just compelled to have to report it to the
police,' and there was some, not much, publicity....

Time magazine gave nationwide coverage to the incident and, in
passing, excoriated the general populace of Alabama as a degraded,
bigoted people.

The first person to the defense of Alabamians was Richard
T. Rives. In his first letter to an editor, which Time published,
Judge Rives isolated the desecration as the work of a misguided individual, unrepresentative of the rest of the citizens of his State,
and admonished that such generalized assumptions about the populace
were both untrue and unfair. Judge Rives never lost faith in the
ability of the average Southerner to adjust, just as he himself had
adjusted, to the recognition of long-overdue Negro rights; as a
realist, though, and a Southerner himself, he knew it would take
time:

It is a complete social revolution in the Deep South, and
it takes a little time for people to get their thinking, even
fair-minded people, to get their thinking turned about, because nobody had ever dreamed of such a complete change
here.

Judge Rives never lost the ability to empathize with Southerners during the years of transition. His chief contribution to the
court's deliberations was a keen appreciation of the realities con-
fronting the southern "fair-minded" man caught between his conscience and the necessity of making a livelihood dependent upon the
good will of the general community. He once advised a young attorney who had come to him expressing a desire to support publicly
the federal courts at the height of public outrage:

I told him, 'Well, if I were in your position, I would not.

Now, you are just committing suicide so far as your law
practice is concerned, and we don't have to have that.
We are protected by life tenure. We are going on and do
our job anyhow. I appreciate your position, but I frankly
don't think you should do it. You don't owe that much
sacrifice to come out and almost destroy your practice,'
which he would have done, I think.

As a member of the federal court sitting in the Deep South,
Judge Rives neither expected nor exacted martyrdom from private
citizens. Judges were to lead the way; public vilification, where it
occurred, and personal sacrifice "came with the territory" of judicial appointment.

'I thoroughly agree,' as Judge Rives later observed, 'that
there should be private clubs and that people are entitled
to select their own private associates. I select my own.
But at the same time, there is no doubt that the law has
a tremendous influence on it and that there is an area in
which law influences how people act in private.'

A function of the law then, according to Judge Rives, was to
make it as easy as possible for "fair-minded" men to act responsibly. Insights gained from his own thirty-seven year general trial
practice echo through countless later judicial opinions. For an example, in the key case establishing the right of a Negro to be tried
by a jury from which Negroes have not been systematically excluded,
Judge Rives noted:

We have called the figures startling, but we do not feign
surprise because we have long known that there are counties not only in Mississippi [the case in point], but in the
writer's own home State of Alabama, in which Negroes
constitute the majority of the residents but take no part in
government either as voters or as jurors. Familiarity
with such a condition thus prevents shock, but it all the
more increases our concern over its existence....
Moreover, the very prejudice which causes the dominant race to exclude members of what it may assume to
be an inferior race from jury service operates with multiplied intensity against one who resists such exclusion.
Conscientious southern lawyers often reason that the preju-
dicial effects on their client of raising the issue far out-
weigh any practical protection in the particular case ...
Such courageous and unselfish lawyers as find it essential
for their clients' protection to fight against the systematic
exclusion of Negroes from juries sometimes do so at the
risk of personal sacrifice which may extend to loss of
practice and social ostracism.

There is not a single area of race relations law which would
remain untouched by Judge Rives's mind and sensibilities. He wrote
seminal opinions in cases involving desegregation, public accommoda-

tions, voting rights, jury selection and the right to demonstrate for correction of grievances, all of which will be discussed in the course of this work. If there may be said to be one salient feature of his judicial contribution to the Court's work, it might be his unfailing sense of the consequences of a particular decision, its "enforceability quotient" in the teeth of southern resistance. Judge Rives was the supreme pragmatist among the court's members; perhaps more than any other single judge, he developed a keen sense of the public mood. His prediction that the City of Montgomery would close its parks to all, rather than allow Negroes to use the facilities, proved true. He was particularly alert to the problem of putting state officers, who might otherwise want to carry out their constitutional duties, in difficulty with the electorate; in one Alabama desegregation case, an opinion of the Fifth Circuit complimented a local school administration which seemed to have decided upon compliance instead of resistance. Judge Rives ruefully remembered, "It put them in a bad political position, as you might imagine. And [they] immediately had to come out with statements that they were as much against desegregation in the schools as Wallace and [their predecessors] or anybody else. We were sorry that we had overlooked the position that we were putting them in."

Perhaps, most significantly, it was Judge Rives who pointed out to his colleagues the practical consequences of further contempt proceedings against Governor Ross Barnett of Mississippi, arising out of the Governor's flagrant disobedience of federal court orders to enroll James Meredith in the University of Mississippi. According to Judge Rives,

> I take the responsibility of bringing that contempt proceeding to an end myself. I had been on the side that was pretty much against Barnett until the Supreme Court said we couldn't do much with it.... Mild punishment would have made him a political hero and would really have been a reward to him. He wanted mild punishment, I think; he would have been willing to stay in for a few months. He would have been a hero from then on. We were constantly faced with the position of having our court sitting there, and Barnett not showing up. He never showed up in person at all, sending his attorneys to represent him. We'd held him in civil contempt.... [W]hatever we did to him was going to be a reward rather than a punishment, and [I thought] it was best to go on and get rid of that proceeding. We then did dismiss it on our own motion. But I was probably the prime mover on wanting to dispose of that proceeding, because we just had got a bear by the tail that we couldn't turn loose, and it was working out just the opposite of what we had hoped for it to work out.

Richard Rives was not the scholar on the Fifth Circuit Court of Appeals, nor the Court's most innovative judge, nor its most colorful figure. He was a courageous, pre-eminently practical man and jurist. While his intuitive knowledge of his region and its people influenced the Court's deliberations, it was finally his integrity that was the Court's mainstay of stability in crisis. In any listing of the "great and near great," he must be included.

The Eisenhower Appointees:
Tuttle, Cameron, Jones, Brown and Wisdom

> The court before which the cause is to come has issued opinions which do more than lay down 'law' on particular points; they also and especially cumulate to show ways of looking at things, ways of sizing things up, ways of handling authorities, attitudes in one area of life--conflict in another. Over a five-year, indeed over a one-year, stretch these facts of the opinions furnish a revealing and appealing study which no appellate lawyer can afford to do without. For one must not forget that a particular bench tends strongly to develop a characteristic going tradition not only of ways of work but of outlook, and of working attitudes of one judge toward another. New judges get broken in to all of this; each normally adjusts largely to the harness which the going tradition seeks to fit upon him. Of course the tradition changes. Occasionally it can change with relative speed.
> --Karl Llewellyn, The Common Law
> Tradition 34 (1960)

In February, 1954, Congress passed an omnibus Federal Judgeship bill which authorized one additional judgeship for the Fifth Circuit Court of Appeals, thus promising some relief from its already overloaded dockets. However, President Eisenhower did not move to nominate a candidate for that new vacancy for almost five months, even though the Court was operating without the services of Judge Russell, who was then terminally ill. Finally, on July 7, 1954, President Eisenhower nominated Elbert P. Tuttle of Georgia. The Atlanta newspapers reported: "There has been some mystery as to why the White House waited so long to fill the vacancy. The explanation can now be given. Administration officials have deliberately withheld making the appointment in the hope of having Tuttle accept."

Elbert Tuttle was a partner of a prestigious Atlanta law firm and a prominent Georgia Republican who, by 1954, passed in most circles as a native Southerner. However, he was born in California and shortly thereafter moved with his family to Hawaii, where his father was an accountant with the Hawaiian Sugar Planters Association. Both he and his brother went stateside to Cornell University for their college education. A friend during the college years later reminisced:

Soon after we got to Cornell we attended a big student
mass meeting. I've forgotten what the subject of discussion was, but it created a hot argument. The snarl got
worse and worse until a slender, modest but poised and
plain-spoken young man arose to his feet. He proposed
a solution to the difficulty; whatever it was; when he finished speaking, the argument was settled. That was Elbert Tuttle. It was the first time I ever saw him....
And from that time to this, I have known that Elbert is
a leader among men.

Tuttle had been a journalism major and a working reporter for two
years after his graduation in 1918. In the meantime, he had met
Bill and Sara Sutherland in Florida during a college vacation when
he lacked the funds to travel to Hawaii for a stay with his family.
Bill Sutherland was a graduate of Harvard Law School who had
clerked for two years for Mr. Justice Brandeis; subsequently Sutherland became Tuttle's long-time law partner and his sister, Sara,
Judge Tuttle's wife.

Elbert Tuttle abandoned journalism as a permanent career
choice in favor of law study, although he supported himself, his
wife and his infant son by news reporting jobs throughout law school
at Cornell. He had a distinguished law school record despite his
family responsibilities, serving his final year as the Editor-in-Chief
of the Cornell Law Quarterly. When he and Bill Sutherland decided
to throw their legal lot together, the question of where to practice
arose. The Sutherlands had originally been from Atlanta but had
grown up in Florida. According to Judge Tuttle, Atlanta was "picked
off the map" for its future potential as a southern boom town, a center of business, and for its high altitude's ameliorative effect on
Sutherland's chronic sinus trouble. It was a happy choice for the
young partnership, the city and ultimately the Circuit.

Though the Depression soon hit, the law partnership flourished;
Sutherland specialized in the new area of taxation law and Tuttle became the firm's generalist. Even though it quickly became a pros-
perous firm, Elbert Tuttle took on a share of free work, even unpopular cases, as a matter of professional responsibility. In retrospect Judge Tuttle cited these cases as his most memorable in a
long career. He later counseled young professional graduates of
Emory University:

The professional man is in essence one who provides service.... His only asset is himself. It turns out that
there is no right price for service, for what is a share
of man worth?
So do not try to set a price on yourselves. Do not
measure out your professional services on an apothecaries'
scale and say, 'Only this for so much.' Do not debase
yourselves by equating your souls to what they will bring
in the market. Do not be a miser, hoarding your talents
and abilities and knowledge, either among yourselves or in
your dealings with your clients.

> Rather be reckless and spendthrift, pouring out your
> talent to all to whom it can be of service! Throw it
> away, waste it, and in the spending it will be increased
> .... It is not enough that you do your duty. The rich-
> ness of life lies in the performance which is above and
> beyond the call of duty.

In 1931, Tuttle, a Major in the Georgia National Guard, was
called out to a rural county to afford protection to a Negro prisoner
accused by a white woman of rape; a mob, threatening lynching, had
surrounded the courthouse where the prisoner was being held. The
cordon of troops led by Tuttle succeeded in masquerading the prisoner in a National Guard uniform and slipping him through the angry
crowd, out of harm's way, late that evening. The following week,
after a trial during which Tuttle's troops were again needed to quell
crowds threatening riot, the young Negro was convicted and sentenced to death. Tuttle's assistance, however, did not end with his
assigned Guard duty; later, he and his law partner successfully intervened on the defendant's behalf and secured a new trial from the
Fifth Circuit Court of Appeals based upon the mob-dominated atmosphere of the first trial. Moreover, even though Tuttle's duty as
appeals counsel in the case had ended and an organization retained
other counsel for the second trial, he did not abandon his client.
After conviction and imposition of the death sentence in the second
trial, Tuttle and others, still believing in the accused's innocence,
personally appealed, although unsuccessfully, to the Governor for a
stay or commutation of the sentence.

Five years later, Tuttle and Sutherland were called by Whitney North Seymour, who asked if they would be willing to represent
a young Negro from New York who had been sentenced to a twenty-
year term for pamphleteering on the courthouse steps in downtown
Atlanta; the distributed literature had been published by the American Communist Party. If there was one type of legal representation more unpopular in the South than representing Negroes accused
of raping white women, it was the representation of avowed communists, Negro to boot. But the firm agreed to take the case and,
after a lengthy legal struggle, the United States Supreme Court declared unconstitutional the Georgia statute under which the pam-
phleteer had been convicted.

Having established something of a reputation as a rare Southern lawyer willing to undertake unpopular causes, in 1937 Tuttle
was approached by the American Civil Liberties Union to represent
a young white Marine who had been tried without the assistance of
counsel in a federal court in South Carolina. This case, Johnson
v. Zerbst, became the most famous in Tuttle's career as a lawyer.
Convinced that an accused was hopelessly prejudiced from a fair
hearing by not having a lawyer at his side, regardless of the magnitude of the possible punishment, Tuttle took the case and even paid
the expenses of a Supreme Court appeal, after losing in the lower
federal courts. Ultimately, Tuttle convinced the Supreme Court to
rule that an indigent had the right to appointed counsel in prosecu-

tions in the federal courts for serious offenses not involving capital
punishment. Johnson v. Zerbst became the landmark precedent
upon which the Supreme Court in the sixties based its extension of
the right to counsel to all criminal prosecutions in state or federal
courts.

Despite involvement in such controversial cases, Tuttle's
firm surprisingly felt very little economic pressure to desist, perhaps because of a largely corporate and taxation practice in which
philosophical predilections mattered little; perhaps because of the
greater general sophistication of metropolitan Atlanta; perhaps because the firm was Republican in politics, making its partners tolerated mavericks in a predominantly Democratic South. Undoubtedly
Elbert Tuttle's unfailing courtesy and quick modesty also blunted the
blows of potential detractors.

Tuttle had become increasingly active in community affairs
and had developed an abiding interest in education. He had been
appointed counsel to the County Board of Education and to the Board
of Trustees of Spelman and Morehouse Colleges, two Negro institutions of higher education in Atlanta. When World War II erupted,
he was called into active duty and commanded the 394th Field Artil-
lery Battalion of the 77th Infantry Division throughout its combat
campaign in the Pacific. He was wounded in fighting on the island
of Ie Shima and decorated with the Legion of Merit, Bronze Star,
Purple Heart with Oak Leaf Cluster and Bronze Arrowhead, prompting a somewhat cynical Washington columnist later to concede that
Tuttle was "an authentic military hero."

After the war, when he returned home, he set out trying to
build the Republican party in Georgia. He described somewhat
facetiously the political situation when he had first come to Georgia
in 1923:

> [T]here were no full-time Republicans who could read and
> write. I mean just none, except a couple of post office
> hangers-on who would organize a group to go to the con-
> vention, and they played a very important part in the con-
> vention but never played any part in the election.... At
> any rate, I saw no reason when I came to Georgia to be-
> come a member of the Democratic Party, a white Demo-
> cratic Party, which was a paternalistic at best, and auto-
> cratic at worst, group of politicians that were running the
> state. Nothing 'democratic' about it at all except the
> name. So I just retained, considered myself a Republican.

Tuttle set about to organize grass-roots county, district and state-
wide conventions to elect the Georgia delegates to the National Convention of 1948, in accordance with the National Committee's rules.
Thereafter, in 1952, in the Taft-Eisenhower struggle for ascendency,
Tuttle was part of a pro-Eisenhower slate which ultimately was
seated at the Convention in a credentials dispute. After Eisenhower's
nomination, Tuttle actively campaigned on Ike's behalf: "In the

debates," Judge Tuttle remembered, "I said, 'Whatever the Republican Party may be elsewhere, in Georgia the Republican Party will be a liberal party because there can't be anything to the right of the present Democratic Party.'" He ruefully recalled, "It was true-- a white Democratic party. We didn't win on that basis, but we got 180,000 votes." As a party faithful and advocate in Eisenhower's campaign, in 1953 Tuttle was named General Counsel of the Treasury Department and served as the Department's representative on the Planning Board of the National Security Council.

But his Washington career was short-lived: when the Congressional authorization came through for an additional judgeship, Tuttle's name from the outset was bruited as the President's choice. While Judge Tuttle could be termed "a political appointment" to the bench, his credentials as a skilled trial attorney and an active liberal in the South were impeccable. The normal rules of conservative federal appointments in the conservative South were suspended when there was a Republican in the White House. Judge Tuttle later observed:

> The district judges in the federal system are really appointed by the United States Senators. They [the Senators] have absolute veto over the appointment of a district judge. And this means frequently that a President will appoint a person who's nominated by Senator Russell or Senator Talmadge or Senator George or he won't get anybody. Now, here on the other hand, a Republican President is in office; in the old 'solid South' the Republican President didn't have to look to the Senators, and they, in a spirit of live and let live, I guess, would not exercise their veto powers over anybody that a Republican President saw fit to appoint.
> I'm quite sure that if he just picked a stumblebum off the street, they'd say, 'Well, this just is too bad for us to take, and we'll undertake to block it.' But no one had to get the approval of the Senators before President Eisenhower appointed me. For instance, I didn't speak to either--it never occurred to me to even speak to [the Georgia Senators]. So this gave the Republican President the opportunity in the South to appoint people who were under no sense, any kind, of obligation, either philosophically or legally, or any other way to the local politicians.

Tuttle's appointment came in July, 1954, scarcely a month after the first Brown decision had been rendered by the Supreme Court. He wryly remembered that his initial reaction to his new appointment was that it would be a welcome contrast to the troubling world of global affairs in which he had been immersed:

> [I]t's a wonderful thing. They have a three months vacation every summer. They hold court around the circuit; our children are gone, and Sara could drive with me.... [On the Planning Board], we had gone through the fall of Dien Bien Phu, and it had been charged that Radford, the

then Chairman of the Joint Chiefs of Staff, had suggested that we drop an atomic or a nuclear bomb on the Ho Chi Minh Trail. We had been through all that ... And I told my colleagues good-bye, I was going to live the peaceful life of a judge in the South, and they said, 'Oh, you haven't been reading the newspapers!'

Judge Tuttle had had no prior judicial experience; however, he brought to the Court twenty-five years' experience in the general practice of the law, with administrative and tactical skills gained as the supervisor of the Treasury's legal divisions and as a Battalion Commander, ultimately a Reserve Airborne Division Commander with the rank of Brigadier General. During his thirteen-year tenure in active service on the Court of Appeals, Judge Tuttle refined a lean prose style learned from his days as a journeyman journalist. His opinions became identifiable by his careful delineation of the legal arguments involved. Early in his judicial career in a tax case, he outlined what he considered the duty of appellate writing: to be as clear and definite as possible in enunciating standards by which the public could guide their conduct:

> It seems to me that we should, therefore, either follow [a particular precedent's] teaching or expressly overrule it, in deference to the right of the taxpayer in this important area to have as much certainty as possible....

Judge Tuttle's race relations case opinions are carefully specific, leaving little doubt as to the Court's directives. Where he felt it was necessary, Judge Tuttle even dictated verbatim the decrees to be entered by district courts. Later, when he became Chief Judge, the Fifth Circuit Judicial Court promulgated an internal rule requiring all reversals to be accompanied by a written opinion. Chief Judge Tuttle's regard for certainty became Standard Operating Procedure. The three values which became the watermarks of all Tuttle's opinions on behalf of the Fifth Circuit were: a concern for clear expression in order that parties and the general public might enjoy as much certainty as possible in guiding their future conduct; a concern for a full exposition of the Court's rationale, outlining all arguments advanced, accepting or rejecting each in an effort to anticipate and avoid future relitigation of the same issue; and a concern for fairness to the arguments advanced by both sides.

No attorney representing even the most politically conservative forces in the community ever charged that while presiding in a case, Judge Tuttle was unfair or discourteous. In 1967 the Savannah desegregation case had again been appealed to the Fifth Circuit and it provides valuable insight on Judge Tuttle's judicial demeanor. Then a Senior Judge, Judge Tuttle was substituted at the last moment for Judge John R. Brown who was absent due to a death in his family. In an extremely awkward moment at the beginning of the hearing, a young attorney for the Savannah school board expressed surprise at the substitution of judges and orally moved that Judge Tuttle disqualify himself for bias in the case. Described by contemporary newspaper accounts as "hesitant in speech," the attorney outlined as a basis for his motion that it was known that while Chief Judge, Tuttle had once written the presiding district court judge to say that if a prompt hearing was not provided in the Savannah case, another judge would be assigned. According to the account, Judge Tuttle "leaned forward, folded his hands, smiled, and said, 'Don't be embarrassed, I'm sorry. I don't suppose any judge likes to sit on a case when it is charged he is biased or prejudiced.'" However, Judge Tuttle patiently explained that since his judicial conduct, the performance of duties which he was obligated to carry out as Chief Judge, was the only thing questioned, he would have to refuse the request: "'My oath of office,' he concluded, 'requires me to sit here.'"

In the tributes which were occasioned upon Judge Tuttle's becoming a Senior Judge, various aspects of his judicial qualities were praised, including his prose style, his fairness, his logic, his industry, his objectivity and his integrity. Yet both students of the Court and his colleagues concur that of all his contributions to the court's work, the most important one was the leadership he provided, beginning in 1959, as Chief Judge of the Fifth Circuit. His responsibility was characterized by Judge Wisdom as "shepherding a court of very unsheeplike judges at a time of social ferment, when the court, as an institution, was exposed to severe stresses and strains." Judge Tuttle's tenure as Chief Judge brought with it momentous changes for the Court as an institution. His leadership and example were to have great impact upon the other four Eisenhower appointees who shortly followed Tuttle on the Court.

* * *

To fill one of the three vacancies, President Eisenhower made his second nomination, Ben F. Cameron of Meridian, Mississippi. Judge Cameron was exclusively a product of the South: he had grown up in Meridian and journeyed only slightly north to Tennessee for college at the University of the South. Thereafter, law and athletics became twin passions which absorbed Cameron throughout his life. Immediately after graduation, he taught Latin and was coach for three years at Norfolk Academy, a prep school in Virginia; subsequently, he supported himself as Athletic Director of Cumberland University in Alabama while there studying law. Upon his graduation in 1914, Cameron returned to open a law practice in Meridian. As a young lawyer in private practice Cameron became quite active in civil affairs: he was a volunteer scoutmaster and ultimately received the Silver Beaver Award, the highest national award attainable by an adult scout leader; he served as President of the Mississippi YMCA; and he became a member of the Board of Trustees and President of the Board of Regents of his collegiate alma mater.

A life-long Mississippian, Cameron was somewhat of an anomaly as a Republican in the Deep South. He would later explain his political affiliation as a consequence of his having been an absolute teetotaler all his life. Dismayed with Al Smith's stand against Prohibition as the Democratic nominee in the Presidential election of 1928, Cameron wrote Hoover volunteering to serve in Hoover's campaign in Mississippi. Although Hoover did not come close to carrying Mississippi in the election, after the national Republican victory, Cameron was appointed United States Attorney for the Southern District of Mississippi, a position he held throughout Hoover's term. When the Democrats were once again in power nationally, upon Roosevelt's election, Cameron returned to his private practice.

By tradition in the Fifth Circuit, each of its constituent states was represented by one appointment to the Court of Appeals. When Judge Edwin Holmes of Yazoo City, Mississippi, retired in November, 1954, a "Mississippi vacancy" on the Court was created. Although Ben Cameron had never been an active organizer for the Republican party in Mississippi, he was, in official affiliation at least, a Republican. Thus, he was a potential appointee when President Eisenhower sought to nominate a candidate from among the few party faithful residing in Mississippi.

By 1955, after the storm presaged by the Brown decisions had broken, political leaders sensitive to the race relations issues in the South had begun to check a judicial candidate's acceptability to the NAACP, then the principal organization leading the civil rights movement. Henceforth, not only was the acceptability of a proposed southern judicial appointment checked through the American Bar Association and the offices of the United States Senators of the nominee's state, but the appointment was also subject to scrutiny by the NAACP.

Ben Cameron was considered acceptable by all constituencies. His NAACP endorsement was to prove an irony of history, as he later became that organization's bête noir on the Fifth Circuit, attempting to block every action of its organizers and lawyers. Judge Cameron is said to have attributed his NAACP support to the fact that he had once made a $100 charitable contribution to Piney Woods College, a Negro institution in Mississippi.

On March 23, 1955, Ben Cameron became a member of the United States Court of Appeals for the Fifth Circuit and thereafter served continuously until his death on April 3, 1964. He was a conservative in judicial philosophy and grew to consider himself the watchdog of conservatism during the Court's increasing activism beginning with Chief Judge Tuttle's administration. Judge Cameron was a conservative not only in race relations cases but in all controversies reaching the panels upon which he sat. He subscribed to the political philosophy that the least government, particularly the least control and intervention by either the executive or judicial branches of the federal government, was the best government.

The consistency of his conservative philosophy is apparent in a comparative study of his opinions. In a labor relations case de-

cided in 1962, Judge Cameron dissented from a decision reached by
Judge John Brown and Senior Judge Hutcheson affirming the issuance
of an injunction against an employer for violations of the Fair Labor
Standards Act. Even though the employer had committed himself
under oath not to violate the Act in the future, the majority was of
the opinion that a formal injunction nonetheless should be entered to
insure against possible future violations. Judge Cameron was incensed that the majority had concluded that the entry of the formal
injunction would subject the employer to "no penalty." In a clear
exposition of his political philosophy, which was echoed throughout
his race relations opinions, Judge Cameron responded in dissent:

> Implicit in this statement [of 'no injury'] is the thought
> that no good citizen should rebel at having an injunction
> stamped upon his back; at being placed in a position
> where federal functionaries will be constantly breathing
> down his neck; where his every action will be suspect.
> In this country many lives have been given in the complete
> repudiation of such a concept as that.... [T]he majority
> would condemn him to the odious status of a constantly
> watched culprit; and in so doing, it holds that there was
> no reasonable basis for the district court's decision....
> The situation thus lightly subscribed to is doubtless not
> unlike that facing Mr. Justice Brandeis when he wrote
> these words:
> 'The makers of our Constitution undertook to secure
> conditions favorable to the pursuit of happiness.... They
> sought to protect Americans in their beliefs, their
> thoughts, their emotions and their sensations. They con-
> ferred against the government, the right to be let alone--
> the most comprehensive of rights and the right most valued
> by civilized men.... Men born to freedom are naturally
> alert to repel invasions of their liberty by evil-minded
> rulers. The greatest dangers to liberty lurk in insidious
> encroachment by men of zeal, well-meaning but without
> understanding.'

Judge Cameron was a firm adherent of the doctrine of states'
rights. Conceding that some governmental control was needed over
the affairs of individuals, he believed that control was best delivered
by the government most responsive to the needs of its constituency:
the local municipality, then the state, and only finally, the federal
union. In a dissent filed again in 1962, this time in a controversial
voting rights case, Judge Cameron drew upon a speech of Mr. Justice Jackson, in which he had noted that states, "which have a greater capacity for self-correction," were thus less likely than the federal government in the long run to transgress upon individual free-
doms. Judge Cameron added his own observations about federal
voting records inspections which had been authorized by the Voting
Rights Act of 1960:

> It is not necessary to conjecture what he [Mr. Justice
> Jackson] would have thought of the unwarranted distortion

by the majority of Congress' words here, and of the spectacle of the invasion by the bright young men from the
North which is taking place in the South today. A kind of
providence spared him the pain of watching groups of
highly trained representatives of the central government,
brought from its seat of power in Washington, backing
their ponderous cameras up to country courthouses in the
rural sections of the South, photographing the records of
the sovereign States and hauling their elected officials into court to answer the variegated charges made by men
who do not understand--the creature turning upon the cre-
ator to rend it--and all with solemn sanction of Judges
who ought to understand.

In his judicial opinions, principally dissents, it was characteristic for Judge Cameron to quote selectively from authorities historically considered within the "liberal camp." The opinions of both
Brandeis, usually touted as an advocate of judicial activism, and
Jackson, who participated in the unanimous Brown decision, served
as grist for Judge Cameron's rationales, as did Lincoln. Judge
Cameron was a well-read man, a careful researcher whose opinions
were second only to Judge Wisdom's in terms of scholarly discussion.

Judge Cameron's early civil rights decisions, from 1955 to
1960, are temperate and well-reasoned. He possessed an unerring
ability to discern weak spots in the cases brought by civil rights
advocates, as well as those in some of the majority opinions of
his brethren on the court. During this period, he became the nettle of the court, warning of the lack of precedent for its escalating
activism and serving as a rallying point, quoted widely, by conservative district court judges. However, as the realization grew that
he could not convince his colleagues to turn from the course of full
implementation of civil rights legislation and Supreme Court pronouncements, Judge Cameron's opinions by 1960 had begun to take
on a strident tone as he grew more frustrated and seemed to tire
of conciliation and scholarly dissent. By 1962, in the James Meredith controversy at the University of Mississippi, Judge Cameron
entered four successive stays attempting to countermand orders entered by his co-equals on the Fifth Circuit, an unprecedented judicial action finally resolved by the intervention of Mr. Justice Black.
The following year, in a dissenting opinion in the Birmingham desegregation case, Judge Cameron launched a public and personalized
criticism of the Court's treatment of race relations cases, terming
the consistent liberals on the Court--Judges Brown, Rives, and Wisdom and Chief Judge Tuttle--as simply "The Four" and impugning
their character as well as their decision making. The controversy
engendered by these accusations widened from congenial accommodation of philosophical differences on the court to a deep chasm of
personal animosity between Judge Cameron and some of his colleagues. In his defense, his memorialist later observed:

Most of us remember Judge Cameron best during the

time that he served as a Judge on the United States Court
of Appeals. We especially know him for the stand that he
took in opposition to the federal regulation and control of
our public school system. He was outnumbered by the opposition on the Court that reached conclusions consistent
with Judicial opinion as it emanated from our nation's
capitol at the time. Due to his failing health, he was requested by loved ones and friends to take a more concilia-
tory position in this matter; however, it has been said
that Judge Cameron was 'long headed,' in that he was concerned with the future consequences of present acts and
felt that he could predict the future consequences of the
acts of the majority of the Court. Above all, however, he
was an idealist and those ideals of truth, courage and
perseverance which were an inseparable part of his personality ... which remained with him always would not allow him to yield to a position that he could not honestly
embrace. If by taking the position that he took and standing firm he was in effect cutting off his nose to spite his
face, his reply was that it 'was a pretty good nose and
not a bad face.'

At his death in 1964, Judge Cameron had almost totally ali-
enated himself from his colleagues on the Court; the personal rifts
engendered by his public denunciation of his brethren, principally
Chief Judge Tuttle, for politicized decisions had left lasting scars.
Even in death, reconciliation proved impossible. Only two members of the Court journeyed to Meridian for his funeral.

*   *   *

After Judge Cameron's appointment, Warren L. Jones of
Florida was nominated to the Court. Jones was born in Nebraska
in 1895 and attended law school at the University of Denver; he
graduated cum laude in 1924 and practiced there for two years. In
1926, he migrated to Jacksonville, in his words "to find his fortune." Although disclaiming that he ever found a fortune, he did
establish one of the largest, most influential corporate firms in the
city.

In his professional life, Warren Jones served as President
of the Jacksonville Chamber of Commerce and President of both the
local and state bar associations. He was an active Mason and
Shriner, an avid student of American history, and in particular, a
collector of Lincoln memorabilia.

When the deaths of Judges Russell and Strum had created
two vacancies on the Court, Jones was one of the first mentioned
among the Florida candidates, but no action was taken for many
months. After Judge Cameron's appointment, Judge Tuttle called
friends in the Eisenhower administration to learn the reason for the
hesitation and delay. According to Judge Tuttle, he asked, "Why in
the world don't you go ahead with Warren Jones' appointment? You

can't get a better lawyer in the state of Florida. He's been President of the Florida Bar Association and headed one of the big law firms in Jacksonville. Thoroughly well-qualified lawyer." The response was baffling: Jones apparently had been temporarily shelved through an unverified misapprehension that he was closely related to a Florida National Committeeman. Judge Tuttle noted, having himself been Chairman of the Republican Party in Georgia, that holding high political rank, much less mere relationship to a political leader, had never before been considered a disqualification. Shortly thereafter, Jones received the Presidential nod and took judicial office on May 6, 1955.

During almost eleven years on the Court of Appeals, Judge Jones was a "swing man," a gray horse on a Court composed of extremes in judicial philosophy. He acknowledged that he identified closely with Chief Judge Hutcheson's philosophy of adherence to stare decisis and felt that certainty in judicial decisions was perhaps more important than any abstract considerations of justice.

In the race relations cases, Judge Jones is a shadowy judicial figure. While he sat on several important civil rights cases-- for example, United States v. Alabama, an important voting rights case, and Gomillion v. Lightfoot, the political gerrymandering case --he rarely wrote the court's opinions, either for the majority or in dissent. Certainly Judge Jones's allegiance to stare decisis as a command of precedent enabled him to join in opinions of the Court where the path was clear, where prior work of other panels dictated the result. So, for example, in 1957 he joined in an opinion with his colleagues Brown and Rives which ordered the entry of an injunction in the Dallas desegregation case, premised upon the Circuit Court's prior decision concerning the New Orleans School system.

Judge Jones described himself as a strict constructionist of the Constitution who considered his obligation as a judge to be to interpret rather than fashion the law as a matter of policy. The oath of a federal judge, Judge Jones pointed out, required him to enforce the law, not "do justice." Thus, Warren Jones stands in contrast to his colleague, Elbert Tuttle, who embraced the goal of securing justice as both a proper and necessary role of a federal judge.

The contrast in view between Judges Tuttle and Jones is never more apparent than when they were both called upon to decide a close set of facts. In 1961, both sat together on a panel reviewing a controversial case between the NAACP and the State of Alabama, which involved the proper relationship between the federal and state judicial systems. Because they disagreed regarding the propriety of federal judicial relief, the interesting background of the case bears reporting.

In 1956, the Attorney General of Alabama brought suit in the state courts seeking to enjoin the NAACP from conducting its organizational activities within Alabama. Alabama subsequently moved for

production of certain records by the NAACP, including its membership lists. The local Alabama court granted a temporary restraining order against the NAACP's activities and ordered it to produce
the demanded records. When the NAACP refused to disclose its
membership lists, the local Alabama court assessed a fine of
$100,000 for contempt of its orders. The Supreme Court of Ala-
bama refused to review the contempt judgment. The United States
Supreme Court granted review and vitiated the contempt citation and
fine, ruling that the state could not require the production of such
records.

On remand from the United States Supreme Court, the Supreme Court of Alabama again blithely affirmed the contempt judgment on the ground that the highest court had been mistaken in its
assessment of the facts on the record. The NAACP again appealed
to the United States Supreme Court and, in addition, sought a writ
of mandamus: an extraordinary remedy which would compel the
Alabama Supreme Court to comply with the mandate in the earlier
case. Reluctant to take such heavy-handed action against the highest
court of a sovereign state, the United States Supreme Court refused
to issue the requested writ, but warned:

> We assume that the State Supreme Court, thus advised
> [by our previous rulings], will not fail to proceed promptly
> with the disposition of matters left open under our man-
> date for further proceedings, and, therefore, deny [the
> NAACP's] application for a writ of mandamus.

The Supreme Court's mandate became final on October 12, 1959,
but eight months later the Alabama Supreme Court still had not sent
an order dissolving the contempt ruling and restraining order to the
local state court. Upon repeated inquiry, the Clerk of the Supreme
Court of Alabama curtly advised the NAACP that "this case will receive attention as soon as practicable, commensurate with the rest of
the important business of the court."

Finally, on June 23, 1960, the NAACP sought relief from the
federal courts. In an action seeking an injunction against the enforcement of any action to harass or oust the NAACP in its activities on behalf of black citizens in Alabama, it asserted that the
"public officials of Alabama, including its judiciary, are committed
to a policy of maintaining racial segregation at all costs, including,
if need be, defiance of federal authority."

In support of its need for immediate relief to avoid irreparable injury, the NAACP alleged that, since the initial action had
been taken by Alabama, it had been forced to close its Birmingham
office, had suffered a loss of membership and contributions within
the state, and had been precluded from supporting black citizens in
Alabama who were attempting to assert their constitutional rights.
Judge Frank M. Johnson, however, declined to issue the injunction,
emphasizing that under the doctrine of abstention federal courts traditionally did not exercise jurisdiction where actions were still pending in the state judicial system.

On review before the Circuit Court of Appeals, Judge Jones, speaking also on behalf of District Court Judge Mize, approved Judge Johnson's rationale and noted:

> The Supreme Court and the district court have assumed that the Alabama courts will proceed in the discharge of their duty to decide this litigation with reasonable dispatch. It is implicit in the assumption of the district court that the State of Alabama and its officers, judicial as well as executive, will recognize and give effect to the federally guaranteed rights of litigants before its courts. We do not think we should indulge in a different assumption. If, as the NAACP fears, the Alabama courts render a judgment which deprives it of a constitutional right, the judgment may be reviewed and corrected by the Supreme Court of the United States. If, as the NAACP suggests as probable, the Alabama courts raise or sanction unjustifiable barriers to a determination of issues, or resort to other deliberate judicial foot-dragging, the NAACP will not be, as we will point out, deprived of a remedy.

However, Judge Jones did rule that the outright dismissal of the NAACP's petition in the federal court was error. Judge Johnson was directed to retain jurisdiction should other evidence come to light to support the NAACP's contention that its "remedy in the state courts was not merely inadequate, [but] is nonexistent."

Judge Tuttle, in dissent, had already had enough of the dilatory procedures of the Alabama state court system. He sharply characterized the ripeness of federal court intervention as follows:

> In this case, I would have not the slightest doubt that the failure of the Alabama Supreme Court to make possible further proceedings in that State's trial court by its failure to take the simple ministerial act of sending down the mandate for a period of more than eight months, and then sending it down only after suit was filed in the United States Court, presented a classic example of a case in which the assumption that the State court would act promptly to permit a trial of the rights of an aggrieved party has been demonstrated to be false.... I disagree with my colleagues ... requiring the appellant NAACP to participate further in the fiction that it had an opportunity to have a reasonably prompt hearing in the State courts.

This litigation between the NAACP and the state of Alabama was typical of most of the race relations cases of the middle period in the years of 1961 through 1968. The cases presented close questions of fact. The gross discriminations which characterized the earlier decisional period had been resolved. Judge Warren Jones chose Chief Judge Hutcheson for emulation: in judicial philosophy, he would withhold the jurisdiction of the federal system until it could be demonstrated without ambiguity that there was indeed no relief

available from the state system. Judge Tuttle, in turn, espoused
the principle that justice delayed was indeed justice denied and, upon
becoming Chief Judge, the Tuttle view became the prevailing force
behind the Circuit's work.

                        *   *   *

        John Robert Brown was the third Eisenhower appointee to the
Fifth Circuit and, like Judge Jones, he received his appointment in
1955. Unlike Judge Jones, however, he became a vigorous, forceful advocate of judicial activism in the protection of civil liberties.

        Though to all appearances a quintessential Texan, with his
bright apparel and engaging affability, John Robert Brown was actually born in Nebraska in 1909. He graduated from the University
of Nebraska in 1930 and two years later was elected to the Order
of the Coif and obtained his law degree, with scholastic honors,
from the University of Michigan. Immediately upon graduation from
law school he was admitted to the Texas Bar and became associated
with a prestigious Houston firm, subsequently to become the senior
partner specializing in admiralty, maritime and transportation law.
Judge Brown later pointed out that although he had grown up in
Nebraska, "twenty miles from water," he somehow "strayed to Texas
where I practiced maritime law for twenty years." When he was
nominated by President Eisenhower to the Court of Appeals, he was
by far its youngest member at age forty-six.

        When the new judgeship was authorized by Congress in 1955
there was great sentiment for a second appointment from Texas, the
largest of the states in the Fifth Circuit. Therefore, when President Eisenhower finally appointed another Texan to join Chief Judge
Hutcheson on the Court in 1955, Texas political forces were mollified. However, it soon became apparent that Hutcheson and Brown
were as different as possible in judicial philosophy: Hutcheson was
a firm believer in judicial restraint, while Brown has become noted
for his judicial activism. At the time of his appointment to the
Fifth Circuit, few observers of that Court could have predicted that
John R. Brown, the Republican-Texas-admiralty lawyer, would become an adept constitutional scholar and would eventually be recognized as one of the Deep South's four great civil rights appeals
judges. Judge Brown's opinions are characteristically direct, always decisive and occasionally eloquent. Typifying his firm belief
in civil liberties, in 1960 Judge Brown appeared for jury duty, refusing to claim the automatic exclusion from jury duty in state
court available to him as a judge. It is reported, however, that
Houston attorneys "wryly rejected him because 'a federal judge's
idea of the requirements for a search warrant is a little different
from ours.'"

        Judge Brown's vigor is not restricted to his opinions; on the
bench his questions to counsel come rapid-fire, are always pointed
and frequently caustic. In the tense hearings on what to do about
Mississippi Governor Ross Barnett's repeated flouting of the orders

of his Court, Judge Brown pierced to the heart of the problem with one question. He recalls the scene:

> We were very much worried about whether the President [Kennedy] really meant to carry out the order [to enroll James Meredith at Ole Miss]. We were going to be involved in public affairs and I told the lawyer for the [federal] government, 'I have to ask you this question: the Court has no means itself to enforce this order. Does the executive propose to support it? We are entitled to know that before we issue an order.'

As the years rolled by without significant progress in desegregation, Chief Judge Brown was usually one of the first on the Fifth Circuit to demand action, not analysis; real integration, not judicial theorizing. In 1965, after welcoming the recently issued HEW guidelines on implementation of school desegregation plans, John Brown cried for an end to delay: "The time for reviewing or redeveloping the undulating administrative doctrines evolved by us for the implementation of Brown is over."

John R. Brown was one of "The Four" condemned by Judge Cameron as the "judicial activists" of the Fifth Circuit. His near-impeccable record, discussed elsewhere, in enforcing Supreme Court mandates and evolving new remedies to combat discrimination--particularly in the voting rights area--will squarely place him, along with Richard Rives, Elbert Tuttle and John Minor Wisdom, among the nation's great appeals judges in the protection of civil rights.

But Judge Brown's contribution to the Fifth Circuit is far broader than the role he played from 1955 to 1967 as one of that court's staunch supporters of civil liberties, important as that role was. After eleven years on the Court, in 1967 he replaced Elbert Tuttle as Chief Judge. With his elevation to the Chief Judgeship, the full range of Judge Brown's talents were to be utilized; it soon became obvious that he was an exceptionally talented judicial administrator. The Fifth Circuit was faced with an alarming increase in appeal filings when John Brown became Chief Judge. Furthermore, almost immediately after he accepted his new duties, the Supreme Court stunned the lower federal courts in the South with peremptory new commands to order immediate, massive integration of the South's public schools. Possessing a gargantuan reservoir of energy and resourcefulness, John Brown was not to be overwhelmed by either his overcrowded dockets or the new Supreme Court integration mandates. Instead, he became a catalyst for action, urging the adoption of innovative new procedures that were to revolutionize traditionally sluggish appellate procedures. Convinced that the opinion writing days for school cases were over, Chief Judge Brown pushed his Court into frenetic activity. Following his leadership in the years between 1969 and 1971, Fifth Circuit panels concentrated on issuing orders mandating more and faster integration. John Brown reflected on that period:

We were desperately trying to dispose of a lot of cases
with genuine movement, an accelerated movement toward
integration--I mean integration, not desegregation--with-
out involving ourselves in a lot of conceptual discussions
about reasons. We were of the view then, and I still am,
that the worst thing you can do [in a school case] today
is write an opinion.

Frequently criticized for being more interested in statistics
than in cases, often charged with pushing his judges too hard and
failing to delegate administrative details, Chief Judge Brown nevertheless got the job done. He piloted his unwieldy court, bloated by
the press of business to fifteen judges, through the eye of a hurricane unprecedented in the annals of the American judiciary. Observers of the federal appellate structure consider John R. Brown
to be one of the premier judicial administrators of this century.

* * *

President Eisenhower's last nominee to the Fifth Circuit was
John Minor Wisdom of Louisiana, in 1957. Blessed with even a
name befitting a judge, he was born in 1905 into a wealthy New Orleans family. Wisdom was sent to Washington and Lee in Virginia
for his college education; however, like most Southerners bent upon
a legal career, he returned to Tulane University in his home state
for law school. He graduated from Tulane in 1929 with scholastic
honors and was elected to membership in the Order of the Coif.
Although he engaged immediately in an active legal practice, he
never abandoned an interest in scholarly pursuits--teaching part-
time as a professor of law at Tulane until his judicial appointment
in 1958.

His practice was interrupted for four years by the second
World War. He served in the Air Force, concluding his military
service with the rank of Lt. Colonel; he received the Army Com-
mendation Ribbon and the Legion of Merit. After wartime service
he, like his colleague Elbert Tuttle, returned to Louisiana with a
peacetime mission to vitalize the Republican Party in his home
state. Prior to the 1952 convention, Herbert Brownell, later President Eisenhower's Attorney-General, and a close friend of John Wisdom, suggested that Wisdom contact Elbert Tuttle, who four years
earlier had pioneered in the process of setting up a grass-roots
organization in Georgia, for advice about how to organize Louisiana.
Wisdom crisscrossed his state helping establish proper local conventions which would elect the Louisiana delegation to the National
Republican Convention. A pro-Eisenhower slate of which Wisdom
was a member was contested at the National Convention, and the
fight was eventually carried to the convention floor, with the available seats finally split between the Taft and Eisenhower forces.
Primarily due to the organizational efforts of Tuttle and Wisdom, the
southern delegations' support of Eisenhower was a sufficient additive
to his solid strength in highly populous states to give Eisenhower the
nomination on the first ballot. After the 1952 Convention, Wisdom

remained active in politics and was an elected Republican National Committeeman from Louisiana, serving from 1952 until his appointment to the federal bench in 1957.

In addition to his political activities, his practice of law and his part-time legal teaching, Wisdom found time to write scholarly articles on legal problems he had encountered in the disparate areas of estates, trusts and admiralty. His civil and community involvement also mirror the interests of a Renaissance man: he served as President of the New Orleans Council of Social Agencies, a member of the New Orleans Urban League, a member of the council of the American Law Institute and a Trustee of Washington and Lee University. He was also named by President Eisenhower as a member of the controversial President's Committee on Government Contracts (chaired by Vice President Richard M. Nixon), a group responsible for insuring that those employers who accepted contract work with the federal government did not discriminate for reasons of race, religion, creed or national origin in their employment practices.

After Judge Strum's death, Louisiana was left unrepresented on the Fifth Circuit Court of Appeals. Through his Republican activities and his friendship with Attorney General Brownell, John Minor Wisdom became a strong candidate to fill that vacancy, despite his involvement in the New Orleans Urban League and in the promotion of non-discriminatory employment practices which caused concern among important conservative Southerners. Although John Wisdom was the National Republican Committeeman of Louisiana, he had the endorsement of the National Democratic Committeeman, Camille Gravel. Gravel had lost substantial political influence due to his public backing of the desegregation mandate, but he was still effective enough to insure that Louisiana's two Democratic Senators would not openly oppose Wisdom's nomination in the Senate on grounds of personal privilege.

However, Wisdom ran into close questioning in the Senate Judiciary Committee, then powered by three arch-conservatives: Senators Eastland, Jenner and Johnston. Although there was a Republican in the White House and senatorial courtesy normally dictated acceptance of his nominees, by 1957 it was clear that the Court of Appeals for the Fifth Circuit would be a critical force in setting the pace and means of achieving compliance with the Brown decisions. Thus, Wisdom's liberal credentials were suspect;* however, the

---

*The events surrounding Judge Wisdom's confirmation for years have provided a lively subject for gossip among Fifth Circuit observers.[1] Prior to his own appointment to the Fifth Circuit, Judge Wisdom was instrumental in securing Judge Cameron's appointment to that same court by running interference for Cameron with Attorney General Brownell. Some feel that Senator Eastland was grateful for Judge Wisdom's intercession on behalf of his (Eastland's) friend Judge Cameron and, for that reason, did not oppose Wisdom's nomination to the Fifth Circuit despite a liberal [cont. on p. 56]

nomination was finally released with a recommendation of appointment.

After his appointment to the Court on July 13, 1957, Judge
Wisdom's first official act was sensational: on the afternoon of
September 25, 1957, scarcely hours before the scheduled grim ceremony, Judge Wisdom granted a stay of execution for Edgar Labat,
a black convicted of aggravated rape of a white woman on the streets
of New Orleans. Not only did the new federal judge extend Labat's
life, but moreover, nine years later Wisdom wrote a landmark opinion in Labat's case which upheld the contention that the defendant
had been denied a fair trial due to the systematic exclusion of
blacks from the trial jury panels in Orleans Parish. Whatever hope
may have been entertained by conservative Southerners that John
Minor Wisdom would not be an aggressive, liberal member of the
Court was thus almost immediately dispelled.

Judge Wisdom joined colleagues Brown, Tuttle and Rives as
one of "The Four" liberals drawing the ire of the conservative Judge
Cameron. But, by virtue of his background as a member of the
social elite of New Orleans, Judge Wisdom was less a victim of adverse community reaction than was, for example, Judge Rives.
While New Orleans was, without a doubt, a hotbed of racial strife,
hostility rarely penetrated the sanctuaries of Judge Wisdom's social
activities or personal friendships. As he later recalled,

> I got all kinds of letters, and I used to get telephone calls
> from two o'clock in the morning until four. And it would
> wake me.... [W]e had two dogs that were poisoned. And
> we had two rattlesnakes that were thrown in our yard, but
> I don't think that I lost a friend. The common greeting
> of my friends would be, for example, 'what have you done

---

record on civil rights and active leadership in the Urban League.
Others delight in repeating unverified rumors that Judge Wisdom
gained acquiescence from Senator Eastland by deceiving both Judge
Cameron and Senator Eastland as to the real nature of his (Judge
Wisdom's) civil rights beliefs. A widespread story has it that,
with his nomination in trouble with Senator Eastland, John Wisdom
called Judge Cameron and asked him to inform Senator Eastland that
he, Wisdom, would go no further in his civil rights opinions than
would Judge Cameron. Thus, the story goes, Judge Cameron called
Senator Eastland, repeated John Wisdom's assurances, and the nomination was confirmed. Thereafter, as he took a liberal position on
civil rights matters, Judge Wisdom allegedly explained that he had
simply changed his mind. The fact that Judge Wisdom seemed to
maintain better relations with Judge Cameron than any other member of the Fifth Circuit's liberal wing substantially undercuts the
veracity of the above story. It should be noted that Judges Cameron
and Wisdom, despite Judge Cameron's caustic denunciations of the
liberal "four," maintained a mutual respect and friendship until Judge
Cameron's death.

to us white folks today?' So it was all done in a kidding
manner. I think most of my friends understood that I was
just calling the shots the way I felt they had to be called.

Judge Wisdom became the Court's scholar-in-residence, elevating the craft of judicial opinion-writing to an art form. Just as
Mr. Justice Brandeis, when an attorney, had developed what became known as "Brandeis Brief" style of argument--the full articu-
lation of the underlying social realities of a case--it may be said
that Judge Wisdom created the "Wisdom Opinion": a characteristically long, detailed exposition of historical development and legal
precedent, with particular attention to factual detail adding local
color, all set in highly articulate prose. More than any other member of the Court, because of his progressive and quotable synthesis
of the issues, Judge Wisdom has become the Court's spokesman. In
every area of race relations law, it is his voice more often than not
which is heard and spread in the work of sister courts. Judge Wisdom wrote seminal opinions, discussed elsewhere, in jury discrimination cases, in voting cases, in public accommodations cases, in
desegregation cases and, for that matter, in landmark cases coming
before the Court in other areas of the law. In writing style, Judge
Wisdom is not a man to mince words. For example, he included
the following passage in an opinion enjoining the Ku Klux Klan and
its members from interfering with the civil rights of blacks in
Washington Parish, Louisiana:

> We find that to attain its ends, the Klan exploits the
> forces of hate, prejudice, and ignorance. We find that
> the Klan relies on systematic economic coercion, varieties
> of intimidation, and physical violence in attempting to
> frustrate the national policy expressed in civil rights
> legislation. We find that the klansmen, whether cloaked
> and hooded as members of the Original Knights of the Ku
> Klux Klan or skulking in anonymity as members of a sham
> organization, 'The Anti-Communist Christian Association,'
> or brazenly resorting to violence on the open streets of
> Bogalusa, are a 'fearful conspiracy against society ...
> [holding] men silent by the terror of [their acts] and
> [their] power for evil.'
> As early as 1868 General Nathan Bedford Forrest, the
> first and only Grand Wizard of the original Invisible Em-
> pire, dismayed by mounting, uncontrollable violence laid
> to the Klan, ordered the Klan to disband and directed
> klansmen to burn their robes and hoods. General Forrest
> was a Confederate cavalry hero, a man without fear and,
> certainly to most Southerners, a man beyond reproach.
> He announced that he would dissociate himself from all
> klansmen and cooperate with public officials and the courts
> in enforcing law and order. But the founders of the In-
> visible Empire had sown dragon's teeth.
> The evil that led General Forrest to disband the orig-
> inal Ku Klux Klan was its perversion of purposes by un-
> disciplined klans led by irresponsible leaders. The evil

we find in the Original Knights of the Ku Klux Klan is an absolute evil inherent in any secret order holding itself above the law: 'the natural tendency of all such organizations ... to violence and crime.' As history teaches, and as the defendants' admissions and the proof demonstrate in this case, violence and crime follow as the night the day when masked men conspire against society itself. Wrapped in myths and misbeliefs which they think relieve them of the obligations of ordinary citizens, klansmen pledge their first allegiance to their Constitution and give their first loyalty to a cross in flame.

Judge Wisdom's lengthy, erudite opinions required meticulous, time-consuming research and preparation. And, sitting on a Court geared to streamlined decision-making, he sometimes had difficulty meeting the deadlines for opinion production. But, for the most part, John Minor Wisdom was not pressured in his pursuits by his more pragmatic colleagues and was the man tapped, when the Court deliberated en banc, to write what it realized would be its most significant opinions.

In an era in which the Fifth Circuit has been the pace horse for the development of race relations law, John Minor Wisdom was the judge on the court who devoted the most thought to the proper role which any Court of Appeals ought to play in the federal judicial system. In a speech he delivered at the Judicial Conference of the Third Circuit in 1967, Judge Wisdom observed,

In this area of conflict the civil rights cases involve accepted customs of the community and the criminal cases involve established state procedures. It is, therefore, an extremely sensitive, difficult area in which federal courts must perform their nationalizing function. This is where localism tends to create wide differences among the judges on our inferior federal courts. Parochial prides and prejudices and built-in attachments to local custom must be expected to reduce the incentive of inferior federal courts to bring local policy in line with national policy. This produces differences in the respective roles of the Supreme Court, the circuit courts, and the district courts, depending on the extent to which the court is capable of establishing policy and the degree of its insulation from localism.... District courts are also understandably loath to change local customs or to appear to be getting ahead of our court or the Supreme Court.
To fill the vacuum, therefore, the circuit court must step in, often with very complete directions to the district judge. It is not that we are more courageous or more enlightened. We are not on the firing line, not as exposed to built-in pressures and allegiances, not as tied by birth, education, residence, professional experience and other ties to a single section of one state, and rarely do we have to condemn and enjoin our golfing and fishing

companions. The Supreme Court, almost wholly removed
from the local scene, is by this criterion, best suited to
carry out the political role of courts....

This district court's function in the body politic is to
stand fast at the pressure points where state policies or
community customs or the local interests of segments of
people press against national policy. When district courts
falter or fail in this mission--and I am sympathetic with
their position--the circuit court must bring the district
courts into line.

I am not suggesting that the court, according to its
notion of justice, may abandon reasoned, principled, neutral decision-making. The integrity of the judicial process
requires a court to respect the requirements of jurisdiction, case or controversy, standing, ripeness, mootness,
stare decisis, and all of the other time-tested restraints
on judicial activism. Beyond and cutting across these is
the natural restraint that comes from the realization of
the magnitude of the problem of balancing the competing
values: how to preserve the value of federalism in carrying out national policies while still giving effect to the
states as political bodies; how to achieve this aim while
protecting the constitutional rights of individual citizens
against government invasions from the Nation and from
the states.

*　　*　　*

These, then, were the men linked by fortune and political
appointment to serve on the United States Court of Appeals for the
Fifth Circuit during the early period of the post-Brown era. Four
of the seven were native Southerners; three were Southerners by
adoption. Oddly enough, in the solid Democratic South, six of the
seven were Republican; one Hoover nominee, one Truman nominee
and five Eisenhower appointees. They were all white, male and
Protestant in religious affiliation: four Episcopalians and three
Presbyterians. Six of the seven had graduated from law school
with scholastic honors. At the time of appointment, they were all
middle-aged, ranging in years from the youngest, John Brown, at
46 to Ben Cameron, at 65. Only one, Chief Judge Hutcheson, had
had prior judicial experience; but, taken collectively, they brought
to the federal bench a total of 204 years of legal practice.

Each had established a lucrative law practice and so undertook the duties of a federal judgeship at a substantial financial loss.
And, far from lionized, each incurred some measure of vilification
at the hands of their contemporaries: for the Court never went fast
enough or slow enough to suit all observers. In sum, all were
highly intelligent men, wise in the temper of the South, willing to
learn, and committed to their responsibility to uphold the Constitution and the Court through a perilous passage.

NOTES AND PRIMARY AUTHORITIES

1. For example, Peltason in his significant early study of the lower federal courts, Fifty-Eight Lonely Men: Southern Federal Judges and School Desegregation (1961) reports at 28: "But when Wisdom told the senators he had served in the Urban League merely to promote harmony and explained his service on the Government Contracts Committee by pointing out the committee had never invoked sanctions against noncomplying employers, Eastland announced: 'I am satisfied.'" The authors are unable to verify the accuracy of this account through any of the primary sources cited.

The definitive account of the history and development of the federal system is Frankfurter and Landis, The Business of the Supreme Court (1928) and Frankfurter, " Distribution of Judicial Power Between United States and State Courts," 13 Cornell L. Q. 499 (1928). Other primary authorities include Hart and Wechsler, The Federal Courts and the Federal System (2d ed. 1973) and Wright, Law of Federal Courts, ch. .1 (1970). The only available historical materials regarding the Fifth Circuit Court of Appeals are contained in Bloch, "History of the United States Court of Appeals, Fifth Circuit," Part I, 18 Ga. B. J. 123 (1955) and Part II, 18 Ga. B. J. 270 (1956) and Leslie, "Recollections of Seventeen Federal Judges," 15 The Alabama Lawyer 426 (1954).

Interviews, additional material:

Personal interviews with Judges Richard Rives, Elbert Tuttle, Warren Jones, John R. Brown and John Minor Wisdom were extremely helpful. Each graciously shared basic autobiographical material upon which this section focuses. A more complete manuscript, with detailed documentation of all sources, is available as indicated in the Preface.

Chapter 2

THE EARLY RETURNS: THE PROGRESS OF PUBLIC
SCHOOL DESEGREGATION: 1954-1962

> I might venture to point out ... that segregation
> is not a new philosophy generated by the states
> that practice it. It is and has always been the
> unvarying law of the animal kingdom. The dove
> and the quail, the turkey and the turkey buzzard,
> the chicken and the guinea, it matters not where
> they are found, are segregated; place the horse,
> the cow, the sheep, the goat and the pig in the
> same pasture and they instinctively segregate; the
> fish in the sea segregate into 'schools' of their
> kind; when the goose and duck arise from the
> Canadian marshes and take off for the Gulf of
> Mexico and other points in the south, they are al-
> ways found segregated; and when God created man,
> he allotted each race to his own continent accord-
> ing to color, Europe to the white man, and Asia
> to the yellow man, Africa to the black man, and
> America to the red man, but we are now advised
> that God's plan was in error and must be reversed
> despite the fact that gregariousness has been the
> low of the various species of the animal kingdom.
> --Judge Glenn Terrell of the Florida Supreme
> Court specially concurring in State v.
> Board of Control, 83 So.2d 20, 27 (Sup.
> Ct. Fla. 1955).

On May 18, 1954, the day after the Brown I decision was
announced by the Supreme Court, the Jackson, Mississippi Daily
News carried a black-bordered, front page editorial of mourning.
Headed "Blood on the Marble Steps," the editorial predicted, perhaps encouraged, violent resistance to the decision and laid all responsibility for any resulting bloodshed upon the Supreme Court.

Angry and resentful, most white southern citizens feared that
the social order in which they had grown up could not survive the
pending revolution, a revolution triggered by a judicial decision which
they could not or would not understand. For the first time in the
lives of most Southerners, a constitutional command became a dominant topic of household conversation. The first half-decade of de-

segregation in the Fifth Circuit became a time of tension, permeated with uncertainties.   No one, including the lower federal courts, had any sure answers about how and when desegregation was going to be accomplished and if, indeed, it was even inevitable.

The chief characteristic of this earliest period of desegregation was deliberation rather than speed.   Negroes had good reason to postpone a general rejoicing.   Just short of a century before, white slave owners had been forced to give freedom papers to their slaves.   Yet, as the newly freed Negro citizens learned soon thereafter, freedom in terms of economic independence was not negotiable. For most, "freedom" still remained a word on a document, only a paper right.   After Brown I, even the most impatient among the South's Negroes proceeded warily to test the viability of this new freedom.   Undoubtedly many Negroes feared a whiplash reaction from whites, igniting a renascence of raids and violent retribution. Other southern Negroes, like their white brethren, gloomily considered the discomfort that might follow such an unfathomable change in the accustomed social order.

Certainly there were a few white southerners who hailed the decision, but they were the same few who even before 1954 had been outspokenly critical of racism and its more subtle progeny, discrimination.   A somewhat larger group had misgivings about the morality, if not the legality, of dual citizenship in a country where equality for all was proclaimed as an immutable principle.   Others, perhaps less analytical, stoutly maintained that casting the paternalistic racial relationships of the South in terms of right and wrong was an oversimplification to be indulged in only by those not acclimated to the daily racial coexistence in southern communities. Of course, there were the vocal southern whites who denied that cultural differences between the races in 1954 could be the result of a century of deprivation and insisted that the members of the Negro race were inherently inferior.   While these were perhaps the archetypal reactions, every blend of these attitudes could be found in the opinion spectrum of both races.

Immediately after Brown I, there were a few glimmerings that the South might acquiesce in the decision.   The day after Black Monday in 1954, the Greensboro, North Carolina board of education publicly pledged that it would obey the law.   Hope for widespread compliance, however, rapidly faded.   Within two years, white resistance to desegregation once again gained respectability.   Segregationist organizations flourished.   Moribund Ku Klux Klan Klavarns were revitalized and white citizens councils mushroomed.   Opposition leaders were encouraged by strong statements of southern congressmen, who vowed to fight to the finish for segregation, and by the deafening silence from the White House, where President Eisenhower refused any public comment on Brown I and was widely rumored to be personally opposed to school integration.   On March 12, 1956, 101 southern United States Congressmen issued what was to be called the "Southern Manifesto."   This document denounced the school desegregation decisions as a "clear abuse of judicial

power [which] climaxes a trend in the Federal judiciary undertaking
to legislate in derogation of the authority of Congress and to en-
croach upon the reserved rights of the states and the people." This
much heralded pro-segregation white paper did more than simply
champion the doctrine of interposition and "states rights" defenses.
Psychologically, it lent the patina of moral rectitude to resistance.
The signatories, including all of the elected Representatives from
Fifth Circuit states, pledged their use of "all lawful means to maintain segregation" and "commended those states which have declared
the intention to resist." In the more colorful vernacular of the
"down home" politician, Georgia's Congressman Jack Flynt termed
the Supreme Court's desegregation mandate "a hydraheaded, five-
fanged, cloven-hooved, and fork-tailed combination of polecat, dog
and rattlesnake." Racial violence broke out in that spring of 1956
at the University of Alabama, spreading the following fall to Texas.
But for the swift and certain condemnation by the United States
Court of Appeals for the Fifth Circuit, greater violence might have
engulfed and even paralyzed the states of the Deep South.

Parallel with the growth of overt white resistance was the
gradual but perceptible change in black attitudes from passivity to
organization and activism. The success of concerted black economic
action, which began with the refusal of Mrs. Rosa Parks to take
the accustomed seat in the back of a Montgomery bus, was con-
tagious and soon spread to the younger generation of southern blacks.
The heralded black student counter-resistance movement began in
Greensboro, North Carolina, in February, 1960, when four fresh-
men at a state Negro college requested and were refused service at
a dime store lunch counter. Their stubborn response gave birth to
the new tactic of the sit-in.

* * *

With responsibility for enforcing the desegregation of public
education in six of the eleven Confederate states, the Fifth Circuit
was at the vortex of controversy. As far as the vast majority of
the general public was concerned, the validity of federal decisions
and court orders was open to debate, if not defiance. Not a single
bar association in any of the six states comprising the Fifth Circuit declared its support for the federal courts. The late Ralph
McGill, Editor of the Atlanta Constitution, was to observe that the
legal profession failed to provide "the people with an alternative to
the peddlers of defiance."

The federal courts in the South were encamped after 1954 in
a no-man's land. Litigants in desegregation cases were rarely
satisfied by the court's decisions, no matter what was ordered.
For blacks, the crucial word in the Brown mandate was "speed,"
while southern school boards accentuated "deliberate." Furthermore, federal judges began their quest of desegregation with very
little guidance from the Supreme Court. Although Brown II listed
specific factors of adjustment to be considered by the local school
boards, the basic direction given reviewing federal courts was the

nebulous observation that these cases "call for the exercise of these traditional attributes of equity power." The Supreme Court did not speak again in amplification of this cryptic mandate until four years later, and thereafter only rarely intervened in the evolution of Southern desegregation.

What Willie Stark, the fictional Louisiana Governor in All the King's Men, said about the law is an apt description of the frustration continually faced by the courts of the Fifth Circuit:

> I know some law.... It's like a single-bed blanket on a double bed and three folks in the bed and a cold night. There ain't ever enough blanket to cover the case, no matter how much pulling and hauling, and somebody is always going to nigh catch pneumonia. Hell, the law is like the pants you bought last year for a growing boy, but it is always this year and the seams are popped and the shankbone's to the breeze. The law is always too short and too tight for growing humankind.

The Texas Example: Peaceful Compliance and Violent Resistance

> The white Southerner is completely at the mercy of his conscience and knows better than we do that segregation is dead. The only thing that concerns the white Southerner now is how costly the funeral of segregation should be and when to hold the burial services.
> --The Reverend Martin Luther King in a speech delivered at Howard University, in April, 1962.

The early years of desegregation, as the law sought to keep pace with its burgeoning problems, are best understood by analyzing what happened in one state which typifies the developments in the states within the Fifth Circuit during the period immediately following the Brown decisions. The first school desegregation cases to reach the Fifth Circuit came from Texas, and, by the end of 1962, more progress had been made in achieving desegregation there than in any other state of the Deep South. Texas typifies all the various reactions to Brown in the early years after 1955, as well as the full gamut of means utilized to accomplish or retard school integration. There was voluntary integration in much of West Texas, organized opposition in East Texas, bitterly contested litigation in Houston and Dallas, and violence at Mansfield. Moreover, Texas gave to the Circuit two of the four Chief Judges during the period of this book's inquiry, beginning with Chief Judge Joseph C. Hutcheson and ending with Chief Judge John R. Brown. For all these reasons, Texas was selected as a focal point.

*   *   *

Texas is the only state that was an independent Republic before joining the union in 1845, and that historical fact flavored its
subsequent transactions with sister states and with the federal government. Texas was deeply split by the question of secession or
loyalty before the outbreak of the Civil War. Though a slaveholding
state, with at least 150,000 slaves contributing to the support of its
agrarian economy, Texas in 1859 elected Sam Houston as its Governor on an antisecessionist platform. In his first general message
to the Texas Legislature in 1860, Governor Houston spoke of matters that were still at issue a century later:

> [N]otwithstanding the ravings of deluded zealots, or the
> impious threats of fanatical disunionists, the love of our
> common country still burns with the fire of the olden time
> ... in the hearts of the conservative people of Texas....
> Texas will maintain the Constitution and stand by the
> Union. It is all that can save us as a nation. Destroy
> it, and anarchy awaits us.

When Houston refused to convene representatives to consider
secession, the Texas Legislature called a state convention. On
February 1, 1861, that convention adopted the Ordinance of Secession. However, because of the bitterness of convention debates, the
ordinance was submitted for ratification by popular referendum, a
singular event among all the Confederate states. Whether because
of fear generated by the Night Riders, resignation, or apathy, less
than half of those eligible actually voted. The final tally showed a
three-to-one sentiment in favor of secession. When Governor Houston still refused to acknowledge the legality of the secession ordinance, he was removed from office.

Though Houston misapprehended the tide of public sentiment,
his prediction of the bloody anarchy that would result from disavowal of the federal constitution cast a long shadow of truth from
the battle of Sabine Pass to the turbulent times of the mid-twenti-
eth century, when Texans once again contemplated the awful consequences of defiance of federal constitutional authority.

*   *   *

In 1955, the Governor of Texas was not a Sam Houston committed to championing adherence to federalism. Governor Allan
Shivers championed segregation in his campaign and in his first address to the Texas Legislature stated: "I recommend that no change
be made in our system of public education until--and maybe not
then--the United States Supreme Court gives us its complete mandate." As a consequence, the 1955 legislature adjourned without
considering any proposals concerning existing state provisions which
required separation of the races in the state's public schools.

Contrary to the Governor's cryptic "wait and see" attitude,

over sixty Texas school boards voluntarily decided to open with bi-racial classes in the fall of 1955. Small Friona, at the extreme western edge of the Panhandle, absorbed its three Negro school-age children into the existing school system. El Paso, with a dual system serving 25,500, quietly merged its Negro students, comprising approximately two per cent of the total school population, into its white schools. However, when the school board in Big Spring, West Texas, moved to integrate its elementary school system, it was met with a legal blocking action by local residents. Their lawsuit sought to prohibit desegregation as being contrary to the Texas Constitution and statutes. This opposition momentum in West Texas was dissipated somewhat when, shortly thereafter, the Texas Supreme Court declared the State Constitution and statutory provisions void insofar as they attempted to require school segregation.

When the Texas Supreme Court ruling removed the threat of loss of state funds to desegregated districts, voluntary school desegregation more than doubled by the close of the 1956-57 school year. Approximately 145 of Texas's 714 school districts were reported as integrated. Austin, the state capitol, adopted grade-a-year plans as did San Antonio, the third largest Texas city. Furthermore, there were many local decisions furthering progress toward desegregation that went unreported.

For those districts which opted for integration, the human problems of social transition remained to be resolved. In some localities, new black students seemed to win instant acceptability; for example, the only black student in Tahoka, Texas High School was elected vice-president of the junior class. Elsewhere, there were difficulties not only in student adjustment but also in inter-action with other still-segregated school systems and with a segregated society at large. A superintendent of another integrated system hadn't worked out the dance problem. The black students "attended one dance only. No incident occurred, but they came no more." In response to a questionnaire sent out by the Dallas Morning News, most superintendents of integrated school systems reported that black students had been fully admitted to extracurricular activities. The problems of social integration arose particularly with functions away from school. Superintendent Carl S. Chilton of Calhoun County noted that "some schools refuse to play games. Lodging and feeding on trips present difficulties and require special arrangements."

*   *   *

Several general observations should be made about the progress of voluntary desegregation in the two years following the first Brown decision. Whether because of a belated sense of responsibility for black children or because of a premonition of the approaching storm of Supreme Court action, many local school boards in Texas, and throughout the South, had taken enormous strides toward equalizing the physical plants of their dual systems. The improvements ranged from the barest necessities to the grandiose. In rural Mansfield, Texas, a dilapidated one-room Negro elementary school, well and privy were replaced by a new four-classroom building with indoor plumbing; in Conroe, a Southeast Texas oil center, a million dollar school with swimming pool, cafeteria "and all the trimmings" was built for the 700 black school children. Modern, fully equipped, attractive school facilities were appealing incentives to children and parents alike. One superintendent's report extolling segregated education in the early years after Brown reported, for example, "Our colored people were given an opportunity to express their wishes [and] they stated that they were satisfied with the schooling that they were getting. Our Negroes are apparently happy." Ordinarily, such self-serving reports should be read with skepticism. However, it is likely that, at least in some systems, blacks were reluctant to exchange the exclusive use of their long-awaited new schools for any sort of sharing arrangement with whites.

Furthermore, prior to 1956, effective resistance to desegregation had not yet developed. Immediately following the Supreme Court's 1954 decision the public appeared to function in a state of shock. However, within those first two years after Brown, anticompliance sentiment was building. In central Texas, the Kerrville School Board had announced a three-year integration plan to begin in September, 1956. The following April pro-segregation candidates won a majority of the school board seats, and promptly rescinded the policy. A random sample public opinion poll taken in May, 1956, by a private survey agency indicated that public resistance to desegregation was stronger than it had been in either 1955 or 1954.

The poll results were confirmed when, in a special two question referendum taken during the Democratic primary elections of July, 1956, Texas voters indicated by a 4:1 margin that they not only favored continued public school segregation but also endorsed the doctrine of "interposition" to halt what the ballot termed "illegal federal encroachment." As a pure expression of public sentiment, the referendum was a telling development; however, the affirmation of "interposition" is probably most accurately analyzed as approval, in coded language, for increased resistance by state officials. Undoubtedly there were few voters who comprehended the import of "interposition," that eighteenth century political doctrine which claimed that the several states had retained the right to "interpose" their sovereignty between their citizenry and federal commands whenever the federal government "exceeded" the limitations imposed upon it by the United States Constitution. All of the states of the Deep South urged interposition as a defense to desegregation orders at one point or another. However, this particular theoretical line of defense proved to be, as characterized in the flamboyant candor of Alabama Governor James E. "Big Jim" Folsom, "like a hound dog baying at the moon--doesn't mean a thing."

Despite the referendum stand, avowed white extremists in the spring of 1956 were only a few in number. The Texas White Citi-

zens' Councils, headed by Ross Carlton of Dallas, claimed a membership of only 20,000 in about fifteen Texas cities.

Another factor which should be kept in perspective in noting
early voluntary desegregation efforts is that they occurred primarily
in western and south central Texas, where there were the lowest
concentrations of blacks. In Huntsville, where, in 1957, the racial
ratio was three black students for every four white students, Superintendent Mance Park announced: "We don't plan to integrate soon--
that is in the next ten years." The largest percentage of black
school children which had been assimilated voluntarily into a local
unitary system in 1956 amounted to only about six per cent of the
total school age population. Statewide it was estimated that by
September, 1957, "integrated situations" would be voluntarily completed by school boards for nearly 500,000 white and 25,000 black
children.

The situation in East Texas, however, was a different story.
Ninety per cent of the black population lived east of San Antonio.
One out of every five children in the Houston School District was
black, and in Dallas the figure was one in six. East Texas was
the bastion of the most conservative political views in the state.
Here desegregation would be finally accomplished only by court
order.

*   *   *

In the summer and fall of 1955, suits were filed to end desegregation in the public school systems of Dallas, Mansfield and
Wichita Falls. The following fall, legal action was begun against
the Houston School Board. Mansfield, a small northeastern community missing from many Texas maps, gained a place in history
as the first school district in the Fifth Circuit ordered to immediately and completely desegregate its high schools. Moreover, because of the hostility that boiled to the surface and successfully
blocked implementation of that order, "Mansfield" became a watchword passed on through the South by the advocates of violent resistance.

Mansfield's population in 1956 was approximately 1,500, of
whom about 350 were blacks. Since 1954, the school system had
consisted of two elementary schools, one white and one black, but
only one white high school. Often overlooked in .the busing furor
of the 1970's is the historical fact that many southern school systems traditionally required busing to out-of-town schools for black
students and thought nothing about the propriety of its use to perpetuate segregation. In Mansfield, black students of high school
age were not only required to attend Negro high schools in Ft.
Worth, some twenty miles away, but the school system neither provided transportation for them nor reimbursed them for the expenses
of public transportation. The black students later testified about
the "inconvenience of early rising and late return," adding that the
bus scheduling precluded those who might wish to participate in extracurricular activities in their Ft. Worth schools.

In 1955, several parents, representing the twelve Negro high
school students, petitioned the local board for their enrollment at
Mansfield High School. The request was a modest one. No attempt
was made to seek the integration of the town's two elementary
schools.

Faced with formal petitions for change from black parents,
this East Texas school board deliberated about alternatives, as
vividly described in the district court judge's opinion:

> ... I see ... a rural school board composed primarily of
> farmers, agents of the State of Texas ... struggling with
> breaking the tradition of generations; opening their meet-
> ings with prayer for solution; studying articles in maga-
> zines and papers; holding numerous meetings; passing reso-
> lutions and appointing a committee to work on a plan for
> integration--making the start toward "obeying the law"
> which their abilities dictated.

Finally, the Mansfield Board announced the results of its deliberations: it would make official intersystem provision for the black
students to attend high school in Ft. Worth and would purchase a
special school bus for their transportation.

Since these administrative steps did not alleviate the burden
of the daily forty-mile round trip to Ft. Worth, the parents of three
black students filed suit in federal court on October 15, 1956, on
behalf of all blacks of high school age. District Court Judge Joe
Ewing Estes, a Ft. Worth Republican who had been appointed only
a few months earlier, dismissed the suit as "precipitate and without
equitable justification." He felt that the school board had made a
good faith beginning effort and, more importantly, held that the Supreme Court had contemplated a period of transition for all school
systems faced with desegregation suits, including Mansfield with its
small black student population.

On appeal before a Fifth Circuit panel composed of Chief
Judge Hutcheson and Judges Rives and Brown, the district court decision was reversed. Judge Estes was instructed to enter an order
that the defendants be "forever restrained from refusing admission
thereto to any of the plaintiffs shown to be qualified in all respects
for admission; and that it retain jurisdiction of the cause for further
orders at the foot of the decree." Chief Judge Hutcheson's opinion
stated that there were "no administrative difficulties" contemplated
in the 1955 Brown decision which would justify the delay of transition; instead, there was "only ... a difficulty arising out of the local climate of opinion." Such negative community sentiment was the
only excuse for delayed desegregation which had been expressly denied local school boards by the Supreme Court: "[I]t should go without saying that the vitality of these constitutional principles cannot
be allowed to yield simply because of disagreement with them."

On August 27, 1956, Judge Estes duly entered an order requiring the immediate admission of all qualified black students to the Mansfield High School. Two days later he refused to stay the order's immediate execution. While the federal courts had done their job, other voices of moderation in Mansfield were silent. Without calm leadership, sympathizers and members of a newly formed White Citizens' Council carried the day. The town's only newspaper published letters from Council members and editorials expressing extreme pro-segregation views. It castigated a handful of local ministers who had attempted to disperse militant crowds as "pin-head preachers who preach the brotherhood of man." Addressing one assembled crowd at the school, the Mansfield superintendent could say only: "Now you guys know I'm with you, but I've got this mandate hanging over my head."

During the week prior to the opening of school, crosses were burned in the Negro section of Mansfield and an effigy of a black was hung over the town's main street. Crowds estimated at from 200 to 400 persons were present during the first two days of registration, waiting for the three black adolescents who were expected to attempt to enroll. Again a black effigy was ceremoniously hanged from the school building; some townspeople carried signs with the message "A Dead Nigger is the Best Nigger." The local constable and county sheriff were present but made no attempt to dispel the crowds or offer escort to the black students claiming their right of entry.

On August 31, 1956, Governor Shivers ordered the Texas Rangers to Mansfield but, in a public statement, he made the motivation for his executive act quite clear:

> It is not my intention to permit the use of state officers or troops to shoot down or intimidate Texas citizens who are making orderly protest against a situation instigated and agitated by the National Association for the Advancement of Colored People. At the same time we will protect all persons of all races who are not themselves contributing to the breach of peace. If this course is not satisfactory under the circumstances to the Federal Government, I respectfully submit further that the Supreme Court, which is responsible for the order, be given the task for enforcing it.... Personally I hope that the U.S. Supreme Court will be given an opportunity to view the effect of its desegregation decision on a typical law-abiding Texas community.

But the Rangers, the constable, the sheriff and the militant crowds waited in vain. No black child arrived to register. With official allusions to shooting, intimidation and community hostility, the Negro parents decided that the two-hour bus ride was a safer alternative. The black litigants did not press for further enforcement of their order. Instead they withdrew their membership in the NAACP.

Governor Shivers later boasted that the Mansfield experience proved that racial controversies could be settled without violence. In a press conference, President Eisenhower responded by characterizing Mansfield's troubles as a local responsibility.

The Texas Example:
Judicial Intervention and Resistance

> Some day curious and shocked Americans will ask history and each other who were these angry and fearful people who reacted so unwisely to a doubtful threat as to be willing to relinquish to politicians the decision as to whether their hard-gained public-school systems would endure or die."
> --Hodding Carter, Editor of the Greenville, Mississippi Delta Democrat-Times, quoted in 65 Time, Jan. 3, 1955 at 42.

AVERY V. WICHITA FALLS:
THE ENIGMA OF INTEGRATION VS. DESEGREGATION

In contrast to the eruption in Mansfield, about one hundred miles to the Northeast in Wichita Falls, Texas, litigation was proceeding quietly which would alter the face of desegregation decisions in the Fifth Circuit for the next decade. The Wichita Falls Independent School District was a comparatively small system with a total enrollment of 13,000 pupils, of whom approximately 1,000 were black. Parents of approximately twenty school-age black children brought a class action in federal court seeking a declaration that they were entitled to enter a desegregated school system. They also sought an injunction prohibiting the school board from denying their right to attend the schools nearest their homes because of their race. Wichita Falls was residentially segregated, with most of the black families living in a geographical pocket served by the all-white Barwise Elementary School. In September, 1955, the parents had applied for admission of their children to Barwise, but their requests were denied.

A suit was filed in federal court in January, 1956. When the case came on the docket for hearing, the Board argued that the Barwise school had been desegregated.

The "desegregation" of the Barwise School provides an interesting insight into the touted compliance of the Wichita Falls Board, as well as the interrelationship between residential and school segregation. A new school was under construction in a white residential area known as "Sunnyside Heights"; it was finally completed for occupancy at the beginning of 1956. At this time, all of the white students in Barwise School were transferred in wholesale lot to the new school. The Barwise School was renamed the A. E. Holland School, in honor of a former Negro principal in the school system, and thus its overnight transformation from a white to a black elementary school was complete, even in name. The Holland School was opened on an announced policy of desegregation, though no white pupils had applied and it operated throughout the 1956 school year as an all-black facility.

The Superintendent of Schools testified that the black plaintiffs' children were now attending a "desegregated" school nearest their homes and that furthermore, "by midterm of 1957 it's altogether possible that the entire school system could be desegregated."

The issue before the district court was whether school board action, which simply resulted in removing the legal barriers to school segregation policy, constituted "good faith compliance" with the Supreme Court mandate. The Wichita Falls case raised serious questions about the duties imposed upon local school boards, questions which were to haunt the Fifth Circuit's deliberations throughout the next twenty years. Was a system truly desegregated within the meaning of Brown II when, although an "open admission" policy was announced, the neighborhood school concept coupled with residential segregation produced uniracial schools? Was the test of compliance the erasure of formal discriminatory policies or was it the actual mixing of the races in public school? Was it permissible for a board to locate schools in areas serving only all-white or all-black neighborhoods and thus minimize the possibility of a racial mixture in schools?

The black plaintiffs argued that, while the court might properly find that some actions had been taken by the Board to undo official barriers to desegregation, they were still entitled to a declaration of their rights, including an injunction requiring the Board to complete the job it had begun "with all deliberate speed." The Board countered by pointing out that the plaintiffs had complained only of having been denied admission to the schools nearest their homes and that situation had been remedied: the Holland School now served blacks without any discriminatory policy in effect there. Furthermore, the Board argued that these beginning steps were sufficient evidence of "good faith" to render the lawsuit premature and any court interference improper. Federal District Judge Joseph B. Dooley granted the Board's motion to dismiss the suit, observing:

> ... I think it would be premature for the court to interfere. Impatience and precipitancy of spirit are not, I am convinced, nearly so reliable a course as that of depending upon these authorities, once you have substantial evidence that they are acting in good faith and with a real and honest purpose to go ahead and without dragging out the plans by any unnecessary or vexatious breaks along the way.

The black parents appealed. However, before the appeal could be argued, the Wichita Falls Board reported facts that further

narrowed the controversy, making the questions for the appellate
court to decide even closer and more perplexing. During the summer session, one of the two formerly all-white high schools was
desegregated as a matter of policy as well as a matter of fact:
411 whites and fifteen blacks attended Wichita Falls Senior High.
At registration the following fall, all student applications were received on a racially nondiscriminatory basis. Yet no black child
applied to any but the three formerly all-black schools in the district.

On appeal the case was assigned to a panel composed of
Judges Rives, Tuttle and Cameron, and the first signal of diverging
philosophies among members of the court appeared in the split decision. The majority opinion subscribed to by Judges Rives and
Tuttle directly confronted only one of the potential issues inherent
in the Wichita Falls case. In affirming the refusal of injunctive relief, Judge Rives concluded that the Board had made "a [sufficient]
prompt and reasonable start" towards desegregation to preclude at
that juncture the entry of any orders. Judge Rives emphasized that
the actions already undertaken by the Board "were steps, but no
more than steps, toward compliance." The answer to the riddle of
what course of conduct would constitute full "good faith compliance"
was left unresolved.

*   *   *

The Rives-Tuttle majority opinion in the Wichita Falls case,
while superficially a mild pronouncement, is exceedingly important
in Fifth Circuit desegregation history. It adopted what came to be
known as the "Briggs v. Elliott dicta." Briggs v. Elliott arose in
South Carolina and was one of the original five School Segregation
Cases consolidated for appeal and argument and decided along with
the only publicly remembered case, Brown v. Board of Education
of Topeka. Upon remand for decision in light of the precedents
shattered by the Supreme Court mandate, the Briggs case was one
of the earliest decided. It was, without doubt, the most significant
post-Brown decision in the early years, until later repudiated in
light of the subsequent evolution of desegregation doctrine.

When the Briggs case was sent back for reconsideration by
a three-judge federal court in South Carolina, the resulting decision
very narrowly interpreted the Supreme Court's mandate. The
Court's opinion observed:

> [I]t is important that we point out exactly what the Su-
> preme Court has decided and what it has not decided in
> this case. It has not decided that the federal courts are
> to take over or regulate the public schools of the states.
> It has not decided that the states must mix persons of
> different races in the schools or must require them to
> attend schools or must deprive them of the right of choos-
> ing the schools they attend. What it has decided, and all
> that it has decided, is that a state may not deny to any

person on account of race the right to attend any school
that it maintains. This, under the decision of the Supreme
Court, the state may not do directly or indirectly; but if
the schools which it maintains are open to children of all
races, no violation of the Constitution is involved even
though the children of different races voluntarily attend different schools, as they attend different churches. Nothing
in the Constitution or in the decision of the Supreme
Court takes away from the people freedom to choose the
schools they attend. The Constitution, in other words,
does not require integration. It merely forbids discrimination. It does not forbid such segregation as occurs as
the result of voluntary action. It merely forbids the use
of governmental power to enforce segregation. The Fourteenth Amendment is a limitation upon the exercise of
power by the state or state agencies, not a limitation upon
the freedom of individuals.

The two most famous sentences of Briggs (the italicized portion in the quotation set out above) became shortened even further to
the shibboleth, "desegregation not integration." That "Briggs v.
Elliott dicta" plagued many later decision writers. Most federal
court judges were convinced that, in fact, the two words--"integration" and "desegregation"--were descriptive of two concepts which
could be differentiated. Unfortunately, the Briggs decision, including its famous dictum, was not appealed. Consequently, the Supreme
Court was not afforded the opportunity of approving or disapproving
the Briggs interpretation of its Brown mandate.

The Rives-Tuttle opinion in Avery v. Wichita Falls concluded,
on the basis of Briggs rationale, that there had been no abuse of
discretion on the part of the district court either in refusing plan-
tiffs' request for a decree declaring the rights of the parties or in
refusing to enjoin future discrimination. Still, they reversed the
grant of summary judgment and dismissal of the case from the
court's docket. Judges Rives and Tuttle held that a cause of action
alleging racially discriminatory policies may properly be dismissed
by a district court as moot only if "in addition to voluntary cessation
of illegal conduct," the court finds that "there is no reasonable
probability of a return to the illegal conduct, and that no disputed
question of law or fact remains to be determined, that no controversy remains to be settled."

In retrospect, several judges of the Fifth Circuit now candidly comment that this adoption of the Briggs theory that there was
no affirmative duty imposed upon the states to eliminate vestiges of
a segregated school system "held us back for years." Yet, there
are others, including judges, lawyers, and laymen, who even today
believe that the Briggs construction of Brown II is correct.

In this earliest stage of interpretation, Judges Rives and Tuttle had signaled the steering of a middle course: while the entry of
formal desegregation orders was not required, the threat of reacti-

vating the case was left hanging over the board to insure its continuing efforts. The Wichita Falls majority opinion was neither radical nor novel. It simply brought the Fifth Circuit in line with previous decisions entered in the Fourth and Eighth Circuits.

Despite the conservative approach to the duties of district courts adopted in the Rives-Tuttle position, Judge Cameron, the third member of the panel, dissented vigorously and at length. This dissent was the first major opinion on a desegregation case written by the judge who was to become the arch-conservative on the court. In this respect, the Wichita Falls dissent takes on added importance.

Here, at the beginning of the ideological struggle within the court, Judge Ben Cameron was at his best. Judge Cameron was a highly intelligent, well-read legal scholar and a stickler for procedure. Although he disagreed with the majority view on several points, the essence of this initial dissent and the crux of his philosophy in all subsequent desegregation matters was his refusal to accept the idea that desegregation cases should be treated any differently than other types of litigation. He was unwilling to recognize any dispositive differences in injuries to the rights of blacks after a century of miseducation or uneducation and those urged by any other aggrieved litigant.

More fundamentally, as is evident from the beginning in his Wichita Falls dissent, Judge Cameron doubted that the social transition required by the Brown mandate could be accomplished by judicial decree over substantial public opposition. He warned that judicial supervision could only exacerbate strained relations between the black parties and the school board, between black and white communities and, in a very pragmatic sense, would not be conducive to voluntary, amicable adjustment of what he termed "the whole delicate problem." In one of his most eloquent passages, Judge Cameron urged a cautious, limited role for the judiciary in the storm of desegregation litigation which was about to break:

> Practically every responsible person in a place of public leadership has stated that this problem will be solved only as men's hearts are reached and touched. Weapons [in the form of court decrees] have never changed the human spirit, or fomented good will, and the threat of force they carry has never nurtured brotherhood. To tempt one litigant to keep his eyes glued to the gunsight, thus provoking the other inevitably to divert most of its energies from constructive and probably generous action to preparations for defense, is to perform a distinct disservice to both and, more important, to the public.... It would be well if we should pause to ponder upon these words written by Mr. Justice Jackson in the last days of his life:
>
> 'It is not idle speculation to inquire which comes first, either in time or importance, an independent and enlight-

ened judiciary or a free and tolerant society. Must we first maintain a system of free political government to assure a free judiciary, or can we rely on an aggressive, activist judiciary to guarantee free government? While each undoubtedly is a support for the other, and the two are frequently found together, it is my belief that the attitude of a society and of its organized political forces, rather than its legal machinery, is the controlling force in the character of free institutions....

'Judicial functions, as we have evolved them, can be discharged only in that kind of society which is willing to submit its conflicts to adjudication and to subordinate power to reason.'

... By leaving the problem before us in litigation, we contribute towards reducing it to a level which assumes that it possesses only a horizontal dimension. The truth is that the vertical dimension is of transcendent importance.

DALLAS: TWO OUTSPOKEN OCTOGENARIANS

The key to how and when the vast majority of Texas schools were to desegregate lay in the ultimate resolution of the maze of litigation that entangled the giant school systems in Dallas and Houston. As one Texas editor accurately observed, "East Texans think of Dallas as theirs, and Houston is the largest city in the South; if these two yield, other holdouts will follow and East Texas itself will be next."

By the beginning of the 1961 school year a handful of black school children in both Dallas and Houston were attending classes with white children. But the process by which this epic, but token, desegregation was accomplished in each of the two cities is a study in sharp contrasts. Second only to New Orleans in duration, the Dallas desegregation litigation was a wearying process involving six years, twelve court hearings and the energies of eighteen different judges. In contrast, the Houston case surfaced only once in reported federal decisions and yet the initial desegregation of its school system was accomplished simultaneously with Dallas!

The district judges who heard the Dallas case, Judges William H. Atwell and T. Whitfield Davidson, were two outspoken octogenarians, both among the oldest federal judges still in active service. Judge Ben C. Connally, who drew the Houston case, was one of the youngest federal judges then in service; a reserved man, he could be severe when his "no publicity" rule was violated by lawyers or their clients. Leading counsel for the black parents in Dallas was the most experienced black attorney in Texas and perhaps in the South, W. J. Durham, Regional Counsel for the NAACP. The Houston litigation was guided by a young man who had only been in private practice for a short period of time; the Houston lawsuit was his first "big case."

Both were rich cities. Dallas was older, more aristocratic. Houston was splashy, the center of a nouveau riche economy created when its shipping channel was cut through to the Gulf. Pro-segregation sentiment was stronger in Dallas. A referendum on the issue showed four-to-one in favor of segregation, in contrast to the two-to-one pro-segregation vote in a similar Houston referendum.

The first official response to the Supreme Court mandate in Dallas was an announcement by the school board that there would be no integration for the 1955 school year. This board was composed of nine elected members, headed by a physician, Dr. Edwin L. Rippy. Dr. Rippy, who described himself as a "bedrock States' Righter," stated that although he "personally doesn't like the idea of integration, with my own emotions out of the way, we knew in 1954 it was coming, and we started preparing." Led by its President, the Dallas Board announced that it had authorized a detailed twelve-point study of the implementation problems and concluded that "it would be impractical to attempt any integration" until these studies were completed.

*   *   *

Dallas had operated a segregated school system for ninety-two years. In 1955, it was the second largest system in the state, with 120 school buildings housing over 93,000 students, of whom approximately one-sixth were black. Unlike Mansfield, a bona fide argument could indeed be made that dismantling segregation in the massive Dallas school system would take time. The attorney for the school board, Andrew J. Thuss, conceded at the first district court hearing "All we want is time.... What does one year amount to when we've had the segregated system for 90-odd years?"

On September 5, 1955, twenty-seven black children applied for admission to white schools despite the board's announcement that segregation would continue. Although they were futile that fall, those formal applications served notice upon both the board and the city that there were blacks who were willing to run the desegregation gauntlet. When the parents filed a subsequent lawsuit challenging the board's policy, it was evident to all observers that black demands would not lie dormant. There would be no respite for Dallas.

Black parents who attempted to register their children later reflected on the reasons for their lawsuit, reasons which could be described as universal parental concerns. They were apparently not interested in protest simply as a cause or symbol. The mother of Shirley Ann Bush, a junior high student, explained: "Negro schools were too crowded to get the training each student should have. The Negro teachers were overworked." The grandmother of another child whose application was rejected commented, "It wasn't just to get into a white school, but to get in one that was near": the black high school was across town, while there was a white high school within walking distance from their home. That grandmother also stated: "There's a difference in training they get, and more facilities for training."

The black parents' petition for declaratory and injunctive relief was assigned to the hearing calendar of Judge William H. Atwell, an eighty-six-year-old Harding appointee to the federal bench. Although Judge Atwell had announced his retirement the previous year, he continued to preside over non-jury trials to help clear the docket for an overburdened district court. While he was specially assigned to certain cases, it remains a curiosity that the desegregation of Dallas, a case of such immense importance with a potential of long-term litigation, was put on the special docket of a judge in semi-retirement. Judge Atwell was an avowed segregationist. He had been censured some thirty years before by the Brooklyn Bar Association for having shown racial prejudice and for having made, while serving as a guest judge, "improper and intolerant" statements to a black attorney appearing before him. In addition, there was evidence that Judge Atwell did not consider the Supreme Court's Brown decisions binding precedent. Three years after the first Brown decision, Judge Atwell declared, "The real law of the land is the same today as it was on May 16, 1954."

The first hearing before Judge Atwell lasted only thirty minutes. The school board attorney stated that he intended to produce evidence showing that efforts had already been undertaken by the board to comply with the Supreme Court decision. His offer of proof was summarily brushed aside by the court as "foolishness." Judge Atwell then asked if the lawyers could agree on the substantial equality of the separate schools for black and for white children. When both attorneys agreed, the board's lawyers asserted that there could be no claim of irreparable damage if the schools were concededly equal. Thurgood Marshall, who as Chief Counsel for the NAACP was arguing the case, replied: "We do not agree the Negro children in Dallas are getting an equal education. We only agree they have equal facilities." Relying heavily upon his finding that "equal school opportunities are furnished to both colored and white," Judge Atwell announced his decision from the bench. He denied the request for an injunction and dismissed the action as premature, stating that the board had not had sufficient time to work out a plan. The black plaintiffs were granted leave "to refile this case at some later date. Give them some time to see what they can work out, and then we will pass upon that equity."

* * *

Judge Atwell's refusal to hear evidence before reaching his decision, dismissing the Dallas case as premature, made the task of appellate reversal easy. Judges Rives and Tuttle combined forces in a majority opinion reversing the district court and directing Judge Atwell to afford the parties a full hearing on the issues. Judge Cameron again dissented. However, here, unlike his dissent in Wichita Falls, his rigid stance is difficult to justify. He took a hard line approach that the choice of remedies available to a district

court was either dismissal or entry of an injunction. He ignored
less drastic options, such as a continuance, that were clearly available. Moreover, he asserted that no right to an injunction was
made out unless the black plaintiffs could prove total inaction by a
school board. According to the Cameron rationale, the mere acknowledgment of the Supreme Court mandate combined with a study
of conditions was sufficient to preclude judicial review.

In 1956 came the second verse of the same song. On June
13, 1956, the Dallas school board instructed the superintendent to
continue planning and maintain segregation for the next academic
year.

The second hearing before Judge Atwell was finally scheduled
six months after the remand order from the Fifth Circuit. At this
hearing, both parties were permitted to put on evidence. The Assistant Superintendent testified that because the white schools were
nearly filled, white children would have to be displaced in order to
let in black children. He further asserted that, according to the
board's statistics, black children were one year behind white contemporaries in elementary school and three and one-half years behind in high school. The superintendent stated that the effect of
immediate desegregation would be mixed classes in all but one of
the senior high schools and in a large number of the elementary
schools.

Judge Atwell again dismissed the plaintiffs' complaint. In
this round, he criticized the Supreme Court for relying upon the
"claims of social scientists." He expressed the view that "the
white schools are hardly sufficient to hold the present number of
white students; that it would be unthinkably and unbearably wrong to
require the white students to get out so that the colored students
could come in." Although the board had previously asserted that the
facilities for white and black children were equivalent, they maintained that desegregation would "displace" white students and leave
them no "suitable" place to go. Furthermore, an assistant principal had also testified that "there were not enough teachers available
to impart adequate instruction to both white and Negro children."

Concerning this latter issue, Judge Atwell queried, incredu-
lously: "There is no complaint against the colored teachers, although we might quite appropriately inquire what would become of
the colored teachers if and when the colored students are taken
away from them. Is it possible, or, probable, that the colored
teachers would be hired to teach the white pupils?" The true test
of the equality of separate systems might well be whether the facilities provided for blacks were suitable for white children. Here,
protestations of the equality of instructional opportunity and buildings
seemed to ring hollow.

Overnight, Judge Atwell became a lionized defender of the
faith in Dallas. The Dallas Morning News editorialized two days
later:

Federal District Judge William H. Atwell handed down Wednesday a decision which may well have jolted the Supreme Court in Washington. Yet he did it in such masterful fashion as to make it both a devastating critique of the Warren line of desegregation opinions and a literal compliance with the latest of those opinions. It should become a historic rebuke to all courts which decree the law instead of interpreting it. [As Judge Atwell put it], 'We have civil rights for all the people under the National Constitution, and I might suggest that if there are civil rights, there are also civil wrongs.' (But if a white school child has any civil rights protected by the Constitution, the Supreme Court has not discovered them.)

* * *

Six months later, the Fifth Circuit delivered its own rebuke. In a per curiam opinion, the panel composed of Judges Rives, Jones and Brown, failing even to comment upon Judge Atwell's criticisms, quickly disposed of the argument that overcrowding could justify the wholesale exclusion of pupils on the basis of their race. Then, in order to insure that a third dismissal did not result on remand to Judge Atwell, the Circuit Court not only directed that an injunction be entered but dictated the form of the decree. Although the Fifth Circuit panel reversed Judge Atwell's decision, it had supportive words for the Dallas board:

We do not impugn the good faith of the Board, of the Superintendent, or of any of the school authorities. Indeed, we note with appreciation the sincere statement of their counsel that 'it is to be hoped that the aftermath which occurred in Mansfield will not be similar in Dallas.'
Faith by itself, however, without works, is not enough. There must be 'compliance' at the earliest practicable date.

The Dallas Board President discounted possible violence as a reaction to eventual desegregation in Dallas; however, he estimated that forty per cent of the citizens would get "unreasonably angry" and, as a result, would no longer support bond issues necessary for the continued development of the expanding system. He also predicted that perhaps twenty per cent of the white parents would pull their children out of public schools and enroll them in private institutions. Dr. Rippy concluded a public statement by observing:

The Dallas Board is somewhat proud of the fact that it has been an exponent of 'gradualism' in this matter, as contrasted with the precipitate desegregation without planning of other communities and the 'never, never' attitude of others. Dallas has no ambition to be the first to undertake this change, but it does have high hopes that when the change is made, it will be done well.

However bright were the prospects of eventual desegregation in Dallas, on August 13, 1957, one thing was certain: there would not be desegregation during the 1957-58 term. The formal announcement of no change was greeted with applause by many of the citizens who crowded into the board room. One of those in attendance was Joe Pool, a Dallas Representative to the Texas Legislature. He was a key figure in a drive during the last session for legislation to cut off State support for any system which desegregated without prior approval by a local referendum on the issue. Representative Pool felt vindicated by the board's decision: "This has proved that Dallas has a school board that has lots of common sense and that knows how to handle the situation.... We've been legislating, telling you folks what to do, now I've come to see how you do it."

Whatever inclination the Dallas board and its superintendent might have had to plan for inevitable desegregation, the legislature had made their job much more difficult. In addition to fears voiced about future local voter disapproval of bond issues, the board had some real reason for concern about the threatened loss of at least $2 million in support from the State if a school system desegregated. The board requested a rehearing from the Fifth Circuit in view of the dilemma it felt it faced. If it complied with the injunction, it would lose funds desperately needed to support the system; if it ignored the injunction, it possibly would be faced with contempt citations and certainly with the loss of control over the timing and methods of accomplishing desegregation. Given the doubtful validity of any statute which would subject a constitutional mandate to popular approval, the Fifth Circuit panel, still composed of Judges Rives, Jones and Brown, discounted the proposition that the board was faced with a true dilemma. As they observed in denying the motion for rehearing, "That Act [of the legislature], of course, cannot operate to relieve the members of this Court of their sworn duty to support the Constitution of the United States, the same duty which rests upon the members of the several state legislatures and all executive and judicial officers of the several states." At least nine other southern states had enacted similar statutes aimed at deterring local initiative in desegregation. In its refusal to grant a rehearing, the Fifth Circuit became the first appellate court to deny the defense of economic retaliation by the states, predating similar decisions by the Fourth Circuit Court of Appeals and ultimately the Supreme Court.

* * *

The Dallas board did not have long to debate the existence of a dilemma. On September 5, 1957, two years to the day after black children had first sought admission to white schools, Judge Atwell entered an order which made all subsequent mandates anticlimactic. In a bizarre move which stunned everyone connected with the Dallas litigation, Judge Atwell ordered system-wide desegregation to commence within four months. Judge Rives subsequently described the four-minute hearing before Judge Atwell as follows:

After he had received the opinion of [this] Court, but before the mandate, Judge Atwell called counsel and made
the following statement: 'It is difficult, Gentlemen, for
me to approve this order, but this is a land of the law
and it is my duty to do what I am ordered to do by the
higher Court, and I therefore ask you ... to prepare an
order ... for the integration to be permitted at the coming mid-winter term of the schools and not before that
time....' [W]ithout inviting suggestions or arguments
from counsel on anything save as scriveners in the drafting of an order to effectuate his prior determinations, the
District Judge thus picked the mid-winter school term of
1957-58 as the time to start system-wide desegregation.

U. Simpson Tate, one of the attorneys representing the black
plaintiffs, was elated and reacted to this unexpected boon by declaring: "This suit illustrates the greatness of America, illustrates
that wherever people have sharp differences they can come into a
public forum, debate in orderly fashion and settle by law." Joseph
Thuss, the school board counsel, was not assured that anything approaching reasoned decision-making had occurred; instead, he later
argued that the order was not only capricious, "no more than a judicial guess," but also "unthinkable and disruptive.... [I]t is critical and precipitate action having no evidence for its support."
The reaction of the public was similarly divided. The President of
the Public Affairs Luncheon Club, an organization which had consistently opposed integration, commented: "We regret that Judge
William Hawley Atwell, who has had such a distinguished career
and who has always fought for the preservation of the highest traditions of the South, was forced to bow to the decision of a higher
court." The President of the Young Democratic Club of Dallas
County reported that this organization "is gratified by the decision"
and noted that as early as the previous February, it had petitioned
the school board to integrate its schools and teachers "immediately."
The board's appeal to the Fifth Circuit was subsequently expedited.
Barely ten weeks later, Judges Rives, Jones and Brown heard arguments on whether Judge Atwell's order should stand. Judge Brown,
in particular, expressed concern over the absence from the record
of any discussion between court and counsel about the particular
date chosen. Mr. Thuss replied for the board, "Judge Atwell just
came in and said he wanted this judgment.... It didn't take but a
few minutes." The following exchange then reportedly occurred:

Judge Brown pressed Thuss as to whether the board was
actually working toward integration. Thuss quoted [school
board President] Rippy as having said that Dallas would
conform to the U.S. Supreme Court ruling, even though
the opinion was not popular, but it would take time to protect the welfare of all children, white and Negro.
'You've taken two years and you're not a step further,'
said Judge Brown.
Judge Warren L. Jones ... asked Thuss when an integration plan would be completed.

'I think this coming summer will produce a plan,'
Thuss replied.

...

Judge Richard T. Rives ... told Durham [counsel for
the Negro parents], 'As I understand it the judge did not
offer an opportunity to the school board to present evidence.'
And Judge Brown observed that Atwell's action 'certainly is not in the mandate' of the appeals court.
The hearing ended with Judge Jones asking Thuss:
'What do you think deliberate speed means in regard to
this situation?'
Thuss smiled, but did not attempt to define the
phrase.

* * *

One month later the Fifth Circuit Court reversed Judge Atwell for the third time, on this occasion observing that his immediate desegregation order had not allowed the board enough time to
prepare for the transition. Slowing the rate of accelerated desegregation seemed anomalous action from a Court surrounded on all
sides by reluctant school boards, intransigent state legislatures and
defiant state executives. This decision generated confusion among
litigants and invited the interpretation that the Fifth Circuit was
backing down from its insistence upon swift compliance. As one national news magazine construed it:

To the layman, the unanimous decision of the 3-judge appeals court might have seemed inconsistent. For originally, Judge Atwell had ruled against integration and he
had been overturned by the same court only last September. But now, after he has set the January date for compliance, the court found him wrong again.... But was
there something more to the decision than pure legality?
Did it, perhaps, presage a softer attitude by the courts of
the South toward the 'all deliberate speed' mandate of the
U.S. Supreme Court? Governor Faubus of Arkansas suggested that the Little Rock School Board should now appeal
the court decision; and Washington observers surmise that
the shock of Little Rock 'undoubtedly had instilled a sense
of caution in the judiciary.'
What the Dallas decision may mean is that the courts
will seek to supply a small 'rule of reason'--reason founded
on the realization that voluntary integration has about
reached its limit and that compulsory integration will take
greater community acceptance. If this is true, then the
South may be in for a breather.

There were in fact enormous problems attendant upon the desegregation of a school system like Dallas, which had now grown to

a size of almost 100,000 pupils and which had 141 school facilities in operation. However, school officials had already taken some steps forward toward compliance. Before reversal occurred, the Superintendent announced that the system would no longer accept black students on a tuition basis from other districts. Further evidence that the board would have met the district court's deadline can be found in contemporary statements issued by the board President. There was an extant survey detailing the amount of desegregation which could be expected in each Dallas school; that survey stated that "all methods of integration have been studied and the techniques utilized in those cities which have been desegregated have been analyzed in detail." Moreover, it appeared that all that remained was for the board to announce the plan already decided. Dr. Rippy acknowledged, "I do not have the authority to announce at this time the method of integration which is felt to be to the best interest of the school children of all races. At the appropriate time such will be announced and the counsel of all qualified individuals and groups will be solicited, and the cooperation of local, county, and state authorities will be requested."

In view of the two-year study and evidence of a plan for desegregation, it may be asked why the Court of Appeals did not let Judge Atwell's order stand? It is true that Judge Atwell had done more than the Fifth Circuit's mandate required. In its remand the Fifth Circuit had fixed no date more specific than "from and after such time as may be necessary to make arrangements for admission of children to such schools on a racially nondiscriminatory basis with all deliberate speed." There is also no doubt that Judge Atwell had misinterpreted not only the command of the appellate court but also the impact of his own order. Perhaps these flaws were sufficient to justify the appellate reversal in an effort to avoid the risk of eventual reversal by the Supreme Court. Undoubtedly, the Circuit panel was also influenced by the necessity of insuring a proper, if painstaking, supervision by its district courts in the future, even at the cost of appearing to condone dilatory conduct by local school boards.

Judge Rives enunciated for the first time, in this third opinion by the Fifth Circuit in the Dallas case, precisely what a district court was expected to do once it had entered a threshold injunction:

> [B]efore a more specific date should be fixed and before
> any orders or judgments should be entered to require compliance with the judgment directed in [the] mandate, the
> school authorities should be accorded a reasonable further
> opportunity promptly to meet their primary responsibility
> in the premises, and then if the plaintiffs ... should
> claim that the school authorities have failed in any respect
> to perform their duty, there should be a full and fair hearing in which evidence may be offered by any and all parties
> and further that the Court should retain jurisdiction to require compliance with its judgment.

*   *   *

The Dallas board enjoyed this reprieve for the next eighteen months; no more was heard about the plan purportedly to be unveiled during the summer of 1958. Finally, in what was termed a surprise move in Dallas, black attorneys filed a motion for further relief on May 20, 1959, in which they demanded immediate desegregation of the system. "The purpose of the motion is obvious," commented one close observer. "All it is, is to get the school board off a dead center course and get it moving."

For this, the fourth round of Dallas litigation, there had been a change in the dramatis personae. A new attorney represented the school board and a new judge presided over the District Court. Judge Atwell had been replaced by his somewhat younger colleague in the Northern District of Texas, Judge T. Whitfield Davidson, an eighty-two-year-old Roosevelt appointee to the federal court, who had been in semi-retirement since 1954. Judge Davidson was to prove no more inclined than Judge Atwell to be the architect of social change in the South. He later observed from the bench, "The southern white gentleman does not feel unkindly toward the Negro .... The Supreme Court has placed your state, your country, and your schools ... to use a street term ... over the barrel."

At the hearing before Judge Davidson on July 30, 1959, the plaintiffs modified their original adamant stance for immediate desegregation, now seeking only that the board present a plan which would provide for the beginning of desegregation by September, 1960. The new Board attorney requested a further delay, arguing, "They are not entitled to the relief they pray for today, they are in too big a hurry." Judge Davidson responded, in an attempt to mollify the board:

> It is not urged before September, 1960. Just what problem will be confronting you ... by the fall of 1960, the court can hardly foresee. I can only say to you, put your house in order for integration, for it is ahead of you.... The School Board should further study this question and perhaps take further action, maybe an election.

Precisely when desegregation would come to Dallas was not spelled out. The district court ordered no plan and scheduled no date for definitive action. Instead, Judge Davidson continued the case and retained jurisdiction until April, 1960.

The plaintiffs again appealed Judge Davidson's non-action on the five-year-old Dallas case to the Fifth Circuit. Their case was argued the following February by Constance Baker Motley who, along with Thurgood Marshall, acted as roving troubleshooter for the Inc. Fund in all its early major desegregation cases. The plaintiffs argued that the school board could "go on indefinitely" delaying desegregation: "We are not asking the whole system be desegregated, but we are asking for an immediate start." Counsel

for the Dallas board countered with a two-pronged defense. He
urged first that until the Texas antidesegregation laws were clarified, the entire school system "would be thrown out of kilter by a
desegregation order. We could never put back the year of schooling deprived the other children." Secondly, and more importantly
from the development of legal doctrine, Board counsel contended that
the Court of Appeals did not have the power to intervene since Judge
Davidson had recessed the previous hearing, postponing a final decision until additional evidence regarding the plan could be submitted.

The question of appellate jurisdiction was intriguing. The
Fifth Circuit's foresight in insisting upon the entry of a threshold
injunction, even of an undated variety, was vindicated by this turn
of events in the Dallas litigation. Courts of Appeals are granted
the power to decide only final judgments and extraordinary district
court orders "granting, continuing, modifying, refusing or dissolving injunctions, or refusing to dissolve or modify injunctions." Here,
appellate jurisdiction could be sustained because Judge Davidson had
refused plaintiff's request that the original injunction now be modified to require school board performance by a certain date. If the
original injunction of September 5, 1957, had not been entered in the
Dallas case, the later action of the district court in simply delaying
further activity might well have been beyond the reach of the Court
of Appeals.

In remanding the case to Judge Davidson, Judges Rives and
Wisdom performed radical surgery on his original order. Curing
what was termed "an error of omission," they inserted into the original injunction the salient requirement that the board submit, within thirty days, a plan for effectuating transition to a racially nondiscriminatory school system. Thereafter, within a second period
of thirty days, a full hearing would be held to determine whether
the plan would accomplish desegregation with all deliberate speed.
It was apparent that time had now run out for Dallas. Judge Rives
observed during oral argument: "We've been engaging in legal literature for five years without action.... [A]ctually the first step has
not been taken on this matter. The school board has not yet come
forward with a desegregation plan. Words without deeds are not
enough."

*   *   *

The hearing before Judge Davidson on May 25, 1960, produced still more unprecedented judicial action. The plan presented
by the school board was the most modest plan then accorded judicial
approval anywhere in any major desegregation cases. It called for
a twelve-year, stair-step plan beginning with the first grade in
September, 1961, and a grade per year thereafter. A twelve-year
plan, the longest transitional period in existence, was in operation
for the City of Nashville and for Delaware's statewide school system.

A second provision of the board's plan, aimed at minimizing
the effects of desegregation, was a transfer provision whereby race

was recognized as an absolute ground for pupil transfers. In a verbatim copying of the "Nashville Transfer" policy, out-of-residence
zone placements would have been approved:

> (1) when a white student would otherwise be required to
> attend a school previously serving colored students
> only;
> [or]
> (2) when a colored student would otherwise be required
> to attend a school previously serving white students
> only;
> [or]
> (3) when a student would otherwise be required to attend
> a school where the majority of students of that school
> or in his or her grade are of different race.

Finally, implementation of the Plan was expressly made dependent
upon an affirmative result from a local referendum.

The attorneys for both sides completed their cases within the
first twenty minutes of the district court hearing. W. J. Durham,
co-counsel with Thurgood Marshall, called the board's proposal "no
plan at all." Thereafter, in an hour-and-a-half speech from the
bench, Judge Davidson refused to sanction the board's plan, not because it was too long a transition or because its potential effectiveness was vitiated by its transfer provisions, but because:

> The 'Dallas Plan' would lead, in the opinion and the light
> of history and unquestionable sources to an amalgamation
> of the races.... In no clime and in no nation have the
> races ever amalgamated that it has not been to the dis-
> advantage of both.... When the President's guard was
> shot, when the halls of Congress were shot up, they were
> not from Negroes that were raised in the South. They
> were from the integrated people of Puerto Rico.

According to one contemporary report, Judge Davidson also repeatedly called for blacks to be "patient," citing the white exodus from
the desegregated schools of Washington, D.C. as an example of
what impatience can cause. But his dissatisfaction with the submitted plan was not manifested simply in rhetoric; Judge Davidson
then produced his own proposal for "voluntary" integration:

> Some educator has advanced the following plan which
> has appeal: That the school authorities set aside schools
> within the city limits in which all those of either race who
> desire integration may be enrolled by placement arrange-
> ment and transportation given to that school and that oth-
> er like schools for different grades be set aside maybe
> elsewhere in the city. Since the children would be there
> together by their parents' consent there is at least one
> reason why good will would prevail in these schools that
> might not prevail in schools where children are brought

together by force and without the approval of their parents. If the plan proved popular, then additional integrated schools would through the years follow, not more than 12 years.

As one observer reported, "Neither attorneys for the school board nor the objecting Negro plaintiffs appeared to understand the judge's unexpected decision.... Thurgood Marshall of New York City, counsel for the NAACP, displayed the most obvious look of surprise. 'I don't know what he [the judge] said,' he declared, grabbing his brief case. 'Just let me out of here.'" W. J. Durham, co-counsel, observed simply, "There can be no integration within segregation."

What had originated as a suggestion became a judicial command: twice the Dallas school board later submitted both its plan and Judge Davidson's so-called "salt and pepper plan," and twice Judge Davidson rejected the school system's plan. His final order approved his own "salt and pepper plan" for Dallas.

* * *

For the fifth time, attorneys for the black school children of Dallas appealed to the Fifth Circuit. While the appeal was pending, Dallas readied itself for the long-awaited local desegregation referendum scheduled for August, 1960. The final tally showed a margin favoring continued segregation of slightly more than four to one. There is little doubt, however, that these figures were skewed as a result of inflammatory misinformation published by the influential Dallas Morning News and issued from other sources. In an election eve editorial, the newspaper warned:

> [E]verybody should be made aware of this--If Dallas now votes for integration in the plebiscite soon to be held, then, following that vote, the court will order a sweeping integration of all schools on a compulsory basis. If, therefore, you favor voluntary integration as the only fair and the only free form of integration, you will vote in the election to be called and vote against compulsory integration.

While the Davidson "salt and pepper plan" may have had certain beneficial side effects such as decentralization and community control, its avowed function was to desegregate public schools only to the extent that desegregation proved "popular." Judge Davidson's proposal was the extension of the notion of desegregation by popular referendum, which had been declared unacceptable by both the Fifth Circuit and the Supreme Court. Argument on the Dallas case was again heard by Chief Judge Rives and Judges Tuttle and Jones on November 15, 1960. Barely fifteen days later, Judge Rives's opinion was published. It is a model of judicial restraint. Only passing reference was made to what was termed the "frustrating history of this litigation," and Judge Davidson's role is relegated to a footnote. The merits of the "salt and pepper plan" were quickly disposed of:

> That plan evidences a total misconception of the nature of
> the constitutional rights asserted by the plaintiffs.... In-
> stead of removing the forbidden classification according to
> race or color, that plan adds another classification.

The opinion then considered the merits of the twelve-year
plan as originally submitted by the Dallas school board, and gave
tentative approval to the time span contained in the plan but ordered
the transfer provisions stricken from its terms. In so ruling, the
Fifth Circuit took a position contrary to the Sixth Circuit and ante-
dating a definitive ruling by the Supreme Court. Judge Rives explained:

> We are so doubtful of the validity of ... [the transfer
> provisions] that we think they should not be included in
> the plan.... [W]ith deference to the view of the Sixth Cir-
> cuit, it seems to us that classification according to race
> for purposes of transfer is hardly less unconstitutional
> than such classification for purposes of original assign-
> ment to a public school.

More importantly, the Fifth Circuit Court served notice that
its approval of a plan proffered by a school board did not mean that
the board had achieved full compliance with the Brown mandate.
Like the issuance of the initial injunction, the plan's approval was
no more than a litigation milestone. First, Chief Judge Rives
warned that the plan must be administered in a nondiscriminatory
manner. Second, the Court observed that the Dallas twelve-year
plan might later be considered too slow a pace for desegregation.
"We reserve the right," Chief Judge Rives cautioned, "to consider
in light of developments whether the twelve-year plan is deliberate
speed." Any plan "insofar as it postpones full integration" was to
be considered suspect and to be subjected to continuous and searching judicial review.

*   *   *

The reaction in Dallas to the Circuit Court opinion was one
of "shock and surprise" that the "vital student transfer provisions"
had been struck. Superintendent W. T. White stated publicly, "It
sounds like more complete integration may result.... I'm shocked
at the deviation from past procedures of [other federal courts] in
approving the same plan. The law is supposed to be consistent. I
just don't understand it." It began to dawn on more than one Dallas observer that the standards of the Sixth Circuit, or Fourth or
Eighth, were not necessarily the standards imposed by the Fifth
Circuit Court of Appeals.

Speculation was rife that the Dallas school board would seek
certiorari from the United States Supreme Court. However, as one
anonymous official warily observed, "Knowing how the Supreme
Court operates, it is possible we would lose what gains we've made
if we appeal. It seems as though we're better off holding what we

have now and not gambling." The deadline for review came and passed. Skeptics predicted that instead of challenging the court's mandate head-on, the board would use a sophisticated interpretation of the Texas Pupil Placement Act to avoid desegregation wherever possible.

On June 27, 1961, Judge Davidson grudgingly issued the order requiring Dallas schools to begin desegregation on the following sixth of September. He commented:

> The court's decree may take effect through the office of the U.S. Marshal or with the soldiers' bayonets. It is forced just the same. The people of Dallas, by a 4-1 majority vote now stand for segregation. They have integration now, not by consent, not by choice, but by force.

He urged white citizens of Dallas to "stand calmly by constitutional authority ... support and cooperate with the board of education in its effort to carry out this order," and admonished black citizens not "to crow over it." Judge Davidson, however, remained unconvinced that even the gradual desegregation implicit in the twelve-year plan could be constructive: "If the medicine is bad and the result, what matter it to those concerned if it is given in twelve doses instead of one?"

*   *   *

September 7, 1961, was a day of tension for Dallas officials as eighteen black children attended the first grade in eight schools. Chief of Police Jesse Curry had prepared for this momentous day for over a year. He had hand-picked a detail of fifty plain-clothes police to monitor the integrated school sites. At the close of the day, these veteran officers reported that the school children seemed "more curious about the police presence than the presence of the Negroes." Geared for any emergency, like the military on maneuvers, school officials grouped at their command post in the board's Administrative Offices. No emergency materialized. The prearranged code phrase "Signal A" was consistently reported throughout the day indicating that "all was quiet." Only one protest was registered by a Dallas parent, an irritated father who called the police department and demanded: "Why couldn't I park in front of my child's school this morning? I've always parked there to let my child out." When he was told that the special "no parking" signs were there only temporarily because of the beginning of integration, he replied simply, "Oh, excuse me." School principals and teachers involved told newsmen that their only problems were the "normal ones of starting out six-year-olds in school for the first time." No distinction between white and black children had been made in any school regarding the lunchroom or other school facilities.

History had occurred, as it sometimes does, in a very ordinary fashion. The <u>Dallas Morning News</u> editorialized the following day,

The News still believes, with thousands of local citizens
and millions in our Southland, that the Supreme Court decree of 1954 was and is premature and without warrant
and law....

If nine men on the bench can deny the right of a state
to declare who can sit next to whom in the school room,
they can deny any state right--and if they can do that then
our republic is gone.

Governmental power will be concentrated in Washington. Dictatorship will have come to the land of the once-
free.

But Dallas handled its problems as sensible men of
God would have us handle it. We fought our legal battle
to the last. The inevitable came. Our only choice was
acceptance in peace.

Men of both races in this city realized long ago that
bayonets and tanks cannot establish good will. Force is
the language of hate. Dallas turned its back on the Ku
Klux Klan--on the one hand--and on the extremists of the
National Association for the Advancement of Colored People
on the other....

The colored citizen of Dallas is proving his worth.
Dallas' challenge is to help him rise in stature, to see
that he gets justice and to restrain the radicals who would
rip the fabric of peace and love.

Judge Ben Cameron had said that "this problem [of desegre-
gation] will be solved only as men's hearts are reached and touched."
If the editorial truly reflected the thoughts of the Dallas citizens,
then the day of solution had not yet arrived. Only eight schools out
of approximately 140 had been involved. None of the original twenty-
seven black student plaintiffs gained any personal benefit from their
challenge: eight had graduated from black high schools; thirteen
were still in segregated classes; one had transferred to a parochial
school; two had moved to Ft. Worth; and four had dropped out of
school. No records were maintained on the whereabouts of the
others.

If the riddle of desegregation had not in fact been solved on
September 7, 1961, at least the first and most difficult step had
been taken towards ultimate solution. Administrators were now taking a harder look at the caliber of instruction they had tolerated
for black pupils, and a rich school system which had been closed to
blacks for a century had been forced open.

HOUSTON: THE DIVIDENDS OF LOCAL ACTION

Houston, the other East Texas giant, provides an effective
counterpoint to the evolution of desegregation in Dallas. During
these early post-Brown years, Houston also stood in contrast to
cities like New Orleans, Montgomery and Little Rock whose more
violent citizenry captured national front-page news coverage. It

would be enormously misleading to imply that defiance of the Supreme Court mandate typified the South. While Houston did not voluntarily integrate its school system, those who opposed integration there fought a hard battle within the bounds of legal argument. When all appeal was exhausted, they turned their energies towards making the social transition work with minimal disruption to the educational process. The United States Court of Appeals for the Fifth Circuit wrote only one opinion in the Houston litigation before desegregation began and, even then, it simply affirmed the work of the district court.

As hoped by the Supreme Court when it handed down the Brown decisions, the desegregation of the Houston public school system was a responsibility recognized and shouldered by local school administrators, community groups and the federal district court. Although most of this work focuses upon the role of the federal appellate courts, a study of Houston's civic involvement is important to an understanding of how desegregation came to many cities and rural areas of the South with little appellate intervention.

Without desegregation cases like Houston, where the district court functioned efficiently and in which parties bowed to judicial mandates, the Fifth Circuit Court of Appeals could hardly have functioned, much less have developed a coherent body of legal doctrine.

To the outsider, Houston has always displayed a curious racial climate.   John Gunther once described Houston as one of the most reactionary cities of the nation.   Yet such reactionary politics does not necessarily equate with racial intolerance.   The NAACP Houston branch was organized in 1915 and since that time has flourished, locally controlled by lifelong black residents of the city.   In terms of public accommodations, the Houston of the seventies is an "open" city.   The process of desegregation of public facilities has been unmarred by violent opposition.   Yet, it is clear that open accommodations resulted, in large measure, from sustained pressure by local black citizens.

In 1955, the Houston School system was the largest segregated system in the entire country, maintaining 173 schools serving 170,000 students.   It was the nation's sixth largest school system. On March 14, 1955, almost two months before Brown II, the Houston school board had set up a biracial commission to study anticipated problems engendered by integration.   That biracial commission recommended, among other things, that the Board prepare for complete integration by September, 1956, with selected experimental integration to begin in the Fall of 1955, if at all possible.   The report and its recommendations were shelved, although in contrast to other Southern cities, there was never much doubt in Houston that desegregation was just a matter of time.   Moreover, this knowledge was not confined to members of the school board or interested parties in potential litigation.   The televised bimonthly meetings of the Houston school board put the populace on notice about the impending changes.   Insiders now differ about whether public attend-

ance at the board's deliberations hindered or aided the course of desegregation, but certainly in Houston there was never a problem of
a public uninformed and unprepared for desegregation.

*   *   *

In 1954, while the board deliberated about the educational problems of transition, the local NAACP sought black parents willing to allow their children to act as plaintiffs in the coming desegregation struggle. George Nelson, a Houston barber and
NAACP volunteer engaged in local NAACP organizational work since
1922, was one of those who during 1954 and 1955 served on a committee charged with this responsibility. Nelson recalled that volunteers worked every weekend scouring black neighborhoods, trying to
find parents willing to send their children to a white school. Using
commitment forms requiring the acquiescence of both parents, Nelson remembered that most contacts resulted in what he termed a
"split decision": one parent would be willing but the other reluctant
for fear of reprisals.

While canvassing the neighborhood near his own home one
Sunday in January, 1956, Nelson knocked at the door of Mrs. Mary
Alice Benjamin, the mother of Delores Ross, then a eight-year-old
second grader. Mrs. Benjamin was interested in allowing Delores
to enter a white school, due to the dangerous route which her daughter had to travel to her all-black school. Although the Benjamins
then lived only one and a half blocks from the all-white Sherman
Elementary School, because of Houston's segregation policies Delores
was required to attend the Crawford School, eleven or twelve blocks
to the East and across two very dangerous sets of railroad tracks.
Nelson was ready to take Delores to the nearby white school the following day. Mrs. Benjamin agreed, asking only that he also take
two male cousins of Delores's who, although schoolboys themselves,
might afford some companionship and protection for her little girl.
Preparing Delores for the fact that there would undoubtedly be jeers,
harassment and rejection at the school, Nelson assured the children
that he would be along to protect them. He also took two other
steps to insure their safety. To secure the protective cover of
publicity, he alerted the newspapers, and he then armed himself
with a loaded .32 caliber revolver carried in a paper bag. Mr.
Nelson later explained that he had acted on advice he inherited from
his father, a man who had defied the Galveston Klan and, as a result, had spent a considerable amount of time guarding his home
and those of other blacks against Klan retaliation. Mr. Nelson's
father had admonished him always to keep a Bible, a world almanac
and a gun: "You keep the Bible to learn how to treat your fellow
man and how to expect them to treat you; the almanac to learn how
men around the world actually treat each other; and the gun to make
sure they treat you right."

The following morning, George Nelson walked Delores and
her two cousins to Sherman Elementary School. As they approached,
a large white man rushed out of the crowd cursing, "You take them

Goddamned black niggers away from here!" Nelson moved his hand
to the handle of the .32 inside the paper bag. The man knocked a
photographer over as he hastened to blend back into the anonymous
crowd of bystanders. Although Nelson had no fear of jeering crowds,
he was concerned about night snipers. That evening he remained
awake at home, fearing retaliation against either his wife or their
three preschool children. Nothing occurred on that or any other
evening. Whatever racial hostility the attempted registration had
generated in Houston was thereafter directed at Mrs. Benjamin.
She became so frightened by threatening telephone calls that she
summoned her mother to Houston. Mrs. Benjamin's mother installed a spotlight in the yard, gave her daughter a gun and told her
she could now fend adequately for herself.

*　　*　　*

Even though the attempt to register Delores Ross had been
rejected, the school board was spurred to set aside a meeting
scheduled for February 27, 1956, to hear grievances from black parents, from an interracial parents' council and from the local white
citizens council. The audience ratings for popular network programs
dropped to an all-time low as Houston residents watched the desegregation presentations. At the meeting, the public was introduced for
the first time to Mrs. Charles White, who subsequently became the
first black elected to public office in Houston since Reconstruction.
As one white resident observed: "Mrs. White gave by far the most
lucid and compelling talk before the school board that night. She
had the facts--statistics on Negro teachers' heavier student loads,
the lack of libraries and kindergartens in many Negro schools, and
many other inequalities--and she delivered them beautifully. [F]or
many whites in Houston it was their first glimpse of an educated,
intelligent, attractive Negro."

Two months later, the Houston School Board issued a policy
statement tying the pace of desegregation to the approval of a $30
million-dollar bond issue. The Board reported that if this proposed
construction program were completed and, if "a liberal policy of
transfer is continued so that no Negro student will be compelled to
attend against his will a school predominantly Negro in student body
and teaching staff," then the problems of the desegregation of Houston would be "largely resolved."

On September 10, 1956, Delores Ross and two other black
children again attempted to register at all-white schools, but were
again rejected. Mrs. Marion Williams, whose child Beneva had
applied for entrance to a white junior high school, remembers the
next six months as a time of harassing letters, telephone calls and
even visits from curiosity seekers. She and her husband also received thinly veiled letter threats which would instruct them to look
on a certain page of a Houston newspaper. There they would find
news accounts of Negro beatings and killings in other parts of the
South. In addition to white harassment, Mrs. Williams received
little support from most other blacks in Houston. Desegregating the

school system was for the most part "considered our own battle." "Other blacks were afraid to rock the boat and afraid of what would happen as a result of the case."

On December 26, 1956, Mrs. Williams and Mrs. Benjamin filed the original desegregation complaint on behalf of their two daughters and all other black children in Houston. They were given an expedited hearing date to be scheduled the following spring.

* * *

As attorneys for both the black parents and school board prepared for their first court confrontation, a side issue simmering during the fall of 1956 moved to the forefront of attention. Triggered by the desegregation lawsuits, the Attorney General of Texas launched an investigation of the activities of the NAACP in the state. Relying upon his power to examine the operation of any private corporation in order to insure compliance with state laws, on September 13, 1956, Attorney General John Ben Sheppard instructed agents to inspect the records of the local offices of the NAACP in both Dallas and Houston. The investigation later spread to several of the 112 other Texas communities with established NAACP branches, including Austin, Corpus Christi and Beaumont, as well as the national headquarters in New York City.

Armed with the results of his blitzkrieg investigation, Attorney General Sheppard filed suit in state court. Alleging that the NAACP was in willful noncompliance with at least three state laws, he sought an injunction against further NAACP activity in Texas. First, the suit charged that the NAACP had made an estimated profit of $100,000 in 1955 as a result of its organizational activities and thus owed franchise taxes on this amount to the state. Second, it urged that representatives of the Attorney General had been wrongfully denied access to all records in the national NAACP office. Third, and most important, was the charge that the members and officers of the NAACP had been guilty of barratry, the unlawful solicitation and stirring-up of litigation. "By preconceived plan," the suit asserted, the Texas chapters of the NAACP had "solicited, recruited and coerced students and parents of students to take steps that otherwise they would not have taken."

While this collateral action against the statewide NAACP organization was pending final disposition, public sentiment regarding NAACP affiliation localized, manifesting itself in action taken by the Houston School Board. In a January 2, 1957 resolution the Board appointed yet another committee to study the problems of transition, expressly stipulating that no one could serve as a member who was then a member of the NAACP "or any other organization of individuals of unreasonable mind on this subject."

In April, the Texas state court granted a permanent injunction against the NAACP and its local branches from "willfully instigating, maintaining, exciting, prosecuting or encouraging the bring-

ing in any court of this state, federal or state, of a suit ... in
which [the NAACP] has no direct interest or financing any such suit"
or from violating any other of the laws of Texas. After the public
controversy engendered by the Attorney General's investigation, the
court's order was anticlimactic. Lists of NAACP contributors were
protected from discovery, and the organization's activities in the
state had not been enjoined as Attorney General Sheppard had hoped.
George Nelson, like many other NAACP members in the South,
freely admitted that there had been a conscientious effort to publicize the need for black children to test segregation. In Houston,
plaintiffs for the eventual lawsuit had indeed been actively sought by
meetings with various black groups and by neighborhood canvass.
It was, however, difficult to urge that the NAACP had no "direct
interest" in the encouragement of such desegregation actions.

Though the ultimate order rendered by the Texas court failed
to impose direct legal restraints upon the NAACP, there is little
doubt that the Texas Attorney General's investigation and the resulting suit had a dramatic effect, intimidating the NAACP membership
and depressing their activities. To many Texas blacks, the NAACP
had been "outlawed." Only the hardy continued to wear membership
buttons or to solicit newcomers to the ranks. Additional growth
was drastically curtailed. The "anti-NAACP" vote was wooed in
election campaigns: in the 1957 Houston mayoralty contest, a pro-
ponent for one candidate urged, "If and when this desegregation
problem comes, our city must have at its head a man who will not
be pushed around or used by the NAACP or, for that matter, any
group."

Controversy over the specific desegregation activities of the
Houston NAACP branch surfaced when attorneys for the school board
took the depositions of the parents of Delores Ross and Beneva Williams, the named plaintiffs in the Houston action. After close questioning of Marion Williams concerning the financing of his lawsuit,
the board attorney extensively probed him about his motivation in
having brought the action:

Q. [by Mr. Reynolds]: I will ask you if it is your position
at this time that you will leave it up to the Houston Independent School District as to what school your daughter is
to go to other than letting her remain in [her all-black
high school]?
A. [by Mr. Williams]: I would have to answer the question
like this: It would be up to the Independent School District
if they did away with the segregated system.
Q. I am asking whether you are interested in doing away with
segregation or are you interested in finding a good school
for your daughter to go to?
A. I am interested in the system.
Q. You are interested in the system? Now, I'm asking if
your primary purpose in this cause is to change the
school that your daughter attends?
A. Well, you have to get to the root of anything to clear it up.

Q. Well now, I believe you can answer that question, Mr. Williams.

A. That is the best I can answer.

Q. Then you are primarily concerned with changing the system, but not changing the school your daughter now attends?

A. I didn't say that. I was partially interested in changing the system.

Q. You didn't say that?

A. Not in the way you stated it, no.

Q. I thought you stated you were primarily interested in seeing that the system in the district was changed, at least, I got the implication from the statement that you were interested in having the system changed from a segregated system to an integrated system?

A. Yes.

Q. That was your primary purpose?

A. Yes.

Q. And that is the reason that you were a party to this law suit?

A. Yes.

Q. And for that reason you were willing to come into this court as a party to this cause in order to see that the system on segregation to desegregation is changed, isn't that right?

A. Yes.

Q. Now that is the purpose for which you were a party to this case.

A. That is part of the purpose.

Q. Is there another purpose?

A. Yes, there are other purposes.

Q. What are they?

A. Well, I know that children in segregated systems don't have it the way that children do in integrated systems.

Q. Now, that is ultimately why you want to change from a segregated system to a desegregated system?

A. That's right.

During the pretrial discovery of evidence in the Houston case, an attempt was made to establish that the black parents, the "test plaintiffs," were only pawns used by the NAACP in the litigation. In particular, school board attorneys sought information about the financial arrangements for funding the costs of the lawsuit, and how and when Thurgood Marshall, U. Simpson Tate and W. J. Durham, NAACP lawyers with national reputations, had entered the Houston case.

Initially, at least, the Houston desegregation case had been totally a local NAACP affair. Three young and relatively inexperienced attorneys in Houston had assumed responsibility for the expected litigation. This was a hopelessly ambitious undertaking for a local organization depending for its sustenance upon donations and two-dollar membership dues, with half of the dues going to the National organization. The regional office of the NAACP in Dallas had revealed that it had spent $33,500 in the single lawsuit to obtain the admission of Heman Sweatt to the University of Texas Law School in 1950. Similarly, it has been estimated that over $200,000 was expended in the litigation which produced the Supreme Court judgment in Brown v. Board of Education. After the first round of the Houston litigation, the three original attorneys for the plaintiffs withdrew, ostensibly because of continuing financial disagreement with the local NAACP. The Inc. Fund, with its cadre of highly experienced civil rights lawyers, was thereafter pledged to the Houston desegregation effort.

It is little wonder, therefore, that the plaintiffs were unsure under cross-examination about who "their" lawyers were or how they were paid. Marion Williams and Bennie Benjamin had joined forces with the NAACP because they wanted closer, better schools for their children and also because they wanted to "see all the system changed." The NAACP organization had provided strength and financial support for them from those in sympathy with their goals. As the Supreme Court later observed in its review of Virginia's efforts to constrict NAACP activities:

> The first amendment also protects vigorous advocacy, certainly of lawful ends, against governmental intrusion .... In the context of NAACP objectives, litigation is not a technique of resolving private differences; it is a means for achieving the lawful objectives of equality of treatment by all governments, federal, state and local for the members of the Negro community in this country. It is thus a form of political expression. Groups which find themselves unable to achieve their objectives through the ballot frequently turn to the courts.... For such a group, association for litigation may be the most effective form of political association.

* * *

While the local NAACP was struggling to steady the litigation it had launched, the Houston school board turned for its defense to highly competent local counsel. Almost from the outset of his legal career after graduation from Baylor Law School in 1947, Joe H. Reynolds had been involved in desegregation litigation. As an assistant Attorney General of Texas, he had represented the University of Texas in Sweatt v. Painter, joining issue against Thurgood Marshall, counsel for the black student seeking admission. Reynolds, who represented the Houston School Board until February 2, 1970, was described by a friend as a "professional segregationist. It's his job, in other words, to stall integration as long as he can. He knows he is going to lose before he starts. His job isn't winning, it's defending the barricades." Even his detractors admitted his skill and were wary of his known ability. One angry black mother once called him the "Perry Mason of the segregation set." In addition to his ability to focus and narrow points of conflict, Reynolds brought another important attribute to the Houston litigation: the ability to control his client. That attribute contributed greatly to the progress of peaceful desegregation. According to Reynolds, one of his prerequisites in accepting the defense of any school system threatened by desegregation was that the administrators agree to abide, at all times, by the decisions of the courts.

*   *   *

The Houston case was allotted four days for argument in late May, 1957, on the trial calendar of Judge Ben C. Connally. The case had originally been set on the docket of Judge Joe Ingraham but, for some reason unexplained in the records and long forgotten by the principals, it was subsequently transferred to Judge Connally.

Judge Connally was thirty-nine at the time of his appointment by President Truman to the federal bench in 1949. His father, Senator Tom Connally, had represented Texas for thirty-three years in Congress, remaining a popular political figure in his home state. The initial reception of Texans to the news of Judge Connally's appointment to the bench is perhaps best exemplified by the Houston Chronicle's headline, "Tom Connally's Boy One of Youngest Federal Judges." Undoubtedly, having a powerful Senator for a father aided his appointment, but Ben Connally had impressive intellectual credentials as well. He had been elected to the prestigious scholastic honoraries, Phi Beta Kappa and the Order of the Coif in his undergraduate and law school careers at the University of Texas and held a Master's Degree in Law from Harvard. Judge Connally also brought to the bench an understanding of the trial lawyer's perspective, having been engaged in private practice in Houston for eleven years. A hallmark of Judge Connally's judicial tenure was his insistence upon in-chambers discussion off the record and out of the headlines, and the negotiation of competing claims in all lawsuits, particularly highly volatile cases. He avoided opinions from the bench and inflammatory prose in written opinions, having concluded that quiet decision-making minimized adversarial friction.

The hearing on Houston's desegregation case opened with testimony from the plaintiff black parents about their children's rejected applications to attend white schools. On the second day of the evidentiary hearing, the President of the Houston board, Mrs. Frank Dyer, testified that the board had no plans for desegregation but had "many plans to mitigate its impact." She characterized immediate desegregation of the system as "impossible" due to the disparity in achievement levels between black and white children. When asked what the board considered to be a reasonable period for transition to a desegregated system, board counsel Reynolds sought a recess during which he could confer with his clients about their response. Upon reconvening, Mrs. Dyer could only state that the board desired "time to complete our school construction program and evaluate what is being done in Nashville, Tennessee, before beginning desegregation in Houston."

Unlike the Dallas litigation, at the conclusion of the first
hearing all parties fully expected that Judge Connally would simply
enter the injunction requiring desegregation with all deliberate speed.
In chambers after the hearing, Judge Connally reportedly urged
counsel for the board to present a plan for desegregation which
would be acceptable to the board and something plaintiffs' lawyer
"could sell to his people."

After keeping the Houston case under advisement for more
than four months, on October 15, 1957, Judge Connally announced
his decision in what was for him a rare written opinion. With little difficulty, he declared unconstitutional those portions of Texas
law which still required racial segregation. Yet in his painstaking
consideration of the equities of both parties as well as the impact
of desegregation upon the community, the opinion reveals a genuine
anguish felt by many southern federal trial judges charged with the
responsibility for ruling in such cases:

> The Board here does not rely upon any assertion that the
> present policy of segregation is lawful or is justified by
> Texas statute.... [However,] it is suggested that the pub-
> lic good flowing from an orderly and planned program of
> desegregation to be adopted and enforced by the board,
> without court intervention, warrants a temporary delay in
> the enforcement of the constitutional rights of the two in-
> dividuals primarily involved here.
>   This argument is cogent and weighty. It cannot be
> denied that the first intermingling of the races of the
> schools of the community is calculated to arouse tension
> and emotional upset. Customs and traditions in which the
> people of this land have been steeped for a century are not
> forgotten in a day. The layman does not readily under-
> stand that what on yesterday had been accepted law for a
> generation is no longer law today. The daily press and
> periodicals show that in many Texas cities [citing San An-
> tonio, Corpus Christi, Amarillo, Austin, Lubbock, El
> Paso and San Angelo] where the local school authorities
> have placed in operation their own carefully devised plans
> for desegregation, the transition has been without incident.
> This is in sharp contrast to the situations presented in
> other cities [citing Clinton, Tennessee, Mansfield, Texas
> and Little Rock, Arkansas] where the enforcement of
> court action in similar cases has led to resentment, riot-
> ing, and disorder.
>   On behalf of the plaintiffs it is argued that the de-
> fendant board is not sincere in this proposition; and that
> its stated acceptance of Brown, and its efforts to comply,
> are but a tongue-in-cheek attitude. It is suggested that
> by dilatory tactics the board seeks only to maintain the
> status quo until the last possible moment, and never in
> fact to admit a Negro student except under court compul-
> sion. These being elective offices, it is suggested that
> the members of the Board then intend to adopt the attitude

of having washed their collective hands of the controversy; and after all possible delay, ultimately to pass on to the courts the task which the board finds odious and unpopular.

During the darkest days of the bloody Civil War, President Lincoln questioned in a letter to a close adviser, "[Is] it possible to lose the nation and yet preserve the Constitution?" Nearly one hundred years later, Judge Connally thought that this was indeed still a real possibility. He did not order immediate desegregation of the Houston schools. Instead, adopting the pattern order approved by the Fifth Circuit in the New Orleans litigation, he entered an open-dated injunction. However, he cautioned the board:

... I am not as yet prepared to find that these public officials are so blind to their duty or devoid of responsibility as to abandon their obligation properly to administer the schools in a time of crisis. If it be true that the board desires to temper the impact of the Brown decision, I do not wish to deny them that opportunity.... In the final analysis the rules adopted by the Houston board dealing with school zoning, the extent to which voluntary transfers from one school to another are allowed, and related matters, will determine the extent to which the races are intermingled in the classroom here.... Any delay will be warranted only if the board immediately comes to grips with its problems. A court of equity will not countenance inordinate delay or evasion where the enjoyment of a constitutional right is involved, though its recognition and enforcement be difficult and unpopular.

This threshold step in school desegregation was achieved in Houston over two months before the Fifth Circuit, in exasperation over the state of the Dallas litigation, entered its own "from and after" decree for that other Texas city. Only one hearing had been necessary to insure the entry of the proper decree in Houston, as contrasted with two district court hearings and two appeals in the Dallas proceedings.

* * *

Despite this early gain in time, black citizens saw few signs of tangible progress toward the realization of desegregation in Houston during the next eighteen months. The board did initiate, in the summer of 1958, what was termed an "upgrading" program for black teachers and principals. Two Negro schools were designated "observation" schools in which one-way glass windows were installed overlooking classrooms. In what must have been a humiliating experience for veteran educators, black teaching personnel were asked to observe white supervisors instructing black pupils. Real political gains were being made, however, by a coalition of blacks and white sympathizers in 1958. In a runoff election that Fall, liberal Democrats had won seats representing Houston and surrounding Harris County in the state legislature. More important for school desegre-

gation, Mrs. Charles White was elected to the Houston board, thereby becoming the first black ever elected to public office in Houston.
As a black Houston elevator operator observed the night of her victory, "It seems that if the school board won't integrate the schools
the people are going to integrate the school board!"

Garnering more than half of her total vote from the white
community, Mrs. White defeated an incumbent who was a staunch
defender of segregation. Subsequently a prominent figure in board
deliberations and a vocal nettle when its other members took delaying action, Mrs. White was a political novice. Like George Nelson,
she had been reared in Houston and was a product of its segregated
public school system. She had graduated with highest honors from
a black college near Houston and had taught school locally before
marrying an optometrist. She soon settled into a life of volunteer
work in the Houston black community and into the comparative ease
of a middle-class homemaker and mother. Mrs. White attributed
her conversion to desegregation activism to her children's experiences. She later recalled,

> When Richard was five or six, he used to ask to stop at
> a place where they had pony rides. I always managed to
> have an excuse. For some reason, I just couldn't tell
> him we couldn't go there because we were Negroes. . . .
> It wasn't until I saw my own children growing up in a
> segregated world that I really objected. The court deci-
> sions had promised so much that was still being withheld
> that I began to wonder if they too would be passed by. I
> guess it's natural for people to be more willing to accept
> injustice for themselves than for their children.

Mrs. White joined the seven-member board with little immediate
chance of becoming an effective policy maker. The board was, in
1958, still controlled by a conservative majority, one of whose members had vowed to go to jail rather than accept integration.

Six months later, the local NAACP finally concluded arrangements for the national organization to enter its stalled litigation.
Inc. Fund attorneys and a local Houston lawyer named Weldon Berry
became counsel of record on May 20, 1959, simultaneously petition-
ing Judge Connally for further relief in the Houston desegregation
case.

In contrast to the corporate image and litigation experience
of board counsel Joe Reynolds, Weldon Berry was a black lawyer
just beginning private practice when he was retained by the NAACP
as local counsel. Berry suddenly found himself a spokesman eagerly sought by journalists. He recalled, however, "We all understood
that this was highly controversial, inflammatory litigation. But the
worst spectacle of all is an emotionally involved attorney. All is
not black and white: there are gray areas--a hard way and an easy
way to do everything. If you are at dagger's point with an attorney
or with the judge, you get nowhere and become ineffective for your
client."

As a result of the renewed attack by the plaintiffs, Judge Connally ordered the board to report by mid-August, 1959, what specific steps it had taken and the plan it had adopted to comply with the injunction. While three fully developed plans had been presented for consideration, the board had neither adopted nor recommended any plan to the court. The board's conservatives balked at this step for political reasons. As Dr. Henry Peterson, (board) member for twenty-two years and then its President, put it, "[I]t is not politically wise for us to desegregate until we are forced to by a court deadline." He added that he estimated "[I]t will take eight to ten years to prepare for desegregation." Past President Mrs. Frank Dyer stated that "[T]he people would regard such a step [integration in the Fall of 1959] as a traitorous act on our part."

Whether or not this reaction was an accurate reading of the will of the Houston populace, the refusal to propose a plan violated the pending court order, a fact not lost upon Judge Connally. In a letter to counsel which was released to the press, Judge Connally stated:

> [T]he defendant Board filed a voluminous reply, the effect of which was to state that it was still confronted with many problems, and had no concrete proposal as to when it might begin to carry into effect any plan for desegregation.... [T]he reply filed in the summer or early fall of 1959, I considered inadequate.... I drew the inference from the reply filed by the defendant Board in 1959 that the Board desired to avoid responsibility for adopting any plan of this nature, and was, in effect, stating to the Court that the Court could adopt and enforce any one of several plans which had been suggested by various interested parties.

During the next few months Judge Connally attempted to work with counsel in chambers, trying to obtain a plan suitable for all parties. Counsel for both sides were in an unenviable position of attempting to negotiate on behalf of clients who were not disposed to compromise and had struck adamant positions. Despite warnings that the court would order district-wide integration unless the board came up with an acceptable plan of its own which would begin integration in the Fall of 1960, the board continued to rehash its alternatives throughout the preceding spring.

Weldon Berry had similar problems with his constituency. The Houston desegregation case was now entering its fourth year, and the local black community was pressing for some real evidence of action. To complicate matters, Inc. Fund attorneys and other legal advisors outside Houston were beginning to talk about bringing a writ of mandamus to compel Judge Connally to rule on the board's obvious resistance to presenting a plan.

There are always enormous built-in delays in litigation,

particularly in the racial controversies during this period. Southern judges were prone to grant delays in hopes of reaching negotiated compromise. Aside from mandamus, an extraordinary order to a trial court that he make a ruling on a pending matter, there was no method to prod a judge into action. Furthermore, seeking a mandamus order, where there is judicial discretion in the ultimate ruling, obviously carries the risk of irritating the judge into an unfavorable ruling. Berry clung to the belief that Judge Connally would eventually order a plan if the board persisted in doing nothing, but time was running out.

Judge Connally himself was not immune from pressure and troubling thoughts about how the controversy should be resolved. Described as a "lawyer's judge," Judge Connally was known to favor a fair compromise, to force retreat from hard-line positions. One lawyer later observed, "nobody ever won" all that was claimed in contested matters before Judge Connally. Judge Connally was perplexed by the suit, feeling that most blacks, like most whites, preferred their own schools. However, he also recognized the importance of establishing the right to attend the school of one's choice. Most important, he was committed to the proposition that the law as announced by the higher courts would be followed. By April, 1960, after almost eight months of meetings, it was clear that the court's patience was wearing thin.

Finally, Judge Connally ordered the board to submit a specific plan for desegregation on or before June 1, 1960. Simultaneously, he took the rather extraordinary step of releasing to the press an explanatory letter, written to counsel for both parties in the Houston case. In the excerpts which follow, he left no doubt in the public's mind that time had indeed run out. He also emphasized that if the court were forced to impose a desegregation plan, it would do so only because the board had refused to act responsibly:

> In our conference of last week ... I advised counsel
> further that I could only consider any requests for addi-
> tional delay in filing some plan or concrete proposal look-
> ing toward the operation on a desegregated basis as an in-
> dication of bad faith on the part of the defendant Board and
> as indicating the intention on the part of the defendant
> Board indefinitely to continue the matter without expecta-
> tion of making a bona fide effort to comply with the agreed
> order of 1957.... The Court advised counsel that the
> Court had no duty or desire to draft or adopt any particu-
> lar plan or program of this nature; that it had been the
> policy of this Court to withhold the injunctive relief which
> the plaintiffs sought (namely, enforcing by Court decree
> complete integration) so long as the Board made a sincere
> and bona fide effort to pursue a plan looking to accomplish-
> ing this objective with a minimum of turmoil and discon-
> tent. I advised counsel further that in the event the Board
> declined to go forward with such plan, the Court had no al-
> ternative but to grant the relief which the plaintiffs have
> sought.

Judge Connally's letter succeeded in provoking action. The board authorized a crash effort by the Superintendent to "use all available means and make whatever expenditures were necessary to circulate petitions calling for the referendum." The board reasoned that a referendum would serve a dual purpose: it would comply with the Texas statute requiring voter approval before desegregation and it would be useful should the board decide to submit its area preference plan. Two weeks before the court's deadline, the board sought an extension, arguing that it was impossible to obtain the approximately 47,000 signatures needed to call the special referendum. Judge Connally denied the extension, warning that any plan drawn up on an area preference basis would be unacceptable.

* * *

On May 25, 1960, Judge Davidson in Dallas issued his ruling requiring only "salt and pepper" integration for that city. It set aside designated schools which could be attended by both white and black who desired integration, leaving the remainder of the system totally segregated. Six days later, Houston board member and arch segregationist Stone Wells introduced a plan whereby "voluntary" integration would be permitted in one elementary, one junior and one senior high school within the Houston system beginning in September, 1964. The plan was hotly debated, with the board badly split in reaction. President Petersen stated that he still considered continuation of segregation the best plan for education, concluding, "Any departure is regrettable." In contrast, Mrs. White charged that "For six years the board has sought to evade, delay and compromise. This plan is an insult to school patrons because only three schools in a system of 170,000 students are integrated." Over Mrs. White's dissent and another member's abstention, the board submitted to the court its preference plan, coupled with the referendum results which were to determine specific school locations for the voluntary desegregation.

The Houston referendum was scheduled for June 5, 1960. Shortly before the election, board member Wells warned, "The people should know that the areas which want desegregation first are going to get it. And the ones that vote for it are going to get it first. That's what this election is for." Wells's statement drew a stern public rebuke from Judge Connally. In a letter to board counsel, which he released to the press, the Judge demanded, "Your clients must recognize that this is not a popularity contest, but is the performance of a duty which the law imposes. In our many conferences and hearings, I have always been led to believe that some plan adopted by other Texas cities, and which experience has shown to be workable, will be submitted here."

On June 5, 1960, with a turnout of less than ten per cent of Houston's voters, the referendum resulted in two-to-one opposition to desegregation. Yet, this protest was totally ineffective to further stall desegregation. On August 3, as might have been predicted, Judge Connally rejected outright the board's so-called "salt-and-pepper" or preferential plan. In the strongest language he had yet used, Judge Connally termed the submitted "plan" a "palpable sham and subterfuge designed only to accomplish further evasion and delay." Finding a continued lack of good faith compliance with the court's previous orders, Judge Connally summarily directed that a twelve-year plan be implemented in Houston beginning that fall.

As continuing proof that desegregation rulings rarely satisfied either party, the school board expressed outrage and blacks were disappointed. Board President Petersen commented:

> [I]t would appear that Judge Connally proposed not only to interpret the ruling of the Supreme Court and secure its execution, but also it would further enlarge his responsibilities to participate in the administration of the schools. In his order to the Board of Education he not only sets the time as to when our schools shall be integrated, but he also gives the Board of Education an assist in the administration by his declaration as to how they shall be integrated.

Weldon Berry, local NAACP counsel, noted only, "We had expected and hoped for a more sweeping program of desegregation, but nevertheless, this does represent progress."

A far more telling comment was registered by board member Wells, who had proposed the preferential plan based upon the Dallas experience: "Judge Davidson in Dallas recommended the very same plan that we as a board submitted to the Judge here. Apparently federal judges differ quite a bit on their outlook on plans." There can be little doubt that for the conscientious district court judge, adherence to the higher court's mandates was made far more difficult because of the aberrant rulings by the few district judges who opposed implementation. The subsequent credibility of Judge Connally's order became publicly suspect because of the clearly erroneous ruling being handed down in nearby Dallas. Judicial orders in volatile desegregation matters were front page news; delay or denial countenanced anywhere rekindled a fading hope in other places that integration might yet be avoided or minimized.

With desegregation only a month away, the board sought a stay of Judge Connally's order from the Fifth Circuit. After hearing counsel's argument on August 26th, 1960, Judges Rives and Wisdom denied the board's request. While returning from the argument in New Orleans, board counsel Reynolds sought an emergency stay of implementation from Judge Connally. Attempting to reach him by the airplane's radio equipment, Reynolds finally located Judge Connally, who was riding circuit, hearing cases that day in Laredo, Texas. Reynolds asked for a stay of implementation until an extraordinary petition for a stay could be presented to the United States Supreme Court. By the time the plane had landed, Judge Connally had listened but refused any additional time.

The board next appealed to Governor Price Daniel for intervention. In a board resolution drafted by a special session on August 30, the board noted that it had "exhausted all of its resources to maintain its school system in accordance with the vote of the citizens of the Houston Independent School District and the State of Texas." The board therefore urged the Governor "to interpose the sovereignty of the State of Texas under the tenth amendment to the Constitution of the United States against such unwarranted acts on the part of the Federal Government and its officials." Despite the fact that Governor Daniel had represented the state as its Attorney General in fighting the admission of a black to the University of Texas Law School and was considered an "outspoken advocate of segregated schools," he declined to act. He simply replied that the state had no power under Supreme Court decisions to invoke interposition in such matters.

The following day, the United States Supreme Court considered the pleas and records in both the Houston and New Orleans cases and by unanimous vote declined to issue stays. In five-column banner headlines usually reserved for matters of international war or peace, Texas newspapers reported "Supreme Court Orders Houston to Integrate." The final hopes for avoidance were extinguished the day before school was to open. The Fifth Circuit affirmed all of Judge Connally's previous orders and the Texas Attorney General ruled that funds would not be forfeited if there was a court order requiring desegregation.

* * *

On September 7, 1960, Houston lost the dubious distinction of being the largest segregated system in the nation, when twelve black children attended formerly all-white schools. It was a day causing at least the temporary reunification of all who were troubled about potential disorder and disruption of the educational process. Superintendent McFarland called the event "a real achievement" and added, "I don't think anybody in the nation expected us to desegregate this school system without incident--including us." And, in a gesture of good will, the board vice-president credited the success of the venture to the "good judgment and understanding of our Negro parents and children."

The Houston litigation had been a long struggle between warring social ideologies. The case had erupted into its most bitter round when board counsel formally charged the NAACP with paying the plaintiffs to bring the litigation. In its only instance of breaking the no-publicity pact, Weldon Berry, counsel for the black parents, replied: "These parents have gotten money from churches, lodges and individuals. I have talked with the NAACP about helping them but I was not hired by that group and not paid by them. These people don't have the 'slush fund' of public funds available to Mr. Reynolds to fight in court. They get their money wherever they can."

Indeed, it had also been a costly struggle for the school

board. Total cost figures do not exist, but board counsel was paid
$100.00 per hour for his expenses in simply attending board meet-
ings. It was reported that, in 1968 alone, board counsel received
$91,000 in legal fees. Houston, like other cities throughout the
country, paid a dear price for waging a futile war.

* * *

In 1960, Houston's transition to a fully desegregated system
was far from complete and many problems of adjustment lay ahead.
Ten years later, Houston desegregation litigation was still pending
on the docket of the District Court of the Southern District of Texas.
However, it was significant that, unlike other southern cities, Houston's first actual desegregation was accomplished in a record time of
three years and was unmarred by violence or public spectacle. The
system of public school education in Houston was never seriously
endangered and the city later accommodated itself to the transition
with minimal friction.

From a historical standpoint, it is instructive to attempt to
analyze Houston's peaceful and comparatively fast-paced desegregation. Several factors may be suggested as possible contributing
elements. Some observers believe that the successful early, albeit
token, desegregation occurred in Houston because the general public
was kept informed of each development through televised board meetings and the publication of the court's warning letters to counsel.
Other observers point to the nonintervention of Governor Daniel as
being the critical difference between Houston and Montgomery, Little
Rock or New Orleans. Certainly, too, the fact that the Houston
school desegregation was considered a local problem, to be resolved
by local efforts, greatly enhanced the enforceability of federal court
orders. Both Reynolds and Berry acknowledge the good faith negotiations and professional respect each had for the other despite their
differing viewpoint. Both counsel are, however, quick to suggest
that the lion's share of the credit must go to Judge Connally. Reynolds stated flatly that Judge Connally "stood between Houston and
disaster." Before his untimely death, Judge Connally observed that
if, in fact, he had anything to do with the success of desegregation
in Houston, if was to keep the developments, concessions and tentative compromises out of the newspapers.

* * *

The development of public school desegregation in the Fifth
Circuit during this earliest period from 1954 to 1960 was fitful and
sporadic, even within the boundaries of a single state like Texas.
The timing of desegregation pressure became the critical difference
between the violence and withdrawal of litigation in Mansfield, the
spectacle of recalcitrance in Dallas and the peaceful if hesitant
compliance with a federal court's orders in Houston. All judges of
the Fifth Circuit later concluded that time had been essential in
most areas of the South in order for the Supreme Court mandate to
be executed.

To those who would scoff at calling the admission of twelve black children into a formerly all-white school system in Houston implementation of the rights declared in Brown v. Board of Education, or discount such developments as tokenism in the much-abused name of progress, these early decisions of the Fifth Circuit might seem insignificant. Certainly these early cases are timid in contrast to the later pronouncements. But, then, law as a matrix for social conduct is not any different in the area of race relations than it is in any other context. Its perfection is never absolute, but always relative to specific facts, specific places and specific times. The comment of two eminent legal scholars about the legal process are apt:

> To be impatient with law because it sometimes fails to do its job well is no more sensible than to be impatient with air because it sometimes gets fouled. Indeed, it is less sensible. For air in its natural condition is pure, and there is some justification for annoyance when it turns out to be impure. But law is the creation of human beings responding to their own natures and the conditions of their environment. It has no tendency to become perfect merely by being let alone. It can never do better than improve upon imperfection, and the degree of the improvement depends upon human intelligence and human effort.

The era of the fifties, illustrated by events in Texas, produced little actual desegregation. Study of this early period of development reveals a federal judicial system gingerly feeling its way in the evolution of the law, faltering at times in the newness of its responsibilities. The United States Court of Appeals for the Fifth Circuit was beginning to sense the peculiar problems it would increasingly face where district courts failed to abide by the Brown mandate. While the Court awaited the full fury of resistance, it was obvious to each judge that the task of grinding the cause of social transition would be awesome.

NOTES AND PRIMARY AUTHORITY

The primary authority for the material contained in this Chapter was:

I. The Texas Example: Peaceful Compliance and Violent Resistance. Valuable statistical information documenting desegregation progress came from Southern School News, beginning with the issue of Feb. 3, 1955 and continuing throughout the period of study, and Wright, Civil Rights U.S.A.--Texas (Staff report to the U.S. Comm'n on Civil Rights, 1963). Primary sources for the Mansfield episode are the cases themselves: Jackson v. Rawdon, 135 F. Supp. 936 (N.D. Tex. 1955), 235 F.2d 93 (5th Cir. 1956), Civ. No. 3152 (N.D. Tex. Aug. 28, 1956) reported in 1 Race Rel. L. Rep. 884 (1956), cert. denied, 352 U.S. 878 (1956); and Griffin and Freedman,

Mansfield, Texas: A Report of the Crisis Situation Resulting from
Efforts to Desegregate the School System (1956).
Primary sources for the Wichita Falls discussion are Avery
v. Wichita Falls Ind. School Dist., 241 F.2d 230 (5th Cir. 1957)
and Briggs v. Elliott, 132 F. Supp. 776 (E.D. S.C. 1955) (three-
judge court).

II. Dallas: Two Outspoken Octogenarians. The primary
sources for the Dallas segment of this Chapter are contemporary
news accounts, principally from the Dallas Morning News, and the
reported federal court decisions: Bell v. Rippy, 133 F. Supp. 811
(N.D. Tex. 1955); Brown v. Rippy, 233 F.2d 796 (5th Cir. 1956),
cert. denied, 352 U.S. 878 (1956); Bell v. Rippy, 146 F. Supp.
485 (N.D. Tex. 1956); Borders v. Rippy, 247 F.2d 268 (5th Cir.
1957); Rippy v. Borders, 250 F.2d 690 (5th Cir. 1957); Dallas Ind.
School Dist. v. Edgar, 255 F.2d 455 (5th Cir. 1958); Boson v.
Rippy, 275 F.2d 850 (5th Cir. 1960), 285 F.2d 43 (5th Cir. 1960).

III. Houston: The Dividends of Local Action. The primary
sources for the Houston segment of this chapter are contemporary
news accounts, principally from the Houston Chronicle and the Houston Post; personal interviews with Joe H. Reynolds, Weldon Berry,
George Nelson, Mrs. Charles White and the late Judge Ben C. Connally; and the reported federal decisions: Houston Ind. School Dist.
v. Ross, 282 F.2d 95 (5th Cir. 1960); Ross v. Dyer, 203 F. Supp.
124 (S.D. Tex. 1962), 312 F.2d 191 (5th Cir. 1963); Britton v.
Folsom, 350 F.2d 1022 (5th Cir. 1965); Broussard v. Houston Ind.
School Dist., 262 F. Supp. 266 (S.D. Tex. 1966), 395 F.2d 817,
403 F.2d 34 (5th Cir. 1968); Ross v. Eckels, 317 F. Supp. 512
(S.D. Tex. 1970), 434 F.2d 1140 (5th Cir. 1970), 468 F.2d 649 (5th
Cir. 1972).

A more complete manuscript, with detailed documentation of
all sources, is available as indicated in the Preface.

Chapter 3

THE SECOND BATTLE OF NEW ORLEANS

The Second Battle of New Orleans, like the first,
in 1815, was fought after the War was over. --J.
Peltason, Fifty-Eight Lonely Men (1971), p. 224.

In contrast to the grudging though peaceful acceptance of the
inexorable progress of desegregation in Dallas and Houston, stands
the record of efforts to end segregation in New Orleans. The New
Orleans litigation is, complete unto itself, an encyclopedia of every
tactic of resistance employed by all other states combined. Over
the relatively short span of time from 1952 until 1962, the Orleans
Parish case consumed thousands of hours of lawyers' and judges'
time: it required forty-one separate judicial decisions involving ultimately the energies of every Fifth Circuit judge, two district
court judges, and the consideration of the United States Supreme
Court on eleven separate occasions. Although the Supreme Court
consistently affirmed decisions of its lower federal courts in the
Fifth Circuit, it never issued a full written opinion during the course
of the litigation.

Backed by the Fifth Circuit, Federal District Judges J.
Skelly Wright and Herbert W. Christenberry lighted the way in this
laborious process. By the end of the decade those two judges had
invalidated a total of forty-four statutes enacted by the Louisiana
Legislature, had cited and convicted two state officials for contempt
of court, and had issued injunctions forbidding the continued flouting of its orders against a state court, all state executives and
the entire membership of the Louisiana Legislature. The desegregation struggle in New Orleans tested the strength of the linchpin of
the Constitution: the supremacy of federal law. The federal courts
of the Fifth Circuit faced attack from all flanks: from the local
state courts and the governor and from the public and its elected
representatives. And yet the federal courts survived, and the Supreme Court's mandate was enforced in Louisiana.

The New Orleans strife is significant not only because the
federal courts demonstrated their flexibility, resiliency, and endur-
ing vitality in crisis, but also because the course of action to be
taken by the other states of the Deep South hung in the balance.
Southerners bent on opposition watched with flagging hopes as, one
by one, the Louisiana Legislature's stratagems were nullified by the

111

courts. Ultimately, even more important was the fact that the yet
uncommitted and uninvolved citizens of other communities of the region and nation were forced to reflect upon indisputable evidence that
the silence of a city's moderates and mediators provides an environment in which immoderation and strife can flourish. As one commentator observed during the New Orleans riots:

> Let Atlanta, Birmingham, Charleston and the other
> Southern cities next in line study well the failure of lead-
> ership in New Orleans, where the moderates failed in turn
> to learn from the experience of Little Rock. As for the
> New Orleans moderates, let them reread Lincoln: 'Let us
> not be diverted by ... gropings from some middle ground
> between the right and the wrong, vain as the search for a
> man who shall be neither a living man nor a dead man....
> Neither let us be frightened from our duty by threats of
> dungeons for ourselves. Let us have faith that right
> makes might, and in that faith, to the end, dare to do our
> duty as we understand it.'*

The Skirmishing: 1950-59

In the fall of 1950, long simmering dissatisfaction with grossly inferior school conditions came to a head in the black community
of New Orleans. On November 6, 1950, an evening meeting organized by the Ninth Ward Civic and Improvement League was held
at the Macarty School, a rambling frame firetrap to which black elementary students had been assigned far beyond any reasonable capacity level.** Dan Byrd, a handsome, charismatic black civil rights
worker with some legal training, then and now employed as a representative of and self-styled "troubleshooter" for the Inc. Fund, spoke
to an overflow audience. Deep frustration over school conditions
had created an atmosphere of crisis: angry complaints were repeated about overcrowded conditions, platooning into daily double
sessions of black children but not white children, shortages of textbooks, out-of-date textbooks, teacher-pupil ratios, and, in most
cases, pathetic facilities. There was an agreement that legal action
should be taken in the federal courts under the auspices of Inc.
Fund attorneys. Byrd reported a plan for a two-pronged attack
against the New Orleans public education system, a system that had
been mandatorily segregated since its inception in 1877.

Although at the time of the Macarty School meeting the Su-

---

*"Moral Blindness," 191 Nation, Dec. 3, 1960, at 426 [hereinafter
cited as "Moral Blindness"].
**Macarty today, on the demolition schedule of the Orleans Parish
School Board for years, still stands and still serves an all-black
student body. It is as dilapidated as it was in 1950, the only "new"
improvements being a wire fence and a blacktopped playground.

preme Court had not yet elected to reconsider its decision in Plessy
v. Ferguson, informed observers were sufficiently encouraged by
recent higher education decisions (see discussion in Prologue) to attempt an all-out attack on public school segregation as unconstitutional in and of itself, without reference to comparisons of racial
treatment in sharing the public purse. Secondly, an alternative fall-
back position was to be pleaded should the Plessy v. Ferguson doctrine of separate but equal survive the concerted attack then being
made in several states. Byrd promised that he would conduct detailed investigations in support of the fall-back position, documenting
the grave disparities in treatment and in expenditure of funds between white and black pupils and schools at every stage of the educational process. Therefore, the suit would demand, in the alternative, that Louisiana be forced to spend massive amounts of money
to equalize the black educational system with the white system. On
reflection, Byrd candidly admitted that prior to Brown I and Brown
II the objective of the Inc. Fund attorneys was to make the dual
system of education so expensive to Southern states that segregation
"would fall of its own weight."

Oliver Bush, father of thirteen children and president of the
Macarty PTA, volunteered to have one of his sons, Earl Benjamin
Bush, act as a named plaintiff. Bush was an insurance salesman
for Louisiana Life Insurance Company, an all-black business concern. At Byrd's insistence, Bush informed the president of his
company of his intentions and, while expressing some concern about
possible attacks on his company's license to do business in the state,
the president agreed that Bush's job would be secure. However,
the president did insist that Byrd agree that the Inc. Fund bear all
the costs of litigation; the president did not want the unusually thrifty
Bush going into debt, even for the worthiest of causes. Thus began
Bush v. Orleans Parish School Board.

After Byrd's completion of the investigation of local conditions, Bush and other black parents filed a formal petition with the
Orleans Parish School Board. At a jammed meeting on November
12, 1951, well-dressed, intense black citizens demanded both an
end to discrimination against their children and their admission to
nearby under-utilized white schools. Mrs. Leontyne Luke, vice
president of the black portion of the Louisiana State PTA, described
the board's reception of the petition as "very cold." Predictably,
the local board denied the petition and after a second demand for
action was also refused, the petition was taken to Baton Rouge, the
state capital. There the Louisiana State Board of Education declined
to intervene, stating that placement policies were within the jurisdiction of the local board. The plaintiffs' administrative remedies
were exhausted. In September, 1952, still two years before Brown
I, Oliver Bush, on behalf of his son Earl Benjamin Bush and the
other black children named as plaintiffs, filed a class action suit in
the United States District Court for the Eastern District of Louisiana.

* * *

The United States District Court for the Eastern District of Louisiana was composed of two divisions, one at Baton Rouge* where Judge Herbert W. Christenberry sat and one at New Orleans presided over by Judge J. Skelly Wright. These two jurists had almost identical backgrounds: both were graduates of Loyola Law School in New Orleans, both were Democrats, both had been United States attorneys, and both were appointed by President Truman. Both are also courageous, forthright judges who felt an obligation to enforce the law as articulated by the Supreme Court in Brown I and Brown II. But the similarities between the two judges are not complete: a one-time English teacher at Fortier High School in New Orleans, Judge Wright is a master of the well-turned phrase who seems better adapted for appellate work than trial work. In contrast, Judge Christenberry, who had a longer experience as a trial attorney, is a blunt, scrupulously impartial man who feels truly alive only in the hurly-burly of the trial court.

Because Orleans Parish** was within Judge Wright's primary jurisdiction, he bore the greater burden of ensuring good faith efforts to desegregate the New Orleans school system. Judge Christenberry's role was as a member, together with Judge Wright and Judge Richard T. Rives of the Fifth Circuit, of the specially appointed three-judge panels convened on five separate occasions to decide the constitutionality of particular state statutes and policies. Judge Wright became the focal point of one of the most intensive campaigns of harassment and abuse ever suffered by an occupant of the bench of a United States court. Known to his colleagues as possessing a temper with a rather short fuse, the square-jawed, articulate New Orleans native was to display the kind of cool determination that amazed both friends and persecutors.

A Catholic and lifelong resident of New Orleans, James Skelly Wright began his legal career as an assistant United States attorney and served in that capacity until the outbreak of World War II. During the war, he served in combat as the commander of a Coast Guard subchaser. He met his wife Helen, the daughter of Admiral Raymond S. Patton, in London during the Blitz and courted her between buzz bombs--perhaps a foreordained conditioning for the anxiety of bomb threats they later faced in his native city. After the war, he became United States Attorney in New Orleans and within two years was appointed, in 1949, to the federal bench at age thirty-eight, becoming then the youngest member of the federal judiciary. During his turbulent years on the district court bench in New Orleans, Judge Wright faced many civil rights battles: he heard cases resulting in the desegregation of the professional schools of Louisiana State University in New Orleans and the desegregation of public buses and city parks, upheld interracial sports events, and restored

---

*Baton Rouge is now located in a newly created Middle District.
**A parish in Louisiana is equivalent to a county in other states.

the names of hundreds of blacks to voting lists. None of those cases, however, touched the raw nerve of the white citizens of Louisiana like the case brought by Oliver Bush against the Orleans Parish School Board.

* * *

Self-touted as "The City Care Forgot," New Orleans was one of the most unlikely of all Deep South cities to be the scene of violent opposition to desegregation. It had less residential segregation than any other major American city and for decades its white and black citizens had lived in apparent harmony, despite obvious inequalities in housing and public accommodations. By 1955, without turbulence, blacks had been hired as law enforcement officers, admitted to the public library, occupied all seats on public buses, and utilized all public recreation facilities in the city. Furthermore, New Orleaneans were considered blessed to have a forward-looking "reform" mayor, deLesseps S. "Chep" Morrison. The school board had for some years been staffed by candidates selected by the reform movement in the city: all were pledged to quality public education.

However, a closer look would indicate that New Orleans might indeed face serious problems. The city was at the mercy of the Governor and a malapportioned state legislature, and its representatives were a minority voice in a state government dominated by rural spokesmen from the northern part of the state.

Like ancient Gaul, modern Louisiana is divided into three parts, separate but not quite equal in political power: the North, the South, and the City--New Orleans.

* * *

After the Orleans Parish suit was filed in 1952, Samuel I. Rosenberg was appointed school board attorney. Seeing a way to put off a fight, he persuaded the overburdened Inc. Fund lawyers representing Bush that consideration of their clients' school case should be suspended pending a decision of the United States Supreme Court in The Segregation Cases later to be referred to as Brown v. Board of Education. Despite the fact that Brown I was decided in 1954 and Brown II was decided in 1955, the only action taken by the Inc. Fund lawyers in 1955 was to appear before the school board, once again requesting that it reorganize the public schools on a nondiscriminatory basis. As with most other school desegregation suits in the early years after the Supreme Court decisions, the Bush case suffered because there were too few lawyers engaged in the task of dismantling segregation to apply constant, sustained legal pressure everywhere.

However, the following year, the school board blundered tactically by formally requesting that Judge Wright dismiss Oliver Bush's complaint. By reactivating the case, the board brought Inc.

Fund lawyers back into New Orleans, where they promptly renewed
their request for a declaratory judgment that compulsory segregation
was unconstitutional. Fortified in the interim by the Supreme Court
decision in Brown I, attorneys for the black plaintiffs were now in
a much better strategic position to fight according to their original
battle plan's first line of attack--an all-out frontal assault on segregation.

For a defendant in any suit, much less a school desegregation case, to take steps to renew legal activity in litigation which
had lain dormant for two full years after Brown I is unusual. This
decision was not made upon the advice of Sam Rosenberg; instead,
he advised the board after Brown II that in his best opinion the
chance of overturning any Supreme Court decision rendered with the
unanimity and finality of Brown v. Board of Education was nonexistent. He frankly told his client that Brown I and II would be applicable to the Orleans Parish School Board, the Louisiana Constitution and all state statutes to the contrary notwithstanding.

One of the five school board members was Emile Wagner, a
generally competent lawyer. However, he was a man "with blinders
on" as far as integration was concerned: he simply refused to accept Rosenberg's counsel. Wagner had become convinced that desegregation would be avoided by New Orleans because support by
the governor and state legislature, in Wagner's judgment, could
"throw the cloak of sovereignty over the edifice of education."

Although members of the Southern bar have been roundly
criticized for their participation in the obstruction of judicial mandates in desegregation matters, Sam Rosenberg stands out as one
of a small group who refused to go along. When he realized that
the Wagner-dominated board was committed to what he felt was
costly and doomed litigation,* Rosenberg asked that he be relieved
of the duty of further representing the board on the Bush case. The
board agreed to hire other counsel to represent it in Bush and relieved Rosenberg from that job, although he continued to serve the
school board on all other legal matters.

The decision to reactivate the pending litigation, and indeed
most of the board's resistive maneuvers from 1956 until 1962,
stemmed from the collective master strategy of the two special attorneys retained by the board to replace Rosenberg. Gerard A.
Rault, a close friend of Wagner and attorney for Hybernia Home-
stead, the New Orleans savings and loan of which Emile Wagner was
president, shared Wagner's enthusiasm for the perpetuation of seg-

_____

*The board had adopted a formal resolution which stated: "It is not
only to the manifest interest of this Board and in accord with its
expressed policy, but also in furtherance of the public welfare of
this community that this suit and any others that might be instituted
with the same objective, be vigorously, aggressively, and capably
defended."

regation. He was also paid an initial salary of $25,000 from the time of his appointment to June 30, 1965, of which the local board had to pay $15,000 (the balance coming from a state "war chest" of $100,000 in public funds to assist local boards in defending segregation suits). In addition, Rault was paid $150 per day for each day in court and another $150 per day for each day he spent outside New Orleans.

The board's second special attorney, Leander Perez, hired to advise Rault, enjoyed a national reputation as the rabid segregationist boss of the adjoining deep delta parishes of Plaquemines and St. Bernard, both rich in offshore oil and minerals. Charges of Perez's involvement in voting irregularities, misuse of proceeds of oil revenues, and plain bullyism had circulated widely for years. Stories of the Perez wars with the federal government, Earl Long, and "niggers" are legion. At one time, he sponsored a scheme to give blacks one-way tickets to move North. Perez was considered the "kingfish of Louisiana's flannel-mouthed racists." He was also for years one of the key political powers manipulating the state legislature. He drove to Baton Rouge two weeks prior to every legislative session and remained throughout the session. While never a member of the legislature, Perez is reputed to have personally drafted most of the resistance legislation passed by the legislature to block desegregation of the Orleans Parish schools. As Perez said, "I always take the offensive. The defensive ain't worth a damn." Thus, in retrospect, the firing of the first volley by the Orleans Parish School Board's special attorneys--and not by the NAACP sponsored plaintiffs in the revived Bush case in 1956--is not surprising.

* * *

Attorneys for the plaintiff class of Negro children amended their original attack on the explicit segregation commandments of the Louisiana Constitution and statutes to include an updated challenge to certain changes made in the 1954 legislative session. To the state constitution, the legislature added what it hoped would be a saving clause: the segregation provision in the state constitution was now expressly premised on exercise of the state police power to protect public health and morals "and not because of race" (emphasis added). After amending the state constitution to command the enforcement of separation of the races in public schools in 1954 (the same year as Brown I was decided), the Louisiana Legislature proceeded to obey its own command. Exercising the state's "police power," the legislature enacted two statutes: the first provided for a fund cutoff (school books, supplies or lunch programs) to any integrated school and closed admission to any state university for the graduates of an integrated school; furthermore, violation of the state policy of segregation was made a crime. The second was the original version of Louisiana's Pupil Placement Act, which became the subject of heated controversy much later in the Orleans Parish litigation.

The plaintiffs asserted challenge to the constitutionality of Louisiana's laws seemed to require the convening of a three-judge panel. Without the benefit of the counsel of two of his judicial brethren, a single federal district judge is normally denied the power to decide alone whether or not state laws conflict with the United States Constitution and, hence, are void. The purpose of this check upon a single federal judge's power is obvious: it prevents undue exacerbation of federal-state relations. Therefore, whenever in a pending case the constitutionality of a state law is challenged, the federal district judge requests the Chief Judge of the Circuit to appoint two other federal judges, usually another district court judge and a circuit court judge, who join him to sit as a panel to consider the constitutional issue. The exception to this normal operating procedure occurs when there is no "serious" question concerning a state law's constitutionality, as where the statute is obviously and patently unconstitutional as written. The exception to the rule is illustrated by this challenge to Louisiana laws in the first round of the New Orleans litigation. However, exercising extra caution and wariness in this potentially explosive case,* Judge Wright requested that the Chief Judge convene a panel composed of himself, Judge Christenberry, and Judge Borah of the Fifth Circuit.

On February 15, 1956, the three-judge district court took just three paragraphs to dispose of the necessity for its continuation as a three-judge trial court. The unanimous per curiam, or unsigned opinion, tersely pointed out that "[i]n so far as the provisions of the Louisiana Constitution and [subordinate] statutes ... require or permit segregation of the races in public schools, they are invalid under ... Brown." Since the case posed no serious constitutional questions not previously decided by the Supreme Court of the United States, the court concluded that a continuation of the three-judge court was not required. The case was returned that same day to Judge Wright for further disposition.

---

*Judge Wright was aware by hard experience that a governmental defendant in a civil rights case can be voraciously hungry for time in which to conjure up any means to avoid, if not escape, undesirable mandates. By convening a three-judge district court immediately, Judge Wright may have been trying to avoid repetition of an earlier, time-consuming mistake. In the first round of the desegregation of Louisiana State University, despite defendant's protestations, Judge Wright had not submitted the request for a three-judge court to the Chief Judge of the Fifth Circuit nor did he in his opinion even refer to the matter, much less set out reasons why he considered such a court unnecessary. Obviously, in the LSU case he believed precedent demanding desegregated higher education facilities was so well established that no real purpose could be served by a three-judge court. However, submitting the three-judge request to the Chief Judge, or at least giving reasons why he would not grant the request in his opinion, could have prevented at least a portion of the three-year time loss to plaintiffs in that case. Judge Wright was not about to make the same "mistake" in Bush.

At the trial before Judge Wright, the school board essentially raised three issues. It first argued that basing a continued policy of segregation on the inherent "police power" of the state rehabilitated the state constitutional commandment of segregation even in the face of the Brown decisions. Secondly, it contended that this lawsuit was a suit by a citizen against the state which is expressly forbidden by the eleventh amendment to the United States Constitution. And, finally, it asserted that the plaintiffs had not exhausted their administrative remedies. Since each of these arguments was advanced countless times by boards bent on resistance throughout the country, perhaps each should be discussed here in some detail, although under established law, each argument was quite properly discounted as a defense by Judge Wright and also by the Fifth Circuit on appeal.

Shortly after the beginning of the Union, when the erstwhile colonies came together as states in a federation, those powers not expressly given the national government or forbidden the states by the Constitution were reserved to the individual states. Such powers are frequently referred to as "reserved powers." One of the powers generally recognized as reserved to the states by the Constitution is the police power. The term "police power" is interpreted as the power, as well as the primary duty, of each state to protect the public health, welfare, safety, and morals of its citizens. Thus, for example, a state can enact health and criminal laws for the governance of all those who reside within its boundaries, and states can differ about the standards of conduct each would exact from its own citizens.

The fourteenth amendment qualified a state's unrestricted exercise of its reserved powers by providing that no state could deprive a person of "equal protection of the law." The equal protection clause of the fourteenth amendment has never been interpreted to require a state to treat all of its' residents equally in every respect. A state can classify its residents and treat different classes of people differently, as long as its classifications are reasonable. For example, a state can prohibit blind persons from obtaining drivers licenses or forbid the purchase of liquor by minors. However, the equal protection clause does not allow unreasonable classifications: a state cannot prohibit all red-headed persons from obtaining drivers licenses or purchasing liquor. Determining whether a state's classification of its residents is reasonable under the equal protection clause of the fourteenth amendment has been one of the Supreme Court's primary sources of business. The equal protection clause of the fourteenth amendment gave rise to the holding in Brown I: classification of school children solely on the basis of race is unreasonable and therefore unconstitutional under the equal protection clause of the fourteenth amendment.

The first argument made by the Orleans Parish School Board was that by amending its constitution to premise continued school segregation directly on the police power of the state to protect the public health, welfare, safety, and morals (rather than explicitly on

race), Louisiana could avoid the Brown decision. In the Orleans
Parish case, Judge Wright summarily dismissed this justification
for segregation. Fifth Circuit Judge Elbert P. Tuttle, on appeal,
probed and ultimately revealed the racist assertion masquerading
under the cloak of the police powers argument. As he pointed out,
nowhere in the briefs did the board attempt to explain why racial
segregation in the public schools of New Orleans was any less the
segregation forbidden in Brown simply because it was expressly
premised on state police powers. Judge Tuttle noted:

> [T]he affidavits introduced on the hearing ... make clear
> what the briefs do not. They deal with the alleged dis-
> parity between the two races as to intelligence ratings,
> school progress, incidence of certain diseases, and per-
> centage of illegitimate births, in all of which statistical
> studies one race shows up to poor advantage. This repre-
> sents an effort to justify a classification of students by
> race on the grounds that one race possesses a higher per-
> centage of undesirable traits, attributes, or conditions.

Leander Perez could quote by memory from a 1902 edition of
the Encyclopaedia Britannica to support his often uttered charge that
the Negro is innately inferior because of an insufficient brain cavity.
Obviously with the aid of Perez, special counsel Rault had submitted
an appellate brief that was as candid an exposition of racism as was
ever filed with a United States appellate court. Twenty-one exhibits
were attached which, according to the brief's conclusion, "establish
only too well that a large segment of our Negro population has little
or no sense of morality and that to intermingle them with the white
children in our public schools could well corrupt the minds and
hearts of the white children to their lifelong and perhaps eternal injury."

With a caustic tone rarely seen in his spare, syllogistic prose
style, Judge Tuttle proceeded in the appellate opinion to annihilate
the police powers rationale:

> Strangely enough, there seems never to have been any ef-
> fort to classify the [white] students of the Orleans Parish
> according to the degree to which they possess these traits.
> That is, there seems to have been no attempt to deny
> schooling to, or to segregate from other children, those
> of illegitimate birth or having social diseases or having
> below average intelligence quotients or learning ability be-
> cause of those particular facts. Whereas any reasonable
> classification of students according to their proficiency or
> health traits might well be considered legitimate within
> the normal constitutional requirements of equal protection
> of the laws, it is unthinkable that an arbitrary classifica-
> tion by race because of a more frequent identification of
> one race than another with certain undesirable qualities
> would be such a reasonable classification.

Thus, Judge Tuttle laid bare the attempt by the board to relitigate the threshold defense advanced before the Supreme Court in Brown-- that classification by race was not arbitrary but rational under the police power of the state in view of certain allegedly inherent disparities between the two races. This is an important argument not because of its credibility but because it was and continued to be the underlying rationale of the opposition to desegregation in the South. Rather than merely chopping off another of the hydra-headed defensive stratagems employed by resistive boards, Judge Tuttle attempted to pierce through to the jugular of racism. The opinion was successful at least to the extent that the issue of the inherent disparities between races was never again raised in the Orleans Parish litigation, although it was repeatedly used out of court to inflame the public to resistance. Variations on this theme were heard in arguments of other southern desegregation cases until 1963 when it was finally silenced by Judge Tuttle once and for all in the Fifth Circuit's reversal of Judge Scarlett's handling of the Savannah, Georgia desegregation litigation.

The school board's claim of immunity to suit was also a stock-in-trade defense commonly asserted, but never relied upon for more than brief-filler by any but the most blindly optimistic or foolhardy. The eleventh amendment to the Constitution, ratified in 1797, provides: "The Judicial power of the United States shall not be construed to extend to any suit in law or equity, commenced or prosecuted against one of the United States by Citizens of another State, or by Citizens or Subjects of any Foreign state." Obviously, a state may elect to waive its immunity or otherwise consent to be sued. However, since 1908 the law has been established that a state may lose its immunity from suit by a private citizen when the state, through one of its officers or agents, acts illegally. Moreover, the specific question of the amenability of school boards to suit by aggrieved citizens was also settled law at least a decade before the Board of Education of Topeka et al. were successfully sued in the Brown decisions. Segregation had been outlawed in Brown I. Any action purportedly taken pursuant to a state policy of segregation thus made the state and its school boards vulnerable to legal challenge by any Negro citizen claiming he had been denied entry to a system yet segregated.

The last and most troubling contention of the school board, and one vigorously advanced, was that the plaintiffs had failed to exhaust their administrative remedies. The doctrine of exhaustion of administrative remedies requires that where an administrative remedy is provided by a state statute, relief must first be sought by a plaintiff from the administrative agency charged with providing the remedy before the courts will act. The public policy reasons underpinning the doctrine are fairly obvious: it is an additional effort by courts to avoid unnecessary friction with administrative agencies, the progeny of the executive branch of government, by not interfering prematurely with their processes. In addition, unnecessary litigation may be avoided if the aggrieved individual first presents his complaint for redress through the supervisory hierarchy. The exhaustion of remedies doctrine, however, contemplates responsible review by administrative decision-makers. If, for example, the plaintiff can show that the appeals process is ill-defined or is simply a rubber-stamping procedure, the doctrine may not be applied to preclude judicial review. The law does not require an individual to pursue an illusory remedy or one predestined as vain.

In considering the board's argument that the plaintiffs had not exhausted their administrative remedies under the Louisiana Pupil Assignment Act, Judge Wright dealt in some detail with the provisions of that statute. Despite an elaborate system of review of a child's complaint concerning placement in a particular school--from superintendent to parish board to Louisiana district court to Louisiana court of appeals--he noted that the Act significantly failed to provide any time limit within which the Parish board's reviewing decision was to be made and also failed to set out any standards by which the different levels of decision-makers were to be guided. Judge Wright held that Oliver Bush and the other black parents had clearly exhausted their administrative remedies, having petitioned the board three times for the adoption of a nondiscriminatory admission policy. To require further hearings, emphasized Judge Wright, "would be a vain and useless gesture, unworthy of a court of equity. It would be a travesty in which this court will not participate." What was not clear from Judge Wright's opinion was whether he had decided the larger issue of the constitutionality of the Pupil Assignment Act, and if so, on what grounds he based his findings.

Perhaps nowhere in all the reported race relations cases reviewed by the Fifth Circuit Court of Appeals is the traditional interplay and division of labor between the federal district and appellate courts better illustrated than in this first reviewed decision in the Bush case. As had been previously discussed, Judge Wright rather summarily dismissed the arguments of "police powers" and "immunity" as bordering upon the specious. As a first level trial court, the federal district court is subject to great time pressures for opinion publication; with a crowded docket and usually the assistance of only one law clerk, the district court judge can rarely indulge in the luxury of long deliberation and polished opinions. Unlike Judges Atwell and Davidson in Dallas, Skelly Wright gave his appellate court supervisors little cause for complaint. He followed the Supreme Court mandate in both letter and spirit; he was alert to an identification of the issues at stake; he was decisive, and even innovative when the occasion demanded.

In contrast to the more hectic life of the federal district court, the Court of Appeals is normally removed from the fray of the trial in both time and distance. Given a reasonable case load, the appellate court is engineered for reflection and consideration of the long-range ramifications of its decisions. With the advantage of full appellate briefs by parties, and occasionally from amici curiae in race relations cases, Courts of Appeals can fully assess the merits of the legal contentions and tailor carefully the design of their opinions.

Among the most painstaking judges of the Fifth Circuit's appellate court, Judge Tuttle, in affirming Judge Wright's decision, clarified and amplified the district court's ruling concerning the Pupil Assignment Act. He analyzed the bases for holding the act unconstitutional because of, in his words, "the role it might have in the future disposition of the case by the trial court." In so doing, he also laid the foundation for future disposition of cases from other school boards within the Circuit; pupil placement statutes and their effect upon dismantling segregated school systems became a dominant theme of much of the Court's later work. Judge Tuttle rejected the alternative of finding the Louisiana Act unconstitutional within the framework of other enactments passed by the state legislature which were obviously aimed at furthering segregation. Instead, the Fifth Circuit held that the Pupil Assignment Law was unconstitutional on its face by either the due process or equal protection standards of the fourteenth amendment, i. e., there were no standards to prevent administrative caprice and the only implied basis for assignment under the act was the prohibited standard of race.

Despite the efficient destruction of all of the school board's arguments in a decision affirmed on appeal, Judge Wright was not insensitive to the difficulties that would be faced by the board. He took pains to point out that under his order Orleans Parish would have time to adjust to the idea of desegregation. While the ultimate goal was desegregation and endless delay would not be tolerated, he explained that the granting of a temporary injunction did not mean that the public schools in Orleans Parish would be ordered completely desegregated overnight, or even in a year or more. He expressly recognized that the problems attendant on desegregation in the Deep South were considerably more serious than generally appreciated in some sections of the country and that integration was a problem which would require the utmost patience, understanding, generosity, and forbearance from all. He eloquently concluded in a strong, deeply felt ending: "But the magnitude of the problem may not nullify the principle. And that principle is that we are, all of us, freeborn Americans, with a right to make our way, unfettered by sanctions imposed by man because of the work of God." Judge Wright then drew the decree that stunned New Orleans and became the prototype mandated by the Court of Appeals in many early desegregation cases. Judge Wright became the first district court judge in the Fifth Circuit to place a school board under an injunction ordering that it no longer require segregation in any of its schools after such time "as may be necessary" to arrange for admission of children to schools on a nondiscriminatory basis "with all deliberate speed."

* * *

Louisa Dalcher wrote:

Waking up with a giant headache after Mardi Gras, 'The City Care Forgot' started cleaning up the debris left by the Lord of Misrule and his merry disporters, went solemnly to Lenten services, and read the early afternoon headlines: Court Orders Desegregation of New Orleans Schools. Six inches of rain fell that day.*

Reactions to Judge Wright's decree were somber. Dr. Clarence Scheps, a member of the school board and comptroller of Tulane University, set the tone for the defiance that later typified the actions of all branches of Louisiana government. "We will not integrate. We will use every legal and honorable means to maintain segregation.... We couldn't integrate even if we wanted to." Eric Severeid commented that the news from the South clearly foretold that the nation faced a period of "official, organized, flat refusal to obey Federal law," which was the most serious challenge to constitutional government since McCarthyism. He prophesied that the country would have to live with such defiance for years to come.

After issuance of Judge Wright's desegregation decree and while the school board's appeal was pending before the Fifth Circuit, the Louisiana Legislature renewed its obstructionist efforts. The legislature passed its first interposition resolution, attempting to interpose the sovereignty of the state of Louisiana "against encroachment upon the police powers reserved to [the] State...." New and interesting constitutional theories were expressed. The legislature stated that the United States Supreme Court had no authority to determine the two Brown decisions and appealed to God and to sister state legislatures to help arrest federal usurpation. The legislature further attempted to grant to itself the power to classify all New Orleans schools as exclusively for the use of white students or the use of Negro students. It passed a series of acts providing for the removal of any public school teacher, school bus operator, or any employee of the school system in Orleans Parish who advocated racial integration in the schools. And it amended the Louisiana Compulsory School Attendance Law to provide for suspension of that law where integration of the races had been required by court or other order (a particularly mischievous action that later was to allow thousands of white teenagers to bolt their schools and riot in the streets without fear of any truancy law).

Consistent with the reaction of the Louisiana Legislature, the Orleans Parish board exhausted every means to obtain reversal of the decision of the Tuttle-Rives-Brown Fifth Circuit panel affirming Judge Wright. On March 23, 1957, the school board petitioned for a rehearing and requested en banc consideration of the issues. Normally, regardless of the number of judges serving on it, a court of appeals divides itself into three-judge panels in order to expedite consideration and disposition of the bulk of its cases. If a party requests reconsideration by the court sitting as a whole and convinces a single judge that the issues at stake are sufficiently important to warrant a reexamination by all, the Circuit Judge then files a request

*Dalcher, "A Time of Worry In 'The City Care Forgot'," 14 The Reporter, March 18, 1956, at 17.

with the Chief Judge that all active members of the court be polled concerning whether an en banc court should be convened. If a majority concurs, the disputed case goes before the entire court for rehearing. An en banc proceeding is a rarity reserved for cases presenting difficult and important questions of law. On April 5, 1957, the Fifth Circuit denied the petition for en banc reconsideration of the Orleans Parish decision and Judge Wright's orders. The school board then petitioned the United States Supreme Court for a writ of certiorari, the procedure by which most cases seeking review reach the Supreme Court. Subsequently, the Supreme Court denied that request for its intervention unanimously.

* * *

If the decision of the Fifth Circuit affirming Judge Wright's decree did not give the more reflective residents of New Orleans a clear indication of the inevitability of desegregation, then surely the tragedy of Little Rock should have removed all lingering hopes for the maintenance of the status quo. Forced by the precipitate actions of Governor Orval Faubus, in September of 1957 President Eisenhower federalized the Arkansas National Guard and dispatched troops to enforce desegregation in Little Rock. In the judicial sequel to Eisenhower's action, in 1958, the Supreme Court, again unanimously, indicated in Cooper v. Aaron that public opposition to school desegregation was simply not to be considered by the judiciary as a reason for postponing or denying the enforcement of fourteenth amendment rights under Brown I and II. The stern condemnation of Faubus contained in Cooper v. Aaron, combined with a firm reassertion of the Supreme Court's role as final interpreter of the Constitution, should have been sufficient proof for any observer, however pro-segregationist, that future resistance was futile.

But the Louisiana Legislature from 1954 through 1962 was anything but perceptive or yielding. At the same time the debacle of Little Rock was being exposed by the media to the eyes of the world, the Louisiana Legislature was gearing up for production of more segregation legislation. The Louisiana School Board Association joined the Louisiana Legislature's Joint Committee* in urging passage of a resolution containing detailed suggestions for legislation to preserve segregation in the state of Louisiana.

Apparently undaunted and despite the less than encouraging results of its first appeal to the Fifth Circuit and its failure to convince the Supreme Court to review the Court of Appeals' decision, the New Orleans School Board began a second appeal to the Fifth Circuit. The grounds of this appeal approached the frivolous. Sixteen months after entry of the decree of the district court, the

---

*The Joint Committee on Segregation was established in 1954, in reaction to Brown I. It was given wide powers, a fat budget, and it largely controlled legislative public expression on the race question, providing a haven for the views of militant segregationists.

Bush plaintiffs had failed to file a nominal $1,000 bond required in that decree. This time Judges Hutcheson, Tuttle, and Jones comprised the panel for the Court of Appeals. Judge Tuttle tersely pointed out for the panel that the injunction entered by Judge Wright required no action on the defendants' part nor did it prohibit specific acts; therefore, the fact that the bond was not executed could not possibly have damaged the defendants. Furthermore, as shown by the first appeal, the injunction was in fact properly granted, and the defendants were not wrongfully enjoined. Incredibly, the school board petitioned for a rehearing, which was denied on March 28, 1958. Pursuing this procedural flyspeck, the school board again petitioned for a writ of certiorari with the United States Supreme Court; that petition was also denied.

When its second appeal failed, the school board, unsatiated, went back to Judge Wright. Under an injunction containing no enforcement date and fighting overextended Inc. Fund attorneys who were desperately trying to stay even with legal battles all across the South, that the school board would again take the offensive--in view of the extreme risk that such action would accelerate desegregation-- is amazing. The new contention was that the board had no power to obey the desegregation decree issued by Judge Wright. The Louisiana Legislature in 1956 had passed a statute that set up a new committee, with two members from each legislative house. By way of this new Special School Classification Committee, the legislature divested local school boards and reserved to itself the sole power and authority to "classify" public schools for the exclusive use of the children of the Negro race and the children of the Caucasian race. On the basis of this statute the Orleans Parish School Board moved to vacate the court's injunction and dismiss the Bush litigation on the ground that the board no longer controlled the classification of public schools; consequently, they simply could not be enjoined. In a concise, much-quoted opinion, Judge Wright summarily disposed of the school board's new contention:

> It would serve no useful purpose to labor this matter. The Supreme Court has ruled that compulsory segregation by law is discriminatory and violative of the equal protection clause of the Fourteenth Amendment.... Any legal artifice, however cleverly contrived, which would circumvent this [Brown I] ruling, and others predicated on it, is unconstitutional on its face. Such an artifice is the statute in suit.

Undeterred by its past defeats, the school board began the process of appealing Judge Wright's latest order. Attorney Rault's major contention on appeal was again that the school board did not have the authority to segregate schools under the school classification act declared unconstitutional by Judge Wright. The appeal was bolstered by the contention that Judge Wright should not have declared the act unconstitutional without first waiting for an authoritative interpretation of the act by the Louisiana Supreme Court.

A Fifth Circuit panel of Chief Judge Hutcheson and Judges
Rives and Tuttle affirmed Judge Wright's latest order on June 9,
1959, in a short per curiam opinion. The Court first reaffirmed
that Bush was entitled to an order directing the board to cease operating racially segregated schools at an unspecified date in the future. The Court then noted that the act in question only purported
to give to the legislature the power to alter the racial classification
of schools; the operation of the schools was still confined to the Orleans Parish School Board. Therefore, the board, as operator of
the schools, was still the proper party to be enjoined and the injunction remained in full force and effect.

Twenty days later, the board petitioned the Fifth Circuit for
a rehearing, again strongly urging that the legislature's School Classification Act should have been interpreted by the Louisiana State
Supreme Court prior to its being reviewed by the federal courts.
Responding to the petition for rehearing, Judge Tuttle wrote a short
opinion for the same panel which had previously considered the matter. In that opinion he patiently explained in simple terms why the
question of the constitutionality of the legislature's School Classification Act was unnecessary for the Fifth Circuit to reach and, therefore, why the consideration of whether there should be a deferral to
wait for a construction of the act by the Louisiana Supreme Court
was unnecessary. Under the statute in question, the local school
board was still responsible for the operation of the school system,
and the original injunction remained in force.

Judge Tuttle's opinion was carefully written; the issue of
whether or not the state's school classification committee members
or the Louisiana Legislature were bound by the terms of the injunction was skillfully avoided for the time being. However, by failing
to meet this statute head-on, firmly resolving the question of its
constitutionality, the Fifth Circuit merely postponed the issue for
the federal courts a year later. Furthermore, by pointing out that
the school board was the proper party to be enjoined because it
still was in effective control of the schools, the Fifth Circuit provided a new strategy for the legislature to use--seizure of total control of all school board functions. Angered to a fevered pitch by
the steady string of defeats handed the school board by the federal
courts, the legislature adopted that tack a year later.

In the meantime, the Louisiana Legislature had been enacting
more pedestrian types of segregation laws common throughout the
South. It passed a statute authorizing the governor to close any public school under court order to desegregate. It passed legislation
authorizing the creation of educational cooperatives to provide private educational facilities; such cooperatives were then authorized
to borrow money from the state and from other sources. And, it
provided for a system of tuition grants for children attending non-
sectarian private schools, where no racially segregated public school
was available.

*   *   *

To fuel legislative fires further, on the same day the decision was issued by the Court of Appeals, denying the defendant's last motion, Judge Wright ordered the local board to present a plan of desegregation by March 1, 1960. He suggested that the board consider desegregating the first grade in the first year, the first and second grades the second year, and so on until all grades had been covered by the plan. In issuing his order, Judge Wright tried to appeal to the good sense of the community's citizens. The choice of whether New Orleans would become another Little Rock, he said, did not depend only upon the deliberations of the school board, but it was a decision which the entire community must face. He expressed the hope that influential citizens would take their place on the side of law and order. On October 9, 1959, Judge Wright changed the date for submission of a plan from March 1, 1960, to May 16, 1960. May 16 became D-day for the board and New Orleans.

The Supreme Court's desegregation order had been a favorite target of Louisiana politicians from the day it was issued, but Judge Wright's deadline of May 16, 1960, for submission of a desegregation plan transformed the theoretical issue of desegregation into an immediate threat. Desegregation of the Orleans Parish public schools became the incandescent issue of the gubernatorial campaign in 1959 and 1960. Any position by any politicial short of diehard defense of segregation was politically untenable. In an eleven-person primary race, among the strongest contenders was State Senator Willie Rainach, an extreme segregationist backed by Emile Wagner, the segregationist member of the Orleans Parish School Board and a prominent figure in the White Citizens' Council. Rainach, with a demonic appeal based on a fanaticism against "mixing the bloods," finished a strong third. Though eliminated, he drew a sufficient vote to remain a key factor in the runoff between Chep Morrison, the handsome mayor of New Orleans, and Jimmie Davis, the erstwhile hillbilly singer and composer of "You Are My Sunshine." Jimmie "I never done nobody no harm" Davis had served a previous term as Governor on a political platform of "peace and harmony." Both Morrison (until the campaign considered a moderate on racial issues) and Davis campaigned as segregationists. As Davis abandoned his previous peace and harmony theme and campaigned on a racial platform, he reminded voters that the Negro precincts in New Orleans had given Mayor Morrison a huge majority in the primary. Morrison was pushed further and further into a segregationist corner, tarnishing his image as a reform mayor and dismaying moderate and liberal supporters. Morrison's flirtation with extremist elements gained him nothing. Despite a healthy lead in the first primary, he was defeated by 54.1 per cent of the vote in the runoff, principally by Davis's blatant racism. During the runoff primary, Emile Wagner transferred his support of Rainach to Davis. Wagner told the public that he had a personal commitment from Davis that, if governor, Davis would prevent the school board from carrying out the pending desegregation order. Citing the traditionally nonpartisan posture of the parish school board, Wagner's fellow school board members asked him to resign because of his extensive campaigning activities first for Rainach, then for Davis. Wagner refused.

* * *

Emile Wagner was not only a thorn in the side of the Orleans Parish School Board; he also caused enormous difficulties for the powerful parochial school system in New Orleans. Approximately two-thirds of the New Orleans population is Catholic and their Archbishop, Joseph Francis Rummel, had a liberal reputation on race relations. As early as 1949, Archbishop Rummel cancelled a holy hour service because the religious procession would be segregated; he ordered white and colored signs removed from the pews in the church; and on the Sunday following Judge Wright's February 15, 1956 ruling that the Orleans Parish public schools would have to be desegregated, Archbishop Rummel proclaimed in a pastoral letter that racial segregation was "morally wrong and sinful." Rummel was subjected to heavy criticism by New Orleans Catholics for his stand. Among other indignities, a cross was burned on his lawn and some priests refused to read his pastoral letter. Worn by pressure and age, Rummel seemed to lose his appetite for the struggle. On October 9, 1960, in the midst of the desegregation crisis involving the public schools, Rummel, then eighty-three years old, fell and broke an arm and a leg. The church bureaucrats acting in his absence had no desire to mount a fight against lay Catholic segregationists. Thus parochial schools in New Orleans were not desegregated until 1962, two years after the public schools had paved the way. Emile Wagner, a devout Catholic and a daily communicant, was one of Archbishop Rummel's most taxing burdens. Wagner was a man of considerable standing in the Catholic community of New Orleans. Although a widower with five children to rear, he had been a former president of the Loyola Alumni Association and a key Catholic civic leader in New Orleans.

After his letter on the sinfulness of segregation, Archbishop Rummel was frontally challenged by Wagner. Within a month of the pastoral letter in mid-March 1956, Wagner persuaded dozens of Catholics to form an organization called the Association of Catholic Laymen. That association took out newspaper ads opposing Archbishop Rummel's position. Rummel ordered the association disbanded. Wagner, obeying reluctantly yet unrepentant, appealed to the Pope in a letter specifically attacking Rummel's charge that segregation was sinful. The Pope did not respond.

* * *

The Orleans Parish School Board is most unusual in the annals of desegregation cases. All five members had been elected through the support of the reform faction in Orleans Parish. The board was a stable unit of citizens: there was no membership change during this decade of the desegregation battle, although by the early sixties there was an unmistakable turnover in leadership within the board. That Emile Wagner dominated the board's decision-making throughout the fifties is perhaps better explained by the fact that he was the only lawyer member of the board rather than by the misleading assumption that the other members embraced segregation as passionately as did Wagner. While publicly supporting segregation, in the context of New Orleans public opinion, the other four members of the board were racial "moderates." They were Theodore Shepard, a shrimp importer; Matthew Sutherland, an insurance company executive who won re-election in 1960 just prior to the desegregation of the schools; Louis Riecke, a lumber company executive; and Lloyd Rittiner, an engineer, who was then president of the board. They were all described as young, honest, civic-minded, nonpolitical businessmen or professionals. Other than Wagner, they did not burn with a segregation-or-else attitude; they believed in public education, and when put to the test, they were willing to fight for it. In the early spring of 1960, in an act of rare personal and political courage, the president of the school board, Lloyd Rittiner, a large, pleasant bear of a man, made a televised statement in which he announced his preference for desegregation rather than closed schools. He said in part, "I am a segregationist--if, however, I am faced with the choice of integrating or closing, I am already on record as favoring integration to the extent that it is necessary to comply with the law...." Mr. Rittiner was the first public official in New Orleans to take this stand.

After Judge Wright set his May 16, 1960 deadline for submission of a plan of desegregation, the four moderate members of the school board began to perceive that the board's position on segregation could no longer be legally supported. They also knew that black children in their city were not receiving equal educational opportunities, even though the Plessy v. Ferguson command of separate but equal was a mandate recognized in Louisiana. In March, 1960, Dr. George Iggers of Dillard University reported that in the previous year white public school capacity utilization was seventy-three per cent as opposed to a black public school capacity utilization of 114 per cent. Furthermore, 1,687 black children were on a daily double-session "platoon system"; no white children attended schools which employed platooning. These facts, damning as they were to the separate-but-equal concept, were confirmed by Emile Wagner. The Orleans Parish School Board found itself caught in the middle between federal desegregation orders and state laws forbidding desegregation. President Rittiner arranged for a poll to be taken of parental preferences in the hope that most parents would support open schools, even if integrated on a token basis, rather than having no public school system at all. The results of the poll were profoundly disappointing to the four moderate members of the board. While a majority of all parents of both races favored open schools, the overwhelming majority of white parents voted for closed rather than open schools. Of white parents, 12,229 voted for closure and only 2,707 for desegregation; 11,407 black parents voted for desegregation, 679 for closure.

New Orleans in the spring of 1960 was a city in desperate need of leadership. While its public education system was threatened by organized diehard opposition to Judge Wright's order, as late as June 26, 1960 the New Orleans newspapers had taken no stand on the desegregation issue. On that late date, content to describe the choice that faced the city as either no schools or desegregation, the Times-Picayune equivocated by supporting neither choice. Thus all through the crucial fall, winter, and spring of 1959 and 1960, when the board should have been preparing a desegregation plan and community leaders should have been preparing the community, no effort was being exerted by the influential citizens of New Orleans to meet the inevitable.

The Battle: 1960-61.

> The crowd was waiting for the white man who dared to bring his white child to school. And here he came along the guarded walk ... leading his frightened child by the hand.... A shrill, grating voice rang out. The crowd broke into howls and roars....
>
> No newspaper had printed the words these women shouted. It was indicated that they were indelicate, some even said obscene. On television the sound track was made to blur or had crowd noises cut in to cover. But now I heard the words, bestial and filthy and degenerate. In a long and unprotected life I have seen and heard the vomitings of demoniac humans before. Why then did these screams fill me with a shocked and sickening sorrow?
>
> The words written down are dirty, carefully and selectedly filthy. But there was something far worse here than dirt, a kind of frightening witches' Sabbath. Here was no spontaneous cry of anger, of insane rage. Perhaps that is what made me sick.... Here was no principle good or bad....
>
> The crowd behind the barrier roared and cheered and pounded one another with joy....
>
> *   *   *
>
> Where were the others--the ones who would be proud they were of a species with the [father who braved the crowd] .... Perhaps they felt as helpless as I did, but they left New Orleans misrepresented to the world. The crowd, no doubt, rushed home to see themselves on television, and what they saw went out all over the world, unchallenged by the other things I know are there."*

On May 16, 1960, the day its desegregation plan was due,

---

*Inger, Politics and Reality in an American City: The New Orleans School Crisis of 1960, at 57-58 (1969), reprinted by permission of Center for Urban Education; quotation from J. Steinbeck, Travels With Charlie in Search of America, at 255-57 (1963), reprinted by permission of Viking Press.

the school board came before Judge Wright empty-handed. Frustrated by a state statute prohibiting any effort whatsoever to aid desegregation and ostensibly blocked by a Louisiana Court of Appeals decision upholding the 1956 School Classification Act and construing it as depriving the board of its power to classify schools, the board simply failed to comply with Judge Wright's order to submit a desegregation plan. A fourth generation New Orleans native, a neighbor of Leander Perez, and a personal friend of several of those involved in the current dispute, including Emile Wagner, Judge Wright knew the dilemma facing the board. Rather than reacting with contempt citations, which were clearly warranted in view of the failure of the members of the board to comply with his order to produce a plan, Judge Wright coolly entered his own plan for the desegregation of the New Orleans schools. In so doing, he became the first district court judge in the circuit to set a specific date for the beginning of desegregation. He ordered that beginning with the first day of school in September, 1960, black children entering the first grade could apply at their option for transfer to the previously all-white school nearest their home and that consideration of their transfer applications could not be based on race. Lulled by the narcotic-like effect of endlessly reitereated promises by the state's legions of Perezes, Wagners, and Rainaches, the white citizens of New Orleans were shaken by the order to desegregate far worse than by any Gulf hurricane.

Seventeen days later, specific counsel Gerard Rault appealed on behalf of the school board to the Fifth Circuit for a stay of Judge Wright's momentous order. The Fifth Circuit, Judge Cameron dissenting, refused to grant the stay. The battle between the federal courts and the state government was joined with fierce resolve. However, the battle lines were no longer drawn between the federal judiciary and the local school board. The legislative, judicial, and executive branches of state government took command of the segregationist forces in the New Orleans struggle.

The Louisiana Legislature sprang into frenzied action. A bill was passed providing that any person, firm, or corporation who furnished school books or supplies without charge to any racially mixed schools, public or private, or anyone who assisted or even recognized such a school, was guilty of a misdemeanor and could be given a fine of any size or imprisoned for any period. An act was literally shouted into law providing that the legislature must approve any school's desegregation plan before such a plan would be effective. The governor was authorized to supersede school boards affected by desegregation decrees and to take over the operation of the schools formerly under the control of such boards. The governor was also authorized to close all schools in the state, if necessary, to preserve segregation.

In addition to legislative interference, the Louisiana judiciary was again brought into the battle. On July 25, 1960, Louisiana Attorney General Jack P. F. Gremillion filed suit in a state court, the Civil District Court for the Parish of Orleans, asking for an injunction restraining desegregation. On July 29, 1960, that court issued the requested injunction. Presumably embarrassed by its flagrantly unconstitutional attempt to enjoin the school board from carrying out a lawful federal court order, the state court suggested that the school board might comply with both the federal court injunction and the countervailing state court injunction by simply closing the schools. Momentarily outflanked by the use of all branches of the state government to frustrate desegregation, Inc. Fund attorneys filed a motion in federal court that both the governor and the attorney general of the state of Louisiana be made additional parties defendant in the lawsuit against the school board; that request was granted by Judge Wright on August 16, 1960.

The next day, the governor announced that he was assuming control of the New Orleans schools. He appointed Dr. James Redmond, then superintendent of the Orleans Parish schools, as his agent.

* * *

Another more significant, but less dramatic event occurred that same day. A group of white parents took legal action to prevent the closing of the public schools. Williams v. Davis, filed on behalf of the intervening white parents, was consolidated by Judge Wright with the Bush case. For the first time, a group of white parents was willing publicly to advocate open schools.

The Williams suit was no fortuity. Lloyd Rittiner, president of the school board, and the other three moderates on the board, could see the inevitability of desegregation after Judge Wright's May 16, 1960 order. They were also painfully aware that neither they nor any other responsible civic leaders in New Orleans had made any preparations for desegregation. Furthermore, any move they made as a board would be reported immediately by Emile Wagner, both to the legislature's Joint Committee on Segregation and to the White Citizens' Council. Therefore, with his back to the wall, Rittiner formed a committee to fight to keep the schools open. The four moderate members of the board, Superintendent Redmond, and Sam Rosenberg, the school board's regular counsel who had withdrawn from the Bush case in 1956, were asked to serve on the committee. Utilization of the committee device allowed meetings to be held in private without inviting Emile Wagner.

Also in August, 1960, Inc. Fund lawyers filed a motion to remove Attorney General Gremillion's state court proceeding to Judge Wright's court. Now actively fighting for open schools against the legislature, Sam Rosenberg concluded--correctly or incorrectly-- that the NAACP was toying with the idea of acquiescing in a school closing to force national opinion to bear on the issue of desegregated schools. He therefore recommended that a lawsuit be brought by white citizens interested in seeing the schools remain open. In taking this step Rosenberg hoped to gain control of the school case, thereby forcing the NAACP out of the fight. With the approval of the board's four moderates, Rosenberg formed a new public group, the Committee to Preserve Education (CPE). CPE had no interest in civil rights as such; the group's only purpose was to battle for the preservation of public education in New Orleans. Rosenberg persuaded another New Orleans attorney, Charles Richards, to act as an attorney for white parents willing to become named plaintiffs and to intervene in Bush. Rosenberg worked all night on August 16, 1960, in Richards' office preparing the Williams suit, and it was filed on August 17, 1960. The strategy in Williams was brilliant. The white parents first publicly disassociated themselves from the NAACP by asking Judge Wright to dissolve his injunction; then, knowing full well that such a request was fruitless, they asked in the alternative that the court enjoin state officials from interfering with the public schools. The actions of CPE and Save Our Schools (SOS), a more liberal group also fighting for open schools, while woefully late, indicated that there were some white citizens of New Orleans who were willing to stand against the torrent of racism spewing forth from Baton Rouge and every parish seat in Louisiana.

* * *

In the face of the Governor's announced seizure of the public schools and the plethora of legislation passed to forestall desegregation, Judge Wright could not sit idle. He convened a three-judge district court consisting of Chief Judge Rives of the Fifth Circuit and Judges Christenberry and Wright. With opinions issued without notation of authorship, but in fact written by Judge Wright, that court sat for months through a storm of abuse both legal and extralegal. On August 27, 1960, shortly before the opening of school, the three-judge court methodically reviewed the chronology of events in the Bush litigation to that date, concluding with an analysis of the statutes passed by the state legislature and the action of the Governor in seizing control of the New Orleans schools. The court then systematically struck down each legal roadblock. The School Classification Act (the decision on the constitutionality of which was deferred by the Fifth Circuit a year earlier) was declared unconstitutional on its face "because it gives the Legislature the right to decide whether a public school shall be segregated or not, and the Brown case teaches that no one has this right." Like the state legislature and state judicial officers, the governor was also held to be bound by Brown.

The various acts giving the governor the right to close individual schools or to close all schools in the state were found "more sophisticated" than the others but "no less unconstitutional." The acts withholding from integrated schools all state funds for such items as free school books, supplies, and lunches were likewise stricken. In total, the court rendered unconstitutional seven acts of the legislature and then issued sweeping injunctions restraining, among others, Governor Jimmie Davis, State Judge Oliver P. Carriere of the Civil District Court for the Parish of Orleans, Attorney General Jack P. F. Gremillion, and State Treasurer A. P. Tugwell.

* * *

At the hearing on August 27, 1960, the three-judge federal court had a firsthand demonstration of the contemptuous attitude of Louisiana officialdom toward the federal courts. In a confrontation with the court, Attorney General Jack Gremillion was cited for contempt. The federal courtroom was packed with attorneys, members of the press, and observers. Thurgood Marshall, A. P. Tureaud, and Marcel Trudeau represented the plaintiffs. Hep Many, the United States attorney in New Orleans, represented the Justice Department and Charles Richards represented the Williams plaintiffs. Gerard Rault, the school board attorney, was making his last appearance for the board. Attorney General Gremillion was present with several members of his staff representing the state of Louisiana. When Charles E. Richards, attorney for the white parents, attempted to introduce several affidavits, Attorney General Gremillion became infuriated. He protested vehemently, claiming he had not been given an opportunity to examine the affidavits prior to the hearing. Even after Judge Rives assured him that he would have a chance to read and respond to the affidavits, Gremillion exploded, "You are violating my constitutional rights.... I do not consider this Justice. You are not playing the game according to the rules. You are running over us roughshod." Slamming a law book to the table, he charged from the courtroom announcing, "I'm not going to stay in this den of iniquity." As he pushed out the door, unseen by the court, he spat at Leontyne Luke and Ethel Young, black representatives of the New Orleans PTA, and several other black women crowded at the rear of the courtroom. In the hallway he bellowed that he had just left a "kangaroo court."

Back in the stunned hush of the courtroom, one of Gremillion's assistants, a career state attorney bent with age and advanced arthritis, rose and requested that the court grant the other state attorneys leave to withdraw since Gremillion had left them no instructions and there was nothing more they could do. Judge Rives granted the request. Judge Christenberry, sitting next to Judge Rives, reports that as Gremillion pushed out of the courtroom, Judge Rives, in his courtly fashion, whispered to Judge Christenberry, "Herbert, we've got to do something about that young man." Judge Rives then proceeded to dictate into the record an order for the United States attorney to prepare appropriate contempt charges. At a hearing held on the contempt citation a few weeks thereafter, Attorney General Gremillion reportedly attempted to explain that the court had misunderstood his parting remarks: instead of calling the courtroom "a den of iniquity," he had actually referred to it as "a den of inequity." Despite the clever sophistry of his explanation, Gremillion was given a sixty-day sentence which was suspended upon his serving eighteen months on probation. Federal District Judge Edwin F. Hunter characterized Gremillion as "a fighter, and the world loves a fighter, but he fought out of bounds." Gremillion sobbed with joy at his close escape from prison.*

---

*As this book is being written, former Atty. Gen. Gremillion is serving a federal prison term for perjury in connection with a commercial fraud. He was reelected to office while under the perjury indictment.

* * *

After the August 27, 1960 order, there was no legal obstacle to enforcement of the decree requiring desegregation to commence with the first day of school in September. Having played out his string of defeats, Gerard Rault resigned, admitting to the board--as the four moderate members had known for months--that there was simply no further legal action he could take. The board was faced with a crisis unparalleled in its existence. No steps had been taken to comply with Judge Wright's order, and precious few days were left before school was to open. The four moderates pleaded with Sam Rosenberg to do something to give them time to comply; however, they did not want Rosenberg, publicly identified with CPE, to appear openly as the board's new counsel immediately on the heels of Rault's resignation. Rosenberg prepared a telegraphic request for a stay to the United States Supreme Court for Lloyd Rittiner's signature as president of the board. Rosenberg called Judge Wright ex parte from Superintendent Redmond's office on behalf of the board and told Judge Wright that, with Rault out of the picture, the board, excluding Wagner, was willing to comply with the court's order but that it was desperate for additional time. Among other things, target schools and black children willing to hazard abuse and perhaps personal danger had to be selected.

The only legal method by which the board could select black applicants was the Louisiana Pupil Assignment Act which established an elaborate testing and interview program governing school transfers. While that act, to be sure, had been adopted as a further barrier to desegregation, it did not specifically mention race as a criterion to be utilized by a school board in passing on transfer applications. Furthermore, the Louisiana Pupil Assignment Act was a verbatim copy of the Alabama Pupil Placement Law upheld by the Supreme Court in the Shuttlesworth case as constitutional on its face, provided it was applied in a nondiscriminatory manner.

The board, through Rosenberg, pledged to Judge Wright that the act would be applied nondiscriminatorily. They realized some black children had to be selected, but because of the complexity of the act, the school board needed time. Convinced of the good faith of the board and impressed by Rosenberg's entreaties,* Judge Wright scheduled a hearing to hear formally the board's motion for a delay. Again, Rosenberg's role was not made public. Lloyd Rittiner appeared publicly on behalf of the board before the three-judge court, announced Rault's resignation as counsel, and said the board was ready to comply but needed time. He requested a delay until after Christmas. The three-judge court publicly announced that, because of evident sincerity and good faith of the board in its desire to carry out the orders of the court, it would stay the order to integrate until November 14, 1960.

---

*It is reported that Judge Wright met privately with the four moderate members of the board at a meeting arranged by Rosenberg.

Critics have argued that the court blundered by granting the delay until November 14. They argue that precious time was given to the White Citizens' Council and the legislature to foment opposition. But they fail to realize that time was also given to the forces supporting the schools. Board member Matthew Sutherland was running for reelection on a platform of open schools. The Nixon-Kennedy presidential election of 1960 was entering the homestretch with neither party anxious for a replay of Little Rock in New Orleans. Finally, the argument made to Judge Wright by Sam Rosenberg concerning the time necessary to comply with the Pupil Assignment Act was valid--the act was complex and it appeared to be binding on the board.

With the delay acquired by Rosenberg, the board had two immediate problems: how to select the black children and how to select the schools. Board members candidly admit that they manipulated the screening process to be employed by Superintendent Redmond to hold to the bare minimum necessary to comply with the federal court order the number of black children who were to be integrated. Furthermore, in order to prevent Emile Wagner from learning the names of the children and schools selected, and concerned that it could not allow certain of its members such information and keep the same information from fellow-board member Wagner, the board instructed Superintendent Redmond to have his staff select the two schools to be desegregated and the children to be assigned and to keep the information secret from the board.

Over 130 black children had applied for transfer to all-white schools; of this number, five six-year-old black girls were selected through the use of a complex screening process. Dr. Robert Coles, eminent child psychiatrist and author, conducted an intensive study of the children selected for integration in New Orleans and Atlanta; in his report, he makes some interesting observations about the effectiveness of even the most sophisticated selection process:

> The irony of human existence is often revealed in striking examples, which upset all the expectations of experience and knowledge. As in war, and as in disaster, a crisis will reveal hidden weaknesses as well as show unexpected strengths, and these both are often hard to predict in advance.
> One child may score high in intelligence tests, may be polite and neatly dressed, but also may come from a home with many tensions below the surface, and may, under stress, respond with nervous overactivity, withdrawal from friends, or severe bodily evidence of anxiety, such as gastric disorders or migraine. Another child may be somewhat dull and of dubious sociability, but may draw in tough times upon a sense of humor or a relaxed disposition which may not be attractive or ingratiating to others, but may be quite resilient and enduring.*

*Coles, "The Desegregation of Southern Schools: A Psychiatric Study," in Integration vs. Segregation, at 201, 206 (H. Humphrey, ed., 1964) [hereinafter cited as Coles].

Fortune attended the intensive search for the black first-graders in New Orleans: as will be seen, they exhibited a serenity which belied their years.

However, the choice of the two schools to be integrated has been widely condemned by almost all observers. McDonough 19 and William Frantz were neighboring schools in predominantly white but nevertheless racially mixed, blue-collar neighborhoods. A concentration of white working class families supplied the bulk of the student population. In retrospect, the schools chosen appear to have been in the very neighborhoods where white hostility to race-mixing would be the greatest and where white parents were the least prepared to cope with the stress of desegregation. Furthermore, the close proximity of the two schools to each other facilitated organized protests. During the bitter white boycott, when the screaming women of New Orleans had reached their pinnacle of rage, the Wall Street Journal reported the statement of a Kennedy administration official that the choice of the two schools was the "worst possible." Why did the board decide to select those two schools rather than readily available middle-class white schools where parents perhaps were more likely to value an education and to abhor violence?

The superintendent attempted to apply the Pupil Assignment Act under policy directives laid down by the board. Under the act, children transferred had to have test scores equal to or above the median for the schools to which they were applying. Consequently, the superintendent's staff restricted their choice of schools to those with low median scores. The staff further projected that, since the two schools ultimately selected were in racially mixed neighborhoods and since the little black girls selected had above average intelligence for the two schools, the girls would not only succeed academically but would also be more accepted socially. The staff was at least partially right: the girls did succeed academically; however, they were not received socially.

* * *

After Judge Wright's postponement of desegregation until November 14, 1960, the state became embroiled in election year politics. In addition to the Nixon-Kennedy election, New Orleans was intrigued by the local school board race. Running on a platform of open schools, incumbent Matthew Sutherland provided a test of the true feelings of New Orleans residents as to whether they favored open or closed schools. His opponents were John Singreen, an insurance executive backed by the White Citizens' Council; Carl Vesy, a young lawyer who seemed to be in favor of closed rather than desegregated schools; and Mrs. Marie McCoy, who indicated that she would do whatever the public wanted on the issue of desegregation. Emile Wagner, the segregationist member of the board, endorsed Singreen and declared that Sutherland had flaunted the desire of the people by agreeing to desegregate schools rather than close them.* Wagner predicted the complete failure of any attempt at desegregation. He based this prescience upon tests which he claimed indicated that forty per cent of all black students were mental idiots.

The New Orleans business community finally began to stir. The Times-Picayune ran an ad containing ninety-eight names and signed by the Business and Professional Men's Committee for Sutherland, asking that he be reelected. The significance of the ad is that anyone at all would have subscribed to it. While timid in tone, indicating only that the signers believed that their children would have a better future "if Matt Sutherland is elected to the school board," it was a surprising step toward support of public education. Finally, after years of silence, even the Times-Picayune editorially supported Sutherland. The election overwhelmingly confirmed that the choice of most New Orleaneans was for open schools. Sutherland won by 55.6 per cent of the vote, with Singreen a poor second polling only 31.4 per cent of the vote.

* * *

At the eleventh hour, Governor Davis called a special session of the legislature to convene on November 6, 1960, to see if there was anything left that could be done to prevent desegregation. The legislature then met in its First Extraordinary Session. Altogether, the legislature met in one regular and five extraordinary sessions between May, 1960, and February, 1961.** On November 8, 1960, then in its First Extraordinary Session prior to the opening of schools on a desegregated basis on November 14, 1960, the legislature suspended the powers of the Orleans Parish School Board and invested them in itself. The state police were also authorized to perform duties imposed upon them by the legislature to prevent desegregation.

A legislative carnival unique in the annals of American lawmaking was under way in Baton Rouge. The following is a contemporary description of the First Extraordinary Session of 1960:

> On the same day, everyone finally learned the details of Davis's legislative package. As soon as the bills were distributed to the legislators, the House, according to plan, voted to suspend the rules and, without discussion, immediately sent the bills to the administration-controlled judiciary committee. Only one representative from New Orleans, Maurice ['Moon'] Landrieu, objected on the floor

---

*Wagner ran as an unpledged elector in the presidential election, calling for defeat of both Nixon and Kennedy as a way of stopping desegregation.
**The fourth and fifth extraordinary sessions were officially labeled the First and Second Extraordinary Sessions of 1961.

to the suspension of the rules, and he was voted down, 93 to 1. Another New Orleans representative, Salvador Anzelmo, described the administration 'steamroller': 'Twenty-nine bills were dumped on my desk, and within 15 minutes referred to a committee, without us having any opportunity to read or digest those bills.' Anzelmo said many members of the House objected to the procedure but dared not speak up for fear of being branded integration- ists. The New Orleans delegation decided, in typical New Orleans fashion, not to work as a unit, but to let each man work on his own. This is how Landrieu was left to make a one-man stand against the suspension of the rules. Throughout the session, Landrieu, with occasional help from some of the others, notably Anzelmo and Senators Robert Ainsworth and Adrian DuPlantier, risked his po- litical career to fight these bills. (Yet even Landrieu felt compelled to assert his attachment to segregation and to claim that he 'wouldn't know a Communist if I saw one.' 'But,' he said, 'I tell you here and now if I had to choose between accepting five Negro children, or closing the en- tire public schools system, I would stand for the open schools.) The steamroller was so effective that within five days all 29 bills had been passed by both houses and signed into law by Governor Davis.*

A "mourners' march," to commemorate "Black Monday," the day black children had entered the Orleans Parish schools, was con- ducted through the chambers of both houses of the legislature to a standing ovation by the lawmakers. The gala procession was high- lighted by a "6-year-old white child, followed by two shirt-sleeved men carrying a coffin in which lay a chocolate colored doll dressed in judicial robes and identified as 'Smelly' Wright."

*   *   *

In the days prior to November 14, 1960, School Board Presi- dent Lloyd Rittiner, fervently tried to persuade the public to support the continuation of public education in Orleans Parish. He spoke at countless PTA and civic meetings and was subjected to constant verbal abuse. Many times a fuming parent told him that he would rather "see my kid dead than go to school with niggers." Rittiner frantically sought community support from influential citizens and groups. A leading businessman invited him to a "private" lunch with two other leading citizens to avoid being seen in public with him, and they asked what they could do. He told them to take out

---

*Inger, supra, at 43-44. In this description of the legislative scene, the name of Senator Robert Ainsworth is listed as one of the few moderates willing to speak. Robert Ainsworth on August 31, 1966, became a member of the United States Court of Appeals for the Fifth Circuit, one of the federal courts so roundly denounced by the leg- islature he was then serving.

an ad publicly supporting open schools and the maintenance of law and order. One of the businessmen demurred that the toilets should remain segregated; another wanted segregation by sex in the class-rooms. No ad was taken. When a Jewish group offered to help, Rittiner suggested they integrate the Jewish-controlled Newman School in September, but nothing was done. A group of ministers also desired to be helpful, but upon the suggestion that they de-segregate their congregations as an example for the rest of the community, they declined. Archbishop Rummel, who had promised years before to desegregate the Catholic schools, feared a loss of funds and refused to order desegregation of the parochial schools to coincide with public school desegregation; he did promise to make an effort to quiet Emile Wagner, his unruly communicant. Governor Davis summoned Rittiner and informed him that while he was not a profane man, he "hated those damn niggers." He then commanded Rittiner not to desegregate the schools. Rittiner advised the Gov-ernor he could not follow that order.

During the months of crisis, Rittiner's engineering business was almost destroyed, and he came perilously close to filing bank-ruptcy; key employees quit, and he was banned from business in St. Bernard Parish. Reportedly, Leander Perez told major oil companies for whom Rittiner had been doing engineering work to cease employing him or face a tax increase. Living alone in a small brick home in the Lakeview area, Rittiner was beseiged for months with hate mail, obscene callers, and threats. One caller persisted in his efforts for years, calling at 3:00 a.m. every morn-ing with the same greeting: "Hello, you nigger loving motherfucker." Rittiner's thirteen-year-old daughter, who visited him occasionally, answered the phone several times and was told in vivid detail how her father was going to be killed. At one point in the hysteria to stop desegregation, rumors reached Rittiner and Rosenberg that state troopers would pick up Rittiner or Superintendent Redmond or both and spirit them to some place in Louisiana where federal marshalls could not find them to serve writs of habeas corpus. When that rumor circulated, the Times-Picayune assigned reporters to spend the entire day and night with Rittiner. In the morning, an assigned reporter, fearing that a bomb may have been planted dur-ing the night, asked Rittiner to start the engine before he consented to get into the car. While the other three moderate board members, Orleans Parish Superintendent Redmond, and Sam Rosenberg fared somewhat better than Lloyd Rittiner, all were the victims of ex-treme harassment.

Not to be outdone by anyone in his zeal for segregation, on November 12, 1960 the State Superintendent of Education, Shelby Jackson, declared November 14, the day of desegregation, a public school holiday. The following day, the legislature followed suit and also declared November 14 a public school holiday and dispatched a force of state police, acting as sergeants of arms of the legislature, to bar desegregation. On D-day minus one, State Superintendent Jackson called Lloyd Rittiner, announced who he was, and told Rit-tiner not to open the Orleans Parish schools. Rittiner, his patience near an end, told Jackson he did not "give a goddamn who Jackson was"--New Orleans would not close her schools. Judge Wright then issued orders restraining the legislature's Special School Committee and over 700 state and local officials from interfering with the operation of the New Orleans schools; he also returned control of the schools to the elected school board. Rittiner telegrammed every principal in New Orleans to open schools on the 14th. Every school in the parish opened; only one principal called in sick. Of all the parishes in Louisiana, the Orleans Parish schools were the only schools which opened that day.

* * *

Desegregation Day finally arrived in New Orleans. On-the-scene accounts portray the events as they happened.

Monday, November 14, 1960:

D-day morning came last week, humid and sultry. By 8 a.m. crowds had begun to gather in front of McDonogh 19 ([o]ne of 22 named for Philanthropist John McDonogh, who bequeathed part of his fortune to establish public schools in New Orleans) and William J. Frantz, the two elementary schools chosen for integrated first-grade classes. Squads of city police stood guard, some joking with the baiters, carefully refusing to answer the taunting question: 'Are the niggers here yet?' Shortly after 9, when the white children were safely in class, patrolmen herded traffic away from the two schools. Up drove several carloads of U.S. marshals with their charges: three neatly dressed, hair-ribboned, six-year-old Negro girls for McDonogh 19, one for William Frantz. The crowds, composed mostly of angry housewives, booed and yelled as the little girls were marched up the school steps by the marshals. Later, when white mothers stormed past police lines to take their children home, the fast-growing mobs applauded and brandished crudely lettered signs, e.g., "WE WANT SEGREGA-TION." But New Orleans' four pioneering Negro pupils stayed in class all day, were escorted safely home at night.*

Tuesday, November 15, 1960:

Next morning a mob of some 350 teenagers from nearby Nicholls High School cut classes and charged toward McDonogh 19, roaring out a football-styled chant: 'Two-Four-Six-Eight. We Don't Want to Integrate.' Police steered the students away from their target....**

---

*76 Time, Nov. 28, 1960, at 19; Reprinted by permission from Time, The Weekly Newsmagazine; Copyright Time Inc.
**Ibid.

While the school superintendent threatened disciplinary action against the truants, legislative leaders in Baton Rouge reminded them that compulsory attendance laws had been repealed. Playing hooky was legalized. Carloads of boys and girls in a holiday mood converged on the two schools where integration had been ordered. Young people and old shouted and cheered, waved Confederate flags, and sang 'Glory, Glory Segregation' to the tune of 'The Battle Hymn of the Republic.'
Things soon got much uglier. Many of the youngsters began to catch the bitter mood of the embattled adults, especially those who attended a wildly racist rally sponsored one evening by the White Citizens Council, where they heard their mayor and Judge Wright reviled in unprintable language. One speaker said the New Orleans police were 'ashamed' that they had to guard integrated schools. There was praise for 'civil disobedience,' which would 'bring the runaway courts to their knees.' And it was announced that 'the Ladies of Frantz School' would lead a protest march to the City Hall the following day.*

One of Leander Perez's most celebrated public speeches was made on Tuesday night, November 15, the day after New Orleans opened its public schools on a desegregated basis. At a mass rally attended by 5,000 at the Municipal Auditorium, State Senator Willie Rainach warmed up the proceedings by stating:

Bring the courts to their knees.... Let's empty the classrooms where they are integrated. A day lost can be made up; a week, a year loss is not fatal.... But once bloods are mixed, that is forever fatal.**

Then Perez, calling for demonstrations against the NAACP, Communists, Jews, Judge Wright, and "'the real culprit, malefactor, and double-crosser--the weasel, snake-head mayor of yours,'"*** concluded, "'Don't wait for your daughter to be raped by these Congolese. Don't wait until the burr-heads are forced into your schools. Do something about it now.'"****

Perez opened "his" schools in St. Bernard Parish to "white refugees" from the two New Orleans schools that were integrated. By this single action he provided for much of the success of the white boycott that was to occur against those schools during the first year of integration.*****

---

*Sherman, "The Nightmare Comes to New Orleans," 23 The Reporter, Dec. 8, 1960, at 24, 26 [hereinafter cited as Sherman].
**Inger, supra at 50-51.
***Ibid.
****N.Y. Times, Nov. 28, 1960, at 34, col. 2.
*****Over a year and a half later, the Justice Department asked for court orders forbidding the St. Bernard Parish School Board from

Wednesday, November 16, 1960:

... 2,000 riled-up teenagers cut classes again ... to make another futile dash at McDonogh 19. Joined this time by a throng of adults, they headed downtown for a protest 'interview' with Mayor Morrison. At city hall police again blocked the way, ordered them to disperse. Instead, the mob moved on to Carondelet Street, headquarters of the city's school board. There fire trucks backed up another police line, finally scattered them with billowing streams of water. All afternoon and evening, gangs of whites and Negroes prowled the narrow, ill-lit streets of the French Quarter, stoning cars, attacking luckless individuals who came their way, tossing homemade Molotov cocktails through darkened windows. Before the rioting ended, New Orleans' tough, alert police, working on extra-long, twelve-hour shifts, had arrested 240 persons (215 of them Negro) on charges ranging from loitering to assault.*

Thursday, November 17, 1960:

The next morning the city was quiet but aghast. Leaders of civic, business, and church groups hurried to join the mayor in an appeal for calm. Even in Baton Rouge, the mood seemed more sober. Governor Davis went before the legislature and said he hoped people of New Orleans 'and all over the state will keep their feet on the ground,' and the legislature passed a resolution condemning violence.**

* * *

On desegregation day, November 14, with racial mixing in the New Orleans schools an accomplished fact, the legislature retaliated with fury. The four moderates on the school board were removed from office, and Dr. James Redmond, school superintendent, and Sam Rosenberg, school board attorney, were summarily dismissed. In an attempt to validate these removals by dodging the Louisiana Constitution which required reasonable cause for dismissal, the legislature cited the action of the school board in obtaining restraining orders against legislative commands and Dr. Redmond's refusal to disclose to the legislature the black pupils' names or their assigned schools.

Legislative anger was not simply addressed to the Orleans

[cont.] providing racially segregated schooling to Orleans Parish students assigned to William Frantz and McDonogh 19.
*76 Time, Nov. 28, 1960, at 19. Reprinted by permission from Time, The Weekly Newsmagazine: Copyright Time Inc.
**Sherman, supra, at 26.

Parish School Board and Judge J. Skelly Wright. In blind frustration, the legislature abused anyone who dared challenge its methods. After an editorial had been published criticizing what were termed "'idiotic pieces of legislation' passed by 'the advocates of segregation,'" a state senator, unidentified in the reports, castigated Louisiana State University administrators for naming "'radicals as editors'" of the student newspaper Reveille. The faculty of LSU also drew fire from the legislature. In a drive sponsored by the Louisiana Civil Liberties Union, sixty-six professors petitioned the special Joint Committee on Segregation of the Louisiana Legislature to defeat proposals for the closing of integrated public schools. Led by Senator Rainach, a committee of the legislature then submitted a questionnaire to sixty-three of the sixty-six signers of the petition asking the following questions: 1) Did the individual listed sign the petition? 2) Did he understand what he was signing? 3) Did he know that the Louisiana Civil Liberties Union was the originator of the petition? 4) Is he a member of: a) the Louisiana Civil Liberties Union? b) the American Civil Liberties Union? c) the NAACP? d) the Communist Party? e) the Southern Regional Council? f) the Southern Conference Education Fund? 5) Does he teach or advocate integration of the races in classes? 6) Does he believe in integration? 7) Does he publicly advocate integration? One of the most outspoken LSU faculty members, Professor Waldo McNeir, was singled out for special attention: by resolution, the legislature authorized its Un-American Activities Committee to investigate him and his university. Professor McNeir had written legislators terming their segregation actions "a disgrace and a national scandal." Representative Wellborn Jack of Caddo Parish reportedly analyzed McNeir in this fashion: "I'm against communism .... He disagrees with everything I stand for; and, therefore, he must be a Communist. I'm for segregation. He must be for integration. I stand for honesty. He must be a crook!" Professor McNeir subsequently resigned from the faculty, citing as his reasons for leaving, "outside threats and inside pressures."

*　*　*

Rioting citizens and a rampaging legislature were not the only agents of harassment. On November 25, school board member Emile Wagner filed a suit against Superintendent Redmond to force Redmond to release the names of all the pupils enrolled at the Frantz School. Two weeks later, Redmond was mandated by the state court to hand over the names to Wagner. Not until February, 1961, when the decision of the state court was affirmed by the Louisiana Court of Appeals, did Redmond finally release the names. Everyone involved knew why Wagner wanted the names: they would have been immediately turned over to the White Citizens' Council and the legislature.

*　*　*

Within the first two days of desegregation, a boycott began at the integrated schools. Each morning New Orleans' screaming mothers gathered outside McDonogh 19 and William Frantz schools for their daily incantations. Like witches, they scratched, screeched and swore at the few who ventured to break through their wall of wrath.

In conversations prior to D-day with school board officials charged with the task of selecting black children for the desegregation effort, Judge Wright had insisted on only one thing: don't put one little Negro child alone in a school. Five little girls were selected--three were assigned to McDonogh 19; two to William Frantz. Just prior to desegregation day, school board officials discovered to their dismay that one of the little girls assigned to William Frantz was illegitimate. Fearing White Citizens' Council repercussions and worrying about the effect of such public knowledge on the child, Judge Wright reluctantly agreed to drop her name--leaving only one little girl to singlehandedly integrate William Frantz. After the first week the white boycott at McDonogh 19 was completely successful; the three little girls assigned there attended school alone for the rest of the year with most of the former white students attending Leander Perez's schools in St. Bernard Parish. The teachers and staff were kept on and given administrative duties by the school board to occupy their time. The teachers in both integrated schools were also subjected to enormous pressures to boycott them. Many were opposed to desegregation but the majority stayed. One teacher ascribed her refusing to honor the boycott to a sense of professionalism: "I didn't like it, but I also couldn't walk out on my job. That would be unthinkable."

But at William Frantz, unbelievably, a few terrified white children, accompanied by frightened but grimly determined parents, began to trickle back. The first to break the boycott was Reverend Lloyd A. Foreman. Later, his home smeared with paint, his church defaced and windows broken, his life threatened, his child shoved and abused, he moved to another part of the city. No arrests were made. John Thompson, an Alabama native and a $73-a-week Walgreen Drugstore employee, also attempted to break the boycott. He moved into the William Frantz area unaware of the trouble. He first sent his two sons, with the other white parents, to the schools thrown open in St. Bernard Parish by Leander Perez to accommodate the boycotters. But Thompson became disturbed when he discovered his boys were studying out of the same books they had used the year before. He then sent them to William Frantz. He was fired by Walgreen's and left town. The parents of three other white children who broke the boycott were also fired by their employers. But still they came. First there were four, then, six white children. In early December, for a short time, the number rose to a high of twenty-three, only to drop back again in the face of the mob's daily fury. A daily box score was kept in the opposing camps to track the boycott's effect. For months attendance bottomed out at seven or eight, to rise a little by the end of the year.

The nation was most captivated by Daisey Gabrielle, a white

mother, and her six-year-old daughter Yolanda. Daily, Mrs. Gabrielle led her little girl past the hysterical mob and the television cameras to William Frantz School. By the end of this first week, the mob had become vicious. Mrs. Gabrielle was followed home by threatening, swearing women. One day over 400 demonstrators closed in on her home, booing, cursing, and jostling. Her daughter Yolanda awaked at night crying about the "horrible women." The Save Our Schools organization had set up a carlift to run the boycott and offered to drive the Gabrielles to school; Mrs. Gabrielle accepted. The carlift began on December 1. The car carrying Yolanda Gabrielle was stoned and manhandled by the mob. Later in the week, it was pursued for two miles by a truck which tried to ram it. Until Wednesday, December 7, the drivers and the women who escorted the children into the school were subjected to the vilest sort of shouted abuse from the daily-assembled crowds. Various individuals and groups also offered financial help; Mrs. Gabrielle declined. James Gabrielle, a worker in the New Orleans sewer and water commission, desperately tried to support his wife's efforts although his job was threatened. Maria, Mrs. Gabrielle's teenage daughter, quit school. One day, James Gabrielle, who had come home early, heard the noise of the mob, came outside, and saw personally the abuse suffered by his wife and child. White with anger, he faced down the mob: "Get out of here, you white scum. Leave us alone!" Another day Mr. Gabrielle was called at work and told his wife had been killed. Rushing home he found her unharmed; on his return to work he was reprimanded for leaving the job. On Thursday, December 15, the Gabrielles moved to Centerdale, Rhode Island, Mr. Gabrielle's parents' home. Before she left, Daisey Gabrielle wrote a letter to the editor of the Times-Picayune. She directed it to the mob around William Frantz School, reminding them: "'For as a man sows, so shall he reap.'"

Several boycott-breaking parents of white children lived in the Florida Housing Project and were subjected to an organized telephone campaign of threats and persecution. Their houses were stoned, as was one of the mothers of a child at William Frantz. The volunteer drivers were threatened with death, arson, and disfigurement. The police were unable or unwilling to prevent the occurrences. With the exception of a couple of juveniles alleged to have stoned Mrs. Marion McKinley, no one connected with the demonstrations was arrested, nor was the mob in front of the school dispersed or told to move on until December 7, when the police guarding the school pushed the crowd behind barricades set up a block from the school.

Mayor Morrison, silent in the spring when Judge Wright handed down his May 17 order, silent when the three-judge court handed down its August 27 order, and silent through the crucial early fall months when leadership was essential, now spoke out. He charged that most of the difficulties at the two schools was generated by the large contingent of newsmen present; he bluntly asked the press to stay away.

Betty Wisdom, one of the mothers who ignored the boycott, in an emotional rebuttal challenged Mayor Morrison's assessment that the trouble was largely caused by the press:

I realize that ex-Mayor Morrison always maintained that the press caused much trouble; I have always believed that he was wrong. The Mayor never visited the disturbed area; he did not talk to any Frantz parents or, indeed, to anyone with first-hand information of events in the area (with the exception of the Chief of Police, who had a disciplinary problem in his force and was reluctant to curb the screamers, even when they stoned cars carrying school children). Morrison was facing, at the time, the necessity of asking the electorate to change the City Charter so that he could succeed himself; he was not anxious to offend a pressure group as strong as the White Citizens Council. Thus, he asked the reporters to form a small coverage 'pool' because their presence was 'causing trouble.' The reporters replied that the trouble had been openly incited by the racists, but said they were willing to try pool coverage, if the mayor [sic] would reduce the number of demonstrators proportionately. This was a fair request; the demonstrators were breaking several city ordinances and a state law against disturbing the peace, to boot. But the Mayor refused, and that was the end of the pool proposal.

Ironically, Mayor Morrison's anxiety to avoid an open clash with the rank-and-file racists backfired; he lost his election primarily because his pusillanimity disgusted many of his former supporters, both white and colored.

IT IS true ... that the crisis might have been covered by our local publisher. If past performance is a useful yardstick, the coverage would have been poor, and the nation would not have really known what was going on in New Orleans. The paper is ultra-conservative; during the school year of 1960-61 it offered virtually no leadership or pertinent information to the beleaguered community; what information it did offer came too late to change many minds. Its editorial position, when that emerged, was that school closing was worse than integration, but that both were evils.

This is in no way a reflection on the reporters who work for the paper. They are conscientious men and women, but they do not control what the paper prints. When a real racial clash nearly occurred on Nov. 16, it was reported in Time and Newsweek, but not in our paper. When, on stage at a Citizens Council rally, tiny white children, half of them made up in blackface, kissed each other while the chairman shouted, "Is this what you want for your children?," it was reported in Southern School News but not in our paper. When facts and figures on a business slump, the result of racial disturbances, were printed, they appeared in the Wall Street Journal and The New York Times, but not in our paper.

. . .

During the darkest days of last year, the reporters from out of town, as well as our local TV people, were kind, thoughtful, quick to warn us of personal danger, assiduous in helping us to secure police protection for badly frightened families. On occasion, when the life of a six-year-old child was continually threatened and her mother was unable to get police protection for her, a wire-service man called headquarters and promised to print a story on police indifference to the safety of the little girl. She was promptly given a round-the-clock guard, and we were once again thankful to the press.

You must remember that we had, literally, no normal support from anyone but our close friends and from the reporters. The Mayor, the business community and the power structure in general ignored us. The local paper was indifferent to our efforts. The legislature was thirst-ing for our blood. Until we began reading the stories and editorials in the outside press (including the Atlanta Con-stitution), we felt cut off from the world. In a crisis like ours, there are few things worse than this feeling of iso-lation. It induces the racists to commit ever more ter-rible outrages, secure in the knowledge that no one but approving fellow citizens will ever see their actions. It induces in moderates and integrationists the feeling that theirs is a Sisyphean task which no one approves or under-stands. We had this feeling for months; we did not stop working, but our task was twice as hard until the outside world, represented by the reporters, suddenly materialized and approved of us. *

*   *   *

One of the few heartening observations about the boycott, the taunts, and the threats that accompanied the desegregation of Frantz Elementary School was that the maelstrom outside had, if anything, a reverse effect upon the atmosphere inside the school. Several teachers described the development of "a kind of school spirit which emerged from a position of beleaguered isolation." A new song was composed and sung during those dark days entitled "Frantz School Will Survive." Indeed, the children should not be forgotten in all the attention and publicity given to the mothers raging outside the school. Dr. Robert Coles commented about the phenomenon of Frantz School and its lesson for integration elsewhere:

Among the young white children in New Orleans, our

---

*"Letter from a New Orleans Mother," 193 The Nation, Nov. 4, 1961, at 353; Reprinted by permission of The Nation.

remembrances about the nature of childhood and personality development will help clarify our observations. Even under the worst situations outside, the children in the schools managed well together. Those white children who remained in the desegregated Frantz school in New Orleans thoroughly enjoyed the increased attention of their teachers, the excitement around them. They often urged their more timid or justifiably frightened parents to keep them in school. In 1961 one of the white children who returned to the almost totally boycotted Frantz school told a little colored girl that she would not play with her because her mother had forbidden this, and then, a few minutes later, did just that.

One hears this over and over from children who obey both their parents and their own natural inclinations of age and whim, by saying words which are ideas to them, and known, and to be remembered, and yet by also doing the deeds which the moments in the playground or classroom suggest.*

*   *   *

In contrast to the strong stand taken by the Orleans Parish School Board in abiding by Judge Wright's orders and in attempting to insure the reality of even the token integration achieved, Governor Davis did not consider himself bound by federal injunction. As previously noted, on November 4, before desegregation day, he summoned the state legislature back for its First Extraordinary Session. Within the space of two days, the legislature had enacted into law twenty-five measures, each of which was an attempt "to halt, or at least forestall, the implementation of the Orleans Parish School Board's announced proposal to [comply with the order of integration]." On November 10, 1960, Judge Wright issued temporary restraining orders against state enforcement of these new stratagems; again, these orders were ignored as the legislature attempted to close the schools for the official holiday, to fire the members of the local school board, and to enact other statutes of blatant defiance.

In vindication of the threatened power of the federal courts, two extraordinary events occurred to counter the legislature insur-

---

*Coles, supra, at 209-10. Dr. Coles' conclusions and observations are based on extensive research. He first visited the four black girls who integrated New Orleans some three to six weeks before desegregation was to begin and thereafter taped monthly interviews with them in their homes throughout the first and second years of their experience. In addition, he similarly followed the development and reactions of a group of white children who remained in the integrated school; the group was evenly divided in terms of those whose parents were initially opposed to integration and those whose parents favored it. Ibid. at 203.

gence: first, scarcely twelve hours before integration was to begin, Judge Wright issued a temporary restraining order against the
entire Louisiana Legislature; and second, the United States Justice
Department entered the litigation on behalf of the federal government.

The judicial restraint of a state's legislative arm was an unprecedented order. With careful wording, Judge Wright limited his
mandate to avoid the grave constitutional questions which would be
engendered by a federal court's attempt to prohibit the rightful power
of a state legislature to enact any laws concerning a given subject
matter. As the three-judge district court later observed in approving this extraordinary action taken by Judge Wright:

> There is no effort to restrain the Louisiana Legislature as
> a whole, or any individual legislator, in the performance
> of a legislative function. It is only insofar as the law-
> makers purport to act as administrators of the local
> schools that they, as well as all others concerned, are
> sought to be restrained from implementing measures
> which are alleged to violate the Constitution. Having
> found a statute unconstitutional, it is elementary that a
> court has power to enjoin all those charged with its execu-
> tion. Normally these are officers of the executive branch,
> but when the legislature itself seeks to act as executor of
> its own laws, then, quite obviously, it is no longer legis-
> lating and is no more immune from process than the ad-
> ministrative officials it supersedes.

As precedent for this distinction, the three-judge court reached back
to Marbury v. Madison, the 1803 case which is the fountainhead of
constitutional law establishing the power of the United States Supreme Court to chasten executive officers when they act contrary to
the mandates of the Constitution. There Chief Justice Marshall declared: "It is not by the office of the person to whom the writ is
directed, but the nature of the thing to be done, that the propriety
or impropriety of issuing a [command to an executive] is to be determined."

But the crises precipitated by the Louisiana Legislature were
far more serious and persistent than that presented by President
Madison when he sought to ignore the Supreme Court's mandate.
Therefore, to further assist in the protection of the federal court's
duly entered orders, the United States Attorney General was invited
to participate as amicus curiae in the Orleans Parish litigation on
November 25, 1960. In justification for this request, the Rives-
Christenberry-Wright court later stated:

> We conclude that the participation of the United States
> at this stage of the proceeding is entirely appropriate.
> We invited the United States to enter the case in an ef-
> fort to find a peaceful solution to the problem created by
> the state's interference with the orders of the court. To

do otherwise was to risk anarchy. Through this procedure, we sought to keep the conflict in the courts. Thus the rule of law was preferred to the law of the jungle. Why the defendants deprecate this choice is difficult to understand. Certainly they were not fatuous enough to hope that the United States would stand idly by and watch the orders of its courts flouted, particularly in this sensitive area of constitutional rights.

Previously the Justice Department had participated in desegregation crises but on a very limited basis. The government had been granted leave of court to present amicus briefs in support of the federal court's powers to restrain the firebrand Frederick John Kasper and other riot-inciting individuals from interfering with the desegregation of the schools in Clinton, Tennessee, and in the Oxie, Arkansas school district. Certainly, the interference by a state legislature presented a greater potential threat to the federal system and to the authority of the federal courts than had the machinations of an individual crowd-baiter; and, even in those earlier situations, the Justice Department's participation was deemed warranted and approved by both the Sixth and Eighth Circuits.

Yet the state of Louisiana objected strenuously to the intervention of the United States Attorney General in what it termed "this private litigation." In support of this contention, the state noted that in the Civil Rights Acts of both 1957 and 1960, Congress had failed to authorize the Attorney General to initiate desegregation proceedings. In extremely restrained language, the Court pointed out that a party entering litigation eight years old could hardly be said to be "initiating" proceedings and countered that there was nothing in the Civil Rights Acts which would indicate a congressional intent to withdraw the right of the United States to intervene in vindication of the inherent authority of its federal courts.

The United States Justice Department responded by immediately seeking an injunction against the keystone of Louisiana segregation architecture, its Interposition Resolution. As has been earlier noted in the desegregation development in Texas, "interposition" was based on the notion that a state could interpose its sovereignty between its citizens and acts of Congress or decisions of the Supreme Court which it felt were unconstitutional. Professing devotion to the Union, Louisiana's resolution demanded that no step be taken to integrate the schools of Louisiana until the United States Constitution had been amended to ratify the holding of the Supreme Court in Brown I; moreover, its enforcing provisions sought to impose criminal penalties against federal judges and United States marshals carrying out desegregation orders.

On November 30, 1960, the three-judge court of Judge Rives of the Fifth Circuit and Judges Christenberry and Wright reconvened to consider the Interposition Resolution and the rest of the legislative package enacted by the Louisiana Legislature in its First Extraordinary Session which had occurred scarcely three weeks before. Reviewing Supreme Court precedent from as early as 1809 through as recent as 1958, the Court concluded that interposition "is not a constitutional doctrine. If taken seriously, it is illegal defiance of constitutional authority." In further deflation of Louisiana's reliance for authority upon the principles of the "Founding Fathers," the Court wryly pointed out that Jefferson, the legendary author of the Kentucky Interposition Resolution, never admitted its authorship, and that Madison subsequently recanted his early support of the doctrine. The Court concluded that all things considered, "interposition" amounted to " 'no more than a protest, an escape valve through which the legislators blew off steam to relieve their tensions.'" In addition, the Court at this sitting invalidated twenty-two other statutory measures enacted at the First Extraordinary Session.

A motion for stay was denied by the Supreme Court, and the decision of the three-judge court was subsequently affirmed per curiam by the Supreme Court.

Despite the complete repudiation of the doctrine of interposition, the undoing of all its previous statutory handiwork, and in the face of the federal court's injunctions, the legislature went immediately into its Second Extraordinary Session at the close of 1960. Representative Ford E. Stinson, a fanatic segregationist, was reported to have called the court's ruling against interposition "clap trap." "We are only saved," he said, "from the hands of these demagogues by the hand of the Lord when he takes them." He called for "full steam ahead. Let's keep going." The legislature proceeded to commend parents who had withdrawn their children from the schools and to condemn federal court contempt citations of state officers. It passed legislation designed to cut off the finances necessary to run the Orleans Parish school system: state funds were stopped, banks were forbidden to allow the board to withdraw its own funds on deposit with them, and one bank was removed as a fiscal agent for the state for cashing the board's checks.

State Superintendent of Schools Shelby Jackson threatened black teachers with the loss of jobs and black students with the loss of education. Jackson--self-styled as being in the same mold as General Stonewall Jackson--was cited for contempt for his efforts to cut off financing of New Orleans schools and appeared before Judge Wright to answer the contempt citations. With segregationists in Baton Rouge daring the federal courts to put him in jail and with Judge Skelly Wright more than willing to oblige, Jackson lost some of his bluster and belied his nickname. When Judge Wright asked Jackson if he intended to interfere with the proper operation of the school system, Jackson meekly answered "no," in a low, quavering voice. Judge Wright then repeated the question, telling Jackson to speak up so everyone in the courtroom could hear. With everyone in the courtroom, including Lloyd Rittiner, straining to hear, Superintendent Jackson then answered in a louder voice, "No," he was not going to interfere with the Orleans Parish school system.

On December 21, 1960, again the three-judge court of Rives,

Christenberry, and Wright was forced to convene. The court nullified all acts of the Second Extraordinary Session while the Third
Extraordinary Session was in progress. Noting that the legislature
had taken "every conceivable step to subvert the announced intention
of the local school board and defy the orders of this court," the
court gave the legislature a step-by-step lecture on elementary constitutional law. The impatience of the court is revealed by its reference to the "singular persistence" of the legislature, its reference
to the setting of a date for desegregation "with what no one dare
term undue haste," and its reference to the legislature's attempt to
have Attorney General Gremillion replace Sam Rosenberg as the
school board attorney as "one of the Legislature's less sophisticated
attempts to preserve racial discrimination." Further injunctions
were issued; particularly important were the injunctions designed to
aid the school board in the monetary crisis brought about by the
legislature's blockage of state funds to the Orleans Parish schools.
School teachers and administrators had gone unpaid, and the city
was threatened with teacher walkouts. At one point Sam Rosenberg
was forced to arrange for private loans to the school board from
anonymous donors to enable the board to meet daily expenses.

*   *   *

Despite the real agony experienced by innocent persons--the
white children and parents who attempted to break the boycott, the
black children who attended the desegregated schools, business and
civic leaders who attempted to speak out, and school board members
--no one faced more continued harassment than Judge Wright. His
life frequently was in jeopardy. Threats became so extensive that
at one point he had to move from his home. A cross was burned
on his lawn. Marshals lived with him twenty-four hours a day,
taking him to and from work. Perhaps worse, he was subjected to
daily public vilification from the state legislature, whose sessions
were being broadcast live to the people of the state.* As now Chief
Judge John R. Brown of the Fifth Circuit commented in reflection,
"Skelly got the bad ones."

From the cauldron of New Orleans, J. Skelly Wright formed
a commitment to the cause of civil liberties probably unmatched by
any member of the federal judiciary. The daily abuse did not weak-
en his resolve but instead seemed to strengthen his fierce determination to see the job through. He wrote in 1965:

> The American Negro is a totally American responsi-
> bility. Three hundred years ago he was brought to this

---

*Judges Rives and Christenberry were not ignored by the segrega-
tionists. At one rally at the federal courthouse in New Orleans,
platoons of screaming mothers were carrying placards with the ini-
tials SOC. A marshal asked one what the letters meant; she retorted, "It's supposed to mean Save Our Children but it really
means Shit on Christenberry."

country by our forefathers and sold into slavery. One hundred years ago we fought a war that would set him free. For these last one hundred years we have lived and professed the hypocrisy that he was free. The time has now come when we must face up to that responsibility. Let us erase this blemish--let us remove this injustice-- from the face of America. Let us make the Negro free.

* * *

Why New Orleans? Why did New Orleans with its history of racial toleration and its cosmopolitan image go through such agonies? Who was to blame? Mayor Morrison blamed the press. Others point the finger at Morrison himself because of his conspicuous lack of leadership. They contrast his conduct in office with the performance of Mayor Victor H. Schiro who, succeeding Morrison, announced before school opened in the fall of 1961: "I am putting all on notice that law and order will be maintained at any cost!" And some blame the New Orleans social and business "elite" who failed to speak out or help prepare the public. One magazine bluntly accused not the vocal racists but the "silent citizens" of New Orleans, and editorialized that New Orleans' failure could be a negative example for other cities still to face desegregation.

But not all of New Orleans' moderate and liberal citizens were silent. The Save Our Schools group, led with fearless courage by Mary Sand and other brave women, shamed the timidity of the male leaders of New Orleans by its show of persistent support for public education. Later, academic and business groups also formed to protect the public schools.

While the organized bars of both New Orleans and Louisiana, by their failure publicly to challenge the patently unconstitutional actions of the legislature, did not distinguish themselves, several leading lawyers in the city did work closely with Sam Rosenberg to defend the school board against the barrage from Baton Rouge. Committees of lawyers were organized to research a host of legal questions and several lawyers allowed their names to appear "Of Counsel" on all school board pleadings for injunctions against the state. But the majority of lawyers in the state did not react similarly. One of the tragedies, not just in New Orleans but throughout the South, has been the general silence of the organized bar to persecution of judges and general perversion of law. The Civil Rights Commission Report on the New Orleans school crisis was especially critical of the Tulane law faculty. The silence of that distinguished group, which could have explained the law with impartiality, was deafening.

The local news media also did not provide leadership. WDSU and WDSU-TV were the only members of the local media to provide any editorial support. The city's two newspapers, the Times-Picayune and the States-Item, kept their silence long past the city's descent into tragedy.

Unfortunately, despite the valiant efforts of a few, overall civic support and leadership for open schools were not widespread at first, and the leadership which emerged came far too late. In the formative period of public opinion, the spring of 1960, the city was all but leaderless--helpless prey for all its most rabid elements.

Finally, the major turning point in public attitude came. On January 30, 1961, a testimonial dinner was held for the long-be-leaguered members of the school board: Rittiner, Shepard, Riecke, and Sutherland, Superintendent Redmond, and board attorney Sam Rosenberg. Emotional speeches were given before an astounding turnout of 1,650 citizens who came to pay tribute. Plaques were presented to the six "for courageous efforts to maintain public education in New Orleans in these years of crisis." Overnight the members of the school board became national heroes. President Kennedy twice publicly praised the board at press conferences, noting their "quiet intelligence and true courage." Although the boycott was effective for the rest of the school year, finances were hopelessly tangled, and legislative abuse continued, the board and the people of New Orleans at that dinner at last recognized that public education in New Orleans would survive.

* * *

But, while the turnaround point had been achieved in the city, the battle with the state government continued unabated. As defeat piled on defeat, the legislature flailed away in every direction. When school board member Sutherland was reelected in New Orleans, the legislature prohibited the Secretary of State from certifying the election and the Governor from issuing the commission of office. Suit was filed for a write of mandamus to force the Secretary of State to perform the purely ministerial act of certifying the election. By the time the Louisiana Court of Appeals decided the case, the statutory period for the Governor's issuance of the commission had expired. The court said the case was therefore moot because under Louisiana law the previous incumbent holds the office until a successor is elected and Sutherland was the incumbent. Sutherland served his next six-year term; he was never issued his commission of office. Similarly, on one of the occasions when the Governor was attempting to seize control of the Orleans Parish schools from the board, he sent two officials to New Orleans, and they seized the school board's official corporate seal. The seal was never returned.

On March 3, 1961, the three-judge court of Rives, Christenberry, and Wright again convened to consider the latest actions of the Louisiana Legislature to frustrate desegregation. In a coldly furious opinion, the court began: "Once again irresponsible conduct on the part of some Louisiana officials compels us to the unpleasant but necessary task of issuing further injunctions." The court doggedly reviewed each new legislative act since its December 21, 1960, opinion and stated: "... we are reluctant to assume that this is defiance merely for the sake of defiance, for it is unthinkable that, without even the excuse of possible success, a state would deliberately expose its citizenry to the unseemly spectacle of lawgivers, sworn to uphold the law, openly flouting the law." In voiding the legislature's latest attempt to remove the school board and fire the superintendent and board attorney, the court excoriated the state's claim that these were harmless personnel changes:

> [w]e are told that the new legislation is pointless, or, at most, constitutes an innocent domestic amusement.
> ... These are not the first blooms of a new spring. This litigation is now in its ninth year and the record is a chronology of delay, evasion, obstruction, defiance and reprisal....
> But it is not only the guilty past that condemns these recent acts. The very circumstances of their birth robbed them of innocence. Indeed, if there were no ulterior motive, no larger purpose to be served, why so much ado about so little? Is such a triviality as the replacement of the attorney for a single local school board, or even a change in the personnel of the board itself, a matter of sufficient gravity and urgency to require a special session of the state legislature?

The Fourth Extraordinary Session of the legislature was abortive. It did commend a private body which had been organized to monitor the news media and to report on those organs of the press that distorted the Southern way of life. The session also commended the Louisiana School Board Association's convention for ousting Mr. Sutherland as its president, two days before his term expired.

Thirty-one days later, on May 4, 1961, the same three-judge court met again. Noting that the Second Extraordinary Session of the legislature commended parents who had withdrawn their children from the public schools and its own officers who had been cited for contempt, the court considered two new Louisiana criminal statutes purporting to create a new crime entitled "Bribery of parents of school children." The first new criminal statute punished the giving to or acceptance by parents of school children of anything of present or prospective value as an inducement to sending their children to a desegregated school. A companion crime was created called "Intimidation and interference in the operation of the schools," which nebulously condemned conduct that would influence any person to do or perform any act in violation of the law of the state. Both statutes promised monetary rewards and granted immunity from prosecution to informers. The state innocently argued that the two new criminal statutes had nothing to do with desegregation. Stating that even the making of such an argument was to "play tricks with the court," the court held the two new criminal statutes unconstitutional. This decision was also affirmed by the Supreme Court.

* * *

Thus ended the 1960-61 school year in New Orleans. Mc-Donogh 19 and William Frantz remained open but the boycott was almost completely effective--most white students fled to Perez's St. Bernard Parish, and by conservative estimates, almost 300 white children who previously had attended the two schools received no education at all. Nevertheless, New Orleans ended the year with a functioning school system.

The Mop-Up: 1962

After the climactic school year of 1960-61, Judge J. Skelly Wright, still vilified in Louisiana, emerged as a national hero. He was the logical choice to fill a new vacancy on the United States Court of Appeals for the Fifth Circuit. Both Judges Tuttle and Wisdom of the Fifth Circuit informed Burke Marshall, Robert Kennedy's civil rights chief, that Wright would be an excellent choice; and, furthermore, that if he were passed over, it would be regarded by all judges as a punishment for his unflinching enforcement of Brown v. Board of Education. Louisiana officialdom, however, reacted angrily to the possibility of judicial promotion for their arch-antagonist. The Louisiana House of Representatives voted 62 to 13 in favor of a resolution asking Louisiana's senators and congressmen to oppose promotion for Wright to the Fifth Circuit "or [any] position of trust." Louisiana Senator Russell Long heard the message; he brought heavy pressure to bear on President Kennedy not to appoint Wright to the Fifth Circuit. Privately, Long told the President that he, Long, could not be reelected to the Senate in 1962 if Kennedy did not blunt the movement urging Wright's promotion to the Fifth Circuit. Publicly Senator Long said Judge Wright would be promoted over his dead body. Instead of appointing Judge Wright to the Fifth Circuit, in a possible effort to placate both Senator Long and those urging Wright's elevation to the Court of Appeals, President Kennedy named Judge Wright to the Court of Appeals for the District of Columbia.

Judge Wright had one more bout with Oliver Bush's case before leaving for Washington, D.C. On April 3, 1962, after his appointment to the District of Columbia Circuit had already been confirmed by the Senate, Judge Wright issued a new decree which again stunned New Orleans and was viewed by many as vindictive. In his order, Judge Wright first declared that the testing program utilized to select black students to attend all-white schools was unconstitutional because it tested only those seeking transfers and did not impartially test all students. He restrained the use of the Louisiana Pupil Assignment Act until New Orleans operated all its schools on a desegregated basis. And, in an order of breathtaking impact, he commanded the integration of the first six grades of school for the fall of 1962. He justified his order on undisputed facts establishing the gross disparity between white and black schools in New Orleans. Over five thousand black pupils were still on the platoon system; no whites were platooned. The average class size for black elementary

schools was 38.3 (the maximum size prescribed by the Louisiana
State Board of Education was thirty-five); the average class size for
white elementary schools was 28.7. He further found:

> Negro classes are conducted in classrooms converted from
> stages, custodians' quarters, libraries and teachers' lounge
> rooms, while similar classroom conditions do not exist in
> the white schools. Even under the separate but equal test,
> these inequalities may not be maintained. It would be un-
> conscionable to compel Negroes, 67 years after Plessy v.
> Ferguson ... to continue to submit to these conditions.

Shortly thereafter, a farewell dinner was held for Judge
Wright prior to his departure to Washington, D.C. Customarily,
upon the promotion of a federal district judge to a higher court,
local lawyers and judges turn out in a public celebration to wish
him well. Judge Wright's dinner at Antoine's was held in a private
dining room with a capacity of less than twenty. In an eloquence
difficult to muster for a small audience, that evening Judge Wright
spoke about the Supreme Court in a manner which perhaps also is
expressive of how he viewed his own responsibility in his desegregation battles:

> The Supreme Court is more than a law court--it is a
> policy court, or, if you will, a political court. It is an
> instrument of government, and while most judges have the
> habit, through long years of precedent, of looking back-
> ward, the Supreme Court must look forward through a
> knowledge of life, of people, of sociology, of psychology
> .... [T]he Constitution [is] a living document. It should
> not be interpreted with reference to the time in which it
> was written but rather in reference to the present, or,
> better still, the future.

*   *   *

In the waning skirmishes of New Orleans' battle over school
desegregation, a change of command occurred. President Kennedy
named Frank Ellis, Kennedy's Louisiana campaign manager, Democratic State Chairman in 1960, and most recently Director of the
United States Office of Civil Defense Mobilization, as a replacement
for Judge Wright. The appointment process involving Judge Ellis
was unusual; officials in Robert Kennedy's Justice Department have
been quoted as stating that Ellis's appointment was "the worst ...
we made." That criticism may be unduly harsh. In the Bush case,
Ellis did stay Wright's order and he did enter a far less demanding
desegregation order for the fall of 1962; however, a close examination of his heavily criticized action indicates that in some important
respects Judge Ellis went further than Judge Wright. Furthermore,
his civil rights record after the first year, while not noteworthy,
was defensible.

On May 1, 1962, twenty-seven days after Judge Wright's

stunning opinion ordering integration of the first six grades of school
for the fall of 1962, Judge Ellis stayed Judge Wright's order and reinstated the order to integrate only the first grade in 1962. On May
7, 1962, the plaintiffs in Bush, for the first time finding themselves
on the short end of a federal court decision, moved to vacate the
stay. Their motion was denied by Judge Tuttle of the Fifth Circuit
because Judge Ellis was scheduled to hear a motion for a new trial
the next day. The next day, May 8, 1962, Judge Ellis heard the
motion for a new trial and on May 23, 1962, he entered a new order
in the case. Judge Ellis reaffirmed Judge Wright's holding that the
Pupil Assignment Act was unconstitutional when applied to a dual
school system providing separate schools for black and white children, but he withdrew Judge Wright's order commanding integration
of the first six grades by September, 1962. Judge Ellis ordered
desegregation only for the first grade and imposed a stair-step plan
desegregating one additional grade per year beginning in 1963.
While his order was universally thought to be a complete retreat,
Judge Ellis did go further than Judge Wright in a most significant
way. He ordered that the school board's dual system of separate
geographical districts governing black and white school assignments
also be abolished as each new grade was desegregated.

Judge Ellis's vacation of Judge Wright's decree stunned the
black plaintiffs as much as Judge Wright's order a month earlier
had stunned the white citizens of New Orleans. On June 11, 1962,
now more vigorous than they were in the early years after Brown I
and II, the plaintiffs filed a brief with the Fifth Circuit to overturn
Judge Ellis's order and reinstate the previous Wright order to desegregate the first six grades. Now under new mayoral leadership
and actively concerned about what happened to its schools, the city
of New Orleans filed an amicus brief supporting the school board's
defense of Judge Ellis's orders. The brief for the board commented
on what had been achieved by the integration of the four black children on November 14, 1960, and responded to the Inc. Fund's demand for reinstatement of Judge Wright's original order. Sam
Rosenberg wrote:

> Appellants seek to belittle this accomplishment, but as
> modest as it was, it constituted such a radical departure
> from local customs, hardened by the time, that it stirred
> deep emotions among many citizens of this community,
> and led a vocal minority to open demonstrations. Appel-
> lants have apparently forgotten that the action of the ap-
> pellee in making this start toward full compliance was not
> so modest as to dissuade the legislature from passing a
> resolution, addressing out of office four of the five mem-
> bers of the Orleans Parish School Board, nor was it so
> modest as to dissuade the legislature in five successive
> extra-ordinary sessions from repealing the Act creating
> the board; from passing two other statutes creating new
> boards; from addressing the Superintendent out of office,
> and even from dismissing the writer of this brief as At-
> torney for the board.... It is respectfully submitted that

never in the history of mankind have there been more local laws and regulations, which had to be revised, than
is revealed in the record of this case.

On August 6, 1962, a three-judge panel of the Court of Appeals, consisting of Judges Rives, Brown, and Wisdom, affirmed
Judge Ellis in part and reversed him in part. In a careful and
diplomatic opinion, Judge Wisdom reviewed the complex background
of the New Orleans desegregation struggle. He then compared the
Wright order and the Ellis order and found that the "area of agreement between the orders ... is larger and more significant than the
area of disagreement." The Fifth Circuit affirmed Judge Ellis's
order holding that the Pupil Assignment Act had been used discriminatorily. Compromising between Judge Wright's order to desegregate six grades and Judge Ellis's order to desegregate one grade,
Judge Wisdom then formulated a new plan ordering that in 1962
second and third graders be given the limited right to transfer to a
school nearest their home under a good-faith, nondiscriminatory application of the Louisiana Pupil Assignment Act.

* * *

The parochial schools of New Orleans, not without considerable difficulty of their own, finally began their process of desegregation in the fall of 1962. For their conduct in opposing the desegregation of the Catholic schools in 1962, three Catholic leaders
of the disturbances in New Orleans were excommunicated from the
church. Excommunication is the most extreme punishment the Roman Catholic Church can mete out. It denies the sacraments of the
church for life and promises irrevocable damnation for eternity.
Two of the three excommunicated were Leander Perez and Mrs.
B. J. Gaillot, one of the most vocal organizers of the screaming
mothers. Although Perez reportedly sought reconciliation with his
church on his deathbed, Mrs. Gaillot has not changed her views.
As recently as December of 1971, she filed a federal suit claiming
that the refusal of hospitals to segregate Negro and Caucasian blood
violated her constitutional rights.

* * *

By 1963, both the federal district court in New Orleans and
to a lesser extent the Fifth Circuit had triumphed in their legal
struggle with the state of Louisiana, though some may wonder if the
victory was not hollow. When measured by the pitifully few black
children actually integrated, the battle seems hardly worth the price.
But before integration could commence in earnest, token desegregation had to be achieved.

Reflecting on those years in New Orleans, Judge Wright has
some strongly held views. He is critical of the lawyers of the
South who could have made the public aware of what the law was
and who should have supported the efforts of the federal courts to
enforce the Constitution. Judge Wright maintains a strong admiration

for the school board officials who finally recognized their responsibilities and kept the schools open. He feels that strong and effective community leadership could have made a difference. He contrasted the New Orleans experience in integrating public transportation with the nightmare that occurred in Montgomery: not one single untoward incident occurred when the buses of New Orleans were integrated. Bus company officials and civic leaders simply made up their minds that New Orleans would not repeat Montgomery's mistakes. Finally, Judge Wright gave high marks to the Fifth Circuit: "They backed me every step of the way."

Contrasts and Conclusions

Judge Wright's response to the Brown mandate can be seen in bold relief when compared with the reaction of Judge E. Gordon West. Judge West was appointed to the federal bench in Louisiana in September, 1961, one year after Judge Wright's struggles in New Orleans. Instead of enforcing the Supreme Court mandate in Brown I and II, Judge West's tactic was to ignore it. Calling the Brown decision "one of the truly regrettable decisions of all times," he asserted that "the trouble that has directly resulted [therefrom] ... has been brought about ... by ... outsiders."

On January 17, 1964, Sarah Louise McCoy, a black co-ed, filed suit requesting an injunction against the Louisiana Board of Education's enforcement of a Louisiana statute restricting attendance at Northeast Louisiana State College to white persons. On February 14, Judge West held a hearing on Miss McCoy's motion for a preliminary injunction. School officials admitted that the only reason Miss McCoy was denied admission was the law prohibiting members of her race from attending the college. Despite repeated decisions requiring district judges to proceed with dispatch in deciding requests for preliminary injunctive relief--particularly in higher education cases--Judge West failed to render a decision until May 18, 1964, three days after Miss McCoy petitioned the Fifth Circuit for a writ of mandamus to force him to act. Judge West dismissed the case, justifying his action by citing a 1907 Supreme Court decision that state agencies are immune from suit. In the process he ignored no less than five recent appellate decisions that such an agency could be sued. He was reversed on appeal. On remand, Judge West again refused to pass on the merits of the case. Again the Fifth Circuit reversed. "For the second time in this case and for the [now] seventh time in recent years, we hold that a state agency is not immune from a suit to enjoin it from enforcing an unconstitutional statute...."

Judge West finally went too far in two school desegregation cases that he, like Judge Ellis, inherited from Judge Wright. A suit against the rural St. Helena Parish School Board began in the early fifties, and one against the East Baton Rouge Parish School remained dormant until 1959. In 1960, Judge J. Skelly Wright

ordered both boards to admit children on a nondiscriminatory basis
"with all deliberate speed." When Judge West inherited the St.
Helena School case, it was still under Judge Wright's all deliberate
speed order. In January 1962, March 1963, and February 1964,
plaintiffs requested Judge West to order the school board to submit
a plan for desegregation. Judge West took no action. In response
to the 1964 request, Judge West's conduct indicated that no order
would be forthcoming until at least the beginning of the next academic
year 1964-65. At this point, the plaintiffs turned to the Court of
Appeals for the Fifth Circuit, represented by the same Inc. Fund
lawyers that represented Oliver Bush. They requested the unusual
remedy of a writ of mandamus to force Judge West to act. Recently elevated to the Chief Judgeship of the Fifth Circuit and speaking
for a panel including Judges Rives and Wisdom, Chief Judge Tuttle
acknowledged that the writ of mandamus (which results in making a
judge a litigant) is an exceptional remedy reserved for "really extraordinary cases." Judge Tuttle stated flatly, "This is such a 'really
extraordinary case.'" In one of the most caustic orders ever issued by a Court of Appeals to a United States district judge,* Judge
Tuttle said that Judge West's response to the petition for a writ of
mandamus "shows startling, if not shocking, lack of appreciation of
the clear pronouncements of the Supreme Court and this Court during
the past year which make it perfectly clear that time has run out
for a district court to temporize for the purpose of making accommodations in order to arrive at solutions that may satisfy a school
board which for ten long years has completely ignored its duty to
'make a prompt and reasonable start toward full compliance' with the
Supreme Court's Brown decision...." Judge Tuttle then said that
where a district court fails in its responsibility to "fashion its own
plan," the Court of Appeals would do the job itself. Judge Tuttle's
reprimand of Judge West is classic:

> The courts can ill-afford the judicial time required to
> consider the case of every municipal, county or parish
> board of education two or three times, through the whole
> gamut of litigation, from the district court to the Court of
> Appeals to the Supreme Court, back to a three-judge dis-
> trict court, thence the Supreme Court, with a return visit
> to the district court and then back to this Court for the
> granting of an order that it was apparent from the start
> was already overdue. This case has run its course. Any
> further delay in granting the petitioners their constitutional
> rights would be abandonment by this Court of its responsi-
> bility. It appears that these rights can be granted now
> only by the extraordinary remedy of mandamus, which
> makes the district judge the respondent and amendable to
> the orders of this Court.

*A reliable source indicates that the first draft circulated by Judge
Tuttle was substantially more tart than the one issued; Judge Tuttle
was persuaded by one of his fellow judges on the Court "to tone it
down."

There would appear to be little to be gained if we were to restrict our order to a requirement that the trial court make a judgment in the matter, without directing the nature of the judgment to be entered. The respondent has had ample admonishment, both from the Supreme Court and this Court, as to what is required of him in the premises. His failure to respect these admonishments makes it reasonably clear that an order from us directing merely that he enter a judgment in the case would mean simply that the case would be back here again because of his clear indication that he does not propose to enter the proper order until directed to do so. Such further delay and such further consumption of judicial time is not only unnecessary but it would tend to destroy the confidence of litigants in our judicial system.

The Fifth Circuit then ordered Judge West to enter an injunction and told him verbatim what the injunction was to provide.

Judge West's reaction to the issuance of the writ of mandamus was pure outrage. In a "Memorandum Opinion and Response to Issuance of Writ of Mandamus," Judge West answered the Fifth Circuit's indictment of him and defended his handling of the suit, his integrity, and his devotion to duty. Judge West's response is also classic:

Ordinarily, as a result of the issuance of a writ of mandamus, nothing is required of the Court to which the writ is directed but to comply with the orders of the issuing Court. The order of the Fifth Circuit Court of Appeals in this instance will, of course, be scrupulously complied with by this Court. However, in this most unusual case, since the opinion rendered by the Court of Appeals is so injudiciously couched in personal terms, and is so written as to directly, and by clear implication accuse me, personally, of refusing to accept my responsibilities as a Judge of this Court, of wasting precious judicial time, of acting in an 'unusual' and 'shocking' manner, and even intimating that I have, in some way, acted unethically in the handling of this case, I would be a poor judge indeed, and less than a man, if I were to let such an obvious attack on my personal integrity go unnoticed. Especially is this true when the opinion, as written by the Court of Appeals, is for publication. It is one thing for that Court to question my judgment, but is quite another for it to question my integrity. Consequently, while I am extremely reluctant to do so, I must of necessity, solely for the completion of the record in this case, make a few brief comments in response to these accusations. Inasmuch as this case will in all probability, be before the Courts for some time to come, the record, in all fairness, should be complete. And I must say that it is only by the exercise of the restraint so necessary, but so often lacking

in the proper performance of judicial functions, that I am
deterred from responding in kind. I question the integrity
of no one. While I might, in certain instances, disagree
with the legal opinions of my brethren of other Courts, I
respect their integrity, their judgments and their right to
disagree. I would not think of questioning their sincerity
of purpose no matter how wrong I might think their judgment to be.

After his emotional defense, Judge West did enter verbatim the injunction against the school board directed by the Fifth Circuit.
Rural Louisiana's deeply felt resistance to integration, seen before
in the actions of the legislature it controlled, was mirrored again
in the resolution passed by the St. Helena Parish School Board in
response to Judge West's order to submit a plan. At a special
meeting, the board requested the court to reconsider its mandate,
among other reasons because, "'We may be persecuted and misunderstood if we were to comply ... [O]ur respective businesses could
and probably would fail ... [W]e beg of this court to understand ...
the humility with which we present these views as free men in a
free society.'" Despite this impassioned plea, Judge West ordered
the board to submit a plan within three days and warned that if it
neglected to comply, he would presume that it favored full and immediate desegregation and had impliedly submitted that proposal as
its plan. The board then immediately began formulating a lesser
alternative.

The contrast between Orleans Parish and St. Helena Parish
is the difference between positive delay to allow time for delibera-
tive preparation and negative delay for the sole purpose of obstructing justice. As one commentator has elaborated:

Substantial delay is to be expected in the creation of
new legal rights. If occasioned by the need for full and
careful deliberation or by the time required to convince
the lawmaker of the merit of the claim for redress of
grievances, it is a not unwholesome aspect of our lawmaking system. But delay for its own sake--obstructionism--
violates the pivotal compact of the open society, the terms
of which are: ungrudging acceptance of the present law in
return for effective access to the processes of orderly
change. Such violation destroys faith in those processes
and constitutes a direct invitation to 'self-help,' that is,
the achievement of desired objectives by force or illegal
pressure tactics. Self-help is the negation of civil orders;
and if employed on a broad scale it brings on the pervasive coercion of the police state.*

---

*Lusky, "Racial Discrimination and the Federal Law: A Problem in
Nullification," in Southern Justice, at 255, 256-257 (L. Friedman,
ed., 1966).

* * *

In the summer of 1973, Bush v. Orleans Parish was still on Judge Christenberry's docket. Since 1967, however, it has been basically quiescent. The federal district court still retains jurisdiction to guarantee faithful compliance by the school board. Under the last court order of October 11, 1967, every November, Sam Rosenberg files with the clerk of court a voluminous yearly report on school population statistics, and every spring he faithfully files another report indicating any assignment changes made by the school board. Orleans Parish is now basically operating a unitary neighborhood school system with fixed district lines. The school system is seventy-five per cent black. When the desegregation struggles began in 1950 at the Macarty School meeting attended by Oliver Bush, there were more whites in Orleans Parish schools than blacks and residential patterns were racially mixed. Now, because of both massive building of low-rent federal housing projects that are almost totally black and massive white flight--for whatever reason-- to other parishes (neighboring Jefferson Parish has an eighty per cent white school system), the dire predictions of Emile Wagner seem likely to become true. Every year the Orleans Parish system tips further toward Wagner's prophesy that the school system would turn "all black." In November, 1969, there were 35,860 white students in the parish and 76,079 black students, for a total enrollment of 111,937. In November, 1972, a short three years later, there were only 26,397 whites as compared to 77,660 blacks, for a total of 104,039 students--a loss of 9,463 whites in just three years. The percentage of black students is even higher in the elementary schools. The faculties of the Orleans Parish schools are now thoroughly integrated. A court order provides for a fifty-fifty black-white teacher ratio in each school, with an allowable variation of only ten per cent in any particular school.

However, despite many all-black schools in the system and the existence of some predominantly white schools, further real integration of students is practically impossible. The "legal" minority, the blacks, are the majority race in the system and the actual minority race, the whites, oppose further integration. In the fall of 1973, two schools were paired, one predominantly white and one predominantly black. New suits have been filed requesting massive busing. But, unless integration is ordered across parish lines* and massive busing occurs, further busing within Orleans Parish will accelerate white flight from the schools.

Oliver Bush is now sixty-two and the operator of a modern service station in the middle of the Ninth Ward, New Orleans' major black ghetto. He has put seven of his thirteen children through

---

*Which appears highly unlikely in the view of the five-four decision of the Supreme Court in Milliken v. Bradley, 418 U.S. 717 (1964) (also known as the "Detroit case"), discussed supra, Part III, Chapter 16.

college, and he feels the school situation in New Orleans is now considerably better than it was in 1951. The struggle, he said, "was worth the price." Gail Etienne and Tessie Prevost were two of the six-year-old black girls who integrated McDonough 19; both are now nineteen and have been to college. Both believe firmly in integration and indicate that their ordeal "was necessary and worth the effort"--they would go through it all again.

NOTES AND PRIMARY AUTHORITY

The primary authority for the material contained in this chapter was:

The Skirmishing: 1950-59. The principal cases relied on were the Supreme Court decisions in Bush v. Orleans Parish School Bd., 366 U.S. 212 (1961), 364 U.S. 500 (1960); Orleans Parish School Bd. v. Bush, 365 U.S. 500 (1960), 356 U.S. 969 (1958), 354 U.S. 921 (1957), 351 U.S. 948 (1956); Tureaud v. Board of Supervisors of LSU, 347 U.S. 971 (1954). West Va. State Bd. of Educ. v. Barnette, 319 U.S. 624 (1943); Ex parte Young, 209 U.S. 123 (1908). Other cases relied on were Singleton v. Jackson Mun. Separate School Dist., 355 F.2d 865 (5th Cir. 1966); Stell v. Savannah-Chatham County Bd. of Educ., 318 F.2d 425 (5th Cir. 1963); 162 F. Supp. 372 (N.D. Ala. 1958) (three-judge court); School Bd. of Charlottesville, Va. v. Allen, 240 S.2d 59 (4th Cir. 1956); Brown v. Board of Educ. of Topeka, 138 F. Supp. 337 (E.D. La. 1956); Briggs v. Elliott, 132 F. Supp. 776 (E.D.S.C. 1955). The report relied on was, The Louisiana State Advisory Committee to the U.S. Commission on Civil Rights, Report of The New Orleans School Crisis (1961). Also used were acts by the Louisiana Legislature reported in volumes 1 thru 4 of Race Rel. L. Rep. Books that were helpful were J. Cook, The Segregationists (1962); M. Inger, Politics and Reality in an American City: The New Orleans School Crisis of 1960 (1969); R. Sarratt, The Ordeal of Desegregation (1966); R. Sherrill, Gothic in the Deep South (rev. ed. 1969). Also used was McGarrick, "Desegregation and the Judiciary: The Role of the Federal Court in Educational Desegregation in Louisiana," 16 J. Pub. L. 107 (1967). Magazine article used was 76 Time, Dec. 12, 1960, at 21; and the newspaper, New Orleans Times-Picayune, June 26, 1960, §2, at 2, col. 2. Also used was the unpublished manuscript of G. Foster, Jr., New Orleans: The Story of School Desegregation (1963). There were personal interviews with Mr. Oliver Bush, Mr. Dan Byrd, Judge and Mrs. Herbert W. Christenberry, Mrs. Leontyne Luke, Mr. Lloyd Rittiner, and Mr. Theodore Shepard.

The Battle 1960-61. Cases used as major sources were: for the Supreme Court, Tugwell v. Bush, 367 U.S. 907 (1961), aff'd sum nom; Marbury v. Madison, 5 U.S. 87, 1 Cranch 137 (1803); for the Fifth Circuit, Rippy v. Borders, 250 F.2d 690 (5th Cir. 1957), Houston Indep't School Dist. v. Ross, 282 F.2d 95 (5th Cir. 1960); for the Sixth Circuit, Kasper v. Brittian, 245 F.2d 97 (6th Cir.

1957), 245 F.2d 92 (6th Cir. 1957); and for the Eighth Circuit, Hoxie School Dist. v. Brewer, 137 F. Supp. 364 (E.D. Ark. 1956), aff'd, 238 F.2d 91 (8th Cir. 1956). Another source was acts of the Louisiana Legislature as reported in 5 Race Rel. L. Rep. (1960). The article by Parham, "Halls of Ivy--Southern Exposure," in With All Deliberate Speed (Shoemaker, ed., 1957) was helpful, as was Wright, "Public School Desegregation: Legal Remedies for De Facto Segregation," 16 Western Reserve L. Rev. 478 (1965). Other sources were: 25 The Negro History Bull., Jan., 1962, at 92. Other sources were: magazines, Taves, "The Mother Who Stood Alone," 152 Good Housekeeping, April, 1961, at 30, 32; Mothner, "Exodus from New Orleans," 25 Look, March 14, 1961, at 53, 58; 76 Time, Dec. 12, 1960, at 20 and Nov. 28, 1960, at 19; Sherman, "The Nightmare Comes to New Orleans," 23 The Reporter, Dec. 8, 1960, at 24, 26; 56 Newsweek, Dec. 5, 1960, at 34; and newspapers, Wall Street Journal, Mar. 6, 1961, at 2, col. 4; New Orleans Times-Picayune, Nov. 1, 1960, $1, at 1, col. 4, Oct. 8, 1960, $1, at 7, col. 2-3, and at 17, col. 1, Aug. 27, 1960 $1, at 2, col. 2; and N.Y. Times, Oct. 8, 1960, at 23, col. 1. There were personal interviews with Mr. Theodore Shepard, Mr. Marcel Trudeau, and Judge J. Skelly Wright.

The Mop-Up: 1962. Helpful sources were: V. Navasky, Kennedy Justice, at 272-73 (1971); and personal interviews with Chief Judge John R. Brown, Judge Lewis R. Morgan, Judge Alvin B. Rubin, Mr. Edward Wadsworth, and Judge John M. Wisdom.

Contrasts and Conclusions. Cases relied on were McCoy v. Louisiana State Bd. of Educ., 345 F.2d 720 (5th Cir. 1965); 332 F.2d 915 (5th Cir. 1964); Hall v. West, 335 F.2d 481 (5th Cir. 1964); Hall v. St. Helena Parish School Bd., 233 F. Supp. 136 (E.D. La. 1964); and Davis v. East Baton Rouge Parish School, 214 F. Supp. 624 (E.D. La. 1963). Other sources were A. Bickel, Politics and the Warren Court, at 73 (1965); Fingerhood, "The Fifth Circuit Court of Appeals," in Southern Justice, at 214, 220-21 (L. Friedman, ed., 1966); and Lusky, "Racial Discrimination and the Federal Law: A Problem in Nullification," in Southern Justice, at 255, 256-57 (L. Friedman, ed., 1966). Also helpful was Delaney, "At 6, Lonely Step Over Color Line," N.Y. Times, May 17, 1974, at 35, col. 1.

A more complete manuscript, with detailed documentation of all sources, is available as indicated in the Preface.

PART II

COMING OF AGE: THE TUTTLE YEARS, 1960-1967

"The test of the moral quality of a civilization is its
treatment of the weak and powerless."
                         --Jerome Frank, 1955

Chapter 4

A DIFFERENT DRUM

In all civilized ... countries, there are judges
who are charged with the duty of saying what
the law means.... When these judges have
spoken, the force behind the law will be used.
--Learned Hand, 1960

Just as 1960 was a watershed year for the nation, with the
election of the young Senator from Massachusetts as the new President of the United States, so also was it a milestone in the history
of the United States Court of Appeals for the Fifth Circuit. On December 5, 1960, Elbert Parr Tuttle of Georgia became Chief Judge
of the Circuit upon the unexpected resignation of Judge Richard T.
Rives. Judge Tuttle assumed his new duties at the height of the
difficulties in New Orleans with a fresh resolve to see the Supreme
Court's Brown mandate finally enforced. During Chief Judge Tuttle's
tenure, the Fifth Circuit became the nation's largest and fastest
growing federal appeals court. The court's case load burgeoned,
with civil rights and desegregation suits being filed across the South
in almost geometric progression. Ten new judges joined the Court
in the turbulent Tuttle years from 1960 to 1967; this infusion of disparate conceptions of judicial duty in civil rights litigation threatened
on more than one occasion to mar permanently the Court's effectiveness as a viable judicial institution. Fortunately, the Fifth Circuit
has had not only more than its fair share of great judges but also
more than its fair share of judges willing, in the final analysis, to
exercise that personal restraint necessary to prevent permanent
fragmentation of the Court.

Ten New Men

Ten new men with richly varied backgrounds and, in com-
posite, representing almost every shade of judicial philosophy, took

Opposite, the 1965 Court, with nine Judges: back row (l. to r.),
Homer Thornberry, Walter P. Gewin, John Minor Wisdom, Griffin
B. Bell, James P. Coleman; front, John R. Brown, Richard T.
Rives, Elbert P. Tuttle, Warren L. Jones.

their places on the Fifth Circuit bench during Chief Judge Tuttle's
seven years. While some, indeed, were more influential than others in the development and evolution of desegregation and race relations law, a few are now rightfully recognized as being among the
premier appellate judges in the nation. However, all contributed to
the Court's rich civil rights history. Each has truthfully left his
own peculiar mark on the fabric of the court's development.

* * *

Born in Americus in 1918, Griffin Bell's background is deeply rooted in Georgia. After a World War II stint as a major in the
transportation corps, he graduated from Mercer Law School, beginning practice in Savannah in 1948. In 1953, he accepted a partnership with the prestigious Atlanta firm of King and Spalding, eventually serving as senior managing partner. In his last two years of
practice Bell served as Chief of Staff to former Georgia Governor
Vandiver. He then was appointed by President Kennedy to the Fifth
Circuit, beginning his service on that Court on October 6, 1961.*

Frequently categorized as the Court's leading conservative
and almost as frequently called the Court's leading moderate, Judge
Bell is, by all accounts, a leader on the bench, time and again apparently able to swing the deciding bloc of votes. Bitterly dismissed
in recent years by civil rights advocates as a "judicial politician,"
Judge Bell has also been criticized by Southern conservatives as one
of the Fifth Circuit's leading judicial activists. He considers himself to be "about in the middle" of the Court in judicial and social
philosophy.

Judge Bell's reputation as the "wheeler-dealer" on the Fifth
Circuit stems, perhaps in part, from his deep belief in a judge's
responsibility to seek accommodation between competing interests.
Judge Bell is a past master of the in-chambers, and out-of-the-pub-
lic eye, conference. On many occasions in the midst of a desegregation impasse, his in-chambers meetings with the principals in a
local school controversy have resulted in compliance with federal
court commands, short of resort to contempt procedures. Judge
Bell's innovative mind and his popularity with his colleagues has
propelled him to a position of national leadership in the development
of reforms in the federal appellate system. John R. Brown calls
him "the father" of many of the Fifth Circuit's innovative screening
and expediting procedures. Judge Bell has served as an influential
member of the American Bar Association's Commission on Judicial
Standards.

---

*After this manuscript was completed, Judge Bell resigned from the
Fifth Circuit in early 1976 and resumed private practice in Atlanta.
He was appointed by President-Elect Jimmy Carter as Attorney Gen-
eral Designate. Despite controversy over his appointment and oppo-
sition by some civil rights groups, he was confirmed by the United
States Senate.

In the evolution of school desegregation law in the Fifth Circuit, Judge Bell has become a controversial figure, not only with the bar but also with his fellow judges. Involved in many of the major desegregation decisions of the Fifth Circuit, Judge Bell's contribution, while exceedingly important, is also exceedingly difficult to evaluate. On the one hand, his record can be read as placing him at the forefront of the liberal forces of his Court in the desegregation struggle; his persistent efforts in Mobile, his steadfastness in the die-hard Mississippi counties and his en banc opinion in one of the epic Singleton v. Jackson rounds are but prime examples of judicial activism that must mark him as a major figure on the side of desegregation enforcement. On the other hand, his alleged behind the scenes involvement in the recent abortive Atlanta compromise plan (for which an ACLU attorney formally demanded that Bell recuse himself from further participation in the case), his continued advocacy of his Orange County Plan as the ideal school desegregation solution (a minority-to-majority transfer plan superimposed over a neighborhood school zoning system), and his retreat from system-wide desegregation in the recent Corpus Christi and Austin cases also are but examples of a much more conservative side that can, perhaps too easily, be read as foot-dragging or even Machiavellian recalcitrance. Judge Bell, in short, is impossible to pigeon-hold by judicial philosophy and impossible to ignore. While torn by the need to vigorously carry out Supreme Court mandates he is just as torn by the fear of the political consequences of judicial over-reaction:

> The danger, this is a big danger as I see it ... someday
> we are going to put a school board in contempt and the
> Justice Department is going to walk away and we are going
> to be like the Andrew Jackson-John Marshall case there*
> .... It will be a terrible thing for our country if that
> ever happens. The courts have got to exercise some re-
> straint.

But Judge Bell also insists that he would have "decided Brown I the same way it was decided." He bristles when his record is criticized by civil rights advocates: "all I can say about that is just look at the results. I'll take my results and back them up against anybody else's results."

Judge Bell's involvement in school desegregation, in both enforcing massive desegregation decrees and in limiting expansive integration doctrine, has provided him with a unique opportunity to judge the effectiveness of court-ordered desegregation plans. In the nearly intractible Mississippi cases involving over thirty counties, Judge Bell charted the success of desegregation and succinctly concluded:

---

*Referring to President Jackson's reputed reaction to one of Chief Justice Marshall's opinions, "He has made his decision, now let him enforce it."

The ones where the blacks are in the minority are all a
success, the ones that were about 50-50, some have
worked out and some have not, and the ones where the
blacks are in heavy majority are all black schools. And
we have the facts to show that on those 30 cases.

*   *   *

Walter Gewin took his Fifth Circuit seat the same day as
Griffin Bell; born in 1908 in Nanafalia, Alabama, he was also a
Kennedy appointee. Educated at Emory and the University of Alabama, he received his law degree in 1935, and then compiled a distinguished record as a small town lawyer in Alabama. He served
for four years as a member of the State House of Representatives
and also later as both the Vice President and President of the Alabama Bar.

A man of humility and deep integrity, Judge Gewin has become a powerful advocate, particularly in judicial council meetings.
Judge Gewin has, at least in race and desegregation matters, mark-
edly shifted from one of the most conservative positions on the court
in the early years of his judgeship to a position that, since the recent Corpus Christi and Austin cases, seems to place him with the
Court's traditional liberals. Many of Judge Gewin's race opinions,
both when he sided with the conservative wing of the Court and recently, when he seems to have shifted to a more liberal position,
are often touched with a rare eloquence.

Judges Gewin and Bell took the bench in the midst of the
Fifth Circuit's monumental combat with Mississippi Governor Ross
Barnett over the matriculation of James Meredith at the University
of Mississippi. Judge Gewin refers to that period as a "baptism of
fire" that taught him "the hard way" that "judges cannot enforce
their decrees if the government does not back them."

While never reactionary in the mold of Judge Cameron, Judge
Gewin in the middle years took a decidedly conservative tack, emphasizing judicial restraint and a belief in the good faith of state officials. However, despite the effect his small town Alabama background may have had on his early race decisions, Judge Gewin has
never been branded a racist. His constant exposure on the bench
to the deprivation of rights, solely on the basis of race, seems to
have had a gradual but an increasingly important influence upon his
personal philosophy. His colleagues point to a public accommodations case that may have sparked a catharsis in Judge Gewin's career, Miller v. Amusement Enterprises. Because Judge Gewin
abruptly joined his liberal brothers in that en banc case and wrote
the majority opinion, the facts--related in Judge Gewin's own words
--which so deeply offended him are worth noting:

Mrs. Miller, in response to Fun Fair's advertisement
that 'Everybody come,' took her two children, Daniel age
12 and Denise age 9, to the park to ice skate. At the

skate rental counter she asked for skates for Denise, who
has a fair or light complexion, and the attendant, thinking
the little girl was white, promptly handed Mrs. Miller a
pair of skates. Daniel, dark-complexioned, who had been
sent back to the Miller's car for heavy socks, then joined
his mother and sister. The rented skates were soon discovered to be too small and Mrs. Miller returned to the
rental stand and placed two skates on the counter. In the
meantime the attendant had discovered that the child was
Negro and he left the skate room to inform the manager
of the situation. As the manager approached the counter,
Mrs. Miller stated to him that the skates did not fit. The
manager snatched the skates off the counter and announced
to Mrs. Miller that Fun Fair did not 'serve colored.' The
people standing in line waiting to rent skates began to gig-
gle, and Denise, frightened and disappointed at not being
allowed to skate, started crying. As Denise stood there
crying others in line appeared to be amused. Mrs. Miller
and her children quickly left the park.

The Gewin opinion in Miller, holding the amusement park was a
"place of entertainment" within the public accommodations provisions
of the 1964 Civil Rights Act, has become a landmark in public accommodations law.

Similarly, in 1966, Judge Gewin wrote the opinions in a pair
of cases which established a student's right to freedom of expression
in the public schools of the Fifth Circuit three years before the
United States Supreme Court reached the same conclusion. By the
mid-sixties, the civil rights movement had seeped down to engage
the interest and energies of high school students and the country's
racial problems became topics of debate both in class and in school
corridors. When Negro students of high schools in Philadelphia and
Issaquena County, Mississippi, sought to publicize a current voter
registration drive by distributing S.N.C.C. "freedom buttons" de-
picting a white and black hand clasped together, they were given the
choice of either removing the buttons or being suspended. The
Court of Appeals directed the entry of an injunction against school
administrators who had prohibited such expression, and Judge Gewin
observed:

We support all efforts by the school to fashion reasonable
regulations for the conduct of their students and enforcement of the punishment incurred when such regulations
are violated. Obedience to duly constituted authority is
a valuable tool, and respect for those in authority must
be instilled in our young people.
But, with all of this in mind, we must also emphasize that school officials cannot ignore expressions of
feelings with which they do not wish to contend. They
cannot infringe on their students' right to free and unrestricted expression as guaranteed to them under the First
Amendment to the Constitution, where the exercise of such

rights in the school buildings and schoolrooms do not materially and substantially interfere with the requirements of appropriate discipline in the operation of the school.

Judge Gewin is a patient man who reveres patience as an important quality in any judge. In school cases he felt it was extremely important to let school boards be heard, "to have the feeling they are listened to." Judge Gewin once persuaded his Court to extend oral arguments on several important school cases from early morning until late afternoon with the comment, "let's let them go on so that they can fully feel that they have told their side of the story." But Judge Gewin's patience was not limitless. One Sunday morning on the way to church, a townsman stopped Judge Gewin with a shrill challenge: "I thought you were on our side.... Why did you write that [Birmingham school] case the way you did?" Judge Gewin asked if the man had read the case and when he replied, "no," the judge retorted, "You can ask me any question you like, but don't ever ask me about a case you haven't even read, because you simply don't know what you're talking about."

Judge Gewin, while more critical of himself then perhaps he should be, refuses to criticize other judges on his Court. He frankly states that he has not "been the best judge that I could have been." When asked about his apparent shift in viewpoint in desegregation matters in recent years, Judge Gewin smiled and commented simply: "I did think at a certain point that more time was necessary [to accomplish desegregation] but now it's like telling a small child 'Don't!' and finally having to draw the line in the sand and say 'It must stop now.'"

*   *   *

In one of the many minor, but nevertheless real, injustices of modern history, Homer Thornberry may well be remembered only as a footnote: the crony of President Lyndon B. Johnson upon whose ill-starred nomination to the Supreme Court Congress never acted. If that is to be Judge Thornberry's fate then, indeed, history will have treated him unfairly.

Homer Thornberry was born to deaf-mute parents in 1909 in Austin, Texas. He attended the University of Texas as both an undergraduate and as a law student, beginning practice in Austin in 1936. The next year he was elected to the Texas Legislature and, except for service as a Lieutenant Commander in the Navy, he held a series of public offices until he was appointed to the bench. He served as a member of the Austin City Council, as Mayor Pro Tempore and then for fifteen years as a United States Congressman. While in Congress he served with distinction as a member of the powerful House Rules Committee and was devoted to legislation to improve education for the deaf.

Less than one month after President Johnson took the oath of

office on an airport runway in Dallas, he appointed Homer Thornberry, a long-time friend and confidant, to the federal district
court bench. After serving little more than a year and a half as
a district court judge, President Johnson elevated Judge Thornberry
to the United States Court of Appeals for the Fifth Circuit. Judge
Thornberry's oath of office was administered at the LBJ Ranch on
July 3, 1965.

Upon Earl Warren's resignation as Chief Justice of the United
States Supreme Court in 1968, Lyndon Johnson again thought of his
old friend in Austin. At the time President Johnson announced his
appointment of Justice Abe Fortas to replace Earl Warren as Chief
Justice, President Johnson also appointed Homer Thornberry to take
the Fortas seat that was to be vacated. Under heavy fire for alleged improprieties in accepting retainers, Justice Fortas resigned
from the Supreme Court. President Johnson left office and Homer
Thornberry's nomination was never acted on by Congress. Judge
Thornberry continued to serve in his quiet, effective way on the
Fifth Circuit.

Homer Thornberry is an unobtrusive, self-effacing, grand-
fatherly man who, after a rocky beginning, has mastered the art
of opinion writing by sheer dint of effort. He is now recognized as
a craftsman on the bench. He has consistently voted for effective
enforcement of Supreme Court decrees and has established himself
as a steady member of his Court's more liberal wing. Since his
elevation to the Fifth Circuit in 1965, he has served on countless
school desegregation panels, tirelessly insisting on greater efforts
by sluggish school officials. His devotion to integration is simply
but powerfully expressed, "I have no doubt that our black children
are entitled to quality education. From what I see and know, I
have no doubt that they will not receive it unless we insist on some
type of integration."

*   *   *

Former Mississippi Governor Coleman was Lyndon Johnson's
second and perhaps most controversial Fifth Circuit appointment.
Born in 1914 in Ackerman, Mississippi, Judge Coleman's judicial
offices are still located in that small town. His background, while
Mississippi country from birth through his undergraduate career at
Ole Miss, was broken by his law school years at George Washington University in Washington, D. C. Judge Coleman's record of public service in Mississippi is one of the most distinguished ever to
come out of that state. Serving in all three branches of state government he was, in chronological order, a district attorney, a state
circuit judge, Commissioner of the State Supreme Court, State Attorney General, Governor from 1956 to '60 and a member of the
Mississippi House from 1960 to '65. At one time he was also publisher of the Chocteau Plaindealer, a weekly newspaper, and a
trustee at Mississippi College.

It fell to Lyndon Baines Johnson to nominate a replacement

for Judge Cameron and the replacement had to come from Mississippi. Finally, in June, 1965, despite his knowledge that Jim Coleman's record as a "moderate" segregationist would be anathema to civil rights supporters of every stripe, President Johnson nominated him to fill the vacancy on the Fifth Circuit. President Johnson's fears were not misplaced. Civil rights advocates lined up to demand his rejection. Congressman John Conyers, a black member of the House Judiciary Committee from Michigan, led the attackers, declaiming Coleman as the "thinking man's segregationist."* Attorney General Nicholas Katzenbach, supporting the nomination on behalf of the administration hotly responded that, in Mississippi, Jim Coleman's consistent insistence on law and order was "worth a hundred [segregationist] campaign speeches."** It was reported to the Sub-Committee of the Senate Judiciary Committee that Coleman now admitted he had made "past mistakes" and he now was convinced that "separation of individuals by color and color alone is dead in this country and it is finished."*** In an article contemporaneous with the Judiciary Subcommittee's hearings and entitled "Mississippi's Best," Time succinctly summarized the dispute over the Coleman nomination:

> To succeed in Mississippi politics since Reconstruction has meant being a segregationist, and James P. Coleman succeeded....
> But Coleman was never a militant racist. He stayed clear of the Citizens Councils, scoffed at the notion of state 'nullification' of federal law, spoke out against violence, and invited the FBI into his state to investigate racial murder. In 1960, he was one of the few Deep South leaders to support John Kennedy for the Democratic presidential nomination. In 1963 this record cost him the gubernatorial election.
> Last month President Johnson nominated Coleman to fill a vacancy on the nine-member Federal Court of Appeals for the Fifth Circuit.... Mississippi is the only state not currently represented on the court. Custom dictated that Johnson pick a Mississippian, and ironbound Senate tradition demanded that his choice be approved by the state's Senators--James Eastland, who happens to be chairman of the Judiciary Committee, and John Stennis. Given all the circumstances, Coleman seemed to be the best available.****

Judge Coleman was finally confirmed by a divided Senate and took office on August 16, 1965. While consistently conservative in voting, unlike his predecessor from Mississippi, Ben Cameron,

---

*Time, July 23, 1965, at 18; Reprinted by permission from Time, The Weekly Newsmagazine; Copyright Time, Inc.
**Ibid.
***Ibid.
****Ibid., at 17-18.

Judge Coleman has become a favorite among his colleagues on the Court. Tall, raw-boned and Lincolnesque, James Coleman's sparkling "good old boy" humor and earthy common sense mask leadership qualities that have gone unnoticed by many critical courtroom observers. While his opinions are unorthodox, frequently sprinkled with family reminiscences and references to home and country, his real effectiveness occurs behind closed judicial chamber doors and in Judicial Council meetings. Mistakenly dismissed by young civil rights attorneys as "another reactionary clown from Mississippi," Judge Coleman has been careful not to repeat Judge Cameron's mistakes. While quick to dissent on most Mississippi race cases, Judge Coleman is not a nay-sayer. In race cases elsewhere and in other judicial matters Judge Coleman rarely dissents, carefully following precedent. Furthermore, his tireless good humor helps prevent divisive intramural struggles typical of Judge Cameron. Judge Coleman has also, even perhaps as the Court's most consistent conservative, faced more than his fair share of abuse from fellow Mississippians. When sitting on the appeal of the civil rights convictions of the murderers of the three civil rights workers in Philadelphia, Mississippi, an explosive device was found in his wife's car. He was so incensed that, doubting his own impartiality, he excused himself from the panel handling the appeal.

* * *

Pragmatic, moderate, meticulous, Robert Ainsworth is a centrist on the Court. Recently, he has been one of the Court's key swing voters, tending to lean ever so slightly toward the conservatives. Born in Gulfport, Louisiana, in 1910, Robert Ainsworth received his legal education at Loyola University in New Orleans. A prominent New Orleans attorney for 29 years, he was Governor Jimmie Davis's floor leader in the Louisiana Legislature during the New Orleans integration crises in 1960. His almost solitary courage in that arena has already been examined, but it was not atypical. When Governor Davis pushed for passage of a one-cent increase in the state sales tax to finance private schools to avoid integration, Robert Ainsworth refused to go along. After that traumatic year of 1960, President Kennedy appointed Ainsworth to the Federal District Court for the Eastern District of Louisiana; in accepting that appointment, Judge Ainsworth gave up a promising political career.

Never really at ease on the trial court bench, Judge Ainsworth was delighted with his elevation to the Fifth Circuit by President Lyndon Johnson on August 31, 1966. By nature reflective and reserved, he has been much more comfortable as an appellate judge. Furthermore, he has established a reputation as a careful, hardworking scholar who consistently tries to avoid sweeping opinions, preferring to confine his decisions to the narrow facts of the case before him. His race and school desegregation opinions, while characteristically narrow, nevertheless reveal his abhorrence for all forms of racial discrimination. Troubled recently by recurring eye problems, Judge Ainsworth's vigorous work schedule has been somewhat curtailed. However, his contributions in the race and desegregation areas have been significant, despite only eight years on the appellate bench.

* * *

John Cooper Godbold took his Fifth Circuit seat the same day as Judge Ainsworth. Now only fifty-four, he has already served eight significant years on the appellate bench, achieving a position of marked leadership among the Court's more conservative members. In the Frankfurter mold, Judge Godbold is considered by his colleagues as one of the Court's most important members, perhaps a future giant.

John Godbold was born in Cory, Alabama, in 1920; a graduate of Auburn, he attended Harvard Law School. He began practice with Judge Richard T. Rives, prior to Judge Rives' appointment to the Court of Appeals and, thereafter, practiced law continuously in Montgomery until appointed to the Fifth Circuit in 1966 by Lyndon Johnson.

He is already recognized as an exceptionally able scholar. His opinions are erudite, exhaustive and often sparkle with a lively, literate style that can be both persuasive and deeply moving.

* * *

Unfortunately, Irving L. Goldberg did not receive his judicial appointment until he was already sixty years of age. In raw intelligence he is, with John Minor Wisdom, one of the brightest members of the Court; however, unless blessed with unusual longevity, Judge Goldberg's full judicial potential may not be realized.

Born in 1906 in Port Arthur, Texas, Judge Goldberg attended the University of Texas and Harvard. A prominent practicing lawyer in Dallas for most of his professional life and a leader in the Dallas Jewish Community, Judge Goldberg has been deeply involved for years in the civic, charitable and religious life of his city. In 1968 he received the Brotherhood Citation of the National Conference of Christians and Jews. He was appointed by President Lyndon Johnson to the Fifth Circuit and took his seat on September 14, 1966.

Irving Goldberg is, perhaps, the Court's most consistent liberal. His record is one of unwavering support for enforcement of civil rights and civil liberties. Furthermore, despite his eight short years, he is a veteran of numerous desegregation battles. On the bench Judge Goldberg is a pepperpot: his intense enthusiasm for his job is likely to bubble over any moment in a barrage of questions for counsel. His irrepressible good humor and deep respect and friendship for his colleagues provides leavening from the left, just as Judge Coleman's winning personality provides needed relief from the right. Judge Goldberg has formed deep personal attachments with his colleagues and, regardless of judicial philosophy, they return his friendship in similar measure.

Despite a liberal voting record, Judge Goldberg is not an ideologist. He is deeply aware of the emotions and fears of parents ordered to bus their children in a school desegregation order. He blames not just Southern segregationists but also unthinking liberals for many of the ugly incidents that have marred desegregation efforts. But he is also committed to the enforcement and, indeed, the rightness of the Brown mandates. He believes it his duty to demand immediate enforcement of desegregation decrees: "the longer you postpone, the heavier the sacrifice."

* * *

Miami's David Dyer is the most urbane member of the Court. Not a native Floridian, David Dyer was born in Columbus, Ohio, in 1910 and attended Ohio State University. However, he soon moved to Florida and enrolled in the John B. Stetson College of Law, never returning North again. An accomplished practicing lawyer for twenty-seven years, at one time in partnership with former Florida Senator George Smathers, David Dyer was a leader of the bar when he received a Kennedy appointment to the United States District Court for the Southern District of Florida in 1961. He served as Chief Judge of his District Court from 1961 until his elevation by President Lyndon Johnson to his Fifth Circuit seat on September 23, 1966, nine days after Judge Goldberg took his seat.

Judge Dyer, like Judge Ainsworth, is considered by most observers to be one of the Court's moderates, a member of neither the conservative nor the liberal voting blocs. However, unlike Judge Ainsworth, if Judge Dyer has a leaning it is perhaps toward the liberal wing of the Court. A veteran of many school desegregation cases, Judge Dyer has become a key swing vote. In the recent Corpus Christi and Austin opinions, discussed in the final chapter of this work, Judge Dyer authored a breathtaking majority opinion, rejecting for the Fifth Circuit the de facto/de jure distinction that has retarded desegregation activity in the North and West. Judge Dyer's Corpus Christi opinion is well ahead of the Supreme Court's doctrinal development in the same area. However, in that same Corpus Christi case, Judge Dyer sided with the Court's moderate and conservative majority to remand the case to the District Judge to rewrite an extensive busing order. Judge Dyer holds a critical vote; his support is wooed with fervor by both sides in civil rights and race cases.

* * *

The last two additions to the Tuttle Court were Bryan Simpson and Claude Femster Clayton. Both were Johnson nominees; both had previously served as federal district court judges in highly volatile civil rights cases in their respective home states of Florida and Mississippi. Judge Simpson was elevated to the Fifth Circuit on November 22, 1966, and Judge Clayton, one year later on November 24, 1967; Judge Simpson is still in active service;* Judge

---

*After this manuscript was completed Judge Simpson retired and

Clayton died only eighteen months after his appointment, on July 4, 1969. Since perhaps the most significant contribution of both of these men stems from their work as district court judges prior to their elevation, they are the subjects of later examination elsewhere in this work.

*   *   *

These then are the ten who joined the Fifth Circuit during Chief Judge Tuttle's middle years: Bell, Gewin, Thornberry, Coleman, Ainsworth, Godbold, Goldberg, Dyer, Simpson and Clayton. With Elbert Tuttle and Judges Hutcheson, Rives, Cameron, Jones, Brown and Wisdom they would all embark in 1960--or join the court between 1960 and 1967--on the nation's most chaotic years in civil rights development and enforcement. Not all would complete the journey but all had a significant role in charting its course.

The Quickening Pace

> Along with his brethren on the Court, Judge Tuttle has devoted unending labor to the mountainous task of assuring the peaceful, orderly, fulfillment under law of the promise of racial equality as swiftly as the processes of justice would permit.... [D]uring his years as Chief Judge, Elbert Tuttle must be recognized as one of the great judges of this era. During his years as Chief Judge, the Fifth Circuit has faced the greatest problems of any circuit in the country, and in the explosive race relations cases themselves, Judge Tuttle has combined these administrative talents with great personal courage and wisdom to assure justice of the highest quality without delays which might have thrown the Fifth Circuit into chaos.... He is richly deserving of the gratitude of his State, his country, and the entire federal court system.
> --The Hon. Earl Warren, Chief Justice

*   *   *

After Chief Judge Hutcheson retired to Senior Status in 1959, Judge Rives became Chief Judge. After serving for slightly over one year, Judge Rives suddenly resigned the position, relinquishing the chief judgeship to Judge Tuttle and assuming his previous role as just a member of the court.

[cont.] assumed Senior Judge status; he was replaced on the Fifth Circuit by District Judge Gerald Tjoflat, whose efforts in the desegregation of Jacksonville's public schools are described in Part III, Chapter 14, "Upheaval," infra.

In addition to personal reasons, prompted by his wife's failing health, Judge Rives later explained:

> Primarily, I felt like Tuttle was an ideal man to be chief judge. He had so much administrative ability, and he was so quick in getting his cases off, there was no burden to him. And if I hadn't been sure that I was turning over the court to someone whom I thought was better qualified to be Chief Judge than I was, I wouldn't have stepped aside.... I timed the thing really, I don't know that I've ever said it to Tuttle, but I timed the time that I stepped aside just because I thought Tuttle had an opportunity of getting on the Supreme Court if Nixon were elected President.... I thought he was Supreme Court timbre, and I thought he had some opportunity. I never did discuss that with Tuttle at all. I called him up once just before then and told him, 'Now, Elbert, I am going to step aside as chief judge today,' and took him by complete surprise. 'I wanted to let you know.' I didn't tell him why, but that was the real reason for my stepping aside.

*   *   *

For convenience in labeling, periods in the life of a court are often referred to, in a patriarchal fashion, by the name of its Chief Judges: thus, there is the "Warren Court," the "Burger Court" and the "Marshall Court." The label does not necessarily imply a singlemindedness of policy or unanimity of decision-making; rarely was there a court more frequently or more bitterly split than the "Warren Court." Furthermore, such a label is not meant to deprecate the contributions of the other individual judges to the creation of the image that a court projects under its Chief. Most legal scholars would point to the contribution of Justices Harlan or Black as being more influential than that of the Chief Justice in the development of the law during the "Warren years." But a strong Chief can assert an influence in a Court's direction even if his is but a single voice in its inner deliberations. Although Judge Tuttle through his opinions added to the development of the substantive   . law, particularly in the race area, his prime contribution was as a leader in the remodeling of his Court's procedures.

It will be recalled that Judge Tuttle had headed the Treasury Department's legions of attorneys and, as a matter of sound administration, he set a high value upon quick response to requests for official opinion. Nevertheless, while Judge Tuttle had been a bureaucrat and a general, his concern about judicial delay came from deeper sources than simply insuring an efficient command. His life-long interest in education, including service as counsel to a county school board and as a trustee of both Southern and Northern universities, caused him to elevate delay to the philosophical concept of injustice. He explained his personal credo:

> I have undertaken to think of these school cases in terms of real personal denials of something that may affect a child or a young man or a young woman's whole life. And when I could visualize that out of the hundreds and thousands of black school children, while maybe all but 10,000 in the Southern school districts and their parents too might have been fairly contented with things as they were, it was also perfectly obvious to any thoughtful person that there would be thousands, or certainly hundreds of young black people, who either would ultimately, if they were very young, or already had arrived at a point where they had an ambition really to make the most of their lives but which would be totally frustrated under the present system. And, therefore, I felt particularly concerned when our court would have a case which we would find came at such a time that we would know that normal delays of litigation would cause a loss of an additional year before anybody could get relief in this system.

Judge Tuttle's recognition of delay as injustice in the denial of access to desegregated public education welled over into such companion areas of black rights as voting. Judge Tuttle has written:

> In the area of voting rights, every election held without participation of Negro voters meant one more term in office for the beneficiary of the old system. There were no effective sanctions to coerce the reluctant official to take voluntary action to comply with what everyone knew was the law. Thus each school district and each county or parish became a separate unit to be dealt with unless it could be demonstrated that time was no longer on the side of the recalcitrant.

The task set before him and the Court was, as expressed by Tuttle, to make "it plain that the prize of delay could no longer be won."

As a consequence of his abhorrence of delay, Chief Judge Tuttle personally set an example of expeditious action for his colleagues during his tenure as Chief Judge. In the University of Georgia case, for example, District Judge Bootle had entered an order finding that the university had pursued a policy of segregation but, unsure of its correctness, had stayed his own order until the Fifth Circuit could review it. Judge Bootle's opinion came down the weekend before the beginning of a new term. Nevertheless, when counsel for the black applicants contacted Chief Judge Tuttle, he agreed to hear the motion to vacate the stay in his offices that very afternoon. At the conclusion of the hearing, he did vacate the stay; the black students appeared for admission the following Monday in time to register for the new term. Similarly, in the area of public school desegregation, Chief Judge Tuttle summarily ordered the readmission of a thousand black children to Birmingham schools pending the Court's full review of the orders entered in the case by District Judge Allgood.

* * *

The machinery for translating the procedural innovations engineered by a single judge into court policy is the Judicial Council of the Circuit, composed of all the active judges of a circuit. Created by Congress in 1939, the Judicial Council's function is to "make all necessary orders for the effective and expeditious administration of the business of the courts within its circuit." The judicial council of a circuit is clearly delegated the power to institute rules concerning the procedures of the circuit court as well as those of the district courts. Furthermore, the prevailing view of the proper function of circuit judicial councils is to amplify this rather ambiguous rule-making power to its fullest. In 1961, the mother of judicial councils, the Judicial Conference of the United States, adopted as policy the following interpretation of a circuit judicial council's responsibility:

> ... The responsibility of the councils 'for the effective and expeditious administration of the business of the courts within its circuit' extends not merely to the business of the courts in its technical sense (judicial administration), such as the handling and dispatching of cases, but also to the business of the judiciary in its institutional sense (administration of justice), such as the avoiding of any stigma, disrepute, or other element of loss of public esteem and confidence in respect to the court system, from the actions of a judge or other person attached to the courts. The councils have the responsibility and owe the duty of taking such action as may be necessary, including the issuance of 'all necessary orders,' to accomplish these ends....

Although the Judicial Council's role had been established for nine years when Chief Judge Hutcheson became the Fifth Circuit's titular leader, he largely ignored it as a crucible for policy. As Judge Rives recalled,

> [T]here's no doubt that the administration of the court is different under every judge. Starting back with Chief Judge Hutcheson, he was a very able administrator himself, but he didn't brook any interference by the judicial council. His usual method of holding a judicial council was to drop into your office and tell you, 'Now, we've had a judicial council meeting as the statute requires.' But he was a strong administrator and handled the matters himself....

* * *

The traditional appellate process is inherently ponderous. Before the circuit court can even begin to consider whether there was error in a trial court's judgment, generally the following minimum steps must occur: the entry of a final district court judgment or otherwise appealable order; the docketing of the appeal with the Clerk of the Court of Appeals; the preparation and furnishing of a written transcript of the trial proceedings and record to the appellate judges assigned for decision; a full briefing by the appellant with an opportunity for the appellee to file a brief in response; and after time for consideration of the written documents of the case by the court members, an oral argument by counsel for both sides. Therefore, in its essence, the appellate process is time-consuming. The Fifth Circuit was wont to observe: "The vindication of private rights by litigation necessarily entails some delay. Laymen and courts alike regret any delay in the vindication of a right that is not the natural and proper result from the orderly handling of the litigation.... [However], [t]he time required to prosecute an appeal in this [traditional] manner is recognized by all to be time well-spent in the ordinary case." Yet, within four years of Elbert Tuttle's elevation to the Chief Judgeship, expedited appellate hearings in race and civil rights cases had become standard operating procedure. On one single day in June, 1963, the Court considered six civil rights cases on an emergency basis, five of which had been docketed for appeal within that very month.

Judge Cameron was distressed by the new policies of accelerating certain cases for review, out of turn and at the expense of pending "routine" work. He publicly aired his consternation in a dissenting opinion:

> The record of this court in hearing and deciding cases is as good as any. That record cannot long endure if certain cases are to be given special attention and considered on a preferential basis. In the vast number of cases now pending before this court are matters of tremendous importance involving business affairs, taxes, property, personal injuries, life and liberty. With deference and full respect, I feel it is my duty to express the opinion that the six cases which were fully argued on June 26, 1963, were not of such overwhelming importance as to take precedence over all other cases then pending in this court.

But Judge Cameron alone could not block the tide: expedited hearings were available to parties who could demonstrate an actual need for immediate relief; sixty-day informally sanctioned deadlines were imposed upon opinion writing assignments of the circuit judges; and, the practice was authorized of issuing the circuit court's mandate effective immediately, instead of after the elapse of twenty-one days.

* * *

Important as new streamlined procedures were to the responsiveness of the appellate judicial system, an infinitely more troubling problem soon emerged. No matter how committed to expeditious handling of its dockets the Fifth Circuit was, it traditionally had little control over a case until a district court had taken

some final action and an appeal had been filed. If a district chose
to simply "sit on" a case or otherwise slow-down the judicial process, what recourse did a Court of Appeals have?

In the normal course of litigation, the jurisdiction of a circuit court of appeals attaches to a case only after a "final judgment" at the district court level: a completed determination of all
issues of facts and law presented by a case. However, as an exception to the general requirement of a final judgment in the trial
court, Congress empowered the Court of Appeals to review certain
temporary orders of a district court in a limited class of actions,
specifically enumerated as those orders "granting, continuing, modifying, refusing or dissolving injunctions ... except where a direct
review may be had in the Supreme Court."

Thus, even if a district judge elected to stall a final decision
on a case, if he had denied or granted a preliminary injunction the
injured party could immediately seek relief from the Court of Appeals. But what if the district court did nothing by way of deciding
requests for even temporary or preliminary relief? The Fifth Circuit's response, engineered by Judges Rives and Wisdom, was to
treat inaction as a refusal to act, thus investing the appellate court
with the power of immediate, interim review. Judge Cameron again
was provoked by what he considered manipulation by the majority of
his colleagues. He asserted that he did not consider it the proper
function of an appellate court to concern itself with "the docket of
the district courts or other minutiae of trials." Judge Cameron
knew that the Rives-Wisdom interpretation of what constituted a refusal to act signaled monumental changes in the Fifth Circuit's interpretation of its powers.

*   *   *

The next step in expansion of the circuit's assumed powers
occurred in 1962. In his opinion in United States v. Lynd, Judge
Tuttle found a new solution to the crisis created when a district
court judge was clearly in error: the Court of Appeals would issue
its own injunction or other equitable relief, freezing the status quo
pending full appellate review. Thus, the "injunction pending appeal"
was born. In declaring power to issue injunctions pending appeal,
Judge Tuttle cited the fountainhead of equitable jurisdiction in the
federal courts familiarly known to lawyers as the "All Writs Act."
That act provided that all federal courts "may issue all writs necessary or appropriate in aid of their respective jurisdictions and
agreeable to the usages and principles of law."

Historically, the "All Writs Act" had been utilized only by
federal district courts to project the vitality of their trial court
jurisdiction. There was, however, no language in the statute precluding the employment of such remedies by the Courts of Appeals,
although very real problems were created when a circuit court, in
effect, assumed the posture of a trial court and issued its own injunctions. The criterion developed by the Fifth Circuit for the

granting of such extraordinary original relief was a demonstration by the applicant that there was "a great likelihood, approaching near certainty" that the Court of Appeals would agree with his position when the case came before it on review. The granting of such extraordinary relief was carefully limited, guarding against its abuse as a total usurpation of the district court's normal responsibilities. However, the fact that the authority had been found by the Fifth Circuit Court of Appeals to issue its own injunctions served to check potential district court abuses. Chief Judge Tuttle is universally credited with the discovery of this authority for the issuance of an original injunction by the Court of Appeals. The United States Supreme Court implicitly approved the practice in 1963.

* * *

Despite the approval of the Supreme Court, discontent within the councils of the Fifth Circuit began simmering over repeated orders involving such novel relief as an appellate court's issuance of direct injunctions. Perhaps due to the growing concern of at least two of its members, Judges Cameron and Gewin, and the difficulties in policing its own orders, in early 1963 the Fifth Circuit somewhat modified its aggressive position. In considering the long-pending desegregation case from Savannah, Georgia, Chief Judge Tuttle, again the spokesman for the Court, stopped short of issuing the Court's own injunction. Instead, the opinion observed:

> It was a clear abuse of discretion for the trial court to deny [Negro] appellant's motion for a preliminary injunction requiring the defendant School Board to make a prompt and reasonable start towards desegregating the Savannah-Chatham County schools.... We have heretofore concluded that this Court has the power to grant an injunction pending the final hearing of the case on the merits in the Court of Appeals. However, it is clearly more desirable for injunctive relief to be granted at the level of the trial court rather than by an appellate court if the same necessary results can be accomplished. Included in the powers of the Courts of Appeal under the All-Writs Statute, is the power of the Court of Appeals to frame the terms of an injunction and direct the trial court to enter such injunction and make it the order of the trial court.

* * *

The action which finally caused both Judges Gewin and Cameron to publish protests about the Court's increasingly aggressive orders in race relations cases was precipitated by the Birmingham desegregation litigation. In late May, 1963, over a thousand school-aged black children participated in what began as a protest march and ended as a disorganized run through the streets of downtown Birmingham. In retaliation, the Superintendent suspended from school all of those students who could be identified as participants. When District Court Judge Allgood refused to enjoin the suspensions,

counsel for the students sought the intervention of Judge Tuttle. He
not only heard the requests in emergency session, but issued, as a
single judge of the Court, his own injunction. It prohibited the dismissal of the students pending appeal of the entire case on its merits to the Fifth Circuit. Judge Tuttle later recalled the event:

> The 22nd of May, 1963 is when I entered this order, or
> when [District] Judge Allgood entered his order. Mine
> was entered the same night. And they were suspended and
> could not be readmitted until the next term. Many of them
> were seniors in high school and would have lost their en-
> tire opportunity to graduate during that year. And in the
> facts of life that we are all familiar with, you question
> how many of these young black children who were seniors
> and had been kicked out a few days before graduation
> would come back and get a high school education. So I
> ... was happy to feel that I had full justification in re-
> instating those thousand school children that close to the
> end of a term which they otherwise would have lost.*

The unusual action taken by Chief Judge Tuttle to block dismissal of the black Birmingham school children in May of 1963 was
a matter of hot controversy among Fifth Circuit judges. The controversy boiled to the surface in July, 1963, when the Birmingham
school desegregation case was before a panel composed of Chief
Judge Tuttle and Judges Rives and Gewin. Federal District Judge
Seybourne Lynne had refused to grant an injunction ordering Birmingham to cease operating its segregated school system. By a two-to-
one vote, the Fifth Circuit ordered that an injunction, pending full
appeal, be issued to end mandatory segregation. The injunction was
modeled after the precedent so recently established in the Savannah
case. Judge Gewin wrote an impassioned dissent: even assuming
that the heady power to issue original injunctions pending appeal resided in courts of appeals, he asserted that such power had been
much abused from over-use in volatile cases involving differing
opinions about what constituted "all deliberate speed."

Judge Cameron, not even a member of the three-judge panel

---

*Outraged at Judge Tuttle's intervention, the school board challenged
his power to issue an injunction pending appeal. A year later, in
Woods v. Wright, a panel composed of Judges Rives, Jones and
Bootle, upheld Chief Judge Tuttle and decided that the trial court
had erred in refusing to enter an injunction pending consideration of
the full appeal. This is an example of the expanding use by the
Court of extraordinary relief in civil rights cases. While normally
the refusal by a district court to grant a temporary restraining order
is not appealable, here it was clear that a full term of school would
be lost to the school children involved absent such relief. Therefore, relying on its very recent development of such unusual remedies, a panel of the Court not dominated by its more activist judges
was willing to continue such appellate intervention.

that considered the Birmingham case, joined in the frey with an
excoriating dissent from the denial, by a 5-4 vote of his colleagues,
to reconsider the Birmingham case en banc. While Judge Gewin's
opinion had a strong, temperately-phrased discussion of what he
considered a lack of precedent for the novel procedures for expediting cases and granting equitable relief approved recently by his
Court, Judge Cameron mounted a personal assault upon the leadership of his brother Tuttle. Both Judges Gewin and Cameron particularly protested the action taken by Chief Judge Tuttle, sitting as a
single Circuit Court Judge, in issuing an injunction pending appeal
in the Birmingham suspension controversy. Judge Cameron asserted:

> [I]n the very nature of things, it was inevitable that the
> [Birmingham] School Superintendent would obey the fiat of
> the Chief Judge of this Court whether it was backed by the
> authority of the law or not. No action could be taken
> which would obliterate the harm done to the Birmingham
> school system by this improvident order.

Furthermore, referring to the Fifth Circuit's four liberals on
race matters, Rives, Tuttle, Brown and Wisdom, as the "Four,"
Judge Cameron charged that he had been "thwarted by the opposition
of the Four" in attempts to have the "legality" of Chief Judge Tuttle's claimed authority ruled on by the Fifth Circuit Judicial Council. Apparently the issue was discussed in its meeting of May 29,
1963; the Minutes of that meeting record:

> The power of a single Circuit Judge to act in certain
> instances including the power to grant injunctive relief
> was next discussed. It was not possible to resolve the
> question of power by rule or otherwise due to an even
> division among the members of the Council as to the
> presence or absence of such power, and because some
> felt that it was not the appropriate subject matter of a
> rule.

Judge Cameron's bitter challenge to Chief Judge Tuttle's aggressive
leadership really began in the Fifth Circuit's consideration of the
James Meredith case, discussed in the following chapter. It continued in the Birmingham case and is further explored in Chapter 6,
"Schism."

* * *

On a more general level of concern here are Judge Gewin's
observations about the change in attitude of his Court of Appeals
toward some of its district court judges.

The gravamen of Judge Gewin's concern was the heavy-
handed treatment of district court judges like Judge Lynne. By way
of preface, Judge Gewin noted in his own dissent:

My brothers of the majority have spoken in such in-
accurate and disapproving terms with reference to the
opinion and order of the distinguished trial judge of the
Northern District of Alabama who tried this case for several days, that I find it not only impossible to agree with
them, but also necessary to write this dissent in order to
inform those who may be interested of my opinion of the
actual holding of the District Court. The cases cited by
the majority condemn the opinion written by them. The
opinion and order of the District Court considered together
as they should be, destroy every reason asserted in the
majority opinion for the unusual action taken in the circumstances of this case....

Certainly the innovative procedural devices adopted by the
Court manifested a growing skepticism concerning the ability or
willingness of certain district court judges properly to adjudicate a
civil rights case. By the early sixties, the reluctance, even intransigence, of some of the district courts to follow the lead of the
Fifth Circuit became noted nationally.

In the calmer times of Chief Judge Hutcheson's tenure, when
there was little doubt of the enforceability of the Fifth Circuit's
mandates, Judge Hutcheson had been most sensitive to the sensibilities of district court judges, even when they were clearly in error.
At least one member of the Tuttle Court, Judge Gewin, felt that the
Court should have continued its practice of softly-worded declarations
of error, for the sake of both internal harmony and public psychol-
ogy. Judge Gewin later maintained that despite the difficulties con-
fronting the Court in directing the course of its district court judges
in the highly volatile race relations cases, reversals should have
been written to create as little acrimony as possible. He said it
was true that "it never helps to scold people"; when any court hails
someone before its bench and says, "You knew better, you did it on
purpose" and otherwise scolds him, "it doesn't accomplish anything."
He strongly believed that the better course of action was to tell
people what they should do in the future, without commenting unduly
on what had gone on in the past.

Chief Judge Tuttle possessed somewhat different views from
those of former Chief Judge Hutcheson and Judge Gewin about the
task of reversing district court judges:

Well, I suppose the most difficult, or the unhappiest task
an appellate judge has is to be faced with a record where
he sincerely believes that an injustice has been done, but
he finds himself, for one reason or another, unable to correct it....
    After being on a court for several years, every cir-
cuit judge, every appellate court judge, does recognize
that some of the judges whose work he's reviewing are
much more apt to be correct than other judges. Just by
statistics we know that some judges are reversed a great

deal more than other judges. In fact, it's not any secret
to say that occasionally you will find a judge where some
member of the court will say, partially in jest, that if
this judgment of the trial court is correct, it is purely
fortuitous! But that doesn't happen often.... I will say
that many of the older judges, Judge Hutcheson, for instance, would always speak about being very careful about
'putting a judge in error,' as if it was the judge that he
was concerned about, rather than the litigant. I think the
Court, at the time I came on it, the appellate judges were
much more concerned about not wanting to put a 'judge in
error,' so to speak; whereas our court really undertakes
honestly to determine the right of the case and is not too
much concerned with which judge it is whose work we're
reversing.

In contrast to the traditional methods of cajoling and admon-
ishing error-prone district court judges, as years of noncompliance
with the "deliberate speed" mandate of Brown stretched into a decade, the opinions written by the majority of the members of the Tuttle Court reflected blunt exasperation with delay. Reversals were
often sharp, non-conciliatory, even threatening. For example, the
following excerpt from a per curiam opinion of Judges Tuttle, Rives
and Bell illustrates the flash of power by the Court:

... [T]here was no abuse of discretion, but with this
caveat. The matter of the grant or denial of the motion
for preliminary injunction, should, as in every case, be
promptly determined. It is the duty of Judge Thomas to
promptly rule on this motion for preliminary injunction.
It appears that the public schools of Mobile are in
fact segregated according to race. This will not do under
Brown v. Board of Education of Topeka.... This decision
is binding on Judge [Daniel H.] Thomas. It is binding on
all District Courts and all District Judges, just as it is
binding on this court.... Thus it is that this court must
require prompt and reasonable starts, even displacing the
District Court discretion, where local control is not desired, or is abdicated by failure to promptly act.

However, on rare occasions, even strongly worded Circuit
Court orders were unavailing. The Fifth Circuit had to resort to its
ultimate sanction, the writ of mandamus; literally, "we command."
In 1962, counsel for black plaintiffs unsuccessfully sought a writ of
mandamus to compel Judge Hobart Grooms to expedite his hearing
of certain matters involved in the Birmingham desegregation case.
But Judge Grooms served simply as the foil in that case; at issue
was an attempt to get the Birmingham case heard by Judge Grooms
instead of Judge Lynne since both were judges serving the Northern
District of Alabama. However, two years later in 1964, a Court
of Appeals panel composed of Chief Judge Tuttle and Judges Wisdom
and Rives did issue a writ of mandamus to District Judge E. Gordon
West of the Eastern District of Louisiana. Though agreeing that

mandamus was an uncommon remedy to be used only in extremes, the Court concluded that almost three years of inaction by Judge West to order the implementation of a desegregation plan for the public schools of St. Helena Parish was sufficient to justify intervention.

* * *

Within the first five years of Tuttle's tenure as Chief Judge, the Court of Appeals, principally moving through a coalition of the Chief Judge and Judges Rives, Wisdom and Brown, had seized control of the now quickened pace of desegregation. Yet, the Court of Appeals, as an institution, showed signs of critical stress, with the greatest test of its resiliency not far away.

NOTES AND PRIMARY AUTHORITY

The primary authority for the material contained in this chapter was:

Ten New Men. The primary sources are personal interviews with Judge Griffin B. Bell, United States Court of Appeals for the Fifth Circuit, in Atlanta, Ga. (June 20, 1972); Judge Irving L. Goldberg, United States Court of Appeals for the Fifth Circuit, Dallas, Tex. (July, 1972); Judge Homer Thornberry, United States Court of Appeals for the Fifth Circuit, Austin, Tex. (Aug. 2, 1972); and, Judge Walter P. Gewin, United States Court of Appeals for the Fifth Circuit, San Francisco, Cal. (Aug. 10, 1972). The following cases were also helpful: Tinker v. Des Moines Ind. Community School Dist., 393 U.S. 503 (1969); Miller v. Amusement Enterprises, 394 F.2d 342 (5th Cir. 1968); Burnside v. Byars, 363 F.2d 744 (5th Cir. 1966); and, Blackwell v. Issaquena County Bd. of Educ., 363 F.2d 749 (5th Cir. 1966).

"The Quickening Pace." The primary sources are the following cases: United States v. Lynd, 301 F.2d 818 (5th Cir. 1962), cert. denied, 371 U.S. 893 (1962); Holmes v. Danner, 191 F. Supp. 394 (M.D. Ga.), motion to vacate denied, 364 U.S. 939 (1961); Armstrong v. Board of Educ. of Birmingham, 323 F.2d 333, 351-52 (5th Cir. 1963) (dissenting opinion); Bason v. Rippey, 275 F.2d 850, 854 (5th Cir. 1963) (dissenting opinion); Greene v. Fair, 314 F.2d 200, 202 (5th Cir. 1963); and, Stell v. Savannah-Chatham County Bd. of Educ., 318 F.2d 425, 427-28 (5th Cir. 1963). The following interviews are also used as primary sources: Chief Judge Elbert P. Tuttle in his offices in Atlanta, Ga. (May 30, 1972) (June 21, 1972); Judge Richard T. Rives in his offices in Montgomery, Ala. (June 29, 1972); and, Judge Walter P. Gewin in his offices in San Francisco, Cal. (Aug. 10, 1972). The following articles are especially helpful: Chapman, "Expediting Equitable Relief in the Court of Appeals," 53 Cornell L.Q. 12 (1967); "The Judicial Performance in the Fifth Circuit," 73 Yale L.J. 90 (1963); Tuttle, "Equality and the Vote," 41 N.Y.U. L. Rev. 245, 264 (1966); and,

Warren, "A Tribute to Chief Judge Tuttle," 2 <u>Ga. L. Rev.</u> 1, 2 (1967).

Secondary sources are 28 U.S.C. §1292 (1970); 28 U.S.C. §1651 (1970); Judicial Conferences of the United States, "Report on the Powers and Responsibilities of the Judicial Councils," H.R. Dec. No. 201, 87th Cong., 1st Sess. 7 (1961); and, Rules of the Fifth Circuit Court of Appeals, No. 32.

A more complete manuscript, with detailed documentation of all sources, is available as indicated in the Preface, <u>supra</u>.

Chapter 5

THE MATRICULATION OF JAMES MEREDITH:
CRUCIBLE FOR THE FIFTH CIRCUIT

The Desegregation of Higher Education:
Preamble to "Meredith"

> A lot of people in the state love the University
> and the University has always been tied up to the
> state. We usually have people here [at the Uni-
> versity of Georgia] from every county--though
> sometimes we fudge a little to get one from Echols
> County or some little bitty place like that. We
> also have five hundred agricultural-extension work-
> ers and home-demonstration workers spread out
> all over the state.... Ernest Vandiver, the last
> governor, was a graduate of the University. Both
> United States senators--Talmadge and Russell--
> are graduates of the University. Herman Tal-
> madge's son is here and he is the fourth genera-
> tion of Talmadges to attend the University. Rich-
> ard Russell went here; his father was a trustee;
> his uncle was here. Why, he was the fourth
> Richard B. Russell here. I went down to speak
> in Greenville not long ago, and nine graduates
> came to hear me speak. Nine graduates right
> there in Meriwether County [with a total population
> of 19,756].
>   --William Tate, Dean of Men at the Univer-
>   sity of Georgia, quoted in Trillin, An Edu-
>   cation in Georgia 44 (1964).

Prior to Brown I, the chain of cases which chipped away at
the separate-but-equal doctrine of Plessy v. Ferguson were all suits
aimed at opening the opportunities of graduate education to qualified
Negro applicants. Certainly strategists working for Negro advancement were correct in their projection that it would be impossible,
as a practical matter, for states to carry the constitutional burden
of establishing separate, substantially equal, state-financed graduate
schools for Negroes. But they were gravely wrong in their prediction that the resistance to the desegregation of colleges and universities would be minimal and non-violent.

The most violent reactions in the history of desegregation

litigation occurred on the campuses of Southern colleges. Southern segregationists fought integration efforts at the state universities of Alabama, Mississippi, and Georgia with a fervor never seen in public school skirmishes. The reasons for such entrenched resistance were not only difficult to forecast, they are still difficult to explain with the hindsight of a decade. Perhaps violence occurred simply because the colleges were the first "white" institutions assaulted. No one will ever know, for example, if the first judicial mandate in Mississippi had been to admit black children to an Oxford elementary school, instead of an order to admit James Meredith to Ole Miss, whether the reaction might have been infinitely more bloody.

Exactly a century ago, Disraeli, speaking to the House of Commons, idealized the university as "a place of light, of liberty, and of learning." According to its own value system, a university indulges in a conscious practice of exclusivity, extending invitations only to the intellectually gifted. Such exclusivity engenders its own peculiar brand of discrimination, ideally cutting across class lines, social strata, economic and political wherewithal to reach those who show promise of becoming future leaders in their chosen fields of study. As the Supreme Court recognized in 1950, when a university is foreclosed from tapping the potentially rich sources of talent represented in the Negro race, it not only frustrates its avowed ambition but threatens the quality of the intellectual exchange of those who are admitted to its community. Yet in 1954, there were approximately sixty tax-supported junior colleges, colleges, and universities in the South and all were exclusively white.

State universities, particularly in the South, are a distinct species in the genus of higher educational institutions, a hybrid of Disraeli's ecumenical ideal and small town political and social parochialism. The Southern state college draws students primarily from its host state and returns many of its graduates to their home-towns. After graduation there continues a pride of association, a personalized and often intensely loyal relationship to the state alma mater among those who at one time shared in its development. Thus, for many Southerners, a challenge to the existing order of the state university was internalized as a personal challenge. Perhaps this, in part, explains the emotionalism rubbed raw which was nowhere more evident than that displayed in the desegregation of higher education.

*   *   *

The earliest cases arising in the Fifth Circuit challenged the segregation policies in force at the University of Florida and Louisiana State University. In 1949, before the Supreme Court pronouncements in McLaurin and Sweatt,* a 48-year-old college graduate named Virgil Hawkins first sought admission to the law school of the University of Florida. Litigated primarily in the state courts,

---

*See discussion in Prologue, infra.

it took ten years and eleven court decisions before the doors of
Florida's higher educational institutions were opened to Negroes.

The Hawkins case amply illustrates the dysfunction of the
normal relations between state and federal judicial systems which
occurred in the area of racial discrimination. It was often forgotten or overlooked during the ordeal of desegregation, by those who
inveighed against the federal courts for their "interference" and
"usurpation of State sovereignty," that in cases like Hawkins the
state courts had turned a deaf ear to the complaints of its citizens,
making federal relief the only recourse of the black litigant. Three
times Hawkins sought relief from the Florida Supreme Court and
three times relief was denied by a majority of that court. Finally,
in its own third review of the case, the United States Supreme Court
indicated that all that could reasonably be expected of a litigant in
first seeking relief in the courts of his home state had been exacted from Hawkins and pointed him elsewhere: "The writ of certiorari is denied without prejudice to the petitioner seeking relief
in an appropriate United States District Court."

Ironically, in the final stage of his lawsuit, Mr. Hawkins had
to abandon his personal claim to entrance, having failed to perfect
proof of his eligibility. However, he did succeed, on June 18, 1958,
in obtaining an order benefiting others of his race who in the future
would seek admission to the graduate schools in Florida.

Charles Dickens once bitterly described a litigant's seeking
court relief as the process of "wearing out the right." A century
later, he might have been moved to make the same observation
about efforts to desegregate higher education in Louisiana. Given
a state commitment to a policy of massive resistance, the legal
process requiring case-by-case determination is ill-suited to provide immediate relief. In pre-Brown litigation, courts were forced
to employ a balancing test of the comparability of white and black
educational opportunities available in each separate field of graduate
instruction. Thus, at Louisiana State University, even though only
a single umbrella university was involved, if a black person were
interested in pursuing a legal education he had the burden of alleging and proving that the legal training which he sought was not available in equal measure at a separately maintained black institution.
In similar fashion, in separate actions by different black plaintiffs,
the school of medicine and the graduate school of arts and science
of LSU were brought under a desegregation order.

In 1953, Alexander P. Tureaud, son of A. P. Tureaud, the
prominent black attorney of New Orleans who represented Oliver
Bush in the desegregation of the Orleans Parish public schools,
sought entrance to the combined arts and science-law program at
LSU. After five appeals by the state the original injunction stood,
but not without having exacted a toll in human terms. Like many
another college student, Mr. Tureaud changed his mind about ma-
jors and, at registration for the fall term 1955, attempted to enroll
in a program leading to a bachelor's degree in education. He was

informed by the registrar that he was only entitled by court order
to entry in the Liberal Arts-Law combined curriculum. As under-
stated in the dry account of a subsequent judicial opinion:

> He [Tureaud] and his father departed, taking entrance
> blanks with them, and promising to advise within a day or
> two whether ... [he] would enroll in the Liberal Arts-Law
> course as covered by the injunction. But they did not re-
> turn. Appellee [Tureaud] instead enrolled in the College
> of Education in Xavier University and has remained there
> during the entire term.

Alarmed that desegregation was inexorably being accomplished,
albeit at a snail's pace, in 1956 the Louisiana Legislature passed,
without dissenting voice, a package of thirteen separate segregation
laws, with two aimed specifically at higher education. The first was
the apparently innocuous requirement that any applicant for a state
college must present a certificate of eligibility and good moral character signed by former principals and superintendents and "addressed
to the particular institution sought to be entered." A second act,
however, provided as grounds for removal from a teaching position
in public education, a teacher's "advocating or in any manner performing any act toward bringing about integration of the races within
the public school system or any institution of higher learning of the
State of Louisiana."

The combined effect of these two statutes obviously prevented
the preparation of any certificate for any black student seeking admission to a white university. A fresh plaintiff took up the cause
abandoned by Mr. Tureaud and filed an action for an injunction
against the enforcement of the requirement that she present such a
certificate in order to be admitted to LSU. Judge Wright, sitting
en banc with Judge Christenberry as the full bench of the Eastern
District of Louisiana, ruled that the certificate requirement statute
"became unconstitutional when applied in tandem with discriminatory
legislation."

In affirming the issuance of that injunction, Judge Tuttle provided additional insight into the human drama of Negro students and
teachers struggling against the snares of segregation statutes. He
quoted from a letter to one of the named plaintiffs from her former
Negro principal:

> I assure you that my refusal to sign the certificate is not
> intended to cast any unfavorable reflection against your
> character. I just cannot take the risk of losing my job.

Judge Tuttle concluded that the statute requiring a certificate was
unconstitutional even without reference to the companion law.

> Either it [the certificate statute] attempts to give desig-
> nated officials the power to exclude students from all state
> supported colleges without establishing objective standards

which they can seek to satisfy or it implies the standard
... of race or color. The requirement ... is in conflict
with the Fourteenth Amendment to the Federal Constitution
and must fall.

Although the Hutcheson-Tuttle-Jones circuit panel did not alter the
form of the Wright-Christenberry decree, they moved to modify its
constitutional base. The trouble with the district court holding of
"tandem unconstitutionality" was that it left both statutes standing if
separately applied. Either could be used in conjunction with a new,
similarly motivated, though slightly different statute. The Fifth
Circuit decision to void each law as unconstitutional on its face is
evidence of the Court of Appeals' growing awareness that endless
litigation was invited when the slightest rein was given to states
bent on obstructionism.

In other Southern states the certificate requirement, as a resistance stratagem, was more subtly devised than its Louisiana
counterpart. By resolution of April 8, 1953, the Georgia Board of
Regents adopted a requirement that any applicant for admission to
a state college or university must furnish certificates of good moral
character and reputation from at least two Georgia alumni of the institution which the applicant sought to enter. While the Georgia requirement was similar to that imposed by the Louisiana statutes, the
Georgia expedient presented a more difficult jurisprudential problem.
The Regents' resolution, contrary to the Louisiana statutes, did not
advert to maintaining an official policy of segregation; furthermore,
neither the Regents' resolution nor the statutes of Georgia sought
to impose sanctions against any alumnus who agreed to certify a
black applicant. Thus, the policy of segregation implicit in the
recommendation requirement in Georgia was totally dependent upon
the voluntary complicity of alumni in the scheme.*

Applications by Negroes seeking admission in the fall of 1957
to Georgia State College, in Atlanta, were rejected by the registrar
for failure to present the requisite alumni recommendations. An
action was filed with District Judge William Boyd Sloan seeking an
injunction against both the recommendation requirement and continued rejection of black applicants solely on grounds of their race.
Despite what would appear to be potentially grave problems concerning the adequacy of proof of state action, the case did not trouble
Judge Sloan. The court took judicial notice of the fact that there

---

*Alumni recommendation requirements were effective blocks to black
candidates. In one of the more determined efforts to persuade
white alumni to break the tacit pact of silence, Clennon King, a
black college professor who had applied to the University of Mississippi to work on his doctorate, inserted a full page advertisement
in a Gulfport newspaper. The ad solicited letters of endorsement
from university alumni: there was no response. R. Sarratt, The
Ordeal of Desegregation, at 127 (1966) [hereinafter cited as Sar-
ratt].

was little social mixing of the races in Georgia and of the consequent lack of opportunity for black students to become acquainted with white alumni of Georgia colleges. In enjoining the Regents and the college administrators from requiring the certificates and from refusing admission to blacks who were academically qualified, Judge Sloan concluded:

> The alumni certificate requirement is invalid as applied to Negroes because there are no Negro alumni of any of the white institutions of the University System of Georgia, and consequently this requirement operates to make it difficult, if not impossible, for Negroes to comply with the requirement, whereas white applicants do not face similar difficulties.

* * *

In 1958, Louisiana became the first state in the Deep South to desegregate its colleges and universities: desegregation had taken ten years of litigation. If attorneys for school boards and the states had become masters of dilatory pleading and other legal delaying tactics, so too the federal courts had begun to develop counterstrategies built upon the experience of the past decade. In the last throes of the LSU litigation, the state opened a new university branch in New Orleans. It thereupon claimed that previous injunctions and orders had applied only to the admission of blacks to the main campus at Baton Rouge. The plaintiffs appealed to Judge Christenberry for an expedited hearing; they asserted that unless a hearing were scheduled within the next ten days the deadline for fall registration would pass, effectively denying their clear right to immediate admission. The board vigorously opposed the motion, contending that more time was needed to prepare briefs and to arrange for a full-scale evidentiary hearing, despite a record that included their own letters admitting a policy of segregation at the new branch in New Orleans.

Judge Christenberry set the case down for an immediate hearing and announced a decision enjoining the board within thirty minutes after the conclusion of argument. The Louisiana State University at New Orleans (LSUNO) board immediately sought a stay of Judge Christenberry's order from the Court of Appeals, but its motion was summarily denied. Thereafter, while the board urged a multitude of defenses on the merits of the case, all of which were overruled, the Fifth Circuit's denial of a stay struck the mortal blow to Louisiana's resistance. One commentator noted that the denial of a stay of execution is one of the most effective spurs to desegregation: once desegregation has occurred in fact, ninety-nine per cent of the incentive to appeal disappears.

Ten days had been required for the Fifth Circuit to quash this last effort to halt the progress of desegregation of higher education in Louisiana. The expeditious treatment of the final round must be compared to the first round, in which almost four years

were consumed obtaining entry of the original desegregation orders.
At this juncture the Fifth Circuit evidenced far more flexibility and
quickened reaction time than did the neighboring Sixth Circuit. In
the Memphis State University litigation in 1959, the Sixth Circuit
refused to order an expedited hearing for black students concerned
about the approach of a fall registration deadline. The passage of
another year was required before relief was finally realized by the
Tennessee litigants.

* * *

Promulgation of statutes and substantial appropriations for
legal defense of lawsuits were not the only shells in the arsenal of
state resistance to the desegregation of its colleges and universities.
The collapse of the segregated system was not accomplished without
legal disarmament of the more ominous weapons of defiance: vigi-
lance, violence, and bloodshed. The effectiveness of mob rule was
first tested when Autherine Lucy attempted to gain admission to the
University of Alabama.

* * *

With the exception of one appeal to the Fifth Circuit, the full
judicial responsibility for the review of this case fell upon Judge
Harlan Hobart Grooms, a 1953 Eisenhower appointee to the district
court for the Northern District of Alabama. Although he was a native of Kentucky, receiving his legal education there, Judge Grooms
had invested his entire adult life in Alabama. He practiced law in
Birmingham for twenty-seven years before being appointed to the
federal bench. Each of his four children attended Alabama colleges,
one daughter subsequently becoming Miss Alabama of 1966. In religious philosophy Judge Grooms is a fundamentalist, having taught
a Bible class at the Birmingham Baptist Church of the Covenant for
nearly half a century. In political philosophy perhaps the only char-
acterization that can be made about him is that he defies categorization. In a feature article published in the New York Times, which
exhaustively analyzed southern federal judges in terms of their being
either "pro-civil rights" or "anti-civil rights," Judge Grooms is nowhere mentioned; although, his nineteen years of sitting on some of
the hottest civil rights cases would seem to lay him open for comment.

Autherine Lucy, the youngest child of a Shiloh, Alabama,
tenant farmer, first applied for admission to the University of Alabama on September 4, 1952. Apparently there was no question as
to her qualifications for admission: nine days after application she
received a form letter from the President of the University which
stated that he had been advised by the dean that she was coming to
the university and wanted to assure her that she would be welcome
on the campus. However, when Miss Lucy appeared in person in
the dean's office on September 20, to matriculate, her application
was summarily rejected.

After the Supreme Court decision in Brown, Miss Lucy sought relief from Judge Grooms in the federal district court. In his decision of August 26, 1955, Judge Grooms enjoined officials of the University of Alabama from denying to the petitioner, and the members of her class, the right to enroll on grounds of race. While there was no statute or written administrative policy or rule excluding blacks from the University of Alabama, Judge Grooms observed that there was "a tacit policy to that effect" which had operated to deny their admission. In handing down his decision, Judge Grooms remarked from the bench, "There are some people who believe this court should carve out a province, man the battlements and defy the U.S. Supreme Court. This court does not have the prerogative" (Sarratt, supra, at 203).

Despite this stated commitment to duty and the decisiveness of the brief opinion, Judge Grooms did agree to a stay of his mandate until an appeal could be taken to the Fifth Circuit. There a circuit judge, unrecorded by name in the reports, continued the stay. Finally, the United States Supreme Court vacated the stay and reinstated the injunction, but its decision came on October 10, 1955, four days after the university's enrollment deadline. The plaintiff sought to have the school officials cited for contempt because of their continued refusal to admit her for the first semester, but Judge Grooms denied the petition, finding that late registration and not race was the university's reason for refusal. The Fifth Circuit, in per curiam opinions, affirmed both the issuance of the original injunction and the subsequent denial of the petition to cite university officials for contempt.

At age 26, in the one hundred twenty-fifth year of the life of the University of Alabama, Autherine Lucy became the first Negro student to attend a class. On that first day, Friday, February 3, 1956, the reaction of white students was one of avoidance and silence: "I was met by hateful stares," she said. "As I sat down several students moved away." That night, made more bold by the conspiratorial cover of darkness, an estimated crowd of over a thousand students marched on the home of President Oliver Cromwell Carmichael, singing "Dixie" and chanting "To Hell with Autherine" and "Keep 'Bama White!" A cross was burned on the front lawn of the dean's house.*

The following day, Miss Lucy attended class and aside from distant catcalls, public resentment was still not personally directed at her. However, again that evening a generalized reaction surfaced. Three cars driven by Negroes were mobbed by angry whites in downtown Tuscaloosa and burning crosses appeared on the university quadrangle. The momentum of frustration and anger was building for a pitched battle: the first full day of classes on Monday, February 6, was described by Autherine Lucy as "a day I'll never want to live through again."

---

*67 Time, February 20, 1956, at 40.

Before she arrived for her scheduled class in children's literature, a crowd of three hundred had gathered in front of the classroom building. The chant of the occasion, still flavored with collegian rhetoric, was "Hey-Hey-Hi-Ho--Autherine must go." By noon the curiosity seekers and jeering crowd had become a mob; the chants had become infinitely more ominous with cries of "Kill him! Kill him!" directed at Miss Lucy's escort, the local Negro owner of a finance company. Although there was no gunfire, eggs and rocks were hurled, and the crowd was menacing and out of control. As one student contemporary later described the incident: "[T]here was no preparation for her ... I got the first edition of the afternoon paper. I looked at it, and there were the riots. She was being stoned."*

In an emergency session that evening, the Board of Trustees expelled the student ringleader of the riots and suspended Miss Lucy "for her safety." President Carmichael explained the trustee's action the following day as necessary in order to prevent "a tragedy far greater than any we have seen."

Almost immediately thereafter attorneys for Miss Lucy brought their second motion for contempt against university officials. The petition asserted that these officials had failed to prepare for the possibility of the riotous reaction to the admission of the first Negro and had failed to provide sufficient police protection to prevent or contain the disorder. The petition further charged that the trustees' suspension of Miss Lucy was a punitive action against the innocent student in violation of the court's order that she be safeguarded in her right to pursue an education there. But, in what was to become the most pivotal allegation, the final charge in the contempt petition asserted that the university administrators and trustees had "conspired to defy the injunction order" and "intentionally permitted persons to mill about ... to assimilate an air of riot ... in order that the same may be used as a subterfuge for refusing to permit [Miss Lucy's admission]." Furthermore, at a press conference called to publicize the contempt petition, Miss Lucy and her attorneys read their allegations, including the charge of the conspiracy involving unversity personnel, and elaborated upon their outrage over the campus riot. This public accusation of the administrators' complicity in the debacle brought to grief four years of effort to integrate the University of Alabama. Shortly after the press conference, at the hearing on the motion for contempt, Miss Lucy's attorney stated for the record that the charges of conspiracy and of the administrators having had any connection whatsoever with the milling crowds "could not be substantiated." He therefore asked, and was granted, the court's leave to amend the motion to delete these charges.

---

*Statement by Charles Morgan, Jr., now Director of the Washington National Office of the American Civil Liberties Union, quoted in Powledge, "Profiles: Charles Morgan, Jr.," The New Yorker, October 25, 1969, at 80, [hereinafter cited as Powledge].

On the remaining allegations, Judge Groom refused to find the defendants in contempt of court. Instead, he found that the university officials were acting in good faith, although they had erred in assessing the extent of protest and the "fury of the mob," and were, therefore, "unprepared to cope with the situation." In substantiation of this finding, Judge Grooms noted that Alabama's failure to anticipate the riot was reasonable in view of the fact that no comparable reaction had developed at any of the other Southern or Southwestern universities upon the admission of their first black students. He concluded that the suspension was justified to prevent great bodily harm or even death to Miss Lucy or others involved. However, university officials were ordered to readmit her on March 5, after having taken all precautionary measures to prevent a reoccurrence of disorder: "This court does not find and does not conclude that law and order in this State have broken down or that the law enforcement agencies of this State are unwilling or inadequate to maintain law and order at the University."

But the die was cast. The board of trustees in action that evening permanently expelled Autherine Lucy. Their resolution cited, as grounds for expulsion, that she had made "baseless, outrageous and unfounded charges of misconduct on the part of the University officials" and that no semblance of discipline could be maintained if students, regardless of race, were permitted to slander administration.

The case thereafter proceeded on the issue of whether the permanent expulsion order was based on "just cause" or was an action discriminating against the plaintiff because of her race. In subsequent hearings, Judge Grooms held that university officials have an "unquestioned right to expel a student for just cause"; that accusing the administration of conspiracies, a crime under both state and federal statutes, was not privileged comment under the first amendment in view of the plaintiff's later concession that such charges would not be substantiated; and finally, that the expulsion was motivated by a legitimate concern for maintaining discipline at the university and not by reasons of racial discrimination.

Although supported in his decision by legal precedent, Judge Grooms has been severely criticized by commentators for his decisions on Miss Lucy's contempt petitions in the University of Alabama case. One political scientist commented:

> Judge Grooms' complacence in the face of the challenge of the mob contrasts sharply with his original handling of the Lucy case. His original injunction not only preserved the constitutional rights of the plaintiffs, but by recognizing the action as a class suit reflected a determination to give full effect to the Supreme Court's desegregation decisions. It has been the last pro-civil rights order Judge Grooms has made.

With the Alabama decision, segregationists lost a lawsuit, but won a battle.*

On the other hand, the contempt power held for use by courts is a two-edged weapon. Judge Grooms later commented, looking back upon his judicial career:

> I've been on the bench nineteen years and I've used the contempt process three times. I fined one lawyer; I've fined some labor union people. I've never used the contempt process in a segregation case.... You make martyrs that way. And you have got to appreciate the problem that they are up against. The superintendents for instance are between the upper and lower millstones.... I don't believe as a general thing in the use of the contempt process except where it's absolutely necessary. Sometimes it's absolutely necessary. But I don't think the judge should just go around and sentence every time he has a chance to sentence somebody for contempt of court.

The appropriate use of the contempt power would continue to plague judges throughout the course of desegregation litigation, ultimately destroying the harmony of the Fifth Circuit Court of Appeals in the University of Mississippi case.

The attempt to integrate the University of Alabama ended with grief for all concerned. There were bomb threats during the hearings and Judge Grooms was inundated with letters from sympathizers for both parties: "I guess I got a peck of letters, most of them abusive, telegrams, flyers, threats, two or three claiming I was a communist, that I had sold out."** At a convocation of 7,500 University of Alabama students, President Carmichael exhorted all "to remove the cloud which, in the minds of many, now hangs over our beloved alma mater.... No great university can afford to defy the laws of the land and thus set an example of lawlessness before its students.... Obviously, society could not long endure it if its institutions of higher learning should array themselves at the side of lawlessness."*** The university officially announced that six professors resigned to protest the expulsion of Miss Lucy; unofficial reports claimed that at least twenty-one were lost as a result. As for Autherine Lucy, after turning down a scholarship offered by the University of Copenhagen, she moved 118 miles away from the Tuscaloosa campus to continue her studies at Talladega College. In retrospect, she observed: "God knows I didn't intend to cause all this violence and agitation among my fellow citizens and fellow stu-

---

*J. Peltason, Fifty-eight Lonely Men: Southern Federal Judges and School Desegregation, at 142 (1961).
**Interview with the Honorable Hobart Grooms, Birmingham, Alabama, July 26, 1972.
***67 Time, February 27, 1956, at 68.

dents. I merely wanted an education ... I will keep fighting until
I get one."*

There can be little doubt, however, that the gross public interpretation of the desegregation effort at the University of Alabama
was that belief in the inevitability of desegregation might be misplaced. Buford Boone, the crusading editor of the Tuscaloosa News
editorialized: "The University administration and trustees have
knuckled under to the pressures and desires of a mob.... We have
a breakdown of law and order and abject surrender to what is expedient." Or, as one Southern attorney has observed: "[T]he
message from Tuscaloosa was 'Violence works.' Nobody was found
in contempt. Autherine Lucy would not be going to school. The
message flashed across the South that violence still works" (Powledge, supra, at 88).

*　　*　　*

The following fall, violent public resistance successfully
stopped the desegregation of a Texas college. The administrators
of Texarkana Junior College were under a court injunction issued
by Judge Sheehy of the Federal District Court for the Eastern District of Texas to admit Negroes. The misinterpretation of the Alabama experience, that violence had been sanctioned as a tool of de-
terrence, was made unmistakably clear in a statement issued by
Texas Governor Allan Shivers on August 31, 1956. He specifically
cited the Lucy case as authority for the exclusion from a school of
"any scholastic [whose admission] ... would reasonably be calculated to incite violence."

On registration day, black students arrived at Texarkana
Junior College only to find a large crowd barring the extrance to
the building and shouting "Kill the niggers!" Governor Shivers ordered in the Texas Rangers, but the Chief Ranger refused to escort
the students through the mob. Sergeant Jay Banks told the students
who had requested his assistance, "Our orders are to maintain order
and to keep down violence. We are to take no part in the integration dispute and we are not going to escort anyone in or out of the
college." The Governor did not alter the standing orders. The
black students simply went home; no contempt action was sought
against demonstrators, college officials, the Governor, or anyone
else. Thus, it is impossible to estimate what indirect effects the
eruption of violence had in discouraging Negroes from seeking admission to segregated institutions or in seeking judicial enforcement
of the Brown mandate.

*　　*　　*

While reviewing the riots which occurred in the desegregation of Central High School in Little Rock, the United States Su-

---

*67 Time, February 20, 1956, at 40.

preme Court in Cooper v. Aaron was doubtlessly also concerned about the violent outbreaks which had occurred in the desegregation of higher education in the Fifth Circuit. Any lingering misperceptions of the Lucy case--that public hostility might postpone or even avoid the desegregation mandate of Brown--were laid to rest in this 1958 Supreme Court opinion. In an unprecedented gesture of unanimity, all the justices signed the opinion, commanding that "The constitutional rights of [Negro students] are not to be sacrificed or yielded to the violence and disorder which have followed upon the actions of the Governor and Legislature ... [law] and order are not here to be preserved by depriving the Negro children of their constitutional rights."

Meredith v. Fair

> It is not the critic who counts, not the man who
> points out how the strong man stumbles, where
> the doer of deeds could have done them better.
> The credit belongs to the man who is actually in
> the arena; whose face is marred by dust and sweat
> and blood; who strives valiantly; who errs and
> comes short again and again; who knows the great
> enthusiasm, the great devotion, and spends himself
> in a worthy cause; who, at the best, knows in the
> end the triumph of high achievement; and who, at
> the worst, if he fails, at least fails while daring
> greatly, so that his place shall never be with those
> cold and timid souls who know neither victory nor
> defeat.
> --Theodore Roosevelt.

James Meredith first ran across those familiar lines while in the Air Force in 1952; he carries a copy with him wherever he goes. While certainly a clue to James Meredith's character and perhaps a hint as to the source of his determination, those lines can also be applied to the United States Court of Appeals for the Fifth Circuit. Prior to its head-on confrontation with the state of Mississippi over the matriculation of James Meredith to the University of Mississippi, the Fifth Circuit had for the most part viewed the civil rights battlefield from afar. In the words of Judge Frank Johnson, the embattled federal district judge in Montgomery, Alabama, being on the Court of Appeals "was something like being in semi-retirement." However, the process of forcing the University of Mississippi to comply with its order to enroll James Meredith at Ole Miss jolted the Fifth Circuit from its traditional reflective appellate role. The Court became a front-line combatant in the most serious federal-state confrontation since the incident at Fort Sumter precipitated the Civil War. The story of how the Fifth Circuit, as an institution, weathered James Meredith's enrollment is the story of how that Court began its journey toward becoming the nation's foremost civil rights tribunal. After Meredith v. Fair, the

Fifth Circuit emerged with "vigor and guts" and a steely determination on the part of the majority of its judges to carry out the mandates of Brown v. Board of Education, unhampered by illusions as to the difficulties involved.

"A MAN WITH A MISSION AND WITH A NERVOUS STOMACH"

There were few things in the early 1960s that the embattled segregationists of the South and the young activists of the civil rights movement could agree on, but there was one truth not open to dispute: Mississippi was the toughest state of all. Segregation was not merely a tradition in Mississippi, or even a way of life, it was a state-supported religion nurtured by prophets of racism from James K. Vardaman and Theodore Bilbo right up to Ross Barnett. In 1959, the new Governor and self-anointed archbishop of segregation, Ross Barnett preached the gospel with undiminished fanaticism: "The Negro is different because God made him different to punish him. His forehead slants back. His nose is different. His lips are different, and his color is sure different.... We will not drink from the cup of genocide."* Apostates and deviationists who would allow even the slightest measure of "race mixing" in Mississippi were not to be tolerated. Mississippi was the citadel of the White Citizens' Council, considered by some to be the most moderate of the segregationist political groups, when compared to widespread and active Klan-type organizations. While massive social changes swirled all around that state, in 1960 the white Mississippian who pinned on his "Never" button in the morning rested secure in the knowledge that the message carried on his lapel was literally true. Mississippi would never accept integration.

* * *

On January 20, 1961, John F. Kennedy was inaugurated President of the United States. The next day a black Air Force veteran twenty-eight years of age, James Howard Meredith, sent a letter to the registrar at the University of Mississippi requesting an application for admission. That letter was received on January 25, 1961, and, with a pleasant form letter, the admission materials were forwarded to Mr. Meredith. On January 31, 1961, Mr. Robert B. Ellis, Registrar of the University of Mississippi, had a first-rate admissions headache arrive in his morning mail. Opening a registered letter containing application materials for admission for the spring term, beginning February 6, 1961, he read that a black Mississippi citizen was seeking admission to Ole Miss and would not be able to furnish the six required alumni recommendations attesting to his moral character.

---

*R. Sherrill, Gothic Politics in the Deep South at 189 (rev. ed. 1969); reprinted by permission of Grossman Publishers, a Division of Viking Press.

James Howard Meredith was born on June 25, 1933, to Moses A. and Roxie M. Meredith. His application materials indicated he was a resident of Koscuisko, Mississippi, the sixth of ten children. He had attended the Attala County Training School until 1950, when he moved to St. Petersburg, Florida, where he graduated from Gibbs High School in June, 1951. He was an eight-year veteran of the Air Force, holding the rank of staff sergeant at the time of his honorable discharge on July 21, 1960. His transcripts of transfer credits showed thirty-four semester hours from the Far East Division of the University of Maryland, six semester hours from the University of Kansas, three semester hours from Washburn University (in Topeka, Kansas), and eighteen quarter hours from Jackson State College in Jackson, Mississippi. Meredith had better than a "B" average on all completed college work. Furthermore, Jackson State had accorded Meredith fifty-seven quarter hours of credit on the basis of tests given to him by the Air Force. But for the fact his cover letter indicated he was black and his application photograph verified that fact, he would surely have been admitted routinely to Ole Miss.

A more complete story of James Meredith's fight to enter the University of Mississippi can be found elsewhere; four books are particularly informative: Russell Barrett's Integration at Ole Miss, Walter Lord's The Past That Would Not Die, James Silver's Mississippi: The Closed Society, and James Meredith's own book, Three Years in Mississippi. Nevertheless, some familiarity with the Old Miss struggle is essential for an appreciation of the role played by the Fifth Circuit and a more complete understanding of the external and internal pressures on the Court.

* * *

James Meredith's ordeal began, quietly enough, that morning of January 31, 1961, when the registrar of the University of Mississippi received the Meredith application for admission. From that moment, Mississippi marshaled her forces and her weapons of war—delay, obfuscation, harassment, and defiance. But Meredith was not unarmed. His litigation was supported by tough, resilient Inc. Fund lawyers, eventually backed first by the federal judiciary and then, albeit reluctantly, by the full might of the executive branch of the United States government.

On the advice of Medgar Evers, the charismatic NAACP chief in Mississippi, Meredith contacted Thurgood Marshall of the NAACP Inc. Fund. After satisfying himself as to Meredith's sincerity and eligibility for admission, Marshall referred the case to Constance Baker Motley, who agreed to represent Meredith within days after his first letter reached her.

The first move in Mississippi's game of delay was a telegram from the registrar to Meredith dated February 4, 1961. Officials at Ole Miss were well aware that the application of a Negro for admission was potentially explosive. While they knew of the legal precedents abolishing racial discrimination in higher education, they also knew only too well the policy of official intransigence at all levels of Mississippi government. With the possibility of litigation in mind, the registrar's telegram to Meredith reported matter-of-factly that the registrar had discontinued processing all transfer applications received after January 25, 1961, ostensibly because of overcrowded conditions. Meredith received the telegram and wrote the Justice Department.

While Meredith decided how to respond to the university's move, on February 7, 1961 the Ole Miss Board of Trustees adopted two new admission requirements specifically directed at the Meredith application. One required that previous college credits submitted by transfer applicants be at institutions acceptable to Old Miss (a method of attacking Meredith's Jackson State transcripts), and the other blocked any transfer in the middle of any quarter or semester (a measure designed again to block a transfer because Jackson State was on the quarter system and Ole Miss was on the semester system). Pursuant to Mrs. Motley's advice, on February 20, Meredith staged a strategic retreat. In a letter to Registrar Ellis, he expressed his disappointment at the discontinuance of consideration of applications for the spring semester of 1961 and requested that his application be considered a continuing one for admission during the summer session beginning June 8, 1961. On February 21, the registrar returned Meredith's $10 room deposit because Ole Miss was "unable to accept [his] application for admission." On February 23, again on Mrs. Motley's advice, Meredith returned his $10 deposit and pointedly reminded the registrar of the request that the application be considered a continuing one for admission to the summer session of 1961.

University officials, now painfully aware that they had a real problem, lapsed into silence. On March 18, 1961, Meredith requested acknowledgment of the receipt of his last letter of February 23; no answer was forthcoming. On March 26, Meredith wrote to the registrar again. On Mrs. Motley's advice, he sent revised recommendation letters that not only attested to his good character but also specifically recommended admission to Old Miss. He further respectfully requested an evaluation of his credits. Again silence. Finally on April 12, with Mrs. Motley still calling the signals, Meredith sent a letter to Arthur Beverly Lewis, Dean of the College of Liberal Arts, citing his unacknowledged letters to Registrar Ellis. Meredith concluded by noting that Mr. Ellis had failed to act upon his application solely because of his race and color, even after he had attempted to comply with all of the admission requirements and without being advised of any deficiencies. Meredith requested that Dean Lewis review the case with the registrar.

Forced to move, the registrar wrote his first letter to Meredith since the aborted return of the room deposit. Registrar Ellis acknowledged receipt of the previous letters and transcripts of credits; however, he indicated that under his preliminary evaluation of the transcripts, he could give Meredith only forty-eight of ninety semester hours of credit he had earned. Meredith communicated with Mrs. Motley and, undaunted, wrote Ellis on May 15, 1961, that he would proceed with the application. To drive home his seriousness, he also requested information about housing for his family, a wife and young son.

Unknown to Meredith and his lawyers, on May 15, the same day Meredith was composing his letter to Ellis, the university's admissions committee adopted another new rule. This time it required that students applying for transfer to Ole Miss receive their academic credits from a college accredited by a regional accrediting agency. While in isolation the new rule appeared innocent enough, it was a direct attack on Meredith's status as a student transferring from Jackson State. While accredited by all appropriate Mississippi agencies, Jackson State was not then accredited by the Southern Association of Colleges and Secondary Schools.

Meredith again wrote on May 21 requesting an answer to his previous letters: had all of the appropriate steps been taken for his admission decision? One observer commented that "[i]f Ole Miss cared for all applications with such speed, it would have no students."*

Finally on May 25, in the words of the Fifth Circuit, "The axe fell." The University of Mississippi formally rejected Meredith's application. The University gave as its reasons that Meredith sought to transfer from a school not accredited by the Southern Association of Colleges and Secondary Schools, contrary to Ole Miss policy; and, his character recommendations from black Mississippi citizens did not fulfill the requirement for alumni recommendations. Meredith was not shocked by the rejection.

On May 30, 1961, Mrs. Motley flew to Jackson, Mississippi, secretly to prepare the first pleading--the complaint--in what was to become an incredible legal struggle. On May 31, R. Jess Brown, a Mississippi Negro attorney willing to sign the complaint with Mrs. Motley, accompanied Meredith and Medgar Evers to Meridian, Mississippi, where Judge Sidney Mize of the federal district court was then sitting. Meredith v. Fair was filed, naming the thirteen members of the Board of Trustees of the University of Mississippi, Chancellor John D. Williams, Dean A. B. Lewis, and Registrar Robert B. Ellis as defendants. The complaint was styled as a class action for the benefit of not only Meredith but also all other Negroes in the state of Mississippi similarly situated. Among other things, the complaint charged that the University of Mississippi was a segregated institution and that the alumni recommendations required in the admissions procedure were unconstitutional as applied to Negroes. It prayed for a speedy hearing to determine Meredith's rights so that he might enter the summer session. Finally, the complaint

---

*R. Barrett, Integration at Ole Miss, at 71 (1965) [hereinafter cited as Barrett].

requested that Judge Mize issue a temporary restraining order (TRO) mandating Meredith's immediate admission, to be followed by a preliminary and then a permanent injunction. A TRO would allow Meredith to be admitted to school prior to a hearing on the merits of the question of whether a preliminary and a permanent injunction should be issued. Hearings take time and the TRO procedure is designed to protect rights that might be lost if the aggrieved litigant must await the results of the time consuming litigation process.

In the teeth of overwhelming precedent requiring an expedited hearing on higher education integration cases--where the "all deliberate speed" standard never applied--and despite Meredith's plea for a speedy hearing, Judge Mize opted to play Mississippi's game of delay. He denied the request for a TRO, and he set the first hearing on the question of whether a preliminary injunction should be granted for June 12, four days after the start of the summer session classes and the last day for late enrollment.

On June 8, Judge Mize allowed attorneys for Ole Miss to take Meredith's deposition.* Judge Mize allowed the attorneys for Ole Miss to conduct an exceedingly wide-ranging inquiry into such matters as who was furnishing Meredith money to prosecute the suit, where the complaint was signed, and even where Meredith had obtained the paper to write his letters to the university. On the other hand, Judge Mize denied Mrs. Motley the right to take the deposition of Registrar Ellis in advance of the first hearing.

On June 12, the first hearing began in Biloxi, Mississippi. Although the Justice Department was not a party and could not intervene in the hearing, without court approval, the presence of a Justice Department lawyer observing the proceedings indicated concern on the part of the Kennedy Administration in the progress of integration in the South. The only other thing of substance that occurred on June 12 was a lengthy questioning of Meredith. Again Judge Mize gave Mississippi's Assistant Attorney General Dugas Shands, an experienced and crafty lawyer from Cleveland, Mississippi, extremely wide latitude in questioning. However, Judge Mize refused to allow the plaintiffs to develop areas of evidence clearly encompassed within the pleadings. At three in the afternoon on that same day, Judge Mize further postponed the hearing to July 10 because of a "calendar conflict."

On July 10, the date the hearing was to resume, the attorneys for the University of Mississippi Board of Trustees were granted a postponement of the time to answer the complaint Meredith had filed until July 19, because of the illness of Assistant Attorney General Shands. It should be noted, parenthetically, that At-

---

*A deposition is a proceeding at which attorneys are allowed to question witnesses under oath in advance of trial; the purpose of a deposition is to allow attorneys to discover information that enables them to be better prepared to conduct the trial of a case.

torney Dugas Shands did suffer from a long standing circulatory problem and his excuse of illness was legitimate, contrary to reports by some sources that his illness was an excuse advanced for the sole purpose of procuring a delay. Judge Mize also set the date for continuation of the hearing on the preliminary injunction back to August 10. By this time any hope Meredith may have entertained of entering the first summer session had passed; the second summer session of 1961 also appeared lost.

Between July 19 and the resumed hearing on the preliminary injunction on August 10, Judge Mize denied four more requests by Mrs. Motley to take the deposition of Registrar Ellis, while at the same time drastically limiting Meredith's request for production of the registrar's records on admissions. Finally, Judge Mize again resumed the hearing on the preliminary injunction on August 10, but the next day he delayed it again until August 15. The hearing was resumed on August 15 and finally concluded on August 16. At the conclusion of the hearing, Judge Mize signaled that he was not about to expedite any decision: he allowed the board until September 5 to file a brief and allowed Meredith until September 15 to file a responsive brief.

Finally, on December 12, after any chance for fall semester enrollment had also passed, Judge Mize decided against the issuance of a preliminary injunction. The holding had an incredible "Alice in Wonderland" quality; Judge Mize blandly held:

> There was a good deal of testimony introduced in the cause, but very little conflict, and the overwhelming weight of the testimony is that the plaintiff was not denied admission because of his color or race. The Registrar swore emphatically and unequivocally that the race of plaintiff or his color had nothing in the world to do with the action of the Registrar in denying his application. An examination of the entire testimony of the Registrar shows conclusively that he gave no consideration whatsoever to the race or the color of the plaintiff when he denied the application for admission and the Registrar is corroborated by other circumstances and witnesses in the case to this effect. Careful consideration was given to the application and in the honest judgment of the Registrar he did not meet the requirements required of all students at the University. This testimony is undisputed and the testimony of the Registrar was not unreasonable, but on the contrary was given openly and fairly; and in addition to his testimony, of course there is the presumption of law that an official will perform his duties honestly. [emphasis added]

Judge Mize further held that the adoption of rule changes by the admissions committee of the university was solely for the purpose of improving the quality of the student body. However, there was at least one minor victory for James Meredith in Judge Mize's decision: Judge Mize did hold that Meredith was a resident of Attala

County despite strenuous arguments by Mississippi's lawyers that his Mississippi residence was in doubt and that he had allegedly made a fraudulent residence affidavit in Hinds County in order to register to vote.

After waiting six months for court enforcement of his constitutional rights and receiving only a denial on his preliminary injunction request, Meredith immediately appealed to the Fifth Circuit. He requested that the Court of Appeals advance the argument of the case on its calendar so that he might still have a chance for admission to the spring semester beginning in February, 1962. He was now one full year behind his requested admission date.

Unlike Judge Mize, the Fifth Circuit did expedite matters. Arguments were heard and a decision was issued on January 12, 1962. While the Court, with Judge Wisdom writing the opinion for a panel comprised of himself, Chief Judge Tuttle, and Judge Rives, denied the request for a preliminary injunction, the Fifth Circuit would clearly march to a different beat than the federal district court in Mississippi. In Judge Wisdom's distinctively crisp style, the opinion begins: "James H. Meredith is a Mississippi Negro in search of an education. Mississippi is one of three states which have not allowed a Negro citizen to seek an education at any of its state-supported 'white' colleges and universities." After that first sentence, lawyers for Mississippi surely must have perceived what the litigation held in store. Judge Wisdom then pointedly repeated the facts of the case. He noted that five attempts had been made to take the registrar's deposition, the last three being denied in Judge Mize's "discretion." He noticed that the district court had severely limited Mrs. Motley's request for production and inspection of records to those of transfer students in the 1961 term. He then emphasized that the narrow question before the Court of Appeals was simply on a request for issuance of a preliminary injunction; no trial had been held on the question of whether a permanent injunction should be issued. Reading the Court's affirmance of denial of the preliminary injunction, a perceptive district judge would surely have known what the Fifth Circuit expected him to do at the trial on the merits. The stinging mockery of Judge Wisdom's observations on the proceedings before Judge Mize on the question of the preliminary injunction is noteworthy:

> This case was tried below and argued here in the eerie atmosphere of never-never land. Counsel for appellees argue that there is no state policy of maintaining segregated institutions of higher learning and that the court can take no judicial notice of this plain fact known to everyone. The appellees' chief counsel insists, for example, that appellant's counsel should have examined the genealogical records of all the students and alumni of the University and should have offered these records in evidence in order to prove the University's alleged policy of restricting admissions to white students.
> We take judicial notice that the state of Mississippi

maintains a policy of segregation in its schools and colleges.

To support its judicial notice of segregation in the state, the Court mentioned the existence of the legislature's Resolution of Interposition; it noticed legislation which required state executive officers to prevent enforcement of the desegregation mandate of Brown; and it pointed out other evidence of intransigent resistance to integration. Despite the Court's unhappiness with Judge Mize's conduct of the proceedings and its blunt judicial notice that Mississippi maintained segregated colleges, the Fifth Circuit held that Meredith still could not be relieved of the burden of proving that Mississippi's segregated policy had been applied to him personally. The Court did take pains to point out to Judge Mize that the five alumni certificates required by Ole Miss for transfer applicants denied equal protection of the law in their application to black students: "It is significant that the University of Mississippi adopted the requirement of alumni certificates a few months after Brown v. Board of Education was decided." The Court concluded:

> Within proper legal bounds, the plaintiff should be afforded a fair, unfettered, and unharrassed opportunity to prove his case. A man should be able to find an education by taking the broad highway. He should not have to take byroads through the woods and follow winding trails through sharp thickets, in constant tension because of pitfalls and traps, and, after years of effort, perhaps attain the threshold of his goal when he is past caring about it.

Several further points are worth observing in the Fifth Circuit's opinion. While formally agreeing with the trial judge's denial of the preliminary injunction, Judge Wisdom issued unmistakably clear instructions to Judge Mize on how to conduct the trial on the merits. He noted that the trial judge had allowed the defendants great latitude in their testimony and on the other hand "so severely circumscribed" the examination of witnesses by Meredith that the record contained irrelevancies as a result of the former practice and omissions as a result of the latter. Furthermore, Judge Wisdom indicated that Judge Mize had been wrong in his limitation on production of Ole Miss admissions records to the summer session of 1961, because the plaintiff had stressed that his application was intended as continuing until the next regular term, making the records for that term equally relevant. Hoping to dispose of the argument about Jackson State, Judge Wisdom reported that it had subsequently been accredited by the Southern Association of Colleges and Secondary Schools. Lastly, Judge Wisdom pointed out to the trial court that the university had given no recognition to Meredith's credits from three prominent and academically impeccable universities: Maryland, Kansas and Washburn.

The case went back to Judge Mize with a brusque command to speed up the proceedings. The hearing on the permanent injunction began on January 16, but again the board moved for a postponement because of Assistant Attorney General Shands' illness. Despite the fact that there were other attorneys for the board present who had had ample opportunity to prepare, Mize granted the postponement until January 24. Finally on January 24, the hearing resumed and was concluded on January 27.

Judge Mize had apparently received no enlightenment from Judge Wisdom's opinion. Indeed, at times he appeared not to have even read it. But, a long, self-serving preamble revealed that Judge Mize may not have been comfortable about the reception his second opinion would receive in New Orleans. He began by setting forth how fairness had been insured to Meredith. He had made several pro-Meredith evidence rulings in conducting the trial. Then, further noting that he had allowed the plaintiff to call as adverse witnesses nearly every member of the board of trustees, Judge Mize got to the point. Brushing aside the Fifth Circuit's judicial notice that Ole Miss was segregated, he doggedly held that James Meredith was not denied admission because of his race:

> The proof shows on this trial, and I find as a fact, that there is no custom or policy now, nor was there any at the time Plaintiff's application was rejected, which excluded qualified Negroes from entering the University. The proof shows, and I find as a fact, that the University is not a racially segregated institution.

Judge Mize did concede that there had been a policy of segregation prior to the Brown case but insisted that "[t]he proof in the instant case on this hearing fails to show that the application of any Negro or Chinaman or anyone of any other race has been rejected because of his race or color." As for the judicial notice of segregation made by the Court of Appeals, that was simply a matter to be considered with all other evidence and was not a conclusive finding of fact. Bypassing the post-Brown Mississippi law requiring maintenance of segregation as a state policy, Judge Mize stated that such laws were an attempt by the legislature to persuade the Supreme Court to return to the doctrine of Plessy v. Ferguson. Those Mississippi statutes and regulations certainly did not require officers of the state of Mississippi to disobey mandates of the Supreme Court.

However, Judge Mize did encounter some difficulty in explaining why the registrar had rejected Meredith's application for reasons other than on the basis of race. He cited the registrar's own testimony on cross-examination that he would still not accept Meredith's application because "... Plaintiff was a rather unstable person; was depressed at times and of a highly nervous temperament; that the Plaintiff had sworn falsely before the Circuit Clerk of Hinds County in making application to register as a voter, swearing that he was a citizen of Hinds County when, as a matter of fact he knew he was a citizen of Attala County, Mississippi...." The judge also noted that the registrar had testified that five of the individuals who signed Meredith's character references had subsequently indicated they were not really aware of the reason Meredith wanted the letters.* Judge Mize, however, did state that since his sole job was to decide whether the registrar had rejected Meredith because of his race and since the registrar had not known about the Hinds County registration dispute and the waffling by Meredith's character references, he had not taken those matters into consideration at the time he decided that Meredith was not denied admission based on race. Judge Mize concluded with the acrid note that Meredith had brought this case as a class action; but since he had failed to show that he had been denied admission to the university because he was a Negro, he could not maintain the suit as either an individual complaint or a class action.

Meredith immediately moved that the Fifth Circuit grant an injunction pending appeal. In short, he was requesting a court mandate ordering his admission to Ole Miss prior to the time the Court of Appeals could formally decide the full appeal from Judge Mize's adverse ruling. Meredith justified his request for the unusual remedy of an injunction pending appeal on the theory that otherwise his case might become moot. He pointed out that if he were not allowed to begin the spring semester at Ole Miss, he could well complete his requirements at Jackson State and graduate before the case could be decided.

Chief Judge Tuttle, Judge Rives, and Judge Wisdom comprised the panel that heard Meredith's request for the injunction pending appeal on February 10, 1962. A per curiam opinion was issued on February 12, 1962, with Chief Judge Tuttle dissenting. The majority determined not to issue an injunction pending appeal because testimony taken before the district court had not been made available to the Fifth Circuit by Judge Mize's court reporter. The majority opinion pointed out that Meredith could, without prejudicing his cause, either not attend college for one quarter or take courses at Jackson State which would not fulfill graduation requirements. However, all parties concerned were directed to expedite the appeal before the Fifth Circuit. Chief Judge Tuttle dissented:

> Undisputed facts, of which we have already taken cognizance when this case was here on appeal from denial of an interlocutory injunction show that the appellant was denied admission on the stated grounds: (1) that he had failed to furnish recommendations from six alumni of the University; (2) that the University policy (adopted after Meredith originally applied for transfer) prevented a transfer from an unaccredited institution (Jackson State College was at that time unaccredited); (3) the letter then stated: 'I see no need for mentioning any other deficiencies.'

---

*These six Negro recommenders were visited by attorneys representing the state and asked about the reasons for their recommendation of Meredith. Considering Mississippi's history, it is not at all surprising that some of the recommenders became less than positive about their recollections of the reasons Meredith wanted their letters.

> In view of our holding in the earlier opinion that 'We
> take judicial notice that the state of Mississippi maintains
> a policy of segregation in its schools and colleges,' and
> our holding that the requirement of alumni recommenda-
> tions was unconstitutional as to Negro applicants, and in
> view of the failure of the defendants to assign any other
> reason for rejecting appellant's application for transfer,
> I am convinced that there is sufficient likelihood that this
> Court will reverse the trial court's finding that Meredith
> was not denied admission on racial grounds that I would
> grant the injunction pending appeal.

Chief Judge Tuttle went on to observe that the majority opinion really required Meredith to drop out of college in his senior year and
lose his GI benefits just to avoid mootness. Chief Judge Tuttle
tartly responded to the majority's contention that there might be possible damage to the appellant himself by rendering an injunction prior
to hearing a full appeal: "I do not think this Court ought to concern
itself with any possible damage to the appellant by granting his motion for injunction. He does not need for us to help him decide
whether he really wants what he is here fighting so hard to get."

After his motion for injunction pending appeal was denied,
Meredith formally appealed Judge Mize's adverse ruling to the Fifth
Circuit. On June 25, 1962, the Fifth Circuit released its third
opinion in the Meredith case. Judge Wisdom again penned the opinion which was joined by Judge Brown. Judge DeVane, a federal district judge sitting with the Court of Appeals by designation, was the
third member of the panel; he dissented.

Judge Wisdom's second opinion is a masterpiece of acid rhetoric.* He began in language strikingly similar to that with which
he began his first Meredith opinion. Perhaps only coincidentally,
Judge Mize's two Meredith opinions each begin with an identical sen-
tence--a sentence which seems to have drawn Judge Wisdom's attention in the beginning sentences of both his opinions. Judge Mize
began both his opinions with the following sentence: "Plaintiff,
James Howard Meredith, is a member of the Negro race and a citizen of Mississippi." Recall that Judge Wisdom's opening sentence
in his first opinion read: "James H. Meredith is a Mississippi
Negro in search of an education." Obviously observing that Judge
Mize from the very first sentence had not budged, Judge Wisdom
this time began:

> The Meredith matter is before us again. This time the
> appeal is from a final judgment after a trial on the mer-
> its. The judgment denied James A. [sic] Meredith, a

---

*Judge Wisdom in an interview candidly acknowledged that his re-
versals of recalcitrant district judges were sometimes tough. He
said a reversal in strong terms can have a circuit-wide effect on
district judges tempted to waiver.

Mississippi negro in search of an education, an injunction to secure his admission to the University of Mississippi. We reverse with directions that the injunction be issued.

Judge Wisdom then proceeded to demolish Judge Mize's findings:

A full review of the record leads the Court inescapably to the conclusion that from the moment the defendants discovered Meredith was a Negro they engaged in a carefully calculated campaign of delay, harassment, and masterly inactivity. It was a defense designed to discourage and defeat by evasive tactics which would have been a credit to Quintus Fabius Maximus.*

Judge Wisdom was at his biting best on Judge Mize's finding of fact that the University of Mississippi was not a segregated institution: "... This about-face in policy, news of which may startle some people in Mississippi, could have been accomplished only by telepathic communication among the University's administrators and the Board of Trustees of State Institutions of Higher Learning." As evidence that Ole Miss was a consciously segregated institution, he pointed to the vigorous fight waged by the university to block Meredith's enrollment and its reliance on specious defenses: "We draw the inference again that the assigned reason for rejecting Meredith was a trumped-up excuse without any basis except to discriminate." Noting that in its earlier opinion the Court had given the university a benefit of doubt, Judge Wisdom stated: "We find nothing now in this case reaching the dignity of proof to make us think we were wrong to take judicial notice of Mississippi's policy of segregation."

In a meticulous rebuke to Judge Mize's handling of the Meredith case, Judge Wisdom dealt one by one with the delays suffered by Meredith in processing his application for admission and awaiting action by the trial court.** He noted:

---

*Quintus Fabius Maximus was a Roman general whose evasive tactics in defending Rome from Hannibal led to the coining of the term "Fabian" to denote cautious waiting.
**"The net effect of all these delays was that the February 1961 term, the two summer terms of 1961, and the two regular terms of 1961-62 slipped by before the parties litigant actually came to a showdown fight. Some of these delays, as in any litigation, were inevitable. Some are attributable to continuances of doubtful propriety and to unreasonably long delays by the trial judge. We refer, for example, to the delay between the end of the trial, August 16, and the entry of the district court's order, December 14. Many of the delays resulted from the requests of defendants. We do not question Mr. Shands' good faith or the fact of his illness, but the Attorney General's Office is well-staffed. And--there are plenty of lawyers in Mississippi ready, able, and more than willing to represent the University. We draw the inference that not a few of the

As a matter of law, the principle of 'deliberate speed' has no application at the college level; time is of the essence. In an action for admission to a graduate or undergraduate school, counsel for all the litigants and trial judges too should be sensitive to the necessity for speedy justice.

Judge Wisdom then examined the reasons given by the state for the rejection of Meredith's application. He refuted the state's claim that Meredith's application was not in good faith and that he was a troublemaker. Referring to Meredith's cover letter accompanying his application material, Judge Wisdom commented: "We read this letter as showing no chip on the shoulder and no evidence of such abnormal concern as to support the defendants' contention that from the start Meredith's letters indicate he was 'belligerent,' a 'trouble-maker,' and had psychological problems. We think it not unreasonable for a Negro to have some concern over his reception on the 'Ole Miss' campus." He also pointed out that Meredith was first refused admission because of allegedly overcrowded conditions. However, the fact was that in February, 1961, when the rejection came, there were 2,500 to 2,600 male students on campus, while in September, 1961, a semester later, there were about 3,000 male students on campus.

Then Judge Wisdom addressed the defense that Jackson State, the school from which Meredith was transferring, was unaccredited. He noted that Jackson State was supervised by the identical board of trustees supervising the program at the University of Mississippi; hence, theoretically, the board of trustees could have insured that Jackson State was never accredited although, by the time of the Court's decision, Jackson State had gained its full accreditation. Turning to the "ex post facto" reasons for the rejection, he refuted the claim that Meredith had falsified his registration as a voter in Hinds County and therefore could be denied admission as a bad character risk. After fastidiously examining that allegation, Judge Wisdom stated: "We hold that the contention is frivolous. We have gone into the facts in some detail only because they show a determined policy of discrimination by harassment." Then Judge Wisdom moved to the contention that Meredith was a troublemaker. After considering the almost complete lack of proof on that charge, Wisdom commented,

> One short answer to the defendants' contention is the Good Conduct Medal. Another short answer is that Meredith's record shows just about the type of Negro who might be expected to try to crack the racial barrier at the University of Mississippi: a man with a mission and with a nervous stomach.

[cont.] continuances and the requests for time in which to write briefs were part of the defendants' delaying action designed to defeat the plaintiff by discouragingly high obstacles that would result in the case carrying through his senior year. It almost worked."

...

> The defendants are scraping the bottom of the barrel
> in asserting that the University should not now admit
> Meredith because he is a bad character risk.

Judge Dozier A. DeVane, a senior district judge from Tallahassee, Florida, dissented:

> Considered as a brief in support of appellant's case,
> the decision of Judge Wisdom is a masterpiece. I agree
> with almost everything he has to say in the opinion about
> the defenses advanced by appellees and I further agree
> that appellees scraped the 'bottom of the barrel' in their
> efforts to keep Meredith out of the University of Mississippi. In so doing appellees weakened their case very
> much before this Court for on every ground save one the
> defenses advanced are not deserving of serious consideration by this Court.

Judge DeVane felt that that one part of Mississippi's case that deserved attention was the "troublemaker" aspect of Meredith's character:

> In passing upon this case, I do not consider that we
> have a right to ignore what the effect of this decision
> could be upon the citizens of Mississippi and I feel that it
> is the duty of our Courts to avoid where we can incidents
> such as the Little Rock case and I fear that the result of
> this decision may lead to another comparable situation,
> particularly for 'a man with a mission and with a nervous
> stomach.' Integration is not a question that can ever be
> settled by Federal Judges. It is an economic, social and
> religious question and in the end will be amicably settled
> on this basis.
> In my opinion Judge Mize was correct in finding and
> holding that appellant bore all the characteristics of becoming a troublemaker if permitted to enter the University of Mississippi and his entry therein may be nothing
> short of a catastrophe.

Judge Wisdom's opinion should have dashed any hope Mississippi retained as to the chances for success before the Fifth Circuit. It was a blunt statement that Ole Miss was segregated by law; that it had discriminated against James Meredith because of his race; and that no valid reasons had been advanced to prevent his enrollment. *

---

*One example of the curtness of Wisdom's opinion is his comment:
"By an ironic twist, the defendants, after Plessy v. Ferguson [and
its separate-but-equal doctrine] has been overruled, seize upon the
inferiority of the facilities-programs of Negro colleges as a reason
for excluding Negroes at Mississippi's white colleges and universities."

While James Meredith must have been cheered by the vibrant tones of the opinion, he would find that this was still not enough to secure his enrollment to Ole Miss.

THE BATTLEGROUND SHIFTS TO THE FIFTH CIRCUIT

After the Fifth Circuit's June 25, 1962 reversal of Judge Mize, apparently nothing further could legally prevent the enforcement of the injunction ordering James Meredith's enrollment at the University of Mississippi. But shortly after the Fifth Circuit's opinion was filed, one of the most bizarre feuds in the history of the federal judiciary erupted publicly.

On July 18, 1962, the Fifth Circuit's maverick conservative from Mississippi, Judge Ben F. Cameron, not even a member of the panel that had reversed Judge Mize, issued a stay of the decision of the Wisdom-Brown-DeVane panel until the Ole Miss Board of Trustees could apply to the United States Supreme Court for a writ of certiorari. Responding rapidly, on July 19, the astounded panel that had issued the injunction mandating Meredith's enrollment ordered the Fifth Circuit Clerk of Court to telegraph all counsel and advise them that for Judge Cameron's stay to be effective, a recall of the mandate issued by the Wisdom-Brown-DeVane panel was necessary. The lawyers were given five days to submit memoranda on the legality and appropriateness of Judge Cameron's stay. On July 27, after review of the memoranda submitted by counsel, Judges Wisdom and Brown--this time joined wholeheartedly by Judge DeVane--set aside Judge Cameron's stay of July 18.

In setting aside the first stay of July 18, Judge Wisdom, again the penman for the panel, began: "In this case time is now of the quintessence. Time has been of the essence since January, 1961, when James Meredith, in the middle of his junior year at Jackson State College (for Negroes), applied for admission to the University of Mississippi." After quickly tracing the chronology of the case, Judge Wisdom demolished Judge Cameron's right to issue the stay:

> The Court is bigger than a single judge. Assuming, but without deciding, that Judge Cameron is indeed a judge of 'the court rendering the judgment,' we hold that the court determining the cause has inherent power to review the action of the single judge, whether or not the single judge is a member of the panel.... A contrary position would allow a judge in the minority, were he a member of the panel deciding the case, to frustrate the mandate of the majority. And, it is unthinkable that a judge who was not a member of the panel should be allowed to frustrate the mandate of the Court. [emphasis is the Court's own]

Judge Wisdom then reported that the other members of the Fifth Circuit agreed that, when a mandate had been issued, it was both logically and legally too late to stay it. Furthermore, Judge Brown and Judge Wisdom went on record as indicating that even if Judge Cameron had the right to stay the mandate, which they denied, such a stay would have been improvidently granted:

> Judge Cameron did not sit on this case. He did not have the opportunity of a sitting judge to study the record, to hear the argument, to discuss the facts and the law in the judges' conference on the case.
> This is not a Chessman case. It is not a Rosenberg case. It is not a matter of life or death to the University of Mississippi. Texas University, the University of Georgia, Louisiana State University, the University of Virginia, other Southern universities are not shriveling up because of the admission of Negroes. There was no emergency requiring prompt action by a single judge. Apparently, however, there was a studied decision by the applicants' [defendants'] attorney not to ask the Court for a rehearing or for a stay.

Judge Wisdom pointed out that the Ole Miss Board of Trustees did have the right to apply for a writ of certiorari, regardless of whether the mandate was stayed or issued. However, in the present case, the denial of the stay was merely a minor inconvenience to the University of Mississippi while the granting of the stay would subject Meredith to the loss of another semester of work. The Brown-Wisdom-DeVane panel then vacated Judge Cameron's stay and reissued the Court's mandate. That mandate stated precisely what injunction should be issued by Judge Mize. But, as shall be seen later, in a most significant step, the Fifth Circuit panel itself entered a "preliminary injunction," the terms of which were to be binding until Judge Mize had actually entered his injunction and it had been fully obeyed. It was because this preliminary injunction was issued by the Court of Appeals itself that later subsequent proceedings against Governor Barnett and Lt. Gov. Johnson were handled by the Court of Appeals and not the district court. The case was then again remanded to Judge Mize with the command to issue the revised injunction.

But Judge Cameron was not finished. On July 28, 1962, the day following the vacation of his first stay, he did the "unthinkable"; he issued a second stay from his home office in Meridian, Mississippi, calling the attempt of Judges Wisdom, Brown and DeVane to set aside his previous stay "void." Judge Cameron did not attempt an explanation for his order. The other members of the Fifth Circuit responded immediately and set aside Cameron's order on the same day it was issued. On July 31, 1962, incredibly, Judge Cameron issued his third stay. On August 4, the three-judge court reaffirmed its previous orders and set aside Judge Cameron's orders of July 28 and July 31, characterizing them as "unauthorized, erroneous and improvident." But Judge Cameron, persistent if nothing else, issued a fourth stay on August 6, 1962. In his fourth stay he reaffirmed his earlier orders and declared the Court of Appeals' orders stayed until disposition of the case by the Supreme Court.

At that point the United States Supreme Court could no longer regard the charade in the Fifth Circuit as a minor internal squabble. Supreme Court Justice Hugo Black, Circuit Justice for the Fifth Circuit,* on September 10, 1962, issued an opinion vacating all of Judge Cameron's stays. Justice Black stressed that the various stays issued by Judge Cameron could only work further delay and injury to Mr. Meredith; he also said that immediate enforcement of the judgment could not harm the university. He pointedly told Judge Cameron that there was little likelihood that the United States Supreme Court would grant certiorari to review a judgment of the Court of Appeals which essentially involved only factual issues. Lastly, Justice Black indicated that although he had power to act alone, he had submitted the matter to each of his brethren for their opinion and as a result was "authorized to state that each of them agrees that the case is properly before this Court, that I have power to act, and that under the circumstances I should exercise that power as I have done here." Thus, the first mini-round of Judge Cameron's war with his own court ended. But, as will be seen from later events, Judge Cameron's appetite for further combat with his fellow judges on the Fifth Circuit had only been whetted.

During the in-fighting on the Court over Judge Cameron's stays, an important event occurred which did not go unnoticed in Mississippi. The United States Department of Justice filed an amicus curiae (friend of the court) brief with Mr. Justice Black supporting the Fifth Circuit's position against Judge Cameron's stays. In commenting on the entry of the Justice Department into the case, Attorney General Joe Patterson of Mississippi compared Attorney General Robert Kennedy to "a 'jackass' braying at 'a great American eagle.'" Of course, Patterson considered Mississippi to be the eagle. Acutely aware of the gathering thundercloud of opposition from Mississippi, the Court of Appeals, on September 18, 1962, followed the Supreme Court's lead and designated the United States Department of Justice as amicus curiae to the Court. The Court hoped that by directly involving the Justice Department in the case its orders would be enforced more vigorously.

After Mr. Justice Black disposed of Judge Cameron's last attempts to block the effectiveness of the Fifth Circuit's injunction, Judge Mize, on September 13, 1962, meekly obeyed his marching orders and entered the verbatim injunction mandated by the Fifth Circuit. It was said of Judge Mize: "He might be a good Mississippian, but the state was going too far. Still, it wasn't easy, and as he handed Mrs. Motley her set of the papers, he sighed that he hoped that he would have no more desegregation cases--he was getting too old and only wanted to play with his grandchildren."**

---

*Each sitting Justice of the Supreme Court is assigned to act as a "circuit justice" for one or more of the United States Courts of Appeal. Mr. Justice Black had for many years been assigned as "circuit justice" for the Fifth Circuit.
**W. Lord, The Past That Would Not Die, at 152 (1965) [hereinafter cited as Lord].

On September 13, the same day Judge Mize reluctantly signed the permanent injunction, Mississippians were enthralled by Ross Barnett's flaming interposition speech delivered on state-wide television. After much vacillation, Governor Barnett had finally decided to throw down the gauntlet. Posturing that he was prepared to go to jail, he called for resistance to "illegal usurpation of power by the Kennedy administration" and vowed that the schools in Mississippi would not be integrated. He then interposed himself, as the embodiment of the sovereignty of the state of Mississippi, between the federal government and the people of Mississippi. Either Barnett did not remember, or simply did not care, that the Interposition Resolution of Louisiana had not been worth the paper on which it was written in the 1960 battle of New Orleans.

* * *

What kind of a man was Ross Barnett? Why was he willing to risk moving Mississippi to the brink of insurrection against the federal government? One of the more caustic descriptions of the man is contained in Robert Sherrill's Gothic Politics:

> Of Ross Barnett, who in 1959, on his third try, won the highest elective office in the poorest state in the nation (at that time, average income: $1,173), the kindest and most accurate thing that can be said is that he is bone dumb. Canny, yes. He started life one of ten children in a poor farm family. After working his way through college and law school as a barber and janitor, he became the most successful damage-suit lawyer in Mississippi, earning $100,000 a year. There was a standard joke around Jackson about the poor yokel who asked another, 'If you was knocked down by a car, which doctor would you call?' Answer: 'Dr. Ross.' Nevertheless, dumb. Well remembered by reporters is that moment when Barnett took over as the registrar at the University of Mississippi to bar James Meredith. Get the scene: Barnett in the doorway. Here comes Meredith, the only Negro within 200 yards, surrounded by a sea of white marshals. Barnett: 'Which of you is James Meredith?'*

Others, closer to the Barnett administration, respond that Governor Barnett was not lacking in intelligence at all; rather, his fault was in his compulsion to try to please everyone. A responsible source, who requests anonymity, argues strenuously that during the whole Meredith affair Governor Barnett wavered continuously between those urging compliance with law and those urging total resistance. He always expressed agreement with the viewpoint of those present at a particular time. In the words of that source: "If old Ross had been a woman he would have been pregnant all his life."

---

*R. Sherrill, supra at 199-200.

Ross Barnett had not been a popular governor in Mississippi until the state faced its Armageddon in the person of James Meredith. In a state which generally viewed his administration as bereft of accomplishment, Barnett scandalized the populace when he put gold-plated bathroom faucets in the governor's mansion. He was even booed at an Ole Miss game in 1960. But Ross Barnett had found the road to glory: he became the new prophet in Mississippi's state-supported church of segregation. He dared the federal government to enforce the orders of its courts.

*   *   *

As events rushed toward the bloodiest state-federal confrontation since the Civil War, frantic officials in the Justice Department began to seek a way out. On September 19, Burke Marshall, Attorney General Robert Kennedy's civil rights chief, called Mississippi Attorney General Patterson and requested a promise that James Meredith would receive the protection of the state. Despite a scalding tongue, Attorney General Patterson was one of the saner segregationists in Mississippi officialdom; he was a close friend of former Governor Coleman, a governor considered to be more moderate than Ross Barnett. Nevertheless, Attorney General Patterson's job was an elective one, and he knew the way the political winds were blowing. Courageously, he assured Burke Marshall that Meredith would receive state protection the next day when he attempted to enroll, and that law and order would be maintained. Patterson made the promise despite the political risks.

Attorney General Patterson's pledge to protect Meredith was dutifully reported to Governor Barnett. Patterson was stunned that evening to discover that the Governor had made undercover plans to have Meredith arrested for the voter registration charge at the time he attempted to register. Valuing his reputation for integrity more than his political future, Patterson called Burke Marshall the next morning and reported that he could no longer keep his promise to provide protection to Meredith. Patterson received several threats that his call to Marshall, which effectively scuttled Barnett's plan, would be used against him politically. His only response was that he had given his word to a fellow lawyer; and, therefore, when he discovered he no longer could keep his word, his duty was to tell the other lawyer.

While not as prolific as its counterpart in Louisiana, the Mississippi Legislature was no less devoted to the holy cause. It passed Senate Bill (S.B.) 1501, providing that no person was eligible for admission to any state institution of higher learning if he had a criminal charge involving moral turpitude pending against him in any Mississippi state or federal court. This legislative attack was a transparent attempt to block Meredith's enrollment because of the specious, but still pending, charge of fraudulent voter registration. The purpose of S.B. 1501 is revealed by a proviso excepting from its terms anyone convicted of "manslaughter as a result of driving while intoxicated"--just prior to adoption of the bill, a white student who planned enrollment at Ole Miss was discovered with such a charge pending.

While the Governor was issuing proclamations of interposition and the state legislature was passing bills designed specifically to bar Meredith's enrollment, the state judiciary was not inactive. A Jones County chancery court, on September 19, 1962, issued a temporary injunction forbidding Meredith, assorted state and university officials, and even the United States Attorney General from performing any act to enroll and register "the Negro, James Meredith."

Events were moving at a pulse-stopping pace on September 20, 1962--the date scheduled for Meredith's enrollment. The Ole Miss Board of Trustees, which had previously removed all powers from Registrar Ellis to enroll Meredith and had conferred such powers on itself, in turn conferred all such powers on Governor Barnett--in effect making the Governor the university registrar insofar as Meredith's enrollment was concerned. On motion of the United States as amicus curiae, the federal district court was requested to enjoin enforcement of S. B. 1501 and to block the arrest of Meredith on the baseless state charge of false voter registration. Earlier that day Meredith had been convicted in absentia by a justice of the peace court in Jackson, Mississippi, for that "crime" and sentenced to pay a $100 fine and spend one year in jail. Judge Mize immediately signed a temporary injunction against the arrest on the voter registration charge, and he enjoined any arrest of Meredith under S. B. 1501; however, the requested general injunction against the enforcement of S. B. 1501 was refused. A Fifth Circuit panel of Judges--Brown, Wisdom, and Bell--already convened in Hattiesburg, Mississippi on another matter, issued a further injunction completely forbidding enforcement of S. B. 1501. The panel specifically enjoined all Mississippi state, county, and municipal officers from taking any action to effectuate the conviction and sentencing of Meredith on the voter registration charge, from attempting to enforce the chancery court injunction of September 19, or from "any other acts which would have the purpose or effect of interfering with the enrollment and continued attendance of James Meredith as a student at the University of Mississippi."

In the afternoon on that same September 20, Governor Barnett flew from Jackson to Oxford, Mississippi, the home of Old Miss, to block personally the enrollment of James Meredith. Meredith was accompanied to the University Continuation Center by James P. McShane, Chief of the Executive Office of the United States Marshals, Justice Department Attorney St. John Barrett, and two marshals. An eyewitness recorded Meredith's first enrollment attempt:

> As Meredith entered there were some boos and mild epithets, and during his twenty-minute stay the mixed crowd of students and outsiders chanted 'We want Ross' and the Old Miss 'Hotty Toddy' yell:

> Hotty toddy, God A'mighty,

Who in the hell are we,
Flim flam, bim bam,
Ole Miss, by damn.

The brief drama inside began as James Meredith said,
'I want to be admitted to the University.' Registrar Ellis
then read the board order which transferred his authority
to Barnett. The governor read his interposition proclamation and denied admission to Meredith. The Department
of Justice attorney then asked, 'Do you realize that this
puts you and the other officials in contempt of a federal
court order?' Barnett replied coldly, 'Are you telling me
I'm in contempt, or does it take a judge?'*

Judge Mize, later on September 20, 1962, issued an order
to show cause why university officials should not be cited for civil
contempt for their failure to obey that court's injunction of September 13 by refusing to enroll Meredith. However, the district court
the next day, September 21, found the university officials not guilty
of civil contempt, presumably because the power to enroll Meredith
had been taken from university officials by the board of trustees
and placed in the hands of Ross Barnett. While no one seemed to
notice at the time, Old Miss was not simply caught in a squeeze between federal and state authorities. Alarmed by the state's blatant
interference with higher education in Mississippi, accreditation
agencies were making threatening noises about the University of
Mississippi's accreditation.

On September 24, 1962, Ross Barnett issued a proclamation
which directed the summary arrest and jailing of any federal official who attempted to arrest or fine any state official. Meanwhile,
on that same day the Court of Appeals for the Fifth Circuit held
another hearing in New Orleans. The Fifth Circuit sat en banc
with all judges but Cameron present. Also present were university
officials, members of the board of trustees, a battalion of attorneys,
Justice Department and NAACP officials.

Charles Clark of Jackson, Mississippi, a highly intelligent,
energetic young attorney who was later to become a member of the
same Court of Appeals, had been appointed as a special attorney
general to represent the board of trustees. Attorney Clark had been
the lawyer who persuaded Judge Cameron to issue his four stays
and was intimately familiar with the Meredith case and with the
pressures back home in Mississippi. He had been originally associated in the case by Mississippi Assistant Attorney General Dugas Shands.

Clark, Attorney General Patterson, and several other Mississippi attorneys faced a barrage of hostile questioning from the
judges: Was the Hinds County justice of the peace who convicted

*Barrett, supra at 107-08.

Meredith in contempt of the Court's previous orders? Was there
any way the Court could enjoin all of Mississippi's chancery judges?
Was it Clark who advised the board that the attempted takeover of
university functions by the Governor was legal? On hearing the university officials' attempted explanation of the role of Governor Barnett and their delegation of the registrar's functions to him, Judge
Hutcheson tartly commented: "That is a misconception of the Governor's powers. In our state we impeach the Governor for interfering, and you all look like you are going to reward him.... What I
mean to say: Were you relying on the doctrine of interposition,
which was knocked out at Appomattox?... I can't see what the
Board got except chicanery and confederation from the Governor...."
At one point Mrs. Motley, on behalf of Meredith, moved in open
court that her client be registered on the spot.

The major issue before the Court, however, remained the
question of whether the university officials were in contempt of
court orders. Attorney Clark pleaded with the Court for understanding: Governor Barnett had threatened to close the University of Mississippi. Judge Tuttle responded curtly, "We have heard that of
every state in the South." The Mississippi attorneys were repeatedly
reminded from the bench that the Court felt that the board of trustees had willfully ignored its orders to enroll Meredith. Clark responded by suggesting the Court proceed directly against the Governor, rather than his clients, the board of trustees. After all, he
deadpanned, his beleaguered board had "had so much help [from
interfering state officials], it has just about been overwhelmed with
it, help it didn't ask for. didn't seek, didn't conspire in getting,
didn't request be done."

The courtroom dialogue between Court and counsel was but
a backdrop to a direct state and federal power confrontation and Attorney Clark urged the Court to understand that the board of trustees
was caught between two irreconcilable forces, neither of which it
could control:

> MR. CLARK: The only thing that I would hope and
> urge that this Court should consider is the propriety of
> proceeding against the Board, and particularly against the
> University officials involved here, before the ultimate is-
> sue has been met.
> JUDGE BROWN: What is that ultimate issue?
> MR. CLARK: And the ultimate issue is whether or
> not the authority of this Court is paramount to the author-
> ity of the Governor of the State of Mississippi to close
> that institution.
> JUDGE HUTCHESON: Listen! Where the Supreme
> Court said it was the duty of the Governor, instead of
> sending his troops to prevent enforcement of the Court's
> order, he should have sent them to enforce it. That is
> the law in Texas and Mississippi, that is the law every-
> where. Governor Barnett hasn't any authority in the world
> to condemn this Court.

JUDGE RIVES: You don't deny the Board and University officials have at least authority now to register Meredith, do you?

MR. CLARK: If Your Honoe please, authority, yes, and may I get back to Judge Hutcheson's question? I would say, Your Honor, that this Board and these University officials lack the power that this Court has to tell the Governor of the State of Mississippi that he can't act, in the same way that we lack the power to tell this Court that you can't act.

JUDGE TUTTLE: Your clients appointed him Registrar with full power to act.

MR. CLARK: Yes, sir.

JUDGE TUTTLE: Can't they revoke that?

MR. CLARK: Yes, sir.

JUDGE HUTCHESON: It is not good politics, too.

MR. CLARK: This is not a question of what is politically expedient, because, if that were so, these men would be honor-bound under oath of office to resign their offices. It might not relieve them of contempt of this Court, but they certainly ought to get out of office and let a trustee take office who will act with regard to the interests of the University and the State of Mississippi.

JUDGE BROWN: This is a curious thing--no personal disparagement, because you do a good job always as a lawyer, but you are standing here as Attorney General of the sovereign State of Mississippi, telling this Court, on behalf of the Board of Trustees, that it cannot perform its duties because of actions taken by the Governor? Is that it?

MR. CLARK: No, sir.

JUDGE BROWN: What is it then? I don't understand you.

MR. CLARK: Judge, what I am trying to say to you is this, that this Board from the night that the Governor of the State of Mississippi made a public proclamation to the people of the State of Mississippi on the 13th day of September as to what action he was going to take, from that moment forward the die was cast on this thing. This entire routine had to be played out to a conclusion in which the men on this Board of Trustees had to act--I think Judge Montgomery expressed it--between Scylla and Charybdis.

The role played by Attorney Charles Clark, representing the board of trustees, and former Governor J. P. Coleman, then representing several individual trustees and later also to become a member of the Fifth Circuit, was important. Clark and Coleman knew that the members of the board, while all segregationists, did not want the University of Mississippi destroyed over James Meredith. The board had been structured originally to provide lengthy, staggered terms for its members for the very purpose of preventing any single governor from appointing a controlling membership. The board's delegation of registrar power to the Governor and its public stance of defiance had been motivated by the urgent fear that any other action would result in the shutdown of the university. Furthermore, some members of the board had been beguiled by the Governor's promises. For months the board had been receiving assurances from Governor Barnett: "Just hold fast, don't admit this man ... I have a plan."

Prior to the trip to New Orleans and while in New Orleans, Clark pleaded with the board to recognize that Governor Barnett had no plan but defiance. They could continue to refuse to obey the Court and face jail and confiscatory fines and still not block Meredith's enrollment. Clark argued,

> Just think of the chancellor who orders a man to convey real property. They're not going to let a man refuse to sign the deed and keep the land from being conveyed. They're going to appoint the Clerk of Court as a scrivener and he's going to write the deed himself and you've all seen that threatened and done. ('Well, yes we have.') Well, they're going to appoing the Clerk of Court or somebody similar as the Registrar of the University of Mississippi and write James Meredith into the University as a student and you'll be pining away in the cell wishing you had your property back.

But Clark's logic did not remove the pressure from home. Charles Fair, the chairman of the board, remembers that while the board was in New Orleans, state legislators who had traveled to the Ole Miss campus sent a telegram to the board asking, "Can we begin to dig trenches and build barricades?"

The board finally faced reality on September 24, in that Fifth Circuit courtroom in New Orleans. Chief Judge Tuttle, addressing the Mississippi lawyers, emphasized that the time for the board to make its position definite could be postponed no longer:

> [Y]ou'd better be prepared before this hearing adjourns to tell this Court whether the clients that you represent, and who are all in court, and who, I express the hope, will not leave the court until the hearing is finally disposed of, will comply with any order touching on the admission of this man in the University, if such order is reasserted and made perfectly plain as a result of this hearing. I don't ask you to state that now, but before the Court adjourns I expressly state the hope that each of you will be prepared to state for your clients whether you will comply with any order the Court makes.

Judge Brown was even more direct: "Are the clients which you represent prepared not to obey [the Court's] order?" Judge Gewin continued the pressure: "Are the men you represent ready to perform the mandates of the decree of this Court's order?" Judge

Hutcheson joined the chorus: "Counsel, excuse me. How can we avoid a finding that the Board had disobeyed our order? How can we avoid it? Suppose we wanted to avoid it. We could not, like I say, wash our hands of it." Chief Judge Tuttle icily summed up: "We haven't fixed it, but I will state to you that I think we have all agreed that, thus far, before this hearing is over we will get a commitment from every member of the Board that is present in the court as to whether he will comply with the order, if the order is made firm and definite on this matter."

After seeing in open court that the judges on the Fifth Circuit were on the brink of issuing contempt citations, the board members, sick at heart but still desiring above all to preserve the university, capitulated. Former Governor Coleman requested a short delay in the hearing; he realized he had to inform his clients that further resistance was impossible and that they had to agree to obey the Court. A twenty-minute recess was ordered by Chief Judge Tuttle and counsel were told to return with an answer from each trustee as to whether he was willing to comply with court orders. After the recess the members of the board returned and Chief Judge Tuttle informed them that the Court had concluded that they had "willfully and intentionally violated the Court's order." Judge Tuttle then said the Court would defer finding them guilty of contempt until they had a chance to report whether they now would obey the injunction. Ashen-faced, the members of the board announced that they were now willing to comply with all court orders.

The Court then issued an order to the board to revoke the action of September 4, relieving university officials from their normal duties and placing authority to admit Meredith in the hands of the trustees. It ordered the board to nullify the action taken September 20 investing the Governor with the board's enrollment power, to prepare notification to all officials of the state that orders of the Court were to be fulfilled, and to instruct appropriate university officials to register Meredith and to permit his continued attendance. The Court also ordered the registrar of Ole Miss, the unfortunate Mr. Ellis, to be available at Jackson from 1 to 4 p.m. on September 25, at the offices of the board of trustees for the purpose of registering Meredith. Lastly, the Court ordered that it be notified by 4 p.m. on September 25, whether the order that Meredith be enrolled at the board of trustees' office in Jackson had been effectuated. The board, belatedly, had displayed courage and good sense.

*   *   *

September 25, 1962, was to be another eventful day. First, taking Charles Clark's hint, the Court of Appeals issued a further restraining order directed expressly to the Governor of Mississippi, prohibiting him from "[i]nterfering with or obstructing by any means or in any manner the performance of obligations or the enjoyment of rights under this Court's order of July 28, 1962, and the order of the United States District Court for the Southern District of Mis-

sissippi entered September 13, 1962." Next, the board of trustees
met as ordered in their offices. Treating the Fifth Circuit's orders
as so much paper, Governor Barnett also appeared at the offices of
the board of trustees and, for the second time, proceeded to block
the enrollment of James Meredith. Backed by a phalanx of state
patrolmen and cheered on by frenzied legislators, the Governor
physically prevented the board of trustees from carrying out the
order of the Fifth Circuit.

As Meredith, again accompanied by Chief Marshall McShane
and also by John Doar of the Justice Department, reached the room
where registration was to occur, he discovered a wild carnival atmosphere. Television cameras had been set up and the Governor
made his appearance to the accompaniment of wild cheering. He
dramatically read another proclamation designed to preclude Meredith's enrollment to the University of Mississippi. There was
raucous applause. James Meredith's impressions after his second
attempt to register are poignant:

> a jeering white women who finally burst into tears was
> sad contrast to a small group of six or seven blacks in
> work clothes who waved to show their enthusiasm and
> friendliness.

After deterring Meredith's enrollment for the second time,
the only thing that tarnished complete triumph for Ross Barnett was
his inability to emerge triumphant on the street in front of the state
office building in Jackson to the cheers of the multitude as planned.
Unfortunately, his elevator stalled on the way down and he missed
his grand exit. James Meredith suspects that the elevator problem
was not the hand of God. He commented drily, "[T]here are a lot
of Negro manual laborers in the capitol building."

Meredith's third attempt at enrollment took place back at Oxford, Mississippi. This time Ross Barnett did not appear. The
official excuse was poor flying weather; some suspect that he simply
wanted to let Lieutenant Governor Paul Johnson, his personal choice
for the next governor's race,* have the exceptional political opportunity of also thwarting Meredith's enrollment. With his now familiar traveling companions, Chief Marshal McShane and John Doar,
Meredith approached the Lyceum Building at Ole Miss, trailed by
a group of federal marshals. The way was barred by Lieutenant
Governor Johnson and a line of hefty Mississippi state troopers.
McShane attempted to serve the Fifth Circuit's court orders on Lieutenant Governor Johnson; Johnson refused the service. Following
instructions, McShane then dropped the documents at Johnson's feet,
generally a sufficient form of personal service on someone who refuses to accept court documents. Lieutenant Governor Johnson told
Meredith and his federal force they could proceed no further. Doar

---

*Mississippi law prohibited a governor from running for consecu-
tive terms.

and McShane then evidently felt some show of opposition was necessary. To show that Mississippi officials could not bluff the federal government, McShane decided to get tough. Moving in on Johnson with clenched fists, he demanded that Johnson step aside. Startled but not faltering, and bolstered by a representative of the Citizens Council, Johnson shook a clenched fist at McShane long enough for newsmen to capture it on film. There was a great deal of pushing and jostling among the state officials backing Johnson and the federal marshals accompanying Meredith. Finally, McShane asked Johnson to step aside to let "Mr. Meredith" through. Johnson retorted that he would not let "Mr. Meredith" through. In so saying, Meredith felt that Lt. Gov. Johnson had committed a fatal political mistake: he had called a black "Mister."

* * *

While the nation openly wondered why President Kennedy allowed a loud-mouthed governor to face down the might of the federal government three times, and while white Mississippians were enthralled with the grand statesmanship of their prophet, a fascinating series of telephone conversations occurred between Governor Barnett and Attorney General Robert Kennedy. Desperately looking for some way out of the impasse and hoping to avoid a rerun of the Little Rock crisis and use of federal troops, the Attorney General of the United States had initiated a series of unorthodox telephonic negotiations with Governor Barnett. A more complete story of those telephone calls is reported at length in Victor S. Navasky's informative book, Kennedy Justice.

While desperate calls were dialed between Washington, D. C. and Jackson, Mississippi, a fourth attempt was made to register James Meredith. The Justice Department announced that Meredith would register at Ole Miss on September 27. A large crowd, estimated at over two thousand, had congregated on the Oxford campus when Governor Barnett and Lieutenant Governor Johnson arrived. Attempts by Lieutenant Governor Johnson to disperse the crowd were ineffective. In desperation, Governor Barnett called Attorney General Kennedy and asked him to call off the fourth enrollment attempt. Attorney General Kennedy agreed and the Meredith convoy, coming down from Memphis and only twenty-three miles from campus, was turned around.

Four separate attempts to register James Meredith had aborted. School was already in session. The state of Mississippi wallowed in self-congratulatory defiance. Hindsight indicates that from the beginning, a massive federal force was patently necessary. The reluctance of the executive branch of the federal government to use force and the resulting delays and comic failures intensified resistance. However, the Kennedy Administration remained convinced that it had to exhaust all avenues of peaceful settlement before using force.

* * *

In this somber context, the Court of Appeals met on September 28, 1962. Previously, on September 25, the Court had issued an order to the Governor to show cause why he should not be held in contempt. A second order to show cause was issued to the Lieutenant Governor on September 26, 1962. The Court convened to hear a response to its orders to show cause and summoned both Governor Barnett and Lieutenant Governor Johnson to appear personally before it in New Orleans. When the Court assembled, neither the Governor, the Lieutenant Governor, nor any attorneys designated as their personal attorneys appeared.* For the first time, a grim court seemed to doubt whether or not its orders would be carried out. Judge Rives remembers feeling that the solemn row of judges had been sitting for weeks, with Governor Barnett "thumbing his nose at us from the sidelines."

The Court first took testimony on the issue of whether or not the Governor had properly been served with the Court's temporary restraining order; service of process had to be shown in order to establish the Court's jurisdiction over Ross Barnett. Oral testimony was taken from a Deputy United States Marshal who had attempted service, and a film of the attempted service was also put in evidence. Then the Court, with uncontradicted evidence of the service before it, took testimony from Chief United States Marshal McShane, who described the attempt to register Meredith at the State Office Building in Jackson and Governor Barnett's physical interference, and the next attempt at Oxford with Lieutenant Governor Johnson's interference. The atmosphere at the hearing was exceedingly tense. At one point when the state of Mississippi's attempt as amicus curiae to take over the defense of the case failed, one of the Mississippi lawyers said: "[T]he State of Mississippi is vitally affected ... bloodshed may result...." Judge Hutcheson shot back, "You are not threatening the Court with bloodshed, are you?"

The judges then turned on the faltering executive branch. At the close of the evidence, which decisively established the Governor's contemptuous flouting of its orders, Chief Judge Tuttle addressed Burke Marshall, Assistant Attorney General of the United States:

> I think I do state the views of the Court that the Court has practically exhausted its powers in the circumstances. I am sure it is a planned policy of our Government that a court have no power to execute its orders. It would be unfortunate no doubt if a court had that power, not only to decide issues but also to execute them. It seems to me

---

*Seven attorneys, led by former American Bar Association President John C. Satterfield of Yazoo City and including Charles Clark, were present to represent the state of Mississippi as amicus curiae. They indicated that they did not represent Barnett personally. After it became clear that the state of Mississippi was attempting to undertake the defense of the case against Ross Barnett, the Court revoked its permission for Mississippi to act as amicus curiae.

that the Court has nearly exhausted its powers to accomplish what this Court has repeatedly said Mr. Meredith is
entitled to, which is admission to the University of Mississippi, and the Court feels that the time has about come,
if what the Court said Mr. Meredith is entitled to he is
going to get, when the burden now falls on the Executive
Branch of the Government.

Now will you help the Court in your discussion this
morning--will you help the Court decide what you think can
be done by the Court to see that its orders are carried out,
and also indicate, if you can, what can be done by the Executive Department to see that the Court's orders are carried out.

Assistant Attorney General Marshall responded that while the efforts
of the federal government had so far failed, "There is no question
that the order of the Court is going to be enforced.... [T]he executive branch ... will use whatever force, physical force, is required
.... Chief Judge Tuttle was not to be mollified: "I do hope and I
assume the executive department has in mind the fact that an order
of this kind may be frustrated by delays as well as by failure to
act." Judge Tuttle's pressures on the Kennedy Administration were
echoed by other members of the Court, frustrated by the seeming
inability of the federal government to enforce the orders of its
courts. Judge Hutcheson commented with exasperation: "Now somebody in the government must have authority and must be willing to
exercise it." Later, as Assistant Attorney General Marshall continued his explanation of the federal government's position, Judge
Hutcheson observed, "[I]f you had one good Texas Ranger, it would
have been all right. You could have gotten the job done." Five
separate times various judges expressed dismay over federal delays
in enforcing its orders and demanded assurances that the government would do its duty.

After the solemn assurance of the Assistant Attorney General that the government would enforce its orders, the Fifth Circuit then, and only then, held Ross Barnett in civil contempt. The
Court ordered that he be committed to the custody of the Attorney
General of the United States, and it imposed a fine of $10,000 per
day unless before October 2, 1962, he had shown to the Court's
satisfaction that he was fully complying with the restraining order
and that he had notified all officers under his jurisdiction to cease
interference with the orders of the federal courts. The Court added
the following cold sentence to its contempt order: "Nothing herein
shall prevent a later assertion of a charge of criminal contempt
against Respondent." While the Court was unanimous in the finding
of contempt, Judges Jones, Gewin, and Bell dissented from that portion of the judgment imposing a fine. The next day, September 26,
the Fifth Circuit, by a three-judge panel, also held Lieutenant Governor Johnson in contempt and ordered him committed to the custody
of the Attorney General and fined $5,000 per day unless on or be-
fore October 2, he had shown full compliance.* Again the criminal
contempt possibilities were left open.

*Further, it is interesting to note the decree provided that if Lieu-

ARMAGEDDON

The fifth attempt to enroll James Meredith was the final showdown. In the continuing telephone dialogue between Governor Barnett and Attorney General Robert Kennedy, a tentative agreement was made that another attempt would be made on Monday, October 1, 1962. President Kennedy himself called Governor Barnett to urge maintenance of law and order. In tapes made public in 1974 by the Kennedy Library, the following conversation occurred between President Kennedy and Governor Barnett late on September 29, 1962. The President said:

... We really want to have from you some understanding ... from you as to whether the state police will maintain law and order. We understand your feeling about the court order and your disagreement with it, but what we are concerned about is how much violence there is going to be and what kind of action it will take to prevent it....
Governor Barnett: We'll take positive action, Mr. President, to maintain law and order as best we can. We have 220 highway patrolmen and they absolutely will be unarmed, not a one of them will be armed.
President: But the problem is--what can they do to maintain law and order to prevent the gathering of a mob and action taken by the mob...?
Governor: ... They'll do everything in their power to stop it.
President: What about the suggestion made by the Attorney General in regard to not permitting people to congregate to start a mob.
Governor: Well, we will do our best to keep them from congregating....
President: Well, just tell them to move along.
Governor: They crowd up on the sidewalks from the different sides of the streets, what are you going to do about it?
President: Now as I understand it, governor, you will do everything you can to maintain law and order.
Governor: I'll do everything in my power to maintain order.
President: Right.
Governor: We don't want any shooting.
President: I understand. Now, governor, what about --can you maintain this order?
Governor: ... I don't know whether I can or not. I couldn't have the other afternoon--there was such a mob there it would have been impossible.... You just don't know the situation down here [sic].*

[cont.] tenant Governor Johnson failed to comply with the order while acting in the stead of the Governor, his fine would be increased to $10,000 per day.
*The Washington Post, Jan. 26, 1974, §A, at 3, cols. 5-8; reprinted by permission.

After a series of preposterous proposals by Governor Barnett, at the last minute Attorney General Kennedy agreed to the suggestion that Meredith be moved to the campus in secret and registered instead on Sunday, September 30. That agreement was only possible after Robert Kennedy threatened to have the President of the United States make public all of Barnett's behind-the-scene dealings with the Kennedy Administration at the time he was making a public stance of total defiance. Pleading for Attorney General Kennedy not to allow such public disclosures, Governor Barnett suggested the Sunday date. In retrospect, the decision to move Meredith to Oxford on Sunday the thirtieth was a serious mistake. One can persuasively argue that he should have been enrolled on Friday afternoon or Saturday morning, after most of the students had abandoned Oxford for Jackson and an Ole Miss football game.

* * *

On Sunday afternoon, September 30, accompanied by several hundred United States marshals, border patrolmen, and other federal employees, James Meredith arrived at Ole Miss. Nicholas Katzenbach, the Deputy Attorney General of the United States (second highest official in the Justice Department), flew in to take command of the federal forces. Mississippi's Armageddon had arrived.

President Kennedy issued a proclamation commanding all persons engaged in obstruction of justice to cease and desist and issued an executive order as Commander-in-Chief authorizing the Secretary of Defense to use such armed forces of the United States as might be necessary to enforce federal court orders. The executive order also authorized the Secretary of Defense to federalize the Mississippi Army and Air National Guards.

From the time of Meredith's arrival on campus until General Billingslea of the United States Army announced at 6:15 a.m. on the eerie morning of October 1, 1962, that the area was secured, Oxford, Mississippi was in a state of insurrection. Following are descriptions of that night of September 30, thru October 1, when the winds of a hundred-year-dead war again blew through the South:

Early Evening:

Within a few minutes after the arrival of the marshals a crowd began gathering at the west end of a tree-filled area called the Circle. This crowd grew steadily throughout the evening, and estimates of its size varied with the time and the imaginative powers of the observer. One reporter stated that it reached four thousand, but a more accurate guess is that it was two hundred at the beginning and eventually grew to about two thousand. Marshal Al Butler, an hour after his arrival, estimated it at five hundred. In the afternoon it was small enough so that individual jeers could be heard, and after reaching the noise level of a football rally, it declined in the late

stages so that individuals could again be heard.
The timing of the crowd's remarks to the marshals is
difficult to determine, except that they became more bitter
and filthy as the crowd grew larger and began to change
to a mob. Early remarks directed at good-natured Al Butler suggested with no attempt at consistency that his wife
was 'home with a nigger' and that he had a 'nigger mis-
tress' and 'nigger children.' A faculty member reported
some unprintable vituperation, but the milder epithets included 'lousy nigger lover,' 'goon squad,' and '_____
_____ son of a bitch.' Some witnesses referred to this
as a 'football' type of cheer, an interesting commentary on
that aspect of American life, and there was indeed the
chanting of the Ole Miss 'Hotty Toddy' yell. There were
several varieties of 'Two, one, four, three, we hate Kennedy.' More menacing were the calls, 'We want Meredith.
Get a rope.' The jeers and threats were reinforced by
scores of Confederate battleflags which draped automobiles
and hung from dormitories, and a variety of bumper stickers along the lines of 'Help Ross Keep Mississippi Sovereign.' The 'rebel' aspect of the scene was heightened also
by the members of the Ole Miss band, who returned from
the Jackson football game in their Confederate-type uni-
forms which some newsmen thought they had acquired especially for the demonstration against Meredith's arrival.
Most members of the crowd during the early period probably were of the 'football set'--rude, boisterous, and smart
alecky, but not violent. But this was no football game.*

7:30-8:00 P.M.:

The crowd became particularly nasty and violent from
7:30 P.M. onward. The patrolmen moved closer to the
Army trucks and the mob swarmed onto the road, while
the patrolmen made no attempt to restrain it. Sometime
between 7:00 and 7:30 the crowd had definitely become a
mob. By this time the photographers who had entered
the campus at 7 P.M. were at work, and many in the
mob were hardly eager to have their actions recorded for
posterity. A group of about thirty-five moved in on a photographer from Dallas who was attempting to reach his
wife waiting in their car. He apparently 'asked for it' by
asking some of the rioters, 'When are you boys going to
start demonstrating?' Considering the events of the last
three hours, the question was hardly appropriate. The
'boys' screamed at his wife (of Jackson, Mississippi),
'Nigger-lovin' Yankee bitch.' A girl expectantly asked her
boyfriend, 'Lord, Joe, what are they gonna do to that
woman?' Her escort replied, 'Kill her, I guess. She's

_____
*R. Barnett, Integration at Ole Miss at 138-39 (1965); reprinted by
permission of Quadrangle Press.

a nigger lover, isn't she?' Reporter Wayne King described the scene: 'Yelling and cheering, they began to rock the car, smashing the windows with rocks and bottles. Some tore off chrome ornaments with their bare hands, while two Mississippi patrolmen made an obvious point of looking the other way, drawing cheers from the mob.' Several patrolmen finally rescued the photographer and his wife. Another photographer was shoved by the crowd and his camera smashed. A faculty member's wife asked a group of five patrolmen to help the injured man. One patrolman told her, 'I don't see anything, lady,' and again the patrolmen smiled at each other. Soon several patrolmen did investigate and two of them grabbed the photographer's arms while the mob continued to attack him, although the patrolmen finally tore him away.*

*   *   *

There is considerable disagreement about the precise time the tear gas was fired. About two-thirds of the witnesses agree with Department of Justice Attorney John Doar that it was at 7:57 P.M., before President Kennedy began his television address. In any case, the disagreement points up the confusion of events; even a few minutes delay indicates that the marshals were willing to wait until the last possible moment before resorting to the use of gas. Lieutenant Colonel Whitney Stuart, Army ROTC commanding officer at the University, told me he was absolutely certain that he was listening to the President's speech on a portable radio at the corner of the Lyceum Building when the first gas was fired. Several witnesses have said that after the first gas they went into the 'Y' building and that the President 'had just started' or 'was just starting' to speak. One significant fact is that the University clocks are always about three or more minutes slow, and anyone who observed the time of the gas firing as 7:57 should have read it as 8 P.M., or slightly after. Having read and listened to a few positive statements and many uncertain ones, I would place the event at the moment the President began speaking or slightly later. One thing is certain: few on the scene thought the question of time was of any importance. John Doar, relying on the Lyceum clock, noted it in a timetable of events which he kept, and Nicholas Katzenbach phoned Robert Kennedy, who in turn attempted to get word to the President, but he was already on the air.**

8:00 P.M., The Presidential Address:

'Even among law-abiding men few laws are universally

---

*Ibid., at 144-45.
**Ibid., at 148-49.

loved. But they are uniformly respected and not resisted,'
the President's calm voice came over a small radio in
the YMCA building on the circle. To the little group
listening his patient tone seemed utterly incongruous against
the background of mounting explosions and breaking glass.
Jeers and howls split the night; somewhere, someone was
pounding on metal. And still the quiet voice talked on,
now addressing the students themselves: 'You have a new
opportunity to show that you are men of patriotism and integrity. For the most effective means of upholding the
law is not the state policeman, or the marshals, or the
National Guard. It is you....'*

Attorney Charles Clark was at his office desk in Jackson,
Mississippi, that Sunday evening, feverishly working on some legal
aspect of the Meredith case. His law partner, Vardamen Dunn,
who had a daughter enrolled at Ole Miss, called the office in great
agitation: "Charlie, do you know that people are being killed at
Ole Miss?" Clark immediately left his office and rushed the short
distance to the Governor's mansion. He was challenged but finally
admitted after convincing the guards that he was one of the Governor's lawyers. The atmosphere at the mansion was electric with defiance. Clark pleaded with the Governor to do something or people
would be killed. He desperately urged the Governor to go on the
air and inform the people of Mississippi that the federal government
had the might to carry the day and that violent resistance was foolhardy. He argued, "Governor, the United States has enough might
to enroll a gorilla at Ole Miss if they want--tell the people Meredith is the federal government's student, tell them anything, but the
situation must be cooled." The Governor seemed to agree; then
other hard-line advisors joined the discussion and the Governor,
following his pattern, equivocated. Finally, at approximately 11:30,
well after the rioters were out of control, Governor Barnett made
his first public gesture toward maintenance of law and order by
broadcasting a request that everyone go home.

8:30 P.M. to 2:00 A.M.:

The highway patrolmen left the scene of the rioting
almost immediately after the gas firing.**

Smoke billowed out from the Lyceum as the marshals
continued pumping tear gas into the night. Shadowy figures in T-shirts raced about the circle in front, pausing
occasionally to hurl rocks and bottles at the federal lines.
This circle quickly became the main battlefield--the first
80 yards served as no-man's land ... the flagpole in the
center was the rioters' front line ... and the Confederate

---

*W. Lord, The Past That Would Not Die, at 211-12 (1965); re-
printed by permission of Harper & Son, Publishers.
**Barrett, supra at 155.

monument on the far side became an appropriate rallying
point. The trees that studded the area--and the comfortable brick buildings surrounding it--gave generous opportunity for cover and strategy. Finally, the new Science
Center under construction nearby offered an arsenal of
bricks and stone that exceeded the dreams of the most
blood-thirsty rioter.

Yells and howls filled the murky night. It was a
setting made for rumor, and the story soon spread that
the federals had killed Colonel Birdsong. The troopers,
now completely out of action and collecting by the gym,
clamored for revenge. They were unarmed, but their guns
were handy in the patrol cars. A quick-thinking Senator
Yarborough hustled the Colonel, alive and unharmed, to the
spot.

Another story couldn't be stopped so easily: the rumor that a coed had also been killed by the opening blast.
Nothing could better fit the popular notion of brave Southern womanhood and federal bestiality; the students struck
at the line of marshals with new fury.*

*   *   *

The riot raged on--a steady hail of missiles crashing
into the embattled line of marshals, who kept mechanically
pumping gas into the night. It did little good, for the
wind was blowing the wrong way. Besides, the boys
seemed to thrive on the danger and excitement; soon they
were even picking up the sputtering grenades and tossing
them back at the marshals. Carried away, they compared
themselves to the patriots of '76 or (and this they especially liked) to a band of Hungarian Freedom Fighters.

'We've got a leader! We've got a leader now!' Suddenly the cry rose above the general tumult. Duncan
Gray glanced across the circle, and there in the glow of
some lights he saw a small cluster of people around a
tall man in a dark suit, wearing a white Texan hat. General Walker** had reached the campus shortly before
9:00 P.M., striding in by the University Avenue entrance,
trailed by Louis Leman and a few other friends picked up
along the street. Halting under a lamp post at the entrance to the circle, he was quickly spotted, and there followed a brief, bizarre reception as well-wishers moved up
to shake hands, request his autograph, ask for his views
on subjects like Cuba and the Constitution while the riot
raged on in the murky darkness.***

---

*Lord, supra at 211.
**A former Army General who commanded United States troops in
Europe and retired to Texas after criticism of his extreme right
wing political activities.
***Lord, supra at 213.

At the White House President Kennedy decided it was time to take a personal hand in the matter. At 11:45 Washington time (9:45 in Mississippi) he again called Barnett, personally urged him to get the Highway Patrol back on the job. The Governor, by now completely out of touch and bombarded with conflicting advice, assured Kennedy that this was being done. Then he begged the President to get Meredith away from the scene. Kennedy said they'd talk about that after peace was restored. Barnett suggested he go to the riot himself: 'I'll get a mike and tell them that you have agreed to remove--'

'Now wait a minute!' broke in the President. He again stressed that nothing of the sort could even be considered with a riot going on. Restore order, and then they'd talk about Meredith.*

*   *   *

At 10:00 a heart-heavy Nick Katzenbach called the White House: he was afraid they'd have to have troops. Technically, of course, the actual decision was the President's, but it was really not that clear-cut. They had been working toward this step for an hour; now they simply agreed together that the time had come. For Katzenbach--believing almost to the end that he could do the job without troops--it was a moment of the bitterest disappointment.

Army Secretary Cyrus R. Vance, standing by at the Pentagon, got the word by scan line a few seconds later. He immediately notified General Abrams in Memphis, who alerted General Billingslea, who would be the field commander. Billingslea passed the orders on to his unit commanders, and in the darkened gym at the Millington Naval Air Station a sergeant's toe ultimately jabbed the side of a sleeping Pfc. Charles Vanderburgh: get up, they were going in.**

Members of the mob brought two odd vehicles into the assault, first a bulldozer and then an old University fire truck, but the marshals repulsed them by what amounted to hand-to-hand combat. Rebel snipers were active with both rifles and shotguns, and they fired at marshals, soldiers, military vehicles, the Lyceum, and almost anything in sight. One faculty member saw a man firing a rifle in the general direction of the Lyceum from two hundred yards away. He asked if the rioter was not afraid of hitting those on his own side, and the man replied, 'I hadn't thought of that.' Two University policemen arrested and identified two men who were shooting out street lights with a rifle, but the Lafayette County Grand Jury after-

*Ibid., at 219.
**Ibid., at 220.

ward failed to indict them. Members of the mob burned a variety of automobiles, all belonging to Mississippi residents, and the owners included a University staff member and four faculty members, two of them staunch segregationists. In addition to the standard bricks, bottles, and rocks, the mob used Molotov cocktails, pieces of concrete from broken blocks and benches, spears fashioned from iron rods and lumber, and acid presumably obtained from the chemistry building. Chemistry professor Bill Herndon had locked the doors early in the evening, but rioters broke through outside windows into two basement rooms, one of which was the physical chemistry laboratory and a probable source of a limited amount of acid. Contrary to some reports, the mob did not gain access to the chemistry supply room. A staff member of the Navy ROTC saw and heard a highway patrolman explaining to some of the rioters how to make a Molotov cocktail.*

It was after midnight now at the White House. The hurly-burly of the early evening was over--the TV people and all their equipment gone. The group in the Cabinet Room and the President's office narrowed down to six-- JFK, his brother, Burke Marshall, Ted Sorensen, and a couple of other aides. The atmosphere was busy but relaxed. As always when the crisis got big enough, the trappings of bureaucracy mercifully vanished, and the scene was strikingly intimate. No special flaps--just six busy people fielding problems as they came, making decisions which might affect the course of federal-state relations for years to come. Sometimes the problems were big: should the marshals be allowed to use firearms? No, said the President; only if necessary to save Meredith's life. And sometimes they were of the small technical kind that hopelessly baffle policymakers: how many gas grenades in a case? The Pentagon finally had to wake up the manufacturer on that one....

In the besieged Lyceum the marshals again asked permission to use their guns. No, said Katzenbach, hang on for five more minutes--the National Guard is coming.

They were indeed. Assured that his unconventional chain of command was valid, Captain Falkner piled his men into three trucks and four jeeps. Knowing nothing of the situation, he told the troops to bring rifles and bayonets, but no ammunition. Happily, he also had a hunch they might need gas masks. At 10:30 the little convoy rolled out of the armory, leaving only five cooks behind. As they headed up University Avenue, a scout car of rioters flashed by them, screaming curses, and sped on ahead to warn the mob.

No trouble till they hit the edge of the circle. Then

*Barrett, _supra_ at 157-58.

a barrage of planks, rocks, bottles. There was gunfire too--one jeep picked up six bullet holes in the windshield. Falkner leading, the convoy plowed on, headed straight for a barricade of concrete benches now blocking the way. The Captain's jeep swung wildly around it; the trucks behind crashed through, scattering hunks of concrete in all directions. A sheet of flame now erupted from gasoline poured across the road ... the men ducked and the convoy roared through, safe at last alongside the Lyceum.*

2:00 A.M. to 6:15 A.M.:

At about 2 A.M. the first regular troops arrived and received the standard greetings of bricks, Molotov cocktails, bullets, and vile language. This platoon of the riot-trained 503rd Military Police Battalion had been flown in by helicopter. One helicopter had circled low over the campus at about midnight in an unsuccessful attempt to find a place to land, and finally went to the Oxford-University Airport instead. After riding to the Northgate entrance of the campus in Navy buses, the soldiers marched to the Lyceum in 'V' riot formation, most carrying rifles with bayonets fixed and some with riot shotguns. These were the men who performed the tiresome and dangerous job of routing the hardcore rioters from the campus. The main body of the 503rd MP's and all of the 716th MP Battalion drove south from Memphis in two convoys. Lieutenant Henry T. Gallagher of the 716th obtained a Mississippi road map from a service station and commandeered a Navy shore patrolman who showed the way as far as Holly Springs, thirty miles north of Oxford. The convoy was impeded by drivers of several private autos, who drove slowly in front of the military jeeps and trucks and would not let them pass. The 503rd went on into Oxford and was partly immobilized when rioters dropped a railroad tie on a truck from a railroad overpass. Other rioters peppered the long line of soldiers with rocks and sticks. Lieutenant Gallagher left the 716th north of Oxford and with the aid of a city map supplied by the Army, drove by a circuitous route to the airport to get orders from Major General Charles Billingslea. Gallagher's driver was hit in the face by a rock on the return trip. One platoon was sent immediately to the campus as reinforcements, while the rest lined up on a street north of the campus to await orders.**

When October 1 dawned and the results of the rioting were made known, Mississippi politicians began the process of placing the full blame for the riot on allegedly inexperienced, trigger-happy

---

*Lord, supra at 221-22.
**Barrett, supra at 161-62.

federal marshals, and, incredibly, on the use of insufficient force by President Kennedy. As late as October 15, the Dan Smoot Report, a Dallas periodical, was still publishing the rumor that a coed had been killed and other students shot by marshals. In an editorial, David Lawrence, in United States News and World Report, accepted and published without question the biased findings of the Mississippi Legislative Investigating Committee. Despite the willingness of professors who were eyewitnesses to testify, the Mississippi Legislative Committee took testimony only from those whose version was favorable to the state of Mississippi. Later, a Lafayette County grand jury placed the entire blame for the rioting on federal marshals, after being instructed by Mississippi Circuit Judge W. M. O'Barr that it could indict "John F. Kennedy, little stupid brother Robert Kennedy ... or any other human being."* Many Mississippians, despite overwhelming evidence to the contrary, still place the blame on the federal marshals.

On one thing all could agree: terrible damage had been done to property, human life, and the reputation of the University of Mississippi. Two men were dead: Paul Guihard, a French newspaperman representing Agence France-Presse, who was shot in the back, and Ray Gunter, an Oxford workman who was shot in the forehead while watching the riots. At least 160 marshals were injured; thirty eight per cent of those sent to Ole Miss. Sixteen of the Mississippi National Guardsmen first led into the riot scene, including Captain Falkner, were injured. No one could be sure of the extent of injuries among rioters, but they were much less extensive--a cold indication of where the balance of force lay. Federal forces took over 200 prisoners, only twenty-four of whom were Old Miss students. No convictions resulted from the rioting.

After a fitful night of sleep in a guarded dormitory room, James Meredith arose and went to the Lyceum Building with John Doar and Marshal McShane. Robert B. Ellis, the shaken registrar whose rejection letter to James Meredith started the chain of events, registered Meredith as a student, majoring in political science.

* * *

The rest of the year was not an easy one for James Meredith. Resisting students taunted and harassed him on his way to and from classes. An underground newspaper, Rebel Underground, appeared and printed vile condemnations of the Kennedy Administration, James Meredith, and the "Kennedy Koon Keepers." Discipline for the first few weeks after Meredith's enrollment was almost nonexistent. Finally, Chancellor Williams, in a get-tough speech to all male students on November 1, 1962, began to take charge of the situation. On November 15, seven Ole Miss students were brave enough to eat with James Meredith in the cafeteria. Two of those

---

*"The Mississippi Battle on Two Fronts," 53 U.S. News & World Report, Nov. 26, 1962, at 4.

students immediately had their rooms wrecked and obscenities scrawled on the wall. No one was punished and only two of the seven students completed their academic programs at Ole Miss.

James Meredith remained stoic throughout most of his ordeal. He did publicly complain about the segregation of the United States troops guarding him on October 4 and, on January 7, 1963, threatened not to return unless changes were made at Ole Miss. His charges prompted Robert Kennedy to criticize the university administration on January 9.

The administration was also subjected to vilification from extreme segregationists. The chancellor was called a "liar" and a "quisling" in the Rebel Underground. Faculty members critical toward the state of Mississippi or friendly to Meredith were not spared. Art Professor Ray Kerciu, on April 7, held a one-man art show on campus, displaying paintings showing his version of the Old Miss riots. In his paintings he used a Confederate flag and some of the bumper stickers and comments heard from the rioters. The Oxford Citizens' Council protested and a law student initiated criminal charges. *

Oddly enough, James Meredith received very few hate letters. He credits that blessing to standard white supremacy doctrine: no black was ever worth writing to about anything. He did receive one outraged letter from Mrs. B. J. Gaillot, Jr., one of the leaders of the screaming mothers during the fall of 1960 in New Orleans who had been excommunicated from the Catholic Church with Leander Perez for protesting New Orleans parochial school integration.

Meredith weathered the harassment. Perhaps his most difficult moment came when his ordeal was almost over: Medgar Evers was assassinated on June 12, 1963, at his home in Jackson, Mississippi. The death of his friend and advisor stunned Meredith, and he issued a bitter statement. Even at the time of Medgar Evers' murder, Meredith showed his aversion to violence by the praise he extended to John Doar for his bravery after Medgar Evers' funeral. Under bad leadership or no leadership, the line of the huge funeral procession for Evers broke for downtown Jackson, bent on destruction. Met by a solid wall of police, the situation was explosive. John Doar stepped out between the police guns and the Negro rioters and brought calm to the scene.

At the end of the summer session 1963, James Meredith, wearing a "Never" button pinned upside down, graduated and the last of the federal marshals left the wounded university. By the end of the year, fifty professors had left Ole Miss.

---

*Barrett, supra at 217-18. The grounds: the paintings were "obscene and indecent" and a "desecration of the Confederate flag." Ibid., at 218.

Surprisingly, in his reflections, James Meredith expressed the view that Governor Barnett was not as dangerous as the more rational and legalistic segregationists that had gone before. He stated that Governor Coleman was much more dangerous, citing the famous Coleman episode involving Clennon King. (King was a Negro professor who had applied for admission to Ole Miss in 1957. Mississippi state patrolmen removed King from the university registrar's office. He was held secretly for two weeks and then committed to an insane asylum for thirty days. He left the state.) In his campaign for reelection to the governorship in 1963, Coleman reportedly boasted, "The point of this story [about King] is not the fact that one man was kept out of Ole Miss. Rather, it shows that we know how to protect your rights in such a way that the federal government could find no excuse for putting hands on the state of Mississippi."

Despite urging from federal officials, Meredith refused to aid the reelection of Coleman by absenting himself from a Coleman rally.

Considered the moderate in the gubernatorial race in 1963, Coleman was running against Lieutenant Governor Paul B. Johnson. In 1963, Paul Johnson was elected Governor on a raging segregationist platform. Despite his public posturing on segregation, some Mississippi moderates close to the Meredith case remember Paul Johnson with respect. Lieutenant Governor Johnson, not Ross Barnett, went to Oxford on the night of the insurrection to attempt to preserve order. In his inaugural address, Governor Johnson took a no-nonsense stand against public disorder.

* * *

Ole Miss was not the only institution that was to suffer turmoil and dissension in the aftermath of James Meredith's matriculation. The Fifth Circuit itself, long after James Meredith had been forgotten by the general public, was tormented by public and private reverberations stemming from that unique federal-state conflict.

Higher Education: Capitulation

With the desegregation of the University of Mississippi, massive violence erupted for the last time on Southern college campuses. Although there had been more federal court litigation over university desegregation in the Fifth Circuit than in all other circuits combined, only ten institutions out of approximately sixty tax-supported "white" junior colleges, colleges, and universities were forced by legal action to accept black students. After the debacle at Ole Miss, the momentum of that last falling domino brought down official barriers in sister Southern states. The desegregation of Southern colleges was hailed as an early "success" of the civil rights movement, but even success is a relative term. Autherine Lucy and Messrs.

Tureaud, Hawkins and Ward never gained access to the state institutions to which they had sought admission.   Even though the legal
obstacles had been removed and the federal courts had stood firm,
there remained enormous personal struggles for those black students
who gained entry to formerly white citadels.   James Meredith ultimately graduated from the University of Mississippi, but endured
harassment which brought him to the verge of a nervous breakdown.
And, certainly, Meredith was more prepared for his mission, from
his eight-year tour of duty in the armed services, than were those
who followed.

*   *   *

The experience of the two young black students who desegregated the University of Georgia was probably far more typical than
Meredith's, exemplifing the life of minority students on a Southern
campus during the first few years after the riots at the University
of Mississippi.

Charlayne Hunter and Hamilton Holmes were twelve years old
when Brown I was handed down by the Chief Justice of the Supreme
Court; they were fourteen when Autherine Lucy was admitted to the
University of Alabama and the riots there began; fifteen, when James
Meredith first applied to Ole Miss.   They were described in a con-
temporary account:

> Both had always been considered perfectly cast for the
> role.   Good-looking and well dressed, they seemed to be
> light-complexioned Negro versions of ideal college students,
> models for an autumn Coca-Cola ad in a Negro magazine.
> Charlayne, a slim attractive girl with striking hazel eyes,
> had finished third in her graduating class at Turner High
> School in Atlanta, had edited the school paper, and had
> been crowned Miss Turner.   The valedictorian at Turner
> that year was Hamilton, who had been president of the
> senior class, and as a smaller than average but effective
> halfback, co-captain of the football team.*

They were both bright, popular, ambitious high school leaders, definitely "college material" according to the standards of any university recruiter.   Each had career plans which would be furthered by
courses offered at the University and not available in such richness
at Negro institutions: Hunter was interested in journalism and
Holmes was planning to be a physician.   When they were ordered
admitted to the University of Georgia by the federal court, despite
an evening of riots,** they were younger and more naive than previ-

---

*Trillin, An Education in Georgia, at 4 (1964), [hereinafter cited as
Trillin]; reprinted by permission Calvin Trillin.
**After they were ordered admitted, the evening of riots occurred;
when the rioting occurred they were "suspended for their own safety"
and another order had to be entered reinstating their right to enroll.

ous test plaintiffs. As a consequence they were somewhat less prepared for the intensity and duration of the social ostracism which
they encountered. On the eve of their graduation from the University of Georgia three years later, Charlayne Hunter, the more outgoing of the two, spoke to an interviewer about her experiences.

> 'We'd always feel little tremors here during things
> like the Freedom Ride and Ole Miss. Then the catcalls
> would start again, but not bad. The first half year, they
> used to let the air out of my tires a lot, but after that
> nothing really out of the ordinary happened....' When I
> asked Charlayne why she came to the Co-op if it seemed
> likely that somebody would say something insulting, she
> said, 'Well, it doesn't happen every day. And it's not
> that bad. It's not the whole group, and I don't sit with
> those boys. And sometimes I get hungry in the morn-
> ing.... It's hard to say how often I hear somebody make
> a remark. I guess I could calculate a way to avoid it for,
> say, a week. But I would have to stay away from cer-
> tain areas--here, in front of the Kappa Alpha house, that
> tree that the law students gather around in front of the
> Journalism Building. But it's not so bad now. The K.A.s
> usually don't yell nasty things now; they just yell my
> name. I might even go a couple of weeks sometimes.
> Last summer, I went for a long time without anybody say-
> ing anything. At the Continuing Education Center, people
> stare a lot, but they never say anything. Oh, one time
> a man kept saying, "There's that little nigger who caused
> all the trouble." He kept saying it quite loud and some
> women with him were trying to stop him. I usually don't
> pay any attention, but that time I got mad. I just stared
> back at him all through dinner. Or for a while. Then I
> just said, "What the heck." '*

She had initially been optimistic about their eventual acceptability.
However, as she ultimately concluded,

> 'I thought there would be coolness for a couple of weeks,
> but I never thought it would last forever, and in some
> ways it has.... Maybe Hamp's way is better. He just
> doesn't get involved. It's more frustrating for me, in a
> way. I get so involved that sometimes I get to thinking
> I'm human.'**

Hamilton Holmes indeed took the opposite tack. Instead of
attempting to penetrate the social life of the campus, he withdrew,
concentrating upon proving his own worth through his academic
studies.

---

*Ibid., at 76.
**Ibid., at 122, 128.

The son of a prominent, middle-class Negro family, Hamilton Holmes was comfortable and admired in northwest Atlanta, a young man with high promise to become a successful physician like his grandfather. In Athens, the smalltown home of the University, he lived off-campus with a Negro family, permitting himself little chance to be rebuffed:

> As Hamilton began his final ten-week quarter at Georgia, he had never eaten in a university dining hall, studied in the library, used the gymnasium, or entered the snack bar. He had no white friends outside the classroom. No white student had ever visited him, and he had never visited one of them. He had, as his father told me, 'lived for Friday,' and had driven the seventy miles to Atlanta every week-end since his enrollment. He could sum up his social life at the university in a few sentences: 'I've gone to almost all the plays--three or four a year. I usually go alone on Thursday night. I've been to the football games. I haven't gone to any basketball games because they're on Saturday night. There's better basketball in Atlanta--plus I'd have to stay here all day Saturday, and I can't be fighting that.... I haven't had any trouble, except a few months ago, I had somebody to flatten all the tires on my car, and they tore the chrome off my door once. But that's about all, except the incident at the frat house.' [That] occurred when he parked his car near the Kappa Alpha house and went into the infirmary down the street to visit Charlayne. He came out to find his car blocked by another car and a crowd of boys in a belligerent mood waiting to see what he would do about it. Hamilton eventually reached into his car for a flashlight and, holding it in his pocket and pretending it was a gun, persuaded the boys to move their car. After the incident at the frat house, Hamilton was bothered even less.*

Even Hamilton Holmes, who turned himself into a seemingly self-sufficient iconoclast at the white University, expressed wishful thoughts that the social life of his college years might have been different.

> 'I've concentrated on getting some good grades; I was so determined to show them that what they said about me wasn't true. I haven't gone out of my way at all to make friends. And I don't expect them to go out of their way-- just go along in the normal way. I'm used to speaking to almost everybody I see. That's the way I was brought up. At home, when I walk down the street, I speak to almost everybody who passes. It's been that way all my life. All week I look up at people, wanting to speak, and people turn their heads. I guess that bothers me more than anything else.'**

---

*Trillin, supra at 83, 85.
**Ibid., at 89.

Charlayne Hunter graduated from the University of Georgia and subsequently became a reporter for the New York Times. Hamilton Holmes graduated with Phi Beta Kappa honors at the University and became the first Negro graduate of the Emory University School of Medicine. Academically, both had been successful in the competitive world of higher education; and, according to most onlookers, Charlayne Hunter and Hamilton Holmes had by their example dispelled the myth of Negro intellectual inferiority. Eugene Patterson, the Editor of the Atlanta Constitution, described their contribution:

> James Meredith has had academic troubles at Ole Miss. Four of the six Negroes at Georgia Tech are struggling to stave off failure. The few Southerners who might be unfeeling enough to try to use this to prove a point for school segregation are simply missing the point of desegregation. This is a land of the lone man, the individual Americans aren't weighed in bulk. They are measured singly. Their rights include the right to fail. But when desegregation gives one single American the right to succeed, whereas segregation of his whole race would have hobbled him, the point of individual rights, and the worth of the U.S. Constitution, is proved.*

NOTES AND PRIMARY AUTHORITY

The primary authority for the material contained in this chapter was:

The Desegregation of Higher Education: Preamble to Meredith. The primary source of cases are: Cooper v. Aaron, 358 U.S. 1 (1958); State ex rel. Hawkins v. Board of Control of Fla., 355 U.S. 839 (1957); Lucy v. Adams, 350 U.S. 1 (1955); Board of Supervisors of L.S.U. v. Tureaud, 228 F.2d 895 (5th Cir. 1956); Adams v. Lucy, 228 F.2d 619 (5th Cir. 1955); Wilson v. Board of Supervisors of L.S.U., 92 F. Supp. 986 (E.D. La. 1950) (three-judge court). Other helpful sources are: Act 15 of 1956, LSA-R.S. 17:2131-35; Act 249 of 1956, LSA-R.S. 17:443; Dickens, Bleak House (1886); Greenburg, Race Relations and American Law (1959); J. Peltason, Fifty-eight Lonely Men: Southern Federal Judges and School Desegregation (1961); R. Sarratt, The Ordeal of Desegregation (1966); With All Deliberate Speed (D. Shoemaker, ed., 1957); speech by Benjamin Disraeli, House of Commons, London, England, March 11, 1873; "Dilemma in Dixie," 67 Time, Feb. 20, 1956, at 65; 67 Time, Feb. 20, 1956, at 40; 67 Time, Feb. 27, 1956, at 68; Powledge, "Profiles: Charles Morgan, Jr.," The New Yorker, Oct. 25, 1969, at 80; Dallas Morning News, Sept. 8, 1956, reported in Sarratt, supra at 159; Southern School News, Sept. 8, 1956, reported in Sarratt, supra at 159; Reed, "Nixon's Rights Effort in South Will Go to Many Judges Viewed as Hostile," New York Times, Oct. 20, 1969, col. 1, at 47.

*Quoted in Trillin, supra at 179.

Meredith v. Fair. A few of the several places where Meredith v. Fair can be found are: 305 F. 2d 343 (5th Cir. 1962); 298 F. 2d 696 (5th Cir. 1962); 202 F. Supp. 224 (S. D. Miss. 1962); 199 F. Supp. 754 (S. D. Miss. 1961); 7 Race Rel. L. Rep. 741 (5th Cir. 1962). Some helpful sources are: Presidential Proclamation and Executive Order, Sept. 30, 1962, 7 Race Rel. L. Rep. 764 (1962); Governor's Proclamation, Sept. 24, 1962, 7 Race Rel. L. Rep. 754 (1962); Governor's Proclamation, Sept. 13, 1962, 7 Race Rel. L. Rep. 748 (1962); R. Barrett, Integration at Ole Miss (1965); W. Lord, The Past That Would Not Die (1965); J. Meredith, Three Years in Mississippi (1966). V. Navasky, Kennedy Justice (1971); R. Sherrill, Gothic Politics in the Deep South (rev. ed. 1969); Silver, "Mississippi: The Closed Society," The Journal of Southern History (1964); Leonard, Harris and Wren, "How a Secret Deal Prevented a Massacre at Ole Miss," 26 Look, Dec. 31, 1962. There were interviews with Chief Judge John R. Brown, Judge Charles Clark, Mr. Charles Fair, Judge Frank Johnson, Judge Richard T. Rives and Judge John M. Wisdom.

Higher Education: Capitulation. The following colleges were desegregated through court order: Texas Western College [White v. Smith, 1 Race Rel. L. Rep. 324 (W. D. Tex. 1955)]; Louisiana State University [Bd. of Supervisors of L. S. U. v. Tureaud, 225 F. 2d 434 (5th Cir. 1955)]; University of Alabama [Lucy v. Adams, 134 F. Supp. 235 (N. D. Ala. 1955)]; Texarkana Junior College [Whitmore v. Stillwell, 227 F. 2d 187 (5th Cir. 1955)]; North Texas State College [Atkins v. Matthews, 1 Race Rel. L. Rep. 323 (E. D. Tex. 1955)]; University of Georgia [Ward v. Regents of the Univ. System of Ga., 2 Race Rel. L. Rep. 599 (N. D. Ga. 1957) and Holmes v. Danner, 191 F. Supp. 412 (M. D. Ga. 1961)]; University of Florida [Hawkins v. Bd. of Control of Fla., 162 F. Supp. 851 (N. D. Fla. 1958)]; Georgia State College [Hunt v. Arnold, 4 Race Rel. L. Rep. 79 (N. D. Ga. 1959)]; West Texas State College [Shipp v. White, 5 Race Rel. L. Rep. 740 (W. D. Tex. 1960)]; and the University of Mississippi [Meredith v. Fair, 306 F. 2d 374 (5th Cir. 1962)].

Also helpful was: Holmes v. Danner, 191 F. Supp. 385 (M. D. Ga. 1960); 191 F. Supp. 394 (M. D. Ga. 1961), motion to vacate stay denied, 364 U. S. 939 (1961) (per Black); 191 F. Supp 412 (M. D. Ga. 1961). Other sources are: Trillin, An Education in Georgia (1964); and With All Deliberate Speed (D. Shoemaker, ed., 1957).

A more complete manuscript, with detailed documentation of all sources is available as indicated in the Preface, supra.

Chapter 6

SCHISM

> Dull Barnett, with his mind half on the poultry
> market, successfully led everybody into the slough
> and thereby became what Hodding Carter accurate-
> ly called 'the dominant political figure in Missis-
> sippi as long as he lives.'*

To a nation deeply shocked by the events of September 30
through October 1 at Oxford, Mississippi, the worst appeared to be
over. James Meredith had been enrolled at Ole Miss and some
semblance of law and order had been restored. However, for the
Fifth Circuit the next few months after the enrollment of James
Meredith were to be the most trying in its history. The Court's
difficulties swirled around the question of what to do about Ross
Barnett and his clear contempt of court orders. That controversy
developed into an unparalleled internal crisis for the Court, deeply
involving every judge and flaring occasionally into acrimonious public conflict. Even the United States Supreme Court was drawn into
the battle. The final resolution of the Ross Barnett affair satisfied
no judge and left a residual bitterness. On occasion, eddies of the
Barnett problem threatened to leave the Fifth Circuit a fractured and
splintered institution. But, miraculously, after the Old Miss crisis
had cooled, the judges on the Court of Appeals seemed, like Shad-
rach, Meshack and Abednego of old, to gather new strength from
the time of testing they had endured together. Tempered by the
fires of conflict and with only Judge Cameron remaining isolated and
aloof, a new court emerged.

"The Man in High Office Who Defied the Nation"

Twelve days after the debacle at Ole Miss, on October 12,
1962, the Fifth Circuit met again for an en banc hearing to consider
the Mississippi situation. Two conflicting legal requests were before the Court. First, there was a federal motion to convert the
temporary restraining order issued on September 25, 1962, against
Governor Ross Barnett and other Mississippi officials, into a pre-

---

*R. Sherrill, Gothic Politics in The Deep South, at 202 (rev. ed.
1969); reprinted by permission of Grossman Publishers.

liminary injunction. Second, there was a Mississippi motion to dissolve the temporary restraining orders and dismiss the contempt proceedings against Ross Barnett and other Mississippi officials, ostensibly on the ground that James Meredith had been enrolled at the University of Mississippi.

In questioning Charles Clark, representing Governor Barnett and the Ole Miss Board of Trustees, the Court expressed grave concern over the continued harassment of James Meredith on the Oxford campus. Judge Brown charged Meredith was "being attacked and roughed up and things thrown, and no effort being made by the authorities to discipline students." Clark responded that Meredith was in federal custody. Chief Judge Tuttle then sharply reminded counsel that high officials of Ole Miss, including the board of trustees, were still subject to court orders and that they had an obligation to provent the abuses mentioned by Judge Brown. Clark assured the Court that its orders were currently being complied with "to the very letter." Judge Rives did not ease the pressure on the young attorney; he asked:

> JUDGE RIVES: Do you think other students have to walk around with a marshal to protect them and be jeered at and holloaed [sic] at as they go about the campus?
> MR. CLARK: Judge, in your question whether or not the people that you directed this injunction to and the people that you could direct this injunction to have complied with your orders, there is not a man--
> JUDGE BROWN: What about the Dean? Why don't they exercise some discipline over students that act this way?
> MR. CLARK: As near as I know, sir, they are exercising all the discipline they can.

A primary concern expressed by the Court was whether or not Governor Barnett would now preserve order, protect Meredith, and obey future commands of the Court. In questioning from the bench, Charles Clark faced one of those rare moments in the life of an attorney where his candor and courage were severely tested. Attorney General Patterson of Mississippi had in the earlier hearing on September 28 stated that Governor Ross Barnett would maintain law and order. The Court pressed Charles Clark as to whether he could still make that assurance unequivocally:

> JUDGE GEWIN: You were present in court, I believe, and had made some statements, and Judge Rives, addressing Attorney General Mr. Patterson, said this:
> 'JUDGE RIVES: I understand, Mr. Attorney General, you assure us as Attorney General of the State and as attorney for the Lieutenant Governor and for the Governor, that to the best of their ability, they will maintain law and order and will comply with the orders of this Court?'
> 'MR. PATTERSON: Yes, sir.'

You remember that?

MR. CLARK: Yes, sir, that is correct.

JUDGE GEWIN: And were you there present, and you and the Attorney General were associated together in--

MR. CLARK: Correct.

JUDGE GEWIN: --in making that statement, whatever it means, to this Court?

MR. CLARK: Yes, sir.

JUDGE GEWIN: And you approved it at that time?

MR. CLARK: Yes, Your Honor.

JUDGE GEWIN: And stated to the Court, you and Mr. Patterson and Mr. Satterfield, that as officers of the Court you made that recommendation to us?

MR. CLARK: Yes, sir.

JUDGE GEWIN: Speak out, sir.

MR. CLARK: Yes, sir.

JUDGE GEWIN: And that was made with the authority of the Governor and the Lieutenant Governor?

MR. CLARK: Yes, sir.

JUDGE GEWIN: And that was your position at that time, whatever the meaning of these words is?

MR. CLARK: Yes, sir.

JUDGE GEWIN: All right, sir.

JUDGE RIVES: But now you retract it?

MR. CLARK: To the extent--

JUDGE RIVES: Or qualify it?

MR. CLARK: If you put a different connotation on it, qualify it to the extent of what I have said to the Court here today.

JUDGE BELL: You have been very candid.

Charles Clark's integrity had been tested by fire. He was being asked directly whether or not he would now associate himself with Attorney General Patterson's promises that the Governor and Lieutenant Governor would obey court orders and preserve order. To associate himself with that assurance would have been the politically expedient decision, but would have misled the Court. To disassociate himself from Attorney General Patterson's statement would have discharged fully his obligations to the Court in the best tradition of the bar, but might have had the potential of being politically disastrous to Clark personally. To make the pressure more unbearable, Attorney General Patterson reaffirmed his assurances:

> JUDGE RIVES: And you this week would give me the same answer, yes, that you gave me last week to that question I asked you?
>
> MR. PATTERSON: Yes, sir.

Charles Clark did not hesitate; he twice disassociated himself from the position of the Mississippi Attorney General, his cocounsel in the representation of their client Governor Barnett, and stated; "I cannot make that assurance [that the Governor and Lieutenant Governor will comply with court orders]." An unimpeachable source, close to the Court, overheard one of the judges remark about Charles Clark to another as they left the bench for a short recess: "That is a young man that can be trusted."

On October 19, 1962, the Court of Appeals issued a new order. Judges Tuttle, Rives, Jones, Brown and Wisdom joined in an order denying Mississippi's motion to dissolve the temporary restraining orders issued on September 25, 1962; instead, they entered the preliminary injunction requested by the federal government. In addition to enjoining Ross Barnett and other named high officials of the State of Mississippi, the Court also enjoined the State of Mississippi as a party. The new order specifically prohibited any attempt to arrest James Meredith or to further interfere with his education.

Concurring in part and dissenting in part, Judges Gewin and Bell agreed generally with the order of the Court but argued that the Court should have remanded its new preliminary injunction to the district court for supervision. They stated: "Our appellate jurisdiction would continue but the remand should tend to restore normalcy in Mississippi, and would comport with good judicial administration under the circumstances." Judges Gewin and Bell did agree that the Court of Appeals should retain the contempt proceedings then pending against Governor Barnett and Lieutenant Governor Johnson for final disposition. However, citing the eleventh amendment to the Constitution, the two judges indicated that they held serious doubts as to the propriety of adding the State of Mississippi as a party defendant to the preliminary injunction. They urged that the temporary restraining order as to the State of Mississippi be dissolved and that the state not be included in the preliminary injunction.

Still smarting from Ross Barnett's defiance of its orders, on November 15, 1962 the Court of Appeals commanded that the Attorney General of the United States prosecute both the Governor and Lieutenant Governor of Mississippi for criminal contempt of court. Sitting again en banc, on January 4, 1963, the Court issued an order to show cause why Barnett and Johnson should not be convicted of criminal contempt. Judges Cameron and Gewin dissented; former Chief Judge Hutcheson was excused from the hearing and decisions of the Court by reasons of his health.

* * *

On April 9, 1963, in an unusually important action, the Court of Appeals split asunder on the question of whether Ross Barnett was entitled to a jury trial on his contempt charges. Following one of the most infrequently used procedures known in appellate law, the Fifth Circuit, for the first time in its history (and one of the few times in the history of the Republic), formally certified a question of law to the Supreme Court for decision. After overruling a series of defense motions, with Judge Cameron dissenting each time, the Court split four-four as to whether the Governor and Lieutenant Governor of Mississippi were entitled to a jury trial on the pending

criminal contempt charges.   Sixty-seven pages in the Federal Reporter were required to report the question certified to the Supreme
Court, to report a meticulously detailed chronology of proceedings
prepared by Judge Brown and to report the opinions of the individual
judges.   Each judge on the Fifth Circuit felt compelled to express
his own viewpoint on the question of whether or not a jury trial was
warranted.   The serious differences between various judges on the
Court and the importance of the question to be decided render the
Fifth Circuit's certification opinion unique in the annals of federal
jurisprudence.

The four judges on the Court with the most liberal voting
records on civil rights matters took a hard line on the existence of
any constitutional right of Ross Barnett and Paul Johnson to a jury
trial.   Recognizing that the granting of a jury trial--which probably
would have to be held in Mississippi and, in any event, would be
held in the South--was the equivalent of acquittal, Chief Judge Tuttle and Judges Rives, Brown and Wisdom argued strongly that the
right of a jury trial did not apply to persons accused of criminal
contempt of court orders.   They asserted that a court had the inherent right to punish persons who were in criminal contempt of its
orders and that the standard right to a jury trial available for other
criminal charges was simply not applicable.

One of the key problems in the case was deciding which
court's order had been violated.   If the order violated was the Court
of Appeals' temporary restraining order of September 25, then Chief
Judge Tuttle and Judges Rives, Brown and Wisdom argued there was
neither a constitutional nor a statutory right to a jury trial.   If,
however, the order violated was the district court's injunction of
September 13, 1962, then, while they would not concede a constitutional right to a jury trial, they concluded there might be a statutory right.   In this case, the four judges opposed to a jury trial
strenuously argued that it was their orders, particularly the temporary restraining order of September 25, 1962, that had been violated
and that: (1) they had the power to issue that order; (2) the issuance
of that order did not convert them from an appellate court into a
district court for purposes of interpreting the statute granting jury
trials for criminal contempt of district court orders; and (3) "it is
now way too late to urge" that the temporary restraining order issued on September 25 was not needed to carry out the Court's opinion of June 25.   The four caustically pointed out that, because of
Judge Cameron's stays, Judge Mize "either was, or thought" that he
was unable to act: "Unless this Court's decision of June 25 was to
be frustrated, affirmative action was needed then and there.   It had
to come from and through this Court, and this Court alone."   Chief
Judge Tuttle and Judges Rives, Brown and Wisdom continued:

It was this Court which made its ruling of June 25.
It was this Court which made its orders of July 27-28.   It
was this Court whose orders were being disobeyed.   It
was this Court which needed the assistance of the sovereign
and called upon it to take appropriate steps for the execu-

tion of the decrees of this Court. The rights of these Defendants are not then to be measured by what might have
been claimed had these asserted acts of defiance taken
place as to the District Court alone.

Those four judges then rebutted Judge Cameron's charges about the
validity of the manner of selecting the three-judge Court of Appeals
panels that issued various opinions and orders throughout the Meredith case.

In expressing his view that Barnett and Johnson were entitled to a jury trial, Judge Cameron essentially argued that the only
valid court order that could have been violated was Judge Mize's
order of September 13 entering the injunction. He said that when
Mr. Justice Black vacated his four stays, the case reverted back to
its posture prior to the issuance of his first stay. At that time the
Court of Appeals, per Judge Wisdom, had reversed Judge Mize and
had ordered the case remanded to him to issue an injunction. Therefore, Judge Cameron argued that if any order was violated, it was
the district court's order and that Barnett and Johnson were thus
entitled to jury trials under federal statutes. Judge Cameron seemed
more interested in establishing that the Court of Appeals had no jurisdiction to issue the contempt orders than he did in the question
certified: the right to jury trial. In addition, he attacked the methods used to select the three-judge panels, a charge he was to make
with far greater vigor later. Judge Cameron asserted that all of the
troubles arose from the Fifth Circuit's attempts to act like a trial
court and to assume the trial court's normal duty of issuing injunctions.

Judge Jones, with a touch of wry humor, began his opinion
in favor of a jury trial:

We have not here made a decision. ... [But] [s]ince
opinions are being written, I will join the cavalcade lest
there be a lurking suspicion that I am neglectful of a duty.

Judge Jones then penned a historical discussion of the right to a
jury trial. He emphasized that the injunctions issued by the Fifth
Circuit had been in the exercise of extraordinary powers. Congress,
he suggested, when it provided for a jury trial on the charge of
criminal contempt of district court orders, could not have been expected to foresee contempt charges also arising from extraordinary
orders issued by an appellate court directly to a person and not
through the usual auspices of a district court. While arguing for a
jury trial, Judge Jones also raised a disturbing question: if Barnett and Johnson were to be tried by the Fifth Circuit, would some
or all of the judges on the Circuit have to be disqualified because
of possible bias to the defendants?

In his separate dissent, Judge Gewin expressed concern
about the active role played by the Justice Department, despite its
status as amicus curiae and not as a real party to the dispute. He

was also critical of what he felt had been undue haste throughout the proceedings since the reversal of Judge Mize's denial of the permanent injunction.

> ... It is easy to yield to the criticism sometimes heard that judicial processes in a democracy are too slow. The truth is that all processes in a democracy are slow compared with the speed with which results are accomplished under some other types of government--the judicial process alone is not involved. Rules of law may serve to protect the rights of individuals in the courtroom as well as in the policeman's office. If expediency is to be the guiding rule in this case, some kind of a decision resulting in a judgment of guilty or not guilty can be rendered at an early date, but I cannot follow such rules of expediency unless such course of conduct is declared to be the law of the land. In my view, there is no end which justifies such means. With all our rush, turbulence, deadlines, speed and excessive zeal, we should remember substantive and procedural fundamentals. In this case, as in many others, procedure protects substantive rights.... Regardless of the parties involved, constitutional and statutory guarantees as they relate to liberty are seriously involved. Conviction of the crimes charged may subject two human beings to serious criminal penalties and interfere with the governmental functions of a State of this Union.

Judge Bell felt that in issuing the extraordinary orders directly to Governor Barnett and Lieutenant Governor Johnson the Fifth Circuit had been acting "as a District Court." Therefore, it had to abide by the jury trial statutes applicable to a district court:

> Under our court system the District Court speaks to litigants, while a Court of Appeals speaks, or should speak, to the District Court. This historical mode lends itself to the maintenance of a judicial dignity and decorum, engenders and preserves respect for law, and avoids an unseemly type of judicial scurrying about that results when there are no rules to follow.
> I regret that the court will not also certify the following additional question, deemed by me at least to be of the utmost importance in the event of jury trial, so as to eliminate more makeshift procedures:
> 'If Respondents are entitled to trial by jury for the criminal contempt with which they are charged, may the order to show cause charging them be referred to the District Court where the alleged acts of contempt were committed for trial?'

*   *   *

While the Court of Appeals awaited the Supreme Court's

decision on its certified question on the right to jury trial, two separate pieces of litigation were filed that also arose out of the Ole Miss tragedy. In the first suit, Virgil Norton, Virgil Wesley and James Chapman alleged that they were apprehended by federal marshals on October 1, 1962, the day of the rioting, on a highway about four miles from Oxford, Mississippi. They charged that they were detained for twenty-one hours and were subjected to indignities by the marshals; they sued Chief Marshal McShane and other federal officers for damage. Judges Rives and Wisdom, with Judge Gewin dissenting, held that the charges against the marshals should be dismissed. Judge Rives stated:

> In that state of the record, we must assume that to the extent the defendants allegedly acted overzealously or maliciously, they were nevertheless acting within the outer perimeter of their line of duty, and the alleged acts had more or less connection with the general matters committed by law to their control and supervision. Moreover, we are of the opinion that the selection of a proper method of enforcing a court's orders in the face of active opposition and obstruction is a decision which it is necessary that these officers be free to make without the fear or threat of vexatious or fictitious suits and alleged personal liability.

In the second suit, the same Fifth Circuit panel, with Judge Gewin dissenting in part, dismissed a complaint brought by an Ole Miss student. The student alleged that he had been wrongfully hit by tear gas projectiles at the time of the riot and had been deprived of his right of free speech and peaceful assembly.

* * *

The United States Supreme Court found the jury trial question no easier to answer than did the Court of Appeals. Almost exactly one year after the Fifth Circuit had certified the jury trial question, on April 6, 1964, the Supreme Court, in a five-four decision, ostensibly held that Governor Barnett and Lieutenant Governor Johnson were not entitled to a jury trial. Mr. Justice Clark, joined by Justices Harlan, Brennan, Stewart and White, delivered the opinion of the Court. The Court held that the statute providing for jury trial in the case of criminal contempt did not apply since the contempt committed was disobedience of a court of appeals' order and not of a district court order. The Court of Appeals did have power to punish for contempt of its own orders; the fact that the conduct of Barnett and Johnson also violated a district court order did not render the court of appeals impotent to punish the offensive behavior. Therefore, the Supreme Court answered the certified question from the Fifth Circuit in the negative: Ross Barnett and Paul Johnson were not entitled to a jury trial.

Mr. Justice Goldberg dissented and was joined by Chief Justice Warren and Justice Douglas; Mr. Justice Black dissented sepa-

rately and Justice Douglas also joined his dissent. The dissenters
would have responded to the certified question in the affirmative:
the defendants had both a statutory and a constitutional right to a
jury trial. Mr. Justice Goldberg acknowledged that the contempts
charged were "extraordinarily serious, among the most serious in
this Nation's history." Therefore, reasoned the dissenters, all the
rights available under the Constitution and statutes accorded to those
charged with serious crimes should apply. The dissenters were
not persuaded by the government's "necessity" argument that the independence of the courts could be undermined if their orders could
be nullified by unsympathetic juries. The dissenters claimed that
this was the "oft-rejected" argument that some guilty men are acquitted by juries and that this is "the price we have chosen to pay
for our cherished liberties."

A casual reader of the Supreme Court's decision could conclude that despite the narrowness of the five-four decision, the Fifth
Circuit had been given the approval to try Barnett and Johnson without a jury trial. However, the real importance of the Supreme
Court opinion is told in the last sentence of footnote 12 to the majority opinion:

> In view of the impending contempt hearing, effective ad-
> ministration of justice requires that this dictum be added:
> Some members of the Court are of the view that, without
> regard to the seriousness of the offense, punishment by
> summary trial without a jury would be constitutionally
> limited to that penalty provided for petty offenses.

That last sentence undercut any hope for effective punishment of
Ross Barnett and Paul Johnson. If a severe penalty was to be invoked, probably anything over six months imprisonment, there had
to be a jury trial. Since four members of the Supreme Court had
dissented and had indicated that there should be a jury trial in any
event, footnote 12 clearly indicated that some members of the five-
Justice majority also felt there should be a jury trial if there was
any penalty imposed beyond that "for petty offenses." The Fifth
Circuit had a most distasteful choice: to impose a light penalty
which would amount to a wrist slapping and make Ross Barnett and
Paul Johnson heroes in Mississippi, or, to conduct a jury trial with
a jury of Mississippians (or, at least Southerners) which would be
tantamount to acquittal.

*   *   *

The final chapter in the Barnett contempt matter was written
on May 5, 1965. The Court, sitting en banc, dismissed all charges
against Governor Barnett and Lieutenant Governor Johnson. At the
time of the dismissal of the charges, the Court was composed of
only seven judges. Judge Cameron had died on April 3, 1964,
three days before the Supreme Court's opinion on the jury trial
question was issued. Judge Cameron's eventual replacement, Judge
J. P. Coleman, the former Governor of Mississippi who had repre-

sented Ross Barnett, was facing heavy weather in Senate confirmation hearings.

The dismissal of charges was a bitter pill for the Court. In making the decision, the seven remaining judges split four-three. The key vote was that of the courtly and courageous Alabamian, Judge Richard T. Rives. For the first time in the entire Meredith-Barnett affair, he failed to go along with the Court's three vigorous civil rights enforcers, Chief Judge Tuttle and Judges Brown and Wisdom. While Chief Judge Tuttle and Judges Brown and Wisdom angrily dissented, Judge Rives joined Judges Jones, Gewin and Bell in dismissing the criminal contempt charges against the Governor and Lieutenant Governor of Mississippi. The majority judges, in a short per curiam opinion, noted that there had been substantial compliance with the Court's orders and also that the 1964 Civil Rights Act had been passed. Feeling that the possibility that others would commit similar acts was unlikely and frankly stating that "no public interest ... [would] be served in continuing the prosecution," the Court said that dismissal of the charges was "an appropriate application of restraint to judicial power." The majority argued:

> ... Jury trial as a matter of right has been ruled out by the Supreme Court. For reasons which need not be stated, jury trial as a matter of discretion would not be granted by majority vote of this Court. For the same acts for which they stand charged with criminal contempt, the defendants have already been tried and adjudged by this Court to be in civil contempt. This Court has already found against them on all of the elements of criminal contempt, excepting only that of intent, willfulness. That state of mind must be determined by inference from evidence, most of if not all of which has been introduced and considered by the Court in the civil contempt proceedings. While we know that every judge of this Court would do his conscientious best to try the criminal contempt proceedings fairly and impartially, we are doubtful, to say the least, whether we and the other judges may not have formed a fixed opinion that the defendants are guilty. Thus some, or all of the present membership of this Court may be disqualified from sitting on a trial on the merits of these criminal contempt charges. The statute makes no provision for any replacement judge to sit on this en banc court and we doubt whether one can properly be devised by judicial invention. It follows that a fair trial on the merits is the subject of doubt, and dismissal of the criminal proceeding is the only course open that is clearly consistent with fundamental fairness.

Judge Rives, on reflection, still makes no apology for his vote. He felt the Court had a "bear by the tail" and just had to let go. Severe punishment was foreclosed by the Supreme Court in footnote 12; anything less would have made Ross Barnett a martyr. Echoing Judge Rives, Judge Gewin believes that any punishment of

Barnett would have made him a United States Senator in the place
of Senator Stennis.

Each dissenting judge wrote his own opinion; all were bitter,
but Judge Wisdom's pen seems to have been dipped in a special vat
of virulent acid: "To my mind, the Court's decision represents the
exercise of judicial license, not of judicial restraint." Judge Wisdom's opinion provides at least a glimpse of the depth of the disagreement on the Court:

> The Court does not purport to base its holding on any
> principle of law. The Court bases its holding on its con-
> fidence in a prescient majority's knowledge of what is best
> for the public. Working with what Dr. Gallup would con-
> sider a statistically small number for a reliable poll, the
> Court dismisses the indictments because its 4/3 poll indi-
> cates that the public reaction would be adverse to a trial
> of the defendants at this time.

> * * *

> The Court is less like a court than it is like St.
> Louis. The good French king used to sit under a spread-
> ing oak tree, not presiding even-handedly as a judge at a
> trial, but dispensing justice subjectively, arbitrarily, hit-
> or-miss, according to his fancy of the moment as to what
> was best for his subjects and when it was best for him to
> tell them about it. Coming closer home, the law in the
> Court's decision is like the law West of the Pecos.

> * * *

> The offense occurred at a time calling for moral
> leadership of the highest order. ... No one can say that
> the rioting and insurrection that took place September 30,
> 1962, in Oxford, Mississippi, and the death and disorder
> that have occurred in many other places in the South since
> that insurrection, were not due, at least in part, to the
> imprimatur the Governor of Mississippi placed on lawless
> defiance of the federal courts.
> The judges in the majority have greater confidence in
> their ability to read the future than I. I cannot say as
> the Court says, '[i]t is highly improbable that other per-
> sons will hereafter commit acts similar to those herein
> charged.' I say that a person who commits the acts with
> which Barnett is charged must be called to account. If
> he should be found guilty and punished, that punishment
> may deter others from committing similar acts. That at
> least is the theory on which criminal penalties rest....

> The confrontation should have been a duel with drawn
> pencils between the Governor of Mississippi and the United
> States Attorney General in the Mississippi Law Journal.

Or it should have started and stopped in the courts, as well it might have, when the University's Board of Trustees, with dignity and grace, agreed in open court to accept Meredith at the University. Unfortunately, Governor Barnett insisted upon a confrontation in the streets of Oxford and on the campus of the University. There was more at issue, therefore, than an affront to this Court's dignity when Ross Barnett, as the head of the State of Mississippi, mobilized sheriffs, highway troopers, and local police officers and by force of arms overcame United States marshals enforcing the law.

The Governor of Mississippi, trained in the law, knew or should have known that the Supremacy Clause makes hash of the so-called Doctrine of Interposition.... But the uninformed, the uneducated, the very persons likely to resort to violence, were certain to be misled when their chief executive 'Interposed' himself between the United States and the University of Mississippi.

Ross Barnett happened to be Governor of Mississippi at an unfortunate time. It would be a mistake to overestimate his place as an obstructionist in the long-run solution of the complex problem of national social adjustment to the changing relationship of the races. What cannot be overestimated, however, in a short-run or long-run solution, is the importance of federal courts' standing fast in protecting federally guaranteed rights of individuals. To avoid further violence and bloodshed, all state officials, including the governor, must know that they cannot with impunity flout federal law.

* * *

There is an unedifying moral to be drawn from this case of The Man in High Office Who Defied the Nation: The mills of the law grind slowly--but not inexorably. If they grind slowly enough, they may even come, unaccountably, to a gradual stop, short of the trial and judgment an ordinary citizen expects when accused of criminal contempt. There is just one compensating thought: Hubris is grist for other mills, which grind exceeding small and sure.

The result of the Barnett contempt proceedings satisfied no member of the Court, outraged some and marked a pivotal point in the history of the Fifth Circuit's enforcement of civil rights after Brown I and Brown II. Up to the time of James Meredith, the Court operated from the traditionally aloof appellate posture that is premised on assumptions about the good faith of lower federal court judges and state officials ordered to carry out federal court mandates. After Ole Miss, a wiser Court could no longer accept face value assurances that state officials would act in good faith or that lower federal courts would follow their orders.

The Judge Who Indicted His Court

One of the unfortunate side effects of the Meredith conflict was Judge Benjamin Franklin Cameron's almost total alienation from his brethren. A life-long resident of Meridian, Mississippi, Judge Cameron seemed always to have been a loner. A non-smoking Episcopalian teetotaler, Judge Cameron was one of the rare Republicans in Mississippi eligible for high judicial appointment during the Eisenhower Administration; he was appointed to the Fifth Circuit in 1955.

Judge Cameron was a tall patrician man in appearance and sported an ever-present bow tie. Deeply religious, he had studied for the ministry at Sewanee before switching to the law. Epitomizing the Protestant ethic, Judge Cameron seemed to excel at everything he attempted by combining his natural talents with plain hard effort. He was an avid sportsman, playing semi-pro baseball and basketball. He was a perennial tennis champion and an accomplished horseman, still finding time to coach the Meridian High School football team without pay while a young lawyer. That high school still presents an annual award to the football player with the greatest fighting spirit: the award is called the Cameron Trophy and commemorates the judge's "fighting heart."

Judge Cameron was devoted to his family and his community. He built a home in Meridian with a small private lake, tennis courts and stables. Much of the work was done by his own hands; the judge himself helped pour the eighteen-inch-thick walls of his impressive home.

An exceptionally well-read man, Judge Cameron, although no glad-hand mixer, had an enormous impact on those who knew him. He was described more than once as "a powerful spirit." Prior to attending law school, Judge Cameron had taught German and Latin and was considered by his colleagues as a classical scholar. He was also a thorough and careful legal craftsman. He was, of course, a segregationist, as were almost all Mississippi's leading citizens at the time. He was not, however, as some have painted him, a race-baiting demagogue; he harbored few, if any, of the racial animosities of many of his neighbors. He was a regular contributor to a local black school and was frequently asked to present its commencement address. Judge Cameron had all the talent necessary to become at least a gifted, if not a great, judge. And yet, his last years on the bench were characterized by acrimony and public controversy. When he died, he was considered by most legal scholars to have been an isolated reactionary with little influence on his own court.

Judge Cameron took the bench with great hopes. His appointment to the court from a distinguished career as a trial lawyer was heralded by those of almost all persuasions in Mississippi. While there had been some initial concern about his racial views, Attorney General Brownell received assurances that Cameron was no racist. John Minor Wisdom, then a private attorney in New Orleans with impeccable credentials as a Republican moderate, called the Justice Department on behalf of Judge Cameron. Reportedly, after the appointment when President Eisenhower met Ben Cameron for the first time, he remarked, "Mr. Cameron, you are the only lawyer I know of in the South nominated to the federal bench who has the endorsement of both Senator Eastland and the NAACP."

Later, Judge Cameron's open rupture with his brothers on the Fifth Circuit and his estrangement from the mainstream of judicial thought on his own court could, perhaps, have been predicted. The strength of his character and his unwavering, almost religious commitment to states' rights seemed to forestall compromise with the other judges. His position on the far right of the Court became apparent within a few months of his swearing-in. In one early, eloquent dissent he wrote, "too much government from too far off has always been counted tyranny." Judge Cameron's dissents became more frequent and more pointed as his years on the Court passed. While consistently a champion of the right of the individual to be left alone whenever the federal government was involved, he took an increasingly conservative, even rigid, view of civil rights claims. During his entire tenure on the Court, he never failed to vote against the position advocated by every civil right claimant. As the years passed, his relationships with his colleagues suffered and his comments at judicial council meetings became more acerbic. Nevertheless, he retained his reputation as a first-rate legal craftsman. In the words of Judge Wisdom, he was "no slight opponent."

Judge Cameron's anguish over what he felt was the pro-civil rights bias of Chief Judge Tuttle and Judges Rives, Brown and Wisdom (whom he publicly referred to as "The Four") became a cause célèbre with his four attempts in the Meredith case to stay the orders of a panel of his own court. By attacking the manner in which panels of his court were selected, he attempted to justify his four stays in his opinion accompanying the certification o f the Barnett jury trial question to the Supreme Court.

After James Meredith's matriculation at Ole Miss and during the pendency of Ross Barnett's contempt proceedings, Judge Cameron became obsessed with the idea that Chief Judge Tuttle had intentionally rigged the selection of panels on all civil rights cases before the Court to obtain favorable rulings for black plaintiffs. He bombarded the Fifth Circuit Clerk of Court with requests for information on the judicial assignment procedures being employed. On July 30, 1963, he filed two dissenting opinions to his court's refusal to grant en banc rehearings in two school integration cases. * Both of those cases had been decided by Fifth Circuit panels of which Judge Cameron was not a member. The most important of his two dissents was in the Birmingham case, Armstrong v. Board of Education.

---

*See discussion of a portion of Judge Cameron's dissent in the Birmingham case in Part II, Chapter 4, infra at 188-90.

Judge Cameron's dissents hit the Fifth Circuit like a thunderbolt. He charged that Chief Judge Tuttle had wrongfully packed the panels deciding civil rights cases with The Four, to deliberately produce a pro-civil rights result. He further charged that the Chief Judge had gerrymandered the composition of three-judge district courts in Mississippi to produce favorable civil rights rulings. The three-judge Mississippi district courts had been sitting to decide the constitutionality of state legislation affecting civil rights. In a personal attack on Chief Judge Tuttle, Judge Cameron flatly charged that the frequent use of extraordinary or expedited procedures in civil rights cases, such as the granting of temporary restraining orders or injunctions pending appeal, had brought on a crisis. He said the Court was besieged by requests for such orders and specifically blamed Chief Judge Tuttle. He alleged that the demand for extraordinary remedies was "set off" by an order of Judge Tuttle granting a motion for an injunction pending appeal, which resulted in blocking the superintendent of schools in Birmingham from expelling or suspending 1,081 black public school students who had been involved in civil rights demonstrations. When Judge Cameron died, he was still personally convinced that Judge Tuttle had rigged Fifth Circuit panels to accomplish pro-civil rights results.

Judge Cameron asserted that only "the Court," meaning the Fifth Circuit as an institution, and not the Chief Judge, had the power to assign judges to panels. He then stated that he had made a two-year study of assignment procedures covering the period from June, 1961 to June, 1963, which supported his charge that one set of procedures existed for civil rights cases and another set for all other pending matters. His study showed that in twenty-two of twenty-five civil rights cases the majority of the panel had been "composed of some combination of The Four." He said in only two cases was a majority composed of the remaining five members of the Court. Judge Cameron also produced evidence which, he alleged, demonstrated that normal procedures had not been followed in convening three-judge federal district courts in Mississippi. He charged that a member of The Four was substituted for the resident circuit judge (himself) and that another member of The Four had been substituted for one of the two resident district judges to create a two-judge majority composed of members of The Four. Judge Cameron stated that a "crusading spirit" was the cause of the "errors" he had exposed.

Judge Cameron's charges were extraordinarily serious. By charging that his own chief judge had deliberately assigned judges to panels for the purpose of achieving results that the Chief Judge favored, Judge Cameron was publicly accusing Chief Judge Tuttle of outrageous and grossly inappropriate judicial behavior. Judge Cameron had, in fact, publicly assaulted the integrity of his court.

Alerted to Judge Cameron's dissents and his study supporting his charges of court packing and gerrymandering, the southern press exploded. Many of the South's newspapers charged liberal judges on the Fifth Circuit with trying to ram <u>Brown v. Board of Education</u>

down their throats. The Houston Chronicle in an eight-column full-
banner headline on August 2, 1963, trumpeted, "Senator to See If
Court Stacked in Integration Cases."

The reactions of the remaining Fifth Circuit judges to Judge
Cameron's charges concerning The Four were no less stormy than
those of Southern politicians. One newspaper openly speculated that
"[t]he revolt of Judge Cameron, couched as it is in caustic terms,
has ruffled the usually placid reserve of his colleagues."*

While the judges who were then on the Court steadfastly refuse to this day to discuss their internal communications at the time
of Judge Cameron's charges, reliable sources who desire to remain anonymous confirm that the following events and communications
did occur. Judge Warren L. Jones of Jacksonville, Florida, a careful precedent-following judge, was reportedly aghast. He called the
Fifth Circuit's new Clerk of Court, Edward Wadsworth, and demanded all of the Court's internal memoranda on assignment of
judges, to determine whether Judge Cameron's charges were true.
Mr. Wadsworth said he could not turn any files over to Judge Jones
without the approval of Chief Judge Tuttle. Judge Jones exploded.
Mr. Wadsworth tried to explain that Chief Judge Tuttle was on vacation in Colorado and could not be reached, but that he, Wadsworth,
would turn the files over to Judge Jones if former Chief Judge Rives
would give his approval. Judge Rives had been Chief Judge prior
to Tuttle and had resigned his Chief Judgeship, after only a year,
in favor of Tuttle because of his [Rives'] dislike for administrative
duties.** Judge Jones called Judge Rives to demand the files.
Judge Rives instantly replied that, of course, Judge Jones, as a
member of the Court, could see any file he wanted. Judge Rives
then called the clerk to check the files; within two hours, Judge
Rives called Judge Jones back. Shaken, he told Judge Jones he
could not authorize the clerk to send the files because they were
worse than he had imagined. Judge Jones had had enough. He
threatened to fly to Washington, D.C., for a conference with Senator Eastland, the Chairman of the Senate Judiciary Committee, to
inform the Senator that a judge on the Court of Appeals for the
Fifth Circuit was not being allowed to see the Court's own files.
The files were then produced for Judge Jones' inspection and Judge
Rives called Chief Judge Tuttle, who was stranded in Denver with
car trouble, to come home immediately.

Meanwhile, sources close to the Court attempted to rebut
Judge Cameron's charges. Judge Rives told the Houston Chronicle

---

*Houston Chronicle, Aug. 11, 1963, at 6; reprinted by permission.
**Judge Jones was next in line of seniority in the Fifth Circuit after
Judge Rives and Chief Judge Tuttle. Perhaps Mr. Wadsworth de-
ferred to Judge Rives, despite Judge Jones' seniority, because he
had been Judge Rives' law clerk for four years prior to becoming
Clerk of Court.

that "no such thing as Judge Cameron has charged has occurred...."*
The Chronicle further reported:

Rives Answers

Aiming a sharp barb in the general direction of Cameron and the federal judiciary of Mississippi, Rives said,
'Chief Judge Tuttle has the responsibility to appoint judges
who will follow the law honestly and fairly and without
prejudice.'
... But a source close to the court felt angry enough
to rush to Tuttle's defense.

Miffed by Cameron

He was especially miffed at Cameron's suggestion:
'If this court is to retain the stature it owned on March
16, 1959, when Judge Hutcheson laid down the duties of
chief judge, it must, in my opinion, forsake the special
procedures which have been discussed....'
'Judge Hutcheson ruled this court with an iron hand,'
said the source. 'It has always been the practice of the
chief judge to appoint the panels and the three-judge
courts as he saw fit. That's the way it was done before
Judge Hutcheson, and that's the way it's done on every
circuit court in the United States.'
... As for Cameron's demand that more southern district judges be appointed to three-judge courts, a source
close to the court said, 'Cameron would not complain
about Judge Tuttle's procedures if the decisions were not
contrary to his views.
'Cameron's views are well known, and so are the
views of the district judges of Mississippi. Cameron is
a mass of predilections.
'The chief judge wants honest judges to decide according to law. Some of the cases in which Judge Cameron
has dissented were cut and dried. There was no longer
any open question.'

A hasty judicial conference was called in Houston for all
members of the Court. All attended but Judge Cameron, who remained in Mississippi because of a heart condition. While the members of the Court refused to state the purpose of the conference,
the press openly guessed that it was called to consider Judge Cameron's charges. Despite the speculation, everyone connected with
the Court remained tight-lipped. When asked the reason why the
conference was convened, Clerk of Court Edward Wadsworth told
one reporter, 'I have no comment and that's off the record.' Because all who attended that fateful conference are understandably
close-mouthed, what occurred is difficult to determine. However,

---

*Houston Chronicle, supra.

that conference did mark a significant turnabout point for the Court. In the face of Judge Cameron's stinging public indictment of its Chief Judge, the Fifth Circuit, still bitterly split over the then unresolved Barnett contempt problem, had to make an effort to pull itself together. It was a court under siege, externally and internally.

Reliable reports indicate that the Houston judicial conference was one no judge would forget. Reports persist that one judge threw his file on the floor and accused others of disregarding their judicial duties. Among other things, the judges discovered that Judge John R. Brown, the assignment judge, had sent a cryptic note to the clerk of court ordering that Judges Bell and Gewin not be assigned to civil rights cases. Upon learning of the note, Judge Bell complained vigorously that he had thought that he was a full member of the Court and now had discovered that he was only a judge under guardianship.

Despite the tension and acrimony of the meeting, the Court did close ranks and did emerge united, at least publicly. Quiet and generally successful efforts were taken to mend friendships on the Court and to rebuild a sense of institutional identity so necessary for a great appellate Court. At least one accommodation was made to Judge Cameron: reliable sources indicate that an informal agreement was reached that Judge Cameron would be placed on three-judge district courts for Mississippi in the future.*

In any event, whatever private settlements were reached, after two days behind closed doors to consider what was described euphemistically as "routine business," the following public statement was released by Chief Judge Tuttle:

> The problems alleged to exist in this court have been considered by the court. The court believes that in no given case has there been a conscious assignment for the purpose of accomplishing a desired result.
> Action has been taken to avoid any appearance of inconsistency in the assignment of judges or the arrangement of the docket.

---

*One of the interesting side results of the alleged agreement to place Judge Cameron on three-judge district court cases in Mississippi occurred in the volatile voting rights area. Judge Wisdom was replaced on the United States v. Mississippi case by Judge Cameron, leaving a panel composed of Judges Cameron, Brown and Cox. Judges Cameron and Cox, true to form, despite overwhelming statistical evidence of discrimination against blacks, agreed to dismiss the Justice Department's case. They issued their order without even informing Judge Brown, the other member of the panel, so that he could dissent. Judge Brown nevertheless appended a mammoth dissent which was later adopted by the Supreme Court when it reversed the Cameron-Cox decision. See discussion, Part II, Chapter 7, on voting rights cases.

Chief Judge Tuttle's public statement, quoted from the Houston Chronicle, was the first ever released in the history of the Fifth Circuit concerning its internal affairs. There is no indication that all of the judges subscribed to the statement, but none made public any contrary viewpoint.

* * *

But what of the substance of Judge Cameron's court-packing charges? Were they true? The figures contained in his study on judge assignment procedures found in Armstrong v. Board of Education appear persuasive and do statistically support Judge Cameron's allegations. Why particular judge assignments to civil rights cases were made from June, 1961 to June, 1963 in the Fifth Circuit is exceedingly difficult to reconstruct at the time of this writing. After an extensive effort to discover what actually did happen, it is suggested that there are at least three plausible theories worthy of consideration. Any one of the three theories, or any combination of them, might be correct; of course, all of the theories might be wrong. Because all judges involved refuse to break the confidence of their judicial council chambers, the following theories are necessarily based on second-hand sources. Nevertheless, these sources are believed to be reliable and, because of the pivotal nature of that judicial conference in Houston, to the history of the Fifth Circuit as a judicial institution, the theories are presented below in the frank recognition that they must be treated as conjectural.

The first theory is that Judge Cameron's charges, with some modifications, were substantially correct. Initially, it must be noted that Judge John R. Brown of Houston, Texas, not Chief Judge Tuttle as Judge Cameron had charged, was responsible for the assignments of judges to panels. When Judge Hutcheson was Chief Judge, Judge Brown had been appointed assignment judge and given the duty of supervising the Clerk of Court in the clerk's administration of judge assignment to panels. Judge Brown, an energetic and efficient administrator, carried out his duties with vigor and assumed new duties involving the calendaring of cases. Because he liked his task and was good at it, both Judges Rives and Tuttle, when each in turn became Chief Judge, continued to use Judge Brown as assignment judge. Judge Brown, one of "The Four" liberal judges attacked by Judge Cameron, may have been anxious to speed up civil rights cases and to enforce Supreme Court mandates. Therefore, in assigning judges and calendaring cases he may have selected judges who he knew would carry out their duties without undue delay and reach results that he, Judge Brown, thought were required by Supreme Court precedent. While this theory retains currency among some knowledgeable observers of the Fifth Circuit, there is no evidence to support it and the writers believe that it is highly unlikely that Judge Brown consciously attempted to gerrymander panels to achieve pro-civil rights results in the blatant manner charged.

A second theory is espoused by at least one generally reliable source. Protracted delays in civil rights litigation had reached crisis proportions during the time period referred to by Judge Cameron's charges. In order to move its docket and to promptly protect constitutional rights, certain Fifth Circuit judges (The Four) had pioneered in various expediting procedures, such as the extensive use of injunctions pending appeal. Civil rights plaintiffs therefore consciously timed the filing of their suits and their appeals so that they could be considered by panels already assigned or convened, which were most likely to be sympathetic to the issuance of such speed-up orders (the majority of which were made up of The Four). This theory is not widely accepted and most observers believe that most civil rights complainants were not that sophisticated in calendaring techniques. Even if they were that highly skilled, this theory could account for only a few such cases.

The third theory is perhaps the most plausible. Judge Brown, as assignment judge, did not deliberately assign pro-civil rights judges to civil rights cases to achieve results which he thought were desirable. Instead, he was faced during the time period selected for study by Judge Cameron with some severe and unusual judicial personnel problems that had to be accommodated. To accommodate those problems, he made assignments by short written or oral commands to the clerk, rather than issue lengthy memoranda to show his reasoning process, which would have exacerbated some of his personnel difficulties. Following are examples of the personnel problems which faced Judge Brown. Judge Cameron himself had told Judge Brown that he preferred not to sit with Chief Judge Tuttle because of their strong disagreements on civil rights matters. On the other hand, other members of the Court were unhappy with Judge Cameron's methods of deciding cases and indicated to Judge Brown that they would prefer not to be assigned to panels with Judge Cameron. For instance, because of his health, Judge Cameron insisted on a nap after hearing cases in the morning. He therefore refused to meet the other judges for their conferences on cases until late afternoon. This was of considerable annoyance and inconvenience to some judges. While seemingly minor, this convenience factor alone caused one judge--probably Judge Jones--to indicate his desire not to be assigned to panels with Judge Cameron. Former Chief Judge Hutcheson was also ill during almost all of the two-year period covered by the Cameron charges and was assigned to very few cases. Furthermore, the two new judges, Gewin and Bell, had only interim appointments from October 5, 1961 to February 9, 1962, while they were awaiting Senate confirmation. Their interim appointments occurred in the middle of Judge Cameron's study, at a time when several civil rights panels were being composed. At the express request of a member of the court and to protect Judges Gewin and Bell from controversial civil rights decisions during this interim period, Judge Brown simply did not assign them to civil rights matters because such assignments might have hurt their chances with the Senate Judiciary Committee chaired by Senator Eastland of Mississippi. The combination of such judicial personnel problems left Judge Brown with four of the eight judges who at no time posed problems when assigned to the same panel: Chief Judge Tuttle and Judges Rives, Brown and Wisdom.

Additionally, at the time Judge Cameron made his charges, there was a vigorous rebuttal of the accuracy of the figures presented in the survey as contained in the Cameron dissent in the Birmingham case. The Houston Chronicle reported at that time:

> The 25 cases over the two-year period Judge Cameron surveyed represent only part of the civil rights cases the court has heard, said clerk Edward Wadsworth.
> The administrative offices of the United States courts in Washington said the Fifth Circuit Court handled 57 such cases in the two years studied by Cameron.
> There are no records available that show which judges sat in those cases.
> Cameron's complaints, in a dissent to an opinion which ordered the schools of Mobile and Birmingham to submit desegregation plans, said that 'The Four sat 55 times; the other five sat 12 times.'

Five Really One

> A study of the 25 cases cited by Cameron shows that five of them--the University of Mississippi-James Meredith controversy--were really one case.
> Two more of the 25, voter registration cases in Mississippi, were actually the same, continuing case.
> Cameron did not mention two appointments of a visiting judge from another circuit [sic].

Even so discounted, unless either or both of the second and third theories considered above are generally accurate, the number of times The Four comprised the majority on panels considering civil rights cases from 1960 to 1963 seems unusually high. Nevertheless, no knowledgeable person, other than Judge Cameron, has indicated that Chief Judge Tuttle had anything at all to do with judge assignments: Despite his innocence, Chief Judge Tuttle took the brunt of the criticism during the period after the Cameron charges were leveled. Chief Judge Tuttle did take steps after the judicial conference to assert more control over the administration of the Court.

After Cameron's intemperate dissents, Chief Judge Tuttle felt he could no longer ignore him. Chief Judge Tuttle was convinced that Judge Cameron had, by his written comments, disqualified himself from sitting on civil rights cases. Therefore, while discussion of Judge Cameron's charges against his court were still buzzing in the corridors of federal courtrooms around the Fifth Circuit, Chief Judge Tuttle deliberately did not assign Judge Cameron, then the only circuit judge from Mississippi, to the next Mississippi civil rights case. That case involved desegregation of the public facilities at the new Jackson airport. In Chief Judge Tuttle's words, Judge Cameron was "fit to be tied" and "ready to start something all over again."*

---

*While he refused to assign Judge Cameron to the Jackson airport

After Judge Cameron's charges were refuted publicly by Chief
Judge Tuttle's press release following the Houston judicial conference,
whatever influence Judge Cameron had left on the Court was destroyed.   Judge Walter P. Gewin, a new judge on the Court at the
time of the Meredith crisis, remembers a conversation he had with
Judge Cameron at that time.   Judge Cameron had become fond of
Judge Gewin and proceeded to give him some advice.   Judge Cameron candidly told Judge Gewin that he [Cameron] had dissented so
much over the years that he had become almost ineffective.   He advised Judge Gewin to dissent only where necessary, to try to work
within the confines of the Court and not to attack the Court from the
outside as he had done.

Judge Cameron died less than a year after making his court-
packing charges.*   Oddly enough, by surfacing his charges and forc-

[cont.]   case, Chief Judge Tuttle did bend over backward to be fair
to Mississippi.   He assigned himself and then took the unusual step
'of assigning two Mississippi federal district judges, Mize and Clayton, to sit with him.   Chief Judge Tuttle immediately learned his
lesson about assigning two Mississippi district judges, who would
therefore make up a majority on the panel, to the same case.   It
was a clear case: an injunction should have been issued to prohibit
the segregation of the airport facilities.   There was no real question
of law; the case had been pending for months.   Chief Judge Tuttle
presided and Judges Mize and Clayton sat on either side of him.
Appearing alone for the petitioners, and prepared, was Constance
Baker Motley.   Five lawyers were present to represent the State of
Mississippi.   One of the Mississippi attorneys stood to say that the
attorney-in-chief was ill and to request another thirty days' postponement.   The case had been set in early June; Chief Judge Tuttle, immediately after the hearing, was to be on his way to California to
see his 88-year-old, critically ill father whom he felt he would never see alive again.   Chief Judge Tuttle was anxious to proceed since
the case was merely an argument on the law which he felt could be
completed in oral argument that day.   He indicated from the bench
that since Mississippi had five lawyers there, and since the case
was not a question of fact but only an argument on the law, one of
the five surely should be able to respond to Mrs. Motley's arguments.
The two district judges sitting with Chief Judge Tuttle then whispered
to him that they wanted a recess.   Both district judges told Judge
Tuttle during the recess that they would be inclined to grant the requested stay.   Chief Judge Tuttle described to them the situation with
his father and said that he wanted to hear the case then.   The two
district judges overruled him and the court reconvened.   For the
first time in his judicial career, Chief Judge Tuttle, after announcing
from the bench that his two colleagues had agreed on the postponement for 30 days, formally dissented from a 30-day postponement.
Later, Judge Rives sat on that same case with the same two district
judges and, over Judge Rives' dissent, they refused to issue injunctions
against the Jackson Airport Authority.   It took two years for the United
States Supreme Court to overrule that opinion.
*Judge Gewin attended the funeral and remembers several black
people seated on the front row in genuine grief.

ing the other members of the court to grapple with their own divisions, Judge Cameron may have provided the catalyst which caused a fractured Court to seek internal cohesiveness.

The Senator Who Threatened the Court

After the trauma of James Meredith and the embarrassment of Judge Cameron's public indictment of his own court, seemingly the years 1962 and 1963 had brought enough grief to the weary Fifth Circuit. Yet, another crisis, also spawned from the agonies of the Meredith case, was to engulf the Court. Mississippi Senator James O. Eastland seethed over the disgrace brought upon his state by the judicial fiats of the Fifth Circuit. As chairman of the powerful Senate Judiciary Committee and wily broker with Presidents over all judicial matters, Senator Eastland's reaction was to lead to further turmoil within the Court. A major prophet of segregation, Senator Eastland was never one to preach that revenge is not sweet.

The appellate workload of the Fifth Circuit in 1972 and 1973 was already heavy and growing more and more burdensome with the passage of time. Several judges on the Court thought that, while some relief was necessary, to merely request more new circuit judgeships--with the Court already at a complement of nine--would create an unwieldy tribunal. Therefore, the Fifth Circuit Judicial Council adopted a resolution urging that additional judge power was needed and, while it was hoped that this would be accomplished without dividing the Circuit, that if a division of the Circuit was the only method by which Congress would correct the deficiency then, in all events, the additional judge power should be provided. Chief Judge Tuttle presented this Fifth Circuit Judicial Council resolution to the United States Judicial Conference where the matter was held in abeyance until the need became so great that the Conference recommended the appointment of four additional judges temporarily.

Publicly expressing concern over the growing size of the Fifth Circuit, Senator Eastland seized on the United States Judicial Conference's recommendation as an opportunity to introduce as proposed legislation what was to become known to some as "The Eastland Plan." He proposed that the Fifth Circuit, the circuit with the most judges and covering the largest geographical area, be split into two new circuits. Specifically, his plan separated Texas and Louisiana into a new circuit, leaving together Mississippi, Alabama, Georgia and Florida as the remainder of the Fifth Circuit. Of course, there were (with the nine authorized judgeships) legitimate questions about the unwieldy size of the Court.* But everyone down home in Mississippi knew that Senator Eastland was not interested in improv-

---

*Today, as is discussed in the concluding chapter of Part III, those same concerns are much more pronounced with the Court at 15 active judges.

ing judicial administration by proposing that Texas and Louisiana be separated from the rest of the Circuit. The Eastland Plan was an attempt to split up "The Four." John R. Brown of Texas and John Minor Wisdom of Louisiana would go with the new circuit; Richard Rives of Alabama and Elbert Tuttle of Georgia would be left with the old circuit, to be outvoted by more conservative colleagues. The control of civil rights decisions by the Court's liberal block would be broken. Apparently, Senator Eastland could think of no greater gift to Mississippi.

Proposed and pushed at the very time the Court was agonizing over the Barnett contempt cases and the Cameron court-packing charges, the Eastland Plan caused new tensions on a Court already badly wounded from internal strife. Several judicial conference discussions were held concerning Senator Eastland's proposal. Five of the judges on the Circuit were willing to support the proposed split in order to obtain some relief from rapidly increasing caseload. Two judges, Richard T. Rives and John Minor Wisdom, fought the proposal tenaciously. Reportedly, at one conference tempers flared to such a point that Judges Rives and Wisdom left by a door different from that used by the rest of the members of the Court, to indicate their profound disagreement with their brethren. Judge Rives bluntly told those present at one conference that he and Judge Wisdom would do everything in their power to prevent a split of the Circuit. He charged that an attempt was clearly being made to destroy the effectiveness of civil rights enforcement in the Deep South. After the conference, Judge Rives contacted Mr. Justice Black, supervising Supreme Court Justice for the Circuit and his close personal friend, and others to enlist aid in blocking Eastland. Judge Wisdom contacted leaders of the American Bar Association to see what they could do to help. District Judge Frank Johnson also made contacts for Judge Rives. A reliable authority reports that at one point Judge Rives personally called a reporter for the Montgomery Advertiser. He told the story of the events at the recent judicial conferences and said the attempt to split the Circuit was for the sole purpose of watering-down civil rights enforcement. That reporter investigated and reported that, although Judge Gewin like Judge Rives was from Alabama, Judge Gewin was one of the supporters of the proposed split and would be Chief Judge in the new circuit. An exposé was printed. Others on the Court reacted angrily. Judge Jones was exceedingly upset; he called Judge Rives and charged that somebody had been talking out of school. Rives responded that he was the one that had talked out of school and that he was going to continue to do everything he could to stop Senator Eastland.

Judge Wisdom was opposed to the Eastland Plan not only because of the effect he feared it would have on race cases, but also because of a broader ground. He took the position that the proper function of the Court of Appeals is to serve as a buffer to adjust the strains between the national government and the state governments and between the state or federal governments and individual citizens. He was convinced that this purpose could be better accomplished with judges drawn from six states. They were more likely to have different backgrounds and different social, educational and political opinions. These differences would widen the viewpoint of the Court, counteracting the possible unconscious representation by a judge of his state's special interests. However, a circuit comprised of only judges from Texas and Louisiana would negate this effect. For example, because both Texas and Louisiana each have a community property system and share a common interest in oil and gas, judges from these states might be more likely to make decisions beneficial to such common state interests and to exclude opposing national and individual concerns. Such special representation could only increase the conflict between these opposing interests, rather than mitigating the strains. Therefore, Judge Wisdom felt that civil rights would not be the only interest affected by a division of the Court.

The Wisdom-Rives efforts to defeat the Eastland Plan were temporarily effective; in the words of one of the members of the Court, Judge Wisdom's campaign "almost drove the [United States] Judicial Conference to its knees." The internal feud over the Eastland Plan seems to have culminated at that same judicial conference in Houston that considered Judge Cameron's court-packing charges. Rumors had circulated to all of the judges that Senator Eastland, incensed by Judge Cameron's charges, was not content with attacking the Circuit through the Eastland Plan. He had reportedly sent an investigator to the Circuit who was either paid by or was working in cooperation with his hand-picked Judiciary Committee staff. That investigator was to look carefully into not only the Cameron charges, but also the personal lives of the judges to see if evidence to support impeachment proceedings could be uncovered. Those rumors gained substance when the Houston Chronicle, in the same headline story that reported the Cameron charges, indicated that Senator Eastland had ordered a "staff study" of the Fifth Circuit under the auspices of the Senate Judiciary Committee.

Reliable sources indicate that at one point in that historic secret conference in Houston, Judge Cameron, who was at home ill in Mississippi, was called by telephone. A proposition was reportedly put to Judge Cameron by Judge Gewin, speaking for the other judges, that if civil rights cases were to assume a normal rotation among all judges, would he, Cameron, call Senator Eastland and ask him to call off his investigators? Judge Cameron reportedly agreed and did call the Senator; in any event the investigation was called off. While some still blame Judge Cameron for stimulating Senator Eastland's investigation of the Fifth Circuit, sources close to Judge Cameron insist that, when he discovered Senator Eastland had investigators in the Circuit to look into the lives of the other judges and the internal workings of his court, Judge Cameron was aghast. Those same sources argue that Judge Cameron detested political interference with the courts and was more than willing to call Senator Eastland to ask that he desist.

While not dead, the Eastland Plan has not been adopted at the time of this writing.

*   *   *

The Fifth Circuit came of age as it passed through the crucible of James Meredith's Ole Miss enrollment, Ross Barnett's contempt, Judge Cameron's charges and Senator Eastland's attacks.
The Court emerged from the historic judicial conference in Houston
a wounded but, at least publicly, a united body. Before James
Meredith, the lonely district judge--the Skelly Wright or Herbert
Christenberry--had to face the daily bombardment of hate, criticism
and harassment from state governmental officials, legislators, citizens and local media. For the most part, no one had heard of Tuttle, Wisdom, Brown or Rives. Thus they could decide cases in the
relative security of their appellate sanctuary. The Meredith case was
the Fifth Circuit's baptism by fire. A scared but stronger Court
emerged. It was no longer a collection of individual judges from a
vast six-state region who met together as a body only on occasion.
After Meredith, the Fifth Circuit evolved into a unified, determined,
and cohesive institution with greater respect and friendship between
the judges. Furthermore, the judges on the Court were no longer
burdened with naive notions about the difficulty of the task ahead.
That task would involve not only the enforcement of the Brown mandate to desegregate the public schools of the Deep South; it would
also involve the enforcement of that most basic of constitutional
rights--the right to vote--and the right to be tried by an impartial
jury.

NOTES AND PRIMARY AUTHORITY

The primary authority for the material contained in this chapter was:

"The Man In High Office Who Defied The Nation."

1. United States v. Barnett, 346 F.2d 99, 105, 106, 107,
109 (5th Cir. 1965) (emphasis is the Court's own).
The primary sources are the following cases: United States
v. Barnett, 346 F.2d 99 (5th Cir. 1965); United States v. Faneca,
332 F.2d 872 (5th Cir. 1964); United States v. Barnett, 330 F.2d
369 (5th Cir. 1963); and, Meredith v. Fair, 328 F.2d 586 (5th Cir.
1962).
The following sources are of particular help: Norton v.
McShane, 332 F.2d 855 (5th Cir. 1964); United States v. Faneca,
332 F.2d 872 (5th Cir. 1964); interview with Judge Richard T.
Rives, United States Court of Appeals for the Fifth Circuit, in his
offices in Montgomery, Ala. (June 29, 1972); and, interview with
Judge Walter P. Gewin, United States Court of Appeals for the Fifth
Circuit, in San Francisco, Cal. (Aug. 10, 1972).

The Judge Who Indicted His Court

2. Houston Chronicle, Aug. 4, 1963, at 6; Reprinted by
permission.

3. Houston Chronicle, Aug. 2, 1963, at 1; Reprinted by permission.

The primary sources are the following cases: Armstrong v. Board of Educ., 323 F.2d 333 (5th Cir. 1963); Davis v. Board of School Comms'rs, 322 F.2d 356 (5th Cir. 1963); Denton v. City of Carrollton, 235 F.2d 481, 494 (5th Cir. 1956) (Cameron, J., dissenting); and, Smith v. United States, 234 F.2d 385, 397 (5th Cir. 1956) (Cameron, J., dissenting); and contemporary news accounts in the Houston Chronicle.

The Senator Who Threatened The Court.

A more complete manuscript, with detailed documentation of all sources, is available as indicated in the Preface, supra.

Chapter 7

IN QUEST OF THE VOTE

The Legacy of Reconstruction

> He says he opposed the Fifteenth Amendment and
> thinks it was a mistake, that it had done the Ne-
> gro no good, and had been a hindrance to the
> South, and by no means a political advantage to
> the North.
>> --President Ulysses S. Grant quoted by his
>> secretary, Hamilton Fish, in his Diary en-
>> try of January 17, 1877.

Perhaps in no chapter of America's on-going revolution in
race relations has change been so effectively entrenched for the future as in the struggle for the right to vote. In retrospect, several judges of the Court of Appeals candidly express misgivings that
despite all their best efforts to implement and enforce school desegregation, that goal has remained ineluctable. In contrast, these
judges cite with pride the durable achievement of equal access to
the ballot.

During the period from 1954 to 1965, the United States Supreme Court wrote only two voting rights opinions. As a result,
the brunt of protecting the Negro franchise was shouldered by the
courts of the Fifth Circuit and finally by Congress in the Voting
Rights Act of 1965. In states of the Deep South, where black citizens represented a substantial percentage of the state's total population, black voters were a massive source of potential political power
which, if united by common cause, could substantially alter existing
power structures from the most remote sheriff's post to the governor's office.

In the area of voting rights, as with school desegregation
and jury selection, the Fifth Circuit Court of Appeals was troubled
by disunity in the ranks of its lower district court judges. One of
the more outspoken trial judges, J. Robert Elliott of the Middle
District of Georgia, observed some eighteen months after his appointment to the federal bench: "I don't want these pinks, radicals
and black voters to outvote those who are trying to preserve our
segregation laws and other traditions."

*   *   *

The bitter roots of racial controversy over suffrage lie deep in Reconstruction. Understanding the emotional fervor of white resistance to Negro suffrage requires appreciation of a major political power struggle that evolved in the century after the Civil War. Ironically, enfranchisement of Negroes had not been one of the war aims of the North, nor was the idea warmly received by even the most ardent abolitionists. William Lloyd Garrison wrote in 1864:

> When was it ever known that liberation from bondage was accompanied by a recognition of political equality? ... Nor, if the freed blacks were admitted to the polls by Presidential fiat, do I see any permanent advantage likely to be secured by it; for, submitted to as a necessity at the outset, as soon as the state was organized and left to manage its own affairs, the white population, with their superior intelligence, wealth, and power, would unquestionably alter the franchise in accordance with their prejudices, and exclude those thus summarily brought to the polls.

Certainly Garrison's prediction of white reaction ultimately proved correct. During the five years immediately after the cessation of hostilities, seven Northern states defeated legislative proposals which would have extended to Negroes the right to vote.

In contrast, the recognition of Negro suffrage in the South was a matter of political expediency, essential to the success of the plans of the Radical Republicans for Reconstruction. President Andrew Johnson urged that the Southern delegation in the House of Representatives be increased by thirteen members, a proposal reflecting the policy that all the freedmen would be counted in the appointment. If the Negroes were not enfranchised, Democrats would very likely fill these new seats, along with those seats they already held representing the Southern states. Consequently, it became not only politically expedient but a matter of political survival for the Republicans to offset this potential disaster to their party by tapping the Negro vote. The leader of the Radical Republicans, Thaddeus Stevens, stated, "If impartial [Negro] suffrage is excluded in the rebel States then every one of them is sure to send a solid rebel representation to Congress, and cast a solid rebel electoral vote. They, with their kindred Copperheads of the North, would always elect the President and control Congress."

In 1867 and 1868, pursuant to this Republican political strategy, the military government in the South undertook the task of creating a new electorate. Approximately 703,000 Negroes and 627,000 whites were registered. At the same time, a great number of white voters were disenfranchised. In Alabama, for example, there were 113,871 white and 92,404 Negro males of voting age in 1860. After the military government conducted the registration, 104,518 Negroes and 61,295 whites were registered. The voting balance throughout the South was altered as Negroes gained a numerical superiority in all the Reconstructed states.

In 1870, the fifteenth amendment was ratified, which placed the right to vote among those most fundamental rights protected by the federal Constitution: "The right of citizens of the United States to vote shall not be denied or abridged by the United States or by any State on account of race, color, or previous condition of servitude." Furthermore, the fifteenth amendment empowered Congress to enforce the right of universal suffrage by appropriate legislation.

Negro suffrage had been imposed by Republicans. Southern whites, allied with the Democratic Party in the South, played no part in the origin of that right and, accordingly, felt no commitment toward its enforcement. Indeed Negro suffrage was viewed as a loathed symbol of the war victor's spoils in the South; its origins in Reconstruction made it a prime target for revision once the political climate again shifted. As Reconstruction ended and Southern whites regained political control of their states, their efforts were directed toward weakening the Negroe's influence. The most effective method was to remove the Negro as a political force, a feat that could only be accomplished by somehow disenfranchising him.

Prior to 1890, no Southern state had enacted requirements concerning literacy, knowledge of constitutional provisions, obligations of citizenship, or even good moral character as a prerequisite of suffrage. However, during the last decade of the 19th century, seven Southern states promulgated new voting qualifications, the clear intent of which was to disqualify as many Negro voters as possible. Because the fifteenth amendment forbade the state from explicitly denying Negro suffrage, Southern legislators sought to skirt the constitutional prohibition as closely as possible by "legal, constitutional means." Called to consider possible means of disenfranchisement, the president of the 1898 Louisiana Convention remarked, somewhat apologetically:

> We have not been free; we have not drafted the exact Constitution we should like to have drafted; otherwise we should have inscribed in it, if I know the popular sentiment of the State, Universal White Manhood Suffrage, and the exclusion from the suffrage of every man with a trace of African blood in his veins.... What care I whether it be more or less ridiculous or not? Doesn't it meet the case? Doesn't it let the white man vote, and doesn't it stop the negro from voting, and isn't that what we came here for?

Two basic statutory methods of depressing the number of Negro electors were devised: the "understanding clause" and the "grandfather clause." As an example of the first, Mississippi amended its constitution in 1890 to require every current and potential voter to demonstrate an understanding of a section of the state constitution by explaining its meaning to the satisfaction of a voter registrar. This "understanding clause" hurdle was imposed in addition to disqualification for nonpayment of a poll tax and for a criminal record. Such "understanding clauses" appeared to be

racially neutral: they seemed on their face to bear a rational relationship to the desire of a state to promote the intelligent use of the
ballot. However, as in Louisiana, the debates of the Mississippi
convention demonstrate that the sole purpose of this requirement
was to disenfranchise as many Negroes as possible. These clauses
were enormously successful. In 1890, sixty-nine per cent or more
of the adult Negro population in the seven Southern states which
adopted such tests were illiterate.

As years went by, the rigor of enforcement of such "understanding clauses" increased as the numbers of educated Negroes increased. It became common for registrars to insist that black voting applicants interpret the most ambiguous provisions of the state
constitution. By the mid-sixties, one observer remarked that the
Alabama "understanding" requirement had become so difficult that
"Earl Warren could not pass it!"

The "grandfather clause" stratagem was less subtle but equally effective in disenfranchising Negroes, until its use was finally
outlawed. The Louisiana constitutional convention of 1898 considered
implementing the "understanding clause" concept but after much debate rejected the idea because it was "based on fraud" and added its
own invention, the "grandfather clause." Thereafter, all citizens
seeking voting registration had to meet certain property and literacy
qualifications, except those citizens who were eligible to vote as of
January 1, 1867, or whose ancestors were then entitled to vote.
Since the touchstone date was prior to the ratification of the fifteenth amendment, only Negroes would be required to meet the new
standards.

The literacy test required an applicant to demonstrate his
ability to read and write by filling out an application form without
assistance. Although less stringent than "understanding clause" requirements, the literacy device, coupled with mandatory reregistration of all voters, achieved a ninety-six per cent disenfranchisement of Negro voters in Louisiana. Within seven years after the
addition of the fifteenth amendment, white voters had regained undisputed control of the ballot in Louisiana.

The "grandfather clause" automatic exemption for white voters enjoyed a brief life. In 1915, it was judicially condemned by
the United States Supreme Court as a ploy to evade the command
of the fifteenth amendment. But the employment of other literacy
demonstrations and "understanding clause" requirements continued
throughout the next sixty years, effectively removing otherwise
eligible black voters from the electorate. The status of black voting strength in selected Southern states in 1950, the year of the
last national census prior to the Brown decisions, was as follows:

State	Potential Black Voters	Registered Black Voters	% of Total
Alabama	516,245	53,336	10.3%
Georgia	633,697	163,389	25.6%

Louisiana	510,090	161,410	31.6%
Mississippi	497,354	19,367	3.9%

Judicial Intervention and Congressional Response

> The [Fifteenth] Amendment nullifies sophisticated
> as well as simple-minded modes of discrimination.
> It hits onerous procedural requirements which ef-
> fectively handicap exercise of the franchise by the
> colored race although the abstract right to vote
> may remain unrestricted to race.
> --Mr. Justice Frankfurter in Lane v. Wilson,
> 307 U.S. 268, 275 (1938)

Brown v. Board of Education obviously had no direct bearing upon black voting rights, but it served as a catalyst in areas peripheral to public school segregation. The case increased awareness among both blacks and whites of the gains possible in other important areas, such as voting. Local branches of the NAACP soon concentrated efforts to register black constituents. Special organizations, such as the Guiding Voice in Ouachita Parish, Louisiana, were formed to encourage and coordinate activity in specific communities. To combat this new momentum within the black populace, intimidation and violence increased; and less dramatically, voting eligibility standards became more stringent. The "understanding clause" was honed to a lethal effectiveness; inquiry into the "good character" of the potential black voter was authorized; and "slow-downs" or "shut-downs" of registration decreased the accessibility of county registrars to blacks persistent enough to attempt the tests. Even where some blacks did succeed in registering, purges of the rolls and challenges for technical irregularities occurred frequently enough to check the threatened upsurge in black voting strength.

As in public school desegregation, fear was a factor in dampening registration efforts. In 1955, a voting registration drive was launched in Belzoni, Mississippi, in anticipation of the gubernatorial primary that fall. One of the local organizational leaders, Reverend George W. Lee, was told by local whites to remove his name from the voting list. He refused. On May 7, 1955, while driving, Reverend Lee was shot in the face by a shotgun fired from a passing car, and later died. According to the sheriff, Reverend Lee had apparently suffered a heart attack and was killed in the crash of his automobile. The verdict from the coroner's inquest was that his death was "accidental." Reverend Gus Courts, the president of the local NAACP chapter, was also warned to remove his name from the list. As Reverend Courts later testified, a member of the White Citizens' Council came into his store the morning following Lee's death and told him: "If you don't go down and get your name off the register, you are going to be next." Six months later, Reverend Courts was wounded when a car pulled up in front of his store and an unidentified assailant fired at him through the store window, striking him in the stomach and left arm. Shortly after the attack, Reverend Courts and his wife moved from Belzoni to Chicago.

Intimidation also occurred in Liberty County near Tallahassee, Florida, where eleven blacks requested that their names be removed from the registration list. In February, 1956, these eleven became the first blacks ever to register in that county. Shortly after the registration, crosses were burned at the homes of two of the voters and one house was hit by shotgun fire. One day before the deadline for the May Democratic primary, all eleven withdrew their names. In all, between 1955 and 1958, 530 reported acts of violence were directed at blacks involved in the voting rights movement.

* * *

Increasing white concern over potential black voting power climaxed in the South in the mid-fifties. Not all blacks were discouraged or intimidated by threats of personal harm. For them, states relied on the voter registration system itself to frustrate black registration efforts.

In those states which functioned politically through the Democratic white primaries, blacks were effectively disenfranchised without resort to any purposeful registration requirements. However, in 1944, white primaries, whether conducted by a political party or by the state, were declared unconstitutional by the United States Supreme Court. The second blow, the Brown decision in 1954, was sufficient to reactivate white interest in reviving the "understanding clause" test which had fallen into disuse as unnecessary.

Most of the "understanding clause" tests were administered orally, hindering any inquiry into what standards were used by local registrars for determining qualifications. According to Attorney General Herbert Brownell, registrars' discretion was abused often and blatantly. He reported that the favorite test questions of one Mississippi registrar to black applicants were "What is due process?" and "How many bubbles are there in a bar of soap?" In Dallas County, Alabama, records revealed that of eleven Negroes who were rejected for giving inadequate answers on the interpretation test, two were high school graduates and three others were teachers.

The validity of "understanding clause" tests was finally decimated in 1963 when a court of the Fifth Circuit reviewed Louisiana's voting procedures. A three-judge district court composed of Circuit Judge Wisdom and Louisiana District Judges Christenberry and West was convened to hear charges that registrars in twenty-one parishes (including the stronghold territory of Leander Perez in East Feliciana, Plaquemines and St. Helena parishes) had used the "understanding clause" to deny the vote to thousands of black voters. In addition to arguing that such tests were unconstitutional per se, because they lacked standards to guide a registrar's assessment of the reasonableness of any applicant's answers, the plaintiffs submitted an exhaustive accounting of specific instances of the clause's discriminatory use against black applicants. As only one example of the testimony heard, Judge Wisdom noted that the following part of the Louisiana constitution was given for interpretation to one black applicant:

> Rolling stock operated in this State, the owners of which have no domicile therein, shall be assessed by the Louisiana Tax Commission, and shall be taxed for State purposes only, at a rate not to exceed forty mills on the dollar assessed value.

The rejected interpretation of this highly technical legalese attempted by a black applicant was: "My understanding is that it means if the owner of which does not have residence within the State, his rolling stock shall be taxed not to exceed forty mills on the dollar." In contrast, "FRDUM FOOF SPETCH" was considered an acceptable written interpretation of Louisiana's first amendment guarantee. That illiterate interpretation, however, was submitted by a white applicant. Moreover, such instances were not exceptional. In its public report, the Louisiana Sovereignty Committee boasted about the effectiveness of such tests:

> We would like to call your attention to the fact that, during this four-year period of time, from 1956 to 1960, 81,214 colored people became of voting age, when the registration figures of colored people actually declined 2,377. Going further during this four-year period, we had 114,529 white people who became of voting age, and, during this four-year period of time, the white registration increased 96,620.

Judge Wisdom's opinion in United States v. Louisiana is a painstaking treatise, tracing the legislative history of voting regulation in Louisiana, the use of the "understanding clause" test throughout the South and voting rights precedents in general. In deciding that case, the three-judge panel was confronted with two apparently inconsistent prior rulings of the Fifth Circuit. In 1949, a three-judge district court panel had declared unconstitutional on its face an Alabama requirement eliminating any applicant who could not "understand and explain" any provision of the federal constitution. Yet, thereafter in 1958, in Darby v. Daniel, a different three-judge panel upheld the validity of a Mississippi provision requiring a voter to "understand ... and give a reasonable interpretation" of any section of the state constitution. The challenged Louisiana provision was legally identical to the Mississippi version upheld in Darby.

Displaying restraint, Judge Wisdom did not point out in his opinion that the Darby case had been decided by the most conservative panel conjurable in the Fifth Circuit: Judge Cameron and District Judges Mize and Clayton. Instead, he distinguished the Missis-

sippi case by observing that in that case counsel had made no showing either of legislative purpose to discriminate or of an arbitrary
and discriminatory use of the Mississippi provision against blacks.
Both factors were demonstrated beyond question in the Louisiana
challenge. Over Judge West's dissent that this decision was "just
another example of 'personal decreeing,'" Judge Wisdom, joined by
Judge Christenberry, concluded that the "understanding clause" test
was unconstitutional on its face because of its unlawful purpose, administration, and inescapably discriminatory effect. The injunction
against its future use by the state was granted.

The United States Supreme Court subsequently adopted in full
the Wisdom-Christenberry rationale. In consigning the "understanding clause" to the oblivion reserved for unconstitutional laws, Justice Black observed:

> As the evidence showed, colored people, even some with
> the most advanced education and scholarship, were de-
> clared by voting registrars with less education to have an
> unsatisfactory understanding of the constitution of Louisiana
> or of the United States. This is not a test but a trap,
> sufficient to stop even the most brilliant man on his way
> to the voting booth. The cherished right of people in a
> country like ours to vote cannot be obliterated by the use
> of laws like this, which leave the voting fate of a citizen
> to the passing whim or impulse of an individual registrar.

* * *

Notwithstanding the use of such tests, registrars so predis-
posed could make voting registration as difficult and time-consuming
as possible for black applicants. For example, Tuskegee Institute,
a highly respected Negro college, is located in Macon County and
generates many highly qualified black voters. To insure against any
large scale Negro registration, for one eighteen-month period during
the mid-fifties, the registrars totally shut down application procedures. District Court Judge Frank Johnson later found that the
Macon County registrars had also routinely and deliberately spent
two-thirds of the time allotted to the registration of voters in the
rural precincts of the County where the demand for black registration was low. Somewhat similar techniques were reported by black
applicants in Forrest County, Mississippi. They were required to
see the registrar personally before registering. When the interview
finally occurred, the registrar allegedly would reply that he not
only could not register them then but also refused to state when he
might later register them.

"Slow-downs" of the registration process were more difficult
to detect and consequently were more effective than some other discriminatory techniques. Occasionally, dissension among officials
brought such abuses to light. In Birmingham, the chairman of the
Jefferson County board criticized the two other members for their
deliberate attempt to slow down the registration process. On one

Saturday, only twenty-nine applicants were processed during the four
hours the office was open. Approximately 125 to 150 more applicants were waiting when the office closed. The chairman stated that
the two other members were "playing for the deadline. If they can
delay registration enough they can keep hundreds of persons from
qualifying to vote in next year's election."

Slow-downs discouraged blacks from even attempting to register. For many blacks who were daily or hourly wage-earners, attempting to register became a hard question of economics. As one
black applicant, who had been waiting in line for three hours, expressed the dilemma: "I'm a service station attendant and I had to
take off work to come up here. If they don't get to me today, it's
costing me money."

* * *

For those blacks who overcame intimidation, who waited out
the slow-downs and the shut-downs, who survived the application
forms and who passed the literacy tests to become registered voters,
there was yet another hazard--the prospect that their certification as
qualified voters would be "challenged" and their names purged from
the lists, forcing them to begin the process anew. The membership of White Citizens' Councils throughout the South was enlisted to
challenge the validity of those blacks on the voting lists. The challenge procedure in Louisiana served as the basis for a celebrated
Fifth Circuit case, Reddix v. Lucky. Under Louisiana law, upon
the sworn statements of two registered voters, alleging that a voter
was improperly registered, the registrar would notify the voter that
his status had been challenged. The voter then had ten days to
produce a counter-affidavit, signed by three voters, attesting that
the registration was valid. The challenges could be based on minor
errors in filling out the registration form, such as mistakes in age
computation or responding to a question of the applicant's race with
a "C" instead of writing out the word "colored." The Colfax (Louisiana) Chronicle conducted a random check of 100 white voters, applying the same challenge standards used by the local Citizens'
Council. Only one white would have qualified under these standards.
None of the members of the Citizens' Council, who had participated
in the purge, nor the local school superintendent, who had figured
his age incorrectly, would have passed.

Registrars also made it very difficult for a challenged voter
to defend himself. In Ouachita Parish, the registrar required the
supporting witnesses to be from other precincts, and a witness who
himself had been challenged was unacceptable. In Caldwell Parish,
a challenged voter had to have a member of the Citizens' Council
and a law enforcement officer accompany the supporting witnesses
to attest to their identity. In Bienville Parish, 560 out of a total
of 595 black voters were challenged and all were purged because
the registrar refused to accept affidavits from any of the supporting
witnesses.

The plight of black voters challenged and purged in Ouachita Parish was the subject of a federal suit brought before District Court Judge Ben Dawkins. Under Louisiana law, voting registration lists were closed to new applications thirty days prior to an election. On April 26, four days after the rolls closed for an upcoming municipal election, Dr. John Reddix and some 2,500 other black voters were challenged. These voters had to disprove the challenge within three days after legal notice was published in the local newspaper on May 11. The plaintiff asserted that during this period there were hundreds of blacks who waited in line and reappeared for the purpose of protecting their rights to remain registered, only to discover that the office was incapable of handling the unprecedented amount of work. One of the three days of Dr. Reddix's allotted response time was a Sunday, during which the office was closed. On the fourth day after publication, when he finally got in to defend his registration, he was told that the time had passed. He was further informed that the rolls were closed, thus precluding the possibility of simply reregistering to correct the irregularity.

Both Dr. Reddix and the Ouachita Parish Registrar filed affidavits squarely contesting certain issues of fact, such as whether the challenges were sworn to before Mrs. Lucky as required by law and whether the office was open at the required time. Despite these unresolved issues, Judge Dawkins granted summary judgment for the registrar, finding that "there were no genuine issues of material fact presented by this record." Furthermore, there is some indication that the district court was influenced in withholding equitable relief because Dr. Reddix had sought judicial relief from the maddening cycle of registration, challenge, counterchallenge and reregistration.

The majority of the Fifth Circuit Court of Appeals panel assigned to the appeal of Reddix v. Lucky took a different view of the relative equities in the case. Expressing his view and that of Senior Circuit Judge Borah, Judge Tuttle found that the complaint stated a cause of action warranting relief and a hearing on the contested issues of fact, reversing Judge Dawkins' order of summary judgment. Moreover, Judge Tuttle concluded that under the circumstances, a plaintiff alleging deprivation of the right to vote under the fifteenth amendment could bring an action in federal court without first attempting to reregister, as had been intimated by the district court. Judge Cameron, the third member of the panel, dissented on all points.

However, the Fifth Circuit decision in the Reddix case proved to be a blow to concerted black efforts to fight discriminatory purges, for the panel in that case also held that such disputes were inappropriate for class action. Although Dr. Reddix had urged discrimination against himself and 2,500 other blacks challenged in the Parish, Judge Tuttle concluded that under current federal law, each voter would have to seek individual relief based upon the asserted irregularities of his own particular case.

Judge Tuttle's construction of the federal statutory law which governed the litigation in Reddix v. Lucky was correct. The fifteenth amendment had left the issue of specific implementation of safeguards against discrimination in voting practices to Congress, and Congress had legislated only once, in 1895, and then in broad terms. It had afforded an individual cause of action in either law (for damages) or in equity (for injunctive relief) for the deprivation of rights, including the right to vote. Federal courts, as creatures invested with statutory jurisdiction, can be only as effective as the congressional legislation which describes their grant of authority. Thus, cases like Reddix v. Lucky spurred Congress to recognize that a serious problem existed in implementing and protecting the black citizen's right to vote under existing legislation. Consequently the Civil Rights Acts of 1957, 1960, and 1965 were enacted.

* * *

In addition to creating a six-member Commission on Civil Rights charged with the investigation of allegations of voting discrimination, the Civil Rights Act of 1957 forbade anyone, acting under the color of law or otherwise, to intimidate, threaten or attempt to intimidate any citizen for the purpose of interfering with the right to vote in any federal election. In addition, the Attorney General was empowered to institute an action in the name of the United States, whenever there were reasonable grounds to believe that a person was engaged or about to engage in any act aimed at the deprivation of the right to vote. The Attorney General was entitled to request appropriate relief, including application for a restraining order and temporary or permanent injunctions. The federal district courts were given jurisdiction over any such proceedings brought by the Attorney General.

In actual application, the 1957 Voting Rights Act still fell far short of being an effective weapon in the implementation of black voting rights in the Fifth Circuit. Under the 1957 Act, there was no authority for bringing a state or its agencies into litigation to challenge voting practices. Only local registrars could be sued and then only in their individual capacities. Thus, a suit brought by the Attorney General under the 1957 Act against the Macon County Alabama Board of Registrars had to be dismissed.

Available remedies for demonstrated irregularities in voting procedures remained inadequate. If each voter had to maintain an individual action for relief, many applicants would not be able to launch such litigation. The federal courts would also be swamped with duplicative challenges. An even more fundamental problem with voting procedures in the late fifties concerned the vast discretion vested in local registrars and the difficulties in ferreting out discriminatory practices posed by inadequate record keeping.

The Civil Rights Commission, in its report in 1959, addressed this last mentioned defect in existing law. The Commission suggested that federal voting registrars be appointed, supplanting local registrars, whenever necessary to secure the rights of blacks to vote in federal elections. Taking a somewhat modified position, the Eisenhower Administration favored a voting referee plan whereby referees could be appointed by the federal courts to investigate complaints.

During the debate on the 1960 Voting Rights Act provisions, Southern congressmen opposed any federal intervention in election procedures. Senator Fulbright of Arkansas charged that the proposed voting referee provision was tantamount to reviving Reconstruction: "[W]e find ourselves embroiled in controversy over whether or not this country should again resort to the use of federally controlled referees. The parallel between this legislation and that of the last years of the 1860s is clear as it is disturbing." Senator Talmadge of Georgia was even more vehement in his denunciation of the proposal. The Southern opponents of the legislation resorted to filibuster which successfully weakened the bill. Among other things, the filibuster blocked inclusion of the galling voter registrar plan from the final act. Instead, Title VI of the Voting Rights Act of 1960 provided for federal judicial appointment of voting referees. Referees were required to expeditiously determine and report to a federal judge whether or not a complaining citizen was qualified to vote, lightening somewhat the burden of conducting hearings from the already overburdened federal judiciary.

The most significant of the provisions in the 1960 Voting Rights Act was the requirement that local registrars preserve federal voting records and make such records available for reproduction and inspection. Prior to this mandate, very few registrars had been willing to voluntarily open their records for inspection, much less preserve evidence that might reveal discriminatory practices. The Act required every election official to retain and preserve for twenty-two months all records and papers relating to application, registration, payment of poll tax or any other voting prerequisite. Upon a written demand by the Attorney General, the registrar had to make such records available. If the registrar refused, the federal district court was empowered to compel the production of the requested records. Criminal sanctions completed the ring of protection now erected around the new requirements. A fine of up to $1,000 and a year's imprisonment was provided for anyone who was convicted of stealing, willfully altering or destroying voting records.

The Voting Rights Act of 1960 was a comprehensive effort to assist aggrieved black applicants seeking redress through the federal courts. It closed the loopholes made obvious in the litigation in the fifties. It permitted the joinder of a state as a party to litigation whenever any official of state or local government was alleged to have practiced discrimination. In addition, upon a finding of a "pattern or practice" of discrimination, any person within the discriminated class and within the affected area would be entitled, without filing a separate lawsuit, to apply for an order declaring his eligibility to vote. Finally, it imposed important limitations upon the discretion of local registrars and made their practices and records subject to inspection and analysis.

* * *

The real effectiveness of the 1960 Voting Rights Act would, however, depend upon the ability of the federal courts, particularly the Fifth Circuit, to handle various tactics of resistance which would undoubtedly be interposed by long-powerful Southern registrars. Deep South states had enjoyed white voting domination since Reconstruction and deeply resented the kind of heavy-handed federal intervention promised by the new congressional legislation. Yet the Voting Rights Act was a tool for finding the truth in the welter of black accusations and disenchantment and white denials and justifications. For the first time since the ratification of the fifteenth amendment, the federal courts were empowered to discover the real dimensions of voting discrimination.

Progress at a Snail's Pace: Judge Cox and Mr. Lynd

Lawyers do not ordinarily like to litigate principles of law already decided against them.
In the whole field of civil rights, however, in some of the states of the Fifth Judicial Circuit, the usual rules have not applied. In resisting change, especially in political and sociological areas, time is what counts. Another school year without compliance with the school desegregation cases has often been considered by local boards a prize worth fighting for, and thus worth litigating for. In the area of voting rights, every election held without participation of Negro voters meant one more term in office for the beneficiary of the old system.
--Chief Judge Tuttle, "Equality and the Vote," the Seventh Annual James Madison Lecture delivered March 15, 1966, at the New York University School of Law, printed in 41 New York University Law Review 245, 264 (1966)

Shortly after the 1960 Voting Rights Act went into effect, the federal government became interested in the activities of Theron C. Lynd, the Registrar of Voters of Forrest County, Mississippi. Little personal history about Mr. Lynd can be gleaned from either the federal cases or from contemporary newspaper accounts. He has been vaguely described as "a huge, 400-pound mountain of a man" who was not a lawyer by profession. Registrar Lynd became the sole target in the federal investigation of Forrest County voting procedures because of his policy of personally and exclusively handling all Negro applications. He explained that "The girls [deputy clerks] didn't want to talk to the Negroes, and I wasn't going to force them."

On February 26, 1959, Mr. Lynd assumed the duties of

official registrar of this southern Mississippi county which had an adult voting age population of 30,000, of whom twenty-five per cent were blacks. In contrast to white registration strength of nearly seventy-five per cent, less than three per cent of the black population had been certified eligible to vote in 1960. The government sought to prove that no blacks had been registered in the county during Lynd's term of office nor had any blacks even been permitted to attempt to register prior to its investigation of reported abuse in August, 1960. Pursuant to the new authority granted under the 1960 Voting Rights Act, the government formally requested that Mr. Lynd make registration records available for inspection and copying. When he refused, the government filed a motion to compel their production on January 19, 1961. No action was taken by the Federal District Court for the Southern District of Mississippi for nearly six months.

In late June, 1961, William Harold Cox was appointed to that district judgeship, the first federal court nomination made by President Kennedy. Shortly thereafter he assumed responsibility for the pending voting registration actions. When Judge Cox's name had been submitted to the American Bar Association's Standing Committee on the Federal Judiciary, he had received its highest recommendation, the "exceptionally well qualified" rating. However, for court watchers sensitive to the political leanings of federal judges in a tense South, there was some cause for alarm in Judge Cox's close friendship with Senator Eastland, an avowed and implacable segregationist.

Cox and Eastland had been classmates at the University of Mississippi in the early 1920s. Since then, Cox had served for years as the Chairman of the Democratic Executive Committee for Hinds County, which includes the state capitol at Jackson. Senator Eastland, the Chairman of the Senate Judiciary Committee, was undoubtedly paying many political debts in the Mississippi political system by urging Cox's appointment upon President Kennedy.

The confirmation of Judge Cox occurred at a time of growing federal concern about the voting situation in Forrest and in several other Mississippi counties. Clarence Mitchell, NAACP Washington chief, publicly charged that the Justice Department "was dragging its feet in Mississippi voting areas." While the request to inspect Lynd's registration records under the Voting Rights Act was still pending, the government soon filed formal suits seeking injunctive relief against Lynd and the Clarke County Registrar. Attorneys for both Lynd and the State of Mississippi filed delaying motions seeking to force the government to allege in greater detail the basis of its claim of discrimination. Specifically sought was the name of each applicant who had allegedly been denied the right to register and dates of such denial, the dates involving any discriminatory mishandling of Negro applications, and the names of white people who, although possessing no better qualifications than Negroes who were denied, had been allowed to register. It was a judicial Catch 22. Judge Cox granted all defense motions, despite the impossibility for the Justice Department to comply while the official voting records were still being withheld from inspection. Then, abruptly on February 15, 1962, Judge Cox dismissed the original enforcement action for the production of records under the 1960 Act as having been "abandoned" because the lawsuit had been filed.

Whatever delays might have been justified because of a new judge's settling into office or because of the unsettled interpretation of the inspection provisions of the recent Voting Rights Act, Judge Cox's order of February 15 was indefensible. The Fifth Circuit had indicated as early as January, 1961, and had explicitly stated ten days prior to Judge Cox's ruling, that Title III proceedings to inspect voting rights records were "investigative" processes requiring only the demand of the Attorney General setting out in a general way the basis and purpose of his request. The Voting Rights Act of 1960 did not contemplate that the demand could be defeated on any showing by a registrar, even upon his affidavit that no black had ever made application to vote. Furthermore, the government had not abandoned its claim under the simplified procedures of the Voting Rights Act. Instead, undoubtedly frustrated by the time consumed in attempting to utilize its procedures, it simply proceeded alternatively and in parallel to seek the traditional remedies available in a civil rights lawsuit for equitable relief.

The fact that access to voting records was the key to successful litigation of voting discrimination charges is clearly established by the Forrest County case. The case was finally set down for a hearing on the government's motion for a temporary injunction on March 5, 1962. Operating in the dark without Mr. Lynd's records, government investigators were able to locate sixteen rejected black witnesses. More surprising, sixteen white witnesses were willing to testify, despite the political climate and despite Lynd's refusal to make any records of white voters available. Only after the government had groped through its presentation, working with the witnesses it had, did Judge Cox order even the records of those particular witnesses turned over to the government for inspection. As the Fifth Circuit panel later characterized the government's case: "Notwithstanding the well-nigh impossible task of showing the true facts, the witnesses produced by the government proved without question that certain serious discriminations had taken place during the term of office of defendant Lynd." One witness called by the government was a black elementary school principal who stated that he had gone to the registrar's office four times before he was allowed to take the literacy test, and then was turned down. Another black schoolteacher testified that she had filled out the forms, but that the registrar had simply pulled out her application and "told me I did not qualify."

The government named a total of sixty-three individuals who had been discriminatorily rejected in their efforts to register to vote. After the government rested its case, despite the fact that Lynd had known that the operations of his office had been under suspicion for almost two years and formal suit had been pending for a

year, his counsel sought a recess of the case for thirty days to
prepare his defense. Judge Cox granted the additional delay. Before the court recessed, Justice Department attorney John Doar
sought an immediate preliminary injunction alleging that Lynd continued to insist upon handling all black registration applications himself, halting process when he was absent from the office on other
business. Judge Cox refused relief, observing from the bench,
"I'm not surprised at Lynd's decision to take Negro applications
himself. You don't know how the Negro people are here. You people up North don't know what Lynd was talking about, but I do. The
girls [deputy clerks] didn't want to be associated with that kind of
influence."

Exasperated by Judge Cox's handling of the case, the government took the extraordinary step of seeking immediate relief from
the Fifth Circuit without waiting for Judge Cox to reconvene the hearing. Under the new regime of Chief Judge Tuttle, the government's
motion for an injunction pending appeal was expedited and the cause
heard one month later by the Chief Judge, former Chief Judge
Hutcheson and Judge Wisdom.

In a succinct opinion written by Chief Judge Tuttle, the contention that the Court of Appeals was without jurisdiction to enter-
tain the appeal because Judge Cox had refused to rule upon the motion for temporary injunction was dismissed summarily. Without
elaboration on that important point, Chief Judge Tuttle simply noted
that declining to issue an order duly and properly requested was
tantamount to a refusal to grant an injunction, and refusals were
appealable under the All Writs Statute. This ruling by the appellate
court served a warning to all district court judges that attempts to
postpone appeals and delay resolution of litigation by simple inaction
would not be tolerated. This holding in the first round of the Forrest County litigation became a key precedent to be followed in public school desegregation cases when similar tactics of delay were
encountered. Further, as if to counterbalance the inordinate delays
already accrued, the panel found sufficient merit in the blacks'
claim of discrimination to enter its own temporary injunction. It is
significant that the Fifth Circuit panel did not direct Judge Cox to
enter an injunction but, instead, under its own authority, the Court
of Appeals issued an injunction against Registrar Lynd and the State
of Mississippi. With no citation of authority, because there was
none, Chief Judge Tuttle reasoned:

> We conclude that the likelihood that the court's refusal
> to grant the temporary injunction will be reversed as an
> abuse of discretion is sufficiently great that we are war-
> ranted in protecting the rights of the Negro registrants
> pending a decision on this issue by this Court.

Such action by a Court of Appeals was definitely a departure
from ordinary, "time tested" appellate procedures. It served to
wrest not only the timing of relief from the discretion of the trial
court but it also made its own orders subject to contempt action

against non-complying parties. Subsequently, in a special concurrence, Judge Bell commented that mandamus might have been a more appropriate remedy than the entry of an original order by the Court of Appeals. Mandamus would have forced the entry of a particular order by the district court, making that district court order the subject of enforcement. If disobeyed, it would have been the district court's duty to conduct contempt hearings for violations of its order. Instead, as happened in this case, the Court of Appeals had to sit as a trier of fact for contempt of its own orders. Judge Bell also expressed concern that the course taken by his brethren in the Lynd case deprived the district court judge of a chance to be heard on the possible reasons for his actions in the case and, in essence, was an appellate "take-over" of the case prior to any decision on the merits by Judge Cox. However, the United States Supreme Court subsequently declined to review the Fifth Circuit's action, perhaps subtly implying some approval of the Court's novel orders. The Court's mandate was entered April 10, just four days after it heard oral argument.

At least the appellate judicial process was moving expeditiously. Scarcely two months later, another panel of the Fifth Circuit reviewed Judge Cox's dismissal of the government's demand to see the Forrest County voting records. The Court of Appeals had decided to consolidate one aspect of the Lynd case with cases from four parishes in Louisiana; Judges Brown, Wisdom and Rives heard argument in New Orleans. United States Attorney Burke Marshall outlined the instances of delay in the case and charged Judge Cox with having put the case "on ice." The Assistant Attorney General of Mississippi hotly defended, noting that the case could be called up at any time and that the government still had pending its motion to discover the disputed records. Judge Rives put an end to the argument. With some acerbity, evoking laughter from the gallery, he asked: "He [Judge Cox] hasn't put it on ice, he's just put it into the refrigerator?"

Within the month, the panel decided the case, rendering the most comprehensive opinion on the nature of the right of the Attorney General to seek production of voting records under the Voting Rights Act of 1960. In brief, Judge Brown noted that all that had been required of the Attorney General was that a written demand be made for official voting records upon the appropriate official, followed by that official's refusal: "the factual foundation for, or the sufficiency of, the Attorney General's 'statement of the basis and the purpose' contained in the written demand, $1947b [of the Voting Rights Act of 1960], is not open to judicial review or ascertainment." Furthermore the records subject to the right of inspection would not be limited to those accumulated during a particular registrar's tenure, as had been argued by Lynd and ordered by Judge Cox. Instead, any record which bore upon the eligibility of any currently listed voter was subject to disclosure. This interpretation of the Act's language, which required only the preservation and retention of "all records for twenty-two months from the date of a federal election," meant that in states such as Alabama, which allowed

permanent registration, records would have to be preserved prospec-
tively until an eligible voter either became disqualified or died. In
addition, the Attorney General could reach all records, including
those, for example, of a sixty-year-old voter who had originally applied in 1921. As a result of its statutory interpretation the Fifth
Circuit gave maximum effect to the reach of the Voting Act's investigatory provisions.

Finally, the panel stated that the Voting Act's investigatory
provisions existed independently of a formal action charging discrimination. The right to disclosure should have been enforced in
the Lynd case, regardless of the suit for injunctive relief; Judge
Cox's ruling that the government "had abandoned" its disclosure action had been clearly erroneous. Noting "there is nothing left in
dispute," the Fifth Circuit remanded the case to Judge Cox with the
direction that he order the inspection of all records sought.

In addition to seeking appellate redress from Judge Cox's actions, the Justice Department attacked on another front in May, 1962.
It petitioned that Theron Lynd be cited for both criminal and civil
contempt of court for having failed to abide by the terms of the Fifth
Circuit's temporary injunction. Thus, Lynd became the first voter
registrar to be so charged under the Voting Rights Act of 1960.

Because the terms of the Fifth Circuit's own order had been
allegedly flouted, Judges Brown, Wisdom and Bell were convened as
a trial court in Hattiesburg in mid-September, 1962. The government asserted that since issuance of the appellate court's injunction,
Lynd had persisted in his discriminatory practices, refusing registration to at least nineteen qualified blacks. A Hattiesburg schoolteacher, holder of two master's degrees, testified that he had visited
Lynd's office four times before he was finally given the voter registration forms, only to be failed on the test twice thereafter. A
black National Science Foundation Fellow at Cornell testified that he
had taken the constitutional interpretation tests, also to be twice
failed. In contrast, a white truck driver stated that he had been
given official advice about how to fill out the application form correctly, as well as hints about what was expected on the tests.
When asked on cross-examination to explain the statistical disparity
between white and black registration, Lynd steadfastly maintained,
"I just know that I turn down anyone, regardless of color, if he
failed. I've had white people get mad enough to fight me and colored people do the same thing." The Fifth Circuit Court of Appeals
adjudged Lynd guilty of civil contempt, leaving open the criminal
contempt charges as a threat of last resort. Lynd was ordered to
comply with the Court's earlier injunction and required to notify any
rejected applicant of the specific deficiency in his application and to
give the applicant an opportunity to correct that defect. The Forrest County Registrar apparently indicated he would comply and
agreed in writing to abide by all terms of the order.

Since adjourning the hearing on the merits of the preliminary
injunction in March, 1962, Judge Cox had taken no further action.

Despite the appellate court's admonition to "move with dispatch," Judge Cox did not schedule the Forrest County case for a hearing on the merits until April, 1964, nine months after the Fifth Circuit's mandate. During this hearing, the simmering ideological conflict between Judge Cox and the Justice Department exploded in an angry exchange. Again representing the government, John Doar addressed the issue of the inadequate staff available to register blacks when they appeared in large groups after "freedom days" rallies. Judge Cox exploded, "It appears that these people went to a church and were pepped up by a leather-lung preacher and they gathered in the streets like a massive dark cloud and descended on the clerk." Doar responded that the blacks had a right to vote and to assemble to do so. Judge Cox retorted, "Who is telling these people they can get in line and push people around, acting like a bunch of chimpanzees?"

Thereafter, Judge Cox's battle with the Justice Department reached out from Jackson to Washington. He wrote letters to Attorney General Katzenbach criticizing the Department's voting actions as "frivolous" and demanded that the government seek perjury indictments against two blacks who had testified in the Clark County voting case.* Judge Cox finally entered an order in the Lynd case four years after the action had originally been filed. His order gave the minimum relief possible and was quickly appealed to the Fifth Circuit. The final round of the case was argued the following summer, 1965, before Judges Brown, Wisdom, and Bell. Of the five assignments of error charged by the government, two were of great significance to the development of the law in the area of voting rights.

In his order Judge Cox had simply ignored the request of the Attorney General that he make a finding on whether or not there had been a "pattern or practice of discrimination." Under the 1960 Voting Rights Act, such a finding triggered extraordinary relief: any person in the class who could prove that he had been erroneously denied the right to vote was relieved of bringing suit but, instead, was required only to seek an order from the court certifying his eligibility. Judge Cox's refusal to rule either way on the government's request for this critical finding of fact had been the subject of a running conflict with the Fifth Circuit.

In an earlier case involving voting discrimination in Clarke County, Mississippi, Judge Cox had specifically ruled that there had been no pattern of discrimination despite what one appellate judge characterized as "gross and flagrant denials" of the rights of blacks to vote. On appeal, the case had been assigned to a panel composed of Circuit Judge Cameron, Judge Edwin Hunter of the Western District of Louisiana and Circuit Judge Rives. In the original opinion by Judge Hunter, dated February 20, 1964, a paean was delivered to Judge Cox:

---

*See Part II, chapter 10, infra at 411.

In our country the courts have a most important obligation
to protect the rights of all and to do it as harmoniously
as possible. In his endeavor to do just this, the District
Judge obviously thought it best not to make a specific finding that there was a 'pattern.' [We omit] ... any definitive action on this facet of the case because we feel it
was within the District Judge's discretion to omit action
on that phase of the complaint.

Judge Rives strenuously objected to this approval of what he had concluded was a mandatory duty imposed upon the district court judge:
the duty to make some finding, upon request, on whether or not a
pattern of discrimination had been proved.

Two months later, on petition for rehearing, the panel's first
opinion on the correctness of Judge Cox's handling of the case was
totally reversed. In a two paragraph per curiam opinion, the panel
ruled that regardless of whether he had discretion or not to avoid
the issue, since Judge Cox had in fact ruled that no pattern existed,
his ruling was subject to appellate review. Furthermore, based
upon the facts in the record, his ruling had been clearly erroneous.
The case was remanded with the direction to Judge Cox to find that
a pattern of discrimination did exist. What caused this abrupt reversal in appellate treatment of the case is indicated in a brief footnote: "Judge Cameron participated in the original decision but died
before the petition for rehearing was decided." Without Judge Cameron as an ally, Judge Hunter was apparently persuadable. With
the death of Judge Cameron, District Court Judge Cox lost his only
supporter on the Fifth Circuit Court of Appeals.

Thereafter, in two other voting cases pending before him,
Judge Cox attempted to sidestep this issue by withholding a ruling
on whether a pattern had been proved, evidently to test the strength
which Judge Rives's opinion carried with his colleagues on the Fifth
Circuit. In those cases, the Fifth Circuit took the position, without
dissenting vote since Judge Cameron's death, that a ruling was mandated. This position was reiterated in the Lynd case. Furthermore, the panel of Circuit Judges Brown, Wisdom and Bell held as
a matter of law that the facts demanded a finding of a discriminatory
pattern.

The second major point at issue in the last round of the
Lynd case was the nature of relief necessary to eliminate discriminatory treatment in Forrest County, Mississippi. The panel quickly
reaffirmed its adoption of the mode of equitable relief referred to
as "freezing." Simply stated, "freezing" meant that in considering
the application of any blacks claiming discriminatory treatment from
either Registrar Lynd or his predecessors in office, the trial court
would measure his qualifications against those used for white applicants at the time the black had sought to register. In essence,
the qualifications for voting were "frozen" to match the often lax
standards used to register whites.

"Freezing" was a revolutionary concept of relief developed
by Judge Frank Johnson of the Middle District of Alabama who,
after the departure of Judge Skelly Wright, became the most influential and innovative federal trial judge in the Fifth Circuit. As
Judge Johnson described the nature of the fledgling concept in 1962:

> In determining whether such applicants are qualified, the
> Court must apply the same standards used by the Board of
> Registrars in qualifying white applicants during the period
> within which the pattern of discrimination is found to ex-
> ist.

The Fifth Circuit embraced the concept and refined it. The United
States Supreme Court subsequently affirmed its legitimacy, elevating
it as the national standard in voting rights actions.

Wary of misconstruction, the Fifth Circuit directed verbatim
the order which was to be issued forthwith by Judge Cox in the
Lynd case. Concerning past abuses, Lynd was ordered to review applications of Negroes rejected during his tenure in office, using as
his only criterion whether they satisfied the citizenship and simple
literacy requirements exacted of white applicants. All blacks who
applied in the future were to be judged only by these standards until either the state could show that the pattern of discrimination
against blacks had been overcome by the use of these less stringent
standards (and no showing would be allowed for at least two years
from the date of this mandate), or that an entirely new registration
of all voters, white and black, had been accomplished using standards approved in advance by the federal court.

As drafted by the Fifth Circuit, the order left little room for
discretion in the running of the Forrest county voting registration
office. Lynd and his associates were required to process applicants
"as expeditiously as possible," including the stipulation that they process at least six applicants at one time, the level of maximum efficiency which testimony had revealed the office could support. Lynd
was further required to rule immediately at the time of application
upon an applicant's qualification. The office was directed to give
the same amount of assistance to black and white applicants alike,
to inform any voter rejected of the reasons for rejection and of his
right to appeal to the federal court, and to make a detailed report
of applications and their disposition each month to the court, with a
copy to the attorneys for the federal government. In the event Registrar Lynd violated these directions, Judge Cox was required to
rule, either personally or through a voting referee, upon any application presented to him by an aggrieved citizen within twenty days
after receiving the request.

The last blow was reserved for Theron Lynd. Having been
found in contempt of the Fifth Circuit's orders on three separate
occasions, he was ordered to notify by registered mail all blacks
specifically found to have been discriminated against, that they had
now been certified to vote; to post in his office "in a conspicuous

place" a copy of the Court's order outlining his duties under the injunction; to sign a statement of compliance with its terms; and--perhaps most important in terms of deterring future contumacious conduct by him or other registrars--Lynd was ordered personally to pay all court costs of the government's action within sixty days.

In 1960, in his last report as Attorney General, Herbert Brownell had predicted trouble ahead for his successor in the implementation of voting rights, even if comprehensive congressional legislation was passed.

> Experience with the 1957 Act impels the conclusion that for some time to come, every action initiated in racial voting and registration cases will be challenged in every possible way to prevent or delay the implementation of the purpose of Congress. The same conclusion appears valid for actions to be taken under the 1960 Act.

The Lynd case demonstrates the accuracy of Attorney General Brownell's prediction. It had taken two years just to procure the official voting records and three more to entrench an injunction against past and future discrimination in one county in southern Mississippi. Theron Lynd's opposition to the new Voting Rights Act certainly might have been one which Brownell spotted for potential problems. One Southern politician observed, "No man ... can be elected to even a minor office [in the South] unless he commits himself in a forthright and effective manner to support the pattern of segregation."

What probably was not envisioned by the Attorney General was a federal judge's defiance of Congress, the Justice Department, and the federal appellate courts. Judge Cox earned a national reputation as a result of his judicial behavior in the Mississippi voting cases. The New York Times reported:

> Judge Cox is probably the Federal judge most dreaded by the lawyers and plaintiffs who initiate civil rights cases. Among them he is nationally known for his unsympathetic handling of Negro voting rights and school desegregation cases. He is also remembered as the judge who once referred to a group of Negroes as 'chimpanzees.'

To counter the resistance of a single district judge, the Fifth Circuit Court of Appeals had been forced to adopt unusual new appellate procedures. It had granted stays pending appeal, expedited appeals, treated lack of a court order as a denial of relief, entered its own injunction, tried cases of contempt, dictated verbatim trial court orders and issued its mandate with immediate effect.

* * *

Judge Cox was responsible for only three voting rights cases. Meanwhile, the Fifth Circuit reviewed actions from Louisiana, Alabama and Georgia as well, putting the flesh of judicial interpretation upon the bare skeleton of the 1960 congressional legislation. The doctrinal contribution of the Fifth Circuit to voting rights law, particularly by its interpretation of a "pattern" of discrimination and its use of "freezing" relief, would have long-range national repercussions.

Pettus Bridge and the Voting Rights Act of 1965

The federal government has demonstrated a seeming inability to make significant advances in seven years' time, since the 1957 law, in making the right to vote real for Negroes in Mississippi, large parts of Alabama, and Louisiana, and in scattered counties in other states.... Does this mean that the basic problem is beyond solution and the simple right beyond realization? The experience of the Justice Department to date would not justify this conclusion.... [T]he harder question is whether the tempo of the civil rights has not quickened to such a degree that there is not enough time left.
     --Burke Marshall, Assistant Attorney General of the United States, "Federalism and Civil Rights," The Negro American, at 389-90.

The handiwork of the United States Court of Appeals for the Fifth Circuit in distilling the spirit of congressional voting legislation into effective remedial action had attracted national support. In its provisions concerning voting, the new 1964 Civil Rights Act incorporated several of the innovations devised by the Fifth Circuit: it mandated "freezing relief"; it prohibited denial of registration for immaterial errors on application forms; it required a presumption of literacy for certain educational grade achievement; and it approved use of statistical presumptions to prove a discriminatory pattern at work. These "new" provisions of the 1964 Civil Rights Act, however, had only limited impact because of the substantial revisions brought about by congressional action the following year.

The Johnson landslide of 1964 was substantially aided by nearly six million Negro votes. Armed with this powerful mandate and a friendly Congress, the new President seemed to have the means for establishing his "Great Society." Whatever long-range planning about voting rights President Johnson might have hoped to undertake became impossible. Violence erupted even before his oath of office had been administered. The events in Selma, Alabama, forced Johnson into action.

On January 2, 1965, Martin Luther King called for a resumption of demonstrations if voting rights were not granted to prospective registrants. With that statement, Reverend King cast the power of the Southern Christian Leadership Conference behind a long-active drive for black voter registration spearheaded by the Student Nonviolent Coordinating Committee (SNCC). On January 25, a dramatic confrontation between Dallas County Sheriff "Big Jim" Clark and Mrs. Annie Lee Cooper over the Alabama voting registration test caused massive demonstrations. During the ensuing week of protests, over three thousand persons were arrested.

The spark that focused national attention upon Selma was a massive march from Selma to the state capital at Montgomery. The march was planned by Negro leaders to protest both the recent fatal shooting of Jimmie Lee Jackson by an Alabama state trooper and the arrests which had followed in the wake of the demonstrations. Despite Governor Wallace's order forbidding the march, it proceeded as planned on March 7, 1965. The marchers had to cross the Edmund Pettus Bridge, and the Alabama State Police were waiting beyond the bridge. The marchers halted twenty-five yards in front of the police and were given two minutes to disperse. At the end of the two minutes, the troopers advanced, using cattle prods to push back the marchers. Suddenly the troopers began to use their clubs and Sheriff Clark's posse, which had been waiting with the troopers, moved in. The marchers were chased back across the bridge, fleeing tear gas and horsemen. Seventy-eight blacks suffered injuries requiring treatment. The march was televised; the shock of the violence was felt firsthand by all American viewers.

On Tuesday night, March 9, three white clergymen who had flown to Alabama to join the marchers in Selma dined at a black restaurant. As they left, they were assaulted outside a white cafeteria by white toughs. All three were viciously beaten, and one, Reverend James Reeb, died in a coma two days later. The nation's sentiment, already stirred against the violence, crested in a wave of revulsion. Sympathy demonstrations occurred all over the country, including a sit-in at the White House.

President Johnson signed orders authorizing the swift dispatch of 700 riot troops to Selma if needed. On Saturday, March 13, President Johnson met with Governor Wallace at the White House. In a press conference held afterwards, the President first announced that he would introduce fresh proposals to guarantee the franchise to all citizens. His new proposals would abolish all bars to voting, including literacy tests. President Johnson commented on his discussion with Governor Wallace: "I told the Governor that the brutality in Selma last Sunday just must not be repeated. I urged that the Governor publicly declare his support for universal suffrage in the State of Alabama and the United States of America." Governor Wallace made no public comment.

The following Monday, President Johnson addressed an emergency joint session of Congress to call for a voting rights bill to "overcome the crippling legacy of bigotry and injustice." Two days later, federal district Judge Frank Johnson lifted an earlier temporary restraining order against further attempts to march from

Selma to Montgomery. Instead, he enjoined Alabama officials from
interfering with the freedom of citizens peaceably to assemble and
petition their state government for a redress of grievances. The
fifty-mile passage was accomplished over a four-day period, March
21-25. It was capped by a rally in Montgomery attended by a crowd
estimated to be from 25,000 to 50,000 people.

* * *

The Selma protest campaign was a watershed of the voting
rights movement. The discriminatory use of tests aimed at excluding black citizens from voting was not generally realized by the
American public. But for the Selma violence, such tests and similar stratagems might have been rationalized by some as a nondiscriminatory protection of the integrity of the electoral process.
However, demeaning human beings who were simply seeking the
vote, and herding them like cattle, galvanized many previously uninvolved television spectators into action. Representatives of most
major religious denominations left the pulpit for the modern day
crusade, committing the power of the church to a modern day struggle. "Going to Selma" attracted many young whites into the ranks
of social protest, spreading the movement to the nation's youth.
But Selma also exacted a toll. At least four protesters had been
killed and nearly a hundred injured, with many more frightened and,
more important, disillusioned by the quick resort to violence by the
resisters. Selma was the final hurrah of a cohesive acceptance of
nonviolence as a race relations philosophy among young blacks.
Beginning that summer of 1965, the black civil rights movement
splintered, leaving the ranks of young followers vastly reduced within the camps of Dr. King and the litigation-oriented NAACP.

Public pressure and Presidential commitment coalesced to
speed congressional consideration of new voting legislation. The
chief thrust of the Administration's bill was to reduce the amount
of time required to implement the right to vote and to end acts of
discrimination. To insure equal opportunity in voting, the leisurely
pace of litigation could no longer be tolerated. Attorney General
Katzenbach testified that the time devoted to each of the seventy-one
cases filed under the Civil Rights Act of 1957 had been staggering.
It was routine to spend as long as 6,000 man-hours analyzing a
single county's voting records, which did not include the time the
government spent preparing for trial. Burke Marshall, Civil Rights
Division Chief, testified about the frustrating problems of delay inherent in litigation in hearings before the United States Commission
on Civil Rights. He noted that 16.33 months was the average
elapsed time between filing of a complaint and the beginning of trial.
Of this, approximately six and one-half months were spent simply
awaiting an answer by state officials.

Even with the streamlined procedures of the Fifth Circuit
and its commitment to minimize all delay within its power, progress
under previous congressional voting legislation had been slow. Appearing before the Senate Judiciary Committee, Attorney General

Katzenbach produced figures illustrating the overall ineffectiveness in total registration achieved. In tabular form his testimony showed:

State	Increase in Negro Voter Registration from 1954-1964	Increase in White Voter Registration from 1954-1964
Mississippi	2. 2%	80. 5%
Alabama	5. 2%	69. 2%
Louisiana	. 1%	80. 2%

Finally, in August, 1965, the Voting Rights Act of 1965 was enacted. The provisions of the act should be examined in some detail because it molded the judicial precedent forged by the Fifth Circuit into statutory law; and because it effectively snuffed out the most blatant forms of official defiance.

The "freezing relief" nourished in the case law of the Fifth Circuit and recognized in the voting legislation of 1964 was further extended. Voting requirements in effect when the great majority of white citizens were registered were frozen for five years, instead of two years as previously required by the Fifth Circuit, in order to allow sufficient time for previously rejected applicants to reapply and for new applicants to seek registration. Secondly, the 1965 Act extended "freezing" relief to state as well as federal elections, thus removing vestiges of double-standard sovereignty. Consequently, the Attorney General was invested with the power to inspect state election records. Any tests used for qualification of voters for state elections had to be administered to all applicants and written copies of tests, results and statistical records of state elections had to be maintained. This provision was important in bringing the internal electoral process of the states within the purview of national scrutiny and standards.

In addition, the problems of proof in voting rights cases were considerably lessened by the new statute. Previously the government had been required to carry the burden of showing that discrimination had been "willful" or "purposeful." Indeed, the requirement of specific intent had been at issue in most of the voting rights cases argued before the Fifth Circuit. As early as 1959, the Court of Appeals had registered its approval of the use of statistics to create a prima facie case of discrimination in a case involving juror selection. The judicial acceptance of statistics to create a presumption of discrimination spilled over into other race relations cases, but its greatest impact was in voting rights litigation. There is a natural relation between voting and jury duty: both are key elements in political power and, in some states, voter registration is even a prerequisite to jury service.

Evidentiary problems in proving discrimination were largely responsible for the thousands of work-hours exacted from government attorneys in voting rights cases. In the first such case in

which the Fifth Circuit directly employed the statistical presumption,
Alabama v. United States, Judge Brown noted that the trial record
comprised over nine hundred pages of testimony taken from fifty-
three witnesses, plus two huge boxes of documentary exhibits. The
government had been hesitant to gamble on its belief that the Court
of Appeals would accept the statistical presumption; therefore, it
also attempted to put into evidence traditional proof of discrimination.
Obviously the easiest corroboration of blacks' assertion of discrimination would come from cross-examination of the principal actors,
the registrars. However, to avoid exposure of the registrars to
federal cross-examination, the state declined to call them as witnesses. The federal attorneys could, of course, call the registrars
as their own witnesses, but by doing so would not have the right to
"lead" or "impeach" that they would have enjoyed on cross-examination. In Alabama v. United States, Judge Frank Johnson had to call
two of the members of the Board of Registrars as the court's witnesses in order to put their account of policies and practices upon
the record. The Court of Appeals panel of Judges Brown and Rives,
over a blistering dissent by Judge Cameron filed shortly before his
death, accepted statistical proof, noting:

> In the problem of racial discrimination, statistics
> often tell much, and Courts listen. Here they are spec-
> tacular. With approximately 17% of the Macon County
> population being white, the balance, 83%, being Negro,
> less than 10% of the Negroes of voting age are registered
> while nearly 100% of the white citizens are.
>   The evidentiary details recited by both colored and
> white witnesses made it doubly clear that these statistics
> were not distorted. They demonstrate also that, for at
> least this time, these figures are reliable in their major
> implication that such disparity could not exist by chance
> alone, that there had to be causes for this result; and
> that a principal cause was conscious racial discrimination
> by those entrusted with the duty of impartial administra-
> tion of the law.

Within two years, the statistical presumption of discrimination in voting rights cases had become conventional in appellate decision making. In reviewing a case out of the Northern District of
Mississippi, in which a county had registered 5,343 whites and only
one black--and he had slipped through in 1892--Chief Judge Tuttle
noted that the trial court had "assumed precisely what we said could
not be assumed"; that is, that the small number of registered blacks
could be attributed only to an intentional choice by blacks not to participate in the electoral process. The statistics alone required the
state to disprove the presumption that officials had failed to freely
and fairly register qualified blacks.

To a limited extent in the voting provisions of 1964, and to
a great extent in the Voting Rights Act of 1965, Congress sanctioned
the use of statistical presumptions as proof of discrimination to trigger different types of remedial devices. Section four, the key pro-

vision of the 1965 Act, became known as the "automatic trigger"
provision. It suspended all "tests and devices" used by any state
where it could be shown that less than 50% of the eligible voters
were registered as of November 1, 1964, or had voted in the 1964
Presidential election. Furthermore, the Act expansively defined
the term "test or device" to include all of the various stratagems
previously used by states to depress black voting. Included within the
application of the automatic trigger remedy was the use by a state of:

> ... [A]ny requirement that a person as a prerequisite for
> voting or registration for voting (1) demonstrate the abil-
> ity to read, write, understand or interpret any matter,
> (2) demonstrate any educational achievement or his knowl-
> edge of any particular subject, (3) possess good moral
> character, or (4) prove his qualifications by the voucher
> of registered voters of members of any other class.

All states in the Deep South used some form of literacy test
and all states in the Fifth Circuit except Texas and Florida had
less than 50% of their eligible adult population registered due to the
high proportion of black population. The "automatic trigger" concept therefore had enormous consequences for voting rights in the
states of the Fifth Circuit. No longer would the government have
to institute suits to end tests that illegally barred blacks or that
were discriminatorily administered. Instead, the states became
automatically suspect given the combination of test usage and low
registration. The Act shifted the burden from the individual to the
states, to bring suit to show why they did not belong in the class
of states whose tests were automatically suspended. While the Act
made provision for states which fell under the automatic trigger
ban to have the suspension lifted, it was an extraordinarily difficult
hurdle for Southern states.

As a result of the use of statistical presumptions enforced
in the automatic trigger provision of the 1965 Voting Rights Act, the
four states of the Fifth Circuit registered impressive gains in black
registration. The biggest gain was in Mississippi when, from 1965
to 1968, the percentage of Negro voters rose from 6.7% to 59.8%.
In Alabama, the percentage rose from 19.3% to 51.6%; in Georgia,
the increase was from 27.4% to 52.6%; and in Louisiana, black
voter registration increased from 31.6% to 58.9%.

The 1965 Voting Rights Act was a stringent measure which
proved an effective means of implementing the mandate of the fifteenth amendment. According to the Department of Justice, as of
May 3, 1967, an additional 416,000 black citizens had been registered since the passage of the Act. Not only was the Act a psychological confirmation of the judicial work of the Fifth Circuit, and
notably of District Judge Frank Johnson, it also offered tangible relief in terms of the case load carried by the Court. The power of
recalcitrant district court judges to delay, illustrated by Judge Cox's
conduct in the Lynd case, was in some measure alleviated by a new
provision which authorized the convening of a three-judge court upon

the request of either party when the government asserted the presence of "pattern or practice" of voting discrimination. Furthermore,
the automatic trigger provisions and freezing relief for five years
drastically curtailed the initiation of new voting litigation.

A few cases were pending in the federal courts at the time
the 1965 Act was passed. In those cases, the Court of Appeals
simply issued its mandate in conformity with the Act, extending
freezing relief to aggrieved voters from two years to five years.
After the Act was passed, the Court of Appeals also reviewed cases
alleging voter intimidation and discrimination arising out of the Selma
voter registration drive. However, the resistance to black voting
through discriminatory registration practices had been broken. Resistance, still alive, instead took on yet another form.

The Last Frontier

> 'Y'see how them niggers do,' a gray-haired
> shopkeeper remarked to me one day as he re-
> called this election. 'They'll always vote in a
> bloc if you give 'em a chance.'
> --Taper, Gomillion Versus Lightfoot: Apart-
> heid in Alabama, at 13 (1962)

The combination of the Voting Rights Act of 1965 and the judicial machinery engineered by the Fifth Circuit secured for the
black citizen the right to register as a prerequisite for voting. Local attempts to cut off access to the ballot, as in the past, appeared
futile. Yet problems in devising remedies to obliterate the vestiges
of discriminatory practices in registration persisted in the federal
courts of the South. By the early seventies, there was evidence of
a shift in the focus of discrimination from an outright denial of the
vote to attempts to neutralize the impact of the "Negro" vote.

A court order employing all the remedies authorized under
the 1965 Voting Rights Act would eventually provide complete relief
in terms of voting eligibility. However, when elections were close
at hand, many potential black voters could not be processed in time
to meet administrative deadlines for registration. As a result,
grave constitutional issues arose.

All states impose registration deadlines in advance of scheduled elections as a matter of administrative necessity, in order to
prepare the official rolls of authorized voters. While time limits
vary, for example, in 1965 under Mississippi law, the cutoff was
set at four months in advance of a general election. On April 8,
black voters in Sunflower County, Mississippi, successfully obtained
an order from federal district court Judge Claude Clayton finding
that the local registrar had discriminated for years against blacks
pursuant to a pattern and practice, and, as a result, future discrimination was enjoined and the appropriate "freeze" order entered. Un-

fortunately, the registration deadline had passed some two months before. Unless the court intervened, the newly certified class of potential black voters would not be able to vote in municipal elections, nor could they be candidates for public office, since candidacy was conditioned upon being a qualified elector. The earliest time black voters could assert the franchise was some four years distant, at the next regularly scheduled general elections. Shortly after receiving Judge Clayton's decision, the black plaintiffs applied to him for a preliminary injunction postponing the upcoming election until they could be processed and registered. On May 4, Judge Clayton denied the requested relief. He pointed out the disruption attendant upon interfering with a scheduled election and noted, among other things, that the ballots had already been printed.

This decision was immediately appealed to the Fifth Circuit for an injunction pending appeal as well as for a preliminary injunction to halt the election. Two things are notable about the Court of Appeals' handling of the Sunflower County case: the responsiveness of the Court and the expansive nature of the relief accorded.

The Court of Appeals historically had shied away from such controversies. In 1948, a disappointed primary candidate obtained a federal court injunction against the appearance of Lyndon B. Johnson's name as the Democratic nominee for the United States Senate on the Texas general election ballot. Johnson, relying upon the equitable powers of the Court of Appeals to grant extraordinary relief, sought from then Chief Judge Hutcheson an expedited hearing on the merits and a stay of the district court injunction. Only seven days remained before the printing deadline and the Court of Appeals was officially in recess. Although he granted a hearing in chambers, Chief Judge Hutcheson subsequently ruled that he was powerless either to hear the case sitting alone or to reconvene an appellate panel before its first regularly scheduled court day, long after the deadline. In that particular case, timely relief was finally obtained from Justice Black, who undoubtedly, by that single judicial action, altered the course of political history.

In striking contrast, in 1966, within six days after the case involving the Sunflower County voters was docketed with the Court of Appeals, a panel composed of Judge Brown and former Chief Judge Hutcheson and District Judge Morgan heard oral argument. Although the panel declined to issue an injunction pending appeal, it expressly reserved a decision on the merits. The black plaintiffs then sought an expedited appellate hearing even though the Court of Appeals was in summer recess as it had been in the Johnson case. The panel again responded, convening for a second time to hear oral argument. The panel declined to rush to a full decision on the merits, with only eighteen days remaining before the slated election and "in view of the many serious legal questions involved in the issue now presented on this appeal." However, in its order denying immediate relief, the Court warned that it would consider itself empowered after considering complete briefs to "grant appellants full relief ... even to the extent of declaring said election to be void."

Subsequently, the Court of Appeals panel did just that. It set aside the Sunflower County elections. The Court held that the injunction should have been granted, despite any pragmatic consequences produced in rescheduling the election. Persuaded by the shadow of influence past discrimination would continue to cast, Judge Brown tartly observed: "Relief, if it is to be had, must perforce come from the Court or the voters must simply be told to wait four more years. That denial of this fundamental right cannot be justified in the name of equity." As is often the case with the assured quality of Judge John Brown's opinion writing, the rationale of the decision is persuasive, logically inexorable and deceptively unextraordinary. That such action was unprecedented can only be gleaned from a study of equitable relief previously utilized by the Court's various panels.

Beginning with Judge Tuttle's tenure as Chief Judge and escalating with John R. Brown's assumption of leadership, the Fifth Circuit rarely avoided difficult decisions while awaiting definitive pronouncements from the Supreme Court. In 1963, for example, the three-judge district court had occasion to consider a disputed Texas election case. The Supreme Court had provided its lower courts with little guidance in Baker v. Carr, its landmark decision concerning legislative reapportionment. Only seven justices had participated in Baker v. Carr, splitting 3-1-3, causing Justice Clark to term it a "bobbed tail court." Four of the justices had concluded that federal courts could intervene to review questions of a state's methods for establishing congressional apportionment. Puzzled by the true dimensions of the Supreme Court's decision, many federal courts simply took the safe path and held pending apportionment cases under advisement. To many judges it undoubtedly seemed precipitous to attempt to expand relief based upon such slender judicial recognition of the basic cause of action. For a century the Supreme Court had consistently held that management of the political process was beyond judicial ken. But, by 1964, the leaders of the Fifth Circuit were not daunted by novel questions nor reluctant to fashion new remedies in protection of their findings.

In Bush v. Martin, a three-judge panel found the Texas congressional districts malapportioned under the tests outlined by the plurality of the Supreme Court in Baker v. Carr. Judge Brown, working against one dissent, fashioned the Court's order enjoining the use of a discriminatory districting statute:

> Granting the existence of invidious discrimination, jurisdiction and justiciability, is this case in its present posture one that either requires or admits of coercive judicial relief? ....
> Of course the easy way out is either to take no action or formally to defer action pending decision by the Supreme Court.... But this Court no less than the Supreme Court of the United States is charged with serious obligations under Art. III of the Constitution and under the implementing statutes of Congress to afford to litigants appropriate relief

in vindication of constitutional and civil rights.... But
when we consider the element of time, it seems clear to
us that there is no basis whatsoever for staying the hand
of equity on the ground that relief can be elsewhere and
otherwise obtained [through reapportionment by the Texas
legislature in 1964].

Judge Brown was right in his prognosis of the Supreme Court's ultimate position on the constitutional guarantee of "one man-one vote."
Furthermore, the use of injunctive relief against unconstitutional apportionment, as ordered by his court in the Texas case, was subsequently affirmed by the Supreme Court on appeal.

Relying upon this Texas precedent and other later apportionment decisions rendered by other three-judge courts within the Fifth
Circuit, Judge Brown justified the further extension of equitable relief in the Sunflower County, Mississippi case. Again, it was Judge
Brown who wrote the panel's far-reaching opinion in a low-key style
that belied the extension of doctrine which was occurring:

There can be no question that a District Court has the
power to enjoin the holding of an election. In State of
Alabama v. United States ... we emphasized the broad
equitable powers of the District Court to mould relief sufficient to wipe out the effects of racial discrimination.
And the recent reapportionment cases remove any doubt
that these powers encompass the power to enjoin an election. To be sure, the Supreme Court ... has held that
in some cases it might be proper not to enjoin an election
to be conducted pursuant to an unconstitutional plan. But
appellee's reliance on these cases is misplaced. The shoe
will not fit. First, the Court clearly warned that it 'would
be the unusual case in which a court would be justified in
not taking appropriate action to insure that no further elections are conducted under the invalid plan.' Second, the
reapportionment cases deal with dilution of the vote. This
case involves a deprivation. Third, in the reapportionment cases the Court is dealing with a legislative function.
Staying judicial relief may give the State a chance to clean
its own house and thus avoid a court-imposed, non-legisla-
tive disruption of its election process.... But the municipal bodies involved in these elections have no power to
eradicate the deprivation of the franchise. Relief, if it
is to be had, must perforce come from the Court or the
voters must simply be told to wait four more years. That
denial of this fundamental right cannot be justified in the
name of equity.

To the "activists" on the Fifth Circuit Court, equitable power
had been lodged in the breast of the Court to be used. It was a
power that could be used to enable the Court to recognize past abuses
by declaratory judgment, to avoid future discrimination by injunction
and even to nullify the results of past discriminations. Accordingly,

given proof of voting discrimination, appellate judicial relief should be available before the fact of an election but, if not, then after the fact: "Our absence of facilities to rectify rapidly should not now prevent us according full relief to the plaintiffs."

The failure to register qualified black applicants could result in a nullification of elections in which they had been precluded from qualifying. But did this extraordinary decision, setting aside a duly conducted election, place all contemporary Southern elections in jeopardy? Throughout every state in the South there were towns and counties where the effects of past discriminations lingered. 1966 was a general election year, and hundreds of political contests could be affected. In order to minimize anxiety about election results elsewhere, the Fifth Circuit in the Sunflower opinion imposed two significant limitations upon the reach of its power to set aside elections. First, the remedy was available only where black complainants had challenged the proposed election before its scheduled occurrences and second, there must be evidence establishing that the complainants had also been diligent in seeking to exhaust judicial review of the challenged political process prior to the election.

Yet, in Bell v. Southwell, a case decided the following year, the Court of Appeals excused pre-election exhaustion of judicial relief where the discriminatory actions took place on election day, too late for outcries. In 1966, a special election was held in Americus, Georgia, to fill the vacant post of Justice of the Peace. The black plaintiff, Mary Bell, was a candidate along with defendant-winner Southwell and four other men. The plaintiffs charged that local officials had conducted the election in a manner that violated the constitutional rights of the plaintiff as a qualified voter. The voting lists were segregated on the basis of race and the voting booths designated "white males," "white females," and "Negroes." There were also other alleged acts of misconduct. Supporters of Mrs. Bell were barred from viewing the voting, and Mrs. Bell was arrested when she attempted to use the white women's voting booth and refused a deputy sheriff's order to leave. District Court Judge William Bootle found that the practices were flagrant violations of the Constitution, but concluded that he could not set aside the election or order a new one. On appeal, the Fifth Circuit again ordered the setting aside of an election. Judge John Brown wrote the opinion for the Court, observing, "Drastic, if not staggering, as is the Federal voiding of a State Election, and therefore a form of relief to be guardedly exercised, this Court [has already] ... expressly recognized the existence of this power." The Court concluded that a new election must be held whenever racial discrimination occurs which is "gross, spectacular, [and] completely indefensible."

* * *

Even though the Voting Rights Act of 1965 had significantly advanced the protection of the basic right to register, it did not reach the "purging" phenomenon which was still used as late as 1970 to disenfranchise blacks. Many states used purging neutrally to win-

now from the official voting lists those who had not exercised the
franchise for a certain length of time and those who had died or
moved from the district.   An election challenge based upon improper
purging in Madison Parish, Louisiana, provided the Court of Appeals,
sitting en banc, an opportunity to review the judicial work of its
panels in the Sunflower County and Americus cases, and consequently,
to reevaluate collectively the appropriate use of judicial remedies
in the political arena.

Louisiana law provided for purging of elector rolls by the
local registrar based upon the patently neutral criteria of a citizen's
failure to vote during the previous four years, failure to report a
change of address, or voting only absentee ballot for the past two
years.   However, implicit in such official authority is the discretion
to discriminate.

Madison Parish, Louisiana had a long history of voting rights
irregularities.   In 1965, the voter registrar had been permanently
enjoined by the Fifth Circuit from discriminating against blacks.   In
1968, the federal court again had to intervene in Madison County,
finding racial discrimination in the distribution of absentee ballots
for a school board election.   The following year, the federal court
held that erroneous instructions on voting machines had the effect of
denying black voters an effective ballot in a special election for
Town Marshall.   In both cases, Judge Benjamin Dawkins, following
the Court of Appeals' decisions, duly set aside the results and required new elections to be held.

In April, 1970, a hotly contested Democratic primary for
Mayor, Village Marshall, Board of Aldermen and Democratic Executive Committee was conducted in the Madison County town of Tallulah.   Flexing newly found political strength, black candidates opposed
whites for every position.   Shortly before the scheduled election, the
registrar challenged the registration of 159 blacks and eleven whites.
However, her purge of voter rolls failed to comply with Louisiana
law.   She was required to give both personal and published notice of
the impending purge to challenged voters, accompanied by the advice that they had the right to respond within ten days in order to
avoid removal from the voter lists.   No notice of the right to defend against the challenge was published.   In addition, the registrar's
office was open for business only five of the ten days before the
books would be closed in preparation for the election.   More importantly, there was evidence of discrimination in the selective filing of the challenges.   Twenty-nine blacks were purged for failure
to report a change of address, although 141 whites who had similarly
moved and an additional sixty-two white absentee voters were not
challenged.

Suit was brought in the Western District of Louisiana contesting the purge procedures and seeking to have the Tallulah elections set aside.   Although the number of black voters allegedly involved was small, the disputed pool of qualified voters might have
turned the election.   White candidates had won the contests by mar-
gins ranging from twenty-four to 140 votes.

Judge Dawkins found that the fifteenth amendment and the Voting Rights Act of 1965 had both been violated and, as a result, enjoined future discriminatory purging practices. Judge Dawkins also set aside the results of the election for Mayor, Board of Aldermen and two positions on the Democratic Executive Committee. Two black candidates who had won the office of Town Marshall and a position on the Executive Committee were not required to run again since their ability to win, despite discrimination, removed the necessity for giving them a second chance.

On review, the appeal was assigned to a panel comprised of Circuit Judges Clark and Simpson and Judge Bailey Aldrich of the First Circuit Court of Appeals sitting by special designation. The panel affirmed that portion of Judge Dawkins's order granting injunctive relief but refused to approve the setting aside of the elections, a clear departure from the tack consistently taken by Judge Brown and by other colleagues on former panels. Upon the request of an unidentified Fifth Circuit Judge, sanctioned by a majority of the judges in active service, all fifteen members of the Fifth Circuit Court of Appeals convened to reconsider Judge Clark's opinion.

At the en banc rehearing on October 17, 1973, the Court of Appeals, by a vote of thirteen to two, vacated the panel decision and, with some modification, affirmed Judge Dawkins's order. Although the district court had found no motive or intent to discriminate on the part of the registrar, the Court of Appeals agreed that, apart from motive, there still had been significant discrimination which tainted the election results. Furthermore, the en banc opinion noted that the alleged lack of diligence in applying for judicial relief, which had troubled Judge Clark in the panel decision, was mitigated here by the brief span of time between purging and the election. Judge Bell characterized the Madison County situation as a "gray area where the discrimination, even if known before the election, was discovered at a late hour." The court shifted the burden of proof to the public officials to demonstrate that the aggrieved voters had deliberately bypassed pre-election judicial remedies.

* * *

In the decade since the 1965 Voting Rights Act, the Fifth Circuit had fully developed its equitable powers, enjoining and even setting aside elections tainted by discriminatory practices. Wielding influence primarily as members of three-judge courts, the judges of the Court of Appeals once more moved to the very frontiers of the law by elaborating upon Supreme Court suggestion and even evolving new remedies.

In addition to coping with discriminatory registration and election practices, the Fifth Circuit also has been faced with more elaborate schemes of disenfranchisement, leading that Court further into the "political thicket." When groups become polarized, as white and black Southerners did in the post-Brown era, each tends to view the other as a homogeneous entity. Individual differences among members of each race become blurred and are lost to sight. So, as Judge Clark had observed in the Madison County case, the misconception arises that voters predictably will make decisions along racial lines. Or, as the white Tuskegee businessman put it, Negroes, at least, vote as a bloc.

In reaction to the feared Negro bloc vote, in many areas of the South the focus of discrimination shifted from denying the vote outright to weakening the effect of the "Negro vote." The major political devices used to dilute black voting strength were reapportionment or redistricting of voting constituencies and the use of at-large elections. The most blatant form of discriminatory redistricting is the "gerrymander." Originating at the turn of the nineteenth century with the political tactics of Governor Elbridge Gerry of Massachusetts, the classic example of discriminatory political exclusion occurred a century and a half later in Tuskegee, Alabama. In 1957, the state senator from Macon County, in which Tuskegee was the principal town, introduced a bill into the Alabama Legislature to redraw the town's boundaries to reduce the number of who could vote in municipal elections. The statute, as passed, altered the shape of Tuskegee from a square to what Mr. Justice Frankfurter called "an uncouth twenty-eight sided figure." That Alabama statute eliminated all but four or five of the town's 400 black voters, without eliminating any of the city's white voters.

Black residents of Tuskegee protested the action by filing suit in federal court. With no precedent to guide him, District Court Judge Frank Johnson concluded that the legislature of Alabama could change the boundaries of Tuskegee, a political subdivision of the state. The issue, as Judge Johnson saw it, was whether the court could review the motive of the legislature's action. Johnson concluded that he did not have that power "by any yardstick made known by the Constitution of the United States."

A three-judge panel for the Court of Appeals comprised of Judges Jones, Wisdom, and Brown heard the case on the appeal. Judge Jones, speaking for himself and Judge Wisdom, stated that this case did not fall into any exception to the general rule that the state legislature has the power to increase or diminish municipal territory. In rejecting the appellants' request for temporary and permanent injunctions to restrain the Mayor and other officials of Tuskegee from enforcing the statute, the majority opinion concluded "[I]n the absence of any racial or class discrimination on the face of the statute, the courts will not hold an act ... to be invalid as violative of the Fourteenth and Fifteenth Amendments to the Constitution of the United States." Judge Brown dissented.

One of the most strongly entrenched principles of judicial review, particularly in the sensitive area of federal-state relations, is the refusal to look for motive behind a legislature's actions when the resultant statute is neutrally phrased and hence, constitutional on its face. Central to the doctrine is the concept that legislators, as members of the coequal branch of government, should be accorded the presumption that they adhere to their oaths of allegiance to the Constitution of the United States and, accordingly, would not purposefully enact laws to discriminate against any segment of their citizenry. But, ignoring the genesis of the legislation, as illustrated by the Tuskegee gerrymander, would make the Court "blind not to see what 'All others can see and understand'." Judge Brown urged, "There is no reason why [Courts] should pretend to be more ignorant or unobserving than the rest of mankind."

On appeal, the United States Supreme Court agreed with Judge Brown's dissent and, in a major decision of first impression, reversed Gomillion v. Lightfoot. The Supreme Court held that if the claims of the black plaintiffs could be proved, the legislation would fall as a discriminatory measure violative of the fourteenth and fifteenth amendments. Justice Frankfurter observed:

> While in form this is merely an act redefining metes and bounds, if the allegations are established, the inescapable human effect of this essay in geometry and geography is to despoil colored citizens, and only colored citizens, of their theretofore enjoyed voting rights.

Consequently, when a state singles out a racial minority for discriminatory treatment, its insulation from judicial review is at an end. The Supreme Court noted: "[S]uch insulation is not carried over when state power is used as an instrument for circumventing a federally protected right."

In 1972, the Fifth Circuit Court of Appeals was again confronted with a case of alleged racial gerrymandering. Two black residents of Adams County, Mississippi filed a class action challenging the county's reorganization plan, claiming it was calculated to dilute the black vote. The County Board had retained a planning firm to prepare a plan for the reorganization of its five districts and, as required by the Voting Rights Act of 1965, had submitted it to the Attorney General who had made no objection. The ostensible aim of the plan was to equally divide the population, as well as the mileage of roads for county maintenance, into a square mile area so that the responsibility of each county supervisor would be equalized. The new plan created districts that started with a broad rural base and converged in "spoke-like" fashion into the city of Natchez, thus dividing up the city. However, as a result of the plan, the blacks lost the electoral majority they had previously enjoyed in two districts. Instead, under the new plan the blacks retained a majority in one district, an equal percentage in another and comprised a minority in the other three districts.

With Judge Dyer writing the opinion, the appellate court panel upheld the district court's denial of relief. Judge Dyer discussed the plaintiffs' burden of proof:

> ... [T]o establish the existence of a constitutionally im-

permissible redistricting plan, in the absence of malap-
portionment, plaintiffs must maintain the burden of proving (1) a racially motivated gerrymander, or a plan drawn
along racial lines or (2) that ... [an] ... apportionment
scheme, under the circumstances of a particular case,
would operate to minimize or cancel out the voting strength
of racial or political elements of the voting population. '

After study of the record, the Court of Appeals concluded that the
blacks had failed to carry the burden of proof cast upon them as
challengers of the new plan.

In 1973, another three-judge panel of the Court of Appeals
heard another appeal taken by aggrieved black residents of Adams
County. Since their last appearance before the Court, the plaintiffs
had submitted an alternative plan for the district court's consideration which accomplished the desired results of equalizing municipal
service responsibilities, while producing less dilution of black voting strength. This time Judge Coleman, on behalf of the Court,
analyzed both the plaintiffs' plan and the County plan and concluded
that there had been no abuse of discretion in upholding the validity
of the County's plan. The two plans were closely matched in population, there being a net difference of .2% in the population ratios
between the two.

A disturbing aspect of this most recent Fifth Circuit decision
is the placing of the burden of proof on the plaintiffs to show either
a racial gerrymander or a dilution of voting strength. In other
areas of voting and in both jury discrimination and public accommodations, the Fifth Circuit had consistently placed the burden of
proof on those who more readily have access to evidence which
could establish or repudiate a discrimination charge. The Fifth
Circuit painstakingly developed and implemented the theory of discrimination pursuant to a "pattern or practice" in voting rights cases,
thus placing the burden on the state to refute the existence of discrimination. It will be recalled that the theory was eventually to
form the basis of that most significant section in the Voting Rights
Act of 1965, the "automatic trigger" provision. However, in cases
of alleged dilution of voting power, to require the plaintiffs to carry
the burden of proof presupposes an absence of even vestigial effects
of discrimination on the part of the state.

The problem with redistricting cases, which will predictably
continue to crop up on the Court's docket, is that redistricting serves
important and even necessary governmental ends. For example, redistricting can balance out shifts in population in order to provide
an adequate tax base for each unit. But, redistricting can also
serve purposefully to dilute black voting strength. The consideration
of allegations of a racially motivated realignment of governmental
units plunges the federal court further into a technical morass of
city planning data, a province once exclusively reserved for the executive or legislative branches of government. Consequently, the
Fifth Circuit's reluctance to enter this new area is somewhat under-
standable.

A second commonly used method which effectively dilutes black votes involves switching to at-large elections within a community. This scheme works where whites preponderate within the class of registered voters. Any black majority in any one district can be outweighed by the cumulative white votes in other districts.

In 1972, the Court of Appeals faced problems engendered by a new at-large system of election in East Carroll Parish, Louisiana, where no black resident had been permitted to vote from 1922 to 1962. Upon charges that the Parish was malapportioned under Supreme Court and Fifth Circuit precedents District Judge Ben Dawkins had ordered at-large elections for police jurors (parish commissioners) and school board members, an acceptable method of complying with the one man-one vote mandate espoused early by courts within the Fifth Circuit. On appeal, another black was allowed to intervene. He challenged the at-large plan as violating black rights under the fourteenth and fifteenth amendments and the Voting Rights Act of 1965. Judge Dawkins had found that the at-large plan did not dilute the black voting strength since there was zero population deviation and since blacks comprised 59% of the total population. If registered, the black majority could vote for and elect all candidates. However, only 46% of eligible blacks were registered. Splitting two to one, the Court of Appeals panel affirmed the at-large election concept, agreeing with Judge Dawkins that the reorganization plan was not racially motivated.

On rehearing, en banc, the Court of Appeals split badly in considering the issues at stake. Judge Gewin, speaking for a majority of nine of the fifteen, reversed the panel's decision and nullified the at-large election plan. The emphasis in the majority opinion was upon the lingering effects of past discrimination in East Carroll Parish. Judge Gewin noted that blacks still had a registered strength of only 46% of those eligible, a suspect statistic under the automatic trigger section of the Voting Rights Act. The majority remained unconvinced of a local change of heart, despite the election of three black candidates for office in the preceding 1971 and 1972 elections. Judge Gewin pointed out that the success of the black candidates could have been attributable to politicians who realized that it was expedient for them, and for the maintenance of the at-large system, for several "token" blacks to be politically successful. In sum, the majority concluded that the black residents of the parish had satisfied the burden of proving that the at-large redistricting scheme would minimize, if not cancel, the voting strength of the registered black population. A statistical population majority was not enough. Vastly under-represented minorities on registration rolls, coupled with evidence of persistent past discriminatory voting practices, satisfied the burden of proof of dilution of political strength. The majority concluded, "[W]e cannot sanction the view that minorities are to be exposed and subject to apportionment schemes otherwise constitutionally infirm because the equal protection clause can be watered down on the basis of population statistics alone."

The split opinion in the East Carroll case may presage difficulties in store for the Court of Appeals in future decisions in this area. The blatant cases of discrimination--the humiliating practices of Mr. Lynd, the obvious gerrymander in Tuskegee--appear to be relics of a recent but now bygone era. At some point, presumptions of lingering discrimination from low black voter registration can fade into presumptions of political disinterest. At some point, Judge Clark's faith will be justified that citizens do not vote strictly along color lines. And, at that point, members of each race in the South can go back to being individuals again.

* * *

Soon after the Civil War, President Lincoln rather hesitantly suggested to the Reconstruction Governor of Louisiana "for his private consideration whether some of the colored people may not be let in [to vote]; as for instance, the very intelligent and especially those who have fought gallantly in our ranks." Neither Lincoln nor abolitionist William Lloyd Garrison, much less white Southerners seething under Reconstruction, could have envisioned that a southern Court of Appeals would lead the way in effectively enforcing universal suffrage without regard to race. The decisions of the Fifth Circuit that guaranteed the right to vote are a monumental contribution to the future political participation of both the majority and all minorities in the United States. Unlike decisions in other civil rights areas such as school desegregation, the Fifth Circuit's voting rights cases show every sign of being a permanent enhancement of the law, the political process and the social order.

NOTES AND PRIMARY AUTHORITY

There are several important sources for the history of voting discrimination and modern day descriptions which served as the basis for this chapter: Woodward, "The Political Legacy of Reconstruction," 26 J. of Negro Ed. 231 (1957); Franklin, "Legal Disenfranchisement of the Negro," 26 J. of Negro Ed. 241 (1957); Ladenburg and McFeely, The Black Man in the Land of Equality (1969); Price, The Negro and the Ballot in the South (1959); Strong, Registration of Voters in Alabama (1956); Schwartz, 2 Statutory History of the United States--Civil Rights (1970); Political Participation, U.S. Comm. on Civil Rights (1968); "Voting Rights: A Case Study of Madison Parish, Louisiana," 38 U. of Chi. L. Rev. 726 (1971); Taper, Gomillion Versus Lightfoot (1962); Watters and Cleghorn, Climbing Jacob's Ladder (1967); Hamilton, The Bench and the Ballot: Southern Federal Judges and Black Voters (1973); and Tuttle, "Equality and the Vote," 41 N.Y.U. L. Rev. 245 (1966).

The relevant federal Voting Rights Statutes are the 1957 Act, Civil Rights Act of 1957, Pub. L. No. 83-315, 71 Stat. 634 (1957); the 1960 Act, Pub. L. No. 86-449, 74 Stat. 86 (1960); and the 1965 Act, Pub. L. No. 89-110, 79 Stat. 437 (1965) [amended and extended in 1975, current version at 42 U.S.C. §§1971, 1973 (1975)].

Judicial Intervention and Congressional Response. Primary sources for materials in this section are the cases, United States v. Louisiana, 168 F. Supp. 170 (S.D. Miss. 1958) (three-judge ct.), aff'd, 380 U.S. 145 (1965); Reddix v. Lucky, 148 F. Supp. 108 (W.D. La. 1957), rev'd, 252 F.2d 930 (5th Cir. 1958).

Progress at a Snail's Pace: Judge Cox and Mr. Lynd. --The primary sources for material in this section are the cases: United States v. Lynd, 301 F.2d 818 (5th Cir. 1962), cert. denied, 371 U.S. 893 (1963); Kennedy v. Lynd, 306 F.2d 222 (5th Cir. 1962); 349 F.2d 785 (5th Cir. 1965); United States v. Penton, 212 F. Supp. 193 (M.D. Ala. 1962); and United States v. Ramsey, 331 F.2d 824 (5th Cir. 1964). Contemporary news accounts were also used such as those contained in the McComb (Miss.) Enterprise Journal, Sept. 18, 1962, the Jackson Daily News, Mar. 8, 1962 and throughout the period of activity in the Lynd case.

Pettus Bridge and the Voting Rights Act of 1965. --The primary source for material in this section was contemporary news accounts such as contained in the New York Times, Oct. 20, 1969, at 47 and Mar. 8, 1965, p. 13, and Time, Mar. 19, 1965, pp. 24-25 and 38. Also used were the cases, Alabama v. United States, 304 F.2d 583 (5th Cir. 1962); United States v. Duke, 332 F.2d 759 (5th Cir. 1964).

The Last Frontier. --The primary sources for material in this section are the cases: United States v. Campbell, No. GC 633 (N.D. Miss. 1965); Hamer v. Campbell, 358 F.2d 215 (5th Cir. 1966); Bush v. Martin, 224 F. Supp. 499 (S.D. Tex. 1963) (3-judge ct.), aff'd, 376 U.S. 222 (1964); Sanders v. Gray, 203 F. Supp. 158 (N.D. Ga. 1962) (3-judge ct.), modified, 372 U.S. 368 (1963); Wesberry v. Vandiver, 206 F. Supp. 276 (N.D. Ga. 1962) (3-judge ct.), rev'd sub nom., Wesberry v. Sanders, 376 U.S. 1 (1964); Toombs v. Fortson, 205 F. Supp. 248 (N.D. Ga. 1962) (3-judge ct.), aff'd per curiam, 384 U.S. 210 (1966); Bell v. Southwell, 376 F.2d 659 (5th Cir. 1967); Brown v. Post, 279 F. Supp. 60 (W.D. La. 1968); United States v. Post, 297 F. Supp. 46 (W.D. La. 1968); Toney v. White, 348 F. Supp. 188 (W.D. La. 1971); 476 F.2d 203 (5th Cir. 1973), 488 F.2d 310 (5th Cir. 1973); Gomillion v. Lightfoot, 167 F. Supp. 405 (M.D. Ala. 1958); rev'd, 364 U.S. 339 (1960); Howard v. Adams County Bd. of Supervisors, 453 F.2d 455 (5th Cir. 1972), cert. denied, 407 U.S. 925, aff'd on rehearing, No. 72-2596 (July 2, 1973); Zimmer v. McKeithen, 467 F.2d 1381 (5th Cir. 1972), rev'd en banc, No. 71-2649 (Sept. 12, 1973).

A more complete manuscript, with detailed documentation of all sources, is available as indicated in the Preface supra.

Chapter 8

JURY SELECTION:
THE RIGHT TO SIT IN JUDGMENT

> There are only two instrumentalities of power--
> the vote and the jury. The jury system stands
> behind the power to vote. How easy is it to cast
> a ballot when you're afraid someone, from the
> sheriff on down, might shoot you and nobody will
> do anything about it?
> --Charles Morgan, Jr., former Southern Re-
> gional Director of the American Civil Liber-
> ties Union, Newsweek, Nov. 8, 1965

In 1958, Lewis Lloyd Anderson, a black minister in Selma,
Alabama, was actively involved in a local voter registration drive.
According to later testimony before the Civil Rights Commission,
Rev. Anderson was a "troublemaker" in the eyes of the white community of Selma. On a rainy day in January, 1959, while traveling
on an unpaved street, Anderson's car collided with another vehicle.
Anderson was dazed and his car caromed down the street, ultimately
killing a pedestrian. The Dallas County Grand Jury indicted Anderson for second degree murder. There was a gross disparity between Rev. Anderson's testimony and the theory of the state's case.
He stated that he had been driving about fifteen miles an hour when
he collided with the second car and had been knocked unconscious.
In contrast, the prosecution charged that Anderson had been reck-
lessly driving at least sixty miles per hour, relying for its evidence
principally upon the testimony of two eyewitnesses, neither of whom
could drive or had ever driven an automobile. In order to convict,
the prosecution had to establish either that the defendant intended to
kill the pedestrian or that his conduct had been so wanton and reck-
less that, as a natural consequence, human life had been endangered.
The key issues at the trial were the speed of Anderson's automobile
and his capacity to function after the first collision. The resolution
of these very critical issues of fact was the prerogative of the trial
jury.

Juries, the ultimate arbiters of disputed facts, play an enormously significant role in the American judicial system. In cases
like the trial of Lloyd Anderson, which involved a politically unpopular member of a minority and where there was conflicting testimony, the composition of the jury took on an extraordinary significance. In pretrial motions, Anderson had asserted that blacks had

been systematically excluded from service as either Grand Jurors or Petit (trial) Jurors in Dallas County. Although it was stipulated that according to the 1950 census of the county's adult male population, there were 7,956 blacks and only 6,940 whites, it was estimated that only about one out of ten "veniremen" (qualified residents from whom trial jurors were selected) was black. In fact, according to the best estimate of county officials, only one or two blacks had ever served on juries during the past twenty years and none had served within the last three years. Rev. Anderson's motions challenging the jury selection system were denied. The all-white jury convicted him of voluntary manslaughter and, in further exercise of its discretion, affixed his punishment at ten years in prison.

At about the same time Rev. Anderson was on trial, a young black man named Mack Parker was confined in a Mississippi jail awaiting trial on charges that he had raped a pregnant white woman. On April 25, 1959, Parker was dragged from his Poplarville jail cell, shot twice, and dumped in the Pearl River. After his body was recovered, the F.B.I. conducted an exhaustive month-long investigation. Among the other items of evidence contained in the F.B.I.'s voluminous report were the admissions of three local white men, stating that they had been involved in events connected with the abduction and listing the names of twenty others who were also directly responsible for the murder. The following November, an all-white, eighteen-member county grand jury was impanelled to consider possible indictments for murder. However, no witnesses were called and the grand jury recessed three days later, declining to take any action. As one resident of Poplarville succinctly concluded: "You couldn't convict the guilty parties if you had a sound film of the lynching."* No person was ever indicted for the murder of Mack Parker. Attorney General Rogers characterized Mississippi's handling of the Parker case: "as flagrant and calculated a miscarriage of justice as I know of."

Four years thereafter, in the late evening of June 12, 1963, Medgar Evers, the leader of the Mississippi NAACP, returned to his home in Jackson after attending a church rally. He was killed by a shot in the back as he was entering his front door. After an intensive investigation by both community officials and the F.B.I., a local white man, Byron de la Beckwith, was arrested first on federal charges of conspiring to violate Evers' civil rights and, subsequently, on state charges of murder.

At the state trial for murder, de la Beckwith based his defense upon an alibi. He produced three policemen who testified that they had seen him near the time of the shooting fifty miles away in Greenwood. However, other accumulated evidence seemed to implicate de la Beckwith as the murderer: the murder gun bore his fingerprint on its rifle scope; the gun was traced to him as its owner, although de la Beckwith claimed it had been stolen from his

---

*New York Times, Jan. 4, 1960, p. 8, col. 6.

car; de la Beckwith had a curved cut over his eye which matched
the sight's eyepiece; and, two carhops testified that on the night of
the murder de la Beckwith was in the vicinity of Evers' home.

After eleven hours of deliberation and twenty ballots, the
jury reported to the court that it was hopelessly deadlocked, seven-
to-five for acquittal. As a result, the court declared a mistrial.
The members of the jury were all white.

The "Impartial Jury": A Paper Right

Trial by jury is an ancient and honored hallmark of Anglo-
American jurisprudence. The jury of one's peers originated as a
shield against royal vendettas. It was a right specifically demanded
by the King's subjects at Runnymede when the Magna Carta was
signed. By the middle of the fifteenth century in England, the trial
jury had been established by custom as twelve "good and lawful
men" of the vicinage, the district in which an offense allegedly had
been committed.

The right to trial by jury was brought with the colonists to
America and was later explicitly guaranteed by the sixth amendment
to the Constitution: "In all criminal prosecutions, the accused shall
enjoy the right to a speedy and public trial, by an impartial jury of
the State and district wherein the crime shall have been committed
.. .."

The Civil War amendments to the Constitution sought to secure for the recently emancipated Negro slaves full political rights,
including the right to equal protection of the laws and due process.
In addition, Congress in the Civil Rights Act of 1875 specifically
attempted to insure the right of trial by an impartial jury by providing that any state official who excluded Negroes from those summoned for jury duty was guilty of a federal crime and subject to a
maximum fine of $5,000.00. Within four years, the constitutionality
of this federal statute was tested in the Supreme Court. Although
a Virginia statute extended jury eligibility to all adult male citizens
and was patently nondiscriminatory on its face, a county judge responsible for juror selection had summarily excluded all black county
residents from consideration. The judge was indicted under the federal statute, arrested, and upon his refusal to post bond, held in
custody. In considering his petition for release, the Supreme Court
upheld the congressional power under the Civil War amendments to
make such discriminatory practices a federal crime, but not without dissent.

The main thrust of the dissenting opinion, in which two justices joined, concerned the friction between federal and state governments which might occur if the federal courts were empowered to
criminally punish state officials. However, Mr. Justice Field also
asked some troubling questions about the nature of the right to jury
trial.

If, when a colored person is accused of a criminal offense, the presence of persons of his race on the jury by
which he is to be tried is essential to secure to him the
equal protection of the laws, it would seem that the presence of such persons on the bench would be equally essential, if the court should consist of more than one judge,
as in many cases it may; and if it should consist of a
single judge, that such protection would be impossible. A
similar objection might be raised to the composition of
any appellate court to which the case, after verdict, might
be carried.

The position that, in cases where the rights of colored
persons are concerned, justice will not be done to them
unless they have a mixed jury, is founded upon the notion
that in such cases white persons will not be fair and honest jurors. If this position be correct, there ought not to
be any white persons on the jury where the interests of
colored persons only are involved. That jury would not
be an honest or fair one, of which any of its members
should be governed in his judgment by other considerations
than the law and the evidence, and that decision would
hardly be considered just, which should be reached by a
sort of compromise, in which the prejudices of one race
were set off against the prejudices of the other. To be
consistent, those who hold this notion should contend that,
in cases affecting members of the colored race only, the
juries should be composed entirely of colored persons,
and that the presiding judge should be of the same race.
To this result the doctrine asserted by the District Court
logically leads.

Nowhere in the Constitution nor in federal statutes was the
term "impartial jury" defined, nor was the meaning of a "jury of
one's peers" settled by common law tradition. Justice Field was
troubled that a Negro could claim a denial of equal protection and
due process because he was not tried by a peer group defined as
those of his own race, and that, by implication, the majority of the
Supreme Court had found that members of one race could not be expected to judge impartially a member of another race.

The following year, in 1880, the Supreme Court considered
its second jury discrimination case and rather gingerly set out some
guidelines governing the jury selection process. In Strauder v.
West Virginia a Negro accused of murder challenged the constitutionality of the criminal process in West Virginia by which Negroes
were explicitly excluded from jury eligibility. The Court declared
the state statute unconstitutional, observing:

The right to a trial by jury is guaranteed to every
citizen of West Virginia by the Constitution of that State,
and the constitution of juries is a very essential part of
the protection such a mode of trial is intended to secure.
The very idea of a jury is a body of men composed of the

peers or equals of the person whose rights it is selected or summoned to determine; that is, of his neighbors, fellows, associates, persons having the same legal status in society as that which he holds.... It is well known that prejudices often exist against particular classes in the community, which sway the judgment of jurors, and which, therefore, operate in some cases to deny to persons of those classes the full enjoyment of that protection which others enjoy. Prejudice in a local community is held to be a reason for a change of venue. The framers of the [fourteenth] constitutional amendment must have known full well the existence of such prejudice and its likelihood to continue against the manumitted slaves and their race, and that knowledge was, doubtless, a motive that led to the amendment.... [H]ow can it be maintained that compelling a colored man to submit to a trial for his life by a jury drawn from a panel from which the State has expressly excluded every man of his race, because of color alone, however well qualified in other respects, is not a denial to him of equal legal protection?

However, the justices also made it clear that states did have the power, absent outright exclusion of any class or race, to proscribe qualifications for juror eligibility. It was, for example, permissible to limit potential jurors to "males, to freeholders, to citizens, to persons within certain ages, or to persons having educational qualifications."

* * *

As a result of the authorization by the Supreme Court in Strauder that some limitations upon juror eligibility were permissible, state legislatures thereafter enacted laws broadly outlining qualifications. These juror qualification statutes have fostered in the twentieth century a jury selection process that combines both objective and subjective standards. The objective standards usually require a prospective juror to be a citizen of the community for a certain period of time, to be of certain minimum age, and to be able to read, write and understand English. Certain groups of citizens are also generally disqualified from jury service by statute; for example, convicted felons and persons with mental and physical infirmities which would render them unable to serve. Finally, certain classes of citizens are typically exempted for jury duty, usually doctors, ministers, lawyers, government officials and mothers with minor children, because they provide critical services in the community.

Virtually all of the states in the Fifth Circuit now have, or have had, additional subjective juror selection standards. Alabama requires jurors to be citizens "who are generally reputed to be honest and intelligent men and are esteemed in the community for their integrity, good character and sound judgment." Georgia requires its jurors to be "upright and intelligent citizens," while Mississippi

requires its jurors to be citizens of "good intelligence, sound judgment, and fair character." Consequently, jury commissioners, like
the voter registrars, for years have enjoyed a wide range of discretion in selecting citizens for jury duty. The stage was set for
a second round of jury discrimination litigation. Although statutes
were racially neutral in selection criteria, at what point did the
actual practices of jury commissioners amount to a purposeful exclusion of classes or races?

The Supreme Court considered this issue for the first time
in 1935, when a black defendant challenged the practices of the jury
commissioners in Jackson County, Alabama. The petitioner, Norris, appealed his conviction for rape on the grounds that qualified
blacks had been systematically excluded from jury service, amounting to a denial of equal protection. He presented evidence which
included the jury book records from 1930-1933 and testimony from
the circuit court clerk and clerk of the jury commissioner, all to
the effect that no black had been called for jury service in Jackson
County. Furthermore, he adduced testimony that there had been
specified blacks who were qualified but were never summoned. In
rebuttal, the state simply presented sworn testimony by the county
officials that they had not used race as a ground for exclusion.

Proving the existence of a discriminatory motive by jury commissioners had previously been an enormous burden which most
criminal defendants could not overcome. However, in the Norris
case, for the first time, the Supreme Court rejected the conclusion
that a simple denial of discrimination by the state was sufficient in
view of the overwhelming statistical showing. As Chief Justice
Hughes noted:

> We think that this [the state's] evidence failed to rebut
> the strong prima facie case which the defendant had made.
> That showing as to the long-continued exclusion of negroes
> from jury service, and as to the many negroes qualified
> for that service, could not be met by mere generalities.

Consequently, states would be required to demonstrate that there
were bona fide reasons--other than race--to explain a long-continued
absence of blacks on juror rolls. In two subsequent Texas cases,
jury commissioners argued that no qualified blacks were known to
them, as a justification for the fact that none had been certified for
jury duty. However, the Supreme court rejected this contention and
cast an affirmative duty upon jury commissioners to familiarize
themselves with all sectors of the community and to avoid any conduct, regardless of intent, which would lead to the exclusion of any
group.

*   *   *

Such was the state of the law by 1950, at the dawn of the
civil rights movement. However, in many areas of the South, jury
selection practices did not reflect the law as it had been clearly

established by the Supreme Court. With the escalation of the civil rights movement, incidents of violence between the races increased. Consequently the jury selection process became a key element in the resulting criminal trials. In testimony before the Senate Subcommittee on Constitutional Rights in June, 1966, Attorney General Nicholas Katzenbach submitted a list of violent deaths resulting from racial conflicts in the South during the period from 1955 to 1965. According to his testimony, the reported incidents demonstrated that blacks charged with murdering whites were more often convicted and received heavier penalties from juries than whites charges with killing blacks. Similarly, after an intensive investigation of Southern justice in racial cases, a reporter for a Southern newspaper concluded that where a black defendant was accused of any offense involving a white victim, he almost invariably received a sentence grossly disproportionate to the usual punishment for the crime.*

* * *

The trials of Lloyd Anderson and Byron de la Beckwith and the refusal to charge any person for the murder of Mack Parker were apparently not simply isolated instances of a breakdown in Southern criminal justice. There was every indication that blacks, traditionally excluded, were continuing to be intentionally foreclosed from participation as jurors in the judicial process in the states of the Fifth Circuit. Thus, civil rights advocates, already litigating civil cases to insure the vote, equal access to public facilities, and desegregation of the public school systems were forced as well to challenge the administration of the criminal process.

The Paper Right Becomes Absolute

Q. Did you, during the time you were Sheriff, if

---

*The following cases gleaned from local records throughout the South were reported as typical of the phenomenon. A teen-age black boy was hunting when a group of white youths, who had been drinking, admittedly tried "to devil" him; one of the white youths grabbed the black's rifle which discharged, killing the white boy. An all-white jury found the black adolescent guilty of murder and sentenced him to life imprisonment. In another example, an elderly white woman, who had been warned repeatedly about jaywalking, was killed when she walked into the side of a car driven by a black. At first, no charges were pressed, but several days later, after pressure from the woman's relatives, the police charged the driver with manslaughter. In another case, involving a traffic accident, a black man was sentenced to eight years for assault with intent to commit murder when a white man received a broken leg as a result of an accident. Charleston Gazette, June 29, 1965, at p. 7 (from the second article of a five part series on the "Negro and Justice in the South," by Jack Nelson).

you can recall, serve any processes or sum-
mons issued by the Clerk of the Circuit Court
of Carroll County for jury service, either
grand or petit jury, to any person of the Negro race?

A. Well, now that's a little difficult question. I
wouldn't say that a man probably had Negro
blood in him, because we have summoned dark
complected people and white complected people,
so I wouldn't say whether a man was or was
not a Negro.

Q. You couldn't tell?

A. I couldn't tell whether he was full blooded
white man or not.

Q. Well, I was asking you a question, has any
person indicated to you that they were members
of the Negro race whom you have served any
processes on?

A. I don't recall any being served on a real black
Negro.

> --Transcript of evidence before the United
> States District Court for the Northern
> District of Mississippi reported in United
> States ex rel Goldsby v. Harpole, 263
> F.2d 71 (5th Cir. 1959)

As late as 1954, no black had ever served on a jury in Carroll County, Mississippi. Fifty-seven per cent of the population of
that county was black, of whom almost 2,000 were adult males; however, state law also required as a qualification for jury eligibility
that an individual be eligible to vote. The tie-in with voting amounted
to an absolute barrier for otherwise eligible blacks, since there
were only two blacks in the county who had ever been registered and
they were both dead. With those facts as a backdrop, Robert Lee
Goldsby, a black, was arrested, tried, and convicted of the murder
of a white couple in Carroll County, and thereafter sentenced to
death.

Federal District Court Judge Claude Clayton had denied
Goldsby's petition for habeas corpus on two grounds. First, Judge
Clayton ruled that his claim of a purposeful, systematic exclusion
of blacks from jury service had not been proved since it might well
be assumed that blacks had voluntarily abstained from registering
to vote. Second, Judge Clayton held that even if such exclusion
could be shown, Goldsby had waived any possible objections he might
have had to the jury selection process when he did not assert a
challenge at his trial. Shortly before Goldsby's scheduled execution,
Chief Justice Warren granted a petition for a stay in order to afford
the defendant an opportunity to appeal his case to the Fifth Circuit.
The Fifth Circuit reversed Goldsby's conviction in what would become one of the court's most significant civil rights decisions.

Speaking for the two other panel members, Judges Brown and

Wisdom, Judge Rives penned a strongly worded opinion in which he characterized the "naked figures" that no Negro had ever been summoned for jury duty as "startling." The court would not indulge in the assumption that blacks had voluntarily abstained from voting, the precondition to juror eligibility, but instead, the court cast the burden upon the state to come forward with proof that officials had freely and fairly registered blacks. In short, the taint of voting discrimination reached out to despoil the state's juror selection practices. In this aspect of the Goldsby case, the Court of Appeals could rely upon Supreme Court precedent allowing statistics to make out a prima facie case of exclusion.

However, the issue of the waiver of the right to challenge allegedly discriminatory selection practices was one of first impression, where the Fifth Circuit had to act without Supreme Court guidance. Although precedent abounded that any alleged waiver of a constitutional right should be closely scrutinized by courts to insure that the relinquishment had been knowingly and voluntarily made, Goldsby had been represented by retained counsel at trial and, thus, objections clearly could have been made. Goldsby had initially retained a black lawyer from out of state to represent him at trial, and that attorney had prepared challenges to the juror selection practices; however, Goldsby's family subsequently hired local white counsel who refused to continue until co-counsel was discharged. For unreported reasons, Goldsby and his family had acquiesced in the demand. The white attorney, who otherwise provided creditable service at trial, did not raise the issue of jury selection.

The Rives' opinion on the waiver issue is an extraordinary one, in view of the facts of this case. Traditionally, constitutional rights are personal to the individual citizen, which he may either insist upon or decline--provided he has been effectively represented by counsel. Furthermore, the legal system recognizes that lawyers may frequently forego raising certain defensive issues as a matter of considered trial strategy. As one federal appellate court expressed the prevailing standard, courts should not intervene unless defense counsel's "errors of judgment" result in rendering the trial a "farce and a mockery of justice." However, under the Code of Professional Responsibility which governs the conduct of all lawyers, quite clearly the waiver of constitutional rights rises above the attorney's individual judgment and requires the informed consent of the defendant-client.

The Fifth Circuit held that there had been no valid waiver of Goldsby's right to challenge the juror selection process. Drawing upon his own thirty-seven years as a trial lawyer in the South, Judge Rives implied that the region's tradition of racial discrimination skewed normal operative assumptions about the legal system. He discounted the possibility that a black charged with a criminal offense would, or could, afford to challenge the status quo. Furthermore, according to the Rives opinion, lawyers--the traditional guardians of defendants' rights--also could not reasonably be expected to challenge the current system in the South:

> [T]he very prejudice which causes the dominant race
> to exclude members of what it may assume to be an in-
> ferior race from jury services operates with multiplied
> intensity against one who resists such exclusion. Consci-
> entious southern lawyers often reason that the prejudicial
> effects on their client of raising the issue far outweigh
> any practical protection in the particular case.... Such
> courageous and unselfish lawyers as find it essential for
> their clients' protection to fight against the systematic
> exclusion of Negroes from juries sometimes do so at the
> risk of personal sacrifice which may extend to loss of
> practice and social ostracism.
>   As Judges of a Circuit comprising six states of the
> deep South, we think that it is our duty to take judicial
> notice that lawyers residing in many southern jurisdictions
> rarely, almost to the point of never, raise the issue of
> systematic exclusion of Negroes from juries.

If neither the black defendant nor his counsel were free to
demand the right to a nondiscriminatory system of juror selection,
then who would or could? Clearly the Goldsby decision represented
an acceptance by these Fifth Circuit judges, on behalf of the federal
judicial system, of that responsibility. The panel did not remand
the case either to the state judicial system or to the Federal District Court for the Northern District of Mississippi. Instead it
ordered a retrial of Goldsby on the murder accusation before a jury
from which blacks had not been systematically excluded and gave the
state eight months to set its processes for retrial in order.

*   *   *

The Goldsby decision provided the foundation for subsequent
Fifth Circuit decisions involving juror discrimination; and the court
reinforced its stand on the waiver issue in the later case of Whitus
v. Balkcom.

In Whitus, two blacks were convicted of murder and sentenced to death by a jury in Mitchell County, Georgia. As proof of
the accuracy of Judge Rives' observations about the Hobson's choice
facing Southern attorneys in challenging jury selection practices, the
defendants' trial lawyer later testified:

> I had hopes that I could obtain an acquittal under the facts
> as I knew them, and I realized that the case had created
> quite a bit of notoriety and to have brought up such a
> question [of discriminatory selection] at the lower court
> would have filled the air with such hostility that an ac-
> quittal would have been almost impossible.

The Fifth Circuit reversed the convictions, finding that there had
been systematic exclusion of blacks from the jury system and that,
under the circumstances, there had been no effective waiver of the
defendants' rights. As Judge Wisdom observed, "The constitutional

vice is not just the exclusion of Negroes from juries. It is also the State's requiring Negro defendants to choose between an unfairly constituted jury and a prejudiced jury."

The evolution of legal doctrine marked by the Goldsby and Whitus decisions exemplifies the blending of judicial talents which the Court of Appeals for the Fifth Circuit had achieved by the mid-sixties. The Goldsby opinion of 1959 was short in exposition of precise constitutional doctrine. It was more of a descriptive essay on an obvious, yet historically tolerated, malfunction of the states' judicial systems. Its credibility stemmed primarily from the fact that it was Judge Richard Rives, the former Alabama trial lawyer, who had written the opinion and had spoken knowledgeably about the human tolls exacted by the South's jury practices. Five years later, in Whitus, Judge John Minor Wisdom, perhaps the most scholarly member of the court, detailed the constitutional theory upon which the court's rulings rested and wove the court's earlier observations into the rubric of equal protection and due process of law. The Whitus-Goldsby rationale, elevating the right to a nondiscriminatorily selected jury to an absolute right--waivable only by a defendant after full discussion with counsel--was, however, to be short-lived. As will be seen in the final period under study, the decade of the 1970s, the composition of the Court of Appeals for the Fifth Circuit changed and the Whitus-Goldsby rationale changed with it.

Jury Selection and the Theory of Probabilities:
Breaking New Ground

I do not count myself among those who are cynical about the capacity of citizens in any sec-tion of the country to rise to the challenge of one of the highest responsibilities of free men--the preservation of law and a just social order.
If I wish to avoid cynicism, so also do I want to avoid the attitude of easy optimism.... The adoption of this amendment holds for me a double significance: not only does it insure that trials will be conducted before juries composed of tales-men selected from all citizens in the judicial dis-trict, but it enlarges the civil rights of citizens who may have heretofore been excluded from jury service under State law.
--Senator John F. Kennedy in floor debate con-cerning the 1957 Civil Rights Act, 103 Cong. Rec. 13306.

As has been seen, both the Supreme Court and the Court of Appeals for the Fifth Circuit had taken uncompromising positions when presented with any case in which a defendant could show by admissions of jury commissions, requirements of state statutory law, or by statistics that blacks had been systematically excluded from selection as jurors. However, the Supreme Court had also ruled that the Constitution did not guarantee to a defendant a trial before a jury in which his race was proportionately represented, nor a trial before a jury on which even one member of his race sat. According to Mr. Justice Reed, "Obviously the number of races and nationalities appearing in the ancestry of our citizens would make it impossible to meet a requirement of proportional representation." What a defendant was entitled to, as a matter of constitutional right, was a potential pool of jurors, selected by color-blind criteria, which would truly represent a cross section of the community and from which his particular jury would be drawn.

Despite a century of case law development, in 1961, after an exhaustive study of discriminatory practices in jury selection, the United States Commission on Civil Rights reported: "The practice of racial exclusion from juries persists today even though it has long stood indicted as a serious violation of the 14th amendment." The earliest decided cases presented blatant evidence of racial discrimination: statutes which excluded non-whites from consideration and jury commissioners' admissions of conscious exclusion. For those early cases, following the lead of the Supreme Court, federal judges pierced through nondiscrimination disclaimers, both statutory and administrative, to find purposeful exclusion where the resulting selection statistics told a story of total or near total exclusion of blacks from jury duty. The Supreme Court noted as early as 1940, "Chance and accident alone could hardly have brought about the listing for grand jury service of so few Negroes from among the thousands shown by the undisputed evidence to possess the legal qualifications for jury service." Similarly, a decade later, the Supreme Court also found it improbable that chance alone, rather than conscious limitation, would explain results where no jury panel ever had more than one black member despite the fact that blacks comprised 6.5% of the population eligible for jury duty. As Mr. Justice Frankfurter observed in a concurring opinion:

> The number of Negroes both qualified and available for jury service ... precluded such uniform presence of never more than one Negro on any other basis of good faith than that the commissioners were guided by the belief that one Negro on the grand jury satisfied the prohibition against discrimination....

In essence, the reasoning process expressed by the Supreme Court welled up from what one commentator has termed the Court's "intuitive idea of probability," a rough-hewn application of the mathematical theory of probabilities. Total exclusion of blacks or a consistent, repeated pattern of limitation offended common sense logic: clearly courts would not be blind to the probable conclusion that, contrary to constitutional principle, jury commissioners were indulging in discriminatory selection practices. But what about evidence of under-representation of blacks on jury lists short of total exclusion or unmistakable pattern? Would a showing of even substantial under-representation permit the presumption of discriminatory selection? Beginning in the late fifties, jury discrimination cases arose which involved more subtle and complicated issues for the Court of Appeals.

* * *

The first such case arose in the Fifth Circuit in 1962. In United States ex rel Seals v. Wiman, a black defendant challenged the jury selection process in one Alabama county in which, although a third of the residents were nonwhite, only two per cent of the veniremen summoned for jury duty were blacks. Judge Rives wrote the panel opinion which held that such substantial under-representation of blacks, like total exclusion, was sufficient to create a statistical presumption of discrimination which the State bore the burden of disproving.

Three years later, in 1965, the Supreme Court considered the issue for the first time in Swain v. Alabama. There was evidence before the Court that while Negro adult males constituted twenty-six per cent of the county's population, only ten to fifteen per cent of the grand and petit jury panels drawn from the jury box since 1963 had been blacks. In a six to three decision, the Supreme Court held:

> We cannot say that purposeful discrimination based on race alone is satisfactorily proved by showing that an identifiable group in a community is under-represented by as much as 10%.... The overall percentage disparity has been small, and reflects no studied attempt to include or exclude a specified number of Negroes. Undoubtedly the selection of prospective jurors was somewhat haphazard and little effort was made to ensure that all groups in the community were fully represented. But an imperfect system is not equivalent to purposeful discrimination based on race.*

In so holding, the majority of the Court recoiled from further extension of presumptions of discrimination where the record reflected an average under-representation of ten per cent, implicitly finding such disparity statistically unconvincing. However, applying standard mathematical computations to the facts of the Swain case, the

---

*Swain v. Alabama, 380 U.S. 202 (1964). Swain is also an important decision on the issue of preemptory challenges to exclude Negroes totally from participating as jurors in a particular trial. No Negro had ever actually served on a trial jury for the past fifteen years in the county. For a discussion of this point, see Id. at 210-28. The Court of Appeals for the Fifth Circuit has consistently, albeit reluctantly, followed the Supreme Court's binding ruling from Swain on the discriminatory use of preemptory Challenges. See United States v. Williams, 446 F.2d 486 (5th Cir. 1971); United States v. Carlton, 456 F.2d 207 (5th Cir. 1972).

intuitive conclusion reached by the Supreme Court appears unsupportable. It is extremely improbable that the panels could have been randomly selected. The composition of the panels appear statistically explainable only as the product of discriminatory design. According to one commentator:

> In Swain, however, venires with five or fewer Negroes appeared in thirty consecutive cases. The probability of this occurrence, applying the product rule, is $0.23^{30} = 4.63 \times 10^{-21}$. This means that, on the average, only one in more than one hundred million trillion groups each containing thirty venires would consist solely of venires which were not more than 15% Negro. If thirty jury venires were selected at random in Talladega County every day of the year, the daily selection would correspond to the facts in Swain only one day in thousands of trillions of years.*

The rejection of the presumption of discrimination in Swain on its facts seems to be a continuation of judicial philosophy first enunciated by Mr. Justice Frankfurter: "The Civil War Amendments did not turn matters that are inherently incommensurable into mere matters of arithmetic."**

There are factors, other than conscious design, that could explain the paucity of blacks contrasted with whites selected for jury service in Swain: a diminished ability to meet eligibility requirements (such as a lower proportion of blacks who met minimal literacy standards or who lacked a criminal record); fewer blacks paid daily or hourly wages who could afford to take time off from employment in order to serve on juries; or, perhaps of greater potential significance, a cavalier or negligent effort on the part of jury commissioners to insure proportional representation of blacks on jury lists.

Perhaps the most troubling aspect of the Swain decision was the Supreme Court's treatment of the latter factor, the standard of duty imposed upon jury commissioners seeking a pool of potentially eligible jurors. There has never been an absolute duty imposed on commissioners to reach every citizen for consideration as a juror. Population growth has made anything more than cross sectional representation of the community an impossibility. However, it was clear prior to Swain that there is an affirmative duty imposed by the Constitution upon jury commissioners to use every means at their dis-

---

*Finkelstein, "The Application of Statistical Decision Theory to the Jury Discrimination Cases," 80 Harv. L. Rev. 338, 357 (1966).
**Cassell v. Texas, 339 U.S. 282, 291 (1950) (concurring opinion). However, it is worth noting that the Supreme Court has subsequently applied mathematical formulae of probability in support of its decision in at least one jury discrimination case. See Whitus v. Georgia, 385 U.S. 545, 552, n. 2 (1967).

posal to tap jurors who in fact reflect a true cross-sectional representation.   Thus, the language in Swain approving an admittedly
"haphazard," "little effort," "imperfect" system of juror selection
was an ominous message for future jury discrimination challenges.

* * *

As a consequence of the new views which seemed to be ema-
nating from the Supreme Court, the Court of Appeals for the Fifth
Circuit took rather unprecedented action.   Six pending appeals, related only by the common thread of challenges to jury selection procedures, were docketed for en banc arguments before the court in
1966.   Of these cases, three were from Louisiana: Scott v. Walker,
Davis v. Davis, and Labat v. Bennett; one from Alabama, Billingsley v. Clayton; and one challenging the federal system of jury selection from the United States District Court for the Middle District of
Georgia, Rabinowitz v. United States.

* * *

In Davis v. Davis, the Court of Appeals confronted the issue
of Swain's effect on the obligations and selection practices of jury
commissioners.   Although adult blacks represented sixteen per cent
of the adult population of Acadia Parish, Louisiana, for the two
years under survey blacks comprised only 7.5% of the persons chos-
en for grand jury duty.   No black had been selected for any of the
petit jury venires.   According to local custom and practice, grand
jurors (citizens charged with general duties of deciding whether or
not to indict persons for crimes) were hand-picked first from the
general venire rather than randomly drawn.   During the period under
study, five of the nine blacks included on the general list were tapped
for grand jury duty; each grand jury during the period had one, but
not more than two, blacks assigned for duty.   Consequently, the
number of available black jurors for petit or trial jury duty was reduced to four.   It was not surprising that after a random drawing
for the trial jury panels from a pool of at least four hundred names,
no black had ever been selected for trial duty.

The petitioner challenged both the petit and grand jury selection systems.   The Court had little problem with the issue of petit
juries; however, since 7.5% of the grand jury panels were black a
variance of less than ten per cent from the general population racial
ratio, the Swain decision seemed to foreclose a finding of discrimination in the selection of grand jurors.   However, in a unanimous
opinion written by Judge Thornberry, the Court of Appeals for the
Fifth Circuit strictly construed the Swain decision and held that it
was not applicable to this case.   The only factual distinction between
the efforts of the jury commissioners in Swain and those in Davis
was that in Davis the commissioners had been slightly more candid.
In Swain the Supreme Court had placed great emphasis upon the fact
that the "record contains no admission by the Alabama commissioners
that they had relatively few Negro acquaintances," although it was
undoubtedly true.   In Davis, the Acadia Parish commissioners ad-

mitted that they personally knew very few blacks and, in fact, one stated that "there were 'a lot' of Negroes who were probably qualified for jury service whom he did not know, but 'I don't go check them to see.'" Relying upon prior precedent of the Supreme Court, and simply ignoring any contrary implications in Swain, the Court of Appeals held that the Parish commissioners had failed to perform duties required by the Constitution to insure representational jury selection.

* * *

In contrast, a second en banc case, Scott v. Walker, was disposed of more easily by the Fifth Circuit. Even under the limitations of Swain the facts in Scott seemed to point to statistical under-representation. Black adult residents made up thirteen per cent of the population of Livingston Parish, and even viewed most liberally, the testimony from the state's witnesses showed that less that one per cent of the jurors available for service were black. Denied access to the official records, the defendant's counsel was forced to dig out information about the numbers of blacks who had been tapped for jury duty by cross-examination of the commissioners. Each official was equivocal, hazy in memory; for example, "[T]here was some [Negroes] on there." ... "More than one." ... "I am reasonably sure that I had one or two in myself, I couldn't tell you about the other commissioners." ... "It's unknown." Thus, hearings on discrimination in juror selection were reminiscent of hearings on the issue of voting irregularities. The availability of a statistical presumption, upon a showing of substantial under-representation, was clearly critical to any petitioner seeking judicial review. In the Scott case, the Fifth Circuit Court realized the defendant's frustration--the practical impossibility of statistically documenting his claims of discrimination to a mathematical certainty. As a result the Fifth Circuit further minimized a challenger's burden of proof. Judge Tuttle wrote for the Court:

> The record discloses that appellant's counsel had some difficulty in having access to the official records prior to the date of trial. An investigator hired on behalf of the petitioner testified that he had requested access to the general venire list of 300, but that this had been denied him. In the state court proceedings counsel sought to have access to the list of names in the then current jury box, which was to supply the panel before whom [the defendant-appellant] Scott was to be tried, but the trial court held that he could not legally make this list available....
>
> While it may be unfortunate that there is no proof in this record as to precisely how many Negroes were listed on the list of 300 for each of the years in question, since this would make much simpler the problem of a court's passing on the question of 'tokenism,' we think the evidence here adduced makes it clear beyond doubt that the number of Negroes' names listed regularly in making up the 12 lists which were subject to inquiry was so small

that it is not necessary that the exact percentages be known.

Also of significance in the Scott opinion is the manner in which the Court of Appeals for the Fifth Circuit treated the Supreme Court's Swain decision. The Tuttle opinion simply emphasized the positive and eliminated its negative implications. The Scott opinion flatly concluded: "The Supreme Court, in the Swain case, did not establish new underlying principles or in any way reverse or over-rule earlier decisions of the court." It is thus apparent from Scott, the first published post-Swain en banc decision, that the Fifth Circuit would strictly construe Swain's potential limiting effect in sub-sequent cases of alleged jury discrimination. This course of action became even more evident when the court reached its decision in Labat v. Bennett.

* * *

In Orleans Parish during the five years under challenge, 1948 to 1953, approximately 25.8% of the population eligible for jury duty were blacks. Of the proposed jury venires during that period the percentage of blacks selected ranged from 4.9% to 16.1%. Under the Swain standard permissible deviation of 10%, the fact that at least one list was less than a deviance of 10% from the general pop-ulation ratio might have been considered dispositive of the issue and sufficient to deny that the black defendant had carried his burden of proof of discrimination. However, the Court of Appeals for the Fifth Circuit instead emphasized that it would look at the average percentage of blacks on the venires during the questioned period, which computed to 6.2%, a variance of over twenty per cent from the general population ratio.

In addition, the Labat opinion, which is a major treatise by Judge Wisdom on jury discrimination, made it clear that the Fifth Circuit would not indulge in what was termed a "wooden" application of statistical computations to any situation involving so serious a challenge to the integrity of the judicial process as juror selection. The opinion noted the testimony of the commissioners that, as a mat-ter of policy, they winnowed from the list of the proposed venire-men all "outside" workers, manual laborers, and earners paid daily wages. It was estimated that forty-five per cent of all black resi-dents of the Parish held such positions and thus were culled from the "final lists" of veniremen. The most relevant statistic, accord-ing to Judge Wisdom, was the fact that the proportion of blacks on the "final venires" was only 3.1%. Thus, as he caustically ob-served, "The system was neutral, principled, and--foolproof: No black ever sat on a grand jury or a trial jury panel in Orleans Parish."

The Orleans Parish jury commissioners had claimed not only that they had not consciously discriminated in the selection of jurors but also that disqualification for daily or hourly wage earners had been practiced for beneficent purposes--to spare such workers financial hardship, since the juror compensation was only four dollars per day in Orleans Parish. Nevertheless, the Court of Appeals for the Fifth Circuit rejected the practice of wholesale exclusion of any economic stratum of the community from jury duty:

> Jury service is a burden on all who serve. And of course it falls most heavily upon wage earners. But this segment of the community is so large and so important that a jury system without daily wage earners simply is not representative of the community....
> A benign and theoretically neutral principle loses its aura of sanctity when it fails to function neutrally. The effect of the exclusion of daily wage earners was to deprive the defendants of a jury of their economic and social peers. But it was much more. The disqualification of all daily wage earners, as it was obviously bound to do, disqualified far more Negroes than Whites and, in final analysis, operated to exclude all but a token number of Negroes from the venires.

The inference of purposeful discrimination by the jury commissioners was further supported in Labat, according to the Court, by the admission of the jury commissioners that they had failed to take any action to compensate for the loss of potential black jurors occasioned by the exclusion of daily wage earners.

In Swain, the Supreme Court had countenanced what it had characterized as a "haphazard" and "imperfect" system of juror selection. The Scott, Davis, and Labat decisions indicated a continued commitment by the United States Court of Appeals for the Fifth Circuit to the ideal that the states within their province would adhere to the Constitution's promise of a fairly selected jury system. Moreover, the Fifth Circuit refused to read the Supreme Court's Swain decision as a signal to soften judicial intervention in the state jury selection processes. Swain was honored as binding precedent but limited as narrowly as possible in potential effect. However, just as these three decisions revealed a federal appellate court intractable in its insistence of a nondiscriminatory state juror selection system, setting standards even higher than the Supreme Court, two other en banc decisions demonstrate the Fifth Circuit's recognition that the Southern states were still in a transitional period. In Billingsley v. Clayton and Brooks v. Beto, the Court indicated that it would decline relief where local officials seemed to be making a bona fide effort to correct past selection inequities.

*   *   *

In Billingsley, it was established that blacks constituted twenty-nine per cent of the adult population of Jefferson County, Alabama, but counsel for the challenger failed to establish the racial composition of the jury lists. Unlike the Scott case, there was apparently no attempt to obtain the official lists for the years under study, and unlike the Davis case, cross-examination of the state's witnesses did not produce evidence from which an inference of statistical disparities could be shown. Furthermore, there was substantial evidence that the Jury Board had taken their duties quite seriously. Although the telephone directory, city directory and tax records had been used as a primary source of potential jurors, the Board had also conducted house-to-house canvassing and had formally requested suggestions for additions from prominent black community leaders. The Court of Appeals affirmed the district court's denial of relief, concluding, "The record reflects a good faith, bona fide effort on the part of the Board to give the Negro citizens of Jefferson County at least an equal, if not a privileged opportunity, to be called for jury service."

Unlike the other cases heard en banc, Brooks v. Beto challenged the purposeful inclusion, rather than exclusion, of blacks on grand jury panels in Van Zandt County, Texas. Like many other areas of the South, in this county in East Texas no black had sat on a grand jury during the twentieth century, although blacks constituted ten per cent of the population. Finally, in 1960, the Texas appellate court handed down a decision dismissing an indictment based on a finding of discriminatory jury practices by county officials. In view of this decision, a Van Zandt County trial judge appointed new jury commissioners, one of whom was a black; and later testified that he charged them that blacks "could not be excluded ... that they couldn't be put on or kept off on account of race." The new Jury Commission proceeded to select sixteen prospective grand jurors, two of whom were blacks, and the defendant Brooks was subsequently indicted by a panel of the two blacks and ten whites.

The only Supreme Court precedent on point, Cassell v. Texas, contained the broad dictum that "An accused is entitled to have charges against him considered by a jury in the selection of which there has been neither inclusion nor exclusion because of race." However, as has been previously noted, an enormously important factor in the Cassell decision was the evidence that while Negroes had sat on grand juries, the commissioners had intentionally limited their selection to not more than one per panel.

The majority opinion in Brooks is a tour de force by Chief Judge John R. Brown. He discussed the dilemma posed for public officials in the transitional period from blatant, deliberate discrimination to the ultimate goal of colorblind governance. He observed:

> In a setting where the presence of the Negro race in the community structure sets in motion the constitutional duty to know [members of that race for selection], a juror selector could fulfill that duty only by being aware of that race and the steps reasonably needed to assure representation of that race in the 'universe' from which jurors are obtained. Not only may he do so, he must....
> Although there is an apparent appeal to the ostensibly logical symmetry of a declaration forbidding race consideration in both exclusion and inclusion, it is both theoret-

ically and actually unrealistic. Adhering to a formula
which in words forbids conscious awareness of race in
inclusion postpones, not advances, the day when this ter-
rible blight of racial discrimination is exterminated. The
challenge is to assure constitutional equality now. This
often means, as it did in this case, eradication of the
evils of the past. That evil of racial exclusion cannot be
ignored. It must be reckoned with in terms which permit,
indeed assure, equality for the immediate future. The
evil and the evil practices are not theoretical. They are
realities. The law's response must therefore be realistic.

While all the members of the en banc court agreed with the
result reached in Brooks, that the Grand Jury had not been unconstitutionally selected, the three special concurrences indicated basic
differences in approach. Like the fabled bears, Judge Wisdom found
the Brown opinion too cold and Judge Bell, too hot. Although in the
majority opinion Judge Brown had made it abundantly clear that purposeful limitation of blacks would not be tolerated, Judge Wisdom,
the court member consistently most skeptical of official discretion,
feared that the Brooks decision would be interpreted as the Court's
acceptance of "benign quotas" of blacks in the jury system. At the
opposite end of the judicial spectrum, Judge Bell issued a personal
blast at the Brown opinion, which he considered too strongly worded.
Judge Bell indicated an even more fundamental concern with his
Court's continued tack away from the Supreme Court's decision in
Swain.

There could hardly be a case where the jury [is] drawn
from a list which reflects a fair cross section of the community. This new standard would result in a finding of
constitutional infirmity in nearly all cases where there is
not a perfect cross section. Anything short of perfect
might well demonstrate negligence or inattention on the
part of the jury commissioners. Yet, we are told in
Swain v. State of Alabama that the jury list need not be
a perfect mirror of the community or accurately reflect
the proportionate strength of every identifiable group.
I pose this problem simply to point up this remarkable new doctrine. I do not do so with any confidence
that my effort will make any great impression on anyone
at this time. However, I would like to be recorded as
being aware of the fact that this newly discovered constitutional principle will be a fertile new ground for postponing the execution of sentences. The long delays that
now inhere in the law will today receive, gratis obiter
dictum in the majority opinion, a wholly new weapon. In
the future careful counsel will not only test the jury list
to make certain that it reflects a fair cross section of
the community; they will test the knowledge and activities
of the jury commissioners.

*　　*　　*

The philosophical differences among members of the Court produced the first dissents in the final of the six cases considered en banc, Rabinowitz v. United States. At issue was the constitutionality of federal juror selection procedures used in the District Court for the Middle District of Georgia, an area composed of eighteen primarily rural Georgia counties. According to the 1960 census, blacks made up 34.5 per cent of the adult population. In the Civil Rights Act of 1957, Congress had imposed new standards for juror selection in the federal court system, requiring basically that the prospective juror be a citizen, twenty-one years of age or older, who had resided within the judicial district for one year. Only three disqualifications from jury selection were sanctioned; (1) unpardoned state or federal conviction of a felony; (2) inability "to read, write, speak, and understand the English language"; and (3) incapacity, either mental or physical, "to render efficient jury service." All members of the Court of Appeals were in agreement concerning the intent of Congress in adopting these quite minimal standards. Congress wished first to enact uniform national standards for service on federal juries, thereby changing the previous requirement that state standards for juror eligibility also govern federal eligibility. Secondly, Congress intentionally set the new standards lower than those of most states in order to increase the number of blacks eligible for service, thus increasing the likelihood of attaining a better cross section of the community.

There was also no dispute on the Court that, in practice, federal jury commissioners had treated the congressional statutory qualifications as minimum standards--to which they were free to apply their own ideas as to good character and intelligence. One commissioner explained:

> [T]here are a lot of people who can read and write and can't understand the kind of proceedings that go on in a courtroom, and we tried to avoid that.... We wanted an outstanding blue ribbon jury list of people who we thought would perform very good service and we did take their character into consideration or tried to; we tried to take their intelligence into consideration as indicated by these standards, and perhaps even went a little further than that; but those were factors that inevitably entered into our thinking.

Since no jury commissioner could personally know all jurors who met both objective and subjective standards, the federal commissioners in Rabinowitz had resorted to a quite common method of supplementation known as the "key man" system. The commissioners sought out citizens considered key men in the community because of their broad range of contacts in and knowledge about the community. The purpose of the system was laudable: to obtain as wide a range and as varied an input of proposed names as possible. But, unfortunately, the key men system was not always effective in reaching all segments of the social structure, as illustrated by this case. The key men were usually personal acquaintances of the jury commissioners, who were white and politically influential community leaders. The key men, in turn, suggested personal acquaintances, perpetuating the vice of tapping a single social stratum. Seldom were prominent black citizens asked to serve as key man referral sources. The result of the key man system in Rabinowitz was to produce a uniformity in jurors where diversity was vital.

The result of the use of subjective standards and the key men selection process was that blacks constituted only 7.4 per cent of the jury lists under study. The federal commissioners testified that they had not purposively sought to exclude blacks; however, as Judge Rives countered for the majority, "If a fair cross section is consistently lacking, then, without more, it is established that the commissioners have failed in their duty." The basis for the majority opinion was that the federal statutory scheme had been violated by the commissioners' "applying the wrong standards and by using grossly inadequate [informational] sources."

The leader of the dissenters from the rationale of the majority, although all concurred in the result, was Judge Bell. He concluded that both the new federal statute and the Constitution permitted the seeking of jurors who were more than marginally literate. He pointed out that according to census figures, only half of the black adult residents of the federal district in question had completed eight or more years of school. He observed:

> Having concluded that the statutory qualifications are minimum only, I would hold that the intelligence standard used was reasonable--to select jurors who could generally understand court proceedings tried to a jury.... In my view it is extremely unreasonable to relate the question to pure racial proportions where it is known that a high rate of illiteracy prevails in the population. It is unrealistic and unnecessary; in fact it would be fatal to the jury system to require that illiterates be permitted to serve on juries. The law makes no such requirement, and illiterates should not be counted in making a result test.

Judge Brown broke the four to four stalemate by joining with the majority in what he characterized as a "weak concurrence." He disagreed that the federal statute imposed maximum standards; the Constitution also governed jury selection and the requirement of a cross section would prevent a juror pool composed only of the marginally literate. The makeweight prompting Judge Brown's concurrence stemmed from the actions of the commissioners, even assuming they were empowered to seek out jurors who were more than minimally competent: "No matter how conscientious they were, the jury selectors did not add enough names of qualified Negroes because they did not know of them.... [Hence] the resulting jury box is defective."

*   *   *

It was clear in 1966 when Rabinowitz, the last of the six en banc decisions, was published that the Court of Appeals for the Fifth Circuit was lighting the way for all courts in the search for standards in jury selection. Two years later, in the Jury Selection and Service Act of 1968, Congress virtually codified the Court's rationale in Rabinowitz for the federal judicial system. The Court had observed, speaking through Judge Brown:

> To fairly represent the community, there must be an awareness of the make-up of that community. Even random selection from broad lists, such as voter registration records, city directories, tax rolls, public utility customer lists, and the like, inescapably require a basic preliminary test: do each, or all, or some, give a true picture of the community and its components? ... In a municipality where, as is frequent, geographical areas--precincts, wards, sections--reflect significant groups, such as laborers, highly educated professional or executives, those of lower incomes, the wealthy, or the like, jury selectors must first 'know' that community. But they must also 'know' the internal structure of such area groupings sufficiently to be able to determine identity and availability of those qualified to serve.

The 1968 Jury Selection and Service Act prohibited any discrimination in the selection process and established that the primary source of jurors was either the voter registration list or the list of actual voters. Yet the 1968 act also required that the primary list be supplemented when necessary by other sources in order to insure a fair cross section of the district. Each district court was authorized to devise and implement its own plan for the selection of federal jurors, consistent with the statute.

Chief Judge Brown thereafter appointed a circuit-wide committee of nine judges, chaired by Judge Gewin, to study the best method of carrying out the statutory mandate. After an intensive study of voter registration statistics in the six states of the Fifth Circuit, the Gewin Committee concluded that these lists now substantially represented a fair cross section of the community, although curative action by supplementation should be taken when a specific deficiency was disclosed. The Gewin Committee's recommendation in 1969 was persuasive evidence of the effectiveness of the implementation of voting rights reforms in the South, and must be considered a direct consequence of the Fifth Circuit's two decades of work in that area. The Judicial Council of the Fifth Circuit adopted the Gewin Committee's recommendations and, by the close of the 1960s, the work of the Court in jury discrimination neared completion.

Portents of Change

The majority do not say that Goldsby was

wrong ab initio. Indeed a group of judges none of
whom was on this court in 1959, and most of them
not even on the bench, are hardly in position to
say that JJ. Rives, Brown (now Chief Judge) and
Wisdom erred in 1959 in considering particular
subject matter to be of such general currency at
that time as to be accepted as true without proof
. . . . It is possible that in some places where
past segregation practices once commanded the
application of Whitus-Goldsby, time and change
have so erased history that the choice--faced by
counsel knowing the facts--of whether to attack the
racial composition of the jury is no longer a choice
between the lesser of two evils. But it is for the
state to prove by objective fact that the particular
jurisdiction is not one of the 'many jurisdictions'
in which Goldsby applies.
--Judge John C. Godbold dissenting in Winters
v. Cook, 489 F. 2d 174, 191 (5th Cir. 1973).

In 1963, after an argument, a black patron named Winters
shot and killed a white tavern owner. Winters was duly indicted by
the Grand Jury of Holmes County, Mississippi, a county with a population about seventy per cent black and thirty per cent white. It
was conceded that at no time in the history of the county had more
than a very small percentage of those on the jury list, if indeed
any, been black, and no challenge of jury discrimination had ever
been pursued in litigation against these county officials. Winters
retained local white counsel to represent him on the charges. Winters' lawyer later admitted that he had intentionally exchanged the
jury discrimination challenge in plea bargaining with the prosecutor
in order to avoid placing his client in jeopardy of facing a possible
death sentence at trial. As counsel elaborated in testimony, the
threat of urging constitutional infirmities in the Holmes County jury
system was the "pry pole" which enabled him to persuade the prosecution, and presumably the trial court who must approve a plea bargain, to offer life imprisonment upon the entry of Winters' guilty
plea. Clearly Winters was never informed nor consulted about his
preference in the decision to forego his right to a fairly constituted
jury, at the risk of being dealt the death penalty after trial. Counsel shouldered full responsibility for the decision-making:

> I was aware that any motion must be filed before ar-
> raignment. I was also aware that in view of the serious-
> ness of the constitutional questions that could be raised,
> that it would be reversible error for the court to overrule
> the motion, probably.... [T]he supreme thing in my mind
> at the time was saving this man's life. I felt then and
> now that I must do and did do at that time all I could to
> save this man from the death penalty.... [I]nsofar as
> making decisions are concerned, I accepted the responsi-
> bility of this man's destiny when I accepted employment.
> I was representing him to the best of my ability, and I

cannot say I would have allowed him to make any decision which I felt would put his life in jeopardy. Before I could do that, I would have asked the court to allow me to withdraw. I could not knowingly allow him to make a decision which would put his life in jeopardy.

Fifteen years before, when the Court of Appeals panel composed of Judges Rives, Brown and Wisdom had considered the record in the Goldsby case, two factors were developed as of paramount importance both to black defendants and to the administration of justice in Southern trial courts. First, the right to a nondiscriminatorily selected jury was a fundamental right personal to every defendant which he alone could elect to waive or assert. Second, given the racial hostilities engendered by the civil rights movement in the South, community pressures to forego the jury challenges effectively precluded the assertion of the right by either Southern lawyers or their black clients. The salient difference between the facts of the Goldsby record and the Winters record was that, in the intervening fifteen years, Southern lawyers were clearly aware of potential jury discrimination issues and not afraid at least to threaten their assertion to a black client's advantage.

When Winters subsequently sought to vacate his guilty plea, conviction, and life sentence before the Court of Appeals, his case was assigned to a panel composed of Judge Rives and Chief Judge Brown, two of the three members of the earlier Goldsby panel, and Judge Clark, the rising young conservative spokesman on the Court. The majority of the panel, Judges Rives and Brown, found nothing significant in the facts of the Winters case to distinguish it from the Goldsby precedent. Judge Rives steadfastly maintained:

> That white lawyers representing black clients often fail to raise an objection to jury composition has been recognized as a problem in this Circuit. Whitus v. Balkcom; Goldsby. The problem has surfaced in this case. Winters' attorney testified that although he has represented many Negro defendants he has never objected to an array of jurors. In recognition of this difficulty we have said that 'the conduct of ... counsel without consultation with his client did not bind [the client] to a waiver of his constitutional rights to object to the systematic exclusion of members of his race from the jury.... We will not, in this case, retreat from that view.

Judge Clark, in dissent, was equally adamant that counsel could, without consultation, waive a client's right to challenge jury discrimination. Furthermore, Judge Clark was persuaded that here counsel had secured a greater benefit for his client as a result of the lever of potential challenge than he probably could have had he actually followed through with an attack on selection procedures. But Judge Clark went even further in challenging the current validity of the Rives-Brown rationale:

Such 'judicial notice' is improper in today's case for
two reasons. First, it is directly refuted by the evidence.
The district attorney, an elected official much more sensitive to community reaction than petitioner's attorney, was
persuaded by the use of this possible defense [of unconstitutional jury composition] to intercede with the court for
a guilty plea and a prison term sentence in an easy-to-
prove case of cold-blooded interracial murder. Second,
this court is in error, and has been since Goldsby, in taking judicial notice of what is no more than judge-created
surmise. A by no means exhaustive examination of the
reported decisions of the Mississippi Supreme Court reveals more than twenty cases decided prior to petitioner's
plea of guilty, where such an objection was raised. In
the years immediately succeeding petitioner's plea the fre-
quency was higher and it is practically certain that the
number of times such pleas or the active use of the lever-
age of such a position by defense counsel took place in unreported trial court situations is much, much greater.
Insofar as this erroneous judicial knowledge would
fault the attorney's judgment here, it is not inappropriate
to note that in Goldsby and other of the cases examined,
the defense was effectively raised, but the defendant was
eventually executed after retrial with a proper jury. A
Pyrrhic victory indeed!

Judge Clark not only filed his dissent to the panel decision
but requested a poll of the active circuit court judges for a rehearing of the Winters case en banc. The entire court agreed to reconsider the case. The sting of the Clark dissent, the move of a
young lion challenging the pride's venerable leaders' opinion as
"judge-created surmise," found its mark.

*　　*　　*

Perhaps nowhere is the contrast in the composition and prevailing philosophy of the Court between the fifteen-man conglomerate
of the 1970s and the smaller cohesive, doughty band of the 1960s
more apparent than in the opinions which issued upon the reconsideration of the Winters case. It is Judge Clark who now wrote
the majority opinion of the en banc court, although he took pains to
soften the barb of his earlier criticism. Twelve members of the
Court joined the Clark opinion, all of whom had been appointed after
1967, the end of the early struggle to entrench the civil rights of
blacks in the South. The remnants of the old guard, Chief Judge
Brown and Judges Rives and Wisdom, attracted only one convert,
Judge Godbold, in dissent.

In the Clark opinion the majority found that there is no substantiation for the conclusion that Winters' attorney had not validly
waived the challenges to the jury array:

[The] language from Goldsby has in subsequent cases

> been construed to support the proposition that this court
> must take judicial notice that white lawyers in this circuit
> almost always will sacrifice their Negro clients' rights to
> be tried by a constitutionally selected jury out of a fear of
> community opprobrium or social ostracism.... [T]he ma-
> jority of the court en banc now announces that it does not
> consider such breach of trust by counsel to be so prevalent
> in any jurisdiction of this circuit that this court should, in
> the absence of proof, place all or even some lawyers in
> this circuit under the cloud of such an accusation. Win-
> ters, and those raising a similar defense in the future,
> may not rely on any court to 'notice' without proof that
> attorneys in this circuit are not to be trusted to make a
> strategic or tactical decision to challenge unconstitutional
> jury discrimination.

The gist of the opinion's rationale was that in the intervening fifteen
years, racial relations in the communities of the Southern states had
ameliorated to the extent that the special rule of Goldsby, discount-
ing real choice to challenge alleged racial discrimination, was no
longer true or needed to insure the constitutional functioning of the
trial system. However, the majority went even further, to announce
that the right to a trial by a constitutionally selected jury "is not
one of the rights traditionally considered so inherently personal that
only the defendant may waive it." Where there is evidence that
trial counsel acted out of a conscientious consideration of what would
be the best course of action for his client's cause, instead of ignorance or provable prejudice, then he may waive the right to jury
challenges in his client's behalf.

The dissenters decried the retreat not only from the Circuit's
own earlier Goldsby-Wiman precedents but also from Supreme Court
precedent implicitly approving the Circuit's stance that the right to
a constitutionally composed jury was so fundamental that it required
a knowing and intelligent waiver personally made by the defendant.
In a case after Goldsby, Wiman and Whitus, the Supreme Court had
said:

> Although trial strategy adopted by counsel without prior
> consultation with an accused will not, where the circum-
> stances are exceptional, preclude the accused from as-
> serting constitutional claims, see Whitus v. Balkcom, 333
> F.2d 496 (5th Cir. 1964), we think that the deliberate by-
> passing by counsel of the contemporaneous-objection rule
> as a part of trial strategy would have that effect in this
> case. *

In conclusion, the dissenting opinion by Judge Godbold observed:

> In this case I do not fault counsel nor do I question the

---

*Henry v. Mississippi, 379 U.S. 443, 451-52 (1965).

bona fides of his conclusions that the case against his client was such that he considered the racial composition of the jury to be immaterial. But these considerations do not solve the constitutional issue. To cite the conclusion about the jury system, or to conclude that faced with the possibility of a 'Hobson's choice' he secured a good plea bargain for his client, is no answer to the principle that the Constitution forbids that the choice be injected into the case in the first instance.... [Winters] was deprived of participation in the decision as to what election to make, and that deprivation cannot be cured by the subsequent reaction of judges that, considering all, he came out remarkably well.

*   *   *

The rub of the Court of Appeal's majority opinion in the Winters case was an assessment of the value which society, reflected by its judicial representatives, accords the Constitution's guarantee of the right to a fair and impartial jury. In an ideal political world racial considerations would play no role in jury selection. Yet, no member of the Fifth Circuit asserted that there was not a discriminatory policy still pursued in Holmes County, Mississippi. Indeed, Winters' trial counsel specifically sought to capitalize upon the system's unconstitutionality in order to secure what was in his estimation a more important, more immediate personal gain for his black client: a good plea bargain. Even if consulted, the black criminal defendant, typified by Winters, would have been in the unenviable position of having to participate in the perpetuation of a system which denied his constitutional rights. But there appears to be more at stake than simply hard choices for black defendants. If the judicial system is powerless to correct malfunctions in the administration of justice unless it has challenges brought to it by injured citizens, and if certain citizens are rewarded by promised personal advantage if they do not seek change, then the prospects for correcting the system for all citizens, both white and black, dim greatly.

At least a partial solution to the dilemma faced in Winters lies in the recognition that the burden of changing any system should not be cast upon one so vulnerable to compromise as a minority citizen accused of crime. In 1966, in Carter v. Greene County, the Court of Appeals had recognized the right of black citizens to bring a class action seeking relief from discriminatory .jury selection practices. The following year the Supreme Court approved the class action procedure, noting:

> This is the first case to reach the Court in which an attack upon alleged racial discrimination in choosing juries has been made by plaintiffs seeking affirmative relief, rather than by defendants challenging judgments of criminal conviction on the grounds of systematic exclusion of Negroes from the grand juries which indicted them, the trial juries that found them guilty, or both. The District Court

[Godbold, Grooms, and Allgood] found no barrier to such
a suit, and neither do we. Defendants in criminal proceedings do not have the only cognizable legal interest in
nondiscriminatory jury selection. People excluded from
juries because of their race are as much aggrieved as
those indicted and tried by juries chosen under a system
of racial exclusion.

* * *

Discrimination in juror selection was one of the most subtle
and elusive by-products of segregation in the South. Indeed, jury
trial, as an institution in the Anglo-American legal system, is difficult to isolate and analyze in terms of the role it plays in the administration of justice. Perhaps the most statistically sound study
yet conducted was reported by the University of Chicago in 1966:
in cases where the defendant received a jury trial the chances of an
acquittal were twice as good as trial before a judge sitting alone.
Furthermore, there appeared to be a tendency on the part of the
juries to convict on a lesser offense or to give lighter sentences.
Yet, on the average throughout the country, racial prejudice also
played its part. Criminal juries were shown to be more sympathetic
to white defendants than to black defendants, as displayed in the
comparative severity of sentences meted out. Negroes were apparently aware of this potential juror bias since they, more often than
whites, waived the right to jury trial. The possibility of jurors'
racial prejudice increased exponentially when, after the civil rights
movement, interracial tensions peaked. Offenses allegedly committed by blacks against whites and offenses generated by interracial confrontations over civil rights were prime potential occasions
for a predominantly white jury's retaliation. It is perhaps significant that of the six cases considered by the Fifth Circuit en banc,
five--Scott, Davis, Labat, Brooks, and Winters--involved either
charges of rape or murder upon a white by a black--and a sixth,
Rabinowitz, involved perjury charges against five blacks and one
white, all members of the Student Nonviolent Coordinating Committee who were actively engaged in civil rights demonstrations in central Georgia.

Aside from speculation about the effect of possible prejudice
when a black is tried by a jury of whites, discriminatory jury selection procedures had a far more invidious effect upon the legal
system itself. For most citizens, their only involvement in the administration of justice is as a juror summoned to sit in judgment.
The wholesale exclusion or token inclusion of blacks, in effect, precluded any participation by that race in the system and in important
community decision making. As with voting, running for public office, enjoying public facilities, attending public schools, the black
race was denied the privileges and power of democratic self-government.

For these reasons, the development of judicially enforced
sanctions against juror discrimination was an important aspect of the

struggle for political and social recognition of black citizens. As in other areas of race relations law, the Court of Appeals for the Fifth Circuit played a leading role in that doctrinal development. Concepts recognized and nurtured in jury discrimination cases, in turn, influenced the course of other areas of race relations law, notably voting and equalization of municipal services.

In the period of 1950-1970, the Court of Appeals moved a region, bound by a time-honored tradition of "whites-only" juries, to neutral selection criteria and enforced a new obligation to seek out qualified blacks for both grand and petit jury service. From its vast experience of guiding the dismantling of a segregated society, the Court recognized: "In the problem of racial discrimination, statistics often tell much, and courts listen." The Court's creation of statistical presumptions, first in the area of juror discrimination, made it relatively easy for a black defendant in a proper case to establish a prima facie case of racial exclusion and shift to the state the burden of rebutting the presumption. The Court also required jury commissioners to come forward with more than mere protestations of good faith or ignorance of qualified Negro residents within the community. In so doing the Court of Appeals for the Fifth Circuit became the first tribunal to impose the requirement of true community cross sectional representation upon state jury systems, even before Congress or the Supreme Court had moved. That Court also developed both the rationale and the juror selection plan which ultimately, through congressional action in 1968, became the prototype for the federal judicial system. But, perhaps the keystone of the Court's doctrinal development was its refusal to find a waiver of the right to a fairly selected jury from a black defendant's failure to raise the challenge at the trial of his case. Without the Court's decisions in Wiman and Whitus, no challenges might ever have been heard by appellate courts, and a malfunctioning judicial system might have continued unchecked and unchanged. Of course, it is equally clear from the majority opinion in the Winters case that the Court of Appeals now has concluded that the earlier era of pervasive, presumptive discriminatory jury practices has ended in the Fifth Circuit.

Chief Judge Brown commented, with justifiable pride in the Court's work to untangle and eradicate jury discrimination:

> Thus, the solution to this problem, as in many other aspects of civil rights, comes from experience born of the rich history of the struggles of the past decade. This Court has not hesitated to fashion judicial remedies to the realities to assure actual enjoyment of the constitutional ideas.... This is the law's response to the problem of today. Today we are dealing with the remnants of a segregated society being compelled to alter its ways to stamp out for all time this invidious distinction. As success is achieved and the constitutional ideal of a prejudiceless society is attained, the law will surely have both the capacity for and the duty of molding its relief to that hoped

for situation.... [O]ur Constitution is vital enough to take cognizance of such changes, and ... it extends its protective arm as the need arises....

NOTES AND PRIMARY AUTHORITY

The primary sources for material contained in this chapter are Kalven and Zeisel, The American Jury (1966); Kuhn, "Jury Discrimination: The Next Phase," 41 S. Cal. L. Rev. 235 (1968); Note, "The Congress, The Court, and Jury Selection: A Critique of Titles I and II of the Civil Rights Bill of 1966," 52 Va. L. Rev. 1069 (1966); Note, "Jury Discrimination in the South, a Remedy?," 8 Col. J. of Law and Soc. Problems, 589 (1972); Hearings on S. 3296 before the Subcomm. on Constitutional Rights of the Comm. on the Judiciary, 89th Cong., 2d Sess. (1966); Finkelstein, "The Application of Statistical Decision Theory to the Jury Discrimination Cases," 80 Harv. L. Rev. 338 (1966); and Gewin, "Jury Selection and Service Act of 1968: Implementation in the Fifth Circuit Court of Appeals," 20 Mercer L. Rev. 349 (1969). Also used were contemporary news accounts such as those contained in the New York Times, Jan. 4, 1960, and Jan. 15, 1960, The Nation, Feb. 24, 1964 at 179-80 and Newsweek, Feb. 17, 1964 at 16-17, and April 27 at 30, 1964. Of particular importance is a five part series on "The Negro and Justice in the South" by Jack Nelson published beginning June 28, 1964 in the Charleston Gazette.

The "Impartial Jury": A Paper Right. The primary sources for material in this section were the cases: Ex Parte Virginia, 100 U.S. 339 (1879); Strauder v. West Virginia, 100 U.S. 303 (1880); Norris v. Alabama, 294 U.S. 587 (1935); Smith v. Texas, 311 U.S. 128 (1940); Hill v. Texas, 316 U.S. 400 (1942); Cassell v. Texas, 339 U.S. 282 (1950); and Akins v. Texas, 325 U.S. 398 (1945).

The Paper Right Becomes Absolute. The primary sources for material in this section were the decisions of the Court of Appeals in United States ex rel Goldsby v. Harpole, 263 F.2d 71 (5th Cir. 1959); Whitus v. Balkcom, 333 F.2d 496 (5th Cir. 1964).

Jury Selection and the Theory of Probabilities: Breaking New Ground. The primary sources for material contained in this section is United States ex rel Seals v. Wiman, 304 F.2d 53 (5th Cir. 1962); Swain v. Alabama, 380 U.S. 202 (1964); Scott v. Walker, 358 F.2d 561 (5th Cir. 1966); Davis v. Davis, 361 F.2d 770 (5th Cir. 1966); Labat v. Bennett, 365 F.2d 698 (5th Cir. 1966); Billingsley v. Clayton, 359 F.2d 13 (5th Cir. 1966); and Rabinowitz v. United States, 366 F.2d 34 (5th Cir. 1966).

Portents of Change. The primary sources for material contained in this section are the cases: Winters v. Cook, 466 F.2d 1393 (5th Cir. 1972) and 489 F.2d 174 (5th Cir. 1973); and Carter v. Greene County, 396 U.S. 320 (1970).

A more complete manuscript, with detailed documentation of all sources, is available as indicated in the Preface, supra.

Chapter 9

PUBLIC ACCOMMODATIONS:
STONEWALL RESISTANCE IN JACKSON

> Conceding the major proposition to be true, that
> Congress has a right to enact all necessary and
> proper laws for the obliteration and prevention of
> slavery with all its badges and incidents, is the
> minor proposition also true, that the denial to any
> person of admission to the accommodations and
> privileges of an inn, a public conveyance, or a
> theatre, does subject that person to any form of
> servitude, or tend to fasten upon him any badge
> of slavery?
> --Mr. Justice Bradley, Civil Rights Cases,
> 109 U.S. 3 (1883).

No accounting of the course of race relations law in the South
would be complete without some attention to the struggle to desegregate public accommodations. This area of the law is tangential
to the desegregation of public education. Yet public accommodations,
like voting rights and jury selection, provides additional perspective
essential to an understanding of the gestalt of racial discrimination
during the post Brown period. However, unlike voting and jury selection, access to public accommodations was more a symbolic campaign than a fight for power. Nevertheless, the sit-ins at Woolworth counters throughout the South ironically engendered far more
public hostility and resistance. While a segregationist might be
outraged in principle if blacks were summoned to jury duty or had
access to the polling place, the effect of this access was relatively
impersonal, and, in the end, was something that could be tolerated.
But such tolerance would not extend to social places of public entertainment, dining and travel. Like the public schools, integration in
these places became vividly personal. One could not ignore that his
children were going to school with black children. One could not
ignore blacks at the local movie theatre or at the town restaurant.
One could not ignore the blacks sitting in the front of the bus. It
was this daily personal awareness that made the civil rights movement real, here, now, instead of a distant legal argument before a
court in New Orleans or Washington recounted in the local newspaper.

In large measure the brunt of securing the rights of blacks
to public education fell upon a cadre of lawyers affiliated with the

353

Inc. Fund or the Lawyers Committee for Equal Rights under the
Law. But the assault on public accommodations was manned by the
rank and file of the NAACP, SNCC, CORE and others attracted to
the cause of the civil rights movement. Without the concerted action of thousands of willing recruits, the Civil Rights Acts of the
sixties might never have been achieved. It should be remembered
that it was the march and confrontation on Pettus Bridge outside
Selma, Alabama, not lawsuits, that precipitated the first congressional response to racial discrimination since Reconstruction.*

In locales of entrenched resistance in the South, entire organizations coalesced to coordinate specific strategies for integration. There was the "Albany Movement" in Georgia and the "Jackson Movement" in Mississippi. The Jackson Movement is illustra-
tive of a concerted campaign to desegregate public facilities, although Jackson was a more perdurable target than most communities. The public accommodations struggle in Jackson also helps to
explain why there was so little early progress in desegregating Jackson's public schools. Local efforts were bent there toward dismantling the symbols of segregation, the "colored only" drinking
fountains and other badges of slavery still present long after other
communities had retreated to more subtle means of separatism.
The story of the Jackson Movement is, above all else, worth telling
because after all the demonstrations, protests, sit-ins, arrests and
lawsuits, the final victory opening public accommodations in Jackson
might well be considered pyrrhic.

* * *

The first congressional action after the ratification of the
thirteenth and fourteenth Amendments, the "Civil War Amendments,"
concerned public accommodations. The Civil Rights Act of 1875
sought to provide that "all persons within the jurisdiction of the
United States shall be entitled to the full and equal enjoyment of the
accommodations, advantages, facilities, and privileges of inns, public conveyances on land or water, theatres, and other places of
public amusement ... regardless of any previous condition of servitude." However, the Supreme Court later declared this statute unconstitutional as an improper attempt by Congress to legislate upon
subjects which are within the domain of states--the regulation of
private rights. Thirteen years later the access to public accommodations issue was again before the Court when Homer Plessy sought
recognition of his rights to ride in the "white only" section of Louisiana's railroads. The Supreme Court dismissed his challenge in
Plessy vs. Ferguson.**

In Brown I, the Supreme Court finally discarded the separate
but equal doctrine of the Plessy case. Despite its apparent emphasis upon public schools in the Brown decision, one week later the

---

*See Chapter 10, infra, "Search for Standards," at 390-92.
**Discussed supra in Prologue, at et. seq. 4-7.

Court made it clear that the Constitution equally forbade state discrimination in its publicly supported public facilities. The Court summarily reversed a Sixth Circuit Court of Appeals decision which had approved a refusal to admit blacks to theatrical performances held in an amphitheatre owned by the City of Louisville. Shortly thereafter, the Supreme Court, again in summary opinions, held that a state could not enforce a policy of racial segregation at public beaches and bathhouses, or at public golf courses.

The Supreme Court later explicitly conceded that "the lower federal courts played a very important role in this ongoing process." In June, 1956, a three-judge court in Alabama reviewed a conviction arising out of the Montgomery bus sit-ins and ruled that statutes and ordinances requiring segregation in public transportation violated the fourteenth Amendment. In 1958, the New Orleans City Park Improvement Association sought to challenge before the Fifth Circuit Court what it urged was an unwarranted extension of the principles of Brown to public accommodations. The Fifth Circuit's per curiam order noted:

> [The Association] takes the completely untenable position that we should ignore the decisions of the Supreme Court because, so it states, they were posited on the ratio decidendi of that court in the school segregation cases which, appellant contends, were based on psychological considerations not here applicable.... [It is contended] that the trial court should have heard evidence to determine whether such psychological considerations are present in the denial of access on a nonsegregated basis to the City Park.

Giving this argument short shrift, the Court of Appeals held that it was bound to follow the lead of the Supreme Court and enjoined the Association from continuing its segregation policies.

* * *

By the early 1960s the work of the federal courts appeared to be complete. Desegregation had been outlawed on a case-by-case basis in every conceivable type of public accommodation: theaters, beaches, golf courses, buses, parks, courtrooms, restaurants in transportation terminals, libraries, swimming pools, tennis courts, zoos, museums and auditoriums. But established law governing segregated public facilities had not filtered down to Jackson, Mississippi. The Mississippi advisory committee to the Civil Rights Commission described the status of blacks in 1960:

> A Negro in Mississippi receives substantially less than his due consideration as an American and as a Mississippian. This denial extends from the time he is denied the right to be born in a nonsegregated hospital, through his segregated and inferior school years and his productive years when jobs for which he can qualify are refused, to

the day he dies and is laid to rest in a cemetery for Negroes only.

The arch segregationist White Citizens Councils were the dominant force in the political and business life of the state. The first such organization in the nation was formed in Indianola, Mississippi, in 1954, and the Jackson Council was created the following year. The Jackson Council's founder promised success if whites were united to preserve segregation.

> In no place has there been integration--even so-called 'token integration'--without the active support of the white people in the community. As long as people are strongly organized on the local level--as long, in other words, as the 'die-easys' are not in control--a community can withstand pressure from Washington regardless of what kind it is.

In 1963, Mississippi was predominantly a rural state with its capital, Jackson, holding a population of about 150,000. Jackson had already endured the riotous integration of the University of Mississippi and the white power structure was determined to avoid further encroachment upon traditional white prerogatives.

Black residents of Jackson had no appreciable political strength. Only 5,000 out of 50,000 blacks were registered to vote and usually less than half of those registered actually exercised the right. Such voting statistics help to explain how Mayor Allen Thompson stayed in power. Before becoming Mayor of Jackson, Thompson had been a lawyer and former professor of Greek. Committed to the preservation of segregation, Thompson once observed that Jackson "is as close to Heaven as any city can get." When complaints were made about the policy that blacks were not allowed to use the benches at the zoo, the Mayor had a quick solution: "I took out all seats and it worked like a charm." In the same vein, Thompson warned in 1961:

> The first time we have a final court decision that says we cannot uphold the law and allow colored people to begin carrying on and taking over the parks and swimming pools--and I frankly think that will be a long time yet--the parks will be closed, the swimming pools will be closed.... If we close down the white facilities, the Negro ones will also be closed.

The staunch segregationist tradition of Jackson was reinforced by the policies of the city's paper, the Jackson Daily News, and its Editor, James Myron Ward. The paper had played a strongly segregationist line for years, a line which was amplified as the civil rights movement became heated. The paper enjoyed a circulation of 43,000 readers and Ward's editorial column was a major source of influence in formulating community sentiment. After the Jackson police used dogs to break up a demonstration, Ward wrote,

"When savages don't know how to behave, it is necessary to resort to some effective method of maintaining order." When the Interstate Commerce Commission established guidelines for the integration of interstate buslines, Ward denounced the regulations as the work of "an organized attempt of swarms of wild-eyed, fanatical crackpots to seize control of the courts and police powers of Mississippi." With its editor so adamant in his opposition to any form of integration, the newspaper could effectively drown out calls for moderation.

* * *

On March 27, 1961, nine black students from Tougaloo Southern Christian College staged a sit-in at the main branch of the Jackson Public Library. Within fifteen minutes, the police had arrived and arrested the students. They were tried in City court for a violation of one provision of a 1960 segregation law package which proscribed the refusal to disperse upon an order of a law enforcement officer.

The trial of these students was a local sensation. On the day of the hearing a crowd of about 100 blacks, including faculty and students from Tougaloo Southern, Jackson State and Campbell, the community's three black colleges, gathered around the courthouse entrance in moral support for those arrested. As the nine student defendants walked up the steps of the building, the crowd began to clap and sing. The police who had been dispatched to the scene quickly moved in with police dogs and used night sticks to disperse the crowd. In the melée, one black onlooker was attacked and beaten; there was some evidence that his assaulter was a white civilian who had simply joined in with the police in the confusion. The Justice Department subsequently called for an F.B.I. investigation of the incident, but the results of the probe were never made public. Although the constitutionality of the law was challenged at the students' trial, the City judge convicted all, fined each $100 and imposed a thirty-day suspended sentence.

The following month, four black college students were arrested for sitting in the front of a city bus. The four refused to move to the back when ordered by a policeman. The four were defended at trial by the NAACP but were found guilty. This time the police took precautions to prevent any recurrence of trouble by posting officers and dogs outside the courthouse. Once the courtroom was filled, police patrolled the area to prevent any crowds from gathering. Although these precautions proved effective in discouraging demonstrations, racial tension in Jackson did not abate. A group of Freedom Riders announced that they would be traveling to protest southern segregation within the next month; their proposed route would include a final stop in Jackson. The first group of Freedom Riders bound for Jackson left Montgomery, Alabama, on May 24, 1961, and arrived the same day. The "ride" had been marked by violence at each stop in Alabama. When the bus arrived in Montgomery, a mob attacked the bus, beating six riders. The violence spread as blacks who had no connection with the freedom

riders were also beaten. The Montgomery police arrived after the
fighting began and were finally able to succeed in dispersing the
mob. The violence in Montgomery increased the tension in Jackson
where the citizens awaited the group's arrival.

Tight security precautions were taken in Mississippi to prevent any outbreaks of violence. Mississippi National Guardsmen
were placed on the buses at the state line. The Highway Patrol
convoyed the buses to Jackson and used helicopters to cover the
buses en route.

Meanwhile, the Jackson police took precautions to secure the
bus station. The block was cordoned off; the police required traffic
and pedestrians to "keep moving." Approximately forty policemen
surrounded the station. After the buses arrived at the station, the
riders got off and entered the white waiting room. The police captain in charge of the station followed the group into the room and
ordered them to move on and out of the terminal. When the group
refused, the captain placed them all under arrest.

The Freedom Riders were charged with having violated the
breach of the peace statute which had been passed in 1960 to prevent sit-in demonstrations. Twenty-five blacks and two whites were
charged. At the trial, the two white defendants were seated in the
white section of the courtroom until their lawyer objected to this
separation; the white defendants were then allowed to sit with the
black defendants. Prior to announcing his verdict and sentence, the
municipal court judge stated that the statutes under which the Freedom Riders were charged were "constitutional on their face." He
added:

> We must bear in mind we're not here trying any segrega-
> tion laws or the rights of these people to sit on any buses
> or to eat in any place.... They were not traveling for
> the purpose of traveling but for the purpose of violence.
> Their avowed purpose was to inflame the public. They
> sought to have people fight out legal issues among them-
> selves.

The Freedom Riders were all convicted; each was fined $200 and
given a six-month suspended sentence.

They appealed their convictions through the Mississippi appellate courts, arguing two issues. The Freedom Riders first asserted that the breach of the peace statute was so vaguely written
and so overbroad in its prohibitions that it was unconstitutional.
However, even if the statute should be held constitutional, they next
argued that it had been improperly applied to govern their conduct
at the Jackson bus station. The defendants relied upon their rights
under the First Amendment to assemble in protest and to travel.
They pointed out that they had committed no acts of violence or
breaches of the peace. Since their purpose was lawfully protected,
they argued they were justified in refusing to leave the terminal.

The Mississippi Supreme Court upheld the constitutionality of the breach of the peace statute and also affirmed the right of the police to order protesters to leave in order to avoid trouble from onlookers. Stirring up racial strife and prompting white violence in reaction was apparently the real crime. The State Supreme Court observed:

> The state's interest in preventing violence and disorder, which were imminent under the undisputed facts, is the vital and controlling fact in this case. If the defendant had been denied the exercise of his right to enter the white waiting room, or to assemble for the purpose of exercising the right to protest or of free speech, his argument (that he committed no violence and was where he had a right to be) would be pertinent. But defendant is in no position to claim that he was merely exercising a constitutionally guaranteed right, for it is manifestly true that he and his associates participated in a highly sophisticated plan to travel through the South and stir up racial strife and violence.

The United States Supreme Court accepted certiorari and reversed the convictions in a per curiam opinion without comment.

Four months later, the Jackson bus terminal was the scene of another attempt at desegregation when it was visited by the "prayer pilgrimage" in September, 1961. The prayer pilgrimage was originally composed of twenty-six clergymen, black and white. The purpose of the pilgrimage was to promote integration and racial equality by visiting religious institutions and other places while traveling from New Orleans to a church convention in Detroit. One of the goals of the group was to attempt to use the segregated facilities in the Jackson bus terminal. Fifteen of the ministers had tickets to Chattanooga and, after arriving the night before by a chartered bus, went to the terminal. The group entered the "white only" waiting room and then moved on to the terminal restaurant. Two police officers, awaiting their arrival, ordered them to move on. When the pilgrims refused to move, they were placed under arrest. There was a dispute in the evidence as to the demeanor of the crowd in the terminal during the incident. Although the prayer pilgrims were tried and convicted in municipal court for disorderly conduct, after appeal new trials were ordered. The first defendant who was retried was acquitted and, as a result, the prosecution decided not to retry the remaining pilgrims.

*   *   *

The Jackson Movement was not formally organized until May, 1963, when local members of the community met together with representatives of various civil rights organizations. A coalition, known as the Mississippi Council on Human Relations, was formed. Committed to attempting negotiated resolution of racial disputes, the Council quickly proposed the appointment of a biracial committee which would work with city officials. Mayor Thompson finally consented to a meeting. The Council presented an eight-point program, which included the following demands: employment of black policemen and school crossing guards, removal of all segregation signs in public buildings, an upgrading of black employment in the city, authorization and implementation of the biracial committee to handle all racial problems and voluntary desegregation of all public facilities and schools. During the brief meeting, Mayor Thompson flatly stated that he would not "bargain on matters which are subject to legal procedures." The only concession offered by the Mayor was an expressed willingness to hire black policemen and crossing guards if the city's blacks rejected "pressure policies and practices of racial agitation, threats of disobedience and violence." After hearing Mayor Thompson's speech, a biracial committee spokesman stated that he did not believe that the two sides would be able to agree on the contested issues. A group of thirteen of the seventeen committee members then walked out.

When these negotiations collapsed, the protests were taken to the streets. Blacks pressed their demands through picketing, boycotting white merchants, sit-ins, protest marches and mass meetings. The remainder of May and June proved to be tense and occasionally violent. On May 28, three black students from Tougaloo Southern entered Woolworth's and sat at the lunch counter. The three ordered food but were refused service. They were directed to a counter at the rear of the store where they could be served. When the group refused to move, store officials turned off the lights over the counter and roped off the area, except where the three were sitting. The three remained there for thirty minutes while a hostile group of spectators surrounded them. A white girl grabbed a mustard bottle and squirted mustard down the back of one of the protesters at the counter. This set off the relatively youthful crowd, numbering between 200 to 300, who grabbed ketchup, salt, pepper, mustard and sugar to shower the demonstrators. One former policeman, after announcing "I'm gonna go up there and push that black bastard off that stool," proceeded to punch the student, knocking him to the floor. The white then repeatedly kicked the student in the head until a detective, who had been standing by, arrested him for assault and the black student for disturbing the peace. More demonstrators arrived and waded through the ketchup and mustard barrage to take seats at the counter. The crowd continued to throw things at the demonstrators while police, who were standing outside, refused to intervene, saying that they could not act unless requested by the store management. After three hours, the crowd finally dispersed when the store officials, seeing the crowd beginning to throw store merchandise, closed the store.

During the next ten days after the Woolworth's sit-in, the confrontations between protesters and police followed a predictable pattern. As soon as demonstrators appeared on either the sidewalks or streets of the city, they were arrested for parading without a permit. Then, on June 11, 1963, Medgar Evers, NAACP Field Secretary for Mississippi and spokesman for the Movement, was murdered at his home in Jackson. The following day, a group of about 150 people marched from the headquarters of the local NAACP office downtown, disrupting traffic. The police arrested all but four for parading without a permit. Violence flared on June 15 during the Evers funeral procession. The march was orderly from the NAACP office to the funeral home, then several hundred people broke away from the procession route and headed downtown. The crowd began throwing bottles and rocks, and the police formed a line across the street. Only the intercession of John Doar of the Justice Department prevented a violent confrontation: he pacified the crowd and persuaded the police to withdraw their lines. The crowd dispersed, but not before twenty-two demonstrators were arrested and fourteen policemen were injured.

The summer of 1963 was long, hot, tense and frustrating for the Jackson Movement. While the grievances and demands of the blacks were publicized by almost daily demonstrations, very little tangible progress was made toward securing voluntary desegregation. The losses sustained by the Movement were substantial. Between May and the end of the summer, 1092 arrests were made. The Jackson Daily News mocked the martyrdom of protesters by running tabulations of arrests headed "Agitation Box Score." A typical entry was:

Arrested:	
Pavement Packers	509
Sign Toters	66
Stool Sitters	19
Curb Squatters	14

The arrest of over a thousand participants in the Jackson Movement imperiled the continued existence of the organization. By the end of the summer of 1963, it was obvious: if anything meaningful were to come out of the Movement, its goals would have to be secured in the courts. They could not be won on the Jackson streets.

*   *   *

The litigation spawned by the Jackson Movement can be analyzed in terms of the targets which were attacked. One group of cases attacked state laws and local ordinances which prohibited picketing and other forms of protest. Another series of cases dealt with segregation in interstate commerce, transportation and travel facilities. Other lawsuits sought the integration of local public facilities.

The Jackson city fathers reacted to the demonstrations not only by authorizing mass arrests under various city ordinances, but also by seeking an injunction in state court to stop both the picketing and a boycott of selected local white merchants which had begun

in the spring of 1963. In City of Jackson v. Salter, the city charged
that various individuals, the NAACP, CORE and the trustees of Tougaloo University were conspiring to engage in an illegal boycott, harassing and picketing business in the downtown area for the purpose
of forcing them to employ blacks, and attempting to paralyze the
economic life of the city. The city claimed that the defendants knew
that these activities would lead to violence and that an intolerable
strain had been placed on the police force. The State Chancery
Court issued a broad temporary injunction on June 6, 1963, which
enjoined the defendants from sponsoring mass marches without a
permit, blocking public streets and sidewalks, trespassing on private
property after being asked to leave, and unlawfully picketing businesses. The following month the state court granted a permanent
injunction to the city prohibiting such activities by the demonstrators.

A year later the black leaders were afforded some relief from
the injunction as a result of a series of appeals to the Mississippi
Supreme Court. In the meantime, the effect of the injunction and
continued arrests had defeated the Jackson Movement. The intense
picketing and boycotts of the early spring of 1963 were suspended
by the leaders of the Movement. Instead, they sought judicial clari-
fication of the permissible bounds of public assembly for protest.
The arrests of civil rights workers in Jackson were based variously
upon charges of parading without a permit, failing to obey an officer's order to disperse, breach of the peace, or, in rare instances,
disorderly conduct. Similar statutes were in force in every state
throughout the nation, but they were pressed into yeoman's service
in southern communities plagued with civil rights demonstrations.
Used routinely as a stock response to stifle public protest, such
statutes often were abused to suppress peaceful assembly protected
under the first amendment.

The civil rights movement forced the Supreme Court to reexamine the boundaries of the state's police powers as activists took
to the streets in exercise of asserted rights of free speech and assembly. In Edwards v. South Carolina, the court reversed breach
of peace convictions of 187 black college student demonstrators who
had walked along the grounds of the state capitol to protest segregation laws. After a large crowd of onlookers arrived, the demonstrators were ordered to disperse and, when they refused, were arrested. The majority of the court emphasized that there was no
evidence of crowd-baiting nor violence by either the demonstrators
or the onlookers. Mr. Justice Stewart concluded for the Court's
majority that "The Fourteenth Amendment does not permit a state
to make criminal the peaceful expression of unpopular views." In
contrast, Mr. Justice Clark, in dissent, noted what he termed "the
almost spontaneous combustion in some southern communities." In
such situations, when officials in good faith believed that disorder
and violence were imminent as a result of demonstrations, Justice
Clark felt that law enforcement officers not only could but should
step in to prevent violence.

Despite the Supreme Court's recognition of the right to peace-

ful assembly and expression, the individual risk of arrest and conviction remained. Even if a demonstrator were ultimately vindicated
in the courts, he had been arrested, jailed, forced to post bond and
to retain counsel. The process of vindication was not only fraught
with the danger that a reviewing court would affirm the conviction
but was also expensive in monetary and human terms. In NAACP
v. Thompson, the leaders of the Jackson Movement sought to minimize these hazards by bringing a class action to enjoin officials
from interfering with peaceful protests against segregation policies
in public facilities. In this same action, the NAACP sought federal
court relief from the denial by Mississippi officials of its right to
exist in the state. The NAACP had been an active leader in demonstrations throughout Mississippi; it had carried on its activities
through unincorporated affiliates while also maintaining an office of
its own. In 1962, it had received notification from the Secretary of
State that an amendment to the state code required foreign nonprofit
corporations to domesticate as a prerequisite to doing business in
the state. The corporation took the ministerial steps required to
comply. Under Mississippi law, the Attorney General reviewed all
applications and expressed an opinion as to whether the application
should be approved, stating reasons for the conclusion. It was no
great surprise when the Mississippi Attorney General refused to approve the NAACP's application. The fundamental reason given for
the rejection of the application was that the NAACP, "like a good
many other corporations of that kind, do not stick to the stated purposes of their corporate charter but go far beyond what their stated
objectives and purposes is [sic]." The Secretary of State faulted
the charter for not clearly stating how the NAACP would achieve
its objectives.

The case was filed on the calendar of federal district court
Judge William H. Cox and the first hearing was held on June 10,
1963. A year later, after a fruitless appeal to the Fifth Circuit to
speed up the process, Judge Cox dismissed both counts of the complaint as totally without merit. In his findings of facts, Judge Cox
recited several of the incidents that had occurred, including the incident at the Woolworth store and the disturbance after Medgar
Evers' funeral. Judge Cox accepted all of the city's contentions at
face value, and found no fault with any official's actions. Judge
Cox concluded that the challenged ordinances were valid and characterized the relief sought by the black plaintiffs as "the unbridled
exercise of [their] rights in violation of valid regulations designed
and intended to protect the rights of the public generally who have
the same rights as the plaintiffs."

The case was appealed to the Fifth Circuit where it was reversed by a panel comprised of Judges Wisdom, Thornberry and
Whitaker (who was sitting by designation from the Court of Claims).
Judge Whitaker prefaced his opinion by noting that both sides had
been in the wrong on occasion. Many of the arrests were justified;
often the plaintiffs could have asserted their constitutional rights
without disregarding municipal ordinances or state law. Judge
Whitaker observed that Judge Cox's findings were brief and failed

to disclose the course of conduct followed by both sides. While some arrests were justified, many that occurred for picketing, parading without a permit, or engaging in prohibited use of the sidewalks were not. Such arrests were part of a general picture which Judge Whitaker concluded:

> ... disclosed a pattern of conduct on the part of the officials of the city of Jackson that leads us to the conclusion that defendants took advantage of every opportunity, serious or trivial, to break up these demonstrations in protest against racial discrimination, and that a large number of the arrests had no other motive, and some had no justification whatever, either under municipal, state, or federal law.

Judge Whitaker was also not optimistic that the course of conduct would change appreciably in the future:

> We have no doubt, from their prior conduct and without any change of heart, that they still believe such demonstrations must be suppressed and that, in order to do so, they intend to take advantage of any law or ordinance, however inapplicable or however slight the transgression, and to continue to harass and intimidate plaintiffs.

Even though the state courts could have protected their rights after arrest, given such a pattern of official intimidation and harassment the plaintiffs did not have an adequate remedy at law.

The panel also reversed Judge Cox's refusal to order the domestication of the NAACP. Judge Whitaker noted that the same arguments advanced by Mississippi officials had been used previously by the Attorney General of Alabama in an attempt to oust the NAACP from doing business there. Two years before this Jackson litigation, the Supreme Court had rejected Alabama's attempts to refuse certification to the NAACP: therefore, the issue was no longer open to debate.

As in other cases involving appeals from orders entered by Judge Cox, the Court of Appeals drafted the injunction which the district court was to issue. State officials were to be ordered to take all necessary steps to authorize the NAACP to do business. Local officials in Jackson were to be enjoined from arbitrarily applying ordinances to discourage or disrupt public protests, at least those of a peaceful and orderly variety.

In its treatment of NAACP v. Thompson, the Fifth Circuit followed the "balancing of private and public interests" test which had been established shortly before by the Supreme Court in the landmark case of Cox v. Louisiana. Reviewing convictions arising out of CORE's picketing of stores which maintained segregated lunch counters in Baton Rouge, the Supreme Court observed:

[T]he State contends that the conviction should be sustained because of fear expressed by some of the state witnesses that 'violence was about to erupt' because of the demonstration. It is virtually undisputed, however, that the students themselves were not violent and threatened no violence. The fear of violence seems to have been based upon the reaction of the group of white citizens looking on from across the street.... There is no indication, however, that any member of the white group threatened violence [or that the officers present would not be able to handle the crowd]....

The rights of free speech and assembly, while fundamental in our democratic society, still do not mean that everyone with opinions or beliefs to express may address a group at any public place and at any time. The constitutional guarantee of liberty implies the existence of an organized society maintaining public order, without which liberty itself would be lost in the excesses of anarchy. The control of travel on the streets is a clear example of governmental responsibility to insure this necessary order. A restriction in that relation, designed to promote the public convenience in the interest of all, and not susceptible to abuse of discriminatory application, cannot be disregarded by the attempted exercise of some civil right, which, in other circumstances, would be entitled to protection.... A group of demonstrators could not insist upon the right to cordon off a street, or entrance to a public or private building, and allow no one to pass who did not agree to listen to their exhortations....

Thus, while laws prohibiting, for example, breaches of the peace were within the legitimate and constitutional powers of state and local governments, they were subject to possible abuses. In contrast, there were some types of laws which, as written on their face, attempted to limit conduct beyond the scope of permissible regulation. In Strother v. Thompson, the Fifth Circuit struck down a Jackson ordinance that required the issuance of a permit by the City Council for the distribution of handbills and other papers. In Guyot v. Pierce, the Fifth Circuit invalidated another Jackson ordinance which required a permit issued by the City Council for all parades and other public gatherings. The vice in both ordinances was the same. The language describing prohibited activity was overly broad and subject to the unfettered interpretation of local officials, lacking any standards which would limit the City Council's discretion. The City Council alone was to decide whether the activity would distract or disturb the normal use of the streets.

* * *

Segregation in transportation and transportation facilities was attacked in two closely related cases, Bailey v. Patterson and U.S. v. City of Jackson. The cases centered around the Jackson trans-

portation terminals and the methods that were used to enforce segregation. Bailey dealt with the over-all question of integration in
travel and use of the facilities, while Jackson dealt specifically with
signs that were used to denote segregated waiting areas.

In Bailey, a group of Jackson blacks brought a class action
to enjoin the city, state officials and the bus and railroad companies from enforcing segregation ordinances or maintaining segregation in any manner, including the use of signs, on the carriers
or in and around their facilities. A three-judge federal court panel
decided to abstain in order to allow Mississippi courts to rule on
the challenged statutes first. The plaintiffs, however, took a direct
appeal to the Supreme Court where the lower court decision was
reversed and remanded.

In a per curiam opinion, the Supreme Court held that although the black plaintiffs lacked standing to enjoin criminal prosecutions under the breach of peace statutes, since there was no allegation of actual or threatened prosecution, they did have standing to
enforce their rights to nonsegregated treatment in transportation facilities as passengers. In its opinion the Court stated: "We have
settled beyond question that no State may require racial segregation
of interstate or intrastate transportation facilities. The question is
no longer open; it is foreclosed as a litigable issue." The case
was remanded to the district court for expeditious disposition regarding the claims of segregated service.

Upon remand, Federal Judge Sidney Mize duly declared the
Mississippi "Segregation Statutes" and a similar city ordinance unconstitutional as violative of the fourteenth amendment. Nonetheless, Judge Mize examined the use of the statutes and concluded
that they were no longer enforced. He also found that there were
only "isolated" instances of misconduct by police officers at the
terminals, that the signs had been removed from the terminal, and
that blacks had full access to all the facilities. For these reasons,
he refused to grant injunctive relief, and simply retained jurisdiction if further relief were shown to be necessary. The plaintiffs
moved to amend their motions and gained a further hearing. Although Judge Mize found that the signs which had referred to race
remained posted and that a certain amount of discrimination continued, he again maintained that corrective action had been taken
and no further relief was required.

The plaintiffs appealed the decision to the Fifth Circuit.
Judge Hays, sitting by designation from the Second Circuit, wrote
the Fifth Circuit panel opinion. Hays stated that injunctive relief
was necessary, notwithstanding the claims that the practices had
ceased, because of the city's course of conduct and its lack of good
faith.

> Notwithstanding the clear pronouncements of the Supreme
> Court in the present case [citations omitted], of this court
> [citations omitted], of the district courts [citations omitted],

and of the Interstate Commerce Commission [citation omitted], to name but some of the pertinent cases, appellees continued to maintain their policies and practices of racial segregation. The record here shows that these policies and practices continued even after the entry of judgment by the district court in the present case.

U.S. v. City of Jackson was a companion case to Bailey in that it also dealt with the signs and the segregated bus terminals that had come under attack in Bailey. The United States and the Interstate Commerce Commission (I.C.C.) initiated the action against Greyhound, Illinois Central Railroad, Continental Trailways, the City of Jackson and its officials, and sought a preliminary injunction to prevent the defendants from maintaining certain signs on the sidewalk in front of the terminals and to prevent enforcement of the sections of the Mississippi Code which dealt with segregation of public facilities. The period of time during which the activity occurred covered approximately five months, from November 1, 1961 to April 9, 1962.

Judge Mize denied the government's motion after a hearing. He found that all the carriers had complied with I.C.C. orders and had not discriminated in the use of any facility. Judge Mize also found that the Jackson police department had placed the signs, which read "Waiting Room for Whites Only - By Order Police Dept.," on the sidewalks near the terminals but had not enforced them. In his conclusions of law, Judge Mize stated that neither the United States nor the I.C.C. had any power or authority to enforce rights under the fourteenth amendment. He concluded that the I.C.C. orders applied only to the carriers and did not control the actions of city officials. Judge Mize also stated that the Constitution did not prohibit a state from authorizing or encouraging segregation. Judge Mize stated that the words "Only" and "By Order - Police Department" were inappropriate and should be deleted from the signs.

On appeal, the Fifth Circuit reversed Judge Mize's refusal to issue a preliminary injunction against the city and its officials as an abuse of discretion. Writing for the court, Judge Wisdom dismissed the city's contentions in a sharply-worded opinion. Judge Wisdom referred to the I.C.C. order, effective on November 1, 1961, which prohibited carriers from using facilities in segregated terminals and to the city's assertions that police were not enforcing segregation and that the signs merely assisted both races in voluntary segregation. Referring to these arguments as "disingenuous quibble," Judge Wisdom noted that in the area of civil rights "federal courts have acquired a thorough education in 'Sophisticated Circumvention.'" Judge Wisdom made it clear that the court would not be impressed by the city's protestations of innocence.

We again take judicial notice that the State of Mississippi has a steelhard, inflexible, undeviating official policy of segregation. The policy is stated in its laws. It is rooted in custom. The segregation signs at the terminals in

Jackson carry out that policy. The Jackson police add muscle, bone, and sinew to the signs.

Judge Wisdom concluded his examination of the city's arguments by stating that a terminal is not an island and that the government's power over interstate commerce is not confined to the terminal but covers the entire state. The city's use of the sidewalks for the purpose of posting signs to encourage segregation, with the resulting harassment of interstate passengers who do not abide by the suggestion, violated the I. C. C. order, the Commerce Clause and the fourteenth amendment. Wisdom also described the city's tactics which feigned compliance:

> Here the record shows that one of the sophisticated methods for circumventing the law is for the local police to eschew 'segregation' laws, using in their place conventional breach of peace or trespass laws as instruments for enforcing segregation, euphemistically termed 'separation.'

* * *

The legal assault on segregated local public facilities was begun in 1962. In Clark v. Thompson, three black citizens of Jackson alleged that they had been denied the use of various public facilities because of their race. Although Judge Mize granted the most limited relief possible, refusing to allow the suit to proceed as a class action, he did declare such segregation unconstitutional. When Judge Mize granted relief to civil rights litigants, the message was clear to all Jackson officials that their course was doomed. Although all public facilities were now in jeopardy, local attention quickly focused on the five public swimming pools as the sanctum sanctorum of separatism. On May 24, 1962, nine days after Judge Mize handed down his decision in Clark, Mayor Thompson stated, "We will do all right this year at the swimming pools ... but if these agitators keep up their pressure, we would have five colored swimming pools because we are not going to have any intermingling." By the following Spring, city officials had become more artful. On May 30, 1963, Mayor Thompson announced that the pools would not open on schedule, "due to some minor water difficulty." When the pools were not reopened thereafter, a group of black Jackson residents brought suit to force the city to resume the operation of the pools on an integrated basis. In this litigation, Palmer v. Thompson, Mayor Thompson filed an affidavit with the federal district court which purported to establish the reasons why the pools had been closed:

> Realizing that the personal safety of all of the citizens of the city and the maintenance of law and order would prohibit the operation of swimming pools on an integrated basis, and realizing that the said pools could not be operated economically on an integrated basis, the City made the decision subsequent to the Clark case to close all pools owned and operated by the City to members of both races.

Judge Cox denied the injunction, concluding, "The Plaintiffs have no constitutional right to require the City of Jackson to maintain or operate specific facilities such as swimming pools...."

On appeal, a panel of the Fifth Circuit Court of Appeals affirmed the denial of relief. However, the members of the full court voted to rehear the case en banc. By a seven-to-six vote, the court again affirmed the denial of relief. Judge Rives wrote the majority opinion, stating while it was true that the city closed the pools, there was no evidence that the decision was made to impede integration. Noting that the other recreational facilities were now completely integrated, Judge Rives found that the reasons for the pool closures were that they could not be safely or economically operated. He pointed out that the operation of swimming pools was not an essential public function in the same sense as conducting elections, operating a public utility or operating schools. Furthermore, in Palmer, there was no showing that the state had contributed money to maintain private swimming facilities. Judge Rives rejected the argument that the closing of the pools was a removal of "a badge of equality" and a denial of equal protection. He stated, "... where the facilities around which the status of equality are removed from the use and enjoyment of the entire community, we see no withdrawal of any badge of equality." Judge Rives further stated that courts, in applying the requirements of the equal protection clause, could not require a city to operate public pools solely because the failure to operate them foreclosed enjoyment of the facilities by those citizens who were financially less fortunate and unable to afford private facilities. The equal protection clause did not guarantee financial or economic equality among the races.

Judge Rives concluded his opinion for the majority by considering the role that motivation may play and by discussing when it can be considered. He argued, "Motive behind a municipal or a legislative action may be examined where the action potentially interferes with or embodies a denial of constitutionally protected rights." A city may, however, take race into consideration so long as it is not for a discriminatory or an invidious purpose. Judge Rives rejected the contention that a municipal policy of continued segregation could be inferred from the closing since the city had put forth the reasons for the closing, and those reasons were legitimate and substantial.

Judge Wisdom, writing for the dissent, began by scolding the majority for its acceptance of the city's reasons:

> Long exposure to obvious and non-obvious racial discrimination has seasoned this Court. It is astonishing, therefore, to find that half of the members of this Court accept at face value the two excuses the City of Jackson offered for closing its swimming pools and wading pools.

Judge Wisdom examined the two reasons and dismissed them both as being without any substantive merit. The city's operation of

the other recreational facilities on an integrated basis without any
disturbances was, in Judge Wisdom's opinion, proof that law enforcement officials were able to preserve peace despite integration.
In rejecting the city's financial contention, Judge Wisdom examined
the operating costs of the segregated pools and found that they had
never been operated at a profit. Thus, in Judge Wisdom's view,
the city's claimed right to close the pools stands in reality on the
alleged right to close a recreational facility on the "grounds of race
and opposition to desegregation."

The argument that the closing equally affected blacks and
whites was summarily dismissed by Judge Wisdom "as a tired contention, one that has been overworked." The fact that closing affected both races was irrelevant since race was the factor that led
to the closing. Judge Wisdom noted that measurable inequality was
not the basis for the Supreme Court per curiam decisions that applied Brown "to public parks and beaches, municipal theatres and
golf courses, buses and courtrooms. In these cases the central
vice in the unlawful state action was the forced display of a racial
badge of inferiority."

According to the dissenters, there was something at stake in
this case which was more important than the loss of recreation facilities or loss of symbolic acceptance in the community. Judge
Wisdom concluded:

> The closing of the City's pools has done more than de-
> prive a few thousand Negroes of the pleasures of swim-
> ming. It has taught Jackson's Negroes a lesson: In Jack-
> son the price of protest is high. Negroes there now know
> that they risk losing even segregated facilities if they dare
> to protest segregation.

The major difference between the majority and dissenting
opinions was a factual one. Both agreed that motivation was a factor to be considered; if the purpose in closing the pools were to
avoid integration, the action would be a denial of equal protection.
The majority had accepted the city's explanation. The dissent was
a good deal more skeptical and felt that the factual background clearly demonstrated that the closing was the result of an established
policy to avoid integration wherever possible.

The Supreme Court granted certiorari to decide the question
of whether the city closed the pool to avoid desegregation, thus resulting in a denial of equal protection. Six of the nine Justices
filed opinions. By a five-to-four vote, the Court affirmed the Fifth
Circuit's decision denying relief to the black plaintiffs.

In the context of the Jackson Movement, the last line on defense was finally drawn in the Palmer case. Local authorities were
free to discontinue nonessential public services and conveniences if
the services were denied to all for reasons ostensibly other than
racial separatism.

The Jackson city officials fought integration as long as and as hard as possible in spite of clear judicial mandates that made total desegregation inevitable. By continually forcing litigation, the city officials, either intentionally or inadvertently, made the Court decide an issue that was in a "gray" area. By a one-vote margin both in the Court of Appeals and in the Supreme Court, the action of closing the pools was vindicated.

*   *   *

The Jackson Movement encompassed a period of ten years, from 1961 to 1971. With the exception of Palmer v. Thompson, the Jackson litigation did not make significant doctrinal contributions to the course of civil rights law. Indeed, the significance of the Jackson story lies in the realization that the law was settled before the court battles were even filed. Yet the city refused to bow until specifically ordered to do so by the Fifth Circuit or the Supreme Court. It was a tedious, frustrating process, "wearying out the right."

The civil rights movement is usually categorized in terms of subject areas such as voting, jury discrimination and school desegregation. One negative result of such categorization is that it retards the ability to observe the cumulative effect which the movement had on a single state or city. Although the Jackson Movement was primarily oriented toward the integration of public facilities, in the span of ten years the Movement had influenced every aspect of community life and irrevocably altered the community's future course. The Jackson story illustrates the frustration and determination required of all who were drawn into the struggle for equality: Jackson's white supremacists, black militants and all those caught in between.

NOTES AND PRIMARY AUTHORITY

1 Dickens, Bleak House, at 3 (1886).

The primary sources for the material contained in this Chapter were the judicial decisions generated by the Jackson Movement: Thomas v. State, 160 So. 2d 657 (Miss. 1964); Farmer v. State, 161 So. 2d 159 (Miss. 1964); Thomas v. Mississippi, 380 U.S. 524 (1965); Pierson v. Ray, 352 F.2d 213 (5th Cir. 1965), 386 U.S. 547 (1966); Bailey v. Patterson, 369 U.S. 31 (1961), 206 F. Supp. 67 (S.D. Miss. 1962), 323 F.2d 201 (5th Cir. 1963); United States v. City of Jackson, 206 F. Supp. 45 (S.D. Miss. 1962), 318 F.2d 1 (5th Cir. 1963), 320 F.2d 870 (5th Cir. 1963); NAACP v. Thompson, 321 F.2d 199 (5th Cir. 1963), 8 Race Rel. L. Rep. 874-75 (1963), 11 Race Rel. L. Rep. 657 (S.D. Miss. 1964), 357 F.2d 831 (5th Cir. 1966); Strother v. Thompson, 372 F.2d 654 (5th Cir. 1967); Guyot v. Pierce, 372 F.2d 658 (5th Cir. 1967); Clark v. Thompson, 204 F. Supp. 30 (S.D. Miss. 1962), 204 F. Supp. 539 (S.D. Miss. 1962), 313 F.2d 637 (5th Cir. 1963), cert. denied,

375 U.S. 91 (1963); and Palmer v. Thompson, 12 Race Rel. L.
Rep. 1468, 391 F.2d 324 (5th Cir. 1962), 419 F.2d 1222 (5th Cir.
1969), 403 U.S. 217 (1971). Also helpful as background information about the Jackson Movement were: Sarrat, The Ordeal of
Segregation (1966); Sitton, "Inquiry into the Mississippi Mind," New
York Times Magazine, Apr. 28, 1963; "Comment, Palmer v. Thompson: Everybody Out of the Pool," 23 Hastings L. J. 889 (1972);
and contemporary news accounts such as, Washington Post, June 6,
1963, at 15; Jackson Daily News, June 19, 1963, at 4, 15, and
July 7, 1961; Delta-Democrat Times (Greenville, Miss.), Mar. 30,
1961, and Mar. 15, 1964, at 22; and New Orleans Times-Picayune,
May 27, 1961. A more complete manuscript, with detailed documentation of all sources, is available as indicated in the Preface,
supra.

Chapter 10

THE SEARCH FOR STANDARDS

The Climate. --Nineteen hundred sixty-three was the penultimate year of the Civil Rights Movement. Americans were treated to a daily news fare of triumph and tragedy on the civil rights scene. Black and white citizens organized, marched, sang and sat-in. With less than two per cent of the non-white residents of Selma, Alabama registered to vote, the Student Nonviolent Coordinating Committee (SNCC) initiated its first direct action and voter registration drive. Sheriff "Big Jim" Clark's response to that Selma voter drive personified the repressiveness of segregationist civil authorities. To alleviate such repression, President Kennedy sent a voting rights act to Congress. Congress did not respond. Using school children as marchers under the leadership of Reverend Fred Shuttlesworth, the Southern Christian Leadership Conference (SCLC) organized demonstrations in Birmingham, America's most segregated city. The over-reaction of Commissioner Eugene "Bull" Conner's police force shocked the nation. A wire service photograph of a snarling police dog unleashed upon an unarmed school boy was called the "moment at which the 1960's generation of 'new Negroes' can be said to have turned into a major social force." After the violence in Birmingham, President Kennedy sponsored new civil rights legislation that would have desegregated public accommodations, given expanded powers to the Attorney General to initiate school integration, and set stringent standards of nondiscrimination in federally financed or assisted programs. Again, Congress did not respond. Acting out the charade promised in his campaign for governor, George Corley Wallace stood in the schoolhouse door to block the enrollment of Vivian Malone to the University of Alabama, and he closed the Tuskegee High School to prevent public school integration. On a Sunday morning, thirteen days after Governor Wallace closed Tuskegee High School, four little girls were killed in the bombong of a Birmingham church and two boys were shot in the violent aftermath.

During the last week of May, 1963, a solitary march by a white postman from Baltimore, William Moore, ended near Attala, Alabama. Moore was found shot dead on the side of the highway still wearing a sign reading: "Equal Rights for All." Medgar Evers, the popular black leader, was assassinated at his home in Jackson, Mississippi. Nineteen hundred sixty-three also saw the beginning of race rioting in Cambridge, Maryland and Danville, Virginia. The Department of Justice reported that during the period of May through July over 186 cities in the South underwent 758 demonstrations. For the entire year there were almost five thousand arrests.

While marked by stark tragedy, 1963 was also the year of the most compelling moment of the Civil Rights Movement: The March on Washington. On one sweltering August day, 1,512 chartered buses and forty special trains brought over 200,000 civil rights "pilgrims" to the nation's Capitol. "[A]n unprecedented and unpredictable confluence of black leaders, white liberals, movie stars, bishops, and tens upon tens of thousands of ordinary citizens [came] to the Capitol to bear peaceful witness to the black American's petition for something called Freedom--Now. It may have been the most romantic single event of twentieth-century America."* Bayard Rustin, one of the organizers of the march and now Executive Director of the A. Philip Randolph Institute, recalls, "There were rich and poor and black and white and Jews and Christians-- all together in unity. It was the most joyous occasion that I have ever experienced." Leonard Carter, the NAACP Western Regional Director and then Midwestern Regional Director, remembers that he "... just watched all the buses and trucks and cars and every kind of vehicle pouring in. I had so many mixed emotions, Dr. King's speech ["I Have a Dream"], all the people sitting around the reflecting pool with their feet in the water. That period is behind us now, but I still consider the march the finest hour of the civil-rights movement. We shook this country to its heels. And that is not an easy thing to do."

On November 22, 1963, John F. Kennedy was assassinated in Dallas, Texas.

Nineteen hundred sixty-three's kaleidoscope of events provides a backdrop to the impatience and frustration of the Fifth Circuit as it attempted to speed up the tortuously slow tokenism of public school integration.

Shifting From "Deliberate" to "Speed"

Embroiled in swirling public and private controversies over Judge Cameron's court-packing charges, the pending Ross Barnett contempt citation, and Senator Eastland's plan to split the Circuit,** the United States Court of Appeals for the Fifth Circuit in 1963 faced the heaviest case load of any federal appellate court. Particularly troublesome were the school cases. Paralleling the pace of the hyperactive civil rights movement, new plaintiffs were filing desegregation suits throughout the Circuit. School cases now received priority treatment on the Fifth Circuit's appellate calendar, with many plaintiffs requesting and receiving extraordinary relief to force foot-dragging district court judges and school boards to proceed expeditiously. Furthermore, unlike an ordinary appellate case where the decision is generally accepted as final, with one

---

*82 Newsweek, Sept. 10, 1973 at 24.
**See Part II, Chapter 6, supra.

opinion resolving the issues, school cases were never finished. The same case would return again and again and again, exacting an enormous toll in judicial time and patience. Each time a case came back, inevitably greater integration was demanded or new mechanisms of delay had to be struck down.

After passage of the Civil Rights Act of 1964, the pace of public school desegregation took a quantum leap, with new case filings seeming to increase almost geometrically every few months. Title IV of the 1964 act required the Commissioner of Education of the Department of Health, Education and Welfare (HEW) to render technical assistance to local school boards in their preparation of school desegregation plans. Title IV also authorized the Attorney General to bring desegregation suits on behalf of complainants unable to sue on their own behalf. Title IV of that same act proscribed discrimination in any program or activity receiving federal financial assistance, under threat of loss of funding. When combined with the Elementary and Secondary Education Act of 1965, which greatly increased the amount of federal money available for the nation's public schools, particularly schools in low-income areas such as the Deep South, Title IV of the Civil Rights Act of 1964 provided federal officials with both a powerful club and a tempting carrot. With one hand they could offer generous amounts of federal aid to recalcitrant school districts, and with the other they could demand that desegregation efforts begin at the risk of the district's losing all of those new-found federal dollars.

To the Fifth Circuit the most disheartening aspect of the school cases was the refusal of many federal district judges to enforce the law at the local level without constant supervision. Cajoling, scolding, complimenting and peremptorily reversing unevenly performing federal district judges frequently unraveled the patience of the Court, seeming at times to stretch its ingenuity to the breaking point. There were disappointingly few district judges courageous enough to mandate compliance with Brown II and follow, without constant prodding, the latest requirements of the appellate courts. Most federal district judges could be classified as negative but passive; they were either unsympathetic, unresponsive, timid or fearful of community reaction and had to be pushed into taking each step designed to increase the pace of integration. Moreover there were also several federal district court judges who seemed bent on using every conceivable legal roadblock to halt integration and who actively sought to frustrate Court of Appeals mandates.

The Brown II hierarchy of enforcement obligations did not work well. School boards had been given the primary responsibility for enforcing the constitutional rights of black students. Yet, with very few exceptions, they refused to budge unless forced by court order, and sometimes not even then. Federal district courts were ordered to act as a second line of defense to ensure compliance; however, most of them were willing to countenance protracted delay. Brown II did not envision the primary enforcement role as resting on the appellate courts, but that is precisely where it lay in far too many cases.

An anonymous Houston attorney, familiar with the work of the Fifth Circuit, wrote an unsigned editorial for the Houston Chronicle in 1963 which severely criticized Southern judges and attorneys for "letting the Fifth Circuit down":

> The overworked Fifth Circuit judges cannot give adequate time to their other challenging cases and still continue to supervise the day-to-day conduct of racial litigation throughout the South. Sooner or later, the enforcement emphasis must shift to those local federal judges who now give grudging effect to the Constitution's commands. By holding one trial judge in contempt for refusal to devise a local pattern for positive action in one civil rights case, the court would do more to support the Constitution than by denying jury trials to a dozen Barnetts.*

After 1963, despite generally successful efforts by the Fifth Circuit judges to pull together, internal divisions persisted and further complicated the Court's handling of school appeals. Prior to Judge Cameron's court-packing charges, most of the Fifth Circuit's three-judge panels were composed of a majority of the Four: Tuttle, Rives, Wisdom and Brown. After the Houston Judicial Council meeting in the summer of 1963, all the Court of Appeals judges on the Fifth Circuit began to see more service on panels assigned school matters. School appeals were frequently handled by panels with a majority composed of the more conservative members of the Court: Jones, Gewin and Bell. Consequently, some of the Fifth Circuit's own decisions in the middle years reflect an unevenness of enforcement, with the panels controlled by the Four generally demanding greater and more rapid desegregation than the panels controlled by the other members of the Court.

As the Fifth Circuit found itself caught in an increasing maelstrom of school desegregation appeals, it desperately searched for uniform standards of enforcement. To enable it to continue to perform its traditional appellate role and handle its own overloaded calendar, the Fifth Circuit sought ways to remove itself from day-to-day supervision over the details of every federal district judge's local school orders. The United States Supreme Court was not necessarily helpful in the middle years. Other than urging its inferior federal courts in the South to move more rapidly, with sharp reminders that the time for transition from segregated to desegregated schools was becoming more limited with the passage of years since Brown, the Supreme Court did not provide guidance on the mechanics of the desegregation process. From 1963 to 1967, with no real assistance from the Supreme Court, with foot-dragging federal district judges, and with inconsistency in its own panel decisions, the Fifth Circuit groped toward standards for compliance with Brown II that would both protect the constitutional rights of black students and remove the Court from divisive day-to-day battles over the details of every school board's desegregation problems.

---

*Houston Chronicle, Nov. 10, 1963, at 6, cols. 1-4.

The painful, halting transition from "deliberate" to "speed" in those far from halcyon years of civil rights activism, 1963 to 1967, can be glimpsed by focusing on a few key cases and judges in four of the states supervised by the Fifth Circuit. The resistance and recalcitrance present in two of the Fifth Circuit's states, Texas and Louisiana, has already been explored in earlier chapters. The more permanent progress achieved in voting rights and jury selection has been traced in chapters 7 and 8. Attention is now directed to school desegregation in the remaining four states in the Fifth Circuit area: Georgia, Alabama, Mississippi and Florida.

GEORGIA

The Scarlett Cases. --While many federal district judges supervised by an increasingly impatient Fifth Circuit were unsympathetic with the plaintiffs in school integration cases, none in retrospect appears more deliberately obstructionist than Georgia's Frank M. Scarlett. A firm believer in white supremacy, Judge Scarlett was unwilling to carry out the mandates of Brown II and openly flouted the orders of his supervisory judges on the Fifth Circuit. His persistent efforts to thwart black plaintiffs in school cases in Chatham, Glynn and Richmond counties, which included the cities of Savannah, Augusta and Brunswick, effectively blocked integration in the Southern District of Georgia long past the time when most other school districts in the Fifth Circuit were obeying court-approved integration plans.

Judge Frank M. Scarlett was born on June 9, 1891, in Brunswick, Georgia. His education was strictly a Georgian one. From 1898 to 1908, he was a student at Glynn Academy, a school whose voluntary integration he later sought to prevent. He then attended Gordon College in Barnesville, Georgia, from 1908 to 1910, and in 1913 obtained his law degree from the University of Georgia at Athens. Frank Scarlett's professional life was spent in Brunswick. He returned there immediately after graduating from law school and remained in private practice until President Truman appointed him to the federal bench. His private practice was supplemented by an appointment as solicitor of the city court of Brunswick from 1919 to 1929. Before assuming his judicial post, Scarlett had been a director of a Brunswick bank, a director of Sea Island Company of Sea Island Beach, Georgia, and president of the Brunswick Chamber of Commerce. His chairmanship of the local Democratic Executive Committee from 1925 to 1945 may explain his federal court appointment on Valentine's Day, 1946.

The capacity of a single federal judge to inhibit the realization of equal educational opportunity in his judicial district by continuous, stubborn resistance to the commands of a superior federal court is best illustrated by the school cases of Judge Scarlett from 1963 to 1968. Those cases also support the charge that it was adherence to his own personal racial views, not legal precedent, that motivated Judge Scarlett in the conduct of his judicial office.

In January, 1962, black students and parents in Savannah and Chatham County, Georgia filed suit in Judge Scarlett's federal district court to desegregate their public schools. They took the typical first step of requesting a preliminary injunction requiring a prompt start toward desegregation of the county schools. Judge Scarlett's attitude toward such cases was evident from his first ruling. Ignoring precedent, he allowed a group of segregationist white parents to intervene as separate parties in the lawsuit between the black plaintiffs and the school board. The white parents intended to take over the lawsuit in order to present evidence that integration of the public schools would be detrimental to both black and white school children. Contrary to the Brown I theory that separate-but-equal schools are inherently unequal, Judge Frank M. Scarlett denied the plaintiffs' request for a preliminary injunction on May 13, 1963, adopting the argument of the white parents that integration would be harmful to their children. In a prompt appeal to the Fifth Circuit, the plaintiffs requested a preliminary injunction requiring the immediate start of desegregation pending the Circuit Court's full consideration of the appeal of Judge Scarlett's ruling.

On May 24, 1963, a panel composed of Chief Judge Tuttle and Judges Rives and Bell granted the plaintiffs their preliminary injunction. The Fifth Circuit panel reasoned that judgments denying preliminary injunctions were appealable as interlocutory orders, and furthermore, that the Court of Appeals could issue the preliminary injunction as a writ in aid of the Court's jurisdiction under the federal All Writs Statute. The panel also pointed out that such extraordinary relief as an injunction pending appeal would be granted only when there was a clear abuse of discretion or a usurpation of judicial power by the lower court. Chief Judge Tuttle's decision found such a clear abuse of discretion in Judge Scarlett's first decision in the Savannah-Chatham County case. Judge Scarlett had found what could not be denied: the Chatham County schools were segregated. In spite of that finding, he had failed to order the remedial action required by Brown II. Chief Judge Tuttle's opinion frankly charged that Judge Scarlett had allowed the intervention of the white parents to provide the intervenors with a convenient forum for a frontal attack on factual assumptions underpinning the holding of Brown I. Chief Judge Tuttle then pointedly reminded Judge Scarlett that both the District Court for the Southern District of Georgia and the circuit courts were bound by Brown I until that case was overruled by the Supreme Court. Therefore, upon his finding of segregation in the public schools of Chatham County, Judge Scarlett had a duty to order the school board to come forward with a plan for desegregation.

Because Judge Scarlett's court would be the court directly responsible for enforcing the preliminary injunction, the Fifth Circuit ordered the district court to enter the order rather than doing so itself. In its order, the Fifth Circuit took an unusual step to avoid further problems with the unresponsive Federal District Court for the Southern District of Georgia. Instead of following normal procedure and letting the district judge frame the preliminary injunction, Judge Tuttle drafted, word for word, the court order and directed Judge Scarlett to enter the order as written.

Soon after the Fifth Circuit's granting of the injunction, Judge Scarlett began the trial on the merits in the Savannah-Chatham County case. In light of the fact that Brown I had been established law for over nine years, his conduct of that trial and his resulting ruling are astounding. First, the black plaintiffs proceeded to support their allegation that school admission was determined solely by race. They established that the Savannah-Chatham County Board had continuously to that date operated racially separate schools. The black plaintiffs then objected to the intervention of the white parent group, arguing that Brown I conclusively established the irreparable injury sustained by black children in segregated school systems. Judge Scarlett reserved his ruling on that objection until the end of the trial. The school board's defense was put on with equal speed and simplicity; the board argued that plans for desegregation were being made and that no requests for transfers had ever been received from black students.

The bulk of the evidence introduced at the trial was produced, not by the black plaintiffs or by the defendant school board, but by the white-parent intervenors. The intervenors claimed that students should be classified as to educational ability, and they asserted that educational ability was a racial trait. In an effort to establish the educational inferiority of black students, the intervenors were allowed by Judge Scarlett to introduce a mass of evidence that clogged his court calendar for weeks. Based on results of intelligence and achievement tests given in the Chatham County schools from 1954 to 1963, a University of Georgia professor testified that there were marked differences between the intellectual capabilities of black and white children. He claimed that blacks scored lower on such tests as a group, with an overlap of fifteen per cent of the black children scoring as high or higher than the lowest white score in the primary grades and an overlap of only one to two per cent in high school. He further alleged that when the factors of economic and social background and segregated schools were controlled the results were similar. A professor of medicine from the University of North Carolina testified that the physiological differences between blacks and whites in brain size accounted for educational differences between the two races, asserting that such differences were hereditary. The intervenors were allowed to present witnesses, qualified by Judge Scarlett as experts, who testified from their own and others' research about the psychological and academic effects of integration. The experts testified that psychological problems for black children could result from an inability to keep up with whites. They warned that if the black children were dispersed throughout the school system, problems could also result from the lack of an identifiable subgroup with which to relate. It was argued by the experts that prejudice would increase if contact between the two groups were forced. Further, it was urged that if only the brightest black students were integrated, the ones remaining in all-black schools would suffer from a loss of leadership. Discipline and truancy problems were predicted.

Judge Scarlett reached his decision on June 28, 1963. He shocked the American legal community by holding that the United States Supreme Court's constitutional holding in Brown I, as to the harm caused to black children by compulsory segregation, was not binding. Because the white parent intervenors in the Savannah-Chatham County case were not parties to Brown I, he determined that the harm judicially noticed by the Supreme Court did not preclude the intervenors from establishing contrary facts in a later case. He decided that the general requirement that inferior federal courts must follow Supreme Court precedent was not appropriate because the principle of stare decisis applies only to questions of law, not questions of fact. Judge Scarlett concluded that Brown I answered a question of fact. He pointed out that the use by the Supreme Court of evidence in the Brown case similar to that offered by the white parents in the Savannah-Chatham County case made the white parents' evidence admissible. Resolving that the evidence in the case before him was more reliable than that used by the Supreme Court in Brown I, Judge Scarlett incorporated the conclusions of the intervenors' evidence into his findings of fact. On the basis of his findings, Scarlett determined that the Fourteenth Amendment had not been violated by the school board in segregating students by race. Judge Scarlett therefore denied the requested injunction, dismissed the black plaintiffs' complaint with the provision that the defendant school board give plaintiffs the same degree of specialized instruction given whites, and ordered that intelligence and achievement tests be impartially conducted. He did not allow the Court of Appeals' preliminary injunction to remain in effect pending a prompt appeal by the black plaintiffs from his decision.

Several comments made by Judge Scarlett in the Savannah-Chatham County trial reveal his personal racial views and help explain his conduct of the case. In his analysis of the reasons for the differences in testimony between the case before him and Brown I, Judge Scarlett commented about a Brown witness who said that differences in intellectual capacity had not been shown to exist between blacks and whites:

> It is difficult for the Court to believe that when Dr. Redfield swore that differences in intellectual capacity or ability had not prior to that time been shown to exist, ... he could have been unaware of such contemporaneous common references on the subject as the Encyclopedia Britannica (14 Ed.) [1902]. There, in the article on "Differential Psychology" a number of studies on the subject are referred to, all to the effect that the variations shown in this case did exist.

Scarlett attacked the credibility of Dr. Kenneth B. Clark, the first expert cited by the Supreme Court in Brown I, and that of other expert witnesses cited in Brown I, because they were asserted to be either "employed or retained either regularly or occasionally by [the NAACP]." Further, Judge Scarlett cited the Senate testimony of one Brown I witness who said that at the insistence of Thurgood

Marshall the Brown plaintiffs were "'using facts, emphasizing facts, bearing down on facts, sliding off facts, quietly ignoring facts, and above all interpreting facts ... to ... get by those boys down there.'" Judge Scarlett said:

> It is rather strange that the Justice Department of the United States Government should exert its powers in an effort to conceal or suppress facts as to discrimination against White people on account of their race and color.
>
> The honest, forthright and objective findings disclosed by this Study ... are apparently the very reverse of that expected. Why such a study should not receive wide publicity and renown is mysterious. The Government that financed the Study has apparently concealed it. It is now said to be 'out of print.'

Finally, of those critics of "tracking" (the grouping of students according to educational ability), Judge Scarlett wrote that tracking was "under violent attack from civil-rights groups and the most sadistic equalitarians."

Judge Scarlett's decision that Brown I was wrong and not binding on the white citizens of Savannah and Chatham County was not made in a vacuum; the schools were not the only focal point for desegregation efforts in Savannah in the summer of 1963. In early June, Savannah theaters were desegregated for one day and then returned to their pattern of segregation. Two months of demonstrations to desegregate the theaters again had led to the use of troops and a motorcade of one hundred members of the White Citizens' Council in counter-protest. Demonstrations continued through July. Desegregation of lunch counters became another issue. During July, violence erupted with the protests. Over the two-month period eight hundred persons were arrested. Finally, by August 3, a truce, arranged through the help of the Roman Catholic Church, called for demonstrations to cease until October and for the city to desegregate some facilities. The truce caused a split in the working relationship between the NAACP and the more activist Crusade for Voter Registration led by Hosea Williams. Judge Scarlett's decision that Brown did not apply to the Savannah-Chatham County case was not simply wrong legally, it was also mischievous. His holding caused deep resentment in an already agitated black community and created false hopes among segregationist whites.

The school board defendant in the Savannah-Chatham County case evidently anticipated a fast reversal of Judge Scarlett's trial decision, and without the usual judicial prodding required in other districts, it attempted to take some minimal steps toward token desegregation. During the summer, the school board adopted a plan to desegregate the twelfth grade effective September, 1963. The plan allowed any student meeting certain requirements to transfer to any senior high school in the system, a proposal similar to the original Atlanta plan. The black plaintiffs in the Savannah-Chatham

County case objected in toto to the plan, and Judge Scarlett refused to approve or disapprove it, claiming he was without jurisdiction. The plaintiffs appealed from Judge Scarlett's refusal to act. While the appeal was pending, nineteen black students actually transferred to white high schools. In spite of the plan's failure to satisfy the black plaintiffs, for the moment at least, Judge Scarlett's inaction had allowed token desegregation to penetrate his defense of segregated education in Southern Georgia.

Judge Scarlett's unusual conduct in school cases was not limited to the Savannah area; every black plaintiff in a school case in the Southern District of Georgia had to face Judge Scarlett. The only thing predictable about his decisions was his opposition to desegregation in any form.

In a calmer Brunswick, Georgia, the Glynn County Board of Education accepted the application of six black students to transfer from the black high school to Glynn Academy, Judge Scarlett's alma mater, for the 1963-64 school year starting on August 28, 1963. Brunswick thus became the first Georgia community voluntarily to desegregate its schools. One day before school was to start, Linda and Brenda Sue Gibson and other white students suing by their guardians obtained a temporary restraining order (TRO), without notice to the black students, enjoining the board from permitting their transfer. Like the white parent intervenors in Savannah-Chatham County, the Gibsons alleged that desegregation was detrimental to both races and sought an injunction against the operation of a "compulsory racially integrated school system"; or in the alternative, they sought an order that the system be reorganized into a tertiary system with some schools for whites, some for blacks and some for both. A request by the County Board to Governor Sanders for legal help in fighting Judge Scarlett's order blocking desegregation was refused because the state was not a party.

On September 6, Judge Scarlett converted his temporary restraining order against the black students into a pretrial order prohibiting them from transferring to white schools during the pendency of the trial. The black students requested that the temporary restraining order be dissolved and that an order be entered requiring the board to submit a plan for reorganization of the school system on a nonracial basis. Judge Scarlett's resolution of that request was to require the Glynn County Board to prepare and submit a plan for reorganization, but only after hearings on the plan had been held, with the board sitting as a court. The effect of this unique holding would have been to require the parties to appeal the school court decision through the superintendent of schools to the State Board of Education.

The black students in Glynn County immediately filed a notice of appeal and by September 12, 1963, the Fifth Circuit had vacated Scarlett's order insofar as it had prohibited the transfers of the black intervenors. As in the Savannah-Chatham County case, the judges specified the exact terms of the injunction in the Glynn

County case (Gibson) and ordered Judge Scarlett to enter it as written.

Judge Scarlett's unprecedented order halting voluntary desegregation in Brunswick was not only unwarranted legally, it was not even necessary politically to appease segregationist whites. Brunswick had a population of 27,000, nine thousand of whom were black; Glynn County had 14,500 blacks out of a population of fifty thousand. In the fall of 1963, black leaders felt the city was responsive to the black community. The library had been desegregated for many years. During the past year there had been voluntary desegregation of lunch counters and parks and the end of segregated signs at the County and City Commissions. With the exception of the swimming pools, all public facilities were expected to be desegregated by the end of 1963. The local NAACP leaders, who had discouraged SNCC and CORE activity in Brunswick, praised the white community for the speed of their reaction to black requests for conferences and desegregation. Although most held menial jobs, there was low unemployment among black citizens, and many were homeowners with home mortgages and loans that were relatively easy to obtain. Many of the residential areas were integrated. Four thousand blacks were registered to vote, with one thousand registered in a drive held during the last twelve months. The black community regarded their schools as generally better than the white schools; they felt they had better-trained teachers, although their schools were more poorly equipped. In the Brunswick climate at that time, Judge Scarlett's strange decision is difficult to explain on any basis but his own animosity toward desegregation of any kind.*

The Savannah-Chatham County and Brunswick cases came together in December, 1963, when a petition for certiorari was filed by the white parents with the Supreme Court from the injunctions granted by the Fifth Circuit. A similar Fifth Circuit injunction had been granted in a Birmingham, Alabama case, and defendants there had also filed a petition for certiorari on December 11, 1963. On February 17, 1964, the combined certiorari petitions were denied by the Supreme Court.

The merits of both the Savannah-Chatham County case and the Brunswick case were decided by the Fifth Circuit on June 18, 1964. While both cases were filled with side issues arising from

---

*Glynn County has become a model of desegregation success. With excellent community and school board cooperation, in 1970-71 Glynn County adopted a school desegregation plan totally integrating the system; the new plan provides for approximately a seventy per cent white and thirty per cent black racial composition for each school in the system. The school board chairman, noting what had been accomplished, indicated he would hate "to go back to the previously segregated system."--"School Desegregation in Ten Communities," A Report of the United States Commission on Civil Rights, at 178, 196-97 (June, 1973).

Judge Scarlett's rulings, the Fifth Circuit saw the central issue to be whether a state could assign children to schools ostensibly on the basis of educational aptitudes while utilizing race as the primary indicia of such educational aptitudes. The Fifth Circuit again openly accused Judge Scarlett of permitting the intervention of the white parents solely to provide a factual basis for overruling Brown I. For this, Judge Bell wrote for the Court: "We reiterate that no inferior court may refrain from acting as required by that decision [Brown I] even if such a court should conclude that the Supreme Court erred either as to its facts or as to the law." Just as it had done in its earlier opinion in the Savannah-Chatham County case, the Court quoted the Brown I principle that segregated schools are inherently unequal and the Brown II duty that, once segregation is found, courts must require remedial action by school boards. Judge Bell concluded, "Thus was the Savannah case ended then, and there it must end now." However, in a seemingly innocuous aside that was to lead to more trouble for the Fifth Circuit from Judge Scarlett, Judge Bell stated that the decision did not mean that children could not be assigned to schools by intelligence if race was not a factor. The discrimination inherent in the Scarlett-approved plan was that capable blacks were placed in black schools because of a racial average and not because of their individual aptitude. Furthermore, the Fifth Circuit made it clear that with the long passage of time since Brown II, grade-a-year plans were no longer acceptable and the timetable for desegregation had to be accelerated.

As the Fifth Circuit was issuing its decision in the Savannah-Chatham and Glynn County cases, another major desegregation suit was beginning in the Southern District of Georgia. In June, 1964, black students and parents began a class action against the County Board of Education of Richmond County to enjoin the operation of a biracial school system in Augusta and surrounding Richmond County. In the fall of 1964, following his fixed pattern despite reversals, Judge Scarlett denied the plaintiffs' request for a preliminary injunction and instead approved a very meager plan of desegregation for grades one, two and three for the 1964-65 school year. An appeal by plaintiffs to the Fifth Circuit was dismissed when the Richmond Board also agreed to desegregate the fourth, fifth, sixth and twelfth grades. Even a request by a black student to take algebra at a white high school in the summer of 1965 had been refused by the school board and by Judge Scarlett; relief had to be provided her by the Fifth Circuit.

Meanwhile in Savannah, the white parent intervenors in the Savannah-Chatham County case were not content with the Fifth Circuit's reversal of Judge Scarlett. They filed a petition for certiorari on September 18, 1964, asking the Supreme Court: "Does [the] Fourteenth Amendment's Equal Protection Clause bar [a] segregated public school system based on tests showing differences in educational aptitudes between races?" The petition was denied on December 7, 1964.

Two years after the original suit had been filed, and still

with no effective desegregation, the defendant board in Savannah-Chatham County filed a new plan with Judge Scarlett prior to the opening of the 1965-66 school year. In his August 24, 1965 decision on that new plan, Judge Scarlett read his 1964 reversal by the Fifth Circuit as leaving open the issues of time and manner of integration. He asserted that the Circuit was mistaken in believing that his decision at the trial of the Savannah-Chatham County case required continued segregation. Picking up Judge Bell's innocuous appearing aside, Judge Scarlett noted that the Circuit had said assignment could be made on the results of intelligence and achievement tests if done on an individual basis. Therefore, Judge Scarlett interpreted the Circuit as approving educational ability groupings if race was not a factor. He concluded that "under the evidence in this case, [ability groupings] should be made." He asserted that Brown I was no bar to educational ability groupings because it required only that "children of 'similar age' and the 'same educational qualifications' ... be classed together." The way to determine the manner of integration, declared Judge Scarlett, was to consider the law in the light of the evidence of black educational inferiority which he had admitted at trial. Such evidence was referred to as "undisputed, credible and convincing." Judge Scarlett found that for effective education to exist there must be separation according to age and mental qualification. He further asserted that the facts he had found to be established at the trial were not subject to reversal. He then proceeded to discuss new evidence, which had not been available at the time of the appeal, that he insisted also demonstrated black racial inferiority.

Judge Scarlett's order that children be separated according to mental ability took the school board by surprise. The board opposed such groupings on the ground that they would cause inferiority and superiority complexes. To Judge Scarlett the board's contention was "unthinkable";

> To restrain bright children in order to keep 'dumb' children from experiencing the urge that goes with an 'inferiority complex' would subvert and nullify the educational process. Excellence is not to be penalized in order to exalt mediocrity.

The board plan was disapproved and the board was ordered to submit a new plan consistent with the trial evidence, the Fifth Circuit opinion, Brown I, and Scarlett's requirement that

> [t]he plan should assure that integration may be accomplished in such a manner as to provide the best possible education for all school children with the greatest benefits to all school children without regard to race or color, but with regard to similarity of ages and qualifications.

At that late date, a new issue was raised by the white parent intervenors: they asked that there be no discrimination against white teachers. They alleged that the mean annual salary of black teachers was higher than that of white teachers while black principals gave their teachers lower ratings than white principals gave their white teachers. Judge Scarlett again accommodated the intervenors by ordering that discrimination against white teachers cease. He also ordered that testing programs be continued and administered so that race would not be a factor in the testing and assignment of students or teachers.

A new desegregation plan approved by the board and the white parent intervenors was submitted to the court for hearing on November 3, 1965, but additional time was granted to the plaintiffs to study the plan. During that delay, the United States intervened through Attorney General Katzenbach on November 12, and filed objections to the plan. Because of the Justice Department objections, the proposed plan was withdrawn and resubmitted with modifications to meet those objections. Desegregation of all grades by September, 1966 was proposed. No action was taken by Judge Scarlett on the amended plan until April 1, 1966. At that time, Judge Scarlett enjoined the defendant board from operating a racial system but mandatorily required them "to maintain [a system] based on age, intelligence, achievement and other aptitudes upon a uniformly administered program."

On April 19, 1966, Judge Scarlett approved a separate plan submitted by the white parent intervenors. It was essentially a neighborhood plan with transfers permissible only if age and mental qualifications were met. Clearly, its aim was to maintain as much segregation as possible. To be eligible for transfer, a student had to meet the academic mean of the school he wished to enter, and parental approval was needed to assign a child to a school or class with a mean IQ less than the child's. New pupils were to be assigned to the neighborhood school, with transfer only in the manner provided for all other students. The proposal to end discrimination against white teachers was repeated. Judge Scarlett's decision was so one-sided and so much at variance with approved plans then in effect in other districts that the black plaintiffs, the school board and the United States all appealed to the Fifth Circuit.

On December 4, 1967, Chief Judge Tuttle, joined by Judges Gewin and Ainsworth, promptly rejected the white parent plan approved by Judge Scarlett. The Court found neither a constitutional right to attend classes based on intelligence nor a constitutional right to teacher salary based on competence. Salary standards for teachers and capability grouping of students were clearly matters for the school boards concerned, and not the courts. The Fifth Circuit then ordered implementation of a plan comparable to those approved at that time in other school districts in the Circuit as mandated by its recent decision in Jefferson II.*

*   *   *

---

*Discussed in Part II, Chapt. 11, infra.

Judge Scarlett's handling of school cases posed a grave threat
to the realization of any degree of desegregation in his district.
Only continuous scrutiny by the Fifth Circuit and prompt and peremptory reversals kept the hopes of the black plaintiffs alive. Despite constant appellate surveillance, Judge Scarlett was able effectively to delay real desegregation in the Southern District of Georgia
far past the time when other districts were operating under court
approved plans. Judge Scarlett's open obstructionism was a source
of constant irritation to the Fifth Circuit. After repeated reminders
that Brown I was binding on Judge Scarlett as well as on all other
federal courts, the Fifth Circuit's exasperation with him was openly
expressed. On the third review of Judge Scarlett in the Savannah-
Chatham County case, the Fifth Circuit opinion began:

> This is the fourth or fifth appearance of this case in
> this court, considering both temporary measures and ap-
> peals on the merits. We simply do not consider it worth
> while to take the time to canvass the exact number of
> times in which we have been called upon to correct the
> actions of the District Court for the Southern District of
> Georgia.... The fact that this appeal now aligns the
> Board of Education ..., the Negro plaintiffs and the United
> States, as intervenor, all as appellants, and Lawrence,
> Roberts and other ... white intervenors as appellees, it-
> self indicates something of the unusual character of this
> litigation.

Chief Judge Tuttle's opinion went on to praise the school board for
its attempts at desegregation but criticized Judge Scarlett and the
intervenors he had allowed to enter the case.

> [T]he Board, in light of the decisions of this court and
> of the Supreme Court, notwithstanding the failure of the
> district court to require any plan to be submitted by it,
> has been moving towards the currently announced desegre-
> gation requirements of this court.... It is plain that
> progress towards the ultimate total desegregation of the
> schools of this city and county would have moved much
> more smoothly, with more certainty, and much more
> promptly had not the trial court, at the instance of the
> Roberts [white parent] group of intervenors, repeatedly
> entered orders, including an order of dismissal at one
> stage of the proceedings, completely in conflict with the
> decisions of this court and of the United States Supreme
> Court.

Judge Scarlett's career on the federal bench was not distinguished.* Aside from the race cases where he was consistently
reversed, his appellate reversal rate on all classes of cases was
far higher than normal. One knowledgeable source, who has asked

*Judge Frank M. Scarlett died on November 18, 1971.

not to be identified, was questioned about Judge Scarlett's general performance on the bench and his overall legal competence. He answered by relating an anecdote: at one time the Fifth Circuit was considering an appeal from a Scarlett ruling and had decided to affirm. A courthouse observer familiar with Judge Scarlett's high reversal rate, remarked to a friend that the decision to affirm was, obviously, "purely fortuitous."

ALABAMA

The Judge and the Governor. --One of the most fascinating sagas to come out of the effort of the federal courts to enforce civil rights in the South is the monumental on-going battle between Alabama Governor George Corley Wallace and Federal District Judge Frank Minis Johnson. Two stubborn, proud men, one elected on a platform of Segregation Forever and total resistance to any form of race-mixing, the other appointed to enforce the Constitution and committed to doing so regardless of opposition, they came to personify their respective positions. Friendly law school classmates at the University of Alabama, George Wallace and Frank Johnson became bitter antagonists in a legal war that inflamed a state. From their struggle, one has emerged as a candidate for the Presidency, and the other has been proclaimed one of the finest trial judges ever to serve on a United States bench.

Frank Johnson was born October 30, 1918, in Winston County, a rare Republican stronghold in the "hill-country" of North Alabama. Winston County attempted to secede from Alabama when Alabama seceded from the Union in 1860, and it has since been referred to by locals as "The Free State of Winston." The son of a one-time county probate judge, Frank Johnson spent his formative years sitting in his father's courtroom, enthralled by the arguments of the lawyers. He now carries the nickname "Straight Edge," inherited from a great-grandfather also known for his fairness. After graduation from Mississippi's Gulf Coast Military Academy, Johnson meandered for a year working as a surveyor and then attending business college. He married a girl from Winston County, Ruth Jenkins, at age nineteen, and they worked their way through the University of Alabama, meeting George and Lurleen Wallace, who were also struggling to obtain an education. Johnson remembers that even then Wallace had "an uncanny ability to sense moves and determine an effective appeal." Both the Johnsons and the Wallaces were separated by World War II, Wallace as a B-29 crewman completing nine combat missions in the Pacific and Johnson as a combat infantry officer in General Patton's Third Army, earning a Bronze Star for gallantry in the Normandy Invasion. Johnson was wounded twice and completed his military duty as a legal officer in England. When Johnson returned to Alabama he entered private practice and became an active Republican, serving as one of President Eisenhower's state campaign managers. After the 1952 election, he was appointed, at age thirty-four, as a United States Attorney. He had a short but impressive career in that capacity and convicted two Alabama planters in one of the few peonage cases successfully prosecuted since the Reconstruction era. In October, 1955, at age thirty-six, he was one of the youngest men ever appointed to a United States Federal District Judgeship. He immediately became embroiled in the adjudication of civil rights questions. His even-handed courage and strong determination have made him almost legendary. Invariably dressed in a freshly pressed black suit, white shirt and black tie, and rarely wearing judicial robes, Judge Johnson has always run his courtroom in a no-nonsense, impartial manner.

Early in his judicial career, Judge Johnson demonstrated that he would not trade his judicial integrity for popular acceptance. He participated in his first major civil rights case in 1956, shortly after his appointment to the bench. In that case, a three-judge court, composed of Circuit Judge Rives and District Judges Johnson and Lynne, was asked to extend the rationale of Brown I to prohibit racial segregation of Montgomery's municipal bus service. Although Judge Lynne dissented vigorously, Judge Johnson joined the majority opinion of Judge Rives condemning such segregation. A dramatic early victory was thus achieved by a young black minister, Martin Luther King, Jr., who had led that historic bus boycott.

The outrage of white Alabamians against Judge Johnson was born with that decision and was nurtured with almost every decision he rendered thereafter in the civil rights area. He sat on the three-judge court that abolished the Alabama poll tax. After one of his rare reversals by the Supreme Court in Gomillion v. Lightfoot, a case that applied the equal protection clause to void the gerrymandered city boundaries of Tuskegee, he handed down the first judicial order requiring the alteration of voting districts established by a state legislature.* Of even greater import was Judge Johnson's work as a member of the three-judge court which decided Sims v. Frink, the case which became Reynolds v. Sims in the United States Supreme Court. Sims implemented the one man-one vote right heralded in Baker v. Carr by requiring the states to reapportion their legislature. When Alabama attempted in its reapportionment plan to prevent the election of black legislators by combining black and white counties to dilute the black vote, the same three-judge court which had decided Sims v. Frink invalidated the scheme in Sims v. Boggett.

Judge Johnson has continued to be at the forefront of develop-

---

*In fairness to Judge Johnson, he first decided the Gomillion case in reliance on the Supreme Court's earlier opinion in Colegrove et al. v. Greene et al. The earlier Colegrove case was penned by Mr. Justice Frankfurter and indicated that "the courts ought not enter this political thicket." In the Supreme Court's reversal of Judge Johnson in Gomillion it did not even acknowledge that its decision repudiated its prior opinion in Colegrove. Gomillion did put the district court in the middle of the "political thicket" and it has not yet emerged.

ing reapportionment law, and has championed the right of women to
serve on state and federal juries.   Judge Johnson's chambers in the
federal courthouse in Montgomery overlook the bus depot where in
1961, freedom riders were attacked and beaten by a mob, while police officers and state officials ignored the violence.   Aware first-
hand of the facts, Judge Johnson enjoined all parties from further
action and reaction pending determination of their rights.   His remark at the time has been widely quoted: "If there are any other
such occurrences, I'm going to put some Klansmen, some police
officials and some Negro preachers together in the U.S. Penitentiary."

Judge Johnson has indicated that his most difficult judicial
decision, from a public acceptance standpoint, was issued during the
1965 Selma to Montgomery civil rights march.   In the seven weeks
prior to the march, Sheriff "Big Jim" Clark jailed 2,000 people, including Martin Luther King, Jr.   A young black woodcutter, Jimmie
Lee Jackson, was shot in the stomach and died after claiming that
a state trooper had shot him.   On Sunday, March 7, 650 black and
white marchers crossing Pettus Bridge outside Selma on U.S. Highway 80 were charged by Sheriff Clark's mounted posse and Colonel
Al Lingo's State Troopers:

> Suddenly the clubs started swinging.   From the side-
> lines, white townspeople raised their voices in cheers
> and whoops.   Joined now by the possemen and deputies,
> the patrolmen waded into the screaming mob.   The march-
> ers retreated for 75 yards, stopped to catch their breath.
> Still the troopers advanced.   Now came the sound of can-
> isters being fired.   A Negro screamed: 'Tear gas!'
> Within seconds the highway was swirling with white and
> yellow clouds of smoke, raging with the cries of men.
> Choking, bleeding, the Negroes fled in all directions while
> the whites pursued them.   The mounted men uncoiled bull
> whips and lashed out viciously as the horses' hoofs tram-
> pled the fallen.   'O.K., nigger!' snarled a posseman,
> flailing away at a running Negro woman.   'You wanted to
> march--now march!'
> 'Please! No!' begged a Negro as a cop flailed away
> with his club.   'My God, we're being killed!' cried an-
> other.   The Negroes staggered across the bridge and
> made for the church, chased by the sheriff's deputies and
> the horsemen.   Many Negroes picked up cans and rocks
> and hurled them at the police.   As the deputies crowded
> in, they were stopped by Selma's Public Safety Director
> Wilson Baker, a bitter enemy of Clark's who has done his
> thankless best to keep peace in the city.   Said Baker to
> Clark: 'Sheriff, keep your men back.'   Replied Clark:
> 'Everything will be all right.   I've already waited a
> month too damn long!'*

*85 Time, Mar. 19, 1965, at 24; reprinted by permission from
Time, The Weekly Newsmagazine; copyright Time, Inc.

National television carried the Selma event and the country was outraged. On Martin Luther King's call, clergymen from all over the nation flew to Selma to stage a protest march to Montgomery to petition Governor Wallace for a redress of grievances. The marchers requested that Judge Johnson enjoin state officials from interfering with their march. The state instead wanted the march enjoined. With an effective tactic which he favors in explosive situations, Judge Johnson temporarily enjoined all parties until he could consider the matter on the merits. King began the mark anyway, but turned back. While awaiting Johnson's decision on a rescheduled march and on an order to show cause why King should not be held in contempt, three white clergymen were beaten by white hooligans in Selma at the Silver Moon Cafe; the Reverend James Reeb died from a blow to the head.

> In Montgomery, lawyers met in Judge Johnson's courtroom to thrash out the claims and counterclaims that had beclouded the week. Hosea Williams testified that on Sunday he had heard Sheriff Clark shouting to his deputies: 'Go get them niggers--go get them goddam niggers!' Questioned closely about the charges that bullwhips were used, Williams said that he saw five or six possemen with the whips. Did he know what a bullwhip was? Replied Williams: 'I'm a country boy. I know what a bullwhip is.'
>
> Selma Lawyer W. McLean Pitts, attorney for Sheriff Clark, demanded that the court cite Martin Luther King for contempt. The judge leveled a cold eye at Attorney Pitts, explained with asperity that contempt is a matter for the court to decide.
>
> Questioning Negro witnesses, Pitts was aggressive to the point that N. A. A. C. P. Lawyer Jack Greenberg, representing King, jumped to his feet to object to Pitts's 'insulting manner.' Judge Johnson sustained Greenberg. 'Everybody in this court, regardless of who he or she is, will be treated with common courtesy,' said he.
>
> Pitts sputtered: 'I'm trying very hard, but ...'
> Johnson shot back acidly: 'Try a little harder.'*

Judge Johnson then allowed the march to proceed, ordering the state to provide protection to the marchers: "'the right to assemble, demonstrate and march peaceably along the highways and streets in an orderly manner should be commensurate with the enormity of the wrongs that are being protested against. In this case, the wrongs are enormous.'" Judge Johnson's decision to let the march proceed brought on an avalanche of caustic criticism and hate mail. One letter, signed "A very dedicated southerner," threatened:

> I will kill and even die before I will let you, the niggers, communist or any other low jacking son of a bitch

---

*Ibid., at 27-28.

take my rights and tramp over me and my family.
I would just like to say that every one of your kind
should be dead and in hell with your dam back broke.

But Judge Johnson's even-handedness was demonstrated later
that very summer. In the spring, 167 had been arrested for demonstrating at the state capital and another group had been arrested on
the same charge at a black college. All were charged with trespassing and other acts of civil disobedience. Thinking that the federal court would protect them from prosecution, they sought to have
their cases removed to federal court. Judge Johnson refused to accept jurisdiction:

> There is no immunity conferred by our Constitution and
> laws of the United States to those individuals who insist
> upon practicing civil disobedience under the guise of
> demonstrating or protesting for 'civil rights.' The phi-
> losophy that a person may--if his cause is labeled 'civil
> rights' or 'states' rights'--determine for himself what
> laws and court decisions are morally right or wrong and
> either obey them according to his own determination, is
> a philosophy that is foreign to our 'rule-of-law' theory of
> government.
> Those who resort to civil disobedience such as the
> petitioners were engaged in ... cannot and should not es-
> cape arrest and prosecution. Civil disobedience by 'civil
> rights workers' in the form of 'going limp' and lying or
> marching in the streets or upon the sidewalks, or march-
> ing around the city hall while night court was in session,
> singing 'freedom' songs, or taking to the streets to do
> their parading and picketing in lieu of using the sidewalks,
> while failing to make any application to city authorities
> for a parade permit, is still a violation of the law.*

Judge Johnson's judicial philosophy is simplicity itself. Flatly refusing to be labeled liberal or conservative, he states: "I'm
not a segregationist ... but I'm not a crusader, either. I don't
make the law. I don't create the facts, I interpret the law.... I
don't see how a judge who approaches these cases with any other
philosophy, particularly if he was born and reared in the South,
can discharge his oath and the responsibility of his office."**

Perhaps Judge Johnson's most inspirational moment on the
bench came in his charge to the jury in United States v. Thomas,
Wilkins and Eaton, the three klansmen charged with violating the
civil rights of Detroit housewife Viola Liuzzo, murdered on a dark
country road after the Selma march.

The first prosecution of Collie Leroy Wilkins, Eugene Thomas

---

*86 Time, Aug. 13, 1965, at 15A.
**98 Time, May 12, 1967, at 72.

and William Orville Eaton was in an Alabama state court; they were charged with murder. The prosecution had a strong witness, Gary Rowe, an informer for the FBI, who accompanied the three men that night. Rowe testified that the men chased Mrs. Liuzzo's car, trying four times to pull even before finally overtaking it. Wilkins and Eaton then emptied their revolvers into the car. The gun that fired the bullet that killed Viola Liuzzo was found in Thomas's home and was the gun that Rowe testified Thomas had given to Wilkins. The three men were defended by Matt Murphy, the lawyer for the Ku Klux Klan. Murphy called six witnesses for the defense, who gave a total of twenty-one minutes of testimony, and then rested his case. In an attempt to influence the all-white jury, Murphy delivered a sixty-seven minute defense summation, which amounted to a racial diatribe: "And I'm proud that I stand upon my feet and I stand for white supremacy. Not black supremacy, not the mixing and the mongrelizing of the races, not the biggest onslaughts of the civil rights movement that has invaded your quiet little county.... And when white people join up to 'em [NAACP], they become white niggers." The jury deliberated two days before asking the court to dismiss them, since they were hopelessly deadlocked ten to two for conviction.

Wilkins was tried a second time for murder in October, 1965, again in a state court. This time, however, Alabama's Attorney General Richmond Flowers replaced the county prosecutor. Flowers concentrated his efforts on the selection of jurors, asking each prospective juror questions about their racial feelings: Was the Caucasian race superior to the Negro? Was any white person who associated with blacks inferior to other whites? Flowers, after he established that eleven of the thirty in the venire felt civil rights workers were inferior, demanded the right to challenge these men for cause. The state trial judge denied the motion, allowing Flowers time to appeal to the Alabama Supreme Court. A four-judge panel of that court denied Flowers' petition for a writ of mandamus, stating that an interruption of the trial for review by mandamus would establish a precedent that would operate to impede the progress of future criminal trials. The jury that was then impanelled for the second state trial was composed of ten men who were either present or former members of the White Citizen's Council, and five who also believed civil rights workers were inferior. This time the jury deliberated only an hour and forty-seven minutes in finding Wilkins not guilty.

Wilkins, Thomas and Eaton did not escape punishment, however. A third trial was held, this time in federal court, where the three were charged with violation of Mrs. Liuzzo's civil rights. In a thirty-page, meticulous charge to the jury, Judge Johnson, presiding at the federal court trial, explained the judicial system and told the jurors their duty, calling the American jury system "a beacon of hope and a last resort for the protection of individual citizens." After the Liuzzo jury reported back "hopelessly deadlocked," Judge Johnson again reminded the jury of their sworn duties and sent them back. They reached a guilty verdict--the first civil

rights conviction in Alabama. "There was ... blank puzzlement on
the faces of Collie Leroy Wilkins and his two accomplices" as the
verdict was read, sentencing the three to ten years in a federal
prison. When asked about the famous Liuzzo jury charge, Judge
Johnson simply acknowledged that it had "a salutary effect."

With the possible exception of Fifth Circuit Judge Richard
Rives of Alabama, and, for a time, Skelly Wright in New Orleans,
no judge in the South has endured more abuse and harassment than
Frank Johnson. Governor George Wallace led the list of public
vilifiers, and his conduct encouraged a flow of hate mail and threats
that would have cowed a lesser man. Calling Johnson an "integratin',
scallywaggin', carpetbaggin' liar," in 200 stump speeches,* George
Wallace developed into a crude verbal art form the politically astute
tactic of roasting the federal courts. He gleefully proclaimed that
the federal bench "doesn't have enough brains to try a chicken
thief."** He told Tom Wicker of the New York Times:

> Of course, if I did what I'd like to do I'd pick up some-
> thing and smash one of these federal judges in the head
> and then burn the courthouse down. But I'm too genteel.
> What we need in this country is some governors that used
> to work up here at Birmingham in the steel mills with
> about a tenth-grade education. A governor like that
> wouldn't be so genteel....***

Wallace's rhetoric may have been counter-productive. Ryan de Graf-
fenreid, Wallace's defeated opponent when Wallace took over the
Governorship in 1962, prophesied, "It's been the same pattern in
every state where you have a loud mouth, rabble-rousing governor.
They have brought the walls of segregation tumbling down on their
heads."**** Nevertheless, Wallace's taunts stirred up an incandescent hate in believing segregationists. They saw Judge Frank
Johnson as the embodiment of a powerful federal force intent upon
forcing integration and destroying the Southern way of life. Judge
Johnson has received a flood of insults, bomb threats and promises
of assassination. Two weeks after he ordered state-wide school integration, the home of his 69-year-old mother was bombed. George
Wallace sent state agents to investigate the school Judge Johnson's
son attended to look for "Communist overtones." A cross was burned
on the judge's lawn and his home has been under periodic federal
guard. Judge Johnson feels that because of his natural reserve--he
is an intensely private man*****--these crushing pressures have

---

*R. Sherrill, Gothic Politics in the Deep South, at 328 (rev. ed.
1969) [hereinafter cited as Sherrill]; reprinted by permission of
Grossman Publishers, Inc.
**Ibid., at 329.
***Ibid., at 312.
****Ibid., at 329.
*****Judge Johnson candidly states: "My life is on the golf course,
or fishing, or in the office or in the courtroom working, and it's
hard to put pressure on someone like that...."

really had very little effect on him. If anything, they have made him more determined "to go ahead and do what was required."

Judge Johnson's flinty determination may have contributed to some of the opposition he has felt. He has not hesitated to scold lead-footed school boards from the bench for failing to act in good faith. From the day he took the bench, Judge Johnson has declined the camaraderie of close relationships with members of the bar. He has made no attempt to explain or sugar-coat his decisions for public acceptance. While giving him credit for doing his duty, another judge charges that by his "stiff-necked" attitude he has brought many of his troubles on himself. His stern, uncompromising public demeanor, however, hides an exceptionally compassionate, humane man. He takes pains to discuss pre-sentence reports with defendants and their families in the privacy of his chambers. In one case, he sentenced four black men convicted of stealing peanuts from a federal warehouse to only thirty minutes custody with the U.S. Marshal after the jury had convicted them but acquitted the white man who had hired them to commit the crime. It is reported that in a recent landmark decision holding that mental patients have a right to treatment, Judge Johnson openly wept from the bench as deplorable conditions in some Alabama mental homes were described.

Those who criticize Judge Johnson for "aloofness" or for failing to fraternize with the local bar, or for not engaging in more community activities, are not aware of the intensity of opposition in Alabama to the federal courts. Blending into community affairs and keeping impartiality is difficult enough for a judge, even in the best of times, but it is almost impossible during times of great stress. The judicial office is a lonely one and perhaps self-sustaining men can best handle its pressures in difficult times. What is forgotten is that men like Frank Johnson, who upheld their oath, were public pariahs in grave and constant personal peril. Following is a sampling of the hate mail received; the threats here were not isolated and they were not idle:

> You must withdraw, rescind, cancel, void, have we made it clear? the order you issued about four weeks ago requiring the schools to integrate further, far beyond the freedom of choice plan as it is working a hardship on every school the order was sent to. You have until Monday Sept. 30 to get the information to the schools affected, every one of them that your order has been canceled, rescinded, withdrawn and for the schools to return to the Freedom of choice plan. We mean every word of this demand and if you ignore or fail to carry out the instructions outlined above your son, an innocent person will pay the penalty first, then your Mother who also is innocent, then will be your time. We will get you regardless of how many bodyguards you have. At home, at the office, in court or in transit from home to the office. You cannot possibly get by us for we have a group plenty capable

for we have had plenty [of] practice picking Viet Congs
off by the dozens. We do not have freedom in the U.S.
anymore but we will soon have some satisfaction of getting rid of some of the bastards causing the trouble.
Signed ..... FIVE VOLUNTEERS.

CIVILIAN ORDER TO THE FOLLOWING:
Judge H. H. Grooms, 2624 Aberdeen Road, Birmingham,
Ala.
Judge Frank M. Johnson, FEDERAL JUDGE, FEDERAL
BUILDING, MONTGOMERY
Judge Richard T. Rives, FEDERAL JUDGE, FEDERAL
BUILDING, MONTGOMERY

   This order you issued must--I mean MUST be re-
scinded--reversed--done away with altogether or you and
your families will pay a mighty big price for it. If you,
by this order force the schools and teachers against their
will to mix in the Alabama schools you will not live to
see the end of this year--Your families will also suffer
severe punishment--possible death due to your efforts.
   Judge Grooms, that fine daughter of your will pay
the penalty along with you.
   Judge Johnson, if your son should survive he will
have to enroll in a public school--not a private school
this year. This had better be arranged at once and The
Advertiser be advised so they can give due publicity of
your action in a news item. We mean NOW.
   Judge Rives, YOU OLD SOB had better get ready also.
You don't have much longer to live and the sooner we get
rid of you the better it will be.
   ALL THREE OF YOU GET READY TO GO OUT LIKE
A LIGHT, if you don't reverse your March 22nd Court
Order. Do you understand?
   We four (4) Armed Services men have spent two years
in Vietnam killing, sniping and going through hell and to
return to this state to find things in such a hell of a fix
as you are making it is more than we will stand for. We
are ready to die for our country if need be but we plan
to save Alabama from you damned Federal [Judges].

   In reflection Frank Johnson refuses to vilify the populous.
He has a deep understanding of the cultural upheaval the civil rights
movement has brought to his fellow white citizens. However, he
does criticize vigorously the performance of the Southern bar.
Leadership from the organized bar, he charges, was nonexistent.
He recognizes the difficulty an individual lawyer would have had if
he spoke out alone. In his view, the bar's failure to act and to
defend its judges was not merely cowardice, but a violation of its
own ethical canons. To the organized bar, Frank Johnson is not
forgiving.

   Frank Johnson is an avid admirer of Abraham Lincoln. He
has a glass paperweight on his desk with the following quotation:

I'll do the very best I know how--the very best I can; and
I mean to keep doing so until the end. If the end brings
me out all right, what is said against me won't amount to
anything. If the end brings me out wrong, ten angels
swearing I was right would make no difference.*

That quotation and the following talk given to some new Americans
at a naturalization ceremony on Law Day in 1967 may explain as
well as anything the complex man that is Frank Johnson:

'It is necessary,' he said, 'now more than ever, that
the responsible American citizen realize and discharge his
obligation constantly to support and defend the proposition
that our law is supreme and must be obeyed. This means
that irresponsible criticism--by those who can hardly read
the Constitution, much less study it and interpret it--must
not be allowed to stand unchallenged.
'When those who frustrate the law, who undermine judicial decisions, run riot and provide uncurbed leadership
for a return to nothing more than medieval savagery, for
the responsible American citizen to remain silent is tantamount to cowardice; it is a grievous injustice to the proposition that in America the law is supreme.'**

Time magazine said of Judge Johnson "[his] impressive record of
calm and considered judgment has stamped him as one of the most
important men in America." Perhaps, however, Judge Johnson
might most appreciate the simple but heartfelt tribute of a former
Montgomery Police Officer and later United States Marshal, Paul J.
Dumas, who said: "I seriously question that a man of more skill,
respect for the law and courage sits on any bench."

*   *   *

George Wallace, in all his rantings against federal judges,
has made it a point over the years to single out Frank Johnson for
his greatest abuse. In his 1962 race for Governor he issued the
following challenge:

This state is not going to be big enough for me as the
elected sovereign of this state and a bunch of Supreme
Court yes-men appointed for life [Federal judges] trying
to run Alabama's school system; one of us is going to
have to go.***

Everyone in Alabama knew that challenge was for Frank Johnson.

Wallace's first great claim to fame in Alabama came in a

---

*83 Time, Feb. 21, 1964, at 76.
**89 Time, May 12, 1967, at 78.
***59 Newsweek, May 14, 1962, at 29.

public defiance of an order of Frank Johnson, although it is alleged that a weak, behind-the-scenes surrender told the real story. When George Wallace was an Alabama circuit judge in 1958-59, the United States Civil Rights Commission, looking into charges of voter discrimination in Barbour and Bullock Counties, asked to see the voting records. Circuit Judge Wallace, with great public gusto, impounded the records. Federal District Judge Johnson ordered Wallace to make the records available to the agents of the Civil Rights Commission, subject to contempt if he refused. In public Wallace continued a stance of defiance, while in private it is reported that he made overtures to the Commission. Wallace furiously denies he capitulated.

> But in reputable circles the story persists that Judge Johnson threatened Wallace with a five-year sentence in the federal penitentiary--long enough to prevent his running for governor in 1962--if he didn't back down, and that Wallace, to escape the contempt conviction, went contritely to Johnson's house at night with his coat over his head so nobody could identify him, and made peace.*

Wallace made a career out of narrowly evading federal contempt proceedings. When he "stood in the school house door" in June, 1963, to block the enrollment of Vivian Malone and James Hood at the University of Alabama, there appeared to be an arrangement with Deputy Attorney General Nicholas Katzenbach to keep the black students in a car parked well away from the door so that he would not "technically" be blocking their enrollment and thus risking contempt.

By 1963, the main battle between George Wallace and Frank Johnson loomed over public school integration, a battle that could not be postponed. Martin Luther King and the Civil Rights movement were pushing on every front:

> We're through with tokenism and gradualism and see-how-far-you've-comeism.... We can't wait any longer. Now is the time.**

* * *

The Alabama School Cases. --The tortuous progress of school integration in Alabama in the middle years, when a plethora of cases was filed across the state, can best be traced by following the progress of the epic Lee v. Macon County Board of Education where George Wallace and Frank Johnson met head-on.

The Macon County School District included the town of Tuskegee. In the 1962-63 school year the system had 970 white students

_____

*Sherrill, supra at 328.
**81 Time, June 21, 1963 at 14.

and 5,317 black students, with seventeen black schools and three
white schools. In compliance with an injunction prohibiting the Macon County School Board from continuing to maintain a racially separate school system, thirteen black students were assigned to the
previously all white Tuskegee High School. Three other Alabama
cities, Mobile, Birmingham and Huntsville, were also scheduled to
integrate in the fall.

While even the segregationist Birmingham press counseled
against violence and spoke resignedly of accepting the inevitable,
George Wallace decided not to capitulate. To the outrage of Tuskegee city officials, on the day the thirteen black children were supposed to arrive at school, Wallace issued an Executive Order closing the school to "preserve the peace" and sent in 108 state troopers. They surrounded the school and blocked entrance to all pupils
and teachers.

> Tuskegee city officials, backed by most of the community's
> citizens, protested Wallace's action as an 'invasion.' But
> the high school stayed shut--and Wallace ordered most of
> his troopers to move on to Birmingham, where integration
> was supposed to start on Wednesday. As the state cops
> were leaving Tuskegee, Wallace's on-the-scene straw boss,
> State Finance Director Seymore Trammell, walked up to
> Mayor Rutherford. Said he: 'You ain't going to have any
> trouble here, Mayor, and if you do, George will send the
> troopers right back.' Retorted Rutherford bitterly: 'Well,
> I have eight thousand angry citizens on my hands.'*

The next day Wallace continued to station troopers around Tuskegee
High School, and they remained for the rest of the week, blocking
the reopening of the school. The night after the troopers arrived
at Tuskegee, the home of a black attorney and civil rights leader
was bombed in Birmingham and a mini-riot followed.

Most of the Alabama press criticized Wallace's action in
closing Tuskegee High School. Nevertheless, on September 9, Wallace issued a proclamation ordering that integration not be permitted
at Mobile, Birmingham, or Tuskegee and an obliging legislature
created a grant-in-aid program for white students. Every white
student in Tuskegee High School was switched to another school.
All the federal district judges in the state, Johnson, Lynne, Thomas,
Grooms and Allgood, joined in issuing a detailed temporary restraining order enjoining Wallace from carrying out his proclamation
blocking integration. The joint action of all the judges was necessary because Wallace's proclamation prevented the enforcement of
previously ordered integration in other school cases in Alabama.

When the white students left Tuskegee High, most transferred
to neighboring Shorter High School or Notasulga High School, the

---

*82 Time, Sept. 13, 1963 at 26.

other two white high schools in Macon County; some transferred to
a new private segregationist school, Macon Academy. Judge Johnson ordered the Macon School Board to cease transporting Macon
area white students who had attended Tuskegee to the other schools.
Wallace then had them transported in state patrol cars and a bus
used by a state vocational school.

In January, 1964, with only twelve black students attending
Tuskegee High with thirteen teachers, Wallace through the State
Board of Education ordered Tuskegee High closed as an "economy
measure." The twelve black students were ordered transferred to
"other high schools in Tuskegee," meaning their return to all-black
Tuskegee Institute High School. Judge Johnson retaliated: on
February 3, 1964 he ordered--not that Tuskegee remain open--but
that the black pupils barred from Tuskegee be transferred to all-
white Shorter and Notasulga "on the same basis" as the white students were allowed to transfer when the blacks first enrolled at
Tuskegee High.

When six of the black students attempted to enroll at Notasulga, the Mayor of Notasulga, James Rea, prevented their enrollment.
Under Rea's influence, Notasulga on February 3, 1964, passed a
"fire" ordinance limiting attendance at Notasulga High to 175, the
exact number of teachers and pupils in average attendance prior to
transfer of the black students. In a terse opinion, Judge Johnson
held that the fire ordinance had no reasonable relationship to safety.
Its only intent being to block enrollment of the black students, Judge
Johnson struck the ordinance and enjoined further interference by
Mayor Rea. Upon enrollment of six blacks at Notasulga and six at
Shorter, all the white students left both schools, and they remained
open for the rest of the year with only twelve blacks in attendance.

In early February, George Wallace began to listen to legal
advice. His blatant manipulation of the State Board of Education
(of which he was ex officio president as Governor), his total control
over the actions of local school boards, as witnessed in Tuskegee,
and his proclamations made it clear that George Wallace ran the
public schools in Alabama. If the Governor and State Board of Education could effectively control local school policies, then why could
not the federal courts, which already had jurisdiction over Wallace
and the State Board of Education by reason of previous injunctions,
order desegregation of all Alabama School districts? That thought
had no doubt occurred to civil rights leaders, the federal courts and
the Justice Department. It also belatedly occurred to George Wallace. The Governor found himself in the embarrassing position of
requesting that the Alabama Supreme Court issue an advisory opinion as to whether any of the actions of the State School Board (under his command) in interference with control of local schools were
invalid. Ostensibly, George Wallace hoped that his own state supreme court would invalidate his actions so that he could avoid a
federal court order directed to the State Board of Education to desegregate all of Alabama's schools. The Alabama State Supreme
Court complied: it declared that no Alabama law authorized the

State Board of Education or the Governor to do any of the acts that they had engaged in at Tuskegee and other cities. But it was too late. The federal courts were cognizant of who controlled Alabama's public schools: George Wallace, through his manipulation of the State Board of Education.

In July, 1964 Judge Johnson found:

> Under the evidence in this case, there is no question that the State of Alabama has an official policy favoring racial segregation in public education. In his Executive Orders of September 2 and 9, 1963, directed to the Macon County Board of Education, Governor Wallace referred to the 'unwarranted integration' being forced by the Federal court. In his Executive Order of September 9, the Governor further said that the threat of integration 'is detrimental to the public interest' and that the 'integration of the public schools will totally disrupt and effectively destroy the educational process.' This is particularly significant in this case in that Governor Wallace is, as stated above, the ex officio President of the State Board of Education. ...

> Further evidence clearly reflecting this official policy is found in one of the State Board of Education's resolutions of February 4, 1964, wherein it was unanimously declared that the State Board would 'defend the people of our State against every order of the Federal courts in attempting to integrate the public schools of this State and will use every legal means at our command to defeat said integration orders and pledges our full support to the local boards of education in supporting the public school systems as now constituted. ... Further evidence of this official policy is reflected by a speech delivered on March 15, 1963, to the Alabama Education Association by the State Superintendent of Education where it was stated, 'We stand a chance to lose millions of dollars in federal aid for defense connected pupils because there is no Judas Iscariot among us who will sell our racial integrity for the proverbial thirty pieces of silver.' A similar statement made in December, 1963, for public release by the State Superintendent of Education was to the effect that 'Teachers, administrators and parents have firmly held the line for our way-of-life and in the opposition to misguided parents who have tried to force the entry of their children into schools for a different race. ...' These public statements in the form of news releases are regularly circulated from the office of the State Superintendent of Education to the various local superintendents of schools throughout Alabama.

Judge Johnson then held that use of the Alabama Grant-in-Aid statutes to support boycotting white students was unconstitutional. He proceeded to the question of whether he should order state-wide de-segregation in all Alabama public schools. He said that:

> [the] admission on the part of these defendants that their
> action was an abuse of their authority and their present
> reliance on the advisory opinions of the Alabama Supreme
> Court of February 18, 1964, to the effect that they had
> no such authority to close the schools and will not 'do it
> again,' places them in an extremely weak position. This
> Court recognizes the authority of the Supreme Court of
> Alabama when it interprets the Alabama law, as it in-
> formally did in these advisory opinions. This Court trusts
> that the Governor, the State Superintendent of Education
> and the other members of the State Board of Education
> will in their future conduct recognize that by their inter-
> ference with the Macon County school board they have vio-
> lated not only the Federal law, but the laws of the State
> of Alabama as well. However, a present recognition of
> their past illegal activity will not--in this case--justify
> this Court's failure to take appropriate action now. The
> Supreme Court of the United States has long since held
> that a state officer who has abused his authority by deny-
> ing due process or equal protection of the laws cannot
> escape responsibility by urging that his action was not
> authorized by the laws of the state and was therefore not
> 'state action' within the meaning of the Fourteenth Amend-
> ment. Furthermore, as pointed out above, there is no
> question that the State Board of Education of Alabama has
> general control and supervision over the public schools of
> this State.

But Judge Johnson went on to say: "However, in this case, at this particular time, this court will not order desegregation in all the public schools of the State of Alabama." Johnson retained jurisdiction and warned that if there was further interference with federal orders he would reconsider his decision not to desegregate the whole state in one dramatic order. Judge Johnson then enjoined further use of the Alabama Pupil Placement Law, approved on its face in the Shuttlesworth case, because it had been used as a device to continue segregation. Lastly, he enjoined Governor Wallace and other state officials from further interference with federal court orders.

Despite Judge Johnson's restraint in 1964, George Wallace continued his interference. Leery of being held in contempt, his actions now were more subtle than simply surrounding a school with state troopers and using squad cars to transport boycotting white students. In August and again in September, 1965, Governor Wallace sent telegrams to school districts that were attempting to comply voluntarily with new April, 1965 guidelines issued by the United States Commission of Education under authority of the 1964 Civil Rights Act. The telegrams urged that boards not go beyond the minimum compliance required by court order. On September 3, 1965, the State Superintendent of Education sent similar telegrams.

On September 6, 1965, Choctaw County succumbed to state pressure and withdrew its voluntary compliance plan.

On July 1, 1966, State Superintendent of Education Meadows extolled the virtues of segregation in a homily sent to all local school superintendents:

> 'Segregation' is a perfectly good word. It has been practiced down through the ages for good results. The Lord set aside or segregated fruit from the apple tree in the Garden of Eden from Adam and Eve, but Eve persuaded Adam to taste the fruit and they were both banished from the Garden of Eden and honest men and women have had to work for their living ever since.
> Segregation has been used by people of the civilized world for man's greatest advancement. Matrimony, the most sacred of all bonds for men and women, is the highest type of segregation. In matrimony, husband and wife bind themselves to cleave to one another, even to the extent of forsaking all others if necessary. A great ministerial commandment has been the public pronouncement at the wedding ceremony 'What God has joined together let no man put asunder.' Without this bond of segregation, there would be no family unit. One of the Ten Commandments forbids breaking this human bond of segregation. Segregation is the basic principle of culture. The good join together to segregate themselves from the bad.
> Segregation is one of the principles of survival throughout the animal kingdom. Animals, in many instances, join their own kind to defend themselves by numbers against other animals that would destroy them without such segregated bond. Birds of a feather truly flock together. Wild geese fly across this continent in 'V' formation, but they never join any other flock of birds. Wild duck fly together and not with other birds. The wild eagle mates with another eagle and not with any other bird. Red birds mate with red birds, the beautiful blue birds mate with other blue birds, and so on through bird life.
> There can be segregation without immoral discrimination against anyone. Integration of all human life and integration of all animal life would destroy humanity and would destroy the animal kingdom. A time of reckoning must come in this United States of America on the fundamental principles of segregation and non-discrimination which can be achieved without destroying segregation in its true sense.

In August, 1966, Tuscaloosa County assigned two black teachers to all-white schools and four white teachers to all-black schools. After telephone calls and public statements by State Superintendent Meadows asking that the assignments be reversed, Governor Wallace threatened at a press conference to use the police power of the state to preserve order and pointedly urged that the controversial teacher assignments be changed forthwith. Nevertheless, the Tuscaloosa board withstood the pressure. Finally, on October 25, 1966, the Alabama Board of Education adopted a new policy providing a new "teacher unit" to counties where white students were provided with a black teacher. Under this unit plan, a white teacher was provided as an alternative for white students assigned to a black teacher.

After a coldly logical point-by-point recitation of the history of Governor Wallace's interference and the control maintained by state officials over local school boards, on March 22, 1967, a three-judge federal court consisting of Circuit Judge Rives and District Judges Johnson and Grooms mandated state-wide desegregation in all Alabama school districts not then under orders to desegregate.

> Not only have these defendants, through their control and influence over the local school boards, flouted every effort to make the Fourteenth Amendment a meaningful reality to Negro school children in Alabama: they have apparently dedicated themselves and, certainly from the evidence in this case, have committed the powers and resources of their offices to the continuation of a dual public school system such as that condemmed [sic] by Brown v. Board of Education.... As a result of such efforts on the part of those charged with the duty and responsibility under the law as announced in 1954 by the Supreme Court in Brown, by the Congress of the United States in the Civil Rights Act of 1964, and, more specifically, by this Court in its July 1964 order, today only a very small percentage of students in Alabama are enrolled in desegregated school systems. Based upon this fact and a continuation of such conduct on the part of these state officials as hereafter outlined, it is now evident that the reasons for this Court's reluctance to grant the relief to which these plaintiffs were clearly entitled over two years ago are no longer valid.

The court then proceeded to describe areas of state control of local policies which frustrated desegregation. Precise findings were made in the following areas: school construction and consolidation, faculty and staff transportation, trade schools, vocational schools and state colleges, and the state tuition grant statute. Particular emphasis was placed on Alabama's efforts to aid private segregated academies:

> ... it is now becoming apparent that the State of Alabama is attempting to make a concerted effort to establish and support a separate and private school system for white students. Twice in less than three years this Court has had to strike down tuition grant provisions designed to achieve this end. Moreover, the Governor has officially encouraged private contributions to support the many private schools throughout the state as alternatives to the

public desegregated school system. Up to this point, this
Court has used its injunctive powers to prevent the State
of Alabama from establishing a separate school system
for white children. It must be made perfectly clear, however, that if the state persists in its efforts dedicated to
this end, and its involvement with the private school system continues to be "significant,' then this 'private' system will have become a state actor within the meaning of
the Fourteenth Amendment and will need to be brought
under this Court's state-wide desegregation order. [Em-
phasis is the court's own.]

In concluding the court said:

This Court can conceive of no other effective way to
give the plaintiffs the relief to which they are entitled under the evidence in this case than to enter a uniform
state-wide plan for school desegregation, made applicable
to each local county and city system not already under
court order to desegregate, and to require these defendants
to implement it. Only in this way can uniform, expeditious
and substantial progress be attained, and only in this way
can the defendant state officials discharge the constitutional
duty that was placed upon them twelve years ago in Brown
v. Board of Education....

Then the court issued its decree, the most detailed by a court to
that date, and foreshadowed the uniform decree mandated in United
States v. Jefferson by the Fifth Circuit.*

The Rives-Johnson-Grooms decree stunned Alabama. In one
giant step all 118 school boards in the state were required to desegregate, while only nineteen had been under court order prior to
the decision. Furthermore, the case marked the death knell for
inferior black schools. The judges supported their decision by noting
that more than twenty-five per cent of the black high schools of Alabama were unaccredited, compared to 3.4 per cent of the white
schools; $607 was spent for each white child as compared with $295
for each black child.

Frank Johnson made the cover of Time. George Wallace
could only fulminate: "You know what we're goin' to tell them when
they ask us to give 'em more in the schools of Alabama this fall?
I'll tell you what we'll tell 'em: 'Goddammit, we jus' ain't.'" Alabama was changing despite George Wallace. In 1966, both "Big
Jim" Clark and Public Safety Director Al Lingo were defeated for
reelection.

* * *

*See discussion, Part II, Chapter 11, infra.

Lee v. Macon County Board of Education, while typical of
many cases illustrating the agony of achieving desegregation in Alabama in the middle years, was by no means the only Alabama school
case, and Frank Johnson was not the only federal district judge in
Alabama who faced difficulty. Judge Daniel H. Thomas, a candid,
straightforward judge, presided over Davis v. Board of School Commissioners of Mobile County, a complex desegregation case featur-
ing almost every form of resistance to integration. The Davis case
has been in continuous litigation since 1963. Judge Thomas, unlike
Judge Johnson, firmly believed that school boards required more
time to comply with Brown than the appellate courts were willing to
give. He was reversed nine straight times in the Davis case for
approving plans that did not go far enough; the tenth time the Fifth
Circuit affirmed and the Supreme Court reversed. He remains convinced that time for compliance was necessary and that his delays
prevented bloodshed.

While no judicial activist and certainly, by the record, a
judge who required constant appellate pressure, Judge Thomas was
not an obstructionist like Judge Scarlett of Georgia or Judge Cox of
Mississippi. He had a running battle with Sheriff Jim Clark over
the Sheriff's conduct in handling the voter registration drive in Selma. In one case he threatened to hold every member of a school
board in contempt and levy a $1,000 per day fine on the board if a
desegregation plan was not produced in three days; the board complied. Judge Thomas also pushed both the school board and the
NAACP into a compromise agreement in the Davis case that has
quieted that litigation. Nevertheless, he remains critical of the
speed of desegregation and feels that the Fifth Circuit's reversals in
some of his cases were precipitate and injured public education.

Judge Seybourn H. Lynne presided over the famous Armstrong v. Board of Education of Birmingham case. A former state
court judge, Seybourn Lynne is an erudite, soft-spoken, classical
scholar. A gracious, personable host and a close friend of Justice
Hugo Black, Judge Lynne, like Judge Thomas, remains convinced
that the delays he granted in Birmingham were essential to preserve
public order. He felt the people in Birmingham had first to see
successful integration in neighboring, more progressive cities like
Nashville, Atlanta and New Orleans. Both he and Judge Thomas
were the laggards of the Alabama federal judiciary. Judge Lynne
has been reversed many times in race and assorted civil rights
cases and yet maintains his reputation as a judicial scholar even
with those who reverse him. He sat on a three-judge panel with
Judges Grooms and Gewin and wrote the opinion which held unconstitutional the public accommodations section of the Civil Rights Act
of 1964. That opinion was reversed by the Supreme Court, but
Judge Lynne personally was complimented by Justice Harlan for having authored one of the best written district court opinions seen in
years. Judge Lynne did enjoin Governor Wallace from interfering
with the integration of the University of Alabama in 1963.

Critical of the Fifth Circuit's heavy reliance on the statistics

of race-mixing in recent years, nonetheless Judge Lynne is complimentary about its work. He and Judge Thomas are perhaps typical
of the federal judges in the South: deeply concerned about Brown II,
anxious to delay whenever possible to avoid local upheaval, but
nevertheless ready to enforce direct appellate court orders. Not
obstructionists, they were also not overly enthusiastic about enforcing civil rights at the expense of antagonizing powerful local opposition.

Judge Harlan Hobart Grooms was discussed in the section on
higher education.* Regardless of the fact that he was not as abra-
sive to local opposition groups as Frank Johnson, he was the victim
of heavy abuse. Threatening letters became so frequent that he
slept for months with a shotgun by his side. Finally, he mentioned
to a local newspaper reporter that he didn't read the letters anyway
and instructed his secretary to throw them out. After that news
article appeared, the letters began to taper off. He sat with Frank
Johnson and Circuit Judge Rives on the 1967 three-judge court which
decided Lee v. Macon County Board of Education, ordering the desegregation of the whole state of Alabama. Grooms was more willing than either Judge Lynne or Thomas to brook local opposition.
He agrees with them, however, that in the state of Alabama, time
for adjustment to the idea of desegregation was necessary. He remains convinced that the Briggs v. Elliott dictum, drawing a distinction between desegregation and integration was valid. But he is
also critical of George Wallace for holding out "false hopes" to the
people and thus intensifying opposition to the inevitable. With a fine
sense of humor, Judge Grooms particularly remembers one case
dealing with the desegregation of a restaurant at the airport in Birmingham. Three black preachers came in shortly after passage of
the Civil Rights Act and demanded to be served. The restaurant
brought out some folding screens and shielded the table used by the
preachers from the rest of the restaurant. When the bill came for
some chicken salad sandwiches, it was astronomically high. Judge
Grooms questioned the attorney representing the restaurant, asking
if he didn't think the bill was exorbitant. The attorney explained
that the blacks had had to pay extra because the restaurant had arranged "private quarters."

*　　*　　*

This was Alabama. From 1963 through 1967, eighty-five
separate judicial opinions were written on school desegregation cases
in that state alone. Paradoxically, desegregation would have been
even more agonizing if George Wallace's interference had not enabled the federal courts in Lee v. Macon County Board of Education
to order state-wide desegregation in 1967. Alabama was the first
Southern state to receive such an order.

---

*See Part II, Chapter 5 at 201.

MISSISSIPPI

The Judges. --In the middle years of 1963-67, Mississippi maintained its reputation as the toughest of the Southern states. Extreme resistance to any form of integration inhibited potential civil rights litigants. Fewer school integration cases were filed in Mississippi and less progress was achieved in those that were filed than in any other Fifth Circuit state. Not the least of the difficulties facing plaintiffs in school cases were the federal district judges of Mississippi.

William Harold Cox is the most famous of the recalcitrant federal district judges in the South; he has already been introduced earlier in the chapter on voting rights.* A former roommate of Senator James O. Eastland at the University of Mississippi Law School, Judge Cox was the first of President John F. Kennedy's judicial appointments to receive Senate confirmation. He took his place on the bench in 1961 and became the source of a series of anguished complaints from pro-civil rights forces. Robert F. Kennedy's Justice Department sustained more criticism over Judge Cox than over any other appointment it approved during the three-year Kennedy Administration. Rightly or wrongly, Judge Cox came to symbolize the widely held belief that Robert Kennedy was a Machiavellian wheeler-dealer willing to barter civil rights to retain favor with powerful Southern satraps on Capitol Hill. Robert Sherrill charged in his caustic book, Gothic Politics, that Robert Kennedy met Senator Eastland in a Capitol corridor and Eastland made Kennedy the following "quasi-threat": "Tell your brother that if he will give me Harold Cox I will give him the nigger" [referring to Thurgood Marshall, now a Supreme Court Justice, whose nomination to the Second Circuit had been held up for almost a year in Senator Eastland's Judiciary Committee]. Victor S. Navasky, in Kennedy Justice, quotes a Kennedy Justice Department official, William Geoghegan, as speculating that the speed with which some of Robert Kennedy's anti-crime measures cleared the Senate might have been "the price for appointing Cox in Mississippi." In fairness to Robert Kennedy's Justice Department, it must be remembered as pointed out earlier, that Judge Cox was rated by an American Bar Association (ABA) committee on judicial appointments as "exceptionally well qualified," the ABA's highest rating. His reputation in Mississippi was excellent; all reports indicated that he was a meticulous, highly accomplished practitioner. And, while almost every lawyer of note in Mississippi professed loyalty to segregation, Cox's public statements on social matters had been subdued and, unlike many contemporaries, he had not been a member of the White Citizens' Council. Robert Kennedy interviewed Cox himself and has stated that Cox promised that "upholding the Constitution would never be a problem." Judge Tuttle is quoted as commenting:

The trouble with that interview is that they were talking

---

*See Part II, Chapter 7, supra at 294.

different languages. When Bobby asked him if he would
uphold the law of the land, he was thinking about Brown
v. Board of Education. But when Cox said yes, he was
thinking about lynching. When Cox said he believed Negroes should have the vote he meant two Negroes.*

Judge Cox is a large man, a conservative dresser whose
formal demeanor discourages friendly banter by companions. He
neither smokes nor drinks and disapproves of those who do; he particularly discourages smoking in his presence. He maintains absolute control in his courtroom and demands compliance by attorneys
with an unusually strict code of courtroom behavior. One notorious
local regulation prohibits attorneys from placing their briefcases on
courtroom counsel tables; Jackson attorneys are frequently amused
by reprimands given out-of-town counsel who inadvertently break the
"briefcase rule." Young, long-haired, casually-dressed attorneys
are a particular source of ire to Judge Cox. But it is his handling
of civil rights cases that has made Judge Cox famous and which has,
according to most observers, permanently marred his otherwise
solid reputation as a stern but careful judicial craftsman.

Many of the actions of Judge Cox which are complained about
by civil rights attorneys and liberal critics seem inconsequential in
retrospect. However, to borrow a phrase from the voting rights
case, they did seem to form "a pattern and practice" of judicial behavior whenever Judge Cox was faced with complaints by black litigants about the denial of basic constitutional rights. For example,
as mentioned, he has been repeatedly charged with referring to
black litigants as "chimpanzees." That charge may not be accurate;
in one voting rights case he did ask from the bench: "Who is telling
these people they can get in line [to register] and push people around,
acting like a bunch of chimpanzees?" He also said they "ought to be
in the movies rather than registered to vote." In 1963, John Doar,
Civil Rights' Chief under Attorney General Robert F. Kennedy, requested information from Judge Cox concerning when a decision
could be expected in a long-pending voting rights case. Judge Cox
scalded Doar in his responsive letter. His intemperance, reduced
to writing, stunned the Justice Department. He called Doar "completely stupid," referred to his "impudence," characterized Attorney
General Kennedy as "boss man" and charged that: "I spend most of
my time in fooling with lousy cases brought before me by your Department in the Civil Rights field...." On November 17, 1963,
Robert Kennedy wrote Judge Cox and informed him that copies of
the Cox letter to Doar were being sent to the Standing Committee on
the Federal Judiciary of the ABA. Four days later, President Kennedy was assassinated and the matter was dropped.

While indeed some of Judge Cox's actions in civil rights matters might be attributed to a quick temper, the consistent effect of
his decisions was unreasonably to delay and frustrate enforcement

*V. Navasky, Kennedy Justice, at 250-51 (1970).

of clear constitutional rights, frequently without legal justification. The following examples of Judge Cox's behavior in civil rights cases provides an indication of the effects a trial judge can produce by his attitudes toward the parties or toward the subject matter of the litigation.

After the Interstate Commerce Commission had ordered the McComb, Mississippi bus terminal desegregated, Judge Cox enjoined the Congress of Racial Equality (CORE) from urging blacks to use it. He charged that CORE's intent was to "taunt and tantalize" and provoke "the tempers of the community." He also refused to issue a clearly warranted temporary restraining order on behalf of John Hardy, a Negro unlawfully arrested for breach of the peace in connection with a voter registration drive in Walthall County where no blacks were registered to vote, although 2,490 were of voting age. In denying the temporary restraining order, Judge Cox accounted for the lack of black registration by noting that blacks weren't interested in voting. Contending that further prosecution of Hardy would intimidate other blacks in their attempts to register to vote, Justice Department attorneys filed an impressive amount of affidavit material showing the trumped-up nature of the charges against Hardy to support their request for injunctive relief. After considerable cost and delay to all parties, Judge Rives wrote the majority opinion in the Fifth Circuit's decision that reversed Judge Cox.

In connection with the 1964 murder of three civil rights workers, Chaney, Goodman and Schwerner, near Philadelphia, Mississippi, Judge Cox dismissed felony indictments against seventeen people, including a sheriff and deputy sheriff. He asserted, "the indictment surely states a heinous crime against the state of Mississippi, but not a crime against the United States." Instead, he ruled that the men should stand charges on a lesser crime which carried the maximum penalty of one year in jail and a one thousand dollar fine. Reversed on appeal, Judge Cox did preside over the trial of some of those charged with the murders. Again, in fairness, it took courage for Judge Cox to preside over that trial, and he carried out his job in that case in a tough and impartial manner. Mississippi was stunned when convictions were obtained. However, as late as 1967, Judge Cox refused a Justice Department request to convene a new grand jury to inquire into the three-year-old murders of the three civil rights workers and the one-year-old murder of Vernon Dahmer, a black leader in Hattiesburg. He said he would grant the request only when the Department of Justice investigated the Head Start program in Mississippi.

As seen previously, Judge Cox's attitude in voting rights cases was consistently hostile to civil rights claimants and the federal government. He wrote Mississippi registrars a letter openly criticizing the federal government for instituting such suits. Perhaps Judge Cox's most notorious voting rights case concerned Clarke County, Mississippi, where only one black had been registered to vote in thirty years. Judge Cox found that there was no "pattern or practice of discrimination," in a decision later called "clearly erroneous" by the Court of Appeals.

A side action in the Clarke County case produced the sharpest conflict between Judge Cox and the executive branch of the federal government. During the hearing on the alleged voting irregularities before Judge Cox, two elderly blacks had testified that seven years before, they had been refused registration although a white man had been registered while they were still in the office. Subsequent testimony established the fact that the white citizen named had been registered for almost two years and on the day in question was simply visiting in the registrar's office. Judge Cox reacted in fury and charged that the testimony given by the black witnesses constituted grounds for perjury charges. He immediately ordered the Justice Department lawyer to seek indictment of the two blacks, saying, "I just want these Negroes to know that they can't come in this court and swear to something as important as that was and is and get by with it. I don't care who brings them here. I think they are fit subjects for the penitentiary." The Justice Department ordered the FBI to investigate. After receiving the agents' reports, the Department stated it could find no grounds for any perjury charge within the meaning of the law. In an attempt to mollify Judge Cox, Attorney General Katzenbach personally called upon him to explain the Department's position.

Judge Cox refused to accept its decision. Judge Cox then sought indictments against the two blacks from a Mississippi grand jury and the blacks were arrested. The Justice Department was forced to intervene, successfully arguing that a state court had no authority to hear a case involving an alleged perjury before a federal court. By this time the case had become a cause célèbre in Mississippi, and Judge Cox refused to back down.

When a Federal grand jury next convened in Jackson on October 23, 1964, to consider indictments in the Philadelphia, Mississippi slayings of three civil rights workers, Judge Cox took the opportunity to instruct the Grand Jurors also to consider indictments against the two blacks suspected of perjury. A young Assistant United States Attorney named Robert Hauberg had drawn the assignment to assist this particular grand jury in its deliberations. He consulted with the Justice Department, and Attorney General Katzenbach instructed him to refuse to sign any grand jury indictments or prosecute the perjury charges. The grand jury duly returned the indictments. Judge Cox recessed his regular calendar in mid-morning to receive the indictments, at which time he was told by the foreman that Hauberg had refused to sign them. Hauberg stated to Judge Cox that he had been personally instructed by Katzenbach that "Neither you nor any of your assistants are authorized to prepare or sign indictments in matters being heard. I direct you to refrain."

When Hauberg had finished reading the statement, the following exchange took place:

Judge Cox: Do you refuse to carry out the court's order?
Hauberg: Because of the instructions, I most humbly have to refuse to comply.

Judge Cox:	You leave me no alternative. I do judge you to be in civil contempt of court. You will be confined in a jail type institution in Hinds County until you decide to comply with the orders of this court.
Hauberg:	I am under instructions of the Attorney General of the United States....
Judge Cox:	I appreciate your position.... I don't think the United States or anybody else has any right to impede the investigation by the grand jury in any case not frivolous.

Judge Cox then ordered Hauberg to prepare a contempt citation against Attorney General Katzenbach and when he demurred, again citing his instructions, Judge Cox fumed, "So that I don't burden Mr. Katzenbach too much, I'll prepare the papers myself." Judge Cox then issued the contempt citation against Hauberg and ordered Katzenbach to show cause why he too should not be held in contempt.

The following day the Fifth Circuit granted an indefinite stay of Judge Cox's contempt order. Holding that the Attorney General was vested with discretion as to when to prosecute, the full Court of Appeals shortly thereafter reversed Judge Cox's contempt citation of Hauberg and dismissed his show cause order to Katzenbach.

One of the most outrageous examples of Judge Cox's hostility to civil rights cases came in the midst of a school desegregation case, where his unwarranted harassment of a black Mississippi lawyer brought forth a sharply critical reversal from the Fifth Circuit and caused Yale Law School Professor Alexander M. Bickel, one of the nation's leading constitutional scholars, to call openly for Judge Cox's impeachment. R. Jess Brown represented several black plaintiffs, including one Ruthie Nell McBeth, in a class action to desegregate the public schools of Leake County, Mississippi. In an appearance before Judge Sidney C. Mize, to Attorney Brown's surprise, lawyers for the school board announced in open court that Mrs. McBeth was withdrawing as a named plaintiff. She claimed she had not consented to be a plaintiff and was withdrawing freely and without "undue influence." Attorney Brown immediately agreed to allow her withdrawal. The case continued and Judge Mize took no further action. However, the next day Judge Cox, who had nothing to do with the Leake County case, summoned Attorney Brown before him. He summarily cited Brown to appear later to answer a charge of contempt, saying that Mrs. McBeth's withdrawal as a plaintiff had just come to his attention. At the contempt hearing, Brown produced a signed retainer from Mrs. McBeth proving conclusively that she had retained him for the suit. Judge Cox, nevertheless, pressed ahead, now threatening Brown not with contempt but with disciplinary action. A lengthy hearing took place and Mrs. McBeth was called. She admitted that she had signed the retainer and that her statement in Judge Mize's court that she had not consented to be a plaintiff was untrue. Judge Cox ultimately found that Brown was not guilty of any professional impropriety; although he had initiated the proceedings, he ordered the cost of the citation be charged to Brown. The Fifth Circuit cancelled the order finding:

> Ruthie Nell McBeth's testimony removed any doubt, if any legitimate doubt there could have been before, about the authority of appellant Brown to have included her name as one of the plaintiffs in the petition in the District Court to desegregate the schools. We think there was no necessity for the taking of the testimony of this woman, but certainly there was no excuse for taking any testimony thereafter. The matter should have ended there, if not before. There was no justification for subjecting appellant to the long and detailed and humiliating interrogation set out on pages 39 to 157 of the record, both inclusive, and for taking the testimony of the other witnesses, and no possible justification for assessing against appellant Brown the costs of the proceeding.
> Whatever may have been Judge Cox's purpose in prolonging this inquisition, the effect of it could only have been humiliation, anxiety, and possible intimidation of appellant, a reputable member of the bar, who was completely within his rights in having filed the suit to desegregate the schools in Leake County, however distasteful this might be to many members of that community and others or, even, however unwise it may have been. He had a right as a member of the bar to seek by all legal means to secure for the members of his race the rights and privileges to which the Supreme Court had held that they were entitled, irrespective of the merits or demerits of that holding, and there was no excuse for punishing him for misconduct in connection with it, of which the evidence of this woman completely exonerates him.

However, Judge Cox's greatest weapon was not harassment but delay. While his erroneous judgments could be corrected, and he did suffer a continuous string of reversals in civil rights cases, appeals took time and cost money, and the endless delays required to correct every wrong decision wore thin the patience of both litigants and the Court of Appeals. Kennedy v. Owen, a voting rights case, is an illustration of the effectiveness of simple delay as a tool of recalcitrant judges like Cox:

> The Civil Rights Act of 1960 provides that the Attorney General may address a demand in writing for the production of federal voting records 'to the person having custody, possession, or control' of them, so that they may be inspected for evidence of discrimination against Negro voters. If the demand is not voluntarily met, the appropriate federal district court is to issue an order for the production of the records. In this case, the Attorney General addressed his demand in writing to the proper persons 'having custody, possession, or control' in several Mississippi counties.

He addressed his demand to them by name, and they received it. But in his letter to them he called them Circuit Clerks, which they are. He omitted to address them also by the title of Registrar, which is also part of their official designation. They refused to comply, and Judge Cox upheld them with respect to records in their possession as Registrars rather than as Circuit Clerks, meaning probably that he upheld them altogether, for it is surely up to them to decide which records are in their possession under which hat. This is farcical. It is straight out of Jarndyce v. Jarndyce, or else Kafka. It is also willful. Judge Cox got himself summarily reversed by the Court of Appeals for the Fifth Circuit. But time was lost. And although there can be no further delay on this score, there isn't a law on the books that is not open to this kind of tactics. *

* * *

While not as arbitrary as Judge Cox, all of the other federal district judges in Mississippi were also masters of delay. Judge Mize was an artist. His conduct is reflected in his handling of the James Meredith enrollment at the district court level.** Judge Mize died on April 25, 1965, and Dan M. Russell, Jr. took his place on the bench that same year. Despite a wide reputation as a segregationist and calls from the national press for a careful examination of his credentials, Russell was confirmed by the Senate without difficulty. Judge Claude F. Clayton, a Democrat who supported Eisenhower, was appointed to the bench in 1958. He had never shown any signs of dissatisfaction with the southern way of life and said at one point about Plessy v. Ferguson, "I had no quarrel with it." Despite his general competence, he also viewed civil rights cases with suspicion. In a voting rights case, black plaintiffs sought the right to look at county voting records. The Fifth Circuit had already ordered that such requests be honored as a matter of course, but it took Judge Clayton four years finally to order the records turned over to the plaintiffs.

Nevertheless, Judge Clayton did gain a reputation for fairness. Eventually becoming an enforcer of civil rights, the pivotal case for Judge Clayton was United States v. Duke. Judge Clayton had ruled that blacks were barred from the voting polls because they were not qualified under Mississippi standards. The Fifth Circuit curtly reversed that decision holding that the real issue was not whether blacks were qualified under Mississippi standards, but whether the standards had been applied equally to both whites and blacks. Judge Clayton, a sensitive man, was affected and ordered a speedup in school desegregation in Grenada, Mississippi.

---

*149 The New Republic, Oct. 26, 1963, at 5; Reprinted by permission.
**See Part II, Chapter 5, supra.

On the first morning of the fall term, a cluster of whites armed with ax handles, lead pipes and chains pounced on the 150 Negro youngsters who showed up, lashing out at boys and girls alike. By noon, the rabble outside had grown to 400. Cheered on by their womenfolk, Grenada's vigilantes savagely attacked terrified Negro children as they emerged from school. They trampled Richard Sign, 12, in the dust, breaking a leg. Another twelve-year-old ran a block-long gauntlet of flailing whites, emerged with bleeding face and torn clothes. Still other Negro youngsters were thrown to the ground and kicked. 'That'll teach you, nigger!' grunted one assailant. 'Don't come back tomorrow.' For good measure, the rowdies pummeled and kicked four white out-of-town newsmen. A pickup truck equipped with a two-way radio helped the mob head off fleeing children. Grenada policemen stood by and grinned. 'These niggers,' explained Constable Grady Carroll, 'is keeping the law-enforcement officers from doing their duty.'*

After the mob violence in Grenada, Judge Clayton immediately ordered the police to protect the children henceforth and sentenced Constable Carroll to four months for contempt of court for his conduct in the beatings. The best of the Mississippi district judges, Clayton was elevated to the Court of Appeals for the Fifth Circuit in 1967, but he died in 1969, having had no real impact on the appellate court.

* * *

The School Cases. --While governor of Mississippi, Judge J. P. Coleman of the Fifth Circuit, predicted: "[A] baby born in Mississippi today will never live long enough to see an integrated school." At the beginning of the middle years of desegregation, 1963-67, Governor Coleman's prediction appeared reasonable. Mississippi had less school integration in those years because it had fewer school suits. It had fewer school suits because of the difficulty of finding plaintiffs. After all, Mississippi was Mississippi. While giving lip service to the wisdom of Plessy v. Ferguson's "separate but equal" interpretation of the Fourteenth Amendment, Mississippi had never come close to enforcing Plessy's requirement that if separate facilities were provided, they had to be equal. As late as 1962, a confidential Mississippi Department of Education report showed "glaring inequities" of treatment at the local level. For every local dollar spent on a black child, four were spent on a white child. In the late 1950s, Mississippi entered a crash program to attempt to bring its black schools up to parity with its white schools; two-thirds of Mississippi's school construction budget was spent on black schools. This attempt to make black schools equal began after the separate-but-equal concept was forever overruled in Brown I.

---

*88 Time, Sept. 23, 1966, at 26.

The Mississippi school case that is perhaps typical of the middle years was Evers v. Jackson Municipal Separate School District, later to be consolidated with the famous Singleton v. Jackson case. This case illustrates the difficulty of school integration in Mississippi. Judge Mize, the federal district judge who had held that Ole Miss was not a segregated institution in one of the early rounds of the James Meredith matter, presided over Evers. Mississippi Attorney General Joe T. Patterson and Assistant Attorney General Dugas Shands, Mississippi lawyers active in the Meredith case, were among those representing the Jackson school board.

The initial complaint in Evers was filed on March 4, 1963, as a class action by black students, and sought to enjoin the operation of a segregated school system in Jackson, Mississippi. The school board immediately filed a motion to dismiss, alleging that the plaintiffs had failed to exhaust their administrative remedies under the Mississippi Pupil Assignment Act. The act had been faithfully copied by the Mississippi Legislature from the Alabama Act that had been approved on its face by the Supreme Court in the Shuttlesworth case. Judge Mize granted the motion to dismiss, reciting the arguments of the school board brief that no black plaintiffs had ever requested transfer to an all-white school under the Mississippi Pupil Assignment Act and, therefore, the plaintiffs had failed to exhaust their administrative remedies. In the process Judge Mize overlooked a series of recent Fifth Circuit decisions dismissing similar exhaustion-of-remedies arguments. A panel composed of Circuit Judges Hutcheson and Bell and District Judge Brewster reversed Judge Mize's decision in a cautious opinion authored by Judge Bell, still appearing to adhere faithfully to the Briggs v. Elliott dictum that the Constitution forbade discrimination but did not command integration. Judge Mize was ordered to grant preliminary injunctions pending a trial on the merits. On March 4, 1964, the same year that SNCC initiated its "Freedom Summer" Mississippi voter drives and the year that the Mississippi Freedom Democratic Party was born, Judge Mize granted the preliminary injunction and restrained the school board, pending trial on the merits, from requiring segregation of the races in any school under their supervision. He also ordered the board to submit a desegregation plan by July 15, 1964. (New Orleans was in its fourth year of integration as the first school district in Mississippi was required to formulate a desegregation plan.)

Judge Mize then proceeded to the trial on the merits. On July 6, 1964, he filed a long opinion stating that because of "difference and disparity" in the achievement and aptitude of black and white children, segregation by race was not an unreasonable classification under the Fourteenth Amendment's "equal protection clause." After a lengthy recitation of "evidence" as to genetic and biological variations between the two groups, including cranial capacity and brain size, Judge Mize indicated that Brown I was wrong. Nevertheless, he felt bound by the Fifth Circuit's opinion in Savannah-Chatham County, Judge Scarlett's case, and ordered that his preliminary injunction be made permanent. In his concluding paragraph, he stated:

In the opinion of this Court, the facts in this case
point up a most serious situation, and, indeed, 'cry out'
for a reappraisal and complete reconsideration of the findings and conclusions of the United States Supreme Court in
the Brown decision, as interpreted by the United States
Court of Appeals for the Fifth Circuit. Accordingly, this
Court respectfully urges a complete reconsideration of the
decision in the Brown case.

The school board appealed, citing Judge Mize's "findings" as
justifying racial separation in the schools. A vigorous attempt was
made to distinguish the Savannah-Chatham County case from the
facts found by Judge Mize in Evers. The school board urged that
"it is shown that the educational or achievement progress of the pupils of the two races always varies widely." The board also argued
that, unlike Savannah-Chatham County, the evidence "proved" that
there was such great disparity between black pupils and white pupils,
"not only in educational aptitudes, but also in scholastic achievement,
learning patterns, mental ability, thought patterns, learning capacity,
traits of temperament, mental maturity and general aptitude," that
these differences could not be changed by environment or betterment
of social conditions or by integration.

In a pointed rebuke authored by Judge Wisdom, the Fifth Circuit on May 14, 1966 summarily rejected the "findings" of Judge
Mize and the arguments of the board and affirmed the issuance of
the injunction. A classic beginning sentence sums up the frustration of the Fifth Circuit in dealing with cases like Evers. Judge
Wisdom wrote: "These cases tax the patience of the Court." The
impatience of the court with Savannah-Chatham County-type arguments was so bluntly stated that after Evers the argument was
abandoned even by the most die-hard school boards. For that reason the opinion is worth quoting:

More than ten years have passed since Brown v.
Board of Education.... Decisions too numerous to mention in this Court and in the Supreme Court show unyield-
ing judicial approval of the legal principle that segregated
schooling is inherently unequal. The principle extends beyond public schools. It is 'no longer open to question that
a State may not constitutionally require segregation of public facilities'....
Yet at this late date, bewitched and bewildered by the
popular myth that Brown was decided for sociological reasons untested in a trial, the defendants and intervenors
attempt to overturn Brown on a factual showing. They assert that innate differences in the races in their aptitude
for educability are a reasonable basis for classifying children by race, demonstrate that separate schools for Negro
children are to the advantage of both races, and justify
continued school segregation in Mississippi. We rejected
this identical contention on an interlocutory appeal in Stell
v. Savannah-Chatham County Board of Education ... less

than two weeks after the court below had sustained the contention. Even before Stell, in St. Helena Parish School Board v. Hall ... we held that a trial judge abused his discretion in permitting an intervention by persons whose sole purpose was to introduce evidence tending to show that the Supreme Court's decision in Brown was wrong.

The Fifth Circuit's second opinion in Evers came three years after the case was filed and should have ended the litigation. Yet the case came back again and again, and at this writing is still in the courts.

FLORIDA

The story of the desegregation of Florida in the middle years is by and large the story of one federal judge who would not be intimidated, Bryan Simpson of Jacksonville, Florida. Now a member of the Fifth Circuit,* Judge Simpson has been described by a Fifth Circuit colleague as "a judge's judge." On the bench for more than thirty-five years, Judge Simpson's first judicial appointment came in 1939, as a judge of the Criminal Court of Record for Duval County, Florida. He was appointed to a Florida state trial court in 1946, and became a United States District Judge in 1950, where he served until becoming a member of the Fifth Circuit in 1966. Whenever one of his brethren on the Fifth Circuit wants the viewpoint of a trial judge, he seeks the advice of Bryan Simpson.

Tall, with a handsome craggy face and snow-white hair, Simpson looks like a judge. A scrupulously fair man, Judge Simpson is forthright, even blunt, and presides with decisive wit and a natural dignity. Judge Simpson was one of the first judges in the South, after Skelly Wright in New Orleans, who faced a baptism by violence in an effort to uphold civil rights. His steely resolve was the decisive factor in restoring normalcy to St. Augustine, Florida, in 1964, after two years of clashes between white ruffians and civil rights activists had reduced the city to near anarchy. In commenting on the St. Augustine situation with quiet pride, Judge Simpson believed his actions there helped Judge Johnson the next year in dealing with Selma, Alabama:

> I think my decisions to let these people parade and strike down the attempt to muzzle them in advance, muzzle speech and petition and assembly and these first amendment rights were ... I don't know what Frank Johnson would say, but they very definitely foreshadowed and gave him something to go on the following spring in March of 1965 in connection with the march from Selma to Mont-

---

*After this work was completed, Judge Simpson retired from the Fifth Circuit and assumed Senior Judge status.

gomery. It was very much the same sort of issue.
Frank Johnson is a man that I admire and I've heard other people say the same thing about him that they would
say about Skelly Wright, that he can't wait to get on that
cross and get the nail holes in his fingers or in his hands,
that he enjoys martyrdom. Well, people who make that
kind of criticism haven't undertaken to be a martyr.
There's nothing pleasant about being a martyr if they
would think about it.

Judge Simpson's ordeal in St. Augustine, Florida demonstrates the perils faced by a federal judge determined to enforce
constitutional rights. An appreciation of that ordeal explains why
there were relatively few Bryan Simpsons, Frank Johnsons, Skelly
Wrights and Herbert Christenberrys sitting on federal benches in
the Deep South.

The St. Augustine troubles began in the early 1960s. Led
by a local black dentist, Dr. Robert B. Hayling, several civil rights
groups had united in St. Augustine to protest segregation of restaurants, beaches and hotels. St. Johns County Sheriff, L. O. Davis,
suppressed many sit-ins and demonstrations in 1962 and 1963. In
September, 1963, Dr. Hayling and three other blacks were badly
beaten by robed Ku Klux Klansmen, but it was Hayling who was arrested for assault. Hayling sued in federal court, alleging that
Sheriff Davis and other officials in St. Augustine were interfering
with his civil rights. Federal Judge William A. McRae, a colleague
of Judge Simpson, dismissed the suit, accusing Hayling of "[display-
ing] a lack of restraint...." Dr. Hayling and his followers again
took to the streets. A Klansman was killed in a nighttime foray
into a black neighborhood. By the spring of 1964, St. Augustine
was a city in siege. Daily sit-ins were met by open attacks by
white thugs. Hundreds of civil rights workers were arrested, including Mrs. Malcolm Peabody, mother of the Governor of Massachusetts. They were confined by Sheriff Davis in an open-air pen
with no toilet facilities and no segregation by sex. They were exposed to sun and rain; high bonds were set, and juveniles were not
released to their parents. The festering St. Augustine situation es-
calated into a national crisis. One Richard "Hoss" Manucy, head
of the Ancient City Gun Club, was appointed a deputy sheriff and
used his group to terrorize civil rights marchers and, later, any
recalcitrant hotel owner who dared comply with the public accommodations section of the new 1964 Civil Rights Act. On May 28, 1964,
a particularly vicious attack was made by white hoodlums on black
night marchers near the city's old slave market. The civil rights
groups again went to federal court. This time Judge Bryan Simpson
was on the bench.

In an unusual move Sheriff Davis was called as a witness for the plaintiffs on June 2, 1964. Tobias Simon,
their attorney, tried to show that the reason for violence
during the night marches was that white toughs were given
a clear opportunity to attack the Negroes, without inter-

vention of any kind by Sheriff Davis's officers. He tried
to show that the deputies themselves were part of 'Hoss'
Manucy's group. Davis's attorney moved to have all these
questions ruled out as irrelevant, but Judge Simpson refused his request. Indeed, Judge Simpson asked questions
himself about Sheriff Davis's recruiting of deputies with a
vigor and pointedness that no southern sheriff has ever suffered at a Federal judge's hands:

> THE COURT: Do you recruit them from the Ku Klux
>   Klan there in St. Augustine?
> THE WITNESS: No, sir.
> THE COURT: Are some of them Klansmen, some of
>   these special deputies?
> THE WITNESS: No, sir, not to my knowledge, if they
>   are.
> THE COURT: Are you a Klansman?
> THE WITNESS: No, sir.

*   *   *

> THE COURT: Are you a member of the Ancient City
>   Gun Club?
> THE WITNESS: No, sir.

After Davis admitted he had deputized a number of
members of the club, Judge Simpson asked:

> THE COURT: I ask you this, isn't the Ancient City
>   Gun Club just the local name for the Klan down
>   there?
> THE WITNESS: I ... I don't think it is, your Honor.
>   I questioned everyone that I've had any contact
>   with....

Judge Simpson ordered Davis to supply a list of his
special deputies to the court. Davis read off a list of
his deputies the next day. When he came to the name of
'Holsted Richard Manucy,' Judge Simpson asked him,
'Isn't he a bootlegger?' Davis admitted that he was.

> THE COURT: He is a convicted felon in this court....
>   Has he had his rights of citizenship restored?
> THE WITNESS: Not that I know of, I don't know.
> THE COURT: He's good enough to be a deputy sheriff?
> THE WITNESS: No, sir....

*   *   *

> THE COURT: You have given them cards saying they
>   are Deputy Sheriffs and asked them to help you
>   keep order in your Easter parade; is that correct?
> THE WITNESS: Yes, sir.

Judge Simpson then remarked:
I think, Sheriff, as a law enforcement officer, you
can appreciate the danger in a situation like this when
you have members of the Klan and allied organizations in
your organization as deputies.*

Judge Simpson found that the violence came not from the
black marchers but from white troublemakers. Therefore, the way
to curb the violence was to be found in effective law enforcement,
he said, rather than in banning the demonstrations. In a second
hearing, Judge Simpson found that the high bonds set by Sheriff
Davis were arbitrary and excessive and that the conditions in his
jail amounted to cruel and unusual punishment. Bail was ordered
reduced and demonstrators were released to march again. The state
of Florida intervened and urged Judge Simpson to reverse his order
allowing the marchers to continue. Careful questioning established
the inadequacies of the state's attempts to maintain order. Judge
Simpson again refused to stop the marchers:

I suggest rigid and strict law enforcement and some
arrests and some real charges to be placed against those
hoodlums that everybody down there seems to be afraid to
move against and I make that [suggestion] with deadly seriousness. If the local law enforcement people are willing
to let them come in there and take over the downtown section of the city without taking steps against them, maybe
it's time for the State to step in and take charge of it.**

Governor Farriss Bryant finally acted decisively, sending
state troopers to St. Augustine. Violence was avoided for a time,
but a new crisis developed. On June 22, blacks who had gathered
at a beach were clubbed by whites in plain sight of state troopers
and on June 25, another large attack on demonstrators occurred.

The state continued to insist that both sides were to
blame. Judge Simpson's comment about this argument
was:
It's a question of taking the view that, when
somebody gets socked in the eye, he's just as guilty
as the man that's on the fist.

At another point he said:

If one group is entitled to march peacefully and to the
right of freedom of speech and the right of petition guaranteed by the First Amendment, it doesn't seem to me at
all that a corresponding freedom to attack with physical
violence goes to another group.***

---

*Southern Justice, at 197-99 (L. Friedman, ed., 1963); copyright
by Pantheon Books, a Division of Random House, Inc.; reprinted by
permission.
**Ibid., at 203.
***Ibid., at 204.

Judge Simpson then pointed to the real source of violence, Manucy's
Ancient City Gun Club. And, under intense pressure from Simpson,
Florida's Attorney General promised that Manucy would be dealt
with. Eighty troopers were sent to St. Augustine. In the process
of quelling the disturbances, Judge Simpson enjoined by name Manucy,
his brothers, the entire Gun Club, the Ku Klux Klan and a long list
of St. Augustine troublemakers. Two persons, one of them a deputy sheriff, were held in contempt for intimidating blacks at a restaurant. Judge Simpson ordered the deputy sheriff removed from
his official position. For the first time, a federal judge had decided who could be a deputy sheriff. Senator Strom Thurmond said
Simpson's decision was the start of a "judicial dictatorship." Sheriff Davis wanted Simpson impeached. However, the troubles in St.
Augustine subsided, in large measure because of forthright judicial
action by Judge Simpson.

Judge Simpson was also effective behind the scenes. In 1962
to 1964, when he was on the district bench, the civil rights attorneys
who represented black plaintiffs were frequently lawyers from New
York or elsewhere in the North. There were vigorous complaints
from the local bar about "these outside lawyers" who were coming
in to try cases in the Florida courts. Some prominent Florida lawyers found an obscure federal court rule prohibiting out-of-state
practitioners from appearing if they had not passed the Florida bar
examination. The Florida attorneys pointed the rule out to Judge
Simpson and urged that he not allow outsiders to practice before
him. Judge Simpson told the attorneys that he was pleased that
they had come to his office, and he would certainly enforce the rule
when Florida lawyers handled their responsibilities. He stressed
that the only lawyers who had represented black plaintiffs in civil
rights actions were attorneys from out of state. The day that the
Florida Bar came forth with a list of prominent local attorneys who
agreed to represent local black plaintiffs to the full extent of their
rights in the Florida courts, he informed them, would be the day
that he would prohibit the appearance of out-of-state attorneys.

Judge Simpson, like Judges Wright and Johnson, was subjected to intense local abuse. Judge Simpson described a typical
incident during the St. Augustine trouble:

> During the St. Augustine demonstrations there were ...
> these ruffians, young toughs with weapons like bicycle
> chains, billy clubs and ball bats, would come in at night.
> They would come from outlying places, from Ocala; they
> might come from west Florida, Lake City or Live Oak.
> They would be in St. Augustine at night to harass the col-
> ored people who were attempting to parade. Well, this
> friend of mine lived in Ocala; he owned one of these big
> truck stops where they have a restaurant in connection
> with it. He called me and told me that some people were
> threatening my life. I said I don't doubt it a damn bit.
> But who? He said, well, I can't tell you who. He said
> the husband of one of the waitresses there was a good

friend of the two people and he had heard them make this
threat that they were going to get me or shoot me or blow
me up or something. I said, well, I wish you could tell
me. He said, I am violating this girl's confidence to tell
you this much, but look into it. So then the next day they
came up from the FBI office and ... they told me that
they wanted to ask me to be careful, and that they would
provide a guard if I thought it necessary. The same people were making the threats, and they knew their names.
So I asked for a picture of the fellows. They said, we
haven't got one. I asked, have they been arrested? Maybe we can get one from a police department if they have
been arrested. They said, no, we can't find one. I
asked if it would be possible to pick them up and mug
them and then release them? I'd like to know who to look
for. They said, maybe. Then they came back in a day
or two and said one of the suspects had moved to Georgia
and not to worry about him. And I remember asking them,
I said, you say be careful, what do you want me to do?
They said, we just want you to be careful. When you sit
in a place, sit with your back against the wall. I said,
do you want me to pack a pistol? I said, I'm not going
to do that. I told them that I had a couple of deer rifles
at the house and a couple of shotguns and that I would
load the guns and place them at all the windows so that if
anybody tried to come in, I could shoot one or two of
them as they were coming. I asked, is that what you suggest I do? They said, just be careful. I said you do
one thing for me. Ask the people in the building, the GSA
people, to keep an eye on my car. (I didn't want anybody
to put something on my car that would blow up when I
went down there.) I had a parking place in the back of
the building. I said, just ask them to watch it. I'm sure
they have my license number by now, and I'll back the car
instead of running it in forward. After a few days you
realize that if they are going to do something to you, they
probably aren't going to broadcast it anyway.

Asked what his reaction to such abuse was, Judge Simpson just
smiled:

Well, I think things like that get to your native stubborn-
ness and make you a little more ... stiffen your resolve,
mainly, that's the effect of it. I like the idea of being
in certain people's SOB book. I never tried to please
everybody anyway. There are certain people that I am
happy to enjoy their ill will.

Judge Simpson is understandably proud of his role in civil
rights cases. Asked if he would change anything he had done in
the civil rights area, he said:

Not for my own part, especially not in the racial field.

I might make them a little tougher. Old Andrew Jackson
in his last days at the Hermitage was asked if he had any
regrets and he said, yes, I should have shot Henry Clay
and I should have hanged John Calhoun. And I think I
might stiffen up a few of [the cases and], insist on my
view rather than being so accommodating. Whenever I
sent a proposed opinion to a brother, he would suggest
that I take this and that out; a few of them, I wish I had
left some of my opinions in the original form instead of
softening them up. That's the only regret.

While on the district court bench, Judge Simpson handled
several school desegregation matters. His most important decisions
were Tillman v. Board of Public Instruction of Volusia County and
Braxton v. Board of Public Instruction of Duval County. He was
the first federal district judge to order an end to faculty segregation, an extremely important milestone on the road to integrated
education. In an opinion by Judge Tuttle, the Fifth Circuit upheld
Judge Simpson's innovation. Judge Jones dissented vigorously, protesting that there had been no finding that assignment of teachers by
race caused injury and noting that Brown dealt with pupil, not teacher, assignment. Many judges, in retrospect, felt that desegregation
would have proceeded more smoothly if the faculties of the schools
had been desegregated first, not last. In a later opinion in the
Braxton case, Judge Simpson was the first district judge to order a
school board to provide a majority-to-minority transfer policy as a
part of its freedom-of-choice plan. Such a policy allowed any student in a school where he was a member of the majority race, on
request to obtain automatic transfer to a school where he would be
a member of the minority race.

The Movement Toward Uniform Standards

A divided and bitter court left Houston after the Judicial
Council meeting that discussed the Cameron court-packing charges.
Caught in the throes of a bitter, publicly-exposed intramural dispute,
threatened with investigation by the chairman of the Senate Judiciary
Committee, and living through the most volatile civil rights year of
all, the Fifth Circuit entered its second era after Brown v. Board
of Education. The early years had been easy in comparison with
what lay ahead.

Brown II had declared an "all deliberate speed" standard. In
the first era (1954-1962) after Brown, most federal district courts
had emphasized the word "deliberate" and ignored "speed." Simple
token integration, a grade-a-year plan involving a few courageous
black students taking the initiative in utilizing complex pupil assignment acts, was the norm in districts where any degree of desegregation had been achieved in the Deep South. Much of the desegregation law that had developed retarded, rather than advanced, the goal
of nondiscriminatory public education. The Briggs v. Elliott dictum,

interpreting Brown as mandating only an end to compulsory segregation but not commanding integration, was continually cited by lower
federal courts as the definitive interpretation of Brown II. In the
Fifth Circuit states, Avery v. Wichita Falls Independent School District engrafted the Briggs dictum onto any effort to desegregate.
The Supreme Court in Cooper v. Aaron, the decision condemning
Governor Orval Faubus for his conduct in the Little Rock desegregation case, had made it clear that disagreement by local authorities
with the constitutional principle involved, or even community hostility, would not serve as a permissible basis for delay. Despite
Cooper v. Aaron, federal district judges for years--with notable exceptions like Skelly Wright, Frank Johnson and Bryan Simpson--
rationalized their own foot-dragging with the excuse that they were
reducing the likelihood of violence and were preserving public education in their districts. And in some cases they may have been
correct.

     After the Houston conference, the judges realized that working
together was necessary in order for the appellate court to perform
its duties. They also knew that the pace of desegregation had to increase, and that their court bore the burden of acceleration. The
Supreme Court in three quick decisions in 1963-64 made it clear
that with the passage of years "deliberate speed" could not be viewed
in the same context as it had been when it was announced. The
problems were enormous. The "easy" districts had already begun
desegregation. Remaining were the die-hard districts in Louisiana,
Florida, Georgia and Texas and the entire states of Alabama and
Mississippi. No longer would a majority of the liberal Four control almost all school panels. Momentum in desegregation had to
be achieved at the time that differences in the composition of different panels on the Circuit threatened any attempt to achieve uniform interpretations of the law. Furthermore, a burgeoning case
load had to be managed, and success was made doubtful by the increasing landslide of civil rights actions. Glimpses of the Fifth
Circuit's journey through those middle years have been seen by the
above focus on the district courts in Georgia, Alabama, Mississippi
and Florida. But the movement of the law from an emphasis on
gradualism and token desegregation to immediate, system-wide integration can be obscured by the very mass of cases, incidents and
judicial personalities. Despite all difficulties, the law did develop
as the Court moved through the maelstrom of those middle years.

     In 1963 the Fifth Circuit was not certain as to the correct
pace for desegregation. In one of the early Davis v. Board of
School Commissioners of Mobile County decisions, the Court reversed Judge Thomas and indicated that the day was almost at hand
when the venerable grade-a-year plan would no longer be adequate.
But the Fifth Circuit was still willing to countenance delay in 1963
and 1964. In Calhoun v. Latimer, the Atlanta school case, the
Court affirmed a decision approving a grade-a-year plan, with Judge
Bell using the following language for the majority: "Gradualism in
desegregation, if not the usual, is at least an accepted mode with
the emphasis on getting the job of transition done." Judge Rives

dissented and the Supreme Court reversed in 1964, remanding the case to the district court for reconsideration of the speed of desegregation in light of its three "speedup" decisions of 1963-64.

The wounds of the 1963 Judicial Council were not easily healed. Some hostilities toward enforcement of civil rights cases can be illustrated by the opinions of that year. Judge Gewin was then one of the more conservative Fifth Circuit judges in school cases (he has in later years become considerably more progressive); in a 1963 dissenting opinion in the Birmingham school case he expressed his pique at what he obviously felt were pushy civil rights attorneys:

> There is another factor which I feel it is my duty to mention as a matter of information to attorneys who appear before our court. The arguments presented in some of the cases mentioned above contained insinuating overtones unfavorably reflecting on both the Federal and State Judiciary, in certain localities, varying in degree from the barely audible tinkling of a distant cymbal to the crashing noise of sounding brass. It is fundamental that lawyers owe full allegiance to their clients and should use their learning, skill, diligence, devotion, and '... all appropriate legal means within the law to protect and enforce legitimate interests.' Lawyers are required in the discharge of their duties to disagree with judges, to allege error, to attack the judges' rulings and decisions, and even to render just and proper criticism of such rulings, decisions and judgments. But the Office of Judge, whether it be Federal or State, requires the respect of the legal profession....

At the same time, Judge Gewin was appalled by the violent public resistance to court orders. Noting that "[c]ourt orders, like constitutional rights, cannot yield to violence," Judge Gewin pleaded for the law-abiding citizens to come forward.

> We have no trouble in taking judicial notice of the fact that there are many upstanding, splendid, law-abiding citizens in Birmingham and throughout the State of Alabama who are so firmly dedicated to the principle of the orderly process of the courts and the law that they refuse to rebel against those laws which displease them. We also take judicial knowledge of the fact that violence and disorder have erupted in Birmingham. There is no indication that the great body of people of Alabama approve of lawless conduct even though such conduct arises out of the enforcement of laws which change customs and traditions. The question now is not approval or disapproval of the law; but whether the law, order, and the educational process will prevail over violence and disorder. The howling winds of hate and prejudice always make it difficult to hear the voices of the humble, the just, the fair, the

wise, the reasonable, and the prudent. We must not permit their voices to be silenced by those who would incite
mob violence. 'The best guarantee of civil peace is adherence to, and respect for, the law....'

The fight of the Court's liberals against excessive gradualism
was led by Chief Judge Tuttle and frequently surfaced in the opinions. Dissenting in 1964 from a Texas school opinion written by
Judge Gewin, who was joined in the opinion by Judge Hutcheson,
Chief Judge Tuttle quoted one of Judge Hutcheson's favorite sayings
back to him: "A court should not 'keep the word of promise to
[the] ear, and break it to [the] hope.' Macbeth, Act V, Scene VIII."
Tuttle's discontent stemmed from the fact that gradualism was inappropriate under the facts of the case. Georgetown, Texas, had
1,300 students, only 173 of whom were black; Chief Judge Tuttle
felt immediate desegregation was possible and gradualism inappropriate.

> ... I consider it necessary to file a dissent to the
> proposition that 'gradualism' may be approved in all cases,
> regardless of the circumstances. Here the court places
> the emphasis on 'gradualism' rather than the devotion of
> 'every effort toward initiating desegregation and bringing
> about the elimination of racial discrimination.'

With prodding from the Supreme Court in 1963, the advent of
Lyndon Johnson and his commitment to civil rights, and the pushing
of its liberal members internally, five major cases involving Birmingham and Mobile, Alabama, and Savannah, Brunswick and Albany, Georgia were decided in 1964. Those cases ordered grade-
a-year plans rapidly stepped-up. Desegregation was started in the
first and second grades and also in the twelfth so that no student
would graduate without a desegregated education. While stressing
that no inflexible standard was intended, the cases did indicate the
importance of a degree of uniformity. The Fifth Circuit, from that
point until its famous Jefferson cases (discussed in the next chapter),
began consistently moving toward a goal of uniform standards that
could be applied throughout the Circuit to avoid endless litigation on
the details of every plan. In the 1965 case of Lockett v. Board of
Education of Muscogee County, Judge Bell set a target date of September, 1968, for all grades to be included in the plan. That date
was applied to other cases and is evidence of the desperate push toward uniform standards.

In addition to speeding up the pace of desegregation, as far
as inclusion of grades, the Fifth Circuit also altered the law in other areas of school desegregation. The Court moved away from
"transfer plans" requiring black students to apply through complex
procedures to initiate their own transfer to white schools. The Supreme Court's decision in Shuttlesworth, approving the Alabama Pupil Placement Act on its face, had retarded a significant degree of
desegregation for years. Finally, it became clear beyond cavil that
the sole purpose of such acts was to retard desegregation. There-

after their application was enjoined. Freedom-of-choice plans replaced pupil assignment plans. The theory of freedom of choice was that every pupil could choose his own school based only on his personal choice and the capacity of the local school. But countless subterfuges to prevent unfettered free choice prevented any significant amount of desegregation under such plans. The HEW guidelines, approved later by the Circuit in the Jefferson cases,* were an attempt to apply rigorous standards to guarantee the workability of such plans. As freedom-of-choice plans were being approved from 1964 to 1966, the Fifth Circuit also began to require contemporaneous abolition of dual attendance zones, separate school attendance zones for black and white children by which they were initially assigned to schools by race. The important Volusia and Duval County decisions of Judge Simpson pointed the way to faculty and staff integration and the Fifth Circuit eventually decided that an all-black or all-white teaching staff was a prime identifying mark of a segregated system and retarded pupil desegregation.

In his Lockett v. Board of Education of Muscogee County decision, Judge Bell succinctly summarized the movement toward desegregation in 1965: "The rule has become: the later the start, the shorter the time allowed for transition." Judge Brown's decision in Price v. Denison also expressed impatience with the delays caused by endless review of legal doctrine. The Circuit began to demand action on effective desegregation. Judge Brown welcomed the new HEW guidelines and pointed out the impetus caused by the 1964 Civil Rights Act: "The time for reviewing or redeveloping the undulating administrative doctrines evolved by us for the implementation of Brown is over."

But perhaps the most compelling statement is Judge Tuttle's in one of the Davis v. Board of School Commissioners of Mobile County decisions. His anguish over endless litigation in lieu of effective desegregation set the stage for the watershed Singleton and Jefferson decisions:

> This is the fourth appearance of this case before this court. This present appeal ... points up ... the utter impracticability of a continued exercise by the courts of the responsibility for supervising the manner in which segregated school systems break out of the policy of complete segregation into gradual ... compliance with ... Brown. ...

NOTES AND PRIMARY AUTHORITY

The primary authority for material contained in this chapter was:

---

*See discussion at Part II, Chapter 11, infra at 437.

The Climate. Bergman, The Chronological History of the Negro in America (1969); Powledge, Black Power, White Resistance (1967); Waskow, From Race Riot to Sit In (1966).

I. Shifting from "Deliberate" to "Speed". Helpful sources are: Goss v. Board of Educ., 373 U.S. 683 (1963) and Watson v. City of Memphis, 373 U.S. 526 (1973). Also helpful are 20 U.S.C. § 236 et seq., 241 et seq., 331 et seq., 821 et seq. (1970) and 42 U.S.C. §§2000c-2, 2000c-6, 2000d (1970).

Georgia. The primary sources are: Roberts v. Stell, 379 U.S. 933 (1964) (sub nom.); United States v. Jefferson County Bd. of Educ., 380 F.2d 385 (5th Cir. 1967); Calhoun v. Latimer, 321 F.2d 302 (5th Cir. 1963); Harris v. Gibson, 322 F.2d 780 (5th Cir. 1963); Acree v. County Bd. of Educ., 294 F. Supp. 1034 (S.D.Ga. 1968); Stell v. Savannah-Chatham County Bd. of Educ., 255 F. Supp. 88 (S.D. Ga. 1966). Also helpful are: 32. U.S.L.W. 3256 (U.S.Jan. 14, 1964); 28 U.S.C. § 1292(a)(1)(1970); 28 U.S.C. § 1651(a)(1970); Ga. Code Ann. § 32-910 (1969); and "School Desegregation in Ten Communities," A Report of the United States Commission on Civil Rights (June, 1973). Of help were N.Y. Times, Aug. 29, 1963, §1, at 14, col. 8, and Handler, "Savannah Is Calm Over Integration," N.Y. Times, Sept. 2, 1963, §1, at 6, col. 1.

Alabama. Major sources of cases are: Davis v. Board of School Comm. of Mobile County, 400 U.S. 815 (1970), aff'd in part, rev'd in part, 402 U.S. 33 (1971); United States v. Albama, 252 F. Supp. 95 (M.D.Ala. 1966); United States v. Rea, 231 F. Supp. 772 (M.D.Ala. 1964); Lee v. Macon County Bd. of Educ., 231 F. Supp. 743 (M.D.Ala. 1964); Gomillion v. Rutherford, 6 Race Rel. L. Rep. 241 (M.D.Ala. 1961); Shuttlesworth v. Birmingham Bd. of Educ., 162 F. Supp. 372 (N.D.Ala. 1958), aff'd, 358 U.S.101 (1958); Browder v. Goyle, 142 F. Supp. 707 (M.D.Ala.), aff'd, 352 U.S. 903 (1956). The book by V. Navasky, Kennedy Justice (1970), was particularly useful. Interviews were held with Judge Harlan H. Grooms, United States District Court for the Northern District of Alabama, in his offices in Birmingham, Ala., July 26, 1972; Judge Seybourn Lynne, United States District Court for the Northern District of Alabama, in his offices in Birmingham, Ala., July 26, 1972; and, Judge Frank M. Johnson, United States District Court for the Middle District of Alabama, in his offices in Montgomery, Ala., June 30, 1972.

Mississippi. Major case sources are: Jackson Mun. Sep. School Dist. v. Evers, 357 S.2d 653 (5th Cir. 1966); United States v. Cox, 342 F.2d 167 (5th Cir. 1965); United States v. Ramsey, 331 F.2d 824 (5th Cir. 1964); United States v. Wood, 295 F.2d 772 (5th Cir. 1961); Stell v. Savannah-Chatham County Bd. of Educ., 333 F.2d 55 (5th Cir. 1964); and, Evers v. Jackson Mun. Sep. School Dist., 232 F. Supp. 241 (S.D. Miss. 1964). Other sources are: Southern Justice (L. Friedman, ed., 1963); 156 The New Republic, Feb. 18, 1967, at 12; Bickel, "Impeach Judge Cox," 153 The New Republic, Sept. 4, 1965, at 13; Time, Nov. 24, 1964, at 80; Time, Sept. 23, 1966, at 26; 85 Time, Mar. 5, 1965, at 25; 84 Time, Nov. 6, 1964, and, 59 Newsweek, Jan. 22, 1962, at 58.

Florida. The major case source was Board of Pub. Instruc-

430 / Let Them Be Judged

tion v. Braxton, **326 F. 2d 616** (5th Cir. 1964). An interview was
held with Judge Bryan Simpson, United States Court of Appeals for
the Fifth Circuit, in his offices in Jacksonville, Fla., July 7, 1972.

The Movement Toward Uniform Standards. The major case sources
are: Calhoun v. Latimer, 377 U. S. 263 (1964); Goss v. Board of
Educ., 373 U. S. 683 (1963); Watkins v. City of Memphis, 373 U. S.
526 (1963); Shuttlesworth v. Birmingham Bd. of Educ., 162 F. Supp.
372 (N. D. Ala. 1958), aff'd, 358 U. S. 101; Price v. Denison Ind.
School Dist., 348 F. 2d 1010 (5th Cir. 1965); Gaines v. Dougherty
County Bd. of Educ., 334 F. 2d 983 (5th Cir. 1964); Stell v. Savan-
nah-Chatham County Bd. of Educ., 333 F. 2d 55 (5th Cir. 1964);
Davis v. Board of School Comm'rs, 333 F. 2d 53 (5th Cir. 1964);
Armstrong v. Board of Educ., 333 F. 2d 47 (5th Cir. 1964); Miller
v. Barnes, 328 F. 2d 810 (5th Cir. 1964). Other sources are:
Tillman v. Board of Pub. Instruction, 7 Race Rel. L. Rep. 687
(S. D. Fla. 1962); Braxton v. Board of Pub. Instruction, 7 Race Rel.
L. Rep. 675 (S. D. Fla. 1962).

A more complete manuscript, with detailed documentation of
all sources, is available as indicated in the Preface, supra.

Chapter 11

THE ZENITH OF FEDERAL COORDINATION

John Minor Wisdom, a small, hawk-nosed, man with piercing eyes, may well be the brightest judge sitting on a federal appellate court. A dominating intellect, combined with a lively, literate style and painstaking research mark him as "the scholar" on the Fifth Circuit and one of America's foremost legal minds.

A former Louisiana member of the Republican National Committee, John Wisdom was an Eisenhower appointee to the bench. Senior partner in one of New Orleans' most prestigious law firms, he was one of the twenty or so key Republicans instrumental in convincing presidential-nominee Eisenhower to name California's young junior senator, Richard Nixon, as his vice-presidential running mate. He also served with Richard Nixon on President Eisenhower's Commission on Discrimination in Government Contracts. Many felt that Judge Wisdom should have been one of President Nixon's first appointees to the Supreme Court. He was a Southerner, a Republican and considered one of the nation's premier appellate judges. But John Minor Wisdom's liberal voting record on civil rights cases clashed with the celebrated Nixon-Mitchell "Southern strategy" and the appointment was never made.

Unlike most circuit judges, who are removed from the direct local pressure faced by the district courts, Judge Wisdom has suffered his share of local abuse. Generally the protests took the form of abusive letters. One particularly "clever" postcard displayed a photograph of Judge Wisdom showing a double exposure with the following message:

> Is this a composite portrait of Dorian Gray, Benedict Arnold and Judas? Notice the double image. Why don't you and Skelly Wright and Christenberry commit suicide, like Judas did. Do you know what a scalawag is? We despise you.
> The 2nd Reconstruction is about ended. The Conspiracy has lost. The Establishment is deteriorating. It's [sic] stooges and puppets have been exposed or will be exposed and disgraced.

However, Judge Wisdom did not suffer the extent of indignities that Judges Wright, Johnson and Simpson faced. He feels he lost no friends, although, as has been mentioned, occasionally one would wryly greet him, "What have you done to us white folks today?"

431

Judge Wisdom's reputation as an innovative judicial scholar is universally affirmed by his colleagues on the circuit bench. Judge Irving Goldberg, a colleague also known for an incisive legal mind, states that "Judge Wisdom lent a scholarship and insight into ... legal history ... that very few judges in any part of the country could bring to this problem of integration." Judge Robert Ainsworth, who sits with Judge Wisdom in New Orleans, flatly asserts that Wisdom is the finest mind on the Court. Judge Wisdom's reputation for exceptional legal scholarship is not restricted to the civil rights cases he has handled, but his contributions to that field alone since Brown I and II mark him as one of the most important men in the history of the modern South. For example, he and Judge John R. Brown helped formulate the "freeze" principle, first used so effectively by Judge Johnson in the voting rights cases--mandating local registrars to register every Negro with the qualifications of the least qualified white on existing voting rolls. In the Poindexter series he struck down increasingly more subtle attempts by Louisiana to destroy desegregation by a tuition grant program. First, tuition grants to white students were declared unconstitutional. Louisiana replied by creating an Education Commission for Needy Children to aid parents not wishing to enroll their children in public schools where there was "an increase in juvenile delinquency, school dropouts and juvenile crime rates." Judge Wisdom found the new program to be the same tuition grant plan with the same purpose-- to thwart desegregation. It was also voided.

However, perhaps Judge Wisdom's most important decisions were in the school desegregation area between 1965 and 1967. His two decisions in Singleton v. Jackson Municipal Separate School District (now referred to as Singleton I and II) and his two decisions in United States v. Jefferson County Board of Education (now referred to as Jefferson I and II) mark the most important doctrinal change in interpretation of the equal protection clause as applied to public education since Brown itself. Judge Wisdom's Singleton I and II and Jefferson I and II decisions marked the end of the middle turbulent years of school desegregation and presaged the era of massive integration. Their importance cannot be overemphasized.

* * *

Singleton I and II and Jefferson I and II revolutionized the progress of public school desegregation in the South. The Fifth Circuit's mounting frustration with tokenism and delay by school boards and federal district courts in the name of deliberate speed grew as the years passed without substantial quantitative progress toward desegregation. Each successive opinion from the Court of Appeals brought only more appeals, more questions, more litigation. Desperately seeking uniform standards that could be applied circuit-wide and which would remove the Court of Appeals from day-to-day supervision of district court decrees, the Fifth Circuit began to view the Office of Education, established pursuant to the 1964 Civil Rights Act by the Department of Health, Education and Welfare, as perhaps the answer to its problems of fully implementing the Brown mandate.

That office had established "guidelines," fixing minimum standards
for use in determining whether a local school board's desegregation
plan would qualify that local school board for federal financial assistance. Could the Office of Education's "guidelines" be the uniform standards that the Court of Appeals had been seeking?

Judge Wisdom's two opinions in Singleton I and II culminated
in his famous Jefferson I and II opinions. Over a year in preparation, Judge Wisdom held in Jefferson I that past ineffectiveness of
individual decrees in producing unitary, racially integrated school
systems, which he felt were required by the Brown mandate, justified the adoption of the Office of Education guidelines as minimum
constitutional standards required of all freedom-of-choice plans in
the Fifth Circuit. Jefferson I was a seminal decision. It broke
sharply with past interpretations of the Fourteenth Amendment's application to school cases by interpreting Brown II as placing on
states an affirmative duty to achieve integrated, unitary school systems, not just to remove legal impediments to desegregation efforts
by individual black students. And that decision held that the test of
whether a school plan was constitutional was simply whether the
plan worked: did it achieve a unitary system.

* * *

The momentum toward the Jefferson I holding was forecast
by Judge Wisdom's opinion in Singleton I, decided on June 22, 1965
by a panel composed of Judges Hutcheson, Brown and Wisdom.
Judge Wisdom explicitly warned in Singleton I that "The time has
come for footdragging public school boards to move with celerity
toward desegregation." He then expressly noted the adoption by the
Office of Education of its minimum standards to determine eligibility for federal financial aid, stating that the Fifth Circuit would "at-
tach great weight" to the new HEW guidelines. While recognizing
that HEW and the judiciary had different functions, the opinion asserted that all three branches of government were united by a common objective: the elimination of segregated education. Judge Wisdom stated that HEW was better equipped than the courts to weigh
alleged administrative difficulties in various desegregation plans.
He warned that judicial requirements in desegregation cases should
not be "less burdensome than HEW guides," or school boards would
flood the courts with desegregation questions in order to avoid HEW's
more rigorous guidelines: "If judicial standards are lower than
H.E.W. standards, recalcitrant school boards in effect will receive
a premium for recalcitrance; the more the intransigence, the bigger
the bonus." The Court then ordered the local board in Singleton I
to "be guided" in the preparation of the details of its plan by the
new HEW guidelines.

In an extremely important footnote, Judge Wisdom provided
the philosophic underpinnings for his favorable recommendation of
HEW guidelines to local school boards. For the first time in a Fifth
Circuit opinion, he attacked the venerable Briggs v. Elliott dictum
as inconsistent with Brown I and II:

In retrospect, the second Brown opinion clearly imposes
on public school authorities the duty to provide an integrated school system. Judge Parker's well-known dictum
('The Constitution, in other words, does not require integration. It merely forbids discrimination.') in Briggs
v. Elliott ... should be laid to rest. It is inconsistent
with Brown and the later development of decisional and
statutory law in the area of civil rights.

Judge Wisdom's footnote observation that the Briggs dictum
"should be laid to rest" provoked a storm of internal controversy
among his brothers on the Court. An impressive series of cases,
all tracing back to Briggs, had interpreted the equal protection
clause application to school cases as essentially negative. Those
cases focused on the "proscriptive" effect of the second sentence of
the Fourteenth Amendment: "No State shall ... deny to any person
... the equal protection of the laws." The negative Briggs interpretation of Brown I said that the decision merely forbade states
from mandatorily segregating public schools and at most required
that artificial legal barriers to desegregation be removed. Judge
Wisdom, however, read Brown I quite differently. He felt that it
implied an affirmative interpretation of the Fourteenth Amendment,
positively requiring a state to provide unitary school systems that
were not racially identifiable. He read Brown I and II as breathing
new life into the three Civil War amendments to the Constitution:
the Thirteenth, Fourteenth and Fifteenth Amendments.

In his Singleton and Jefferson reasoning, Judge Wisdom
placed emphasis on the first, positive sentence of the Fourteenth
Amendment that, "All persons born ... in the United States ...
are citizens," rather than the negative interpretation of Briggs.
He read the Thirteenth Amendment as not only abolishing slavery
but "all badges and indicia of slavery," and he viewed segregated
education as an indicia of slavery and racial inferiority. Reading
the Thirteenth, Fourteenth and Fifteenth Amendments in concert, he
argued that the Constitution created an affirmative right of black
citizens to enjoy all the benefits of full citizenship without special
treatment by reason of their race. Judge Wisdom argued that those
states that had erected legal impediments to full citizenship, by
creating "badges of slavery" like segregated schools, did not satisfy their obligations by removing segregationist laws. Retreating to
a neutral corner and placing on individual black citizens the full
burden of initiating desegregation was not enough. The states that
had segregated blacks by law had to assume the primary burden of
desegregation through the creation of unitary school systems that
treated all citizens equally without regard to race. Later, in Jefferson I, Judge Wisdom expanded his argument to attack "the popular
myth" that Brown I and II were premised on sociological studies that
asserted that segregation caused psychological harm to black children. Rather, he argued, the Brown holdings were directly premised on the mandatory language of the Fourteenth Amendment which
prohibited unreasonable classification by a state of its citizens.
Classification of school children by race was per se unreasonable

without a showing of harm. Therefore a state had not only a duty to proscribe past segregation laws but it also had an affirmative duty to prescribe an integrated education for all its citizens where race was not a factor.

Judge Wisdom's footnote attempt in Singleton I to destroy Briggs v. Elliott seriously wounded the dictum but did not kill it. Judge Rives, a solid member of the liberal "Four" and one of the circuit judges who had suffered the most abuse because of his staunch enforcement of constitutional rights, had written the first opinion in the Fifth Circuit adopting the Briggs dictum, Avery v. Wichita Falls Independent School District. He felt strongly that the Fourteenth Amendment had only a negative or prohibitory effect. In judicial council he took issue with his brother Wisdom, with whom he had agreed so often in the past, and chastised him for an attempt to overrule a case as entrenched in decisional authority as Briggs v. Elliott by a simple aside in a footnote. However, Judge Wisdom remained convinced that Briggs v. Elliott was the single most important legal roadblock to full implementation of the Brown mandate.

*   *   *

Seven months after Singleton I, Judge Wisdom, sitting on a panel with Judge Thornberry and Senior Judge Whitaker, who was sitting by designation, wrote Singleton II. An extremely complex procedural background caused Judge Wisdom to refer to Singleton II as a "tangled web." Nevertheless, the case involved only one matter: "judicial approval of a lawful and effective desegregation plan for schools in Jackson, Mississippi."

Noting the weaknesses of freedom-of-choice plans, Judge Wisdom again pointed out, as in Singleton I, that the Court attached "great weight" to HEW guidelines promulgated by the Office of Education and designed to make freedom-of-choice plans more effective. However, to assuage rising criticism over his Singleton I comments about HEW's guidelines, he made it clear that "we do not abdicate our judicial responsibility for determining whether a school desegregation plan violates federally guaranteed rights."

Judge Wisdom then began a careful frontal assault on Briggs v. Elliott, raising his barbs from the footnotes to the text:

> The Constitution forbids unconstitutional state action in the form of segregated facilities, including segregated public schools.... The school children in still segregated grades in Negro schools are there by assignment based on their race.... They have an absolute right, as individuals, to transfer to schools from which they were excluded because of their race.
> This has been the law since Brown v. Board of Education, 1954.... Misunderstanding of this principle is perhaps due to the popularity of an over-simplified dictum

that the Constitution 'does not require integration' [citing Briggs v. Elliott]. But there should be no misunderstanding now as to the right of any child in a segregated class to transfer to a formerly all 'white' class, regardless of the slow pace of systematic desegregation by classes.

In Singleton II the Briggs dictum was, at last, held not to bar the right of any black child to transfer to a white school. But that dictum's final death knell, first sounded in Singleton I, then repeated more directly in Singleton II, had to await Judge Wisdom's monumental effort in Jefferson I.

*   *   *

United States v. Jefferson County Board of Education (Jefferson I) is, with Brown I, Brown II, and Swann v. Charlotte-Mecklenburg decided in 1971,* one of the four most important school desegregation cases yet decided. Covering seventy-four pages in the Federal Reporter and a year in gestation, it has had enormous impact on both the law and the pace of desegregation. An understanding of Jefferson I is necessary for an appreciation of how the federal courts moved from token desegregation to massive integration. Although mortally wounding the Briggs v. Elliott dictum, as a side effect it also nurtured the new "de-facto/de-jure distinction" that still frustrates the movement of integration to the ghettos of the North and West.

Judge Wisdom's Jefferson I opinion is divided into seven parts. In a preamble section, the need for a new approach to desegregation is dramatically stated:

> When the United States Supreme Court in 1954 decided Brown v. Board of Education the members of the High School Class of 1966 had not entered the first grade. Brown I held that separate schools for Negro children were 'inherently unequal.' Negro children, said the Court, have the 'personal and present' right to equal educational opportunities with white children in a racially nondiscriminatory public school system. For all but a handful of Negro members of the High School Class of '66 this right has been 'of such stuff as dreams are made on.'

Judge Wisdom noted that in the seven separate cases consolidated for hearing in Jefferson I, not one of the school districts before the Court made a start toward desegregation until 1965, eleven years after Brown. They then moved only after a court order was obtained over vigorous opposition. The Southern Education Reporting Service revealed that in Alabama, in December, 1965, for example, there were only 1,250 Negro students, out of a state-wide total of 295,848, actually enrolled in schools with the state's 559,123 white students.

---

*Discussed at Part III, Chapter 16, infra.

In the preamble to his decision, Judge Wisdom then tersely laid to its final rest the troublesome Briggs v. Elliott dicta:

> Decision-making in this important area of the law cannot be made to turn upon a quibble devised over ten years ago by a court that misread Brown, misapplied the class action doctrine in the school desegregation cases, and did not foresee the development of the law of equal opportunities.

To emphasize the new test by which courts were to judge the constitutionality of school board desegregation plans, Judge Wisdom penned the following resounding paragraph:

> The only school desegregation plan that meets constitutional standards is one that works. By helping public schools to meet that test, by assisting the courts in their independent evaluation of school desegregation plans, and by accelerating the progress but simplifying the process of desegregation the HEW Guidelines offer new hope to Negro school children long denied their constitutional rights. A national effort, bringing together Congress, the executive, and the judiciary may be able to make meaningful the right of Negro children to equal educational opportunities. The courts acting alone have failed.

Judge Wisdom then emphasized that the new HEW standards were substantially the same as those that had evolved in the difficult middle years from the Court's own cases. By mandating the standards as new minimum constitutional requirements for racial integration, the Fifth Circuit attempted to block school boards from seeking court orders that were less rigorous.*

After the preamble to his opinion indicating that Briggs was overruled and that the HEW guidelines were being mandated circuit-wide, Judge Wisdom--having urged in Singleton II that school boards "grasp the nettle" and begin real desegregation--stated: "We grasp the nettle." He then plunged into the seven parts of his opinion justifying his abrupt departure from past precedent, both as to the

---

*The issuance of HEW's new guidelines caused a number of recalcitrant school boards, "that had not moved an inch toward desegregation," to seek weak court orders so that the Commissioner of Education would not cut off their federal funding.

The following statement appeared in the Shreveport Journal for July 1, 1965: "The local school boards prefer a court order over the voluntary plan because HEW regulations governing the voluntary plans or compliance agreements demand complete desegregation of the entire system, including students, faculty, staff, lunch workers, bus drivers, and administrators, whereas the court-ordered plans can be more or less negotiated with the judge." This was not news to the Court.

pace and method of desegregation, with the comment that, " 'No army is stronger than an idea whose time has come.' " The importance of Titles IV and VI of the Civil Rights Act of 1964 was discussed in Part I of the opinion. Judge Wisdom asserted that a new national policy had emerged from the 1964 Civil Rights Act: "The national policy is plain: formerly de jure segregated public school systems based on dual attendance zones must shift to unitary, nonracial systems--with or without federal funds."

Part II of Judge Wisdom's opinion reviewed in detail the slow pace of desegregation and issued a new clarion call for a change in both the speed and manner of desegregation in the Deep South. Judge Wisdom charged that misplaced reliance on the Briggs dictum had given rise to the most serious obstacle to real desegregation: the pupil placement acts. Those acts placed the full responsibility for desegregation on the individual black citizen rather than the state. However, with congressional recognition in 1964 of a national goal of integration, Judge Wisdom held that both the executive and the judicial branches had a duty to bring about uniform standards for desegregation. He said that the executive branch had done its part by promulgating the new HEW guidelines. Now, he continued, the courts must do their part. The Court, then, not only decided that the new HEW guidelines were authorized by the Civil Rights Act of 1964; it also apparently viewed the new HEW guidelines as a godsend. Now, maybe, the courts could remove themselves from the school business and let the executive branch administer a uniform school desegregation program. Judge Wisdom was acutely aware of the tremendous burden placed on the Court by never-ending school cases. He also deplored the lack of any development of clear and uniform standards by the lower federal courts, thus placing a premium on delaying tactics by local school boards.

> What Cicero said of an earlier Athens and an earlier Rome is equally applicable today: In Georgia, for example, there should not be one law for Athens and another law for Rome.

The Fifth Circuit had high expectations for the HEW guidelines. It thought relief was in sight. But relief was not to come. The Jefferson decree was not self-executing, and over 100 school boards were already under court orders less rigorous than the HEW guidelines. The NAACP Inc. Fund, therefore, had to take the initiative to reopen all of those cases--causing more litigation. Furthermore, when HEW finally seemed ready for a vigorous push toward desegregation, Richard Nixon was elected President. The Fifth Circuit then began to sense that its newly found HEW and Justice Department allies were beginning to falter. Nevertheless, on December 29, 1966, when Jefferson I was written, faith in the new guidelines was strong in the Fifth Circuit.

Part III of the Wisdom opinion is a brilliant and scholarly excursion into the meaning of the Brown mandate, the Civil War amendments to the Constitution and the evolving school case law.

Judge Wisdom systematically destroyed the last vestiges of support for the Briggs v. Elliott dictum. Briggs was a negative view of the fourteenth amendment. It only prohibited states from interfering with an individual's rights. Under Briggs, once legal barriers were removed a state's duty was exhausted--the individual then had the responsibility to assert his rights. Judge Wisdom struck hard at the basic fallacy in the Briggs argument: he insistently reiterated that Brown I and II were class actions, to benefit all blacks similarly situated.

If Brown had been an individual action, then once the plaintiffs were admitted to white schools the case should have ended. Why did Brown II formulate the "all deliberate speed" remedy directing all states to reorganize their dual school systems? Judge Wisdom's vigorous assault on Briggs answers this question in the following compelling passages:

> The gradual transition the Supreme Court authorized was to allow the states time to solve the administrative problems inherent in that change-over [to a unitary system]. No delay would have been necessary if the right at issue in Brown had been only the right of individual Negro plaintiffs to admission to a white school. Moreover, the delay of one year in deciding Brown II and the gradual remedy Brown II fashioned can be justified only on the ground that the "'personal and present'" right of the individual plaintiffs must yield to the overriding right of the Negroes as a class to a completely integrated public education.
> . . . .
> The position we take in these consolidated cases is that the only adequate redress for a previously overt system-wide policy of segregation directed against Negroes as a collective entity is a system-wide policy of integration.

As illustrated above, the reasoning of Judge Wisdom in Part III that the Constitution imposes an affirmative duty to desegregate was impeccably documented. However, to persuade his brothers to adopt his view, knowing full well that his Jefferson I opinion would be considered by a full court sitting en banc because of its sweeping changes, Judge Wisdom carefully restricted his opinion to "de jure segregation," segregation that had been required by state law prior to Brown. Aware that all states in the Fifth Circuit had a de jure background and also aware that it was persuasive to argue that those states had an obligation to correct affirmatively the vestiges of a segregated school system that had been imposed by law, Judge Wisdom limited his holding to de jure segregation. The issue of the applicability of the fourteenth amendment to "de facto segregation," segregation caused by housing patterns and typical of that existing in the North and West, was not reached in Jefferson I. Ironically, therefore, while destroying one distinction that had plagued the progress of integration for years, Judge Wisdom, in differentiating between de facto and de jure segregation, created another distinction that would be used to justify differential treatment

between the South and North. And, that distinction still retards integration in the North.

The Fifth Circuit in two landmark 1972 decisions dealing with
Corpus Christi and Austin, Texas, had to again grapple with its de
facto/de jure distinction and again its decision predated the Supreme
Court in doctrinal development of desegregation law.*

Part IV of the Jefferson I opinion was devoted to demonstrating that a specific provision in the Civil Rights Act prohibiting assignment of children to schools "to overcome racial imbalance" was
meant to apply to de facto, but not to de jure segregation, further
entrenching the new distinction. Judge Wisdom also interpreted the
Civil Rights Act not to prohibit teacher desegregation. He said,
"As long as a school has a Negro faculty it will always have a
Negro student body."

Part V of the opinion upheld the HEW guidelines' use of percentages as legitimate goals by which the efficiency of desegregation
plans could be evaluated. Judge Wisdom also urged local boards
and district courts to use the technical assistance offered by HEW
under the new 1964 Civil Rights Act in preparing their new integration plans.

Part VI discussed at length the serious shortcomings present
in most freedom-of-choice plans. It detailed the elements necessary
to make a free-choice plan work. The discussion focused on such
items as speed of desegregation, mandatory annual free choice, notice, transfers, services, facilities, activities, programs, school
equalization, scheduled compliance reports and desegregation of
faculty and staff.

Part VII attached a detailed decree to be entered with respect to each of the school boards consolidated before the Court in
Jefferson I. The Court indicated that "the provisions of the decree
are intended, as far as possible, to apply uniformly throughout this
circuit in cases involving plans based on free choice of schools."
Then Judge Wisdom pointedly added, "As the Constitution dictates,
the proof of the pudding is in the eating: the proof of a school
board's compliance with constitutional standards is the result--the
performance." Lastly, the Court mandated continuing judicial surveillance by the lower federal courts in measuring performance of
school boards in their compliance with the new decree, stressing
again that the goal was "'to disestablish dual, racially segregated
school systems.'" Judge Wisdom concluded:

> Now after twelve years of snail's pace progress toward
> school desegregation, courts are entering a new era. The
> question to be resolved in each case is: How far have

---

*See discussion of the Corpus Christi and Austin cases at Part III,
Chapter 16, infra.

formerly de jure segregated schools progressed in performing their affirmative constitutional duty to furnish
equal educational opportunities to all public school children? The clock has ticked the last tick for tokenism
and delay in the name of 'deliberate speed.'

* * *

The reaction to Jefferson I was immediate, and it was intense. Praised by most legal commentators in the North, the decision was roundly condemned by politicians, school boards, some
federal judges and most of the white populace in the South. Mississippi's District Judge Cox, sitting by designation with Judges
Wisdom and Thornberry on the panel in Jefferson I, dissented vigorously. Referring to the majority as "impatient ... trailblazers"
(and later as "distinguished associates"), he called the opinion a
"mailed fist decision" that would twist "[t]he rope of liberty ...
[into] a garrote" and "in the name of protecting civil rights of some
[would] destroy civil rights and constitutional liberties of all our
citizens, their children and their children's children." He vigorously decried the overruling of the Briggs v. Elliott dictum and disagreed with the notion of an affirmative duty on the part of the states
to integrate.

The second installment of Jefferson came shortly. Because
of the revolutionary nature of the opinion in Jefferson I, an en banc
rehearing was granted. The March 29, 1967 decision of the en banc
court became known as Jefferson II. The Fifth Circuit had grown
to twelve judges, the largest appellate court in the land. They were,
in order of seniority, Tuttle, Chief Judge, and Brown, Wisdom,
Gewin, Bell, Thornberry, Coleman, Goldberg, Ainsworth, Godbold,
Dyer and Simpson, Circuit Judges. For two of the new judges,
Dyer and Simpson, Jefferson II was their first en banc decision.
All twelve judges participated in the rehearing. Although the opinion of the majority in Jefferson II was issued in a per curiam for-
mat, it is well known that Judge Wisdom was again the penman for
the Court. The per curiam opinion adopted as its own the full opinion of Judge Wisdom in Jefferson I, correcting only a few technical
matters in the Part VII attached decree. The Jefferson I holding
was succinctly summarized:

Freedom of choice is not a goal in itself. It is a
means to an end. A schoolchild has no inalienable right
to choose his school. A freedom of choice plan is but
one of the tools available to school officials at this stage
of the process of converting the dual system of separate
schools for Negroes and whites into a unitary system.
The governmental objective of this conversion is--educa-
tional opportunities on equal terms to all. The criterion
for determining the validity of a provision in a school desegregation plan is whether the provision is reasonably related to accomplishing this objective.

However, the Jefferson II per curiam opinion seemed to go even further than Jefferson I in one important respect. Not only were the currently issued HEW guidelines mandated for circuit-wide use, but district courts were also told to give "great weight" to future guidelines, "when such guidelines are applicable to this circuit and are within lawful limits." In Jefferson II, the existence of any affirmative duty to desegregate in de facto situations was expressly reserved.

Three of the twelve judges, Gewin, Bell and Godbold, vigorously dissented and Judge Coleman wrote a concurring opinion. Stunned by the sweep and impact of the new doctrine, Judge Gewin, joined by Judge Bell, protested in a powerful, articulate dissent that: "The thesis of the majority, like Minerva (Athena) of the classic myths, was spawned full-grown and full-armed. It has no substantial legal ancestors. We must wait to see what progeny it will produce."

The de facto/de jure distinction was particularly disturbing to Judge Gewin, remaining a sore point with him until the 1972 Corpus Christi and Austin decisions.* "[T]he opinion and the decree are couched in divisive terms and proceed to dichotomize the union of states into two separate and distinct parts." Judge Gewin could not understand how the Constitution could apply differently in different parts of the country. He protested:

> The Negro children in Cleveland, Chicago, Los Angeles, Boston, New York, or any other area of the nation which the opinion classifies under de facto segregation, would receive little comfort from the assertion that the racial make-up of their school system does not violate their constitutional rights because they were born into a de facto society, while the exact same racial make-up of the school system in the 17 Southern and border states violates the constitutional rights of their counterparts, or even their blood brothers, because they were born into a de jure society. All children everywhere in the nation are protected by the Constitution, and treatment which violates their constitutional rights in one area of the country, also violates such constitutional rights in another area. The details of the remedy to be applied, however, may vary with local conditions. Basically, all of them must be given the same constitutional protection. Due process and equal protection will not tolerate a lower standard, and surely not a double standard. The problem is a national one.

Judge Gewin also argued that the HEW guidelines, at at issue when the cases consolidated in Jefferson I were at the district

---

*Discussion on Corpus Christi and Austin cases is found at Part III, Chapter 16, infra.

court level,* should not have been adopted without evidentiary hearings in the appropriate district courts. He also felt that the detailed nature of the decree undercut the dignity of the district courts. Judge Gewin was further disturbed that the Jefferson I opinion called for race-mixing even if contra to the express wishes of all parties involved, including the black student. Judge Gewin also took strong issue with Judge Wisdom's conclusion that the 1964 Civil Rights Act prohibiting school assignment solely for the purpose of racial balancing applied only to de facto and not to de jure situations.

After joining in Judge Gewin's dissent, Judge Bell wrote a dissent of his own, which Judge Gewin also joined. He agreed that the goal of Brown II was a unitary system but did not agree with the compulsory integration language contained in Jefferson I. Calling Judge Wisdom's mandate of HEW guidelines on all systems "new fuel in a field where the old fire has not been brought under control," Judge Bell argued for a freedom-of-choice plan superimposed over a strict neighborhood school zoning practice. Each child would have a choice as to the school he would attend, and all children not exercising a choice to attend a school out of their neighborhood would be assigned to the school closest to their home. Judge Bell contended that serious due process problems were presented because the guidelines had been approved without lower court hearings. He argued that the new legal test of an integration plan--"one that works"--was unconstitutionally vague. And, he asserted that the de facto/de jure doctrine was unfair. He also disagreed sharply with the overruling of the Briggs v. Elliott dictum.

Judge Coleman, in a separate opinion, worried about how "not [to] wreak irreparable injury upon public schools while executing the sentence of death against compulsory segregation." Judge Coleman agreed with Judge Gewin that Briggs v. Elliott had been decided correctly and that all areas of the country should be treated the same. In a homespun but deeply felt conclusion, Judge Coleman referred to his own background:

> In conclusion, I wish to say that in my own case a burning desire to obtain an education in the face of impossible circumstances is not a theoretical experience encountered only by others. I did not have an opportunity to attend school until I was eight years of age. The delay was quite unavoidable; there simply was no school to attend at that particular time. My mother taught me how to read and write, to add and subtract. My total sympathies are with the cause of education freely available to all. This, of course, under the Constitution requires no special privileges for any group or segment of the population. I regret that where once the concern was for schools to attend we now have so much strife about the details of utilizing those so readily available.

*Prior to oral argument in Jefferson I, however, counsel had been specifically asked to brief the issues regarding the guidelines.

> What I have said herein is with the greatest deference
> for my Brethren who think otherwise. We must and shall
> continue to work together according to our individual judg-
> ments of the law. The en banc decision may portend
> more problems ahead than we have theretofor encountered.

Judge Godbold expressed fear that the percentages of integration suggested in the guidelines would become fixed requirements of
mandatory mixing. He was convinced that the Constitution does not
require race-mixing if against the wishes of all concerned. He protested:

> The collision is head-on between individual freedom
> and paternalistic authoritarianism. No more invidious
> discrimination, or improper government objective, can be
> imagined than national power setting aside the valid exer-
> cise of choice by members of a class in the name of the
> constitutional objective for which the choice was granted to
> the class in the first place.
> . . . .
> Whether Negroes are entitled to move, and wish to move,
> from the back of the bus is one thing; whether the power
> of the state is to be employed to require them to move is
> another.

Furthermore, charging that the majority had "succumbed to the
temptation to reach all issues within its sight and thereby present
a total package--complete, neat and with all corners square," Judge
Godbold asserted that the imprimatur given the guidelines was premature.

*   *   *

As is the case with many things in the Fifth Circuit, Chief
Judge John R. Brown had perhaps the last word in the Jefferson
case. In another school opinion a year after the en banc decision
in Jefferson II, he underscored the reason why Jefferson I had
adopted the HEW guidelines and why the Fifth Circuit was willing to
risk such a revolutionary departure from past school doctrine. The
Court, Chief Judge Brown said, was simply weary of the school case
struggle and hoped Jefferson I would provide a way out:

> Finally, we think it appropriate to sound these com-
> ments. We do not seek the burden or responsibility of
> school operation. We ought not to have it. By now the
> law is clear. These cases bear many service stripes in-
> cluding many trips to this Court. The aim of Jefferson
> is to lay down sufficiently definitive standards so all can
> understand and apply them. Now it should be up to school
> boards either alone in taking the initiative so obviously
> called for, or in conjunction with cooperative (it is hoped)
> efforts of parent, race or similar groups to achieve the
> goal of race-less public schools. To be sure, this puts

burdens on all sides but this too, is part of constitutional democracy. The Judiciary is not, cannot be, the universal salvor. In saying this we believe we express for the District Judge--indeed all of them--a like hope that the schools soon run without orders of any kind from Courts, Federal or State.

NOTES AND PRIMARY AUTHORITY

The primary sources for the material contained in this chapter were the decisions in Singleton I and II and Jefferson I and II, themselves: Singleton v. Jackson Mun. Sep. School Dist. (Singleton II), 355 F.2d 865 (5th Cir. 1966); Singleton v. Jackson Mun. Sep. School Dist. (Singleton I), 348 F.2d 729 (5th Cir. 1965); United States v. Jefferson County Bd. of Educ. (Jefferson II), 380 F.2d 385 (5th Cir. 1967); and United States v. Jefferson County Bd. of Educ. (Jefferson I), 372 F.2d 836 (5th Cir. 1966). Personal interviews with Judges John Minor Wisdom, Irving Goldberg and Robert Ainsworth were also helpful. Secondary sources such as Wisdom, "The Frictionmaking, Exacerbating Political Role of Federal Courts," 21 S.W.L.J. 411 (1967); Comment, 28 La. L. Rev. 455 (1968); Comment, 28 Rutgers L. Rev. 753 (1967); and Comment 77 Yale L.J. 321 (1967) were consulted.

A more complete manuscript, with detailed documentation of all sources, is available as indicated in the Preface, supra.

PART III

THE BLOODLESS REVOLUTION:
THE BROWN YEARS, 1967-1973

Judge John Minor Wisdom of New Orleans. Photo by H. J. Patterson, reproduced by permission of The Times-Picayune.

Chapter 12

THE ERA OF THE SUPER COURT

[In previous controversies we decided] that
functions of educational officers in states, counties
and school districts were such that to interfere
with their authority 'would in effect make us the
school board for the country.'
... Such Boards are numerous and their ter-
ritorial jurisdiction often small. But small and
local authority may feel less sense of responsibility to the Constitution, and agencies of publicity
may be less vigilant in calling it to account....
There are village tyrants as well as village Hamp-
dens, but none who acts under color of law is beyond the reach of the Constitution.... [T]his is
a field 'where courts possess no marked and certainly no controlling competence.'
... But we act in these matters not by authority of our competence, but by force of our
commissions. We cannot, because of modest estimates of our competence in such specialties as
public education, withhold the judgment that history
authenticates as the function of this Court when
liberty is infringed.
--Mr. Justice Robert Jackson in West Virginia
State Board of Education v. Barnette, 319
U.S. 624, 637-40 (1943).

From 1967 forward, the day arrived when, in fact, federal
courts were performing many of the functions traditionally reserved
for school administrators. Federal district judges assigned both
students and faculty to particular schools, closed schools with inadequate facilities, approved site selection for new facilities and
arbitrated grievances. By the end of this era, federal courts quite
commonly retained their own experts to draft desegregation plans
which were designed to accomplish interracial school systems, according to whatever happened to be the latest Supreme Court guide-
line. Because of "permanent" assignments to certain pending school
cases, Fifth Circuit judges became more familiar with the facilities,
demographic statistics and internal politics of their assigned systems
than they had been with their own children's schools.

In retrospect, the work of the Fifth Circuit during this third and final period under review was its most frustrating. Beginning in 1968, then in 1969, 1970, 1972 and 1973, the United States Supreme Court reasserted its prerogative of setting the pace of desegregation, and the pace it set was by no means constant or consistent. The Supreme Court provided leadership by fits and starts, difficult and even hazardous to follow. But perhaps even more significant than losing control of the pace of the South's desegregation, the United States Court of Appeals for the Fifth Circuit had to function virtually alone, without the support of many of its former allies within the executive branch of the federal government. With the advent of the Nixon administration in 1968, the Justice Department and the Department of Health, Education and Welfare lost any zeal to enforce the mandate of desegregation in the teeth of Southern political resistance. After the debacle of Mississippi cases in 1969, moreover, federal executive action might realistically be viewed as even antagonistic to the implementation of carefully wrought desegregation decisions of the Fifth Circuit.

* * *

Instructed each year in a new Supreme Court rhythm, threatened with the retreat of its valuable federal allies in enforcement, the Fifth Circuit still had unfinished work to do. There were enclaves of segregation, untouched by decisional law, which yet stood in southern Louisiana and Georgia and northern Florida, and school cases docketed in the fifties and reviewed steadily thereafter showed every sign of being permanent responsibilities. In 1967, the caseload of the Fifth Circuit had reached a critical point. It was unable to dispose of all the cases that had been filed yearly and its docket was falling further and further behind. In addition to a heavy increase of cases in every category of federal jurisdiction, the Court was instructed by the Supreme Court in 1969 to move immediately-- even in mid-year--to establish unitary school districts for all the formerly segregated school systems in the six states of the Deep South. Moreover, the expeditious treatment of civil rights cases on the Fifth Circuit dockets was a legacy of the Tuttle years. The desire to continue that Tuttle tradition, coupled with the increase in school cases, threatened to convert Court hearings into perpetual emergency sessions, exhausting the energies of even the most hardy judges. One member of the Court later remembered, "For two or three years, we never took a vacation."

Elbert Tuttle attained senior status in 1967. The mantle of Chief Judge then passed to his heir, John R. Brown of Houston, Texas, by right of seniority of service. No federal appellate judge was perhaps better suited to manage such an overburdened Court than John R. Brown. The Fifth Circuit no longer needed as its primary motivating force the personal courage of a Rives or the activism of a Tuttle, although John R. Brown indeed possessed both qualities in large measure. It needed as its leader an organizer and administrator. As Chief Judge, John Brown was to undo the Gordian knot created both by the backlog of school cases and by the

press of rapidly increasing judicial business in all areas. He
brought efficiency and phalanx battle strategy to bear on the new
crises of his Court. During his eleven years on the Court, he had
acquired far more experience than any judge before him about its
inner workings. Even as early as Chief Judge Hutcheson's rule of
the Court, Judge Brown had assisted his senior colleague from Texas
in the duty of docketing case assignments, a responsibility which he
continued to exercise under Chief Judge Rives.

Possessing a gargantuan reservoir of energy and resourcefulness, John Brown is alternatively characterized by his colleagues
as "peppery" and "warm," "sarcastic" and "charming," "forceful"
and even "pushy." But all concede the enthusiasm and wit which
he brings to all his responsibilities. His humor is often irrepressible and frequently crops up in his opinions. Sitting on a relatively
routine per curiam case concerning the question of whether a state's
attempt to regulate the marketing practices of a detergent manufacturer had been preempted by pre-existing federal regulations, Chief
Judge Brown could not restrain himself. After concurring with two
other judges in a flavorless holding that federal law was supreme
and that the contrary state regulations were thus void, John Brown
wrote a short concurring opinion which parodied the majority opinion which he had just joined:

> Clearly, the decision represents a Gamble since we risk
> a Cascade of criticism from an increasing Tide of ecology-
> minded citizens. Yet, a contrary decision would most
> likely have precipitated a Niagara of complaints from an
> industry which justifiably seeks uniformity in the laws
> with which it must comply.

It is rumored that while writing that concurring opinion Judge Brown
sent a law clerk out on an uncommon mission; to obtain from the
local supermarket a list of the names of every soap and detergent
product on its shelves.

In contrast, like Judge Wisdom, when Chief Judge Brown
feels that the legal process is being abused, he does not hesitate
to flay the offending parties with blunt language. In a Florida desegregation case, marred by years of delay, the school district
contended in 1972 that it could not comply with the district court's
injunction for immediate implementation because it did not have a
formal definition of the term "Negro." In a caustic opinion of the
Court, Chief Judge Brown commented:

> In the long march from Mansfield [the Court's earli-
> est desegregation decision] this court has seen, heard,
> or heard of everything--everything, that is, until today....
> [The Superintendent's] argument is that he cannot en-
> force the District Court's order because it contains no
> definition of what is a Negro and therefore, he contends,
> the order is vague and uncertain. Justice Douglas's state-
> ment ... sufficiently answers that argument--'One thing is

not vague or uncertain, however, and that is that those who discriminate against members of this and other minority groups have little difficulty in isolating the objects of their discrimination.' The record indicates that in the past the School District has apparently had no difficulty identifying Negroes for the purposes of segregating them. For desegregation they can be identified with similar ease.

* * *

Although the Court had lost the active services of Judges Rives and Tuttle, shortly after John Brown became Chief Judge, Congress in 1968 approved four additional judgeships for the Fifth Circuit. Thus, by 1970, with fifteen active judges, the United States Court of Appeals for the Fifth Circuit, the "Brown Court," became the largest constitutional court in the history of the Republic.

Lewis R. Morgan of Georgia. --The first new appointee to the Court was Lewis R. Morgan, he took the Georgia seat vacated when Chief Judge Tuttle attained Senior Status in 1967. Born in LaGrange, Georgia, in 1913, he completed his pre-law work at the University of Michigan and obtained a law degree from the University of Georgia. After two years of private practice in his hometown, he was elected a member of the Georgia House of Representatives in 1937, serving until the outbreak of World War II. He returned to his hometown and engaged in public service, first as City Attorney and thereafter as County Attorney until 1961.

In 1961, President Kennedy appointed Lewis Morgan a district judge for the Northern District of Georgia. Despite strong criticism from liberal quarters concerning the quality of Kennedy appointments to the federal bench, Judge Morgan has always been considered an excellent choice. While he handled no school desegregation cases as a district court judge, he shared the burden of decision-making in controversial cases in the related areas of public accommodations and voting district reapportionment.

Shortly after assuming his new judicial duties, Judge Morgan participated as a district court member in two of the three decisions rendered by three-judge courts specially designated by Chief Judge Tuttle to consider the volatile issue of a politically malapportioned Georgia. Judge Tuttle concluded that to have any chance of even minimal acceptability by politicians and citizens, a federal judicial decision declaring that the rural-dominated Georgia legislature must be reapportioned had to be issued by a court constituted with great care. Therefore, Chief Judge Tuttle designated, as the members of the three-judge court, himself, the former Republican Chairman of the state, Griffin Bell, a former executive assistant to Senator Talmadge, and Lewis Morgan, a former state legislator from a rural county. Judge Morgan also was assigned the first challenge to the constitutionality of Title II of the Civil Rights Act of 1964, which proscribed discrimination in public accommodations. An Atlanta motel owner desiring to continue his policies of not accepting

Negro guests brought suit and Judge Morgan sustained the federal statute; the United States Supreme Court later affirmed.

From these years as a district court judge sitting in a maelstrom of civil rights litigation, Judge Morgan emerged as a dependable mainstay, if somewhat conservative in judicial philosophy. In the panels on which he sat with Circuit Judges Bell and Tuttle, including the controversial refusal of the Georgia Legislature to seat Julian Bond, its first Negro member since Reconstruction, Judge Morgan aligned with Judge Bell rather than Chief Judge Tuttle. On his record, therefore, Judge Lewis Morgan was acceptable to both President Johnson and to the southern Democratic caucus; and on August 2, 1968, he was elevated to the Fifth Circuit. A latecomer to that appellate court's labors with desegregation, Judge Morgan experienced, first-hand, school problems which had festered by permitting certain areas to maintain segregation long after Brown had been proclaimed the ruling law. In Judge Morgan's own metaphor, it is more difficult to guide and discipline an adolescent who had passed through childhood with little or no interference with his activities than it would be had discipline been exacted in the child's formative years. After his appointment, Judge Morgan inherited, with Judges Bell and Thornberry, the intractable Hinds County case involving 33 segregated Mississippi counties. He also became deeply involved in the Pinellas County (Florida) case in which Governor Claude Kirk threatened to mimic George Wallace's stand in a schoolhouse door to block integration. Judge Morgan is a firm yet affable man, a favorite among colleagues, both liberal and conservative; he is a believer in consensus, rarely dissenting and usually found with the majority on most panels.

* * *

With the new Nixon administration came the famous search for "strict constructionists" of the Constitution; that search was to affect not only Supreme Court appointments but also the Fifth Circuit vacancies. Once again there was a Republican in the White House, but President Nixon, unlike President Eisenhower, felt that politically he could not afford to ignore the influence of southern Democratic Senators. Although ultimately President Nixon filled four appointments to both courts, because of the greater size of the Fifth Circuit's membership the Nixon appointments there had a lesser impact than those made to the Supreme Court. In order, the four men selected by President Nixon for appointment to United States Court of Appeals for the Fifth Circuit were Charles Clark of Mississippi, George Harrold Carswell of Florida, Joe M. Ingraham of Texas, and Paul H. Roney of Florida. Three of the four men were elevated from the federal district court bench and all were thought to be conservative in judicial philosophy.

Charles Clark of Mississippi. --The first Nixon nominee, Charles Clark, was already well-known to older members of the Court. He had appeared before the Court many times as the lawyer for the Board of Trustees of the University of Mississippi during the

James Meredith cause célèbre. While certainly a vigorous defender
of his client's policies of segregation, Clark had then earned the respect of the Court's membership in the forthright manner he disassociated his clients from the intransigent Governor Barnett.

Born in Jackson, Mississippi, Clark attended Millsaps College and Tulane University before returning to the University of
Mississippi for his law school degree in 1948. For twenty-one years
he practiced law in Jackson, serving as a special assistant to the
State Attorney General during the James Meredith struggle from
1961 through 1966. On October 17, 1969, he was appointed to the
Fifth Circuit by President Nixon.

A tall, handsome man, since his appointment Judge Clark
has become perhaps the most articulate and powerful spokesman for
those on the Court who urge adherence to the doctrine of judicial restraint. Not hesitant to dissent from a panel decision, he nonetheless thereafter generally concedes that it controls as precedent for
future cases on which he sits in judgment. Moreover, as the only
member of the Circuit Court with school-age children, Judge Clark
is personally sensitive to the impact of the Court's school decisions
on public education in the South. He was sending his children to
public schools in Jackson at the time of its system's massive integration and is acutely aware of some of the troubling academic and
disciplinary problems that can follow forced integration.

Joe McDonald Ingraham of Texas. --At the time of his appointment as the third Nixon nominee to the Court, Joe McDonald Ingraham was 66 years old. He was a native of Pawnee County, Oklahoma, and received his legal education from National University in
1927. Shortly thereafter he moved to Ft. Worth and became a member of the Texas Bar. He was named to the District Court for the
Eastern District of Texas by President Eisenhower in 1954. By the
fates of docketing, he escaped the controversial Houston desegregation case which was instead assigned to Judge Ben Connally, the
other member of the East Texas federal court. Thus, Judge Ingraham's early judicial career aroused little notoriety. In judicial
philosophy, he may be considered a moderately conservative judge
both at the district and circuit levels. Because of his advanced age
and short active service on the Court, he has had only a limited
impact on decisional law in the area of race relations. He took
senior status in the summer of 1973 and was replaced by Thomas
G. Gee of Austin, Texas, also a Nixon appointee.

Paul H. Roney of Florida. --The last Nixon nominee was Paul
H. Roney of St. Petersburg, Florida. Born in 1921, he attended
the University of Pennsylvania's Wharton School of Commerce and
Finance, where he obtained a degree in Economics. After service
in World War II, he graduated from Harvard Law School and practiced in the prestigious Wall Street firm of Root, Ballentine for
two years. He then returned to his hometown of St. Petersburg
and ultimately established his own law firm in 1957.

By nature, Judge Roney is a quiet man with a crackling dry sense of humor; he rarely speaks from the bench, instead deferring to the questioning of his more volatile colleagues. By reputation he is considered a highly intelligent, quick judge with a still unformulated judicial philosophy. Due to the new procedures of the Court under Chief Judge Brown, whereby standing panels were assigned to long-pending desegregation suits, Judge Roney has participated in only two major en banc desegregation cases, Austin and Corpus Christi, discussed later. As is the case with Judge Clark, because of his youth at the time of his appointment, Judge Roney's place in history lies still in the future.

* * *

These were four of the five new men appointed to the Brown Court, at least two of whom could be expected to serve well beyond the 1970s. The fifth appointee, Judge G. Harrold Carswell, coming chronologically between the nominations of Judge Clark and Judge Ingraham, would become probably the Circuit's most famous member, not by dint of his work as a member of the Court but because of his defeated nomination to the United States Supreme Court. The swirling public controversy in 1970 over the elevation of one of its members to the nation's highest Court caused serious internal dissension among Fifth Circuit judges, at a time when they were desperately searching for unity in implementing new Supreme Court mandates. Many misperceptions were engendered by the Carswell appointment, yet its impact upon the Court and the aspirations of other southern lawyers and judges was quite clear. In the Carswell case, the political appointment process of federal judges is perhaps most vividly portrayed.

The Carswell Fiasco

The real basis for Judge Carswell's opposition is not whether he is a white southerner, but what kind of a white southerner he is. On the nomination of Justice Thurgood Marshall, I received letters opposing him because he was a Negro; I rejected all such opposition as unworthy. Opposition is heard to Judge Carswell because he is a white southerner. I likewise reject it as unworthy. I reject all attacks based on race, religion, regionalism, or national origin....

It is unfortunate that the President by the Carswell appointment, adds to the myth that all white southern conservatives are mediocre men, or are highhanded and intolerant toward lawyers of differing views when they are placed on the Court.

--Senator Ralph Yarborough of Texas reported in Volume 116 of the Congressional Record, at page 10596 (1970).

George Harrold Carswell was born and grew up in the small town of Irwinton, Georgia. Attending Duke University in Durham, North Carolina, he graduated in 1941 and went on to the University of Georgia Law School in Athens. His law training was interrupted for three years in 1942-45 while he served in the United States Navy. After the war, he returned to law school, transferring to Mercer University in Macon, Georgia, where he graduated in 1948. He was admitted to the Georgia bar in 1948, and returned to his hometown Irwinton to run the Irwinton Bulletin, which he had also operated during his years as a Duke undergraduate. In 1948 Carswell ran for Congress against an incumbent who attacked him as "too liberal." Losing the race, he moved to his wife's hometown of Tallahassee, Florida, and associated with Ausley, Collins & Truett, the law firm of Florida's then Governor LeRoy Collins. In 1951 he and two other young attorneys formed the firm of Carswell, Cotton & Shivers. During the 1952 presidential campaign, Carswell, a Democrat, was persuaded to take Eisenhower's side in a local radio debate. Thereafter he became known as an Eisenhower spokesman in Florida. After the election he was appointed United States District Attorney for the Northern District of Florida (sitting in Tallahassee) and formally became a Republican. His Republican appointments continued without opposition; in 1958 he was appointed a Federal District Judge for the Northern District of Florida. In June, 1969, after eleven years on the district court bench, he was promoted to a seat on the Fifth Circuit. Scarcely seven months later, he was nominated by President Nixon to become an Associate Justice of the United States Supreme Court.

Given the essential outline of Judge Carswell's public career, his nomination was not surprising. President Nixon's publicly expressed nomination criteria called for a Republican Southerner presently sitting on a federal bench who was a strict constructionist, under sixty, and not personally known to Nixon. In the words of the chief talent scout for nominees, Attorney General John Mitchell, "He's just too good to be true."

Hearings on Judge Carswell's nomination began quickly, with the expectation that confirmation would follow. Even Senator Birch Bayh, who would eventually lead the Carswell opponents, felt his confirmation was assured. In questioning Judge Carswell he said, "[y]ou know that you are going to be on the Supreme Court if this nomination is confirmed, which I think it will be." Likewise, news reports contained confident predictions of confirmation: "he will very likely become the ninth and youngest member of the Supreme Court."

But before the confirmation hearings began, the national press uncovered two damaging pieces of information overlooked by the FBI and the Administration in their investigations of Carswell's background: in his abortive 1948 congressional race, Judge Carswell had made a speech containing strong white segregationist language; and, in 1956, he had been a subscriber of a corporation that was organized to take over municipal golf facilities for use by a

segregated, private country club. The nominee was questioned on
both points in the hearings.

The segregationist speech had been made 22 years previously
to the American Legion and had been reprinted by Carswell in his
newspaper. In it, Carswell declared:

> I am a Southerner by ancestry, birth, training, in-
> clination, belief and practice. I believe that segregation
> of the races is proper and the only practical and correct
> way of life in our states. I have always so believed, and
> I shall always so act. I shall be the last to submit to
> any attempt on the part of anyone to break down and to
> weaken this firmly established policy of our people.
> ...
> I yield to no man as a fellow candidate, or as a fel-
> low citizen, in the firm, vigorous belief in the principles
> of white supremacy, and I shall always be so governed.

When first confronted with the speech by CBS news, Carswell ex-
claimed "God Almighty, did I say that? It's horrible!" Later he
recanted more formally:

> Specifically and categorically, I denounce and reject
> the words themselves and the ideas they represent.
> They're obnoxious and abhorrent to my personal philoso-
> phy.

Before the Judiciary Committee, Carswell rejected the statement
again.

> I am not a racist. I have no notions, secretive, open,
> or otherwise, of racial superiority. That is an insulting
> term in itself and I reject it out of hand.

Inclined to regard the statement as political rhetoric, most
senators accepted Carswell's challenge that he be judged on the intervening years of public service. His opponents were convinced
that intervening events did not establish that Carswell had ever
really rejected his youthful segregationist philosophy; his proponents
could find nothing that convinced them he still held such beliefs.

Perhaps more troubling was Carswell's role in the establishment of a Tallahassee country club. To avoid a 1955 Supreme Court
ruling which required desegregation of public facilities, a common
practice of converting them into private facilities had grown up in
the South. There was evidence that such a practice had been followed when Tallahassee's public golf facilities were leased to a private corporation for $1.00 in 1956. Carswell had been District At-
torney at that time and was asked by the private corporation for a
subscription of $100, which he paid. He was given a certificate in
return and was listed as one of the original directors. He withdrew
six months later and received a $72 refund. He did not participate

as an officer or director or attend any meetings, although he did later join the private club for a period of three years to enable his sons to play golf. He testified that he did not discuss the segregation purposes of the corporation with anyone and that the only purpose mentioned to him at the time he subscribed was that of rejuvenating deteriorating facilities. He insisted that he had contributed out of a sense of civic responsibility.

Opposition to Judge Carswell's elevation on grounds of past support of segregation was remarkable in view of the past course of other judicial appointments. On the Supreme Court itself sat Justice Hugo Black, a long-converted, long-forgiven former member of the Alabama Ku Klux Klan. Perhaps had a Hugo Black been proposed thirty or even twenty years later than 1937, his past indiscretions would have worked the undoing of his appointment. Blacks and civil rights activists now had a strong voice in the assessment of candidates for the Supreme Court. Closer to home in the Fifth Circuit, and then sitting as a senior judge was Richard T. Rives, one of its most universally respected, much beloved liberals on civil rights issues. Yet Judge Rives had in his past law practice given legal advice to a private club of which he was a leading member about how to exclude Negroes from membership, and had counseled an Alabama Board of Registrars about how to prevent Negro voting registration. Furthermore, currently sitting beside Judge Carswell on the Fifth Circuit bench was the newly appointed Charles Clark, the former lawyer who had given aid and comfort to the official forces of segregation during armed battle over the admission of James Meredith to Ole Miss. It is ironic that those concerned about evidence of past racism in a lawyer's career would rally to prevent a Supreme Court appointment but allow an appointment to slip through to the Fifth Circuit Court of Appeals, the more influential court in the day-to-day struggle for civil rights. Furthermore, the examples of judicial metamorphosis represented by Justice Black and Judge Rives would seem to discount the certainty of any presumption that Harrold Carswell also could not rise above these ashes of racism.

However, there was some evidence that unlike Justice Black and circuit colleagues Rives and Clark, Judge Carswell had continued to display discriminatory attitudes while sitting as a federal district judge for eleven years. Several civil rights attorneys testified that Judge Carswell had exhibited disrespect to them and the Negro plaintiffs whom they represented in his courtroom. As the supervisor of NAACP's Inc. Fund attorneys in Florida testified:

> ... whenever I took a young lawyer into the State, and
> he or she was to appear before Carswell, I usually spent
> the evening before making them go through their argument
> while I harassed them, as preparation for what they would
> meet the following day.

Other testimony raised the argument that Carswell as a federal district judge had been reversed frequently in the civil rights and habeas corpus cases that he had handled and that he had moved slowly in his school desegregation cases.

Moreover, to the aid of NAACP opposition came other voices less concerned about Judge Carswell's racial attitudes than about his overall judicial record. Three distinguished law professors argued that he did not have sufficient intellectual stature to merit elevation to the Supreme Court. The most damning testimony was given by Duke Law School Professor William W. Van Alstyne who, in contrast, had previously testified for the nomination of Clement Haynsworth. In reviewing Judge Carswell's decisions, Professor Van Alstyne concluded:

> ... [I]n the cases generally ... there is simply a lack of reasoning, care, or judicial sensitivity overall, in the nominee's opinions.
>
> There is, in candor, nothing in the quality of the nominee's work to warrant any expectation whatever that he could serve with distinction on the Supreme Court of the United States.

Yet the American Bar Association's Standing Committee on the Federal Judiciary had found Judge Carswell "qualified" for appointment. Thus such derogatory assessments of Judge Carswell's judicial calibre might have passed as contrived, drawing little notice, had President Nixon's floor leaders not ignited a storm of furor in their brazen defense of the assumed quality of their candidate's "mediocrity." In a radio interview repeatedly quoted thereafter, Senator Roman Hruska of Nebraska asserted:

> Even if he were mediocre, there are a lot of mediocre judges and people and lawyers. They are entitled to a little representation, aren't they, and a little chance? We can't have all Brandeises and Frankfurters and Cardozos and stuff like that there.

Or as Senator Long of Louisiana put it:

> Does it not seem to the Senator [Bayh] that we have had enough of those upside down, corkscrew thinkers? Would it not appear that it might be well to take a B student or a C student who was able to think straight, compared to one of those A students who are capable of the kind of thinking that winds up getting us a 100 per cent increase in crime in this country.

Coalescing under the banners of suspect racial attitudes and mental mediocrity, by early March, 1970 the forces of public opposition had swelled. Unprecedented numbers of lawyers and law teachers publicly objected to the elevation of this particular nominee to the Supreme Court. Some 350 lawyers signed a petition circulated by a former judge of the New York Court of Appeals and by the president and past presidents of the Association of the Bar of the City of New York; the petitions cited Judge Carswell's civil rights attitude as the basis for opposition. Among the signers were the deans and faculty members of 42 law schools and numerous partners of prestigious law firms. Senator Yarborough presented the letters from 14 University of Texas professors against the nomination; only one letter, from Professor Charles Allen Wright, favored Carswell. Headed by Dean Acheson, a group of 206 former law clerks to Supreme Court justices sent a letter opposing Carswell's confirmation because "[t]he records show him to be of mediocre ability."

Although the nomination had been favorably reported out to the floor of the Senate by the Judiciary Committee by a vote of thirteen to four, the hearings belied a protracted struggle. On March 19, the Senate's lone Negro, Republican Edward Brooke of Massachusetts, made a Senate speech eloquently opposing Carswell's confirmation:

> We are all politicians in this body. We make speeches and sometimes we say things that, perhaps, in quieter or saner moments we might not have said. But I read that 1948 statement closely, as did the Senator from New York. I tried to put myself in the position of this man as best I could, under the circumstances prevailing at that time, to see if these were just political words or whether they went deeper.
> I found that they were deeply felt words.
> Then I examined the age of the nominee at the time the statement was made. He was 28 years old. I know we are considered to be men at 28 years of age.
> At that age, I had spent 5 years in war. In many respects, Judge Carswell and I were passing through a similar period, since we were both coming out of military service and had both gone to law school at the same time.
> I think that I was pretty much a man at 28 years of age. Today the question of lowering the voting age to 18 is being considered in this country, so that the young people can anticipate decisions, and vote in Federal, State and municipal elections at the age of 18. We now believe that young people are mature and responsible. Certainly they are intelligent and aware of their surroundings. And I do not believe the times were so different 20 years ago. Thus, I do not believe a man is or was immature at 28. There may be some exceptions, but Harrold Carswell was a man who had been trained in the law.
> Then I said, 'Well, a man can change.'
> Men do change.
> Great social changes have taken place in this country. The spirit of the time of Pope John XXIII and the Ecumenical Council changed the minds of many people in this country as well as in the world. I said, 'Let us look for that change.' As I am sure the Senator from New York did, I searched the record looking for that change. But I must confess, regrettably, that I did not find any. In fact, I found considerable evidence to the contrary. I found that in periods along the way in Judge Carswell's public career,

he had made statements and had acted and conducted his
court in a manner which indicated to me that there was no
change, that he still harbored racist views.
Then I thought about our country. Where is our country going today? Many things that have been happening in
this country recently, including the statements of some of
our highest political leaders made me think, Are [sic] we
really moving, as the Kerner Commission report suggested,
toward two societies, one black and one white?
Do we really want war between the races of this Nation?
Did President Nixon really mean it when he said he
would bring us together?

This speech was new inspiration for those opposing Judge
Carswell's nomination. It accentuated the questioning in the minds
of those yet uncommitted about where the other judges of the Fifth
Circuit stood on the issue of the elevation of their colleague. Surely these men who had reviewed Judge Carswell's decisions for eleven
years, and who had known him for almost a year as a fellow Circuit Judge, could be a decisive influence upon the debated issues of
Judge Carswell's judicial behavior. There was precedent in the
Fifth Circuit for involvement by the judges in confirmation proceedings involving one of their own. When Judge Homer Thornberry
was nominated by President Johnson to the Supreme Court (to fill
the vacancy which would have been created by the proposed elevation of Associate Justice Abe Fortas as Chief Justice), Chief Judge
Brown had written a strong letter of support to President Johnson.
Impressed with Chief Judge Brown's letter, President Johnson requested that Senator Yarborough place a copy in the Congressional
Record. Judge Brown's letter on behalf of Homer Thornberry had
stated that, while he could not speak for his Court on a matter as
important as the nomination of one of their members to be a Supreme
Court Justice, he could indicate his own personal support for Judge
Thornberry which he felt would be shared by his brothers. When
the Carswell nomination was first announced, several judges on the
Fifth Circuit indicated their willingness to testify in support of their
brother, despite his brief tenure on the Fifth Circuit bench. One
of the Fifth Circuit judges who was supporting Judge Carswell actively requested that Chief Judge John R. Brown circulate a proposed telegram, to be signed by all Fifth Circuit members, en-
dorsing the nomination. Judge Brown replied that he would favor
such a telegram if it were unanimous; he pointed out that less than
unanimous support would hurt Judge Carswell.

Support was less than unanimous; Judge Wisdom reacted
strongly to the proposed telegram and indicated that not only would
he not sign it but he would disassociate himself from it publicly if
it were sent. The opposition of Judge Wisdom ended the telegram
proposal as far as Chief Judge Brown was concerned. Unfortunately
for Judge Carswell, the Press discovered that a telegram of support
might be forthcoming. Reporters pursued Chief Judge Brown from
a Washington, D.C. judicial meeting to Abilene, Texas, where he

was to attend the funeral of a family member. In Abilene, Judge
Brown issued a statement which revealed the split in opinion of his
colleagues on the proposed elevation of their brother to the Higher
Court. He indicated that some judges supported the nomination and
some did not; therefore, the judges as a group would not take a
stand on the matter. Consequently, in contrast to the Thornberry
nomination, the lack of public support given by the Fifth Circuit
judges, as a body, to their colleague became significant.

As embarrassing as the lack of united support from colleagues
on the Fifth Circuit was for both the Court and Judge Carswell, the
most excruciating episode concerned the withdrawal of public endorsement by former Chief Judge Tuttle.

With several other judges of the Fifth Circuit, Judge Tuttle had sent a letter dated January 22, before the battle became intense, to Senator Eastland, offering to testify before the Senate Judiciary Committee on behalf of Harrold Carswell. He wrote then:

> I have been intimately acquainted with Judge Carswell
> during the entire time of his service on the Federal bench,
> and am particularly aware of his valuable service as an
> appellate judge, during the many weeks he has sat on the
> Court of Appeals both before and after his appointment to
> our court last summer. I would like to express my great
> confidence in him as a person and as a judge.
> My particular reason for writing you at this time is
> that I am fully convinced that the recent reporting of a
> speech he made in 1948 may give an erroneous impression
> of his personal and judicial philosophy, and I would be pre-
> pared to express this conviction of mine based upon my
> observation of him during the years I was privileged to
> serve as Chief Judge of the Court of Appeals for the Fifth
> Circuit.

Five days later, however, the press reported a story, dealing with the segregated Tallahassee country club, which lent considerable doubt to the issue of Judge Carswell's candor and integrity
in his appearance before the Senate Judiciary Committee. Apparently this new development was sufficient to sway Judge Tuttle to
withdraw public support. On that day, January 28, 1970, Judge
Tuttle telephoned Judge Carswell and told him he would not come to
testify. But quietly and privately withdrawing his support proved
more difficult than the giving. At the close of the proceedings just
the day before, Senator Eastland as Committee Chairman had placed
Judge Tuttle's letter, along with other endorsements, into the official record. Despite his having personally communicated his withdrawal to Judge Carswell, Judge Tuttle had not talked to spokesmen
for Judge Carswell or officially retracted his endorsement of record.

Because of former Chief Judge Tuttle's distinguished record
as a champion of civil rights, the recorded Tuttle endorsement of
Carswell had been constantly used in rebuttal to the attacks mounted

by lawyers and law professors. Finally on March 3, a report appeared in the Atlanta Constitution that Chief Judge Tuttle had informed Carswell he could not testify for him, but did not want to hurt his chances publicly. The article stated that Judge Carswell had solicited Judge Tuttle's help but that Judge Tuttle had withdrawn his support because of the revelation concerning Judge Carswell's involvement in the country club and land development covenants. Hearing of this article a few weeks later, Senator Tydings asked Tuttle to confirm his position. In a series of telegrams from Judge Tuttle, released to the press by Senator Tydings, the public disavowal of support by the former Chief achieved disproportionate importance on the eve of a mounting momentum to block confirmation of Judge Carswell in the Senate. Two days later Judge Wisdom's private refusal to endorse Judge Carswell became public knowledge. Judge Wisdom flatly told a television interviewer that he never intended to support Carswell. "I stand with Tuttle," he said.

The Congressional Record contains a letter solicited by Deputy Attorney General Kleindienst listing 50 of the 58 active district judges and seven of thirteen retired district judges as supporting the nomination. In addition, just before the vote for confirmation, the Carswell forces succeeded in persuading ten of the fourteen active Fifth Circuit judges to write President Nixon supporting Judge Carswell. However, the silence of Chief Judge Brown, and the public refusal of support by Judge Wisdom, and the highly publicized retraction of Judge Tuttle, as the Court's stalwart liberals, may have overshadowed the endorsements of other judges of less renown and national influence.

Subsequently, as history records, the Carswell nomination was defeated in the Senate by a vote of 51-45, just three votes shy of the majority needed for confirmation. The elevation of Judge Carswell had been defeated by a curious combination of forces and events no one of which, taken alone, would have been sufficient to block his appointment. Judge Carswell's own testimony kindled concern about his integrity, and his own spokesmen, by failing to confirm endorsements and hasty retorts about mediocrity, did perhaps more than his antagonists to engineer his defeat.

But there were portents of greater concern to the South and its federal judges latent in the defeat of Harrold Carswell. While few judges would decline a Supreme Court nomination, some were more openly ambitious. The federal bench is a reservoir of talent and experience from which many judges have been tapped for elevation to the Highest Court. Furthermore there had been a Southerner on that tribunal since its earliest days, beginning with the appointments of Justices John Blair and James Iredell in 1789-90. With Mr. Justice Black in failing health, a position seemed, in equity, to belong to a Southerner. Yet with the defeat of the Carswell nomination, the Supreme Court aspirations of any judges in the Fifth Circuit seemed dashed. For those conservative Republican judges who, like Judge Carswell, had a past record of involvement in the South's segregated society, the prospect of surviving close scrutiny

seemed extraordinarily hazardous. For those Republican liberals
still on the court, notably Chief Judge Brown and Judge Wisdom,
their activist stance on civil rights disqualified them even from
Presidential consideration. The Republican landslide of 1972 and
the disarray of the national Democratic party over the question of
minority representation seemed to remove even the possibility of
consideration for those Democratic judges in the Fifth Circuit. The
civil rights movement had exacted another toll from the judges embroiled in its battles.

*   *   *

The Spring of 1970 was fresh with renewed problems for the
Fifth Circuit judges. The internal acrimony created by the Carswell nomination and rejection reopened philosophical antagonisms
that observers believed had been forgotten in the intervening years
since the James Meredith affair. Residual bitterness over Judge
Carswell's humiliation would linger between certain judges, concealed only by the façade of judicial decorum. But the principal
victim was Carswell himself. Although originally upon his denial
of confirmation Judge Carswell had announced he would remain on
the Fifth Circuit, two months thereafter he abruptly resigned to
seek the Republican nomination for the United States Senate in the
Florida Republican primary. Defeated in his political bid, G. Harrold Carswell again became a federal judicial officer, assuming a
post as a Referee in Bankruptcy in Tallahassee, Florida. In 1976
Judge Carswell's name again surfaced in the national press; it was
reported that he was arrested on a morals charge involving an off-
duty police officer.

Court Congestion and the Conservation of Judicial Energy: Summary Disposition and Standing Panels

Those courts are wise who make a standard
practice of sorting out some proportion of their
cases for memorandum opinions, thus mobilizing
resources for more solid effort where more solid
effort is needed....
But the easing of the load by way of sifting
and non-discussion comes at a price in care and
responsibility--a price which reminds us of the
reason for both the older practice and those statutes which demand opinions. The candor which in
a full opinion forbids ignoring an uncomfortable
authority must scorn equally its disregard in silence by way of a Per Curiam. The task of
smithying discordant materials into some working
harmony is not to be ducked by pretense that it
is not there; nor does it square with appellate judicial duty to make new law, deliberately without
open accounting not only to the fact of the old but

to the reason for the new. Summary Per Curiam
is properly the portion only of a case which is in
essence clear not only as to outcome but as to adequate ground as well; and no line of worry about
our Supreme Court seems to me to compare in
solidity with the fear that in Per Curiams, there
may be developing some leak in the dike of restraint
against unwarranted resort to unaudible secrecy.
--Karl Llewellyn, The Common Law Tradition,
312-313 (1960)

The key to understanding John R. Brown's administration as
Chief Judge of the Fifth Circuit is to recognize his almost compul-
sive desire "to get the job done." With Singleton I and II and Jefferson I and II on the books and with the Supreme Court demanding
immediate enforcement of its desegregation mandates, Chief Judge
Brown took command with marching orders, in his own words, to
"ride roughshod" to complete the job of school integration in the
Deep South.

Borrowing liberally from experience in other circuits and
combing scholarly literature, John Brown became a judicial administrator without parallel in the federal appellate system. His court
evolved into a matrix of new expediting procedures. His persistence
brought his court's docket up to date, prodded his colleagues into
better use of their time, and enabled the Fifth Circuit to meet the
new demands of the Supreme Court in the school area. Out of its
"crisis" the Fifth Circuit became a beacon to all courts with overcrowded dockets. In his definitive work on "Screening and Summary
Procedures in the United States Courts of Appeals," Professor
Charles R. Haworth flatly states, "[T]he Fifth Circuit has established
the most far-reaching screening and summary procedures of any
circuit."

One of the most time-consuming aspects of appellate litigation is the hearing of oral argument from counsel. Traditionally,
each side in an appeal from a district court judgment is accorded
between 30 to 45 minutes of oral argument before a panel of three
sitting judges. Moreover, due to the large area encompassed by the
Fifth Circuit, almost every schedule of oral argument requires extensive travel to assemble the judges in panels of three. The random assignment of judges to certain panels and allotting time for
oral argument in every appeal was only by tradition circuit court
policy; nowhere in the federal statutory law governing appellate procedure were such practices mandated. In fact, the Federal Rules
vested broad powers of self-regulation to the circuit courts. Chief
Judge Brown appointed a Committee composed of Judge Bell, as
Chairman, and Judges Ainsworth and Dyer, to make proposals for
new case screening procedures.

The resulting changes were comprehensive, touching virtually
all of the Court's daily operations. First, the mammoth fifteen-
judge Court was divided into five standing panels, each composed of

three judges. Ultimately, through Chief Judge Brown's insistence, three-judge panels were assigned to particular school cases and were told that they would remain on that case until its final disposition. Therefore, on complex school matters, a circuit judge knows that his responsibility for a particular case will not end until the school district has adopted an effective unitary plan. Even Judge Cameron might have been less tolerant of delay and evasion had he known that he would have to review a particular board's diversionary practices, virtually limitless in configuration, ad infinitum.

Permanent case assignments represented an enormous saving in judicial energy since panel members could draw upon their own prior study of the controversy as background for current problems demanding resolution on appeal. Thus, over years of review, panel members became experts on the peculiar problems of Jackson, Mississippi, Savannah, Georgia, or whatever their particular assignments included. One potential hazard, at least, in the new system of standing or permanent panels was the loss of cross-fertilization of ideas and insights among all fifteen members who, under the traditional method of random assignment, would sit at one time or another with all colleagues. Similarly, the new system, unchecked, might also permit a "runaway" panel--a panel whose control of the progress of school desegregation in particular cases was inconsistent with the prevailing stance assumed by other panels, unilaterally either demanding too little or demanding too much of a local school district.

To guard against these possible dangers in the new system of standing panels, the practice was adopted whereby each panel would circulate its tentative desegregation opinions among all circuit judges on other panels. This modification allowed the various standing panels assigned to school cases to keep abreast of the law as it was being simultaneously developed by other panels in the Circuit.

Secondly, the Court of Appeals under Chief Judge Brown established elaborate case screening procedures. Under the new system, shortly after an appeal is docketed, it is assigned, on a strict rotation basis, to a single judge on each panel who assumes responsibility for screening the merits of the particular controversy. After review of the appellate record and briefs, the screening judge classifies the case into one of four major categories: those which appear totally frivolous; those which do not seem to demand further presentation by oral argument (regardless of whether or not a substantial question of law is presented); those in which further oral explication is warranted but fifteen minutes per side seems adequate for presentation; and finally, those that will require full exploration in the traditional manner of allocating thirty minutes of oral argument to each side.

The new screening procedures, adopted by the Fifth Circuit through John Brown's urging, have been important in enabling the Circuit to stay abreast of its case load in all categories of appeals.

Furthermore, as the Fifth Circuit has become more confident of its screening procedures and more and more appeals have been filed, those procedures have been more extensively utilized.* Only by extensive use of screening procedures has the Court been able to catch up and stay abreast of its caseload.

While it seems clear from the statistics involved that the Fifth Circuit could not continue to function with its present case load without screening devices, strenuous objections to screening procedures have been raised by lawyers throughout the Circuit. They charge, perhaps unfairly, that John Brown's court is more concerned with efficiency and disposition of filed cases than with administering justice in each and every controversy. Many lawyers have complained that oral judgment is an essential part of the appellate process and that they are being shortchanged, and their clients inadequately represented, when oral argument is not available. In support, they cite the court's own statistics which indicate that there has been a marked drop in the reversal rate of district court decisions, by the Fifth Circuit, since extensive employment of the various screening procedures began. Some lawyers also charge that a drop in reversals is evidence that their clients are receiving a lower quality of justice. Others, however, candidly concede that the decrease could just as accurately be interpreted as evidence that there are many less than meritorious appeals filed by litigious counsel.

Moreover, many of the Fifth Circuit judges are also concerned about the number of cases that are decided without oral argument. Nevertheless, the procedures do seem to insure that exceptional caution will be taken before a case receives that disposition. Furthermore, without the efficiency brought to the Court by such procedures, John Brown's circuit would be hopelessly backlogged. Chief Judge Brown reacts with some impatience to the adverse criticism: because of the number of cases entitled to expedited treatment, including criminal cases and many categories of civil rights cases, he asserts that without such screening devices, the appeal of a normal civil matter might never be decided.

In addition to case screening innovation, by mid-career Chief Judge Brown had become a convert committed to brevity in opinion-writing. After fifteen years of desegregation cases, Judge Brown concluded that all that could be written about school litigation had already been written. He therefore urged his colleagues to write a

---

*For example, of the 667 cases filed between December, 1968 and June, 1969, the first full year the procedures were in effect, 32.7 per cent of 218 cases were assigned to Classes I or II--the categories not requiring oral argument. In fiscal year 1970, 38.1 per cent of the 1,187 cases filed were decided without oral argument. In fiscal year 1971, 45.7 per cent of the 1,428 case filings were decided without oral argument; in 1972, 59.1 per cent of the 1,777 case filings were decided without oral argument.

minimum of opinions and to enforce school desegregation mandates by "opinion orders," most of which consisted of preemptory reversals on statistics showing prima facie an insufficient amount of desegregation had been achieved by the means used. Chief Judge Brown also repeatedly cautioned against the use of contentious verbal symbols in school orders. As a result of concurrence in this advice, emotionally laden terms such as "busing" and "racial balancing" are conspicuously absent in the Court decisions in 1968, 1969, and 1970. Chief Judge Brown argued that loaded terms and written opinions only drew dissents, split the Court, and unduly prolonged litigation. It was his firm conviction that now was the time to enforce overdue mandates, not plow new legal fields.

As a result of Chief Judge Brown's influence, and his strong skepticism of the value of opinion writing in the Grand Manner, the Circuit also adopted local Rule 21--which became its most controversial procedural change. Rule 21 provides that lower court judgments or orders may be affirmed or enforced without written opinions by the appellate panel. Rule 21 dispositions have never been used in school cases; however, its existence has enabled the Fifth Circuit to dispose of other cases more rapidly, thus allowing it to devote more attention to school matters. The one-sentence Rule 21 appellate decisions have, however, been used by the Court in other race relations decisions and obviously such a procedure has great value in expediting the rendition of the Court's mandate.

The proponents of such a short-hand opinion assert that many appeals are of such a nature that the federal district court decision is either clearly correct or, at least, is based on a factual determination that is sufficiently supported by the record. In such cases the Fifth Circuit simply affirms the lower court with a reference to Rule 21. That reference means that the Fifth Circuit is adopting the lower court opinion as its own. On the other hand, the Rule 21 procedure remains a target for vigorous criticism by attorneys. They frequently charge that Rule 21 is a ruse which allows the Fifth Circuit to avoid its homework; they argue that the Fifth Circuit should be required in every case to explain the rationale supporting its decisions. The Supreme Court has indicated that its lower appellate courts should not resort to such summary dispositions, without opinion, where they are reversing, as opposed to affirming, district court decisions. However, since the Rule 21 procedure is explicitly limited to affirmances of a district court decision and accompanying opinion, presumably the Supreme Court would sanction it as an available alternative to the traditional appellate opinion.

During 1968, the year in which John R. Brown's circuit first adopted Rule 21, there were only twenty-four cases decided without an opinion. After two years of operation under that rule, Judge Brown reminded his court that it "must be sparingly used." However, by 1972, 488 decisions were disposed of without opinion under Rule 21 procedures. By 1974, with an almost unmanageable caseload, Rule 21 procedures have come to be utilized by the Fifth

Circuit far more extensively than even Judge Brown anticipated when he urged its adoption as a tool leading to judicial efficiency.

In the early sixties, when Chief Judge Tuttle urged his colleagues to accept what were then novel procedures of emergency hearings and expedited appellate review, an enormous controversy flared, with protests filed from both within and without the Court. By the end of the decade, expedited scheduling in school cases had become the express policy of the Court; and, in 1969, the pace of appellate review was accelerated almost to its outer limit of capability. In a new court policy adopted by the Fifth Circuit Judicial Council, effective December 2, 1969, an expedited record and briefing schedule was imposed on the district judges as well as on counsel and the parties. The new schedule assured that school cases would reach the Fifth Circuit within thirty to forty days after the trial court's order and in a posture for immediate decision by the Circuit Court. School cases were then placed on a school roster by the clerk and assigned to one of the standing three-judge panels for disposition. As has been indicated, each panel assigned a school case was responsible for that case for whatever number of appeals, months or years were necessary to desegregate fully the particular district involved and transform it into a unitary school system. The expedited procedures in school cases also drew attorney criticism. At one point the Justice Department even suggested that the Court drop expedited time schedules in school cases, arguing that while some plans could be implemented without delay, others contained legal problems that deserved more extended treatment. Despite such criticism, expedited procedures for school cases remain in effect in the Fifth Circuit.

* * *

As a consequence of the combined effect of these procedures, the Brown Court took giant strides toward massive desegregation of school systems of the Deep South. From December, 1969 to September 24, 1970, the Fifth Circuit handed down 166 opinion orders involving eighty-nine separate school districts (see Appendix C, for more complete statistics). Some of those school districts had two or three separate appeals in that same time period. For example, in the Mississippi cases involving Hinds and Alexander counties, the standing panel of Judges Bell, Thornberry, and Morgan may have set a judicial record that will never be surpassed: they wrote fifty-seven opinions in those Mississippi cases alone. In contrast to the Fifth Circuit, the next closest circuit in school assignment case load was the Fourth, which had 18 school cases during the same time period, only three of which were handled on an expedited basis. Moreover, the new screening and abbreviated opinion procedures have had enormous impact upon the efficiency of the members of the Court. In 1968, the average Fifth Circuit judge wrote 61 opinions. In 1969, he wrote 72; in 1970 he wrote 82; in 1971 he wrote 107 and in 1972 he wrote 116. In short, the judicial output in the Fifth Circuit has increased 90.1 per cent since 1968 when Judge Brown initiated his screening and summary procedures in the Fifth

Circuit. And the monumental procedural changes adopted by the
Circuit Court have not gone unnoticed by the Supreme Court. Chief
Justice Burger, also an advocate of efficiency in judicial administration, has given high praise to the screening and summary procedures
developed in the Fifth Circuit.

The Fifth Circuit Court of Appeals, from 1967 forward, entered into a new era of streamlined judicial decision-making. In
contrast, the Tuttle Court of the previous decade, geared up then
far beyond anything contemporary court-watchers had seen in the
past, seems slow and ponderous. The Tuttle era may be characterized by its agonizing en banc decision-making, a collegial rift
with doctrinal disputes which spread out over hundreds of pages of
the Federal Reporters in majority opinions, special concurrences,
and dissents. Its experimentation was tentative, on a case by case
basis, seeking out the consensus which would bring the Court together and yet render speedy justice. In the era of the Brown
Court, the en banc hearing had become an endangered species: the
new Chief urged that convening the full fifteen-member Court exacted enormous tolls in precious time, expense, and dislocation of
judges, caused endless opinion writing delays, splintered the Court,
exposed its internal differences, and was an anachronistic process
in a time in which further delay in integration would no longer be
tolerated by the Supreme Court.

Within ten years and with a change of command, a quiet
revolution had occurred almost imperceptibly and yet inexorably.
Chief Judge Brown's passion for efficiency, his enthusiasm for
statistics and sound administration, and his willingness to expand
upon the innovative experimentation begun by his predecessor, not
only enabled the Court to meet the enormous demands made upon it
in the area of school desegregation but also created the most efficient appellate court in the United States.

NOTES AND PRIMARY AUTHORITY

The primary sources for the material contained in this chapter were: Interviews with judges on the United States Court of Appeals for the Fifth Circuit; the Congressional Record; Hearings on
Nomination of George Harrold Carswell Before the Senate Comm.
on the Judiciary, 91st Cong., 2d Sess. (1970); The Federal Rules of
Appellate Procedure; Haworth, "Screening and Summary Procedures
in the United States Court of Appeals," 1973 Wash. U.L.Q. 257;
Burger, Report on Problems of the Judiciary 93 S.Ct. (see miscel-
laneous section) (1972); Wright, "The Overloaded Fifth Circuit: A
Crisis in Judicial Administration," 42 Tex. L. Rev. 949 (1964);
Note, "Judicial Performance in the Fifth Circuit, 73 Yale L.J. 90
(1963); and contemporary news accounts, such as those contained in
95 Time, Feb. 2, 1970, at 9; and the Atlanta Constitution, March
3, 1970, §A, at 8, col. 1. Reported decisions of the Fifth Circuit
and other courts were also utilized.

The book Decision, by R. Harris (1971), is an excellent source for those interested in a more detailed treatment of the Carswell nomination and subsequent rejection; it has been of significant aid to the writers of this work in this brief treatment of the Carswell matter.

A more complete manuscript, with detailed documentation of all sources, is available as indicated in the Preface, supra.

Chapter 13

DO IT NOW!

Less than a year after John Minor Wisdom's monumental opinions in Singleton I and II and Jefferson I and II mandated uniform HEW guidelines on all federal district courts in the Fifth Circuit, the Supreme Court changed the ground rules for school cases. In the early years after Brown II, the Supreme Court appeared content to observe from the sidelines as its lower federal courts in the South evolved methods of desegregation under Brown II's "all deliberate speed" standard. However, during the sixties, the Supreme Court grew increasingly impatient with the slow pace of desegregation in the South. Supreme Court Justices became incensed by the innumerable delays and obstructions placed in the path of effective desegregation. There were repeated signals that the Supreme Court would soon reexamine its "deliberate speed" language in Brown II and order the pace of desegregation accelerated. At last, the Supreme Court acted. On May 27, 1968, eleven months after John R. Brown became Chief Judge of the Fifth Circuit, the Supreme Court decided Green v. County School Board of New Kent County. That case initiated a major new emphasis on immediate integration and marked the end of freedom-of-choice plans as a judicially sanctioned method of desegregation.

The "Green" Case: Freedom of Choice's Death Sentence

New Kent County was a small rural county in eastern Virginia with no residential segregation and a student population divided almost equally between blacks and whites. Traditionally operating a dual school system, New Kent County had been subject to a court-ordered freedom-of-choice plan since 1965. There were only two schools in the entire system: the school on the east side of the county for whites; the school on the west side of the county for blacks. No attendance zones existed in the county. White students were bussed from one end of the county to the other, as were black students. At the time the Supreme Court decided the case on May 27, 1968, no white students had ever chosen to attend the black school under the New Kent County's freedom-of-choice plan. Only 115 black pupils had enrolled in the formerly all-white school. This left eighty-five per cent of the black students in the school system attending the one all-black school. Mr. Justice Brennan, on behalf of a unanimous Supreme Court, stated that those facts established that Virginia

472

... acting through the local school board and school officials, organized and operated a dual system, part 'white' and part 'Negro.'

The Supreme Court further held that the purpose of the Brown decisions was to command a transition from a dual system of segregated schools to a unitary nonracial system of public education. Noticing that during the first years after Brown II the principal focus of federal courts had been to require local school boards to provide a desegregated education for those few Negro children "courageous enough to break with tradition," the Supreme Court said that token desegregation was only the beginning step in the process toward unitary nonracial education. The Court indicated that it would measure New Kent County's freedom-of-choice plan by its effectiveness in reaching the goal of a unitary nonracial educational system for all school children in the county. School boards that had operated state-compelled dual systems were "charged with the affirmative duty to take whatever steps might be necessary to convert to a unitary system in which racial discrimination would be eliminated root and branch" (emphasis added).

The Supreme Court then reformulated the Brown II mandate in imperative terms, heralding the beginning of a new era of desegregation: "The burden on a school board today is to come forward with a plan that promises realistically to work, and promises realistically to work now." In addition to its emphasis on immediacy, the reformulated Brown II mandate in Green v. New Kent County crippled the further utility of so-called freedom-of-choice plans which were being uniformly adopted throughout the South. The Court held that where a freedom-of-choice plan offers real promise of achieving a unitary nonracial system there might be no objection to allowing it to be proved in action. But it further indicated that under the facts in Green, the New Kent County freedom-of-choice plan offered no reasonable hope of achieving a unitary nonracial system; therefore, freedom of choice was not acceptable. New Kent County had an obligation to use other methods of desegregation that would be effective: "The Board must ... fashion steps which promise realistically to convert promptly to a system without a 'white' school and a 'Negro' school, but just schools."

Two other school cases decided by the Supreme Court the same day as Green reemphasized the obligation of school boards to move forward with integration plans that promised "realistically to work now." Both a freedom-of-choice plan in Arkansas, similar to the New Kent County plan, and a "free-transfer plan" in Jackson, Tennessee were held ineffective. Under the free-transfer plan, school zones were established but any child not content with his assigned zone could transfer to another school. All white children residing in Negro school zones in Jackson, Tennessee, had transferred to the nearest white school. Only a very few black children in white zones stayed in white schools.

*   *   *

After Green, the Court of Appeals for the Fifth Circuit knew that its well-laid plans in Singleton I and II and Jefferson I and II were in serious jeopardy. If freedom of choice did not "work," despite meticulous adherence to HEW guidelines, the federal courts would be forced to reevaluate those school systems. New plans would have to be adopted which in fact did work. Close scrutiny of the Supreme Court opinion in Green indicated that the freedom-of-choice plan there was held ineffective essentially because it produced integration of only fifteen per cent of the Negro students into the all-white school. After Green, therefore, federal courts naturally focused their attention on the percentage of race-mixing already achieved. Statistics became the prime indicator of whether a de-segregation plan promised "realistically to work now." Of deep concern to the Fifth Circuit was the fact that the fifteen per cent integration figure achieved in New Kent County, Virginia was sub-stantially above the integration percentages achieved under most freedom-of-choice plans in operation in the Deep South. Therefore, the efforts of the Fifth Circuit in Singleton I and II and Jefferson I and II had a very short life indeed as far as the applicability of HEW guidelines to freedom-of-choice plans was concerned. The Fifth Circuit realized that it had not escaped from school cases, as hoped, but rather it was back in the school business under far more imperative requirements.

The Supreme Court's decision in Green created grave new problems of interpretation for the Fifth Circuit. While it was clear that freedom-of-choice plans which did not "work" would not suffice, the freedom-of-choice concept was not expressly disapproved. A new wave of litigation testing the continued viability of freedom-of-choice plans followed. Further, the Supreme Court had not defined what was meant when it said that a plan had to "work." Were statistics showing the percentage of race-mixing to be the sole cri-terion of workability of desegregation plans? The term "unitary school district" also was not defined with particularity. Any ambi-guity that could be found which might conceivably justify further liti-gation and delay implementation of new desegregation measures was exploited by the polished procrastinators running local school boards. Placed by Green under new marching orders to require adoption of desegregation plans that "promised realistically to work now," the Fifth Circuit was not given a clear mandate which would enable it to enforce more effective integration without a tangle of further liti-gation.

The Circuit did receive some enlightenment from the Su-preme Court a year after Green in United States v. Montgomery County Board of Education as to one of the factors necessary in the establishment of a unitary school district. In that case the Su-preme Court reviewed Judge Frank Johnson's desegregation orders affecting Montgomery County, Alabama. The Fifth Circuit had previously reviewed Judge Johnson's meticulous order and affirmed it for the most part. However, in one part of his orders Judge Johnson had issued explicit guidelines on faculty desegregation. He basically ordered that the faculty of each school in the school district be required to have the same ratio of black and white teachers as the ratio of black and white teachers employed in the entire district. Judge Gewin, in a cautious opinion joined by District Judge Elliott, reversed Judge Johnson's order as to the required faculty ratio, holding that such a "quota" system was too explicit. The Fifth Circuit then held that the school board need only strive for greater faculty desegregation. Judge Thornberry dissented from the panel's reversal of Judge Johnson's faculty desegregation order. The Supreme Court reversed Judge Gewin's opinion for the Fifth Circuit and reinstated Judge Frank Johnson's faculty desegregation order in toto. Thereafter, as far as faculty integration was concerned, the Supreme Court obviously approved of absolute racial balancing of a faculty as a valid step toward desegregation. Chastened by its reversal, the Fifth Circuit began mandating Frank Johnson-type faculty ratio desegregation orders throughout the Circuit.

Even before the Supreme Court's Green opinion, there were signs that some of the judges on the Fifth Circuit were becoming impatient with the obvious ineffectiveness of freedom-of-choice plans. While normally applying the Jefferson II decree rigorously, the Fifth Circuit occasionally approved methods of desegregation other than freedom-of-choice. Judge Homer Thornberry, new on the bench but becoming from the beginning a consistently strong supporter of rigorous civil rights enforcement, mandated a strict neighborhood school plan in Davis v. Board of School Commissioners of Mobile County. That case dropped all freedom-of-choice provisions.

Furthermore, some judges on the Fifth Circuit became concerned with side effects of school plans that reentrenched segregated school practices. Judge Rives and District Judge Connally approved a district court order allowing Houston to go ahead with a major school construction program financed by a large voter-approved school bond issue, even though location of many of the new schools would solidify segregation. Judge Wisdom dissented vigorously:

> There is a bridge under construction, resting on the Constitution, connecting whites and Negroes and designed to lead the two races, starting with young children, to a harmonious, peaceful, civilized existence. That bridge is a plan for equal educational opportunities for all in an integrated, unitary public school system based on school administrators affirmatively finding ways to make the plan work.
> Black nationalists and white racists to the contrary, school integration is relevant. It is an educational objective as well as a constitutional imperative.

The kind of commitment evidenced by Judge Wisdom's dissent in objecting to the location of new schools began to permeate the Circuit. In exasperation, Chief Judge Brown exploded openly in United States v. Board of Education of the City of Bessemer:

> [The Court] has the right--indeed it has the duty--in the

face of facts showing little, if any, compliance to cry out
in a juridically scriptural way to those on whom its orders
pin the burden: 'When, oh when? What is being done?
What, exactly what are you going to do? Not what are
your hopes?'

* * *

In Chief Judge Brown's view, the period between Green and
the next burst of activity in the United States Supreme Court was the
most interesting in the history of the Fifth Circuit's school desegregation efforts. Certainly, it was the most frantic. In that seventeen-month period between Green and Alexander v. Holmes County
Board of Education, the Fifth Circuit reached its peak in both activity and inventiveness. Vigorously pushing desegregation pursuant to
the Green mandate, it was at the same time seeking innovative ways
to force school districts to come forward with plans that promised
"realistically to work now." The Circuit focused more and more
on the "figures"--what would be the percentage of integration if a
particular proposed school board plan were approved? Because of
Green's indication that fifteen per cent integration was not enough,
the percentage of black children attending previously all-white schools
became the critical factor. Dissenting from the Fifth Circuit's refusal to rehear en banc Judge Gewin's reversal of Judge Johnson
when he ordered faculty ratios in Montgomery County, Chief Judge
Brown stated succinctly what was to become the overriding concern
of the Circuit: "The result is in figures."

One of the techniques that was extensively employed in the
Fifth Circuit resulted from the Florida desegregation cases. The
Fifth Circuit developed in those cases desegregation plans providing
for a mandatory majority-to-minority transfer option. Such an option guaranteed that any student in a school where his race was in
the majority had an absolute right to transfer to another school
where his race was in the minority. Thus any black child had the
right, if he so wished, to transfer to any predominately white
school. The Fifth Circuit found the majority-to-minority option extremely attractive. It guaranteed any black child whose constitutional rights had been impaired by segregated schools the right to
attend a white school, regardless of the kind of desegregation plan
selected. A clause providing a majority-to-minority option increasingly appeared as a required part of approved desegregation plans
in the Fifth Circuit. Later, the Fifth Circuit began to require that
any student exercising such an option had to be given preference in
case of overcrowding and also had to be guaranteed any necessary
transportation. The Fifth Circuit sensed that freedom-of-choice
plans had been effectively removed as a realistic school board option. Therefore, that appellate court became critical of school
boards and district judges who continued to advance such plans.

One of the most telling criticisms of the free-choice plan was
made by Federal District Judge Heebe. His criticism was cited extensively and favorably by the Fifth Circuit.

If this Court must pick a method of assigning students to
schools within a particular school district, barring very
unusual circumstances, we could imagine no method more
inappropriate, more unreasonable, more needlessly waste-
ful in every respect, than the so-called 'free-choice' system.

Under such a system the school board cannot know in
advance how many students will choose any school in the
system--it cannot even begin to estimate the number. The
first principle of pupil assignment in the scheme of school
administration is thus thwarted; the principle ought to be
to utilize all available classrooms and schools to accommodate the most favorable number of students; instead,
this aim is surrendered in order to introduce an element
of 'liberty' (never before part of efficient school administration) on the part of the students in the choice of their
own school. Obviously there is no constitutional 'right'
for any student to attend the public school of his own
choosing. But the extension of the privilege of choosing
one's school, far from being a 'right' of the students, is
not even consistent with sound school administration. Rather, the creation of such a choice only has the result of
demoralizing the school system itself, and actually depriving every student of a good education.

Under a 'free-choice' system, the school board cannot know or estimate the number of students who will want
to attend any school, or the identity of those who will
eventually get their choice. Consequently, the board cannot make plans for the transportation of students to schools,
plan curricula, or even plan such things as lunch allotments and schedules; moreover, since in no case except
by purest coincidence will an appropriate distribution of
students result, and each school will have either more
or less than the number it is designed to efficiently handle,
many students at the end of the free-choice period have to
be reassigned to schools other than those of their choice
--this time on a strict geographical-proximity basis ...
thus burdening the board, in the middle of what should be
a period of firming up the system and making final ad-
justments, with the awesome task of determining which
students will have to be transferred and which schools
will receive them. Until that final task is completed,
neither the board nor any of the students can be sure of
which school they will be attending; and many students
will in the end be denied the very 'free choice' the system is supposed to provide them.

In experimenting with new methods of integration that promised "realistically to work now," one of the methods first considered was mandatory zoning. However, neighborhood school zoning
was no panacea for all school districts. While zoning might produce a great degree of integration in some locales, in other communities with heavily concentrated black residential areas, neighbor-

hood school zoning cemented existing segregation. Therefore, the Fifth Circuit invalidated school zoning plans, as readily as it struck down free-choice plans, where zoning perpetuated segregation; in both situations it cited Green as authority.

Judge Wisdom identified six indicia that became the criteria by which the effectiveness of desegregation plans were to be judged. An effective plan had to produce 1) a desegregated student body, 2) desegregated facilities, 3) desegregated staff, 4) desegregated faculties, 5) desegregated transportation, and 6) desegregated school activities. The Court rigorously struck down all excuses advanced for implementation of less than effective desegregation plans. One of the excuses most frequently voiced by lagging school boards was that adoption of an effective desegregation plan in a particular school district would result in white flight. White flight from many integration plans did indeed occur, particularly in districts with heavy black populations. Nevertheless, the Fifth Circuit continued to demand compliance with Green regardless of the reaction of whites, and even in some cases in the face of "wholesale withdrawal" on the part of whites.

*   *   *

Methods used by opponents of integration to avoid "race-mixing" were not all legalistic. Documented cases of extreme intimidation and coercion of black students are plentiful. In fact, one of the reasons for the popularity of freedom-of-choice plans in many Deep South school districts may have been the requirement in such plans that individual black students come forward and select white schools, thus making themselves public targets for abuse and harassment from white extremists. Other desegregation plans which required school boards to shoulder the primary duty of integration, rather than placing the burden on individual black students, provided far less occasion for intimidation.

United States v. Farrar contains a terse chronicle of examples of coercion of blacks who were attempting to exercise their constitutional rights to attend integrated schools in Noxubee County, Mississippi. Howard and Eugenia Spann, black grandparents of three children who had chosen to attend white schools, were told by a local white that there would be "trouble" if they did not persuade their son to withdraw his children from white schools. Spann was specifically warned that he would lose his job. The same white who threatened the Spanns told Sally Mae Beck that if she did not withdraw her children she would not be able to sell her farm products. Other blacks who enrolled their children found that they were subjected to lawsuits for small debts that were slightly overdue, contrary to long-standing, lax credit policies. Nelson Short, who had enrolled his four black children in previously all-white schools, was warned by one white carrying a pistol in his back pocket that there would be trouble if he did not withdraw his children. Writing for the court in Farrar, Judge Ainsworth outlines several other incidents in that same county involving black parents who lost jobs, had suits filed against them, or were physically intimidated into withdrawing their children from white schools.

One of the more extreme examples of official intransigence occurred in Leander Perez's Plaquemines Parish in Louisiana. In Plaquemines Parish School Board v. United States, the Fifth Circuit specifically complimented beleaguered District Judge Herbert Christenberry for his detailed findings of fact. Judge Christenberry's opinion found that there had been a persistent conspiracy by Plaquemines Parish officials to destroy their own public school system, and thus drive all whites into local private schools. If that plan had not been exposed and enjoined by Judge Christenberry, all chance of education for most black students in Plaquemines Parish would have been destroyed along with the parish's public schools.

* * *

That seventeen-month period between Green and the Supreme Court's next decision in Alexander v. Holmes County Board of Education marked a high point in innovative desegregation experimentation in the Fifth Circuit.

"Alexander v. Holmes County Board of Education": A Political Sellout Boomerangs

On October 29, 1969, the Supreme Court again shook its lower federal courts in the South with a new peremptory order in Alexander v. Holmes County Board of Education. Fearful of alienating powerful Southerners on Capitol Hill and, despite protestations to the contrary, apparently lacking a basic commitment to civil rights, Robert Finch, the first Secretary of Health, Education and Welfare in the Nixon Administration, either blundered or was forced into waffling on desegregation deadlines involving several die-hard Mississippi counties. Finch's intervention resulted in the Supreme Court's Alexander decision. That case had a shattering new impact on the Fifth Circuit's handling of desegregation matters and triggered a plethora of new school orders mandating massive integration across the South.

Implementation of Green infuriated segregationists across the South. For the first time real integration of the public schools-- as opposed to token desegregation--appeared as a distinct probability. Encouraged by lukewarm statements on civil rights by Richard Nixon during the Presidential Election of 1968, Southern politicians prepared a last-ditch fight against integration by addressing their protests directly to the highest levels of the new administration. Following is the story of how politics affected the background of a stunning reversal of the Fifth Circuit, a reversal directly attributable to the failure of the executive branch of the federal government to enforce the law as articulated by the Supreme Court.

* * *

After Lyndon Johnson decided not to seek reelection in the spring of 1968, civil rights enforcers in the Justice Department and in HEW became fearful that the strong pro-civil rights stand of the executive branch might not be continued in the next administration. Using Green as a spring-board, desegregation suits were filed throughout the South and the executive branch pushed the courts for more effective desegregation orders. After the Nixon Administration took office, civil rights groups were cheered by the appointment of Robert Finch as the new Secretary of HEW. Finch had a distinguished civil rights record and was considered to be the most progressive member of the new Nixon cabinet. John Mitchell's appointment as the new Attorney General, however, was not greeted as favorably. Nevertheless, the suits filed during the last months of the Johnson Administration were generally pursued with vigor by Justice and HEW staffers during the first few months of the Nixon Administration. However, danger signals from the Justice Department, HEW, and the White House began to appear. Recurrent rumors picked up by the press were that the architects of the President's "Southern Strategy" were particularly upset by HEW's continued emphasis on school desegregation. Heavy political pressure from South Carolina's Republican Senator Strom Thurmond reportedly was received sympathetically in the White House.

Southern politicians and, as the spring of 1969 progressed, some high-level White House staffers began to focus their attacks on the hated HEW guidelines, mandated uniformly across the Fifth Circuit states by Jefferson I and II. HEW Secretary Finch initially resisted efforts to mitigate the guidelines, arguing that they were the minimum requirements necessary to comply with court decisions. However, the pressure proved effective. On July 3, 1969, Secretary Finch issued a statement announcing "new, coordinated procedures" for achieving desegregation. The statement, at one point, seemed to do away with HEW deadlines:

> Accordingly, it is not our purpose here to lay down a
> single arbitrary date by which the desegregation process
> should be completed in all districts, or to lay down a
> single, arbitrary system by which it should be achieved.
> A policy requiring all school districts, regardless of the
> difficulties they face, to complete desegregation by the
> same terminal date is too rigid to be either workable or
> equitable. . . . *

The Finch statement also contained rhetoric about continued commitment to "the goal of ending racial discrimination in the schools" and included the assertion that the "terminal date must be the 1969-1970

---

*From Bring Us Together, by Leon Panetta and Peter Gall, at 216. Copyright © 1971 by Leon E. Panetta and Peter Gall. Reprinted by permission of J. B. Lippincott Co.

school year." By and large, the press read the Finch statement as a major retreat. Most commentators interpreted it as an easing of school desegregation guidelines even though the Finch statement expressly said that no new guidelines were announced--only "new, co-ordinated procedures." A few newspapers recognized the deliberate confusion contained in the statement. The Washington Daily News called it "a policy statement that seemed deliberately calculated to confuse liberals and Southerners alike into believing each had won." The Saturday Review flatly called it a "victory" for "Senator Strom Thurmond and his segregationist allies."

In the news conference immediately following the statement, the Justice Department supported the idea that some leniency should be afforded as to the time element--despite the Green mandate of "desegregation now." In contrast, HEW representatives at the news conference emphatically declared that their department favored the fastest kind of desegregation enforcement. Leon Panetta, head of the Office for Civil Rights of HEW (the body responsible for enforc-ing HEW policy in the area of school desegregation), announced to his disheartened staff that vigorous enforcement would continue. He told his people that a letter confirming his interpretation of the Finch statement would be going to all school districts to make them aware that the guidelines had not been changed. Those districts that had negotiated plans would be held to those plans; exceptions to the deadlines already in effect would be few. In short, Panetta as-serted that HEW guidelines and deadlines were not changed by the Finch statement.

Panetta spent a good part of Independence Day that year in-forming Spencer Rich, a reporter for the Washington Post, of his interpretation of the statement. In an article which appeared in the Washington Post on July 5, Rich reported: "Panetta said the Thurs-day statement ... may have suggested to some that the deadlines were being relaxed or that renegotiation was possible, but this simp-ly was not the way HEW intended the statement." Rich indicated that a letter would be sent to all districts clarifying the fact that the guidelines had not changed. In Rich's view:

> The 'crunch' for the Nixon Administration, and the true test of its intentions would come ... when Southern-ers presented themselves in the Capital to demand ex-tensions of the deadline for their individual districts: Would the Justice Department and the President then stand behind the tough interpretation contained in the Finch let-ter, or would they force Finch to yield and grant exten-sions time and again?*

Panetta's proposed letter never went out. On the same day that Rich's article appeared, John Ehrlichman, Presidential Assist-ant for Domestic Affairs, telephoned Panetta from the Key Biscayne

*Ibid., at 229.

White House, and told him that "the President just read the story about the possible letter HEW may send out and we're not quite sure this is the right time for that." Ehrlichman then rather strongly advised Panetta that "things should be allowed to settle now," and ordered that he not do anything until Panetta had talked to Ehrlichman personally on Monday, July 7. On Monday, Panetta was told by Secretary Finch not to see Ehrlichman about the letter. Finch told him "things just have to be allowed to settle," and implied that he would try to work things out himself. Panetta helped things "settle" by sending memoranda to his regional offices advising them in dealing with local school board representatives to refer to HEW's interpretation of the July 3 statement. Guidelines were unchanged. Attorney General Mitchell allegedly "blew up" when he found out about Panetta's memoranda.*

In the weeks following the statement, HEW took enforcement action against districts not in compliance in three different states by terminating funds. In a prepared speech given before an educational research group on July 17, Secretary Finch seemed to toughen:

> The 1969-1970 school guidelines will remain in force. There will be no renegotiation of agreed plans. There will be no concessions granted except for compelling, bona fide reasons.**

Copies of his speech were sent to regional offices. HEW continued its established enforcement proceedings.

During the spring and early summer of 1969, when HEW Secretary Finch was fighting his battle to keep HEW's guidelines intact, an important but generally unnoticed internal policy change occurred at John Mitchell's Justice Department. Reviewing past Johnson administration efforts in desegregation, Nixon appointees became convinced that part of the unpopularity of desegregation was due to enforcement of desegregation plans hastily drawn by government lawyers that failed to take cognizance of local conditions. Therefore, in 104 cases in five states the Justice Department asked the local federal district court to order the defendant school boards to seek expert assistance from HEW's Office of Education in drawing their desegregation plans. The feeling was that the professional educators would draw up more acceptable plans than the lawyers in the Justice Department who were unfamiliar with local educational problems. Focusing on the drawing of plans to meet local problems, the new Justice Department policy tended to undercut the theory of Jefferson II that uniformity was necessary.

* * *

---

*Ibid., at 231.
**Ibid., at 232.

In the spring of 1969, in Mississippi, Green was still a theory. On May 13, 1969, the federal district court in Mississippi upheld freedom-of-choice plans in thirty-three Mississippi counties, ignoring Green. Mindful of Green's "do it now" command, a Fifth Circuit panel of Chief Judge Brown and Judges Morgan and Thornberry reversed the district court on July 3. Picking up the new Justice Department policy, the court ordered that new plans be drawn up utilizing the assistance of Office of Education experts. The new plans were to be submitted by August 22, 1969, with full desegregation to be implemented by August 27.

The HEW plans for those Mississippi districts were largely the work of Title IV (Office of Education) teams headed up by HEW veteran Greg Anrig. The Title IV teams had worked closely with officials of the districts involved. The new plans allowed four of the thirty-three districts until 1970 to desegregate completely; the remaining districts were to begin in 1969 at the start of the school year, just three or four weeks away. In nineteen of the districts, optional interim steps for 1969 had been included in case the court felt that 1970 should be the appropriate termination date, although HEW desired compliance by September. It was expected that the court would require most of the districts to comply immediately. Secretary Finch unqualifiedly approved the HEW plans for all thirty-three Mississippi districts prior to their submission to the court. The plans were, in large part, a compromise on the part of HEW; nevertheless, they were felt to be effective and practical.

Because the HEW plans filed with the court on August 11, 1969, involved districts already under court order, HEW's only involvement should have been in providing Title IV assistance to the districts in their formulation of new plans. But in Washington, D.C., enormous pressures had been building on HEW Secretary Finch. The fate of those Mississippi districts was under the jurisdiction of the federal courts; therefore, the Justice Department--not HEW--should have been the responsible federal agency representing the interests of the United States. Nevertheless, despite the fact that those Mississippi counties were under court-ordered--not HEW-initiated--plans, on August 20, Secretary Finch inserted himself directly into the Mississippi controversy. Finch's action presaged his own eventual resignation as HEW Secretary, destroyed his image as a forceful advocate of civil rights and precipitated Alexander and its massive integration decree.

On August 20, Chief Judge Brown received an ex parte communication from Secretary Finch, personally delivered by "safehand" courier, requesting additional time for those Mississippi districts to submit new and overdue terminal desegregation plans. The Finch letter stated:

> I have personally reviewed each of these plans. This review was conducted in my capacity as Secretary of the Department of Health, Education and Welfare and as the cabinet officer of our government charged with the ultimate responsibility for the education of the people of our nation.

In this same capacity, and bearing in mind the great trust reposed in me together with the ultimate responsibility for the education of the people of our nation, I am gravely concerned that the time allowed for the development of these terminal plans has been much too short for the educators of the Office of Education to develop terminal plans which can be implemented this year.

The administrative and logistical difficulties which must be encountered and met in the terribly short space of time remaining, must surely, in my judgment, produce chaos, confusion and a catastrophic educational setback to the 135,700 children, black and white alike, who must look to the 222 schools of these 33 Mississippi districts for their only available educational opportunities.

I request the court to consider with me the shortness of time involved and the administrative difficulties which lie ahead, and permit additional time during which experts of the Office of Education may go into each district and develop meaningful studies in depth, and recommend terminal plans to be submitted to the court not later than December 1, 1969.*

Judge Brown was stunned. He had never received such a communication from a cabinet officer. Furthermore, the communication had been directed to him personally. Copies had not been given the other parties. He didn't know what to do.

The next morning he communicated with Judges Morgan and Thornberry, the other members of the standing panel on the Mississippi cases. The panel decided that an order should be issued immediately to the three Mississippi district judges, Cox, Russell and Nixon, setting forth verbatim Finch's letter and ordering an immediate hearing in Jackson, Mississippi. Copies of that order, incorporating Finch's letter, were sent to all parties. The district court judges were told to forward their findings to the Court of Appeals.

The reaction to Finch's letter was one of disbelief. Justice Department attorneys handling the cases had not been consulted. Finch had not consulted his own Title IV experts; he had not visited the districts; he had acted without any real personal knowledge. HEW staffers were astounded and rebellious. Civil rights forces were galvanized into action. HEW hurriedly issued a press release quoting a line or two from the letter in an attempt to diminish the hail of criticism. The destruction caused by Hurricane Camille to the Mississippi school districts was emphasized. The hurricane, which had struck the Mississippi coast on August 17, actually had not disrupted any of the schools in the districts involved.

The HEW officials and Office of Education experts responsible for developing the August 11 plans were appalled at Finch's

---

*Ibid., at 255.

interference. Led by Greg Anrig, they flatly refused to testify at
the Mississippi district court hearing called to consider the delay
request. In Panetta's words:

> The Secretary had publicly repudiated the work of his
> own employees, had asked for a delay that was not justi-
> fied by any previous standard.... Worst of all, he had
> committed a symbolic act of retreat on school desegrega-
> tion which couldn't help but infect all such programs.*

Panetta also refused to testify. Further, the Justice Department
attorney in charge of the Mississippi cases refused to prepare the
motion for delay. Jerris Leonard, head of the Civil Rights Division of the Justice Department, had to prepare the motion himself, undertake an intensive search for people who would testify
for the government, and argue the case.

According to Panetta, HEW people who refused to testify
were threatened with loss of their jobs. The "experts" who eventually agreed to testify were Jesse J. Jordan, HEW regional director for Title IV in Atlanta, and Howard Sullins, a former school
superintendent from HEW's regional office in Charlottesville. Both
Jordan and Sullins had promotions forthcoming soon thereafter.
Neither had been involved with drawing up the Mississippi plans,
which Secretary Finch had claimed would cause "chaos" and "confusion."

Largely on the basis of the Finch letter and the hurried,
perfunctory testimony by Jordan and Sullins, the three-judge Mississippi district court found that the facts justified the Finch delay
request and recommended that the Fifth Circuit grant the delay. On
appeal, Jerris Leonard urged before the Fifth Circuit that the findings of the district court should be affirmed and a delay granted;
he confessed during his argument to the Circuit judges that he was
"somewhat embarrassed" about the delay request. Unwilling to overturn the district court findings of fact and obviously impressed by
the urgency of the allegations in the Finch letter, the Fifth Circuit
accepted the district court's recommendation and ordered a delay until December 15, 1969, when new plans were to be submitted. The
NAACP Legal Defense Fund, a comrade with Justice Department
civil rights lawyers in numerous desegregation battles, for the first
time since Brown II openly and abruptly split with the Justice Department. The Inc. Fund lawyers bitterly charged that "the United
States Government for the first time has demonstrated that it no
longer seeks to represent the rights of Negro children." The NAACP
appealed the delay granted by the Fifth Circuit to the United States
Supreme Court, initially requesting a stay of the Fifth Circuit's delay.

The South's segregationists were elated by Finch's interven-

*Ibid., at 256.

tion. It was seen as an eleventh hour reprieve that might be broadened to include other districts under court-ordered integration plans scheduled for implementation that fall. The New York Times reported that:

> Within days after the Administration called for a delay in requiring 33 Mississippi districts to integrate, a few school boards elsewhere in the South began to reverse their decisions to abolish their dual systems this September.
>
> Some of the blacksiding [sic] districts are not bothering to inform the education department. The Wheeler County, Ga., board simply announced in the local newspapers that it was returning to freedom of choice this September and abandoning the ambitious plan for integration that H.E.W. had approved.

Bombarded with requests for similar intervention in other cases, Finch retreated from public view.

On September 5, 1969, Supreme Court Justice Hugo Black refused to interfere with the August 28 Fifth Circuit order granting the delay requested by Finch. However, Justice Black, in a five-page opinion, expressed open sympathy for the black appellants and urged them to place their case before the full Supreme Court "at the earliest possible opportunity." He further stated:

> I fear that this long denial of constitutional rights is due in large part to the phrase 'with all deliberate speed.' I would do away with that phrase completely.

When Alexander v. Holmes County Board of Education was orally argued before the Supreme Court, Jerris Leonard, for the Justice Department, symbolically sat--for the first time--at the same counsel table as the lawyers representing Mississippi. Courtroom observers openly commented on the difficulties which the experienced Leonard had before the Supreme Court, while in the same breath complimenting the performance of Jack Greenberg for the NAACP.

On October 29, 1969, just six days after the oral argument, the Supreme Court reversed the Fifth Circuit's order delaying integration in the 33 Mississippi counties and ordered immediate desegregation. In a blunt per curiam order, the Supreme Court stated:

> The question presented is one of paramount importance, involving as it does the denial of fundamental rights to many thousands of school children, who are presently attending Mississippi schools under segregated conditions contrary to the applicable decisions of this Court. Against this background the Court of Appeals should have denied all motions for additional time because continued operation of segregated schools under a standard of allowing 'all

deliberate speed' for desegregation is no longer constitutionally permissible. Under explicit holdings of this Court
the obligation of every school district is to terminate dual
school systems at once and to operate now and hereafter
only unitary schools.

The Supreme Court then "ordered" the Court of Appeals to vacate
its delay order and to give the Mississippi cases "priority." It was
an unusually terse and stern reversal for the Fifth Circuit, a court
that had labored earnestly to implement Green. Chief Judge John R.
Brown frankly admits that he considers the delay granted by the
panel in Alexander as his "worst mistake" in all his long years of
handling school desegregation cases. The Fifth Circuit was deeply
affected by the Alexander reversal.

* * *

What may be the real story behind the Finch letter did not
surface until two weeks after the Court of Appeals affirmed the district court's granting of the requested delay. When the behind-the-
scenes story did surface, it did not attract great public attention--
perhaps because other national issues were in the forefront. The
story however, should be retold, not so much because of the fact
that a delay was granted at the request of Secretary Finch, but because of the way Finch was reportedly "motivated" to write his controversial letter.

Reliable sources assert that political pressure brought by Senator Stennis on the White House was translated into a political command to Secretary Finch. However, Secretary Finch has insisted
that he received no undue political pressure; that his sole reason
for requesting the delay in the thirty-three Mississippi cases was
his sincere belief that the HEW-sponsored plans submitted to the
Fifth Circuit on August 11 were unworkable and would have been
detrimental to the local schools if implemented immediately. One
reliable source, in supporting the Finch position, reports entering
Secretary Finch's office a day or two prior to the day the Finch letter was hand carried to the Fifth Circuit. Finch was found scrutin-
izing stacks of files on the thirty-three Mississippi cases, mutter-
ing to himself "this is really bad" and "we've got to do something
about this." Despite the fact that Secretary Finch may have been
distressed by some aspects of the HEW plans on file with the Fifth
Circuit, something had to have prompted his personal focus on those
thirty-three Mississippi counties at a time when similar orders were
on file for districts across the South. Furthermore, even if Secretary Finch was genuinely upset by those plans, why did he feel he
had to interfere? Close advisors repeatedly insisted that those
cases were not HEW's problem. If there was something wrong, the
Justice Department had the responsibility to seek relief, not HEW.
After all, none of those plans were HEW-initiated; they all involved
school districts under court orders that originally had been sought
by the Justice Department. HEW's only role had been to provide
technical assistance in response to a request of the Justice Depart-

ment. Further, Secretary Finch himself had previously approved the plans. Greg Anrig and other HEW experts remain convinced that those plans were workable and effective. Those technical experts, not Secretary Finch, had investigated local conditions. After Deputy HEW Secretary Patrick Gray drafted the letter for Secretary Finch's signature, Finch sent it prior to informing either his Office of Education experts or his Office of Civil Rights enforcers. What prompted that unusual letter by Secretary Finch?

In August, 1969, Mississippi's Senator Stennis, as Chairman of the Senate Armed Services Committee, had great influence at the White House because of his vital role in legislation involving the military. At that time, a bitter struggle over deployment of the ABM (Anti-Ballistic Missile) system was being waged in the United States Senate. A vote on the ABM issue occurred on August 6. The Administration forces won, with the help and vote of Senator Stennis, 51 to 49. This vote, following lengthy and heated debate, rejected the Cooper-Hart Amendment which would have limited the ABM bill to research and development of the missile. The fight for deployment of the missile was to continue; the Administration expected that Senator Stennis would be significantly embroiled. Furthermore, Senator Stennis was also a member of the Senate HEW appropriations subcommittee which had jurisdiction over the funds for Mr. Finch's department.

After desegregation plans were submitted for the thirty-three Mississippi districts on August 11, Senator Stennis communicated to "people in high places" in the Administration that he was considering stepping down as floor manager of the still-pending ABM bill. He reportedly complained that, because of the intense pressure he was under from his constituency concerning the impending mixing of the races in Mississippi, he might have to return home. This meant that Senator Symington, next in seniority on the Armed Services Committee, would have assumed the floor leadership of the bill. Significantly, Senator Symington had voted for the Cooper-Hart Amendment on August 6. The "message" from Senator Stennis to the Nixon Administration was clear: Do something about your desegregation orders in Mississippi, or face defeat on the ABM issue.

In fact, there is good evidence that the pressure applied by Senator Stennis was less subtle than that described above. On September 11, 1969, George Overby, a former Stennis aide and at that time a reporter for the Jackson (Mississippi) Daily News, reported "the Nixon administration's decision to ease desegregation efforts in Mississippi schools was made by President Nixon himself, who intervened after Senate Armed Services Committee Chairman John Stennis threatened to quit as floor manager of the controversy-riddled Military Authorization Bill." The Overby story said that after the Stennis ultimatum was delivered to San Clemente, three cabinet officers called Stennis on Saturday, August 16, to achieve a "workable solution." The Overby story asserted that:

Attorney General Mitchell called Stennis first and re-

lated that Finch and he had discussed the matter and that
Finch would be calling shortly.... Within the hour Finch,
also in California, called Stennis and advised him the guidelines [sic] HEW had been insisting upon had NOT been reviewed or approved in Washington and were being recalled.
... Following the Finch conversation, Stennis was called
again by Mitchell and then Laird, whose aid Stennis had
sought earlier in the summer as an intermediary with the
President.

Overby had left as a Stennis aid only scant weeks earlier.   His
sources were good.

    In the Chicago Daily Tribune, also on September 11, Willard
Edwards reported in his column that a letter written by Senator
Stennis was hand-delivered to the White House in mid-August and
relayed by courier plane to President Nixon in his western headquarters at San Clemente.   The letter threatened that Senator Stennis would turn over his leadership chores to Senator Symington if
the Administration did not slow down the Mississippi desegregation
pace.   The Edwards story asserted that:

    Nixon summoned Melvin Laird, secretary of defense, and
    Robert Finch, secretary of the health, education and wel-
    fare department, for a conference.   The price exacted by
    Stennis would have political repercussions, they realized.
    Telephone calls to Stennis from Atty. Gen. John Mitchell,
    Laird and Finch burned the wires.   They found him [Sen-
    ator Stennis] adamant, and gave in.

Willard Edwards is a respected columnist with a reputation for dramatic but accurate reporting.

    In the final analysis, only a very few people actually know
whether a letter-ultimatum was sent by Senator Stennis to high administration officials, or to the President directly.   Neither Senator
Stennis nor his aides have ever denied that such a letter was sent.
White House aides have refused to discuss the matter.   In fairness,
a failure to deny cannot be regarded as an admission.   The point
remains, however, that pressure was brought to bear upon the Nixon
Administration, in substance, to act "illegally" in regard to the Mississippi desegregation cases by disregarding its constitutional obligations to enforce the law.   This has been established, even in the
absence of any Stennis letter, by the statements of numerous HEW
officials.

    The Finch letter was a minor irritant for the Nixon Admin-
istration, and a major disaster for Secretary Finch.   By reason of
the Supreme Court's peremptory reversal of the Fifth Circuit in
Alexander, the letter also resulted in the issuance of a flood of
massive integration orders across the South.   The delay in the thirty-
three Mississippi districts precipitated a rebellion among civil rights
lawyers in the Justice Department.   The Finch letter triggered a

demand by over 1000 employees of HEW that Secretary Finch appear publicly and explain his action. (Finch promised to appear and then was hospitalized; the meeting was cancelled.) The Finch letter damaged the relationship of mutual trust and respect that had developed between the judges of the Fifth Circuit and the Justice Department attorneys who had appeared so many times before them. The apologetic argument made by Jerris Leonard in pleading for a delay deeply disillusioned members of the Court. Several judges felt that they no longer knew or could trust the position of the United States on desegregation. Others doubted whether the Nixon Administration had developed any policy other than one of political expediency.

* * *

On September 16, 1969, a very unusual step was taken prior to convening an en banc hearing in Houston on Singleton III, a consolidated case involving sixteen separate school districts. The Fifth Circuit ordered its clerk to write the Justice Department and specifically request both that it appear as amicus, and that the government attorney sent to argue be able to state "the views" of the government. The letter also informed the Government that a court reporter would be present to record the oral presentations of counsel. Clearly, the Circuit was bluntly telling the Government that it must publicly state its position on desegregation, and that its statement would be preserved. The text of that letter follows:

September 16, 1969

Mr. Jerris Leonard
Assistant Attorney General
Department of Justice
Washington, D.C. 20530

Re: No. 26285 - Singleton v. Jackson Municipal
School District
(Scheduled at Houston - October 15)

Dear Mr. Leonard:

This letter is written at the request of the court in connection with the above captioned case. The court requests the government to fully express its views and state its position in this case by timely filing an amicus curiae brief. If the government is unable to comply with this suggestion for some appropriate reason, please advise this office as soon as practicable.

Further, if the government wishes to appear and argue as amicus curiae, a request to argue should be filed with the clerk forthwith. It may be assumed that the request to argue as amicus curiae will be favorably considered; and if such a request is made, the government is advised that the court desires to have its argument reported and for it to make arrangements for such reporting.

You are requested to give notice to counsel for all parties by sending a copy of the amicus curiae brief to counsel for the parties. If you propose to argue as amicus curiae, you should give a similar notice to counsel for the parties of such intention.

Yours very truly,

EDWARD W. WADSWORTH, CLERK

By _Audrey D. Glynn_
Deputy Clerk

The Finch interference boomeranged. It resulted in more integration, not less, and in more "do it now" orders, not more deliberation. It destroyed Secretary Finch's strong civil rights reputation, and led to his eventual resignation as HEW secretary. It also led to charges that in domestic affairs there were no matters, not even the civil rights of black children, that were not "up for sale" by a politically sensitive administration.

The Justice Department and HEW desperately tried to recoup their lost credibility. In the summer of 1970, Jerris Leonard and Stanley Pottinger traveled throughout the South on behalf of the Justice Department to carry the message to school boards that they could expect no further delay: they would have to integrate. Deputy Attorney General Kleindienst bluntly told a meeting of United States Attorneys in Atlanta that they would have to support the Administration on school integration cases, or get out of their jobs. But the damage had been done. No one representing the civil rights movement or representing Southern school boards would forget that in the pressure and power game played between Senator Stennis and the Nixon Administration the forgotten pawns were the thousands of black school children in Mississippi whose civil rights were ignored.

On September 13, 1969, within two weeks after the delay granted to the Mississippi districts by the Fifth Circuit in response to the Finch letter, the United States Civil Rights Commission, chaired by Father Theodore M. Hesburgh, the President of Notre Dame, issued a statement, deeply critical of the Nixon administration, which called for a new example of moral leadership from the President.

* * *

Alexander v. Holmes County Board of Education marked the end of judicial patience with litigation as a means of delay. School districts were commanded to establish unitary school systems immediately. Legal questions were to be decided after school districts had already begun to operate as unitary systems. The Brown II allowance of "deliberate speed" was no longer constitutionally permissible.

"Carter v. West Feliciana Parish School Board":
The Second Slap

On January 14, 1970, the Supreme Court reemphasized its determination to force immediate desegregation in Carter v. West Feliciana Parish School Board.

While Alexander was pending before the Supreme Court, the
Fifth Circuit had scheduled sixteen major school cases for en banc
hearings on successive days. While those en banc arguments were
being heard, the Supreme Court announced its decision in Alexander.
The Fifth Circuit responded to the Alexander mandate with alacrity.
The sixteen cases then before the Court had been consolidated for
hearing under the already famous name of Singleton v. Jackson Municipal Separate School District. Therefore, the first en banc decision after Alexander, which was decided in response to that decision, came to be known as Singleton III. The Fifth Circuit's good
faith determination to order massive integration in the South without
undue delay is apparent from the language in Singleton III:

> Following our determination to consider these cases
> en banc the Supreme Court handed down its decision in
> Alexander v. Holmes County Board of Education.... That
> decision supervened all existing authority to the contrary.
> It sent the doctrine of deliberate speed to its final resting
> place....

Despite its desire to implement Alexander without delay, as
ordered by the Supreme Court, the Fifth Circuit judges could not believe that the Supreme Court intended for them to issue orders that
required the relocation of hundreds of thousands of school children
in the middle of an on-going school year. The Circuit decided to
desegregate as much as possible immediately while still allowing the
school year to be completed without total disruption. Consequently,
in Singleton III it responded to Alexander by dividing integration into
a two-step process:* part one of the process required desegregation
of faculties, facilities, activities, staff and transportation no later
than February 1; part two permitted postponement of massive integration of student bodies until the beginning of the new school year
in September of 1970.

Carter v. West Feliciana Parish School Board was one of
the sixteen cases consolidated in the Fifth Circuit under the Singleton III heading. The NAACP's Inc. Fund lawyers immediately appealed the Singleton III holding, taking the case to the Supreme
Court under the name Carter v. West Feliciana Parish School Board.
The Inc. Fund lawyers argued that postponement of student desegre-

---

*Fifth Circuit Judge Irving Goldberg warned his brothers privately
that, while he would join their opinion, he feared that any delay in
any aspect of desegregation would be reversed by the Supreme
Court.

gation until September to avoid massive student upheaval in midterm was nevertheless an avoidance of Alexander. In Carter, the
Supreme Court peremptorily reversed the Fifth Circuit.

With that blunt Carter reversal, the Fifth Circuit--which had
been the most diligent court in America in desegregating public
school facilities--was wrist-slapped a second time for delaying
massive student desegregation for a short four-month period to
avoid disruption in the midst of a school year. After the remand
of Carter to the Fifth Circuit, that Court in Singleton IV ordered
immediate massive integration in mid school term across the Deep
South.

* * *

In the closing months of 1969 and the spring of 1970, the
Court of Appeals for the Fifth Circuit found itself facing a judicial
crisis unique in the history of the federal judiciary. The Supreme
Court had peremptorily reversed any suggestion of delay whatsoever in desegregation. Immediate massive desegregation orders
had to be issued for all school boards in active litigation in the
Fifth Circuit area. Legal questions were to be postponed for consideration until after institution of unitary school systems. In this
context, Chief Judge John R. Brown and members of his court came
to a tacit agreement that no further en banc hearings would be held;
opinion writing by three-judge panels would be avoided where possible. As John Brown preached over and over to his judges, "All
that can be said about school cases has been said; there is no point
in writing further words." The Fifth Circuit, prodded by the Supreme Court and pushed by John R. Brown, adopted the practice of
issuing opinion-orders and urgently sought innovative ideas to manage the new crisis in school desegregation.

NOTES AND PRIMARY AUTHORITY

The primary authority for the material contained in this chapter was:

The Green Case: Freedom of Choice's Death Sentence. The princi-
pal cases relied upon were The Supreme Court decisions in United
States v. Montgomery County Bd. of Educ., 395 U.S. 225 (1969);
Green v. County School Bd. of New Kent County, 391 U.S. 430
(1968); Raney v. Bd. of Educ., 391 U.S. 443 (1968); and Monroe v.
Bd. of Commr's, 391 U.S. 450 (1968). The principal Fifth Circuit
cases relied on were United States v. Greenwood Municipal Sep.
School Dist., 406 F.2d 1086 (5th Cir. 1969); Henry v. Clarksdale
Mun. Sep. School Dist., 409 F.2d 682 (5th Cir. 1969); United States
v. Farrar, 414 F.2d 936 (5th Cir. 1969); Plaquemines Parish School
Bd. v. United States, 415 F.2d 817 (5th Cir. 1969); Carr v. Montgomery County Bd. of Educ., 289 F. Supp. 647 (M.D. Ala. 1968),
aff'd in part, 400 F.2d 1 (5th Cir. 1968) Gewin, J., dissenting, 402
F.2d 782 (5th Cir. 1968); Davis v. Bd. of School Commr's of Mobile

County, 393 F.2d 690 (5th Cir. 1968); Broussard v. Houston Indep. School Dist., 395 F.2d 817 (5th Cir. 1968); and United States v. Bd. of Educ. of the City of Bessemer, 396 F.2d 44 (5th Cir. 1968).

Many other cases were also relied on, including District Court opinions such as Moses v. Washington Parish School Bd., 276 F. Supp. 834 (E.D. La. 1967). Interviews with Circuit and District Judges also provided useful background.

Alexander v. Holmes County Bd. of Education: A Political Sellout Boomerangs. In addition to the Alexander case, 396 U.S. 19 (1969), the background of Alexander comes primarily from facts reported by Leon Panetta and Peter Gall in their book Bring Us Together (1971). The Panetta-Gall account has been supplemented by interviews with them, and with key governmental and judicial figures who had first-hand knowledge of the facts. Most of those interviewed expressed the desire that the information they gave not be attributed to them. "The Federal Retreat in School Desegregation," Southern Regional Council, Inc., 30-37 (Dec. 1969), is a contemporary account that supports the Panetta-Gall account. Other sources included The Congressional Record; Orfield, "The Politics of Resegregation," 52 Saturday Review, Sept. 20, 1969; Rosenthal, "Stennis Linked to Desegregation Delay," N.Y. Times, Sept. 19, 1969, $1, at 36, col. 3; N.Y. Times, Sept. 13, 1969, $1, at 28, col. 7-8; Chicago Tribune, Sept. 11, 1969, $1, at 18, col. 3; Reed, "Pupil Integration Spurting in South," N.Y. Times, Sept. 2, 1969, $1, at 1, col. 7, $1, at 37, col. 2; Rosenthal, "In Washington: Showdown by the Administration," N.Y. Times, Aug. 31, 1969, $4, at 1, col. 1-2; and Rich, "Schools Policy Defended," Washington Post, July 5, 1969, $A, at 1, col. 2, $A, at 10, col. 2.

The cases relied on were Alexander v. Holmes County Bd. of Educ., 396 U.S. 1218 (1969) (Black, J., Issued in chambers, Sept. 5, 1969); United States v. Hinds County School Bd., 1 Race Rel. L. Survey 110 (S.D. Miss. 1969), rev'd, 417 F.2d 852 (5th Cir. 1969) and United States v. Hinds County School Bd., 1 Race Rel. L. Survey 166 (S.D. Miss. 1969), aff'd, 1 Race Rel. L. Survey 116 (5th Cir. 1969).

Carter v. West Feliciana Parish School Board: The Second Slap. The principal sources were the Carter case, 396 U.S. 290 (1970); Singleton v. Jackson Mun. Sep. School Dist., 425 F.2d 1211 (1970) (Singleton IV); and Singleton v. Jackson Mun. Sep. School Dist., 419 F.2d 1211 (5th Cir. 1970) (Singleton III).

A more complete manuscript, with detailed documentation of sources, is available as indicated in the Preface, supra.

Chapter 14

1970: UPHEAVAL

As far as the average citizen of the Deep South was concerned, for fifteen years since Brown I in 1954, the predicted upheaval in social relations had been a matter for mere conjecture and debate. However, after the Supreme Court reversals of the Fifth Circuit in Alexander and Carter, the long-feared revolution began. Massive integration came to the public schools of the Deep South.

The efforts of the Fifth Circuit to implement the Supreme Court's new edicts are reflected primarily in the extraordinary number of opinion orders issued in school cases.* However, in the period following Carter, a few opinions were written and a few dissents were recorded--enough to allow a glimpse of the tensions that persisted on the Court concerning the vast social changes stimulated by its orders. The Fifth Circuit's legal activity following Carter will first be examined in this chapter. Then the impact of massive desegregation orders on the Deep South will be discussed by focusing on two widely separated Southern areas: three rural parishes in Louisiana and the large Jacksonville-Duval County school system in Florida.

The Fifth Circuit's Implementation of Carter

One of the first major cases after Carter was Bivins v. Bibb County Board of Education, the same case in which the Fifth Circuit instituted many of its expediting procedures. Bivins indicated a commitment by the majority of the Fifth Circuit's judges to carry out the Alexander and Carter mandates for immediate massive desegregation. However, despite Alexander and Carter, Fifth Circuit judges were still not in concert on the methods to be adopted to effectuate the Supreme Court's mandates. The Bivins panel of Judges Wisdom, Simpson, and Coleman reversed two freedom-of-choice plans that had been reinstated, with modifications, by an obstinate district court after Singleton III. Mississippi's Judge Cole-

---

*See discussion in Part III, Chapter 12, supra, concerning the number of opinion orders issued under the Fifth Circuit's new expediting procedures.

man, however, was deeply disturbed by what he termed the majority's continued effort to strive for racial balance; and, he did not
conceal his frustration:

> We are never going to get out of this worsening problem
> by continually saying, 'This is not enough.' We should
> say what is enough, in affirmative language, and let us
> get back to educating children of all races in an atmo-
> sphere of learning.

Judge Coleman's strong disagreement with what he felt was an attempt to achieve integration by focusing on race-mixing percentages
was seen again in his dissent in Hall v. St. Helena Parish School
Board, one of the several decisions involving the balky St. Helena
Parish School Board:

> I would concur if it were not for the wholly unreason-
> able requirement that these schools be torn up in the mid-
> dle of a semester. Everyone seems to overlook the fact
> that this works as great a hardship and is educationally
> as damaging to the black children as it is to the white.
> It is educationally a folly and in general the results have
> been glaring failures.

After the Fifth Circuit's decision in Singleton III had been
reversed by the Supreme Court in Carter, the same school boards
that had been before the Court in Singleton III again found themselves
before the Fifth Circuit. In a very brief order enforcing the mandate in Carter, the Fifth Circuit in Singleton IV voided its delay of
student desegregation until September, 1970, and ordered immediate
student desegregation in midterm on February 1, 1970. Although
Judge Coleman conceded that the Supreme Court's ruling had to be
obeyed, he protested vigorously the Fifth Circuit's failure in Singleton IV to provide detailed instructions to its federal district courts:

> What I dissent from is the continuing failure of this
> Court to provide a lighthouse in the new storm which is
> upon us. The school authorities and the District Judges
> need something to steer by.

* * *

While expressing reticence to dissent because of his newness on the Court, Judge Charles Clark, the other member of the
Fifth Circuit from Mississippi, joined Judge Coleman's dissent in
Singleton IV and appended a moving dissent of his own, which in
turn was subscribed to by Judge Coleman:

> Of all the tasks to which we have been set as judges,
> certainly this action is the most sensitive for we deal with
> the central lives of literally hundreds of thousands of chil-
> dren, parents, teachers and others, each one of whom has
> a most important right to be heard and to be equally pro-

tected in his or her constitutional rights as an individual person. If ever there was a time for the court to bend every effort to be credible and persuasive to those affected by our order, it is now. The central aim of courts is to solve problems--not create them. The brief order we here use to enforce the mandate lacks even the smallest spark of compassionate understanding.... We simply issue another cryptic edict....
... we must secure popular acceptance for what we here decree if it is ever to become truly effective. This is put forth without in the slightest way advocating that we become a populist court. My concern is not with the popularity of the court's orders, but with the function of such orders in a way that has some chance to bring about the result intended.

* * *

After its reversal in Carter, most of the Fifth Circuit's work was comprised of opinion orders that reversed federal district courts for failure to achieve a sufficient amount of desegregation. As has been indicated desegregation was measured primarily by the statistics on race-mixing. Nevertheless, the Court occasionally took time to write an opinion and to comment on the performance of the federal district courts it supervised. In Carr v. Montgomery County Board of Education, Judge Irving Goldberg painstakingly detailed the duties of school boards and federal district courts under the new Supreme Court mandates. Judge Goldberg also took the time to compliment Federal District Judge Frank Johnson, personally, as exemplifying the kind of diligence expected of district court judges. At the same time he extended a rare kind word to a school board:

> In conclusion, we take note of the fact that since 1964 the Montgomery County school system has been under sensitive judicial surveillance. The record indicates that the responses of the Board of Education have not been animated by excessive reluctance, recalcitrance, or a desire to frustrate. Moreover, just as the Board has been responsive to the mandates of the district court, so the district court has been sensitive to the mandates of this court and of the Supreme Court.... If more district courts and more school boards had been as sensitive as those here involved to the requirements of the law, the path to the goal of school desegregation in this circuit would have been infinitely smoother than it has been.

In contrast to the complimentary tone of the Carr opinion, the Fifth Circuit expressed extreme impatience with district judges who failed to respond to the immediacy of the Supreme Court's directives in Carter. When Dallas's elderly Federal District Judge Joe Ewing Estes, instead of immediately ordering desegregation of several major Texas districts, established a date after the beginning of the 1970 school year for only the consideration of trial motions, the Fifth Circuit reversed with unusual heat:

Courts all over this Circuit have labored through this summer, and are still laboring, to bring into uniform reality the compulsions of Alexander, Carter, and Singleton for conversion of dual systems to unitary school systems. Singleton requires that in 'these and all other school cases now being or which are to be considered in this or the district courts of this Circuit' that desegregation plans are to be implemented which 'accomplish a unitary system of pupil attendance with the start of the fall 1970 school term.'

Accordingly, we grant the appellant's motion for summary reversal....

* * *

On February 17, 1970, seventeen days after Singleton IV was implemented, one of the most important and controversial Fifth Circuit desegregation opinions was issued by Judge Griffin B. Bell of Atlanta. Speaking for a panel including Judges Ainsworth and Godbold, Judge Bell's decision in Ellis v. Board of Public Instruction of Orange County was to provide a continuing source of controversy for other panels mandating school integration in the Circuit.

The Orange County school system sprawled across a wide geographic area; it covered the whole of Orange County, Florida, including the urban areas of Orlando, Winter Park, Winter Garden, and Apopka, as well as rural areas in the county. The land area consisted of 910 square miles, almost the size of the state of Rhode Island. Orange County had 83,000 public school students, eighty-two per cent of which were white and eighteen per cent black.

The Orange County Board of Education had met five of the six criteria of a desegregated school, but complaints were still raised about the amount of student desegregation achieved. The Board had adopted essentially a strict neighborhood school zoning plan containing a majority-to-minority transfer option. After some criticism of the zoning lines, the Bell panel approved the neighborhood school concept. The court held that requiring children to attend the schools nearest their homes, as determined by districts drawn without regard to race, was an acceptable method of integration meeting the Green admonition that the plan must promise "realistically to work now." Judge Bell argued that an iron-clad, majority-to-minority transfer option allowing any child the right to transfer from a school where he was in the racial majority to the nearest school where he was in racial minority--super-imposed over the neighborhood school concept--would result in a fully integrated school system for Orange County. Judge Bell's Orange County plan became a rallying point for many school districts who were opposed to more drastic forms of desegregation, such as busing of students and clustering and pairing of schools.

Firmly convinced that the Orange County plan still offers a sane, logical, and neutral method of desegregating the school districts

of the Deep South, Judge Bell is deeply disappointed that the Ellis
case was never appealed to the Supreme Court. He remains convinced that it would have gained Supreme Court approval. He vigorously argues that if Ellis had been followed by other opinions, the
politically explosive issue of busing in the presidential election in
1972 would have been nullified. Judge Bell has spoken out both publicly and privately on the merits of the Orange County plan; he
charges that in bypassing that case, the Fifth Circuit missed a
chance to solve the school integration problem of the Deep South,
avoiding much of the trauma caused by other methods of desegregation.

     Other judges on the Fifth Circuit dispute Judge Bell's claim
that the Orange County plan met the mandates of the Supreme Court
in Green, Alexander, and Carter. They contend that while a strict
neighborhood school system, with a majority-to-minority transfer
option might well work in Orange County, it was not applicable to
all other school situations. The Supreme Court command was to
order plans that promised to convert previously de jure segregated
school systems into unitary systems immediately. Opponents of the
Orange County plan argue that ordering a neighborhood school system in Southern school districts which have heavy racial concentrations in certain areas would perpetuate segregated education. The
split in the Circuit over the Orange County idea developed almost
immediately after the decision was rendered.

     In Henry v. Clarksdale Municipal Separate School District, a
panel consisting of Judges Wisdom, Simpson, and Coleman--with
Judge Coleman vigorously dissenting--found that an Orange County-
type plan would not disestablish a segregated school system in Clarksdale, Mississippi. There were more blacks in the system than
whites, and the system included only the urban area of Clarksdale,
Mississippi. Other desegregation devices, such as the clustering
and pairing of schools, were found to offer a better chance of creating a unitary, nonracially identifiable school district. The majority judges, Wisdom and Simpson, rejected the use of the Orange
County plan based on the facts existing in Clarksdale. The majority
emphasized that the Orange County plan was not meant as a panacea
but only as a solution for Orange County under the facts as they existed in that case: "The answer in each case turns in the final
analysis, as here, on all of the facts including those which are peculiar to the particular system" (emphasis added).

     Judge Coleman, asserting that the Clarksdale plan was "a
simon-pure Orange order," objected that if a strict neighborhood
school district, with a majority-to-minority transfer option, was
good enough for Orange County, Florida, it should have been sufficient for Clarksdale, Mississippi. Angered by what he felt was
favorable treatment for a Florida school system over a Mississippi
school system, Judge Coleman requested an en banc hearing of the
decision in the Clarksdale case. A majority of judges on the Circuit denied the en banc request. An anguished Judge Clark, not a
member of the panel in the Clarksdale case, dissented from the

Fifth Circuit's denial of Judge Coleman's request and charged that massive desegregation orders were creating havoc in public education:

> As I write these words (August 31, 1970), news comes that the highly-regarded progressive superintendent of the State's largest school system [Jackson, Mississippi] has found it physically necessary to resign less than two weeks before school was to start. He left with these words:
>
>> With deep regret I have found it necessary to request the Board of Trustees to accept my resignation as Superintendent of the Jackson Public Schools. As everyone is well aware the Jackson schools have been in a continuous series of litigation involving numerous court orders requiring the Superintendent to administer drastic changes. Professionally and personally I cannot continue as superintendent under the existing situation.
>>
>> I regret that I cannot be involved in developing the outstanding school program that I am confident could exist in Jackson. I assumed the position of superintendent here to develop such a program. Unremitting disruption has prevented the accomplishment of that objective.

* * *

Thus, the Fifth Circuit's massive integration orders changed the face of the Deep South. Despite enormous dislocation, most systems complied with federal orders and desegregation did occur smoothly in most school districts. However, in some school districts, particularly where there was a majority of black students, whites fled the public schools. For example, the Woodville Attendance Center in Wilkinson County, Mississippi closed when all white students left the school system; there were insufficient pupils to justify continuing to keep the Woodville Center open.

The Fifth Circuit's extensive use of the opinion order device and the reversal of district judges based primarily on racial percentages did implement the Green, Alexander, and Carter mandates. However, some of the judges on the Fifth Circuit remain convinced that in its haste to obey the Supreme Court's commands, the Fifth Circuit actually moved beyond the Supreme Court doctrinally. The result of the Fifth Circuit's orders was a form of racial balancing that, they argued, has never been required by the Supreme Court. In Ross v. Eckels, the famous Houston school case, Judge Clark bitterly dissented to a Fifth Circuit order which disapproved an Orange County-type plan for Houston. He bluntly charged that the Court was requiring racial balancing beyond any Supreme Court requirement:

It is rapidly becoming apparent that despite express dis-

claimers ... the special school case panels of this circuit
are now out ahead of the requirements laid down by the
Supreme Court and have adopted sub silento some unmen-
tionable standard of numerical pupil racial balance to
govern the affirmance or reversal of school case decisions.

The true principle that underlies the reversal of the
district court here is that the neighborhood school system
ordered for Houston did not achieve that degree of racial
balance some judges of this circuit have declared is
'enough.' We do nothing but delude ourselves when we
adopt such a premise. Like chasing the pot of gold at the
end of the rainbow, this reasoning embarks us on a course
without an end. Unless someone would be boldly foolish
enough to assert that courts can deprive school district
patrons of their freedom, then it follows as the night follows the day that the courts will never finish litigating
such 'numbers game' cases.

Despite the disputes on the Court that surfaced in the few
written opinions, the real story of the effect of massive integration
on the South can only be glimpsed fleetingly by focusing upon the
judicial opinions of the Fifth Circuit. The severity of the rent in
the fabric of Southern life is perhaps best appreciated by examining
the impact of Fifth Circuit orders on the cities, towns, and counties
of the Deep South. Following are accounts of the arrival of massive
integration in two isolated, but perhaps typical, areas.

Massive Integration in Iberia, Evangeline, and St. Landry Parishes

The problems faced by Federal District Judge Richard J.
Putnam in implementing "do it now" desegregation orders in eight
rural Louisiana parishes were typical of those encountered in numerous small towns and sleepy counties throughout the Deep South. A
native Louisianan, former district attorney, and state trial judge
prior to acceptance of a federal judicial appointment from John F.
Kennedy, Judge Putnam is a soft-spoken, gracious Southern gentleman. Personally of the opinion that desegregation should have occurred through congressional action rather than by the judicial fiat
of Brown I and II, Judge Putnam was not a judicial activist in the
mold of Frank Johnson or J. Skelly Wright. Instead, he was one
of those unswaying federal district judges who, while opposing the
jarring effects of massive desegregation orders and desiring to avoid
the limelight, nevertheless was determined to carry out his judicial
obligations to the best of his ability. He was not an obstructionist.

Judge Putnam's ordeal occurred in the fall of 1969, in the
pervasive atmosphere of hostility among the white citizens of his
parishes to any form of desegregation. Throughout the 1969-70
school year, white pressure groups demanded a return to freedom-of-

choice plans that had utterly failed to accomplish any significant degree of desegregation. Of course, those same vocal "supporters" of free-dom-of-choice desegregation were past masters in the application of both subtle and not-so-subtle methods designed to discourage any child, of either race, who tried to make freedom of choice work. Intimidation and coercion had transformed freedom of choice into a cruel joke for the black children of the eight Louisiana parishes presided over by Judge Putnam. For example, in the 1968-69 school year, the New Iberia High School had only twenty blacks enrolled under freedom of choice. Under the massive desegregation order to be mandated by the Fifth Circuit and implemented by Judge Putnam, that same high school would have 500 black students. To groups that viewed the twenty black students as a federal threat to the "Southern way of life," the impact of the order that was implemented by Judge Putnam can hardly be overestimated.

In 1969, prior to the time in August when it had to grapple with HEW Secretary Finch's request for a delay in desegregation in the thirty-three Mississippi counties, the Fifth Circuit had deter-mined that under the Green mandate, freedom of choice was not working in thirty-seven Louisiana school districts. It had ordered those districts to implement more workable plans. In order to car-ry out the new Fifth Circuit directive, Judge Putnam ordered each of the school boards in his eight parishes to submit new desegrega-tion plans to him in the summer of 1969.

* * *

Meanwhile, threatened with real integration in their public schools for the first time since Brown, white citizens throughout Louisiana were forming Citizen's Committees for Quality Education (CCQE), headed by Dr. Donald Roberts. The purpose of CCQE was to present a focal point around which white resistance to desegrega-tion could rally. Ostensibly, however, the whites joining these CCQE groups were merely defending their right to send their chil-dren to the school of their choice. A fully financed CCQE organiza-tional drive was underway by July 20, 1969.

In addition to the strident demands of CCQE's neo-segrega-tionists, Judge Putnam's parishes were also subjected to inflam-matory agitation by black militants. Charles Bryant, a teacher and President of the St. Landry Chapter of the NAACP, was painted by the press as a local firebrand. However, Bryant's real position seems confused. At times he sounded as if he were a black separa-tist claiming that the rising majority of blacks opposed all forms of integration. At other times he called for ramming the HEW school integration plan down the white man's throat.

In a heavily editorialized news report of a Charles Bryant press conference, the local Opelousas Daily World signaled the tor-ment of the coming fall in Judge Putnam's parishes. Bryant had called the conference to announce that the local black community, for which he claimed to speak, was willing to accept the HEW plan, with modifications. That HEW plan, submitted to St. Landry's

school board on July 5, had already been rejected and returned to
HEW along with twenty reasons why it allegedly could not be put into effect. Judge Putnam summarily rejected the St. Landry board's
request for continuation of freedom-of-choice and ordered submission of a new plan. The threat of impending conflict increased on
August 22, as the opening of schools neared. CCQE groups across
Louisiana sponsored a mass march on the state capital to protest
the imminent implementation of new HEW desegregation plans. St.
Landry citizens were among the 3,000 in attendance, some carrying
signs proclaiming "HEW Smells Like Communism."

*　　*　　*

By the opening of school in late August, the six parishes in
the Lafayette Division of Judge Putnam's court had complied with his
order to submit desegregation plans which did not depend on student
freedom of choice. The school boards' desegregation plans in Lafayette, Acadia, Vermillion, St. Martin, and St. Mary, which were approved by Judge Putnam substantially as written by the boards,
worked relatively well. In Vermillion, for example, approximately
sixty per cent of the black children in the parish were sent to integrated schools--with eighty per cent of all the children in the public
schools attending integrated schools. HEW officials were complimentary, no appeals were taken, and the only item worthy of report
is the success achieved. The success in those parishes supports
the thesis that even with overwhelming public opposition to desegregation, integration is possible when a school board firmly carries out
its obligations and community leaders support the continued operation
of public schools.

However, desegregation was not achieved as easily in three
of Judge Putnam's eight parishes: Iberia, the sixth parish in the
Lafayette Division, where the school board did submit a plan, and
St. Landry and Evangeline, the two parishes in the Opelousas Division of the court, where the school boards did not submit plans.
While the following accounts pinpoint Judge Putnam's difficulties in
these parishes, it must be emphasized that for every school district
torn by conflict over desegregation, there were many more where
cool heads in responsible positions assured that the schools stayed
open and the law was obeyed.

Both of the school boards in the Opelousas Division parishes,
St. Landry and Evangeline, would not cooperate with HEW or submit
plans of their own. They simply refused to act unless ordered to
do so by the court. Judge Putnam recognized that in these two parishes there had been so much agitation by militants on both sides
that the boards had become paralyzed. Therefore, with no other
option before him, he ordered implementation that fall of the HEW
plans. Based on the attitude of those two school boards, as opposed
to that of the boards in the other six parishes, Judge Putnam was
reasonably certain that if he had trouble with desegregation it would
be in St. Landry and Evangeline parishes.

Ironically, however, the first crisis of the 1969-70 school year occurred at New Iberia High School in Iberia Parish, one of the parishes which had complied with Judge Putnam's order and submitted its own plan.* The situation was brought about by the closing of formerly all-black Henderson High School. About 500 black students who had attended Henderson until the end of the 1968-69 year were assigned to New Iberia, where there has been only twenty blacks the year before. On August 27, the first day of school, fighting broke out between black and white students. According to the local newspapers, bands of black students attacked single white students. The accuracy of those reports has not been verified, and the general quality of objective local journalism during this period provides some ground for skepticism. However, at some point a large group of black students decided to march to Henderson High, several miles away, and occupy it. This plan was thwarted en route by a blockade of police who broke up the march with tear gas, arresting several people. During the day a hastily called conference was held between Acting Governor C. C. Aycock (Lieutenant Governor acting as governor while Governor John McKeithen was out of state), General Wade of the Louisiana National Guard, Judge Putnam, District Attorney Knowles Tucker and the school board. Thereafter, Acting Governor Aycock imposed a strict curfew on the area for the night of the 27th, which was later extended to include the night of the 28th.

* * *

On that same evening of the 27th in Evangeline Parish, several thousand citizens attended a rally in City Park in Ville Platte. Fifteen hundred people signed a petition and $6,000 was collected to finance court action to stop integration. Several teachers signed the petition after members of the school board assured them that no action would be taken against them. The teachers were urged to sign by Preston Aucoin, an attorney who was to handle the suit.

---

*The smoldering racial tensions in New Iberia, and elsewhere in Judge Putnam's parish, is captured in the following New York Times report: "Here in New Iberia, in the heart of Acadia, the peaceful land of Evangeline, Longfellow's heroine, there is little escape.

"Wilfred Lambert is a black Baptist clergyman who has tried both as a pastor and as a member of the local chapter of the National Association for the Advancement of Colored People to serve as a moderate force among Negro youngsters.

"Thursday, after a tense day and night caused by fist fights at the local high school between black and white students, the Rev. Mr. Lambert answered the phone at his neat brick church on Weeks Street.

"'Hello,' he said.

"A white woman's voice responded: 'How many sticks of dynamite will it take to blow that damn church to hell?'" Wooten, "In the South, the Face of Die-Hard Segregation," N.Y. Times, Aug. 31, 1969, §4 at 1, col. 6.

Aucoin had represented the Evangeline school board in the summer of 1969, before resigning to represent white citizens bringing suit to enjoin the school board from integrating.

The next day, two lawsuits were filed in state courts. One sponsored by the Evangeline Parish group was filed by attorney Aucoin in the Thirteenth Judicial District Court of Louisiana, Judge Joe Vidine presiding. That suit asked that the defendant school board be enjoined from implementing the "illegal" HEW plan and that the plan be declared unconstitutional. Judge Vidine set a hearing for 9:00 a.m., August 29. The Freedom of Choice Committee of New Iberia filed a suit in the Sixteenth Judicial District Court against the Iberia Parish School Board and HEW Secretary Robert Finch to require that freedom of choice be allowed.

The Justice Department filed a motion in Judge Putnam's federal district court asking that the case in the Thirteenth District be removed to federal court and consolidated with the original desegregation unit. Judge Putnam agreed and issued a stay order to Judge Vidine the night of the 28th, telling him not to hear the case the next day. Judge Putnam notified all involved in the case not to promote a school boycott. He also denied a request by the Evangeline Parish School Board for a new trial on the freedom-of-choice issue, terming it futile.

On August 29, Dr. Donald Roberts announced that CCQE would continue to apply pressure on the state legislature to call a special session to repeal the state's compulsory attendance law. The Catholic Bishop in Lafayette called for moderation, asserting that boycotts and demonstrations would harm and deprive the children of their right to an education.

On September 2, New Iberia High School was reopened peacefully; the situation in Iberia Parish had returned to near normal and remained so throughout the fall. On that day, ten black students had been suspended as a result of the disturbance the previous week.

*   *   *

Events were moving in the opposite direction in Evangeline Parish. On September 3, the school board convened at its offices. A crowd of 2,000 citizens gathered outside and demanded that the meeting be moved to the Ville Platte High School gym; the board moved the meeting. The white citizens made four specific demands on the board: 1) recess the schools, 2) join in their suit to seek remand of the case filed in state court back to that court from its previous removal to federal court, 3) join as co-plaintiffs in the suit to prevent implementation of the HEW plan, and 4) ask that both cases be set for speedy trial. One board member said, "They're here with blood in their eyes, and we're not going to be able to leave this place until their demands are met." Attorney Aucoin, representing the group, issued a veiled threat of violence. The board capitulated and accepted all four demands after a heated two-and-a-half hour meeting.

* * *

In St. Landry Parish on September 3, the schools opened under an August 8 order of Judge Putnam. The expected enrollment was 22,300, but 2,000 black and 6,000 white students failed to enroll. Of those who did, 9,300 were black and 5,000 white.

On September 4, the Iberia Parish School Board, whose members were evidently more persevering, took a surprising step in changing four elementary schools from freedom of choice to pairing. The vote was seven to six, with the newspaper naming those voting against, but not those voting for the change.

On September 6, the St. Landry School Board held a meeting which was almost an instant replay of what had happened in Evangeline Parish three nights earlier. The board began the meeting in its offices. A crowd of 3,500 gathered outside and demanded that the meeting be moved to the Opelousas High School auditorium.* Once there, a telegram from Jerris Leonard of the Justice Department was read to the crowd. The message was apparently a reaction to events in Evangeline Parish. It advised the board that the Justice Department was aware that citizens might pressure the board to close the schools. The Department went on to say that it had enforcement responsibility and it would not hesitate to use "whatever legal means" were necessary to enforce the order of Judge Putnam. After much oratory by Sylvester, a public school principal, and other CCQE leaders, the St. Landry board, in the face of a very hostile crowd and following the example of its counterpart in Evangeline, also agreed to recess the schools. The board returned a telegram to the Justice Department requesting a representative to survey conditions.

The next day, the Justice Department requested a hearing before Judge Putnam on September 15, to require the Evangeline Parish School Board members to show cause why they should not be held in contempt for refusing to comply with a federal desegregation order issued by Judge Putnam on August 5. The hearing was ordered.

On September 9, Jerris Leonard flew to Lafayette for a closed conference with the St. Landry School Board. Leonard offered federal law enforcement assistance but Superintendent Dupre declined. Instead, his board again refused voluntarily to reopen the schools. Leonard then asked Judge Putnam for a restraining order to reopen the schools. It was issued late that day, along with an order to the members of the St. Landry School Board to appear September 18, to show cause why they should not be held in contempt.

---

*"I won't be responsible for what's going to happen this afternoon," the board was told by Sidney Sylvester, President of the parish Citizens Committee for Quality Education, if the board did not move to the high school.

On September 10, Evangeline Parish filed a request with Judge Putnam for a stay of the integration order. The Evangeline attorneys eagerly seized on the delay granted in the thirty-three Mississippi counties by the Fifth Circuit. They claimed their situation in Evangeline Parish was indistinguishable and demanded similar treatment. They sent copies of their request for a stay to Attorney General John Mitchell, requesting that the Justice Department join in their action.

On September 11, Judge Putnam ordered both St. Landry and Evangeline parishes to reopen their schools by September 12. Jerris Leonard said that there was no chance that Louisiana's public schools would get a delay similar to that in Mississippi because "[T]here is no similarity to the situation in Mississippi." Interestingly, Leonard did not, or perhaps could not, elaborate on just what the differences were. Perhaps Louisiana's senators had put less pressure on the White House or perhaps they were simply not in as good a bargaining position.

Judge Putnam's show-cause order generated considerable pro-school board sentiment in Evangeline Parish. A police jury declared a "holiday of concern" to permit citizens to march in favor of the board on September 15, the date of the hearing on the contempt charges.

The St. Landry and Evangeline schools were reopened on September 12, in accordance with Judge Putnam's orders. White student attendance was almost nil, but the opening was quiet.

In view of the peaceful school reopenings, the Justice Department moved that the contempt hearings for St. Landry and Evangeline boards be indefinitely delayed; Judge Putnam granted the motion. To emphasize his determination, however, Judge Putnam ordered the board members to be prepared to proceed with the contempt hearing on twenty-four hours notice. Since the hearing was postponed, the parade scheduled for September 15 to show support for the board was cancelled.

* * *

Apparently resigned to the fact that their public schools must become integrated, the white citizens of Evangeline decided to seek an alternative to public education. On the evening of September 16, 2,500 white citizens gathered in the courthouse square in Ville Platte to investigate the feasibility of establishing a private school. They began to look for facilities, teachers, and funds. All seemed readily available. Sheriff Elin Pitre offered the use of "his" Town and County building west of Ville Platte for the school. No one seemed concerned about whether or not this use of state facilities would constitute "state action," thus destroying the school's private status. Teachers were to be hired from the ranks of recently retired and resigned members of the public school staff. Each student would be required to pay a $150 entrance fee plus tuition. By the time the meeting broke up, $88,500 had been collected in cash and pledges. Reverend Melvin Plauche, fund raising chairman, said that he hoped to have $200,000 in pledges from local businesses by the end of the next day. The group also petitioned the Evangeline School Board to recall a special one cent sales tax which had apparently been passed with the proceeds earmarked to aid the public schools. Thus, from its inception, the private school movement reflected an attitude of indifference to the fate of the now black public schools. The legality of such a recall was not considered. The group proudly dubbed their new institution of learning "Evangeline Academy."

Once again, an instant replay occurred in St. Landry Parish on September 24, where citizens met in the courthouse to discuss the feasibility of a private school. St. Landry, however, was a little more professional in its approach. A private consulting firm from Pennsylvania was hired to make a feasibility study. A $5,000 amount was raised at the meeting to pay for the study, and a drive was started to raise $500,000 for school buildings. Sidney Sylvester of CCQE promised his group's support.

The Opelousas Daily World ran an editorial on October 12, in which it said to the federal judiciary. "We told you so"; that is, that white students would flee public schools if the courts pushed too hard. The editorial writer praised the establishment of the private schools as a healthy development but cautioned that public schools should be maintained as well. The newspaper did not note that in many cases whites who desired to keep their children in the public schools were afraid to do so because of threats by CCQE supporters. Judge Putnam recalls one lady calling him in the evening and reporting:

> 'I'm a white widow, I've got six children and I run a little business and I've got to send my children to the public schools and they are calling me up and threatening me. They are going to burn my house, they'll burn my store if I send them to the public schools.' She said, 'What must I do?'

* * *

The never-say-die attitude of white Louisianans flared up again on November 4, when 4,000 gathered in Opelousas carrying signs and waving flags protesting integration. Sound trucks moved along the streets playing Dixie. The gathering had been sponsored by the newly organized Citizens for Local Control of Education (CLCE). The CCQE boycotted the affair, referring to the CLCE as a "splinter group." There is no hint as to what caused the split, but presumably the CLCE was dissatisfied with the complacency of the CCQE. However, the top three elected officials of the state were on hand to lend moral support to the citizens' battle against the "federals." Governor McKeithen threatened that if HEW plans were ordered in all schools, the state legislature would refuse to "vote a dime for public education." The Governor called upon the federal government to treat Louisiana no differently than the northern parts of the country where segregation existed. Lieutenant Governor Aycock, viewed as a likely replacement for McKeithen in 1971, said that he was "tired of seeing the South constantly being made the whipping boy of the country." Apparently reflecting a growing public dissatisfaction with the legislature's inaction, Lieutenant Governor Aycock assured the crowd that he had not come to defend the legislature but to show that "we stand with you and your cause is our cause." Attorney General Gremillion, who had jousted with J. Skelly Wright in New Orleans, stated with some truth that he had dedicated his life to fighting the federal government and federal controls. Although all the members of the legislature had been invited to attend the rally as a demonstration of their solidarity with the people, only two legislators attended. The master of ceremonies challenged: "If the present members of the Legislature will not help the people, then we will have to get some that will."

In December 1969, the Supreme Court refused to hear an appeal from thirty-four Louisiana parishes asking for freedom of choice in the public schools. The Daily World quoted several educators' statements that the Court was destroying public education. Charles Bryant, the NAACP activist, viewed the causation issue differently. He said if white citizens had allowed freedom of choice to work, the high court would have held it constitutional.

On December 4, 1969, the St. Landry Parish School Board asked Judge Putnam to declare their system unitary so that the board could operate it without continuous judicial supervision. It also rescinded its September 5 "recess" resolution and asked the court to remove the permanent injunction which was still in effect against the board.

* * *

By late June of 1970, the full effect of the fall's events could be seen. The whites in Evangeline Parish had succeeded. Of 2,000 available white children in the Ville Platte area, 1,800 were in private schools. The public schools were almost totally black. During the spring, a sober biracial committee was formed in Evangeline Parish to try to restore the badly damaged public school system. The committee attempted to draft a plan which would replace the HEW plan, satisfy the court, and attract white students back to public school. The first plan submitted called for zones which extended beyond the town's limits, but the new zone lines met with opposition from rural property owners. The plan submitted to the court would result in a slight white majority in one school while making another all black. Students would be assigned by zones if they were city residents but would have freedom of choice if living outside the city. The plaintiffs and interveners in the original school case attempted to discredit the committee, charging that the proposals would recreate a dual system. Judge Putnam stated in open court: "It is an unfortunate thing when the

races become so polarized." He also charged: "There are some
elements in Evangeline Parish that don't want the public school system to work." The judge wasn't quite correct; there were some elements in Evangeline Parish that didn't want an integrated public
school system to work. The judge then took under advisement the
board's request for modifications of the HEW guidelines he had imposed on the board the previous year.

Massive Integration in Jacksonville

Difficult as they may have been, the school integration problems faced by the South's rural counties and small towns seem relatively simple when compared to the almost intractable difficulties
facing the region's segregated metropolitan areas. One of those
metropolitan areas was Duval County, Florida, including the city of
Jacksonville. Unlike its sister Miami to the South, Northern Florida's largest city, Jacksonville, is Deep South to its core. Containing almost one-fifth of the state's black population, mostly residing in concentrated black ghettos, Jacksonville appeared in the
1969-70 school year to be an integrationist's nightmare. But Jacksonville .did integrate, and the story of that endeavor is a tribute
to a harassed but effective school superintendent, a vigorous, young
federal judge, and scores of citizens of both races who refused to
give up on the public schools.

*　　*　　*

On December 6, 1960, the first legal action was taken to
implement Brown II in Duval County. Federal District Judge Bryan
Simpson, now a member of the Fifth Circuit, found that the responsible officials were operating a racially segregated system. He
ordered submission of a desegregation plan to correct the situation.
As was typical of other courts that year, Judge Simpson approved
a plan in 1963 providing for integration of one grade per year until
1974, coupled with a freedom-of-choice system.

By March of 1965, when only sixty black children out of
30,000 in Jacksonville-Duval County were attending integrated schools,
plaintiffs succeeded in forcing the board to accelerate the integration
process. However, the modifications adopted were also not satis-
factory. In January, 1967, Judge Simpson's patience seemed
strained. He found that the board was frustrating desegregation by
gerrymandering attendance zones and refusing to allow black students
to transfer to white schools. Faculties were still totally segregated.
He ordered the board to correct these deficiencies and he abolished
freedom of choice. He further ordered that those in the racial majority in a school be permitted to transfer to another school only
when they would be in the racial minority in the new school. Thus,
black students in black schools could transfer to white majority
schools, but white students in those schools could not flee to all-
white schools.

By August of 1967, Judge Simpson realized that the board
was either incapable of implementing his January order, or unwilling
to do so. He then ordered the board to request the assistance of
the South Florida Desegregation Center at the University of Miami;
the center's report was submitted to the court January 8, 1969.

*   *   *

Important political developments during 1968 and 1969 were
to effect integration in Jacksonville and Duval County. The city
and county governments were found to be so thoroughly corrupt in
the early sixties that an outraged citizenry abolished both city and
county governments by referendum and established the Consolidated
City of Jacksonville, encompassing all of Duval County. On October 1, 1968, the new government took over. Under the old system
the school board had been partisan, paid and political. Under the
new city-county government, it was to be non-partisan, non-paid,
and non-political. The Superintendent of schools, who had been
elected, was now to be appointed by the non-partisan board.

In January, 1969, the new school board began operation,
dominated by eager but inexperienced members dedicated to a re-
juvenation of Jacksonville's public school system. They set out to
find the best superintendent available. After a vigorous search they
persuaded a highly respected and experienced California educator,
Dr. Cecil Hardesty, to head up the new system. Dr. Hardesty, at
61, was recognized as one of the nation's premier school administrators. He had supervised a top-flight school system in San Diego
for over 16 years and had only recently lost the race for California
Superintendent of Public Instruction to Max Rafferty, an extreme
conservative. Dr. Hardesty ruefully recalls that in the summer of
1968, while being wooed by Jacksonville's new board members, he
asked about desegregation. He was assured that "there are no integration problems in Jacksonville." After taking the job, Dr.
Hardesty estimated that eighty-five to ninety per cent of his working hours were spent on integration difficulties.

*   *   *

During the period of governmental change-over in Jacksonville, Judge Simpson was elevated to the Fifth Circuit and Judge
William A. McRae, Jr. inherited the Duval County School case. On
August 29, 1969, at the time the Fifth Circuit granted Secretary
Finch's request for a delay in the thirty-three Mississippi counties,
Judge McRae ordered the Jacksonville board to submit a new plan
by December 1, designed once and for all to achieve a unitary school
system. No sooner had compliance with that order been attempted
by the school board in Jacksonville than the Fifth Circuit issued its
landmark ruling in Singleton III, in response to the Supreme Court's
reversal in Alexander.

Singleton III required that unitary school systems must be
established immediately by implementation of a two-step plan. By

February 1, 1970, faculties were to have the same black-white ratio in each school as existed in the system as a whole. Student bodies were to be fully desegregated by the start of the fall 1970 term. On December 30, 1969, Judge McRae ordered reassignment of faculty in Jacksonville-Duval County to comply with Singleton III.

Dr. Hardesty vividly recalls that spring of 1970, calling it "the most dramatic experience for the Jacksonville faculty in its history." After receiving Judge McRae's December 30 orders to desegregate his faculty immediately, Superintendent Hardesty put a team of school administrators together over the New Year's holiday and they worked around the clock. They adopted a plan requiring a basic ratio of seventy per cent white teachers and thirty per cent black teachers for every school in the district. For some junior and senior high schools as many as sixty white teachers might be transferred out, with a like number of black teachers transferred in, or vice versa. Faculty integration for Jacksonville, as for many areas of the South under Singleton III and then Singleton IV orders, created acute personnel problems. It proved to be a wrenching, highly emotional period for affected teachers and administrators. While causing less public turmoil than massive student reassignment, in many ways it posed a greater threat to the continued viability of the public school structure.

Jacksonville approached its teacher desegregation problems with sensitivity, considering the imperative requirements of the Singleton III mandate. Dr. Hardesty decided that only the most capable young black teachers would be sent to the white schools. No teacher, black or white, was to be transferred without a year of experience, and then the youngest teachers with over a year of experience were to be transferred on a reverse seniority basis. Each principal was allowed to freeze ten per cent of his faculty in order to retain key people. A grievance procedure was established to consider hardship cases. School was cancelled for a full week between terms to allow sufficient notice to transferees. Despite all their efforts, the Duval County administrators faced a torrent of personnel problems all spring. Teachers quit, many flatly refused to transfer, and chaos resulted. Later in the spring, in order to keep the schools staffed until the end of the school year, the school board--knowing it could not keep the promise--passed a resolution guaranteeing that it would transfer back any teacher who so desired if that teacher would just remain with the new assignment until school was out. By September, 1970, the personnel crisis began to subside; principals had now worked with teachers of both races, teachers had weathered the difficult transition period, new teachers were hired who knew what they faced, and older teachers who would not accommodate left the system. There were some striking examples of community cooperation. One group of forty to fifty black citizens offered to host coffee hours for white parent groups in order to set a positive tone of cooperation. Superintendent Hardesty was able to use that offer to coax white groups into similar acts.

The basic cause for the personnel crisis over faculty desegregation was the great disparity in quality between the black and white
schools, entrenched by a century of mandatory segregation and ne-
glect of black teachers and students. The typical black teacher had
attended an all-black grade school and an all-black high school, both
of inferior quality. By the time he graduated from high school he
had no better than a fifth or sixth grade reading ability. He then
had attended an all-black, understaffed and underfinanced college
where he obtained a B.A., and perhaps even an M.A. and Ph.D.
After his formal education he still was woefully behind his white
counterpart in all basic educational skills. He then went back to
an all-black school system to teach the next generation. Most all-
black schools therefore were glutted with middle-aged, tenured but
incompetent black teachers who--as the products of a segregated
system--perpetuated the cycle. To make matters worse, the preva-
lent corruption of the previous governmental systems in Jacksonville
had infected the black schools. For years it was common knowledge
that kickbacks and bribes were necessary to secure teaching positions in Jacksonville. The going rate for retention was reportedly
$500 per year.

The typical white teacher was also a Southerner who, while
generally better educated than his black counterpart, was also a
victim of a segregated system. He had never attended schools with
blacks and, as a "beneficiary" of a segregated society, he had only
been exposed to blacks who served him in menial roles. He had no
notion of black language, black deprivation, or black pride. Both
white and black teachers were terribly unsuited for the shock of
ratio-faculty desegregation.

White female teachers--unfamiliar with everyday ghetto language and loose discipline standards--complained bitterly about black
students who would refuse instructions with a curt "I ain't a'gonna
do it, you mother-fucker" or who would give them a friendly pat on
the bottom as they negotiated crowded hallways. White teachers
who had been accustomed to holding their students up to a high
level of achievement could not fathom the lack of accomplishment
or desire to achieve in many black students. Scores of white teachers simply quit out of frustration, disgust, or racial animosity.

Black teachers were equally bitter about impudent white students who ridiculed their knowledge of their subject matter or their
ability to teach. They were also resentful of white colleagues who
snubbed them in the dining hall or joked about them in the faculty
lounge. One story made the rounds in Jacksonville about Miss Q.,
a middle-aged black teacher who had been transferred from an all-
black high school to a predominantly white school. An irate white
parent stormed into Superintendent Hardesty's office clutching her
teenage daughter's English notebook. One page in the notebook was
covered with a list of profanities that would have made a Jacksonville stevedore blush. The parent insisted that the daughter had been
told by Miss Q. to copy the words from the blackboard. After investigation, it was discovered that Miss Q. had heard one of her

new white students say "damn." Drawing on her ghetto teaching
background, she decided to write all of the words on the blackboard
that she considered inappropriate for classroom usage. The students
were told to copy the words down so that they would know which
ones were forbidden. While the technique had worked for her in
the ghetto, she failed to perceive that many white students had never heard some of the words; needless to say, the exercise was a
source of great hilarity for her students, although it was greeted
with less than humor by some white parents. There were countless
complaints from white parents and students about black teachers who
could not spell or write complete sentences. It was alleged that
many could not do the multiplication tables. One persistent story
concerned a black tenured faculty member who could not tell the
story of the Little Red Hen in sequential order. Counter complaints
from black parents and students about discriminatory discipline,
racist remarks, and a hostile environment were legion. In retrospect, Superintendent Hardesty feels that the spring of 1970, when
faculties, staffs, and facilities were integrated, was worse than the
massive student integration, which did not arrive in Jacksonville until the fall of 1971.

*   *   *

On January 19, 1970, after Carter, Judge McRae ordered
Superintendent Hardesty to request further assistance from the Florida School Desegregation Center on how to implement the next step
in the desegregation plan: full student integration. After considering the Center's report in August, Judge McRae ordered nine black
schools desegregated by pairing them with neighboring white schools.
However, he left eighteen other black schools in the core city untouched. Neither side in the Duval County case was pleased and
both appealed.

While the Duval County case was on appeal, the United States
Supreme Court decided the famous Charlotte-Mecklenburg case,
which, among other things, specifically condemned one-race schools
unless the school board could overcome a presumption that such a
situation had resulted from conscious discrimination.* Subsequently,
the attorneys for the parties, the chairman of the school board, Dr.
Hardesty, and the members of the Court of Appeals panel assigned
to the case, met in Atlanta to discuss a settlement. Fifth Circuit
Judges Bell and Godbold pushed all of these parties toward some
accommodations. Judge Bell told the school board that it had an
affirmative duty to submit a plan within the Charlotte-Mecklenburg
framework. He turned on the NAACP attorneys and told them flatly
that their request for mandatory racial balancing would not be
granted. Judge Bell then called the district judge in Jacksonville
and set up an appointment the next day in the district judge's offices
for all parties to work further on the details of an acceptable plan.

---

*Swann v. Charlotte-Mecklenburg Board of Education is discussed
in the following chapter.

At this point in May of 1971, Judge Gerald B. Tjoflat assumed control of the case, having just assumed the federal bench
in October of 1970. The judicial change was necessitated by an extended leave of absence granted Judge McRae for health reasons.
Called "boyish and outgoing ... every bit the extrovert," Judge
Tjoflat at forty-one was one of the nation's youngest federal judges.
Considered able and something of a "workhorse" by his colleagues,
Judge Tjoflat assumed control of the Duval County school case at a
time of extreme pressure.* The Fifth Circuit had allowed the district court only until June to adopt a desegregation order to bring
Duval County into compliance with Singleton IV and the Charlotte-
Mecklenburg case. Even without such a deadline, Judge Tjoflat
could be expected to move quickly. His philosophy was that "the
more you drag a school case out and the more indecisive a judge is,
the worse off he is and the worse off the community is."

Judge Tjoflat's first step in the case was to attend the meeting arranged by Judge Bell, with the NAACP lawyers representing
the plaintiffs, the school board lawyers, the board, and the superintendent to discuss a timetable for disposition of the case. The
judge stressed that the Charlotte-Mecklenburg case required a dismantling of the dual system. He also impressed upon the school
board that the burden rested with it to devise a plan to accomplish
that goal. "The impression was created that we would solve the
problem within twenty days ... come hell or high water. You can't
leave the impression that the problem won't be solved." Judge
Tjoflat also recognized his own role; he knew that a judge must be
prepared to take the entire "monkey on his back": "this is because
both representatives of the blacks and the whites must satisfy many
conflicting interests within their groups. Every move they take
must be ordered by the judge so that neither side must accept political blame for the respective shortcomings of the eventual compromise."

About a week before the deadline, Judge Tjoflat held two days
of hearings on proposed plans. The black member of the school
board presented a plan acceptable to the black community. A white
member of the board did the same. Each seemed to present a plan
which had no real chance of success, but which would please the
constituency represented.

*   *   *

In earlier years of desegregation, a federal district judge
had generally been able to rely on the NAACP Inc. Fund attorneys,
and later on Justice Department or HEW lawyers, to provide help
in drafting desegregation plans. However, as the civil rights movement fragmented, local factions developed in the black community.
No longer was there monolithic support for desegregation, and those
groups that did support the integration goal warred openly over the

---

*Judge Tjoflat has since been elevated to the Fifth Circuit.

methods for achieving it. The NAACP lawyer became less and less a support to the local judge when requested to submit proposed plans. He either resorted solely to demanding "more" integration, without suggesting how his demands could be met, or he submitted impossible schemes designed to please all factions in the black community. The Justice Department and HEW lawyers had never been initiators of desegregation cases in the large metropolitan areas of the South. Both the Johnson and Nixon Administration policies appeared to consciously avoid the big cities and concentrate on the easier rural areas. Government lawyers entered such suits only when requested to come in as an amicus. They seldom supported bold desegregation steps that required any extensive student transportation. Therefore, in Southern cities like Jacksonville, in the 1969-71 years of massive integration, the federal trial judge frequently had to draw his own desegregation plan. He had never been able to rely on school board lawyers to propose anything but minimal steps; now he could no longer rely on useful help from either the plaintiffs or the government. In Jacksonville, Judge Tjoflat proceeded to draw the final judgment.

The final order was a masterpiece of judicial diplomacy. In plain language, Judge Tjoflat carefully developed the entire case history, the relevant legal precedents, and the current local school situation so that the basic law and facts could be understood by concerned Jacksonville parents. Their support--or at least the absence of their concerted opposition--was vitally necessary to the success of the plan. Judge Tjoflat was convinced that by candor and education, boycotting might be avoided. While his final order had to be legally correct to avoid reversal, he felt it should also serve an important informational purpose.

Of particular concern to Judge Tjoflat was his decision to order the closing of seven core-city black schools and the busing of the former students to suburban white schools. He feared reversal. The action looked discriminatory on its face. Black children would be forced to ride buses out, but white children would not be forced to ride buses in. Therefore, in his order Judge Tjoflat made meticulous findings of fact, describing in detail the wretched condition of the schools to be closed, to assure the appellate court that the schools in question were not fit for the education of any child, black or white:

> The South Florida Desegregation Center described Forest Park (#104) in these words: 'One Negro school is particularly displeasing in terms of location. Forest Park Elementary No. 104 is a large (1,080 capacity), relatively new building on a 1.72 acre site. The school is "surrounded by a City incinerator on the East, a polluted creek on the North, and a meat and poultry (abattoir) company on the West. This has caused a serious problem with regard to stench and sewage backing up in the school plant." In urging that this school should remain open, the attorney for plaintiffs presented evidence that the incin-

erator was no longer in operation. However that may be,
it is undisputed that the slaughter house and McCoy's
Creek are still producing highly noxious odors which even
permeate the school cafeteria.
    ... Across the Expressway lie Isaiah Blocker (#135)
and Darnell-Cookman Junior High School (#145). These
schools are located in the area of the highest crime rate
in the city, where eighty per cent of the hard narcotics
are trafficked. Influences in the neighborhood make quality education at these schools a virtual impossibility. The
school buildings are frequently invaded during school hours
by vandals and trouble-makers, mostly consisting of truants and teenage drop-outs. Fences and locked gates have
been no deterrent, nor have 'administrative assistants'
whose sole function is to patrol the halls. It is customary
to lock the teachers and students in the classrooms for
their safety. Even this procedure has not precluded as-
saults on teachers and students. The conditions are such
that the Superintendent has been unable to maintain a sufficient number of certified white teachers at any of these
schools to comply with the seventy-thirty white-black
teacher ratio.
    In sum, this Court finds that the School Board acted
in good faith in resolving to close the seven elementary
schools. The action does not constitute invidious discrimination proscribed by the Fourteenth Amendment. The
closing of these schools 'is simply a reasonable part of a
workable plan of desegregation.'

    In the last section of his order, Judge Tjoflat ordered the
board to acquire 250 additional buses to carry out his plan. Due to
supply problems, the court ordered that only 100 of these need be
acquired before final disposition of the case on appeal.

    The final order was issued June 23, 1971. In an extraordi-
nary stroke of thoughtful judicial administration, Judge Tjoflat persuaded the local newspaper to publish it in its entirety in a special
section of the paper the next day. The paper also quoted the school
board attorney as saying that the board was pleased and planned no
appeal. The attorney also expressed confidence that any appeal by
the plaintiffs would be unsuccessful.

    That prediction proved accurate; on August 16, the Court of
Appeals affirmed the order. Two days later, Judge Tjoflat vacated
that portion of his order allowing delay in the acquisition of the
final compliment of 150 buses and ordered the board to submit by
August 27, 1971, a report detailing the earliest date upon which the
full plan could be implemented. On September 2, following receipt
of this projection, the court ordered the full plan to go into effect
at the start of the 1972-73 school year, by which time all buses
were to have been acquired. In addition, to insure follow-through
on the order, Judge Tjoflat set several reporting dates through the
1971-72 school year and during the summer of 1972 to check the

progress of the bus purchases. The court order specifically provided that the buses were to be acquired whether or not outside
(federal) funds were available to the board. Busing was an integral
and essential part of the Jacksonville plan. In a school district as
large as Duval County, with impacted racial concentrations, no effective integration could have been achieved without extensive student
transportation.

* * *

Judge Tjoflat's precautions and Superintendent Hardesty's tireless efforts were successful. School opened in September of 1971
with relative calm, despite extensive local criticism of federal courts
and integration. Interestingly, some blacks who had previously
moved to suburbs and had enrolled their children in integrated
schools joined the shrill criticism of massive integration. Reportedly, some charged that the "riffraff" from the ghettos would lower
the quality of the schools--they had moved out, they said, to avoid
sending their children to school with just such people.

As expected, there were more problems in the high schools
than the elementary schools. The process ran more smoothly at
Raines, a formerly all-black school, than it did at nearby Ribault,
a formerly all-white school. The black principal at Raines, a
strict disciplinarian, had sufficient rapport with the black student
leaders to head off most of the racial conflicts. Reportedly, he
told his potential troublemakers that their job was to protect the
white students and to keep the peace; his gamble proved highly successful.

With the coming of the Florida presidential primary, the relative calm that initially greeted massive integration vanished. Busing
of "little children" had become a political football. Presidential
aspirants, like Senator Henry "Scoop" Jackson from the State of
Washington, greeted little children at bus stops, with ever-ready
television cameras standing by, to remind them how bad it was to
have to catch a bus every morning to school.

The problems became critical at Ribault High School. On
Friday, February 18, 1972, fighting broke out between black and
white students at the school and a faculty member was beaten by
black students. About forty uniformed police were required to restore order. Superintendent Hardesty closed the .school to protect
students and prevent further damage. There was difficulty in getting
some of the black students to leave the school, with several adult
black males reportedly arriving to add to the confusion.

The school was reopened on Monday, February 21, with thirty
additional school personnel on the campus and several law enforcement officers on standby in the immediate vicinity. Only 1,000 of a
total enrollment of 1,700 were in attendance--the atmosphere was
extremely tense. After school, there was an off-campus meeting of
black students; black adults in attendance urged a "walk out" of
school on Tuesday.

School opened Tuesday morning with the same personnel and a hostile atmosphere. School officials were warned that black students had planned disruptions. An incident surrounding the removal of an Angela Davis poster in the cafeteria heightened the tension. When classes changed, about fifty white and 125 black students gathered in the courtyard between two wings of the school. A free-for-all ensued which resulted in the hospitalization of two students and injuries to many others. Following this fighting, a full-fledged riot erupted with 400 students rampaging through the halls, yelling and breaking windows. The forty policemen standing by were called and were able to restore order in twenty minutes. School authorities again ordered the school closed and later suspended thirty students who were identified as participants in the disturbance.

On Wednesday, Thursday, and Friday, the school administration tried without success to bring the various groups together to solve the problem. The meetings broke up in outbursts as the blacks walked out. The faculty also met in workshop sessions and an announcement was made on Thursday that school would be resumed on Monday, February 28. Black groups held meetings to plan a school boycott.

On the afternoon of Friday, February 25, a class action suit was filed in state court against Dr. Hardesty to prevent the reopening of the schools on the grounds of danger to the students. The state court judge refused to issue the injunction and the school reopened Monday, February 28, with about 500 students in attendance.

On Monday, Tuesday, and Wednesday, representatives of both races met to consider ways to return the school to normalcy. Gradually increasing enrollment indicated the measures adopted had met with some success. However, on Wednesday afternoon and Thursday morning, a small group of militant blacks stepped up their efforts to achieve a complete black boycott of the school, using threats and coercion in some cases. In addition, a crowd of blacks stirred up by the same small group completely disrupted a meeting which the school had attempted to hold Thursday night with parents of the suspended students.

Alleging a concerted effort to prevent operation of Ribault High School, Superintendent Hardesty and the local sheriff petitioned Judge Tjoflat for an order enjoining those responsible for the disruptions from further preventing implementation of his desegregation decree. Judge Tjoflat responded swiftly; he found that the alleged acts of disruption had occurred and would continue to occur unless the requested injunction was issued. In response to a courtroom charge by an attorney representing various black groups that he was attempting to "restrain the world," Judge Tjoflat reportedly leaned across the bench and retorted, "that's exactly what I'm trying to do--nobody is going to interfere with the schools and that means nobody."

On Sunday, March 5, Judge Tjoflat enjoined anyone from

committing certain enumerated acts as well as "any other act to disrupt the orderly operation of Ribault Senior High School...." Personnel permitted on the school grounds were strictly limited. The order was read over the school's public address system on Monday morning, copies were mailed to each suspended or expelled student, and copies were personally served on seven individuals specifically named in the decree. The named parties were members of a small, but militant, group that had instigated many of the problems at Ribault. One member of this group was later convicted of criminal contempt for violation of the order, as were a number of students who continued to engage in disruptive activities. Disruptions ceased for a time and then, as if certain students were testing how far they could go, incidents began to reoccur. Dr. Hardesty was forced to close the school once again on April 7, 1972. However, when it became clear that both the school officials and the court meant business, the students settled down, order was restored, and the educational process resumed at Ribault High School, with only isolated incidents sporadically reoccurring.

* * *

Spurred by debates in the Florida primary, in the late spring and early summer of 1972, a nationwide tide of public opinion developed against the use of busing to achieve school desegregation. This development encouraged the school board to petition Judge Tjoflat for a stay of execution of the second phase of his busing order, scheduled to go into effect for the 1972-73 school year. Superintendent Hardesty warned the board that further legal action could only result in even sterner orders and that hope of relief was futile; it appealed anyway. The board cited public opinion as one of its reasons for requesting relief from busing in the petition filed July 27, 1972. Also cited as reasons were the unavailability of federal funds, risks to the health and safety of the children, impairment of the educational process, and new legal criteria established by the Charlotte-Mecklenburg case. In his order denying the motion on August 10, 1972, Judge Tjoflat deftly disposed of each reason in turn. He reminded the board that it had committed itself to busing as ordered by not appealing the July 23, 1971 order, and its commitment was made with or without regard to the presence or absence of federal funds. As to the safety and risk arguments, Judge Tjoflat held that the board had not convinced him as a factual matter that safety and health could not be maintained unless the busing order was modified. Finally, Judge Tjoflat rejected the board's legal arguments by pointing out that the Supreme Court still required desegregation, and if the board could propose a method to accomplish that end without busing, he would at that time consider staying the order.

* * *

Overcoming what appeared to be nearly insoluble personnel and student problems, Jacksonville's experience with integration can be read, at least, as a success story. While 15,000 whites did leave the school system, it did not become all-black. Although bitter complaints occurred about the decline in instructional quality because of the influx of black teachers into white schools, white achievement rates held at substantially the same level as existed prior to integration. Significantly, after the influx of white teachers into formerly all-black schools, achievement levels, while still woefully below the national average, did increase substantially. While diverted from his initial goal of substantially improving the Jacksonville public school system by court orders demanding immediate desegregation, Superintendent Hardesty did contribute as much as any man to the survival of the system--he left a viable structure on which others could build. He is convinced that while integration in Jacksonville was disruptive, it will prove in the long run to be the salvation of the black child.

A positive thinker, Superintendent Hardesty--in the midst of threatening letters, abusive phone calls, teacher resignations, and student disruptions--always sought out the success story to inspire his harassed school system employees. When besieged with complaints about busing, he would report on a survey he had conducted among the students showing most to be enthusiastic about busing: many said they enjoyed the ride. When told that black students were under-achievers and hated school, he would tell of the experience of a white principal in a suburban white elementary school: she left school at the end of the day and, as the last bus left carrying black children back to the center city, she saw two little black children come around the side of the building. Thinking they had missed the bus home, she began to chide them. She discovered, however, that they had not missed the afternoon bus home; they had instead missed the morning bus to school. They then had walked from home to school, fifteen miles, five of them along a busy freeway. They had just arrived, bone-tired, when the principal saw them. As she drove them home, she inquired why they had walked all that way. Both eagerly replied that they liked school and didn't want to miss their classes.

NOTES AND PRIMARY AUTHORITY

The primary authority for the material contained in this chapter was:

<u>The Fifth Circuit's Implementation of Carter.</u> The primary sources are the cases, cited in the order they are mentioned in the text: Bivins v. Bibb County Bd. of Educ., 424 F.2d 97 (5th Cir. 1970); Hall v. St. Helena Parish School Bd., 424 F.2d 320 (5th Cir. 1970); Carr v. Montgomery County Bd. of Educ., 429 F.2d 382 (5th Cir. 1970); United States v. Texas Educ. Agency, 431 F.2d 1313 (5th Cir. 1970); Ellis v. Bd. of Pub. Instruction of Orange County, 423 F.2d 203 (5th Cir. 1970); Henry v. Clarksdale Mun. Separate School Dist., 433 F.2d 387 (5th Cir. 1970); United States v. Hinds County School Bd., 433 F.2d 598 (5th Cir. 1970); and Ross v. Eckels, 434 F.2d 1140 (5th Cir. 1970). Allen Bd. of Pub. Instruction, 432

F. 2d 362 (5th Cir. 1970), collates and describes the thrust of the desegregation decisions of the Fifth Circuit in 1970.

Massive Integration in Iberia, etc. The primary sources are personal interviews and contemporary reports in local newspapers such as the Daily Iberian, Opelousas Daily Advertiser, and the Opelousas Daily World. A lengthy interview with Judge Richard J. Putnam was particularly helpful.

Massive Integration in Jacksonville. The Jacksonville school case is styled as Mims v. Duval County School Bd.; the history of that case is reported in 329 F. Supp. 123 (M.D. Fla. 1971); other portions and documents of the case are found in the District Court file, Civil No. 4598-Civ-J (M.D. Fla. 1971); 447 F. 2d 1330 (5th Cir. 1971); and 338 F. Supp. 1208 (M.D. Fla. 1972). The state court action associated with the case is Radford v. Hardesty, Civil No. 72-1832 (Cir. Ct. of Fla., 4th Cir., 1972); and the criminal action associated with the case is United States v. Hall, Criminal No. 72-65-Cr-J (M.D. Fla.). Interviews with Judge Gerald R. Tjoflat, Judge Griffin Bell, Judge Bryan Simpson and Dr. Cecil Hardesty were particularly helpful as were contemporary news accounts in the Jacksonville Florida Times-Union.

A more complete manuscript, with detailed documentation of all sources, is available as indicated in the Preface, supra.

Chapter 15

THE WORD FROM MOUNT OLYMPUS

Throughout the desegregation battles from 1955 to 1970, the Supreme Court of the United States had been content with prodding its lower courts toward more rapid compliance with its mandates. Even in its decisions in Green, Alexander, and Carter, the Supreme Court issued terse "do it now" commands, it did not provide "how to do it" instructions. Lacking firm directives from the Supreme Court on how to accomplish desegregation, the lower federal courts --with the bulk of the activity centering in the Fifth Circuit--were abandoned to their own devices in determining appropriate methods of compliance. Much of the on-going struggle from the early years after Brown II until mid-1970 had centered around evolution of means of implementing Supreme Court mandates. From pupil placement acts to freedom-of-choice to neighborhood zoning to majority-to-minority transfer options to clustering and pairing of schools to busing, the federal courts of the South had struggled with the "how" of integration while the Supreme Court had been content with "hurry-ups."

Swann v. Charlotte-Mecklenburg Board of Education

On June 29, 1970, the Supreme Court granted certiorari in a series of desegregation cases directly raising--for the first time --questions about the "how" of desegregation: Should courts order racial balancing? Is widespread busing permissible? The chief case in which certiorari was granted was Swann v. Charlotte-Mecklenburg Board of Education. In that case, a feisty federal district judge, James McMillan of Charlotte, North Carolina, had used a racial-balancing concept in formulating a desegregation plan requiring widespread busing in metropolitan Charlotte and surrounding Mecklenburg County. The Fourth Circuit had reversed the busing portion of Judge McMillan's plan as being overly harsh. When the Supreme Court decided to review Judge McMillan's case, waves of anticipation and dread spread throughout the lower federal courts in the South. Finally, perhaps, the Supreme Court would give some answers to its lower courts on the "how" of accomplishing the herculean task so peremptorily ordered in Alexander and Carter.

When certiorari was granted in Swann, Chief Judge John R. Brown of the Fifth Circuit reacted with alacrity. In the only press

release he has ever issued, the Chief Judge indicated that the Fifth
Circuit would freeze all but the most essential desegregation activity in the circuit until it had received instructions from the Supreme
Court in Swann as to "how" to implement its mandates. The great
integration revolution sweeping the South since Carter was suddenly
halted. The federal courts waited for the Supreme Court to drop
the next shoe.

The Supreme Court took nine suspense-filled months to issue
its opinion, an unconscionably long delay by the same Court which
had ordered peremptory reversals of the Fifth Circuit for three-
month delays to accomplish massive desegregation orders in Alexander and Carter. On April 20, 1971, the long wait ended. The
Swann opinion satisfied no one. It dismayed almost all parties involved in the desegregation struggle, and raised more questions
than it answered.

*   *   *

Mr. Chief Justice Burger wrote the opinion for a unanimous
court. He began by reaffirming that certiorari had been granted to
review two important issues raised by Supreme Court desegregation
mandates: "the duties of school authorities and the scope of powers
of federal courts." From the onset of his opinion, Chief Justice
Burger made it clear that the Court's holding was to apply only to
schools systems with a background of de jure segregation (schools
systems that prior to Brown I had been mandatorily segregated by
law).

The Chief Justice examined the facts of the Swann dispute.
The Charlotte-Mecklenburg county school system was the 43rd largest in the nation. It included the city of Charlotte, North Carolina,
and all of surrounding Mecklenburg County, an area of 550 square
miles. The school system served 84,000 pupils in 107 schools; approximately seventy-one per cent of the students were white and
twenty-nine per cent were black. Two-thirds of the black students
attended just twenty-one schools which were either totally or more
than ninety-nine per cent black as of June, 1969. After the Supreme
Court's decision in Green, Judge McMillan held "numerous hearings
and received voluminous evidence." The district court ordered the
school board to come forward with a plan for both faculty and student desegregation. The school board, after vigorous prodding,
came forth with only a partially completed plan. In light of the
board's failure to comply with the court's mandate, Judge McMillan
appointed Dr. John Finger, an expert in educational administration,
to prepare a desegregation plan for the court. Therefore, when
Judge McMillan acted, he had before him two alternative pupil assignment plans: the finalized "board plan," which was patently inadequate, and the "Finger plan." The Finger plan was most controversial in the method of which it dealt with the desegregation of
junior and senior high schools. Finally, on February 5, 1970, after
the Supreme Court's decisions to accelerate desegregation in Alexander and Carter, Judge McMillan adopted the board plan as modified

by Dr. Finger's plan for the junior and senior high schools. The approved plan required extensive busing in the secondary schools, and employed the technique of pairing and grouping of elementary schools. Fearing that the pairing and grouping of elementary schools would place an unreasonable burden on the board and the system's pupils, the Court of Appeals remanded the district court's decision for reconsideration. At that point, the Supreme Court granted certiorari.

After reviewing the facts, Chief Justice Burger emphasized that the Supreme Court was not retreating from its holding that state-imposed racial segregation in public schools denied equal protection of the law. He reaffirmed the prior Brown I and II decisions, pointedly reminding school authorities that they carried the primary responsibility for eliminating all vestiges of state-imposed segregation. Federal courts were to act only after school boards had defaulted; when forced to intervene, they were to be guided by equitable principles.

The Court repeated the goal of all desegregation plans: "The objective today remains to eliminate from the public schools all vestiges of state-imposed segregation." The task of the district court was to balance individual and collective interests, and to develop a remedy that repaired the denial of constitutional rights. The power of school boards in desegregation matters was plenary; the power of federal courts was limited to correcting constitutional violations when violations were found to exist. Mr. Justice Burger then quickly disposed of objections to busing based on Title IV of the Civil Rights Act of 1964.

The Supreme Court then proceeded to define "with more particularity" the elements of an acceptable school desegregation plan. In addition to student assignment, the Supreme Court emphasized again--as it had in Green--that existing policy and practices with regard to faculty, staff, transportation, extracurricular activities and facilities were also important indicia of a segregated system. School authorities had an immediate and nondelegable duty to eliminate invidious racial distinctions in all of those areas. The Court cited with approval Judge Frank M. Johnson's famous Montgomery County case, which required each school in the system to have the same ratio of white to black faculty members as was present throughout the school system. The Supreme Court only briefly discussed desegregation of transportation, staff and activities; implementation of a desegregation plan in those areas was ostensibly simple. The school authorities were only required to eliminate existing invidious racial distinctions. The Supreme Court also recognized that school construction should not be ignored in any desegregation plan. School construction and school abandonment policies were not to "perpetuate or reestablish [a] dual system."

The Supreme Court then gingerly examined the central issue --the problem of student assignment--in the Swann case and in all school cases. Again specifically confining its attention to de jure

situations, the Court turned to the explosive question of the appropriateness of racial balancing. The Supreme Court pointed out that
while Judge McMillan had utilized the twenty-nine per cent to seventy-one per cent black-white ratio in the Charlotte schools, he had
done so only as a starting point for review of the two plans before
him. The Supreme Court held that racial balancing was not required by the Constitution:

> If we were to read the holding of the District Court to
> require, as a matter of substantive constitutional right,
> any particular degree of racial balance or mixing, that
> approach would be disapproved and we would be obliged
> to reverse. The constitutional command to desegregate
> schools does not mean that every school in every commun-
> ity must always reflect the racial composition of the school
> system as a whole.

Almost immediately the high Court seemed to undercut the holding it
had just announced a few lines earlier:

> We see ... that the use made of mathematical ratios
> was no more than a starting point in the process of shap-
> ing a remedy, rather than an inflexible requirement.
> From that starting point the District Court proceeded to
> frame a decree that was within its discretionary powers,
> as an equitable remedy for the particular circumstances.
> As we said in Green, a school authority's remedial plan
> or a district court's remedial decree is to be judged by
> its effectiveness. Awareness of the racial composition of
> the whole school system is likely to be a useful starting
> point in shaping a remedy to correct past constitutional
> violations.

Consequently, the Supreme Court's decision in Swann on the racial-
balancing issue has been both intentionally and unintentionally misunderstood by all sides in the myriad of school cases pending before the lower federal courts. While the Supreme Court specifically
indicated, on the one hand, that racial balancing was not required
by the Constitution; nevertheless it indicated, on the other hand,
that a school's black-white ratio was a logical starting point for reviewing the effectiveness of desegregation plans.

The Court next turned its attention to the problem of "one-
race" schools. The Court held that there was a presumption against
one-race schools, but it refused to hold that the existence of one-
race schools constituted a per se violation of the Constitution. Significantly, in its discussion of one-race schools the Court specifically blessed the majority-to-minority transfer provisions seen in so
many Fifth Circuit cases. Judge Bell has wondered aloud if the
Supreme Court's favorable comments about the majority-to-minority
option might breathe life into his Orange County opinion.

The Supreme Court then confronted the problem of remedial

altering of attendance zones. The Court said that the following weapons were within the arsenal of the lower federal courts: gerry-mandering of school districts, "pairing, 'clustering,' or 'grouping' of schools, with attendance assignments made deliberately to accomplish the transfer of Negro students out of formerly segregated Negro schools and transfer of white students to formerly all-Negro schools."

At least from a political standpoint, the last issue that the Court faced--busing--was perhaps the most troubling. The Court specifically approved busing as a tool of desegregation. It pointed out that bus transportation had been an "integral part of the public education system for years, and was perhaps the single most important factor in the transition from the one-room schoolhouse to the consolidated school." The Court noted that in Charlotte, where there had been impassioned protests against busing, the school board had bused children for years to maintain a dual system of education. But the Court also noted that there might be limits beyond which busing orders would become unreasonable:

> An objection to transportation of students may have validity when the time or distance of travel is so great as to either risk the health of the children or significantly impinge on the educational process. District courts must weigh the soundness of any transportation plan.... It hardly needs stating that the limits on time of travel will vary with many factors, but probably with none more than the age of the students. The reconciliation of competing values in a desegregation case is, of course, a difficult task with many sensitive facets but fundamentally no more so than remedial measures courts of equity have traditionally employed.

After reviewing all of the issues raised by the Swann case, the United States Supreme Court held that the district court's order was not unreasonable but was both feasible and workable. Then, in a very strange conclusion to an already confusing holding, the Court seemed to indicate that there was perhaps a way out of school desegregation problems:

> At some point, these school authorities and others like them should have achieved full compliance with this Court's decision in Brown I. The systems would then be 'unitary' in the sense required by our decisions in Green and Alexander.
> It does not follow that the communities served by such systems will remain demographically stable, for in a growing, mobile society, few will do so. Neither school authorities nor district courts are constitutionally required to make year-by-year adjustments of the racial composition of student bodies once the affirmative duty to desegregate has been accomplished and racial discrimination through official action is eliminated from the system. This

does not mean that federal courts are without power to deal with future problems; but in the absence of a showing that either the school authorities or some other agency of the State has deliberately attempted to fix or alter demographic patterns to affect the racial composition of the schools, further intervention by a district court should not be necessary.

* * *

Three companion school desegregation cases were decided by the Supreme Court the same day as Swann v. Charlotte-Mecklenburg Board of Education. In a case arising in the Fifth Circuit, Davis v. Board of School Commissioners of Mobile County, the Supreme Court reversed the Fifth Circuit for failing to achieve a sufficient amount of desegregation in Mobile County, Alabama. The Fifth Circuit had approved a desegregation order that did not require the busing of students across a major highway which divided Mobile, Alabama into district zones. The Supreme Court's reversal implicitly indicated that the Fifth Circuit should have ordered more busing to achieve more desegregation. The Davis case, when read in tandem with Swann, gave proponents of busing substantial authority to insist that this remedy had been judicially endorsed. Both decisions added fire to the busing controversy that dominated the 1972 presidential primaries.

In McDaniel v. Barresi, the Supreme Court reversed a foolish Georgia Supreme Court holding that a desegregation plan violated equal protection because it treated students differently because of their race. The Supreme Court tartly commented that, in compliance with its duty to convert to a unitary system, the local board of education of Clarke County, Georgia had properly taken race into account in fixing attendance lines in order to achieve desegregation mandated by Brown I and II. In a fourth case, North Carolina State Board of Education v. Swann, a companion case to Swann v. Charlotte-Mecklenburg Board of Education, the Supreme Court held unconstitutional North Carolina's anti-busing law, which had attempted to forbid assignment or transportation of any student because of race, or for the purpose of creating a racial balance. The Court held that the North Carolina statute was an attempt to prevent implementation of desegregation plans required by the fourteenth amendment, and was thus unconstitutional.

Reactions to "Swann"

The reaction of legal writers to Swann was muted. Noting that many questions had been left unanswered by the Supreme Court, law journal writers generally felt that the Swann case did not substantially change the law of desegregation as it had been developed by lower federal courts. The increasingly divisive de facto/de jure distinction had not been resolved; the South apparently would continue to bear massive school integration orders while northern de facto segregation would go unrectified.   While conceding that the Swann decision might accelerate the pace of desegregation initially, one perceptive legal writer questioned its real impact on dismantling a dual school system:

> For the present at least, its impact should be to accel-
> erate the pace of desegregation in many states primarily
> because the lower courts will be less reluctant from a
> legal standpoint to utilize busing and racial quotas to
> achieve the racial balance called for in Brown I.... Re-
> gardless of the early indications of compliance, however,
> it is still premature to conclude that the Supreme Court
> has taken a significant stride toward the elimination of the
> dual school system, and toward the realization of equal
> educational opportunity.   In view of the current public re-
> sponse to the instant decision, the opposite conclusion
> seems to be the more likely result.   The controversy re-
> volves around one central point: busing and the use of
> racial quotas are highly unpopular measures, especially
> among whites.   As the ultimate desegregation weapons in
> a court's arsenal, they unquestionably will have a dramatic
> impact upon every community in which they are used, po-
> tentially affecting every school age child, irrespective of
> wealth, race, or place of residence.   It is this prospect
> that most alarms opponents of busing and racial quotas.
> Not only does it prompt them to withdraw their children
> from the schools, but it also might influence them to with-
> draw their leadership and financial support from public
> education altogether.   Worse still, if whites continue to
> abandon the public schools, the schools will be unable to
> promote the interaction among students of different races
> that Brown I found to be so essential to the development
> of racial tolerance and a sense of equality in a democratic
> society.   In short, the side effects of assaulting racial
> discrimination in the public schools are jeopardizing the
> very goal of equal educational opportunity that is being
> sought.   This is the underlying irony of the desegregation
> movement, and the courts are now caught squarely in the
> dilemma.   Constitutionally bound to dismantle the dual
> school system, they possess desegregation weapons that
> they dare not use to the fullest extent for fear of destroy-
> ing the good characteristics of public schools along with
> the bad. [1]

Newspaper reaction across the nation to the Swann decision was more varied but not nearly as restrained as the reaction of legal commentators.   The conservative Richmond Times Dispatch was outraged:

> Following a grotesque logic, the court arrived at the
> unanimous conclusion that there is, in effect, a dual stand-
> ard on school integration in this country.   While busing

> may be required in the South, it may not be required in
> the North. Neighborhood schools are probably acceptable,
> and even desirable, in the North, but they are to be for-
> bidden in the South. Serenity in Boston, said the court,
> and chaos in Richmond.
>
> Yes, the South is occupied territory, the victim of a
> relentless federal oppression that seems to be nurtured by
> the incomprehensible notion that the South must pay eter-
> nally for the sins of its past while the North may be for-
> given the sins of its present. [2]

The Times-Picayune, perhaps having learned its lesson from the
1960-61 chaos in New Orleans, was considerably more restrained,
warning that despite continued inequities, strong support of public
schools was necessary.

Unlike the Richmond-Times Dispatch and the Times-Picayune,
the Atlanta Constitution took an upbeat attitude, pleading for compliance with the law. It is significant to note that the Charlotte Observer, the newspaper in the city where the Swann case originated,
painstakingly explained the decision to its readers, pointing out that
Judge McMillan's decision had been justified. Judge McMillan had
been a much vilified figure in Charlotte. The attempt of the local
newspaper to explain the decision and to support the judge showed
a high level of journalistic responsibility.

Elsewhere in the nation reactions varied. In contrast to the
outrage expressed in many Southern newspapers over the differing
treatment between the North and South, the New York Times emphasized the history of recalcitrance in the South. The Christian Science Monitor used the decision to criticize obliquely President Nixon's comments on busing; the Cleveland Plain Dealer stressed the
political implications of the decision on President Nixon.

*   *   *

Swann was the last of a long line of unanimous decisions by
the Supreme Court in the school integration area. The decision was
not innovative; it restated much of the development of prior desegregation law in vague and general terms. The pressing question of
whether the Constitution applies in the de facto segregated ghettos
of the North and West was not answered. Precise guidelines on the
permissible extent of busing as a remedy were avoided. While racial balancing was not constitutionally required, it was a permissible
starting point--thus obscuring, rather than solving that volatile issue. Lastly, the opinion tantalized the lower courts by indicating
that they could get out of the school business once school systems
were unitary--not defining when or how that would be determined.

The most common reaction of lower federal judges was frustration and confusion. In the Fifth Circuit, where activity had been
held up for nine months awaiting a decision that was to answer definitively all questions, there was not only confusion but lingering bit-

terness. Now composed of fifteen members, the Fifth Circuit found itself divided as to the meaning of Swann. Unable to give any more direction to its lower courts than the vague generalities of Swann, the Fifth Circuit continued its practice of reversing lower courts primarily on statistics showing insufficient racial mixing. In recognition of the Delphic Swann decision, the Fifth Circuit simply appended to its opinion orders reversing lower courts the cryptic comment that the reversal was "in light of Swann v. Charlotte-Mecklenburg Board of Education." Many federal district court judges who had been hopeful of receiving considerably more advice became hostile not only toward the Supreme Court but also toward the Fifth Circuit. Swann was an opinion for all litigants. It provided language readily adaptable to the position of almost any party in a desegregation battle. The decision added to the woes of the overburdened lower federal courts by stimulating further litigation in an area where there had already been entirely too much.

The long-awaited word from Mount Olympus had been muted and was to be universally misunderstood.

Post-"Swann" Massive Integration in Savannah and Augusta

Judge Alexander Lawrence replaced Judge Scarlett in the Southern District of Georgia, and inherited both the Richmond County (Augusta) and the Chatham County (Savannah) cases. Integration efforts in both counties had been frustrated for years by Judge Scarlett's obstructionism.* Massive integration did not arrive in Savannah and Augusta after Alexander and Carter as it did in many areas of the South. However, after Swann even those two cities, long considered by their white citizens to be somehow immune from the integration revolution sweeping the South, were forced into compliance by federal judicial fiat.

Like Judge Scarlett, the new district judge had spent his entire life in the Georgia city whose desegregation became his responsibility. Alexander Lawrence was born in Savannah in 1906 and received his A.B. magna cum laude degree from the University of Georgia in 1929. He was admitted to the Georgia Bar in 1930, and practiced in Savannah until his appointment to the bench on August 2, 1968. One of Georgia's leading trial lawyers, Judge Lawrence once ate a cockroach during a trial to demonstrate the lack of ill effects. He was a member of the American College of Trial Lawyers, a past president of the Georgia Bar Association and a member of the Georgia Board of Bar Examiners from 1951-58.

A noted Southern historian, Judge Lawerence seemed an improbable choice to enforce massive desegregation decrees. He has had a long and active interest in history, especially that of Georgia

---

*See discussion, supra, Part II, Chapter 10.

and Savannah. He was a member of the Georgia Historical Commission from 1951-67, a past president of the Georgia Historical
Society and active in the preservation of historical buildings in
Savannah. He is the author of five historical books,* and is a popular speaker in Georgia. He was named one of four outstanding
citizens of Savannah in 1968, and was awarded the Thomas H. Gignilliat Award for contributing to cultural programs in Savannah and
Chatham County.

Judge Lawrence's appointment to the federal court came after
a long struggle between his chief supporter, Georgia Senator Richard
Russell, and Attorney General Ramsey Clark. In September, 1959,
at a Constitutional Week speech in Atlanta, Lawrence stated:

> Tyranny is always versatile. It has ridden with the sword.
> It has borne the scepter. We have seen it in the cassock.
> It has carried the mace. Today it appears in a new garb
> --black robes.

That and other similar statements opposing court intervention in
school cases were used against him when his nomination was suggested. Both the NAACP and the Chatham County Human Relations
Council opposed his nomination; Attorney General Clark reportedly
stated he would resign if Lawrence was nominated. The six-month
struggle between Senator Russell and Attorney General Clark was
finally resolved at a face-to-face meeting with President Johnson.
After Lawrence was nominated, Senator Russell, whose brother had
been Lawrence's roommate at the University of Georgia, asked
President Johnson to return the letter of support Russell had written
for Judge Lawrence, so strongly worded were the terms of Russell's
defense. No opposition appeared at the Senate hearings; Judge Lawrence was confirmed after receiving the American Bar Association's
top rating, highly unusual for a nominee over sixty.

When the Richmond County (Augusta) case was transferred to
him in November, 1968, Judge Lawrence faced immediate hearings
on proposed plans for integration. Under Judge Scarlett's tutelage,
the Richmond County (Augusta) school system had placed only 7.7
per cent of its black students in white schools and 0.2 per cent of
its white students in black schools. The situation was no better in
Chatham County (Savannah): out of a public school total of 42,500
students, there were only 1,620 black students in white schools and

---

*James Moore Wayne, Southern Unionist, 1943, the biography of a
Georgia associate justice of the Supreme Court from 1835 to 1867;
Storm Over Savannah, 1951, reprinted 1969, the story of Count d'Es-
taing and the siege of Savannah in 1779, for which Judge Lawrence
researched materials in the Archives Nationales and Service Hydro-
graphique de la Marine in Paris; James Johnston, Georgia's First
Printer, 1956, a monograph; A Present for Mr. Lincoln, 1961, an
account of Savannah from secession to Sherman; and Johnny Leber
and the Confederate Major, 1962, a fictional book.

589 white students in black schools. At a time when the Supreme Court was calling for effective, immediate integration, Savannah and Augusta's token integration evidenced the effectiveness of Judge Scarlett's prior delay tactics. The white citizens of Savannah and Augusta had been lulled by Judge Scarlett's intransigence, making Judge Lawrence's role all the more sensitive.

*   *   *

The Richmond County (Augusta) board proved to be the most troublesome for Judge Lawerence.

Judge Lawrence first held hearings in Augusta on December 17, 1968. In August the board had promised to present a zoning plan; the plan was not forthcoming. Instead, the board urged that a plan containing a possible combination of attendance zones and freedom of choice be used. The black plaintiffs moved for adoption of a unitary plan based on nonracial zoning, with pairing of contiguous schools to be implemented on February 1, 1969, the start of the second semester. Unlike Judge Scarlett, whose orders in school cases had not been issued until several months after hearings, Judge Lawrence made his decision within nine days. His December 26, 1968 order found that the existing plan was constitutionally impermissible and ordered geographical zoning to be used. Implementation was delayed until the fall of 1969, the beginning of the next school year.

Several attitudes of the new judge were apparent in his first reported school desegregation case. He repeatedly asserted that he had a duty to act under the mandates of the Fifth Circuit, the Supreme Court and the Fourteenth Amendment. His careful reliance on precedent and invocation of his duty to follow the dictates of higher courts established that he, unlike Scarlett, was not going to be controlled in his judicial behavior by personal whim.

Judge Lawrence also emphasized that the school board had duties to perform. In response to the Richmond County superintendent's argument that he could not achieve faculty integration because many teachers refused reassignment, Judge Lawerence pointedly quoted Jefferson II:

> 'Obviously, the fulfillment of the Constitution cannot rest on the willingness of people to abide. The School Boards do not meet their duty by soliciting volunteers for the fact remains that the responsibility for faculty desegregation ... lies ultimately with the board, not the teachers.'

However, as a novice to the bench and to school cases, Judge Lawrence was not ready to surrender on freedom of choice entirely. He recognized that under Jefferson II no student had a constitutional right to choose a school, but still he thought, "the free choice of attending comparable schools is something which should not be obliterated (and I do not intend to do so) in one

Olympian judicial gesture." The new judge was painfully aware of
the disorder wrought elsewhere by massive integration and desired
to avoid it: "Chaos is as much to be avoided as strict legality to
be sought."

The Richmond board first appeared to adhere to Judge Lawrence's timetable. On June 16, 1969, a hearing was held on its
proposed plan. The black plaintiffs objected to the plan in toto,
alleging that on its face it showed that little effort had been exerted
by the board to achieve real integration. The board did not know
how many children were in each zone; freedom of choice remained
in three areas where black schools were adjacent to white schools;
the faculty remained segregated. Superintendent Roy E. Rollins defended the plan by asserting that the criteria for drawing the zones
were natural boundaries, the proximity of pupils to schools and the
maximum use of buildings.

In his order a month later, Judge Lawrence approved the
plan temporarily for the 1969-70 school year. He ordered the board
to consult with HEW officials in drawing up another plan; he further
ordered the integration of the faculty and staff. Judge Lawrence
stated that the board had acted in good faith but "did not approach
geographical zoning with the purpose of producing greater integration."
He also expressed skepticism about the vestiges of freedom of choice
remaining in the plan.

His first bout with integration in the Richmond County (Augusta) case illustrated Judge Lawrence's initial uncertainty in handling school cases. Sensing that the plan had weaknesses and was
vulnerable if reviewed by the Circuit, he approved it only temporarily for the 1969-70 year. He further directed that the Richmond
County board contact and cooperate with HEW officials in formulating
a better desegregation plan. Judge Lawrence's personal agony in
his first school cases is candidly disclosed in his opinions. The
duty of the court and board was clear to him:

> The school desegregation mandates of the Fifth Cir-
> cuit, as I said in a recent case, beat out in cicadian and
> circadian refrain ... a tom-tom ostinato of 'affirmative
> duty,' 'unitary, nonracial system,' 'failure of freedom of
> choice;' 'wiped out root and branch,' 'meaningful and im-
> mediate progress,' 'not tomorrow but now....'

But how to proceed was not so clear.

> I am in a quandary. Here it is mid-July and the
> next school year starts at the end of August. Time is
> running out. What to do under the circumstances has
> caused me much concern. In my December decision I
> said that 'Chaos is as much to be avoided as strict legal-
> ity to be sought.' I will follow that principle.

Initially careful not to antagonize the board, Judge Lawrence stated

that the plan had been presented in good faith. Yet, he also stated
that zoning had not been approached with the proper purpose and
that his own experience told him that the other portion of the plan--
freedom of choice--was unworkable. Judge Lawrence's humility in
his early opinions may have mesmerized Augusta school officials
into believing that he lacked the iron determination he would later
display. He was perhaps too frank in expressing his frustrations
and lack of expertise:

> I will add that I do not at all relish the job thrust
> upon me of deciding how public schools should be run. It
> is far beyond my competence. I cannot think of anyone
> less qualified to administer school systems. Moreover, I
> do not have the time to go around telling school boards
> how to operate schools. This Court has the second heavi-
> est weighted case load of any federal district court. The
> Acree case alone has consumed about 9 days of my time
> during the past six and one half months. And no matter
> what I do there will be new motions, more objections and
> hearings ad infinitum. '[B]ut we glory in tribulations also;
> knowing that tribulation worketh patience; and patience ex-
> perience.' The trouble is 'experience' does not always
> worketh the 'hope' mentioned in Romans, 5.

Not satisfied with his cautious approval of the school board
plan with modifications, the black students, in March, 1970, filed
a notice of appeal from Judge Lawrence's decision the previous July.
With the Alexander and Carter reversals fresh in their minds, the
Fifth Circuit judges were not satisfied with the situation in the Richmond County schools. A new plan was ordered formulated. Judge
Lawrence was given explicit instructions that "prompt and immediate"
action was necessary.

In compliance with the new Fifth Circuit order, Judge Lawrence held new hearings on July 30, 1970. He approved the HEW
plan with modifications on August 3. It was essentially a neighborhood zoning plan similar to that adopted in Judge Bell's controversial
Orange County case. An appeal was taken from Judge Lawrence's
decision while Swann was pending. After the wait for Swann, a per
curiam opinion of the same Brown-Morgan-Ingraham panel vacated
Judge Lawrence's judgment of August 3, and remanded with directions to require a plan complying with Swann, Carter, and Singleton
IV and to require semi-annual reports of the school board.

At this point, Judge Lawrence first faced the total intransigence of the Richmond County school board. He also discovered
that his erstwhile allies in HEW and the Justice Department had
deserted him. He was literally one lone judge directed to accomplish the near impossible. His anguish is evident in his next opinion:

> To my amazement, the H.E.W. officials did not show
> up at the August 26, 1971, hearing. Without notice or ex-

cuse and at whose behest I do not know they did a disap-
pearing act. The Board's behavior was no less contempt-
ible. They passed the buck to the Superintendent of
Schools, who, no doubt under instructions, presented a
'plan' to the Court on behalf of the Board. What this individual did recommend does not surprise me in the light
of his statement to this Court at the hearing held in Augusta on December 16, 1971. I inquired of him what
plan he would suggest to the Court for the integration of
the school system and his reply was, 'Freedom of Choice.
The plan presented by the School Superintendent at the
'hearing' on August 26th last was to keep the school zones
as they were except for two or three minor changes as to
boundaries. One of them would have transferred about
100 white students to an all-black high school. This plan,
so learned counsel for the Board informed me, made the
system a unitary one, if it was not already such.

Judge Lawrence suspects that HEW officials were directed not to
cooperate with any of his plans which envisioned busing. Desperately seeking help that he was not receiving from the school board, the
federal government, or the plaintiffs, Judge Lawrence hired two
school experts from Rhode Island, Mr. Munzer and Mr. Herman,
on August 31, 1971. Their alternative plans were filed on September 27. In October, white parents intervened, claiming to be opposed only to busing and not to integration. The white intervenors
submitted a freedom-of-choice plan. On October 8, 1971, the
Rhode Island experts presented their plans in court. Evidentiary
hearings were held on all proposed plans on December 16 and 17.
A twenty-day extension was granted to the parties to agree on a
plan of their own, but none was presented.

After eight years, a constitutional desegregation plan was
finally approved for the Richmond County (Augusta) schools on January 13, 1972. In 1970-71 figures for the elementary schools indicated that seventeen schools were predominately white (having eighty-
five per cent or more whites) and nine were predominantly black.
There were four all-black schools and one all-white. Eleven elementary schools had five per cent or less of a minority group;
three had ten per cent or less. Richmond County had seventeen
secondary schools. One was all-black; two were ninety-nine per
cent black. Six were predominantly white, with ten per cent or
less blacks; two were predominantly black with six per cent or less
whites; two were eighty-eight per cent white. The statistics were
similar for 1971-72, since the same plan had been in effect. There
were forty-one white schools with a total of 24,721 students, 26,648
of whom were white and 4,073 of whom were black. Eighteen black
schools with 12,941 students had 360 whites (2.8 per cent) enrolled.
Hopeful of improving those dismal statistics, Judge Lawrence selected one of the Herman-Munzer plans for the desegregation of the
Richmond County elementary schools; the plan called for pairing,
clustering and zoning of schools. Decisions about classroom space,
classes for exceptional children and the closing of schools were left

to the school system for determination so long as resolution of those problems did not change the racial ratio significantly. The elementary schools were to be desegregated in three phases beginning on February 15 with two clusters of schools; others were to be desegregated on March 15, and the remainder in September. Judge Lawrence realized that the middle of the year was a poor time to start desegregation; but, because of the long delays, he felt an immediate start had to be made. However, he did allow desegregation of the high schools to be postponed until the next fall and did not order a secondary school desegregation plan, desiring that the parties work one out together.

Judge Lawrence's total exasperation with the school board, the superintendent, and the white intervenors was expressed in his opinion:

> The Richmond County Board and its Superintendent have abdicated their responsibility. They have been contemptuous and intransigent. They have chosen to ignore the Constitution and the courts. Apparently, they, together with a segment of the population of Richmond County, deem themselves above and beyond the law. The Fourteenth Amendment is not to apply to those who find it not to their liking.
> ...
> The Board's response [to the Herman and Munzer plans] was of expected quality and content. It raises every carping, contumacious objection conceivable. It is a mishmash and embranglement of letters from individual members of the Board, the Superintendent and principals opposing desegregation of the system. There are resolutions, letters, speeches, newspaper clippings, et cetera. The response contributes less than nothing to the difficult problem the Board faced but fled.
> ...
> At my suggestion, the Intervenors presented a plan for my consideration. It is entitled 'Quality Education Plan for the People of Richmond County, Georgia.' The plan is nothing more than Freedom of Choice both for students and faculty. Since the Intervenors have a right of appeal from this Order the higher court can enlighten us as to my evaluation of the 'plan' proposed.

In August, 1970, with implementation of his massive desegregation order now an immediate threat, public resistance in Richmond County became intense. Large crowds picketed the courthouse during hearings with signs, "Go Home, Lawrence." Judge Lawrence believes members of the school board or others thought that the presence of those opposed to busing and integration would have an effect on his decision. Letters, telegrams, petitions and resolutions came to Lawrence by the thousands; threats by letter and phone were received. An organized telegram and letter writing effort was obviously underway; many of the letters received from

Augusta were mimeographed and the same phrase, "The emotional and mental balance of our children should take precedence over racial balance in schools," appears over and over. Members of the school board helped organize the Citizens for Neighborhood Schools (CNS). Many white teachers and principals as well as parents were members. School Board Chairman John Fleming admitted contributing money; his wife was a leader in the group. Fleming or another board member, David Smith, was always present at the steering committee meetings of CNS in a thinly veiled attempt to coordinate board and citizen opposition. An organized boycott kept sixty per cent of the Richmond County students home on the Monday after the first phase of elementary desegregation began. Judge Lawrence enjoined the boycott, admitting ruefully that he was perhaps stretching the First Amendment. School board member David Smith was ready to be jailed for contempt; he carried his toothbrush in his pocket. His attitude toward Judge Lawrence is reflected in a statement to a newspaper reporter:

> Sunday afternoon I was so mad I would have poked him in the nose. It would have been worth $1,000 to me for just one good lick. It's like shadow boxing. You know you're right but there is nothing you can do about it.

Chairman Fleming had convinced the board to hire his law partner as the school attorney. He described the legal tactic employed as one of inaction and delay, forcing the judge to order the board to take every new step. He was proud that "[a]ll the ideas originated with Mr. Beazley and me."

The appeals that followed the January, 1972, order had no effect on the start of desegregation. Judge Lawrence had ordered that there be no stay pending appeal. The Fifth Circuit's quick response on March 31 not only affirmed the order of January 13, but also modified it to require the immediate development of a secondary desegregation plan. The Fifth Circuit also joined Judge Lawrence in his criticism of the school board. The plaintiffs were outraged and immediately filed certiorari petitions with the Supreme Court. The petitions were denied on November 13, 1972.

Elementary school desegregation had been accomplished in Augusta and surrounding Richmond County. Judge Lawrence did initiate contempt proceedings against Richmond County school board officials, but excused himself from presiding because of his emotional involvement. Coming to the aid of his embattled colleague, Judge Bell of the Fifth Circuit held an informal meeting with the bellicose school board. The board was apparently shaken by Judge Bell's remarks; Judge Lawrence found the board cooperative thereafter and the contempt charges were dropped. In June of 1972, a chastened board presented a plan for secondary desegregation which Judge Lawrence approved over the plan of the experts. With the fall of 1973, the schools of Richmond County (Augusta) were finally operating in accordance with constitutional standards.

* * *

Generally, Judge Lawrence had an easier time with his hometown Chatham County (Savannah) school board. In 1970 or 1971, he
felt "it finally awakened to the fact ... realized it was their duty,
affirmative duty, to desegregate the system."

Interestingly, the Savannah-Chatham County Board of Education had to call upon Judge Lawrence to help them continue their
plan of desegregation against an interfering state legislature. At a
special session, the Georgia General Assembly had passed the
"Savannah-Chatham County Freedom of Choice School Assignment
Law" which required the board to establish a system of primary and
alternate choices for the parents for school assignment. The assignment at the chosen school would be mandatory as long as capacity
permitted. The law would be effective in the second semester of
the 1971-72 school year. The board asked Judge Lawrence to res-
cue them from the quagmire of obeying federal law only to violate
the state law. Lawrence ordered the board to "do nothing in the
way of compliance with legislation which from the constitutional viewpoint amounts to nothing." The decision to Judge Lawrence was
clear: the state was attempting to amend the Constitution as construed by the Supreme Court and to nullify orders of the federal
courts in an effort to resegregate the public schools. Noting the
unconstitutionality of similar laws in Alabama in 1970, and a similar state-wide Georgia law in 1970, which Judge Hooper had invalidated without opinion, Judge Lawrence scathingly remarked:

> A mere glance at North Carolina State Board of Edu-
> cation ... v. Swann ... should convince all but the self-
> deluded that any such concept of constitutional law is the
> quintessence of hallucination and wishful thinking....

After a ten-year struggle, the Savannah-Chatham County
schools, like their more obstinate counterparts in Augusta-Richmond
County, were desegregated, with the exception of one school.

* * *

The debilitating personal pressures faced by Judge Lawrence
in integrating Savannah and Augusta can hardly be overestimated.
Deserted by HEW and Justice Department allies, subjected to public
vilification from fellow citizens of his lifelong place of residence,
and the target of an organized harassment campaign, Judge Lawrence endured. Particularly troubling to Judge Lawrence were the
thousands of letters, telegrams and petitions that poured into his
office. While few letters contained personal threats--his wife received most of those when she answered the telephone at the peak of
the Savannah case--many spoke of compelling personal hardships.
During a Fifth Circuit Judicial Conference in Savannah in April,
1972, large protest marches were held during which Judge Lawrence
was burned in effigy and symbolically buried. Congressman Fletcher
Thompson, who was running for the Senate, called for Lawrence's

impeachment. Lawrence's response was like that of other beleaguered colleagues. The pressure was only irritating: life tenure
gave comfort.

Judge Lawrence moved too hesitantly at first. Though cognizant of his duty, he did not invoke his full authority until deserted
without help from other sources. Finally, when he could no longer
ignore a bald threat to the authority of the federal courts, he moved
swiftly and effectively. At first, he tolerated too much delay from
the Augusta board: his approval of the board's plan in July, 1969,
as a temporary plan for 1969-70, was in retrospect a mistake. The
plan he approved in 1970 was also unsatisfactory. Lawrence admits,
"It did not achieve any real degree of integration ... I think I was
naive to have swallowed the excuses of the enormous cost of cross-
town busing and the lack of buses because I got the same from
Savannah. Yet when they were forced to bus they were able to do
it...." After HEW had disappeared and school officials remained
belligerently uncooperative, Judge Lawrence proved his mettle in
the Richmond County case.

When asked how he answered the complaints of fellow Southerners, who could not understand why they had to bus their children
when Northerners did not, Judge Lawrence's overriding sense of
duty is evident in his response:

> I don't have to answer to anyone. I tell them that I
> went along with freedom of choice, I went along with
> every conservative approach, but when I am told to do
> something, I'm going to do it. And I am going to follow
> what the higher courts say regardless of what's happen-
> ing in the North.

In addition to his sense of duty, Judge Lawrence's ever-present
sense of humor was an aid. He penned a prayer that was presented
to the Atlanta Lawyer's Club and has become a classic in the Fifth
Circuit:

> Dear Lord, on bended knee I pray you, tomorrow send
> me a plain old tort case. Or if you can't do that, a
> suit on a simple contract in writing will do just as well.
> That's a little enough favor to ask even if I have gotten
> rusty on the common law since I've been on this Court.
> And deliver me, oh Lord, from any 2254's or 1981's,
> 1983's, 1985's, or any 2000's. You got troubles, I know,
> in enforcing Chapter 20, subsections 3-17, inclusive, of
> the Book of Exodus.... And if you care about me, Lord,
> don't send me any class actions, whatever they are.
> It's not that I mind work, You know me better than
> that, Lord. It's just that I'm not a pedagogist, penologist,
> theologist, sociologist, tonsorialist, restauranteur, liter-
> ary censor or personnel director.
> And another thing, please don't put me on any more
> three-judge courts. Lord knows, I got enough trouble

agreeing with myself--much less trying to convince two
other damn fools.

Now I know you don't have much contact with the
United States judges in the Northern District of Georgia.
You can't be everywhere. We realize that. But for your
information, Chief Judge Smith's got six district judges
besides himself in that District. And down here in the
Southern District I got nobody but me. I'm a Chief with
no Indians and it looks like everybody's on the warpath
against me.

. . . .

Now, Lord, I'm not trying to run your business. But
some day you've got to put an end to the invidious discrimination against me and give me the equal protection of
the Ten Commandments and all the recent amendments
thereto.

Letters from Savannah and Augusta, 1971

In 1971, when it became apparent that massive desegregation
and increased busing would soon be ordered, citizens of Savannah
and Augusta inundated Judge Lawrence with letters, telegrams, petitions, resolutions and even a few threats. Most letters were signed
with names, addresses and phone numbers; many expressed regrets
at intruding upon the judge's time; many recognized that he operated
under mandates of higher courts. Some people suggested their own
plans for desegregation; others sent him newspaper clippings or inspirational verse. In Savannah, many of the letters asked that rising seniors not be required to transfer in the first year of desegregation or requested personal exceptions from their new school assignments. Common to both cities were similar concerns: the long
time spent on buses, small children far from home, fear of ghetto
areas, loss of school spirit, lost participation in school activities
by parents and children, and fear of white girls being molested by
black teenagers. A few political cranks charged that Judge Lawrence's orders were the result of a socialist or United Nations
conspiracy. Some people reported violations of the orders; others
thanked the Judge for more white classmates for a child who had
been the only white in a class at a black school.

The following are all authentic, unedited letters received by
Judge Lawrence and school board officials from concerned parents
and citizens in response to massive desegregation orders in Savannah and Augusta. Only names and addresses have been removed.
These letters are typical of those received by all federal district
judges in the South implementing massive desegregation mandates of
higher courts. The letters speak for themselves and tell, perhaps
more graphically than any other way, the poignant human drama of
the effect of massive desegregation on individual citizens.

Sept. 8, '70

Hello Buracurat,

I feel you are a coward, Negro Lover. And that you have Betrayed All People. You Are Scum. I would like to get my hands on you. The people are tired of you. The concerned citizens wont to talk to you. You are the Biggest coward of all time. Nigger or Hippie you love. You are not decent to Juge no one. I could kill you myself and you brother W. W. Law. as well. Youre time will come, you had better bet it will. Keep your damn Federal Marshal. But you alone listen to HEW. And you alone will cause the street to flow with blud afore long. I wont you personally when it start. damn any Federal Government that backs this up. Take a deep look at youreself at nite. You Comminist Devil. Mr. Bevil is Wright. You are a Hipporicrit.

A Federal Juge HATER

October 12, 1970

Dear Judge Lawrence:

... I have just returned from taking my 14-year-old and his friends to Wilder Jr. High School. Since I will be worrying from now until 3:00 about the safety of this child and an older son, who is a student at Savannah High School, I would like to share some of my concern with you.

Rumor has it that there will be more than the usual trouble at Savannah Hi today------let's hope not. The fact that the students waiting for the start of school at Wilder seemed to be divided into large groups of blacks did nothing but increase my concern.

You see, my real worry stems from the fact that although I'm a loving mother, I neglected to see that my sons received training in hand-to-hand combat or gang warfare. Until now, I never thought they would need this specialized training until Uncle Sam made soldiers of them....

Sincerely,

August 20, 1970

Dear Mr. Lawrence:

... I am in tears over this situation this very minute, I hope I don't smear this letter, this is not the first time I've cried over this thing; but I feel like I should feel better, because I registered (2) two of my children in private school yesterday.

I guess I'll have to look for work to help pay for
their schooling, because we can't afford the extra expense.
We have to scrape to find lunch money everyday even for
public school. I'm not really able to work as I am a
heart patient under the care of Dr. _____, but we
knew we had to keep them out of that undesirable neighborhood where I'd worry every day that they may be raped
or killed or both. And Dr. _____ doesn't like me to
worry a lot. I'm surprized I was able to take what I've
been through this last month. I feel like I am fortunate
in spite of my bad health, I have a husband that is able
and willing to work to pay our other expenses. I shudder
to think of the widows and divorce's that will be forced to
send their children into the neighborhood of Spencer
School. It is cruel and those are the ones I'm crying for
today....

Sincerely,

September 7, 1970

Dear Sir:

I am one of the mothers who is sending her daughter
(white) to an all black school.
My objection is that there is not enough white children
assigned to Tompkins High. There are enough white children in this district to make it more equal.
I obeyed your order because I believed the races
would be more equal. My child is the only white one in
some of her classes.
The Board of Education could have made districts so
that integration would have been total. I believe your
office has the duty to see that it is done. Have someone
go to the schools and see how many of each race is at
school. The white schools is just as unequal.

Yours Sincerely,

September 14, 1971

Dear Mr. Lawrence,

Enclosed is a picture of my 9 year old son Adam.
He is very small and very vulnerable. He spends 2 solid
hours getting home from school. The first thing he did
yesterday upon arriving home was throw-up. He was
naseated from riding 2 hours, four children to a seat in
the extreme heat. Do you or your husband ever ride a
bus four to a seat? No! You ride an air conditioned car.
Do you care about Adam? Do have an ounce of compas-
sion for a small boy? I love him.

September 30, 1971

Dear Sir:

Not only is the current bussing situation unfair and a general nuisance, but it is a great hardship on the children involved, and is causing problems which have not been made public. In most of the schools in Savannah today, many of the busses are bringing the children late for classes.

From the beginning of the school year, my child and others on his bus have been deprived of being in school on time three quarters of the time! They have been left standing at the bus stop for 1 to 1-1/2 hours waiting for a school bus which seems to break down regularly 3 or 4 times a week. His bus number has been changed indiscriminately almost every other day without notification. The first week they were brought home as late as 1 hour after school had ended, close to 6 P.M.

Last week for three days he was assigned to the only bus which seems to run on time in the Windsor Forest area, a fairly new one. The rest of the 4 weeks of school, there has been a discrepancy in the time the bus was supposed to pick the children up and when it actually showed up. Yesterday, after waiting 1 hour, he and his friends finally went home at 9:30, when their school was supposed to start. I was working and did not know that he was not in school until my return. Today the same bus was again 'broken down' as well as 'out of gas,' which seems to be the daily excuse, the 3rd time this week alone. Yet the school board members are informing the news media that problems have been worked out.

How can these children be expected to do any lessons when they have so far missed the equivalent of 2 or more days of school by being so late? There are also high school students being bussed to Beach and elsewhere who have had this same experience. It is general!

The poor 1-4th graders from the Jackson school area who are being bussed to Windsor Forest Elementary have to be away from home at least 8 hours each day because they leave for school to be there at 9:30 and are kept there until busses arrive for them near 5 P.M. The teachers who have to 'baby sit' for free after their usual school day is over are unhappy and are quitting. More than anything, this is hard on the little children.

On Wilmington Island, young 6-year-olds are put out on a corner to transfer to a bus that will later come for them from Savannah Beach to carry them to their school. This purely an outrage! Surely you cannot condone this! If you sleep with this on your conscience, I can't understand you. Please do something at your earliest convenience to relieve this stupid situation which is helping no one and injuring your coming generation.

Yours truly,

Petitions against busing were sent by the Port Wentworth's Lions Club, the Savannah Trinity United Methodist Church and the Port Wentworth Mayor and Council.

Dear Judge Lawrence,

I am opposed to the massed busing of our school children. Maybe my reasons are not valid to a Judge but to a mother they are.
I have three children [in] school and one at home. My little girl was to be bussed to a school about six miles away. This means she would leave her home a little before nine and she would not get back home until after 5 P.M. She is only 10 and in the 5th grade. When does she have time for dancing lessons or Girl Scouts? Maybe this isn't important to the Courts but it is to my little girl.

October 21, 1971

Dear Judge Lawrence,

I know you have been hearing many pleas for and against busing. I must enter my plea against it. I think it is terribly unfair to the children who must be separated from brothers and sisters. It is most inconvenient for the parents too.
This year our two smaller children must ride a bus for nearly an hour in order to get to a school which is twelve minutes away by car and twenty minutes away by school bus (if they could go the route they went last year). Now they have to go all the way to Pooler School before they get to their school in Bloomingdale.
... Next year according to the plan our schools are operating under now, we would have children in 3 different schools. These schools all dismiss at different times in the afternoon. Having children in so many schools also makes it difficult for parents to attend the school meetings, such as PTA, or others. When the school has a program or show of some kind for parents to see, it usually included all the grades at one time. As you can see it would be much harder for a mother to go to three different schools than to one where she could see all the children at one time. I am afraid this situation will prevent many mothers from taking the proper interest in school activities. Mothers who would otherwise be in walking distance of school, will especially be affected. The situation I have just pointed out will affect some of the colored children and their parents even more than the white ones....

Sincerely,

July 28, 1970

Mr. Thord Marshall
Superintendent of Schools
208 Bull Street
Savannah, Georgia

Dear Mr. Marshall:

This is to advise that J has been a patient
of mine for several years. She has a condition known as
regional enteritis which is definitely aggrivated by emotional stress.

She has attended Savannah High School for two years
and is presently being transferred in her senior year to
Beach High School. The emotional impact of this impending transfer has caused a flare-up of her enteritis.

I think it is extremely important that she continue at
Savannah High School in order to alleviate this problem.

Thank you for your cooperation in this matter.

> Very Sincerely,
> Dr. M.

July 29, 1970

Dear Dr. M

Your letter of request concerning J has been
fowarded to our school board, Mr. Basil Morros. He
will probably be in touch with you in the near future.

The recent court order handed down on July 18 by
the United States District Court makes no mention of such
a privilege as you refer to in your letter. However, Mr.
Morris will give you an official answer.

> Sincerely,
> Thord M. Marshall
> Superintendent of Education

August 1, 1970

Dr. Thord M. Marshall
Superintendent of Education

Dear Dr. Marshall:

In reply to your letter of July 29, 1970, a photocopy
of which is enclosed, I have not the remotest idea whether or not the United States District Court makes any mention as to the privilege of a transfer of a student from one
school to another for health reasons. I am glad that you
have referred this to the school board attorney, Mr. Basil
Morris, but I am not terribly interested in his opinion.

I will state unequivalently that any fundamentally disturbing emotional events may result in this girl becoming seriously, or even fatally ill.

I am writing you to re-emphasize my request that she continue to attend Savannah High School. I am not the least bit interested in compromising this girl's physical health because of political or a psycho-social considerations which are outside her control.

Very sincerely,
Dr. M

August 9, 1971

Dear Judge Lawrence:

I realize you are a very busy man with many important cases to make decisions on. However, I am writing you in hopes that you will help me with a problem that is very close to my heart.

Your Honor, I only have one child. Her name is M   and she is seventeen years old, and a senior in high school. For the past two years she has attended Groves High School in Garden City, Ga., where she maintained a B average and hoped to graduate this coming year. As far back as I can remember, this was her one dream and desire. One hundred and eighty more school days would have seen this dream come true....

Your Honor, I would like to request an exception in her particular case because of medical reasons. Unfortunately, M   has a very serious kidney disease, (Nephrosis, complicated by varying degree of Nephritis.) I won't go into all the medical technology now, but this does include high blood pressure among other serious symptoms. She is restricted to a diet without the use of salt, plus has to take medication for her high blood pressure. The change to another school is worrying her considerable and I believe emotional stress does not help high blood pressure any at all. It is my understanding from her physicians that eventually in the next year or two, she will have to have a kidney transplant in order to try and save her life.

Sir, I believe you to be a man with a very understanding heart. Otherwise I don't think you would be in the high position that you are. I know when you make judgments that affect other people's lives it is a tremendous responsibility and requires many serious thoughts. That is the reason I have written to you, m   's outlook at the very best has many IF'S. Current Statistics show that a transplant with the donor a close relative is 90% success. If one has to depend on a cadaver as a donor, it is only 50% success. Since I am the only close relative M   has it depends on me. I need not tell you Sir, that she is

55effort5

fort5rt5

my life and her happiness means all the world to me.

In view of these facts I sincerely pray Sir, that you will be lenient and can find it in your heart to grant her permission to return to Groves High School.

I ask you Your Honor to please keep this out of the newspapers and other news media. We are not seeking publicity, only help and happiness.

Sincerely yours,
Mrs. A

P. P. S. Incidentally, M 's father is a deceased Veteran. He died when she was age 6. I am solely responsible and limited finances prevent moving as being unfeasable. Sir, I am completely in your hands.

August 18, 1971

Dear Mrs. A

I have read with interest and with sympathy your letter of August 9th. You will understand that I am not running the public schools. The Board of Education does that. They have consistently taken a hard-line position on individual hardship cases. This is such a case.

You apparently lack an understanding of the function of the federal court. I have no power whatsoever to grant exceptions in instances such as the unfortunate case of your daughter. If I were to do this, I would have time for nothing else.

The most I can do (and I have done this) is to send a copy of your letter to the School Board with a request that they give it all the consideration it deserves. I regret that I cannot be of more assistance.

With kind regards,

Sincerely,
Chief Judge, U. S. District Court

Dear Judge Lawrence,

I do believe in integration but when it has to jeopardize me from a subject I need for my major in college it is unreasonable.

I have been planning since I don't know when to major in Spanish. Now I have been transferred to Beach Senior High I am told I can no longer continue Spanish. Spanish III is not offered at Beach.

Secondly as I said at the beginning of the letter I do believe in integration but not the way it has been handled. To put the percentage 10 to 90 or 20 to 80 in a school just to say it is being integrated is rediculous. Shouldn't it be based on fifty-fifty?

Sincerely,

August 21, 1970

Dear Miss C

I have your letter of August 20th. I hope you understand that there are over 100,000 students in schools in this district now under plans of desegregation. I cannot take up individual hardship cases, no matter how compelling the circumstances or how personally sympathetic I may be.

Certainly, the Board of Education should make it possible for anyone like you, who in good faith wishes to receive instruction in Spanish, to get it. It should make every effort toward that end. After all, the Board of Education runs the schools, not I, and your problem must be resolved at that end.

Sincerely,
Chief Judge, U.S. District Court

July 26, 1970

Mrs. Saxon P. Bargeron
Board of Public Education
208 Bull Street
Savannah, Georgia   31402

Dear Mrs. Bargeron:

I will be a senior this year and for the past two years I have attended Windsor Forest High School. I live in Paradise Park, under the new zoning change, I would attend Jenkins High School.

I have a high scholastic average in my school work and I am a charter member of the W.F.H.S. Beta Club. However, I can only attend college with the aid of scholarships. My parents are divorced and I live with my mother, who supports my brother, sister, and me as a teacher in Chatham County.

The counselor at W.F.H.S., Mrs. D   , assured me that scholarships are dependent on scholastic averages plus extracurricular activities. On this information, I campaigned and was elected Chaplain-Parliamentarian of the Windsor Forest Student Council for the 1970-1971 school year. My field of interest is journalism, and I was also elected Co-Editor of the school newspaper, 'The Oracle,' by the newspaper staff. Both of these positions were to give me the opportunity to serve in elected positions for the experience and to better my chances for a scholarship to college.

As a new student at Jenkins I would have no opportunity in a leadership role. For these reasons, I would appreciate your consideration in allowing me to attend Windsor Forest this last year.

I realize the purpose of the rezoning, but Windsor Forest and Jenkins are still both predominantly white schools.

My sister, who will be in the tenth grade, and my brother, who will be in the sixth, are to go to new schools this fall and will attend these schools because of the rezoning. My request is solely due to my elected positions, the first time I have ever been elected to serve in any position in my eleven years in school.

I would be glad to discuss this with you in person if you could spare me the time.

Yours very truly,
Mr. H

August 14, 1970

Dear Mr. H

I have your letter of July 29th. I hope you understand that there are over 100,000 students in schools in my District which are under plans of desegregation. I cannot consider individual hardship cases, no matter how compelling the circumstances or how personally sympathetic I may be. The School Board is supposed to run schools, not this Court.

I wish that I could be of assistance in hardship cases involving high school seniors who have been transferred. The number of seniors affected by the H.E.W. plan is considerable and exceptions cannot be made by the Board.

In my opinion, if you maintain your scholastic average, the matter of extracurricular activities in your senior year is not going to affect the award of any scholarship to you. If you desire me to do so and should the occasion arise, I will be glad to write a strong letter in that respect on your behalf.

Sincerely,
Chief Judge, U.S. District
Court

August 5, 1971

Dear Judge Lawrence,

Provided it is acceptable to the Court, I wish to request the approval for a 'Senior Option' ruling under which rising senior students in the Secondary Schools of Chatham County would have the privilege to return to the same senior high school, where they matriculated during the 1970-1971 term.

As a parent, it seems to me that it would be advantageous for a student to complete the final two years of high school work in the same educational institution. It is very important for a college-bound student to maintain his class standing, to continue his contacts with the same counselors and to participate in the same extra-curricular activities under the same faculty advisors. Also, college recommendations are most effective when given by teachers who have known the pupil longest and most intimately.

I make this appeal because I know that the schools are not equal educationally or in physical facilities. This ruling, if granted, would apply only to present seniors (1971-1972 term); as subsequent classes would automatically spend the final two or more years in the same institution....

Very sincerely,

August 30, 1971

Dear Judge Lawrence,

There have been many opinions expressed over the segregation/desegregation problem in the southern schools. This letter is another opinion expressed by a very confused and concerned sixteen year old student.

I would like to begin, if I may, by telling you that I am not a racist or a segregationist. The best example of ignorance I have found is a person who believes that segregation is right (After all, is God going to have a different heaven for each group of people He created? Does he love one racial group more than He does another?) I am an American who believes that all men are created equal and that all are entitled to life, liberty, and the pursuit of happiness (does that ring a bell?)....

Sir, do you remember: being an eighth grader, just entering junior high school, faced with the prospect of finding classes and being termed a 'junior high dog'; being a sophomoric tenth grader caught up right in the middle--definitely not junior high, but not quite good enough to be considered high school; the excitement of being a junior, ordering your class ring, and sponsoring the Junior-Senior dance; your senior year, being the top class at your school--the school you grew up in, with the kids you've known since you were a confused and lost eighth grader, the school whose alma mater you sang and whose football games you attended. Even though there were struggles, both physical and mental, you loved every minute of

it. Do you remember the year your school beat every
other school in the county in the spirit contest? Do you
remember the year books you helped edit and the dances
you helped plan?

Judge Lawrence, these things may not mean anything
to you and the Fifth Circuit Court of Appeals, but they
do to a teenager who goes from adolescence to adulthood
in five very short, but memorable years. Adults are constantly telling us that our high school years are the best
years of our lives and that we should enjoy them. When
we try to follow this advice, the main thing that makes
these years so great is distorted.

What good is it to learn where Health I class is,
when a few weeks later one has to find a different Health
I in a different school. Just when a sophomore gets used
to the period of transition he is undergoing at his own
school, he is forced to readjust at another school. What
good is a Glenn Hills Class of '73 ring when one is forced
to graduate from ARC?

Separating students from their own schools, especially
six weeks after the beginning of school, will disrupt student councils, football teams, annual staffs, honor societies, cheerleading squads, friends, and innumerable other
clubs and organizations that are all a significant part of
school life. Most important of all, the education of thousands of students will be hindered. Surely, you can see
that.

The preamble of a very famous American document
begins, 'We the people of the United States....' Unless
there is a new definition of 'people,' teenagers would be
considered people--human beings with emotions and feelings, silly though they may seem.

Therefore, sir, I beg of you, I plead with you, please,
please, don't separate Spartans from Glenn Hills, Eagles
from Jasey, or Muskateers from Richmond unless they request to be transferred. (I believe that's called freedom
of choice, which is connected with liberty, which is contained in 'life, liberty, and the pursuit of happiness.')

I would like to submit a plan: 1) Let each student
choose the school he wants to attend. 2) If the student
cannot provide his own transportation, send one of those
buses you plan to use in the 'massive busing to achieve
desegregation and racial balance' to take him to the school
of his choice. 3) Students will be happy, parents will be
happy, and Judge Lawrence won't have an Excedrin headache....

I have doubts that my opinions have been expressed
effectively. I'm hoping that you aren't the heartless man
we have a tendency to picture you as, and that maybe,
just maybe, you'll see our (the students') side of this controversy. I realize that many of the people who were at
the hearing Thursday, September 26, want segregation.
They are merely showing their ignorance. Do you honestly

feel that by forcing their children to be bused to a different school to achieve racial balance can change what is in their hearts? Sir, I think we both know that this will only cause hard feelings and broken hearts. Instead, we should act on the knowledge that education is the cure for ignorance. As a better educated generation arises, this ignorance will be alleviated....

Sincerely,

A Prayer For Older People printed in The Calendar of the First Baptist Church of Savannah was anonymously sent to Judge Lawrence.

... RELEASE ME from the craving to straighten out everyone's affairs.

TEACH ME the glorious lesson that occasionally I may be wrong. Make me thoughtful but not nosy--helpful but not bossy. With my vast store of wisdom and experience it does seem a pity not to use it all. But thou knowest, Lord, that I want a few friends at the end.

(Mimeographed form letter--hundreds received)
Dear Judge Lawrence:

The emotional and mental balance of our children should take precedence over racial balance in schools. As a parent, I believe that forced bussing from neighborhood schools will jeopardize the welfare of all children in Richmond County.

Sincerely,

Telegram
Would you kindly die painfully of cancer.

Signed

Judge,

I have just read that you have employed the notorious team of Child Molesters, Herman and Munyer. These two perverts specialize in the immoral practice of child mixing and in my opinion represent the fowlest type of humans. How low and lothesome are you capable of sinking? I can't imagine you unleashing such a pair of fanatics on the people of your area. I'm sure it must be the thrill you derive from the exercise of such power, while cowardly hiding behind a lifetime tenure to prevent from being thrown from office.

Such men as you are creating a cesspool within the Federal Judiciary which needs a swift and complete cleaning. In closing, the only comment that I can make and carry out, is that I wouldn't let one of you Bastards order a child of mine to the toilet!

February 12, 1972

Dear Congressman Gallagher:

... Not too long ago, Professor Rubin Fox, an influential dedicated Boas disciple at Rutgers University, in a long essay in The New York Times Magazine (6/30/68), counselled the nation--that racial differences ... 'should be eliminated by vigorous interbreeding and move on to better things.'

Your concern about Dr. B. F. Skinner's behavioral tripe is timely. Dr. Skinner's techniques are widely used in departments of government, especially in the Department of Health, Education and Welfare. Secretary Elliott Richardson is the bell-sheep of the reformers seeking the goal of mass-hybridization. Note the shenanigans re 'sensitivity' and 'racial awareness' training in HEW--enforced by Secretary Richardson.

HEW's forced-busing to achieve racial balance in our schools is the most important phase of the grand design. You get at the young in the moulding stage. HEW now see to it, in already integrated schools, inside the classes, that the Black boys sit next to the White girls and the White boys next to the Black girls.

And make no mistake. Secretary Richardson is doing nothing contrary to the wishes of President Nixon. Under the tutelage of his counsellor, Daniel Patrick Moynihan, Mr. Nixon has swung over to Liberalism. Mr. Moynihan, as a sociologist, knows well that you cannot have successful integration without full-scale intermarriage. Mr. Moynihan emphatically recommends intermarriage between the races (New York Times, 12/17/67, pp. 70). He is for a hybridized society.

So, Mr. Gallagher, a grand design does exist ... promoted by the left-wing Boas-Myrdal-Skinner school of social scientists and their dedicated followers.

The best guess, however, is that you will not be successful in getting your hearings in motion. Too much is at stake. An investigation in depth would reveal more than forty years of organized deceit.

Very truly yours,

September 4, 1971

Dear Judge Lawrence:

I beg you to consider every side of the issue of the

integration of Richmond County schools. Please think of the children, black and white, and how their lives will be affected. The blacks don't want their children bused away from their neighborhood schools any more than the whites do.

Our forefathers were wrong in the treatment of the blacks but, Sir, why must our little children have to pay all at once for this three hundred [year] old sin.

If our children are bused at the other side of Richmond County to achieve racial balance in schools that are in predominately black neighborhoods and many miles from their homes how can there be any school pride and spirit or any of the extracurricular activities that make the long hours of school exciting for our children. I know that learning takes precedence over other school activities but the children need the other activities to make them well rounded citizens.

It is very hard for the average person to understand why the Court says Freedom of Choice doesn't work. I don't see how anyone could complain if they were told to take their pick of schools and the county would provide transportation to the school of their choice. The majority of the blacks chose to remain in their neighborhood schools. This alone should prove that they don't want any massive busing to achieve racial balance.

Sir, you can tell from the tone of my letter that I am white and a native Georgian but I am Christian first and I know that God is no distinguisher of races and I want all children to have equal opportunity at education and life.

Why can't the money that busing would cost be spent to assure that all schools are equal in facilities and faculty and give back the Freedom of Choice with busing provided and leave our neighborhood schools intact.

I pray that you will consider this matter very, very carefully and have mercy upon our little children because they are the ones who will be hurt and affected. My heart aches for you and the heavy burden you carry and I pray you will ask God's guidance in making your decision.

Sincerely,

August 31, 1971

Dear Judge Lawrence:

My husband was recently appointed to the faculty of the Medical College of Georgia and we moved to Augusta from Albany, New York.

We are quite concerned over the forced bussing away from neighborhood schools in order to make the racial balance equal in all schools. We have lived in Albany, New York; Lincoln, Nebraska; Belleville, Illinois; and St. Louis, Missouri where the schools are integrated the same

as in Augusta, Georgia. There is no forced bussing in
any of these northern cities. We cannot understand why
it is being forced upon the people in Georgia now.

Our daughter was in an accelerated program in New
York State and we want her to be able to continue such a
program. We bought a home in Augusta near schools that
we want our children to attend and do not want them bussed
to another area of the city.

We are not opposed to integrated schools; but are very
much opposed to forced bussing and would appreciate anything you can do to enable our children to go to our neighborhood schools.

Sincerely yours,

September 1, 1971

Dear Judge Lawrence:

... Could you put your six-year-old child on a school
bus to be taken miles away when a school is less than
two blocks from his home? Surely not. Allow me to
pose this question: if I filed suit in federal court opposing the fact that only 2% of my son's school was Baptist--
even though Baptists were welcome to attend and not barred
because of their religion--would you, in turn, order massive changes and/or massive bussing in order to achieve
'religious balance'? This is ridiculous! In the same manner, the situation we now have on hand is also ridiculous!
Our constitutional law specifically states that a child cannot be bussed in order to achieve racial balance; it also
states that a child cannot be assigned to a specific school
because of color. I am sure that you are familiar with
our constitutional law, since you are a Federal Judge, and
that you will do everything in your power to uphold this
law.

Sincerely,

September 2, 1971

Dear Judge Lawrence,

Why did you turn down the Richmond County, Georgia
school desegregation plan for 1971-72?

Chief Justice Berger has said racial balance is not
required in all schools, according to law.

Who is right--you or he?

I am opposed to bussing students to achieve integration. I am for freedom of choice and neighborhood
schools. ...

Sincerely,

August 31, 1971
Judge Alexander Lawrence

Sir:

The emotional and mental balance of our children should take precedence over racial balance in schools. As a parent, I believe that forced busing from neighborhood schools will jeopardize the welfare of all children in Richmond County.

Granted you have not stated that massive busing would be effected, only massive changes, which to me means massive bussing. How you can hand down rulings like you do, especially over an issue that is so unpopular with black and white parents, is beyond me.

We have a duly elected school board which you have set aside. We did not elect you to run our school system. I definitely feel that you are infringing on my civil rights by taking my elected representatives power away.

I urge you to use common sense and an equal fairness for white parents in your future rulings.

June 26, 1972
Dear Judge Lawrence:

I'm sure that each day you are swamped with a deluge of mail and I hate to bother you, but I feel that I have a problem that only you can help me solve.

I am the Mother and sole supporter of three very intelligent children and I feel that the new ruling on zones for the Richmond County schools will jeopardise the future education of my young son, J   . The new zoning has placed us just one house below the Richmond Academy attendance area, even though we are just one block away from the school.

My husband, a Georgia Tech graduate, was for twenty-one years a fine engineer here in Augusta, having served as the _____ and later was co-owner of _____, a consulting engineering firm. This year, at a very early age, he was stricken and the victim of Leukemia. My children have also lost both their grandfathers this year, so this leaves me with the responsibility of rearing these three children alone, and naturally, I want the best for them. It was one of my husband's last wishes, that I keep the children in Augusta, so J could get a good education at Richmond Academy.

Judge Lawrence, I'd like to tell you about my son, J   , for I am most proud of him. He was fifteen years old on June the third, and he has had an excellent academic record, as well as being an outstanding athlete. He earned very good grades in elementary school, and I'd like to list some of his accomplishments in Jr. High:

1. President of Student body-
2. Received the plaque for the student who had contributed the most to his school-
3. One of the ten top students in his school-
4. Membership in President's All American team (Physical Fitness)-
5. Member of numerous school organizations-
6. Captain, and voted most valuable player on football team-
7. Captain, and voted most valuable player on basketball team-
8. Athlete with the highest scholastic average-
9. Earned letters in football, baseball, basketball, and track in eighth and ninth grades--

At age fifteen, he now has thirty-one trophies and many medals and certificates he has earned in sports. One of his trophies is a Jr. All American Basketball trophy, presented to him in Pennsylvania, when he played in the National tournament. As you can see, he has been an ambitious young man, and I am very anxious that he continue to have the education which will give him a challenge....

Judge Lawrence, the only way that my children are going to be able to further their education in college will be through earning a scholarship, consequently, I feel that J   must attend Richmond Academy, almost out of necessity. In conclusion, with the one car, and my working, it will be so much easier for us if he can walk to Richmond Academy each morning, rather than ride several miles on a bus to attend Lucy Laney. I honestly have no animosity toward my children attending school with the blacks, but Judge Lawrence, J   has been such an outstanding student, I feel that Richmond Academy present the greatest challenge for him. At the crucial age of fifteen, without a father or a grandfather to guide him, I feel it is most important that he be near such fine men as Mr. R   , Principal of Richmond Academy, and other fine teachers and coaches there, who are familiar with J   's outstanding record, and our family's unusual circumstances. I think that it is very important at this age, that J   have the encouragement of the fine men who knew his father. At Laney, no one would know J   and it would be difficult to bring out his potential there.

Judge Lawrence, in this case, and under these circumstances, could you possibly allow J   to attend Richmond Academy this Fall? I will appreciate so much any consideration you will give us.

Thank you very much.

Sincerely,

September 5, 1971

Dear Judge Lawrence:

It is near the time for the 'massive changes' you plan for the Richmond County School System and I feel that I have waited until the twelfth hour to write to you; however, I should like to be heard, for I have five children to be affected in the changes, representing three schools. Attorney Ruffin has none.

I am not a segregationist. as evidence that I served as Secretary to the _____ here for four and a half years, until the time I felt more needed here at home.

If you think of the possible consequences as a result of the white children being sent to the predominantly black schools, you would not order this to come about. Already the blacks who attend the predominantly white schools carry switchblades concealed in their hair and knives and blackjacks in their pockets. The boys think nothing of inviting our white daughters 'to the bushes and woods' with them, nor the black girls cursing and yelling obscene remarks to the whites in the hallways. I know--my kids are there now--and this is happening in the predominantly white schools. They will not be subjected to slashing and raping in the predominantly Negro schools--I will go to jail first.

Do you have grandchildren, Judge Lawrence? Perhaps you have a beautiful granddaughter or niece in the Public School System. Would you send one of them into a Negro neighborhood just to please the minority in Savannah? Search your soul, your heart and your mind before you say 'Yes' for I don't really believe you would. Then PLEASE don't send mine there.

When you review the plan submitted by your 'experts' from Rhode Island, take my points into consideration, plus the fact that they will not be near their Mothers when they need us, before you hand down your Order. You will not only have to answer to the Supreme Court, but to God Himself some day.

Sincerely,

August 31, 1971

Honorable Alexander A. Lawrence
U.S. District Judge
P.O. Box 9029
Federal Building
Savannah, Georgia 31402

Dear Sir:

I am writing to you concerning the desegregation plan

for Richmond County Schools.

As a parent of a senior, I beg of you to consider the possibility of permitting the seniors to graduate from the school which they have been attending previously. My daughter ordered her senior ring last spring and we paid a deposit on it. She will soon be receiving it, and I am sure that the company from which they are purchased will not make a refund since it will already be made to order for her.

During the summer vacation, she worked very hard selling ads for the Butler Annual, the yearbook at the school she has attended for the past two years.

Also, she has participated in two Car Washes during the summer which were promoted by the 1972 Senior Class of Butler High School as fund raising programs for their Senior Council.

Last night as she was making preparations for beginning school today, I walked into her room and found her in a very depressed mood. When I inquired of the trouble, her reply was, 'I had looked forward so much to this year of school and now they have just ruined it for me. I just don't care if I never go to school again.'

Please, Sir, consider our children and the mental strain that they will be subjected to if they are forced to transfer to another school at this time of their education.

Your consideration in this matter will be greatly appreciated.

Very truly yours,

September 5, 1971

Dear Judge Brown:

I am a 17 year old Senior at Butler High School, Richmond County, Augusta, Georgia. I feel that my civil rights will have been violated if Judge Alexander A. Lawrence, U.S. District Judge, decides that I should be bused to another school to achieve racial balance, despite the fact that I have already bought and paid for my class ring and will get it within two weeks, and will graduate in the spring of 1972.

May I remind you that in November 1972, I will be old enough to vote and so will everyone else my age. Maybe then we can elect someone who will care enough to see that we have a quality education rather than busing or racial balance and maybe they will appoint judges that care about quality education as well.

Sincerely,

['I'm not against busing,' said Mrs.   B   But she

said she hoped any busing would involve students of both
races because 'there are only eight white children in
Clara Jenkins School and four of them are my grandchildren. ']

Please Bring Racial Balance To Richmond County Schools.
You Are The Only Hope For Justice Against The School
Board.

February 22, 1972
Dear Judge Lawrence:

You may have been informed that on the day of your
Augusta decision an add appeared in the Augusta papers
calling on the citizens of this community to support the
legal authorities of this country, no matter what your decision might be. As sponsor of this add, my name appeared first. I mention this history to indicate my support in the past for our legal system....
I have restrained myself from writing, realizing that
you are very busy. At this time, I feel compelled to call
to your attention that the citizens of Augusta, especially
the blacks and the young people, are waiting to see whether due constitutional authority will rule or whether John
Fleming has been right in the speeches he has been making at every opportunity. My black friends and students
tell me that if they can no longer depend upon the Federal
courts to implement their restraining orders that they can
no longer with integrity tell their friends to restrain themselves in response to the racist activities of many in this
community.
Augusta and Richmond County needs very much your
leadership and sense of direction at this time. Thank you
for your consideration of these remarks.

Sincerely,

March 2, 1972
Dear Judge Lawrence:

Don't worry ... this is a friendly letter. We're sure
you've had entirely too many of the other kind.
My husband and I have done our own soul-searching
on the busing issue and would like for you to see the
statement which we've mailed to the House Judiciary Committee. Perhaps it will help to see that there are white
Augustans who feel you have acted fairly and who are personally distressed that you have had to endure so much
emotional criticism.
We met at a tea for newly-naturalized citizens in
Augusta last December, and at that time I told you that

in another 50 years you'd be a hero. Maybe you won't
have to wait that long!

Sincerely,

NOTES AND PRIMARY AUTHORITY

The primary authority for the material contained in this chapter was:

Swann v. Charlotte-Mecklenburg Board of Education. The primary
sources are the following Supreme Court cases: McDaniel v. Barresi,
402 U.S. 39 (1971); North Carolina State Bd. of Educ. v. Swann,
402 U.S. 43 (1971); Davis v. Bd. of School Commr's of Mobile
County, 430 F.2d 883 (5th Cir. 1970), 430 F.2d 889 (5th Cir. 1970),
402 U.S. 33 (1971); and Swann v. Charlotte-Mecklenburg Bd. of
Educ., 311 F. Supp. 265 (W.D. N.C. 1970), rev'd in part, 431
F.2d 138 (4th Cir. 1970), district court opinion reinstated, 402 U.S.
1 (1971).

Reactions to Swann.

1. Recent Cases, 24 Vand. L. Rev. 1243, 1249-50 (1971);
reprinted by permission.

2. Richmond Times-Dispatch, Apr. 21, 1971, §A, at 12,
cols. 1, 2.

The following law review articles were helpful: Note, 46
N.Y.U.L. Rev. 1078 (1971); Comment, 23 Baylor L. Rev. 555
(1971); Comment, 49 Texas L. Rev. 884 (1971); Comment, 39 U.
of Chi. L. Rev. 421 (1972). For other newspaper reactions, see
The Times-Picayune, Apr. 22, 1971, §A, at 12, col. 1, 2; Atlanta
Constitution, Apr. 21, 1971, §A, at 4, col. 2; The Charlotte Observer, Apr. 21, 1971, §A, at 18, col. 1, 2; New York Times,
Apr. 22, 1971, §1, at 40, col. 1; Washington Post, Apr. 22, 1971,
§A, at 18, col. 1, 2; The Christian Science Monitor, Apr. 22,
1971, at 20, col. 2; and The Cleveland Plain Dealer, Apr. 22,
1971, §A, at 12, col. 2.

Post-"Swann" Massive Integration in Savannah and Augusta. The
Augusta case was styled Acree v. County Bd. of Educ., and is reported in several different opinions; 429 F.2d 387 (5th Cir. 1970);
301 F. Supp. 1285 (S.D. Ga. 1969); 294 F. Supp. 1034 (S.D. Ga.
1968); Acree v. Drummond, 409 U.S. 1006 (1972); 458 F.2d 486
(5th Cir. 1972); 336 F. Supp. 1275 (S.D. Ga. 1972); 443 F.2d 1360
(5th Cir. 1971). The Savannah case was styled Stell v. Bd. of Pub.
Educ., 334 F. Supp. 909 (S.D. Ga. 1971).

Of particular help was a lengthy interview with Judge Alexander Lawrence. Contemporary newspaper accounts were also examined.

A more complete manuscript, with detailed documentation of all sources, is available as indicated in the Preface, <u>supra.</u>

Chapter 16

THE UNCERTAIN FUTURE OF INTEGRATION AND
THE UNCERTAIN FATE OF THE FIFTH CIRCUIT

The third decade of the doctrinal development of desegregation law began with the Supreme Court's decision in Swann v. Charlotte-Mecklenburg Board of Education in 1971. Like its earliest
decisions, Brown I and II and the Little Rock riot case, Cooper v.
Aaron, the Supreme Court's opinion was unanimous; nonetheless, the
Swann decision confounded legal scholars and confused the lower federal courts. Unlike previous Supreme Court desegregation precedents, the unanimity of Swann seemed to have been purchased by
such a compromise of disparate judicial interpretations that the ultimate opinion was near meaningless as coherent doctrinal guidance
from the Court.

Since Brown II in 1955, desegregation had been exclusively a
Southern problem. Unsympathetic to a region that had compelled
the separation of the races in public schools by force of law, the
rest of the nation ignored the existence of de facto segregated schools
in the ghettos of its large cities. However, after the Supreme Court
in Green articulated the right of every child to obtain an integrated
education and placed the duty on school boards to come forward immediately with plans that promised realistically to integrate the public schools, most prescient observers realized that a decision day
for the North and West could not long be postponed.

In the next four years after Swann five major cases were
decided, two by the United States Court of Appeals for the Fifth Circuit and three by the Supreme Court. Those five cases substantive-
ly divided the pronouncements of the Fifth Circuit from the national
policy enunciated by the Supreme Court. Furthermore, there was
every indication that the future of integration in the Deep South
might differ drastically from integration in the ghettos and barrios
of the North and West.

The first two cases were from Texas cities, Corpus Christi
and Austin. Both decisions were rendered en banc by the Fifth Circuit; and, although the Court was badly split, those cases moved
that Southern federal appellate tribunal into the vanguard in the evolution of integration law. Subsequently, the Supreme Court decided
cases from Richmond, Denver and Detroit, and disavowed the doctrinal lead of the Fifth Circuit. Furthermore, in a parallel development, a Congressional Commission has now recommended as a solu-

tion to the staggering caseloads of the nation's federal courts of appeals that the Fifth Circuit be split into two separate circuits, thereby terminating the present form of that great civil rights tribunal. It is an appropriate if regrettable end to this history that, for the first time, the United States Court of Appeals for the Fifth Circuit seems cut off by the Supreme Court's retreat from the Fifth Circuit's doctrinal advances. As a final irony, the Fifth Circuit may even cease to exist as an institution in the future.

The holdings in these five post-Swann decisions provide perhaps the last opportunity to consider the three great issues that have remained unresolved since the federal judiciary first responded, ever so tentatively, to the clarion call of Brown I: 1) the continued viability of the de facto/de jure distinction in desegregation matters; 2) the breadth of the remedy in desegregation decrees--to encompass a single school, an entire school district or a combined county-city area; and 3) the use of busing as a specific desegregation remedy.

Five Cases in Five Cities

The Corpus Christi and Austin cases were decided on the same day in 1972 by the Fifth Circuit. The following year the Supreme Court issued its "nondecision" in Richmond, and shortly thereafter, its ruling in Denver. After an extended delay, the Supreme Court's five-to-four holding in Detroit was finally released on July 25, 1974.

*   *   *

A city which has a tri-ethnic population composed of Anglos, Mexican-Americans and Negroes, Corpus Christi, Texas, is segregated residentially along ethnic lines. The school board employed a neighborhood school system that, when superimposed over an ethnically divided city, resulted in a system in which the schools were identifiable by racial or ethnic origin. But Corpus Christi and Austin posed a new problem for the Fifth Circuit: Mexican-American children, unlike black children, had never been segregated by law. In contrast, black children in Corpus Christi, segregated by law until 1954, could demonstrate de jure segregation. Hence they could claim all the benefits of the Supreme Court's desegregation decisions: Green, Alexander, Carter, and Swann. While every bit as segregated and educationally deprived as their black counterparts in the same city, Mexican-American children in Corpus Christi had never been segregated by force of law; instead, their segregated schooling had developed from residential housing patterns, school locations, private choice and school board action. In short, they suffered from classic de facto segregation. De facto segregated Mexican-American children lived side by side with de jure segregated black children.

Could a federal court order integrated education for blacks

in Corpus Christi while ignoring the Mexican-American children,
solely on the basis of an artificial legal distinction spawned in an
earlier case? Furthermore, even if a federal court ordered integration of both black and Mexican-American children, could a federal court legally order busing of as many as one-third of the
school-age children in Corpus Christi, given the residential concentrations of black and Mexican-American children there? Those
were the hard decisions facing the federal district court in Corpus
Christi during the divisive national debates over busing led by
George Wallace in the 1972 presidential primaries. Woodrow B.
Seals, the district court judge, did not equivocate. He held that
Mexican-American as well as black children had been unconstitutionally segregated; that Corpus Christi was operating a dual school
system; and, that one of the remedies that had to be employed was
extensive busing. Mr. Justice Black stayed the implementation of
Judge Seals's order until the Fifth Circuit could consider the case
en banc.

The fifteen judges of the Fifth Circuit split badly in their en
banc decision in Corpus Christi. Six separate opinions were written.
A ten-judge majority affirmed the district court's findings of fact and
its statement of the law but disagreed with the remedy, remanding
with instructions on busing: the district court was to order extensive busing only if absolutely necessary. This majority opinion
was written by Judge Dyer and he was joined by Judges Bell, Thornberry, Coleman, Ainsworth, Godbold, Morgan, Clark, Ingraham
and Roney. Five judges--four known liberals, Chief Judge Brown
and Judges Wisdom, Goldberg and Simpson--joined an opinion by
Judge Gewin, concurring in part and dissenting in part; they would
have affirmed Judge Seals's order in toto. Judge Coleman dissented, arguing that the Court should not have filed an opinion at
that time. Chief Judge Brown and Judges Wisdom, Gewin and Simpson also joined an opinion by Judge Goldberg protesting that the majority's remand of the case to the lower court to reconsider the
remedy would only result in further desegregation delay. Judge
Ainsworth, joined by Judges Bell and Roney, concurred in the result and in the remand on the remedy. Judge Godbold, joined by
Judges Coleman, Morgan and Clark would have stayed the Court's
opinion until the Supreme Court decided Denver.

While disagreeing about the remedy to be invoked and whether any implementation should await the Supreme Court's anticipated
Denver decision, there was marked unanimity or at least lack of
dissent in one key area: the de facto/de jure distinction should be
abrogated.

*　　*　　*

Decided the same day as Corpus Christi was an appeal from
Austin, Texas, presenting similar issues. Austin is also a tri-
ethnic community; residential segregation and the use of a neighborhood school assignment plan had resulted in racially and ethnically
identifiable schools. Like the action of Judge Seals in Corpus

Christi, in Austin the federal district judge found that there was a history of de jure segregation as to black children and ordered a remedy involving limited busing. However, the judge held that there had been no de jure segregation affecting Mexican-American children, and therefore refused to order any relief that would ameliorate their segregated status. The Fifth Circuit reversed on the de facto/de jure issue, holding that Mexican-American children were as entitled to constitutionally protected equal educational opportunities as black children. The school board's past actions had ostensibly maintained segregation as to Mexican-American children; therefore, there had been sufficient state involvement in such segregation to require that relief be accorded to Mexican-Americans as well as to blacks. Although the segregated situation of Mexican-American children arose by school board action and not by force of prior state law, the Fifth Circuit held that such school board action could also give rise to de jure segregation without requiring a finding of intent to segregate.

However, the Fifth Circuit again was divided on the remedy issue, just as it had been in Corpus Christi. Only fourteen of the judges sat on the Austin case; Judge Thornberry had excused himself because Austin was his home town. Seven of the fourteen (Judge Godbold, joined by Judges Bell, Coleman, Morgan, Ainsworth, Clark and Ingraham) wanted to hold the case in abeyance without reaching the merits, in order to await the anticipated Denver decision. But, on a parliamentary rule, the seven votes were not enough to delay reaching the merits: a decision had to be made. Seven different opinions were written by the fourteen judges, which prompted the district judge later to comment that he frankly did not know what had been decided. Judge Wisdom wrote an opinion joined by Chief Judge Brown and Judges Gewin, Goldberg, Dyer and Simpson. They found that de jure segregation had existed in regard to both blacks and Mexican-Americans because of the past conduct of the school board, and they disagreed with the district court's manner of providing relief. Judge Bell wrote an opinion specially concurring, joined by Judges Coleman, Ainsworth, Godbold, Morgan, Clark, Ingraham and Roney. The Bell opinion was a discourse on the powers of the court in fashioning relief in school cases and the steps to be considered by district courts in formulating remedies. Judge Wisdom, joined by Chief Judge Brown and Judges Gewin, Goldberg, Dyer and Simpson, penned an opinion highly critical of Judge Bell's opinion on the relief to be accorded, calling the opinion so general that it had no specific application to the case. Judge Gewin, joined by Chief Judge Brown, and Judges Wisdom, Goldberg and Simpson, also dissented from the majority's remedy. Judge Godbold, joined by Judges Bell, Coleman, Morgan, Ainsworth, Clark and Ingraham, wrote an opinion urging a delay in hearing the merits until after the Supreme Court's decision in Denver. Chief Judge Brown, joined by Judges Wisdom, Gewin, Goldberg, Dyer and Simpson, sharply responded to Judge Godbold's delay argument. Judge Clark, joined by Judge Coleman, would have certified the case to the Supreme Court in the same fashion that the jury trial issue was certified in the James Meredith Case. As further evidence of the strength of their disagreement, the Fifth Circuit judges rejected a later request to clarify their holdings.

*   *   *

On the day the Austin case was appealed from the district
court by the Justice Department, President Nixon personally inter-
jected himself into the dispute, criticizing the plan filed by HEW
for Austin which had recommended clustering and pairing of schools
and busing of students. Instead, the President apparently preferred
the plan that had been advocated by the Austin School Board, which
required almost no busing and achieved very little actual integration, except some innovative "cultural" afternoons where the races
would be mixed. The school board's plans had been approved substantially as written by the district court. When the Justice Department's civil rights lawyers appealed the Austin case, urging
adoption of the more rigorous HEW plan discarded by the trial court,
the President angrily reacted. In an unprecedented statement, the
President himself attempted to dictate school policy in a specific
school integration case, criticizing two of his own departments in
the process: HEW and the Justice Department. On August 3, 1971,
the President stated that Attorney General Mitchell had personally
assured the President that an appeal was necessary in Austin because the desegregation plan, as approved by the district court, was
inconsistent with recent Supreme Court decisions. However, the
President asserted:

> The Justice Department is not appealing to impose the
> H. E. W. plan. In the process of the appeal, the Justice
> Department will disavow that plan on behalf of the Govern-
> ment.
>   I would also like to restate my position as it relates
> to busing. I am against busing as that term is commonly
> used in school desegregation cases. I have consistently
> opposed the busing of our nation's school children to
> achieve a racial balance, and I am opposed to the busing
> of children simply for the sake of busing. Further, while
> the executive branch will continue to enforce the orders of
> the Court, including court-ordered busing, I have in-
> structed the Attorney General and the Secretary of Health,
> Education and Welfare that they are to work with individual
> school districts to hold busing to the minimum required by
> law.
>   Finally, I have today instructed the Secretary of
> Health, Education and Welfare to draft and submit today
> to the Congress an amendment to the proposed Emergency
> School Assistance Act that will expressly prohibit expen-
> diture of any of those funds for busing.

Prior to his public statement, the President had brought
pressure on the Justice Department to drop any plan for appealing
the Austin case. Despite public presidential opposition, the case
was nevertheless appealed. The fact that the appeal occurred at
all was openly viewed by many Justice Department lawyers as a
signal victory over the White House. They felt it demonstrated
their commitment to continued enforcement of Supreme Court mandates in school cases.

The Nixon statement did nothing to ease the rigors of oral argument for Justice Department lawyers who presented the Austin appeal to an en banc session of the Fifth Circuit. They were peppered with questions from the bench, probing the executive branch's policy on busing. The lawyers unsuccessfully tried to respond that busing was only a political question, attempting vainly to direct the Court's questioning back to the facts of the case before it.

* * *

In the meantime, the United States Court of Appeals for the Fourth Circuit was considering a case from Richmond, Virginia. The three school districts servicing the city of Richmond and the two neighboring counties, comprising the metropolitan Richmond area, had been drawn along existing city and county boundaries. After extended legal struggles typical of those that had occurred in other cities of the Deep South, Richmond and the two adjoining residential counties had basically achieved unitary systems within each existing school district. However, black students were heavily concentrated in the core city and, if the entire Richmond metropolitan area were considered as a whole, the schools would remain racially identifiable depending on which side of the county line they were situated.

Considering Richmond and the two surrounding counties as encompassing the same basic community of interests, Federal District Judge Robert Merhige boldly ordered a metropolitan-wide desegregation plan that would have effectively merged the two county school districts and the city district into one large district. The Fourth Circuit reversed Judge Merhige. Judge J. Braxton Craven, writing for a Fourth Circuit panel split two to one, held that the obligation of the city and two counties to take affirmative action ended when they had achieved a unitary system within their districts. Therefore, he reasoned, the district court lacked the power to order further relief.

The Richmond case created a heated debate over the extent of the powers of federal courts to ignore the boundaries of existing state governmental entities in ordering desegregation. The issue was controversial and ripe for definitive resolution. The United States Supreme Court issued certiorari in Richmond, but was unable to reach a decision. Associate Justice Powell, a native of Richmond and familiar with the facts and parties, had excused himself. The remaining eight Justices split four to four. Therefore, the Supreme Court being equally divided, the Fourth Circuit's reversal of Judge Merhige was affirmed without opinion.

* * *

Since the Brown case from Kansas, the Supreme Court had not considered desegregation cases arising in the western states. The day arrived for Denver, Colorado, on June 21, 1973, when the Supreme Court issued its opinion in Keyes v. School District No. 1, Denver, Colorado.

In early 1969, the Denver School Board had adopted three resolutions designed to desegregate the schools in the black Park Hill area of their city. After a local election produced a board majority which was opposed to the three integration resolutions, the plan was scrapped.

At that point, black plaintiffs filed suit. Initially, the plaintiffs in Denver sought a limited goal; they sued only to desegregate the schools in Park Hill. However, upon achieving success in that endeavor, they expanded their suit to secure desegregation of all of the schools in the Denver school district. The federal district court at that point balked. It denied further relief, holding that the fact of deliberate segregation in Park Hill by past school board action-- which the court considered to have been established--did not prove that the school board had followed a similar segregated school policy for the rest of Denver. The district court held that the plaintiffs had failed to prove de jure segregation for the other areas of Denver, particularly the core city.

Denver, like Corpus Christi and Austin, was to some extent a tri-ethnic community. The district court did treat Mexican-American students as a separate minority group; but, as to both blacks and Mexican-Americans, the lack of finding of de jure segregation in the rest of Denver was held sufficient to block relief. In an unusual gesture, the district court did find that the core city schools were inferior to other schools; and, on the theory that the Brown I and II holdings applied only to de jure segregation and were not applicable to the core city's de facto segregation, the court breathed new life into Plessy v. Ferguson's separate-but-equal doctrine by ordering that substantially equal facilities be provided to core city students. The Tenth Circuit affirmed the holding denying relief based on the de facto/de jure distinction, but reversed the district court's order requiring that better facilities be provided for the center city schools.

After the unfortunate non-decision in Richmond, when certiorari was granted in Denver, most observers believed that the Supreme Court would grapple with the de facto/de jure distinction, provide guidelines on the extent busing could be employed as a remedy, and formulate policy on whether system-wide remedies were required when only portions of a system were segregated. It will be recalled that seven of the Fifth Circuit judges in Corpus Christi and Austin had wanted to defer their holdings in those cases because they were certain that the Supreme Court's Denver decision would provide new answers. The Supreme Court in Denver, however, did not definitively resolve any of those issues.

Mr. Justice Brennan authored the majority opinion in Denver; Chief Justice Burger concurred in the result; Mr. Justice Powell filed a lengthy, but compelling opinion, concurring in part and dissenting in part; Mr. Justice Rehnquist dissented; and Mr. Justice White, from Denver, did not participate. Without any real discussion on the issue, the Supreme Court preserved the de facto/de jure distinction, holding that there had to be a finding of <u>intentional</u> governmental segregation on the part of the state or its <u>agencies</u>, such as local school boards.   The Supreme Court, nevertheless, reversed the Tenth Circuit and remanded the case by holding that proof of a segregationist intent by the school board in the Park Hill area created a presumption that a similar illegal intent was behind the segregation found elsewhere in the Denver system.   The school board, not the plaintiffs, must prove--not merely allege--that their actions in the rest of the Denver system were dictated by a neutral neighborhood school policy and were not motivated by any segregationist intent.   If the school board could not meet the burden of proof, then the remedy had to be system-wide; the remedy was not sufficient if it dealt only with the schools that had been the victims of discrimination.   In his separate opinion, Mr. Justice Powell eloquently attacked the continued existence of the de facto/de jure rationale, citing favorably the Fifth Circuit's recent <u>Austin</u> and <u>Corpus Christi</u> decisions.   He then wrote at length on the disruptive effects of busing as a remedy, urging basically that it be used sparingly. Mr. Justice Douglas joined Mr. Justice Powell's condemnation of the de facto/de jure distinction and the futility of imposing on the lower courts the duty of seeking out evidence of school board "intent" before protecting constitutional rights.   In an opinion that seems to hark back to the discarded <u>Briggs v. Elliott</u> distinction between desegregation and integration, Mr. Justice Rehnquist argued that remedies should be applied only in those schools where de jure segregation was proven.

*   *   *

Long awaited with trepidation by most metropolitan area school boards of the North and West was the Supreme Court's reaction to the much publicized <u>Detroit</u> decision of the late federal District Judge Stephen J. Roth.   Released on July 25, 1974, the <u>Detroit</u> decision drew anguished response from civil rights advocates and rejoicing from those who opposed massive integration in large metropolitan areas.

The Detroit city school board had passed a plan for voluntary integration.   The Michigan Legislature responded by passing Act 48 of 1970 which in effect prevented Detroit from implementing its voluntary plan.   The plaintiffs in the <u>Detroit</u> case subsequently went to federal court, seeking to enjoin enforcement of the new Michigan law and to implement the school board's integration plan. Judge Roth denied the plaintiff's request for a preliminary injunction, but on appeal the Sixth Circuit declared the state law null and void. Then a complex series of legal events occurred, culminating in an order by the District Court directing immediate implementation of a temporary plan.   Again, there was an appeal, but the Sixth Circuit upheld the decision; furthermore, the Court of Appeals ordered the district court to proceed immediately to the merits.

Detroit did not have a history of statutory segregation.   But there was a long history of public and private discrimination that, combined with other factors, had produced residential segregation. Detroit's neighborhood schools mirrored the city's racial residential segregation. The plaintiffs in Detroit claimed, as had their counterparts in Denver, that imposition of school attendance zones over the existing segregated residential pattern had produced a dual school system. They cited the school board's policy in school construction, its approval of optional attendance zones, and other factors to urge that Detroit's school system was a de jure segregated system subject to constitutional attack. Judge Roth agreed and found for the plaintiffs. Instead of restricting his remedy to the Detroit city schools, Judge Roth found that heavy black concentrations doomed any intradistrict integration plan and ordered integration of the entire metropolitan area, holding that "[s]chool district lines are simply matters of political convenience and may not be used to deny constitutional rights." Judge Roth thereafter ordered fifty-three suburban school districts in the three counties surrounding the city to be joined with Detroit in order to accomplish an effective conversion to a unitary system. The desegregation plan was based on fifteen clusters, each containing part of the Detroit system and two or more suburban districts.

With visions of mass busing into and out of Detroit's violence-ridden ghettos, the defendants appealed immediately. The Sixth Circuit Court of Appeals sitting en banc, held, however, that it was "within the equity powers of the District Court" to order an interdistrict remedy, even though the district court had received no evidence of de jure segregation in the suburban districts:

> [A]ny less comprehensive plan would result in an all black school system immediately surrounded by practically all white suburban school systems, with an overwhelmingly white majority population in the total metropolitan area.... [T]he only feasible plan involves the crossing of the boundary lines between the Detroit School District and adjacent or nearby school districts for the limited purpose of providing an effective desegregation plan.

After months of waiting for definite answers to those great questions that went unanswered in Richmond or were only fleetingly answered in Denver, and on the last day of the 1973 term, the Supreme Court's five-to-four decision in Detroit was issued. It seemed to some observers to mark the end of this nation's great integration experiment, born with such high promise in Brown I. The Supreme Court overruled the metropolitan-wide remedy ordered by Judge Roth. The majority opinion penned by Chief Justice Burger held that Judge Roth erred in ordering a multi-district, metropolitan-wide remedy for Detroit when he had only made findings that showed de jure segregation in one district involving the Detroit core city.

Division in Doctrine: Three Issues in Synthesis

> [M]en seeking right and justice both perceive
> the facts and turn for standards to the body of met
> and organized experience with which they are
> equipped. These 'experience spectacles' must of
> necessity yield differing results both of intake and
> of applicable standard, must yield results which
> differ increasingly as our modern variegated world
> dilutes community of experience among the indi-
> vidual members of the bench and multiplies and
> differentiates the situations out of which conflicts
> emerge to be adjudicated.
>   So that the Style of Reason which once could
> be hoped--even despite the conflict of Federalist
> and Republic, or of Jacksonian and the Solid Citi-
> zen--to yield some relatively single way of seeing,
> and then of judging, for addition to the brew of
> 'the authorities and justice'--that style, today, must
> give a wider range of result. Queer, and lovely,
> I should argue, that after the years it yields dis-
> senting opinions only one time in seven, or at most
> in four.
>   --Karl Llewellyn, The Common Law Tradition
>   463 (1960).

In the cases from Austin, Corpus Christi, Richmond, Denver and Detroit, bare majorities of the judges assigned to their consideration decided the critical issues at stake. Split decisions are unsettling to both laymen and lawyer: not only is the stability of the particular decision suspect but also such open disagreement on basic principles fuels more intense criticism of the prevailing rationale. But, if nothing else was learned from the Swann decision, it seemed clear that judicial unanimity could exact too high a price. The power that apparent unity lent to that opinion was rendered hollow by the confusion of its rationale. Swann did not reconcile the differences in opinion among the justices; it only disguised internal disputes in a solution of broad and incompatible concepts and postponed their inevitable precipitation.

Twenty years is but the bat of an eye in the normal evolutionary course of the law. Perhaps it should not be expected that any tribunal, either the Fifth Circuit or the Supreme Court, should or even could speak with one voice about issues of such current and future impact as the constitutional distinction between actual and law-imposed segregation and the nature and scope of constitutionally permissible remedies. However, despite possible prematurity, some analysis of the implications of these five decisions seems in order.

The De Facto/De Jure Distinction. --The most fundamental issue confronted by both the Fifth Circuit in its Austin and Corpus

Christi cases and the Supreme Court in its latest triad of decisions is the constitutional relevance of how segregated schools came about in a particular school system. Should the duties of states be affected by whether racially identifiable schools resulted from the force of state laws or from voluntary residential associations? De facto versus de jure segregation is not a new issue suddenly injected into the desegregation litigation of the seventies. As early as 1958, in the Fifth Circuit, black plaintiffs had sought relief from a segregated neighborhood school system in Palm Beach, Florida, which had resulted from the city's patently neutral residential zoning for taxation in 1912. Although the case was decided on other and more narrow grounds, Judges Rives, Brown and Wisdom had focused upon the fact of segregation as controlling: "by whatever means a completely segregated public school system was and is being maintained and enforced."

If the constitutional guarantee of equal educational opportunity continues to be limited only to states, cities and counties with a history of legally mandated segregation in the public schools, then only the South can be subjected to desegregation decrees. The black child in a Northern ghetto or the Chicano child in a Southwestern barrio will be forever relegated to that separate and "inherently unequal" education condemned in Brown I. A historical quirk will have determined the application of constitutional guarantees. As Judge Gewin observed in his dissent in Jefferson I, the evils of segregated education are just as real to a black child in Harlem as to his brother in Jackson: one child, however, will receive the protection of all of the remedies that have evolved since Brown II, while the other will remain in a segregated school. Furthermore, if the de facto/de jure distinction is maintained, once a Southern city achieves a unitary school district, by simple inaction, it can thereafter avoid further federal court interference with its schools. For example, should resegregation of Southern schools occur through white flight or other causes, as long as the resegregation is not attributed to the force of law, there will no longer be a de jure history to evoke constitutional guarantees; that is, the resegregation at worst will be de facto. Consequently, much of the effort of the last twenty years to achieve desegregation could become wasted effort. It will be recalled that Mr. Chief Justice Burger's opinion in Swann, which expressly avoids reaching the de facto/de jure issue, seems to hold out hope in its last paragraphs that, indeed, once unitary systems are achieved the business of the federal courts with Southern schools will have been completed.

On the other hand, if the Constitution is interpreted to apply to any segregated school, as long as there is identifiable school board involvement in fostering or condoning segregated education-- without regard to the school's history as being either de facto or de jure--then integration must move North and West. Furthermore, if there is any state or school board involvement in resegregation of the schools in the South, after they are declared unitary, the federal courts can reenter the picture to protect those efforts already expended to achieve unitary school systems. Thus, the monumental importance of the de facto/de jure issue is evident. Resolution of that issue may determine whether integration is halted at the Mason-Dixon line, or whether integration will become a national reality policed by vigilant federal courts.

The treatment of the de facto/de jure distinction in the five major cases since Swann is, therefore, of extraordinary interest. Perhaps the boldest of the decisions is that of Judge Dyer in Corpus Christi, a case which puts the Fifth Circuit well ahead of the Supreme Court's treatment of the same issue in Denver. Judge Dyer bluntly declared for an aroused Fifth Circuit that the sword of the Fourteenth Amendment extends not only to repulse segregation statutorily imposed, but it also extends to actions and policies of the state, as represented by its school boards, which have the same effect of denying equal protection as statutory segregation. The school board in Corpus Christi had argued that, even if the Fourteenth Amendment reached its past actions, there was no violation of constitutional rights because segregated schools did not result from such actions or policies, but rather from socio-economic factors such as housing patterns. Further the board strenuously asserted that before there could be a finding of de jure segregation, there had to be a finding of intention to discriminate. The board then pointed out that because they were operating a neutral neighborhood zoning plan there could be no basis for any finding of intent.

Judge Dyer's doctrinal breakthrough lay in his answers to the board's arguments. He first identified the specific board action which brought about the constitutional violation: "The Board imposed a neighborhood school plan, ab initio, upon a clear and established pattern of residential segregation in the face of an obvious and inevitable result." That action of the school board was state action and was not placed beyond the remedial power of the courts by attempting to classify the resulting segregated schools as de facto. Judge Dyer declared: "Thus, we discard the anodyne dichotomy of classical de facto and de jure segregation." He indicted the use of the distinction as mistakenly shifting the court's focus away from the results of the state action. Judge Dyer then quoted favorably Judge Gewin's dissent in Jefferson II that it mattered little to the child who suffers the discrimination whether segregation results from de facto or de jure history.

Disposing of the de facto/de jure distinction, Judge Dyer then held that intent to segregate is not necessary. He argued that the focus should be on the result of the school board's action and not on its thought process at the time it took the action.

In place of the distracting de facto/de jure distinction, Judge Dyer substituted a new two-step test:

> First, a denial of equal educational opportunity must be found to exist, defined as racial or ethnic segregation. Secondly, this segregation must be the result of state [school board] action.

The Dyer opinion left unanswered how much school board action is necessary, other than saying that there must be a real and significant relation between the board's conduct and the resulting discrimination. It must be emphasized that no dissent was registered by any of the other fourteen Fifth Circuit judges to Judge Dyer's attempt to abrogate the de facto/de jure distinction.

* * *

The Austin case, decided the same day by the same Fifth Circuit judges, absent Judge Thornberry, also dealt with the de facto/de jure distinction. This time Judge Wisdom wrote the opinion on that issue and his treatment also drew no dissents. Judge Wisdom's treatment is different from Judge Dyer's only in theory, not in effect. Rather than attempting to destroy the de facto/de jure distinction, Judge Wisdom simply defined de jure segregation broadly enough to encompass almost all situations that previously had been considered classic de facto segregation. He declared that every action or inaction of a school board which causes or maintains segregation is sufficient state involvement in discrimination to invoke constitutional sanctions--and all such actions or inactions amount to de jure segregation. Judge Wisdom's opinion in Austin coincides with Judge Dyer's in Corpus Christi in the holding that it was unnecessary to prove that a school board had a discriminatory intent when it took the action or inaction resulting in discrimination --the discriminatory result was all that was important: the board is liable for the natural and foreseeable consequences of its acts. In Austin, Judge Wisdom found that the board's choice of school sites, its construction and renovation of schools, and its drawing of school zones together constituted sufficient state action to invoke the Fourteenth Amendment. Those school board actions foreseeably perpetuated ethnically identifiable schools and a dual school system. Thus, although Judge Wisdom did not attempt to abrogate the de facto/de jure distinction as did Judge Dyer, his treatment in practical effect appeared identical to Judge Dyer's. He emphasized the importance of the school board action and focused on the foreseeable results of those actions and inactions in the same manner as Judge Dyer.

Despite the boldness of the Corpus Christi and Austin treatments of the de facto/de jure distinction, in the Denver case the Supreme Court ignored the Fifth Circuit's open invitation to destroy that much maligned obstruction to Northern integration. Instead, Mr. Justice Brennan for the majority specifically reaffirmed the distinction. However, the Supreme Court did retreat from the strict requirement of some past cases which defined de jure segregation as resulting only when schools were segregated by force of state law. The Supreme Court held that de jure segregation could also result from action, and presumably inaction, of a school board that was intended either to segregate or to perpetuate segregation. Thus, Denver continued a differential treatment of the same constitutional guarantees as applied to the North and the South.

In the South, with a history of legally imposed segregation, there was an automatic de jure finding and the federal courts moved immediately to the consideration of appropriate remedies. In the North and West, the Constitution could be invoked--but only after a factual showing that by its past actions the school board had intended to promote or to perpetuate segregation. The difficult showing of intent to segregate could take months and years, consume enormous amounts of court time and result in widely differing results in neighboring communities. Thus, despite its wounds in the Fifth Circuit, the de facto/de jure distinction was resuscitated by the Supreme Court in the Denver decision, and in its new viability it could delay and confuse integration in the North and West for years.

The Denver case did, however, increase the momentum of integration in the North and West in one important respect. Once discriminatory intent has been established by the plaintiffs in any portion of a school district, the burden of proof is shifted to the school board to prove that the board did not practice that same discriminatory intent in other segregated portions of the district.

There are those who defend the continuation of the de facto/ de jure distinction. In particular, some lawyers at the Justice Department have argued that integration poses so many problems in the large cities of the North and West that some degree of public support for school desegregation is essential. They assert that without some measure of support, public opinion will be so aroused that proposed "anti-busing" constitutional amendments would stand a real chance of adoption. They contend, therefore, that requiring the legal exercise of proving acts of past intentional segregation on the part of former school boards can be used to arouse the public conscience, thus providing a measure of support to integration efforts. However, despite such arguments, the reaffirmation of the de facto/ de jure distinction in Denver did in fact continue a disparate constitutional treatment of identically segregated black children, depending entirely on the section of the country in which they reside.

In the Denver case, Mr. Justice Douglas indicated in a short opinion that he would abolish the de jure/de facto distinction. Favorably quoting Judge Wisdom in the Austin case, Justice Douglas would focus on the results of state action. He argued that to allow de facto segregation is to legitimize the more subtle school board action which caused it. To Justice Douglas, the continued use of de jure and de facto labels only identified different levels of impermissible school board action.

Mr. Justice Powell's treatment of the subject in Denver was impressive. The theory of his dissent on that issue is rooted in Judge Wisdom and Judge Dyer's earlier opinions in Austin and Corpus Christi. He would abolish the de jure/de facto dichotomy. He argued that its use has placed the burden of desegregation unevenly on the South. Under the present system, he pointed out, the courts need only to consider the existence of segregation in the South to impose a duty of affirmative action. Yet, in the North, the courts ask not only for proof of segregation but also require proof of intent. Mr. Justice Powell questioned how intent can ever be convincingly established when the board actions spoken of usually took place over a number of years and were directed by boards of changing composition. In addition, he argued that much of what was remedied in Swann was caused by factors existing in all cities, North and South: migration patterns, housing restrictions, unequal job opportunities and other social and economic forces. There is, Justice Powell asserted, no reason for ordering relief from segregation caused by such factors in the South and failing to order the same relief in the North.

In examining the duty imposed by the fourteenth amendment, Justice Powell noted that the law had evolved over the years. He asserted Brown I was a negative decision, imposing a neutral responsibility on school boards. However, since Green, school boards have had the affirmative duty to operate integrated school systems. Justice Powell would now place the burden on all school boards to demonstrate that they are operating integrated systems.

Mr. Justice Rehnquist, on the other hand, took a very different and decidedly conservative approach. He maintained that the de jure/de facto distinction was valid. In the very kind of dichotomy to which Justice Powell objected, Justice Rehnquist would require proof of intent in the absence of a history of statutory segregation. However, Justice Rehnquist would not allow the shift of the burden of proof to the school board, as ordered in Justice Brennan's majority opinion.

* * *

The recent Detroit decision reaffirms the Denver holding that only de jure segregation is prohibited by the Constitution. The Supreme Court pointed out that Judge Roth had made no findings: 1) that the school district boundary line in the Detroit metropolitan area had been made with the intent to segregate; or 2) that the outlying school districts (other than the core Detroit district) had failed to operate unitary school systems; or 3) that the outlying school districts had committed acts that effected segregation within the core city district. A fair reading of the Detroit opinion indicates that that to find de jure segregation, there must be either past segregation by law or proof of action or inaction on the part of the state or the affected school districts, taken with the intent of segregation. The combined weight of both the Detroit and Denver holdings is to maintain the de facto/de jure distinction. The doctrinal advance made by the Fifth Circuit in Corpus Christi and Austin was ignored by the Supreme Court and can, perhaps, be viewed as having been disapproved, sub silentio, by Denver and Detroit.

The Breadth of the Remedy. --In the en banc arguments in Corpus Christi and Austin the Justice Department surfaced a new and restrictive approach to the application of desegregation remedies.

Perhaps responding to President Nixon's criticism of the HEW plan submitted in Austin, or perhaps to hold down the sweep of controversial busing orders, the Justice Department argued that rather than impose system-wide remedies when illegal segregation had been found in a school district, the court could identify "pockets" or "incidents" of segregation in the system and apply more localized remedies. While never specifically referring to the Justice Department's arguments, Judge Bell in the Austin case seemed to accept that contention in discussing the steps to be taken by the district judge in formulating a remedy on remand of the case.

The clear implication in Judge Bell's opinion for the majority of eight is that, after a finding of segregation as to specific schools in the Austin school district, school board authorities could limit relief to those specific schools. The opinion in Austin by Judge Godbold, joined by Judge Bell and five of the judges who had subscribed to his opinion, urged that the Fifth Circuit defer decision until Denver had been decided. In the Godbold opinion, criticism of the wavering position of the executive branch was expressed. Therefore, even though seven judges seemed to accept the Justice Department's arguments about the legality of less than system-wide remedies, they, with their more liberal brothers, were also critical of the performance of the Nixon Administration:

> This court has committed itself to giving deference to desegregation plans and proposals emanating from agencies of the executive branch of the government that possess expertise in the field, and we have required district judges and school officials to give similar deference. But we have seen those agencies become divided within themselves, their policies and recommendations changeable and changing from case to case and even in the same case.

Judge Wisdom sharply dissented from Judge Bell's generalized discussion of the remedy to be employed by the district court on remand. After castigating his eight colleagues for a remand order that could only result in continued delay when "[t]he questions cry for settlement," Judge Wisdom was severely critical of Judge Bell's evident approval of less than system-wide desegregation remedies:

> The most destructive feature of Judge Bell's opinion is its ambiguous treatment ... of the Justice Department's about-face. Ever since Brown the Department has taken the position that school segregation is system-wide in nature and must be remedied by system-wide measures. Infection at one school infects all schools. To take the most simple example, in a two school system, all blacks at one school means all or almost all whites at the other. Up to now, neither the Department of Justice nor this Court has ever spoken of 'incidents' or 'pockets of discrimination' or required the district court, as Judge Bell puts it, 'to identify the school or schools which are seg-

regated' or stated that the 'identification must be supported by findings of fact'; or asserted that some 'one
race schools ... are the product of neutral, non-discriminatory forces.' These are blatant euphemisms to avoid
desegregating the system, preserving the whiteness of
certain schools.

Most previous opinions support Judge Wisdom's stinging dissent. There is a reciprocal effect between school locations and
housing patterns--if minorities all live in one area, then the schools
in that area will be racially or ethnically identifiable while schools
in other areas will be relatively free of minorities. Given the interaction between housing patterns and segregated schools, past
cases support the motion that attempting to create a unitary school
system by remedying only the "pockets" of segregation is unrealistic.

*   *   *

The willingness of eight members of the Fifth Circuit to remand the Austin case with generalized instructions amounting to a
rehash of Swann, accompanied by the expressed desire of seven
members of his court to defer any action until the Denver case,
exasperated Chief Judge Brown. His responsive opinion to Judge
Godbold's arguments that action should be stayed pending the decision in Denver capsulized the Court's building frustrations:

... [W]aiting is not the privilege of a Federal Judge.
He must act in the face of the day's challenge to constitutional denial. Indeed, the very Court to whom the dissenters look for guidance has in no uncertain words made
it plain to this Court--one whose record in school cases
exceeds all in volume and, hopefully, history will recognize with comparative quality--that we should get on with
our job--job being the street's description of duty.
    In response to a modest request delivered safehand by
air courier by the Secretary of HEW to the Chief Judge at
his home for a 60-day extension of the effective date of a
plan for some 20 Mississippi school districts, the Supreme
Court summarily reversed this Court. Alexander v.
Holmes County Board of Education ... [cite omitted].
    When we met in November 1969 to hear a dozen school
cases en banc, this decision was fresh on our minds. On
en banc consideration of those cases and in recognition of
the late time in the school year, we again thought that
there was a reasonable basis for a postponement of pupil
assignment until the next September at the commencement
of the next school year. With the ink scarcely dry on our
order, we were told again in positive terms to get on with
the business--the business we had tried so hard to prosecute since 1957! Carter v. West Feliciana Parish School
Board, 1970 ... [cite omitted]. Not a Judge on this Court
disparaged either summary reversal. Indeed, the rever-

sals were consistent with everything we had done in the
long march from Mansfield.

These decisions were sharp, peremptory reminders
of our duty to decide--not just rubber stamp after getting
the word from Mount Olympus.

Now we must heed this call again. A realist knows
that we will not get the answers if we wait. With all
deference, Swann is proof of that. More important, to
delay means that identifiable children--now Mexican-Americans, not primarily Blacks--will leave the last year of
their public education without ever experiencing a single
year of education free of racial/ethnic discrimination....

Surely, after the 19 years (1954-1973) since Brown
there must be a better answer than this.

* * *

The Supreme Court in Denver deals extensively with the issue of whether desegregation remedies had to be system-wide. Mr.
Justice Brennan's reasoning for the majority on the de facto/de jure
distinction influenced his resolution of the issue concerning the
breadth of desegregation remedies. He argued that where there was
statutory segregation in a jurisdiction at the time of Brown I, the
affirmative duty to desegregate fell on the entire system, without
any need to investigate the effects on the entire system. However,
where there was a finding of de jure segregation of a non-statutory
origin in a substantial portion of the district, the procedure for
application of remedies became considerably more complex. The
school board had the duty to prove that the segregated section was
so separated from the rest of the district by physical and geographical boundaries that the entire district was not tainted. Where the
board failed in this showing, de jure segregation in a substantial
portion of the district made the entire district a dual system. However, if the board was successful in showing that the parts of the
system were separable, the examination did not stop. Where there
was de jure segregation in a substantial portion of the district--
even a separable and distinct area--it shifted the burden of proof
to the board to show that the segregation in the remaining portion
of the district was not also de jure. If the school board failed to
prove absence of a segregationist intent, its last defense was that
the relation between its past intentional acts and the present condition of segregation was so attenuated that it could not be considered
the source of the segregation.

Mr. Justice Powell's opinion emphasized the importance of
system-wide remedies in school districts where segregated schools
are found to exist. Again Mr. Justice Rehnquist's opinion was the
most restrictive. In the absence of statutory segregation, Justice
Rehnquist's approach was to identify the actual areas affected by the
discrimination. Discriminating against some people in a district
"does not necessarily result in denial of equal protection to all
minority students within that district." Only those who are actually
affected by the de jure segregation have a right to a remedy. He

rejected Justice Brennan's view that a finding of segregation in a substantial portion of the district shifted the burden. Justice Rehnquist pointed out, as did Justice Powell, the weakness in interpreting intent from acts taken at different times by a board composed of changing members. Since Justice Rehnquist's approach continued to require a showing of intent for a finding of de jure segregation, he necessarily rejected any "part-infects-all" notion. He also rejected Justice Powell's concept of an existing duty on the part of school authorities to operate an integrated system. Justice Rehnquist argued that such a duty existed only where there has been a history of statutory segregation. Where segregation of a non-statutory nature existed, Justice Rehnquist would have imposed on the board a duty to desegregate only the specific schools affected. In Justice Rehnquist's view, if the use of neutral principles resulted in segregated schools there was no duty to integrate, absent a history of statutorily imposed segregation. Only Mr. Justice Rehnquist of the sitting Supreme Court Justices adopted such a restrictive view. Acceptance of the Rehnquist approach would stultify desegregation efforts in the North and West.

*   *   *

The Richmond non-decision left standing a Fourth Circuit reversal of a district court approved metropolitan-wide remedy that would have effectively merged two county school districts with the core city district. The Supreme Court's four-four split in Richmond left undecided the legality of plans that ignore existing school district boundaries in order to reach an effective level of integration. That issue was again before the Court in Detroit.

*   *   *

Judge Roth had found that the Detroit schools were impermissibly segregated. He held that Detroit had a duty to "achieve the greatest possible degree of actual desegregation, taking into account the practicalities of the situation." Because of residential patterns, time, distance and transportation problems, he determined that the achievement of desegregation within Detroit alone was impossible. Therefore, he ordered desegregation carried out on a metropolitan-wide scale. He reasoned that a federal court has the power to remedy a constitutional violation caused by a school board since it is a subdivision of state government, and that the state's use of geographical boundaries did not prevent implementation of the only effective remedy--metropolitan-wide integration. Judge Roth's holding was sweeping: if it had been upheld, scores of outlying independent school districts would have been subject to his desegregation order, without any showing of illegal segregation by them and without any showing that the school district lines as originally drawn were unconstitutional.

While the Supreme Court's reversal of Judge Roth's multi-district remedial order did not rule per se that all metropolitan-wide desegregation plans that ignored school district lines were overly broad, that opinion can only be read as casting serious doubt on future metropolitan plans involving more than one school district. The Supreme Court ruled that, before school district lines can be ignored, de jure segregation must be found to infect all of the districts subject to the integration plan.

In addition to disapproving Judge Roth's multi-district remedy for desegregating Detroit's ghettos, the Supreme Court majority opinion indicated that Judge Roth and the Court of Appeals had applied an "erroneous standard" by seeking a racial balance in Detroit metropolitan-area schools. Reaffirming language in Swann that racial-balancing was not required, the majority also stressed the historical importance of local control over schools and the administrative problems that would result in multi-district plans.

The Detroit holding split the Supreme Court badly; four of the Warren Court Justices--Douglas, Brennan, White and Marshall--dissented and Mr. Justice Stewart, the other Warren Court member, in a concurring opinion attempted to narrowly confine the Detroit holding to its facts.

In a separate dissent, a deeply troubled Mr. Justice Douglas argued that Detroit, read with San Antonio Independent School District v. Rodriguez, which basically held that poorer school districts "had to pay their own way," meant that not only would core city black children be left in segregated schools but that they would be left in inferior schools. "So far as equal protection is concerned we are now in a dramatic retreat from the 8-to-1 decision in 1896 [Plessy v. Ferguson] that Blacks could be segregated in public facilities provided they receive equal treatment."

Mr. Justice White dissented (joined by Justices Douglas, Brennan and Marshall) and Mr. Justice Marshall dissented (joined by Justices Douglas, Brennan and White). Mr. Justice White essentially argued in his dissent that the State of Michigan was responsible for the segregationist acts of the Detroit School District; that the plan of Judge Roth was administratively feasible; that only a multi-district plan was likely to provide any effective integration; and that the outlying Detroit school districts were subdivisions of the State of Michigan whose boundaries could be ignored in devising a plan to rectify constitutional violations.

In a powerful, strongly worded dissent, Mr. Justice Marshall, who had been Counsel for the plaintiffs before the Supreme Court in Brown I and II, began:

> After 20 years of small, often difficult steps toward that great end, the Court today takes a giant step backwards. Notwithstanding a record showing widespread and pervasive racial segregation in the educational system provided by the State of Michigan for children in Detroit, this Court holds that the District Court was powerless to require the State to remedy its constitutional violation in

any meaningful fashion. Ironically purporting to base its
result on the principle that the scope of the remedy in a
desegregation case should be determined by the nature and
the extent of the constitutional violation, the Court's answer is to provide no remedy at all for the violation proved
in this case, thereby guaranteeing that Negro children in
Detroit will receive the same separate and inherently unequal education in the future as they have been unconstitutionally afforded in the past.

Mr. Justice Marshall emphasized that restricting the remedy in the
Detroit case would not result in desegregation of those schools. He
argued that the State of Michigan, not just the Detroit School District,
was responsible for the segregation in Detroit's schools; therefore,
mere school district lines drawn by the State should not block an
effective remedy. Mr. Justice Marshall also argued that Judge Roth
was not attempting to racially balance all of the schools in the Detroit metropolitan area. He gloomily concluded:

> Today's holding, I fear, is more a reflection of a
> perceived public mood that we have gone far enough in
> enforcing the Constitution's guarantee of equal justice
> than it is the product of neutral principles of law. In the
> short run, it may seem to be the easier course to allow
> our great metropolitan areas to be divided into two cities
> --one white, the other black--but it is a course, I predict,
> our people will ultimately regret.

Busing.--Among available methods for alleviating segregation,
by far the most politically charged is busing. Today the very term
"busing" has taken on so many emotional connotations that judges
often gingerly refer to this particular desegregation remedy simply
as "transportation." That busing of children to designated schools
has become such a watchword of resistance in rallies, mother's
marches and similar protests is a major irony of the evolution of
desegregation. Certainly when populations were less concentrated,
publicly supported transportation of scattered children of farming
families to a nearby schoolhouse was considered a boon of an enlightened, progressive society. Furthermore, as far as black children were concerned, there was no great outcry when they were
bused past the nearest schoolhouse to a more distant segregated
facility. For example, in 1955 when the Mansfield, Texas, school
board was faced with a petition from black parents that their children be permitted to attend the town's all-white public schools, the
board's response was to set aside sufficient funds to purchase a
school bus to transport the Negro children twenty miles away to a
black school in Ft. Worth.

The Fifth Circuit majority opinions in Corpus Christi and
Austin, bold and forthright on the de facto/de jure issue, are vague
and indecisive on the busing issue. In Corpus Christi, District
Judge Woodrow Seals's plan called for extensive busing and the con-

version from a walk-in to a busing system. Judge Dyer, for the
majority judges, cautioned that federal courts should first seek
remedies that do not require busing. He suggested clustering and
pairing, arguing that it would involve no more than the expansion of
the neighborhood school system. Judge Gewin, dissenting to the
remedy, found Judge Dyer's suggestion ironic since the majority
opinion had already identified the use of a neighborhood school system as the source of the violation in the first place. Judge Dyer's
opinion warned of the dangers to health and education if busing was
extensively used, and specified in his remand order that if transportation was undertaken, it must fall on Anglo, Mexican-American
and Negro children equally. Judge Dyer's opinion in Corpus Christi
can be fairly categorized as broadening the scope of violation (his
abrogation of the de facto/de jure distinction) but narrowing the
means of remedying the violation (his restrictions on busing).

Ten of the Fifth Circuit's fifteen judges joined the Dyer opinion. Judge Gewin dissented, joined by the Court's traditional liberals. The fact that Judge Gewin, long considered as one of the
more conservative members of the Court in school matters, joined
the liberals in both Austin and Corpus Christi indicated a significant
shift in his judicial position on integration questions. Judge Gewin
criticized the Dyer opinion for its failure to answer the key question:
how much busing is too much. Judge Gewin reminded the majority
judges that since the Green case, the test of any remedy is its effectiveness in providing desegregation. In saying that busing must
be minimized even after other means have been exhausted, Judge
Gewin charged that the majority had undercut the Green test. Judge
Gewin acknowledged that busing poses financial and administrative
hardships; but he argued that such hardships cannot be used as reasons to avoid desegregation, if other remedies prove ineffective.

In his two opinions in the Austin case, Judge Wisdom expressed his dissatisfaction that the district court had identified
busing as the key issue in the case. The eight-judge majority in
Austin, after listing all the well-known disadvantages of busing, had
ordered the interested parties to formulate a plan in such a way
that "transportation problems ... may ... be minimized." Judge
Wisdom rejected that treatment of the issue. He noted that the plan
approved by the lower court provided for the busing of blacks, but
not whites. Noting tartly that apparently busing does not interfere
with black education, Judge Wisdom pointed out that busing is a
legitimate tool in fashioning an effective remedy. Busing has been
used throughout the nation for many years, often to maintain segregated schools. The use of busing was an inherent adjunct to several of the tools necessary to convert a dual system to a unitary
system. He argued that where busing was necessary to achieve a
unitary school, the court should not dismiss it as a remedy. Judge
Wisdom was particularly caustic in condemning the busing of blacks
but not whites: "there is no basis in the record for the district
court's order requiring the busing of two-thirds of the black students, a few Mexican-Americans, and no whites." Judge Wisdom
saw the Justice Department's proposed treatment of "incidents" and

"pockets" of segregation and Judge Bell's vague reference to one-race schools as attempts to avoid the busing issue: "These are blatant euphemisms to avoid desegregating the system, preserving the whiteness of certain schools."

Judge Bell's treatment of the volatile busing issue for the eight-judge majority in Austin was similar to that of Judge Dyer's in Corpus Christi. Judge Bell ordered that techniques not requiring busing be exhausted before using noncontiguous busing; and, even then, the busing technique should only be used to the minimum extent possible. While pointing out the familiar evils of busing, Judge Bell did state that if busing was undertaken it must fall equally on both races.

In his Austin opinion, urging his brothers to defer reaching the merits until Denver, Judge Godbold also discussed busing. Recognizing the current emotional outcry over busing, Judge Godbold believed its use was tied up in the complex issue of de jure/de facto segregation. He pointed out that only if integration moved North and West would busing affect the rest of the nation; the nation at large was only outraged when busing affected their schools and not just those of the South.

* * *

Busing played only a minimum role in the majority opinion of Justice Brennan and the concurring opinion of Justice Douglas in the Denver case. However, Mr. Justice Powell devoted a large portion of his separate opinion to that issue. He reiterated the fears and counter-fears expressed by the judges of the Fifth Circuit in Corpus Christi and Austin. He saw the main issue to be, simply, at what cost to other rights and valid concerns may busing be ordered. In Mr. Justice Powell's view busing is a legitimate tool; however, extensive use of it, while perhaps appropriate in rural areas, might be extremely disruptive in an urban setting. Mr. Justice Powell expressed fear that the lower federal courts had read Swann as requiring extensive busing solely to achieve the greatest possible integration. He indicated if that, in fact, were the correct reading of Swann, then he was in disagreement with it: "Nothing in our Constitution commands or encourages any such court-compelled disruption of public education." Swann, in Mr. Justice Powell's view, laid down a "broad rule of reason under which desegregation remedies must remain flexible and other values and interests be considered." Mr. Justice Powell was troubled that federal courts in their zeal for busing would overlook other valid local concerns: parents can have a legitimate interest in having their child attend a neighborhood school; neighborhood schools can serve a broader function than just education by providing a social, community affairs center; and extensive busing can disrupt the educational process and be a danger to the health and safety of children.

Justice Powell emphasized that federal courts cannot anticipate the long term societal effects of busing. Busing in some situations could precipitate white flight and lead to a deterioration of public support for schools. Also, the burden of busing might fall unevenly on districts according to the degree of financial resources, the degree of urbanization and their racial composition. The great economic burden of massive busing also bothered Justice Powell. He argued that busing was unique among desegregation remedies in that the burden of the remedy fell on one group, the children; whereas the source of the constitutional deprivation was another group, the school board.

Despite his forceful argument against busing, Mr. Justice Powell would not discard it as a remedy. However, he urged that its use be limited to that necessary to correct the unconstitutional evil involved; courts, in ordering a busing remedy, should remain flexible and give proper consideration to valid local concerns. Justice Powell's argument left unanswered the key question: how much weight should be given to those other valid community interests when the court determines that massive busing is the only effective remedy for the deprivation?

The Detroit case provided no fresh discussion of the busing issue; nevertheless, anxiety about that issue was perhaps one of the motivating factors behind the ruling of the five-judge majority overturning Judge Roth's multi-district integration plan.

The End of the Super Court

MR. MADISON observed, that, unless inferior tribunals were dispersed throughout the republic ... appeals would be multiplied to a most oppressive degree.... An effective judiciary establishment, commensurate to the legislative authority, was essential. A government without a proper executive and judiciary would be the mere trunk of a body, without arms or legs to act or move.
    --5 Elliot, Debates on the Adoption of the Federal Constitution 159 (1896)

I am not sure but that it will be found highly expedient and useful to divide the United States into four or five, or half a dozen districts; and to institute a federal court in each district, in lieu of one in every state. The judges of these courts may hold circuits for the trial of causes in the several parts of the respective districts. Justice through them may be administered with ease and dispatch; and appeals may be safely circumscribed within a narrow compass. This plan appears to me at present the most eligible of any that could be adopted, and in order to do it, it is necessary that the power of constituting inferior courts should

exist in the full extent in which it is seen in the
proposed constitution.
--The Federalist Papers, No. 81

Madison and Hamilton would undoubtedly have been amazed
that the federal judicial system would subsequently include ninety
district courts and eleven courts of appeal which, by the time of the
nation's bicentennial, would still be inadequate to meet the needs of
litigants. For more than a decade legal scholars, judges and Congress itself have become increasingly concerned with the ability of
the eleven United States Courts of Appeals to handle almost exponentially growing case loads. In all eleven circuits in 1960, only
3,899 appeals were filed--providing a yearly work load average of
fifty-seven appeals per federal appellate judge. By 1973, 15,629
appeals were filed in the circuits, increasing the average annual
appeals per judge to 161 filings. That time period, then, saw a
301 per cent increase in filed appeals while federal district court
case filings in the same period increased only fifty-eight per cent.
In addition to that astronomical increase in appeal filings, Congress
has increased the subject matter reviewable by federal courts. New
volumes of litigation in previously unknown areas now burgeon dockets: sex discrimination, consumer protection and environmental
protection being only the most obvious examples. Congress also increased the number of federal district judges serving the nation;
and new judges stimulate more appeals until they learn their jobs.

In response to the spiraling crisis in its courts of appeals,
Congress created a Commission on Revision of the Federal Court
Appellate System* to examine the problem and to propose solutions.
That Commission began its work by recognizing that a special situation existed in the Fifth Circuit. While the entire federal appellate
court structure appeared to be jeopardized by the alarming increase
in business, a particularly severe crisis existed in the Fifth Circuit. With fifteen judges, the Fifth Circuit remains the largest federal appeals court, with the largest number of appellate case filings.

The Commission was given the following two mandates by
Congress: 1) to consider the geographical division of the circuits;
and 2) to consider the structure and internal procedures of the circuits.

Since its first mandate was to consider the possible geographic splitting of the Circuit--before considering structure and internal
procedures--the Commission began hearings in August and September in both the Fifth and Ninth Circuits, the first and second courts

---

*The Commission began its work in the summer of 1973 with six-
teen members, four appointed from the Senate, four appointed by
the President, four appointed by the House and four appointed by the
Chief Justice. Senator Roman Hruska was appointed Chairman of
the Commission and Professor A. Leo Levin of the University of
Pennsylvania Law School was named its Executive Director.

in terms of case load. Four public hearings were held in Fifth Circuit cities: Houston, New Orleans, Jackson and Jacksonville.

The hearings began in Houston, Texas, and Chief Judge John R. Brown of the Fifth Circuit was invited to make an opening statement. From the onset of the hearings in Houston, Chief Judge John R. Brown was obviously opposed to splitting his mammoth court. Proud of the enormous task accomplished by the Fifth Circuit in all of its judicial business, not just its civil rights and desegregation cases, Judge Brown was well-known as an excellent judicial administrator. He enjoyed a widespread reputation as an innovator of many of the most promising reforms in appellate court administrative structure. He took great pride in chairing what he termed "the largest constitutional court in the history of the Republic." While stressing the immense work load on his court and the vast increase in cases, Chief Judge Brown insisted from the beginning of the hearings that the Fifth Circuit was not in a crisis situation and that it could indeed continue to conduct its business. Most of the members of Chief Judge Brown's court, however, openly opposed his viewpoint. They urged that an immediate split of the Fifth Circuit was essential to enable that court to continue to conduct its business.

As the hearings progressed, at each hearing location, lawyer representatives of the bars of all Fifth Circuit states presented their own views on circuit realignment and internal operations of the Court. While the lawyers were split among themselves on whether the Fifth Circuit should be divided geographically, they almost uniformly criticized their Circuit for many of its expediting and summary calendar procedures. Several charged that some of the changes adopted by the Fifth Circuit, particularly the screening and Rule 21 (affirmance without opinion) procedures, were not only offensive to lawyers but resulted in lowering the quality of justice. The more outspoken speculated openly whether denial of oral argument in over forty per cent of the cases did not mean that the standard of justice in the Circuit was adversely affected. Law professors and judges also testified. All the members of the Fifth Circuit Court of Appeals expressed viewpoints and opinions with the exception of its then newest member, Thomas G. Gee.

All of the Fifth Circuit judges agreed that without screening and other expeditious procedures, products of the innovative genius of Chief Judge Brown and Judge Griffin Bell, Chairman of the circuit's administration committee, the Court could not have kept abreast of its work. In fact, several judges argued that the screening and Rule 21 procedures would be of permanent value to the appellate structure. While such procedures were conceived in a crisis atmosphere as methods of expediting the court's work, they had intrinsic value and were not a threat to the quality of justice administered in the Circuit. In many ways, the Commission hearings were an educational forum where the judges informed the lawyers of the Circuit of the pressures on the Court and the reasons for the procedures that had been adopted.

*   *   *

The interaction between the judges of the Fifth Circuit, and their differing viewpoints on splitting the Circuit, proved fascinating, partly because the subject of splitting the Circuit first occurred in the schism period following the James Meredith imbroglio. At that time, it will be recalled that Senator Eastland proposed splitting Texas and Louisiana from the rest of the Fifth Circuit, ostensibly because of the Court's overcrowded dockets. However, the issue of splitting the Circuit was intertwined with civil rights problems. Judges Rives and Wisdom successfully led the earlier fight against splitting the Circuit, at least partially on the theory that the Eastland Plan was motivated by a desire to separate the liberal judges who then controlled the Fifth Circuit.

By 1973 and the Commission hearings, civil rights issues had by and large been divorced from the issue of whether or not the Circuit should be split. While echoes of that famous divisive court dispute could be faintly heard in subtle nuances in the testimony of some of the judges, most of the judges stuck to the issue at point: should the Circuit be split because of the work load. The contrasting viewpoints of the judges on the issue of dividing their own court is not only instructive, but revealing.

Chief Judge John R. Brown defended his court's expediting procedures against the charges of his lawyer critics and attacked what he considered the most threatening charges to the continued existence of the Fifth Circuit, that his court was both too large and too overburdened to properly handle its business. Asserting that his court was not "helter-skelter, confused or mismanaged," Judge Brown fought back. He refuted the charge frequently made that a court of fifteen fostered so many internal conflicts that a prohibitive number of en banc hearings were required to settle conflicts between panels. He analyzed each of the en bancs participated in by the Fifth Circuit for the preceding three years to show that most were called because of the importance of the matter at issue and not because of conflicts between various panels of different judges on the same Circuit.

Throughout Judge Brown's testimony ran the theme that the number nine had no magic; he attacked the insistence that a court of appeals should not go beyond nine in number. Judge Brown challenged the Commission directly on the issue of whether or not a circuit realignment would provide any solution to the complained of problems. He insisted that the first step had to be an understanding of the capacity of both the appellate court and appellate judges.

After a rigorous defense of his innovative procedures and his assertion that splitting his court was not a solution to its problem, Chief Judge Brown did concede that the work load problem in the Circuit was severe. He then suggested several new ideas that, in his view, held more promise than circuit splitting. He urged that a group of career lawyers be hired to help the Court with such items as screening and other administrative matters, thus freeing the judges' time for judging. A bold pitch was made that Congress should provide other new and updated services to the Court and he urged all judges to make more rigorous use of law clerks and other supporting personnel. After commenting on a wide variety of proposed solutions, Judge Brown again emphatically concluded that "There is nothing resolved by the drawing of a line or the shifting of a state ... the problem requires radical solutions." Finally, he opposed allocation of more than fifteen judges to his court and said that the present judges could handle the job: the Fifth Circuit was not near collapse.

After his presentation Chief Judge Brown submitted to questions. One of the reasons Judge Brown had opposed splitting the Circuit was, he had argued, because the two split circuits--within a year or two--would have an equal or even greater case load than the present circuit. He further argued that the new circuits would also require more judges. A very telling point was made in the questioning by Professor Leo Levin, the Executive Director of the Commission. Professor Levin quietly asked what would be the judgeship requirement in 1981 in the present Fifth Circuit if 100 dispositions per judge were considered the optimum case load per appellate judge. Judge Brown estimated between forty-six to fifty judges would be required to handle the projected case load. The point was shattering to Chief Judge Brown's previous arguments. While Chief Judge Brown might be quite correct in contending that splitting the Circuit would only create two new circuits of the same size as the present Fifth, failure to split the present circuits would result in a court that by 1981 would be a monstrosity, requiring forty-six to fifty judges. Judge Brown seemed to surrender on the circuit-splitting issue. He ruefully smiled and stated, "I predicted that at 3:00 P.M. today I would have to throw in the sponge. I desperately want you to leave the Fifth Circuit alone, but I know that's not possible."

* * *

An even stronger opponent than John R. Brown to splitting the Fifth Circuit was Judge John Minor Wisdom. He opposed the split for substantive reasons that contained echoes of the arguments in 1963 over the Eastland Plan:

> As I see our system, a federal circuit court has a federalizing function as well as a purely appellate function of reviewing errors. We do not just settle disputes between litigants. The federal courts' destined role is to bring local policy in line with the Constitution and the national policy. Within the framework of 'cases and controversies' and subject to all the appropriate judicial disciplines, federal courts adjust the body politic to stresses and strains produced by conflicts (1) between the nation and the states and (2) between the states and private citizens asserting federally-created or federally-protected

rights. The United States Supreme Court cannot do it all. When it acts, inferior courts must implement the Supreme Court's decision, must put flesh on the bare bones of such mandates as requiring schools to desegregate with 'all deliberate speed.'

The increasing importance of this function of federal courts is not caused by activistic tendencies on the part of some federal judges to intrude into state affairs. Events beyond the control of judges have thrust the federal courts into a larger and more active role than their predecessors played--but not a role unanticipated by the authors of the Constitution....

For the most part the friction-making cases in the federal courts are not those over the allocation of power between the states and the nation. They are the cases between the states and its citizens involving civil rights and fair criminal procedures. These contests arise from state courts' employing different constitutional standards in their criminal procedures from those federal courts employ, or from a state's failure to give effect to constitutionally created or federally guaranteed rights, when these rights conflict with state laws and customs. Civil rights cases reflect the customs and mores of the community as well as the legal philosophy of the individual judges called upon to adjudicate the controversies. This area of conflict therefore is the most sensitive and difficult one in which federal courts must perform their nationalizing function. This is where localism tends to create wide differences among our courts. Parochial prides and prejudices and built-in attachments to local customs must be expected to reduce the incentive of inferior federal courts to bring local policy in line with national policy.

The handling of civil rights matters, while no longer a central point of dispute in the circuit-splitting controversy, was obviously still an important motivating factor in Judge Wisdom's opposition to an immediate circuit split.

In a carefully thought out series of recommendations, Judge Wisdom suggested methods of handling the crushing case burden presently resting on the Fifth Circuit, short of dividing that Court. He advocated: 1) curtailing federal jurisdiction at district and appellate levels; and 2) providing more effective administrative assistance to the federal appellate courts, with particular attention to the development of the new central administrative staff concept, suggested by Chief Judge Brown. In advocating the curtailing of federal jurisdiction, he suggested abolition completely of the three-judge federal court, abolition or at least heavy curtailment of diversity jurisdiction, the use of an ombudsman-type approach in some criminal cases, and complete abolition of the petition for rehearing. On the idea of setting up a central staff of supporting administrators, Judge Wisdom argued that adoption of such a program would endorse screening proceedings as a legitimate method of administering appellate case loads in the federal courts.

After he learned that the majority of his fellow judges on the Fifth Circuit supported a split of the Circuit, Judge Wisdom filed a supplemental statement reasserting his own opposition in ringing terms:

> I respectfully suggest to the Commission and to all interested in preserving American Federalism that partition of the Fifth Circuit now is a step toward destruction of the effective functioning of the federal judicial system. If the Commission and Congress think that statistics argue for realignment now, consistency requires that this same remedy be resorted to again in 1974, 1975, and again in 1978. As long as no court may consist of more than nine judges, and as long as the appellate process is not revised, the federal circuit court system will have to be divided, sub-divided, and re-subdivided, until there is one circuit for the Southern District of New York and one circuit for Mississippi. If numbers control, in a few years there will be a circuit court for most states, but two or more for New York, California, Texas, Florida, Pennsylvania, and many other states.

Joining Judges Brown and Wisdom, Judge Ainsworth also expressed reservations about circuit splitting and indicated a desire to see the maintenance of the existing circuit alignment.

*   *   *

However, eight of the Judges of the United States Court of Appeals for the Fifth Circuit--Judges Gewin, Godbold, Dyer, Simpson, Coleman, Clark, Bell and Morgan--submitted a strong statement urging an immediate circuit split as an urgent first step to any consideration of revision of the appellate court system:

> It is our considered conclusion that the Fifth Circuit is geographically too large and that 15 Judges is definitely 6 too many. It is extremely difficult for an appellate court composed of 15 Judges to function with maximum efficiency. The sheer weight of administrative problems and the necessity of one Judge having to deal with 14 others impairs the judicial process. It is very burdensome for each Judge to read and carefully analyze all of the slip opinions of the other 14 Judges. Moreover, it is only natural that intracircuit conflicts multiply when there are 15 active Judges....
> It is the considered opinion of the Judges who join in this statement that the public interest demands immediate relief for the Fifth Circuit. Jumboism has no place in the Federal Court Appellate System. This statement applies both to geographical area and the number of judges

serving the court. In spite of innovative procedures, long hours of work and the decision of over 125 cases per Judge per year, on the average, it is apparent that the Fifth Circuit cannot keep abreast of its mounting caseload. The populations of both Texas and Florida are expanding very rapidly. Much of the litigation in the Fifth Circuit originates in these two states. It appears to be almost impossible for one circuit to accommodate two states which are growing at such a rapid rate which results in ever increasing litigation.

Some have expressed the fear that any remedy is objectionable. This fear seems to be based upon the concept that any remedy which may be adopted will result in parochialism, provincialism and a lack of cross-pollination amongst Judges of different backgrounds which will seriously interfere with the court's traditional role as a national court. The undersigned Judges reject out of hand this expression of fear.

Echoing a strong reaction against any charge that circuit splitting this time around was motivated by racial considerations, the eight judges appended the following paragraph which dealt specifically with the school integration question.

The undisputed record demonstrates that the Fifth Circuit hears as wide a variety of cases as any circuit in the nation. In addition it is recognized that the Fifth Circuit has been the active battleground of school integration cases, suits involving the integration of public accommodations, attacks on jury discrimination and other civil rights litigation. By innovative procedures we shortened the time for perfecting appeals, filing briefs and reaching decisions in school integration cases.... For example, in the Fifth Circuit we heard 166 appeals in school integration cases alone between December 2, 1969 and September 24, 1970--a period of slightly over nine months....

We believe it is fair to say that the six states which (in addition to the Canal Zone) comprise the Fifth Circuit are far more integrated on all levels than any other six states in the nation. We have rendered more integration decisions than all of the other appellate courts of the nation combined. A very high percentage of those decisions were rendered by three-judge panels, but during the critical period mentioned, all opinions were circulated to the entire court for possible objections prior to release. This practice is still followed in school integration cases.

Possibly with the acrimony over the 1963 Eastland Plan in mind and sensitive to charges that their support of circuit splitting was motivated by anything other than concern for the Court's case load, the eight judges attached a table to their statement. The table indicated that two judges were then eligible for retirement; within three years, an additional five members of the Court could retire; and in five

years, two more members could also retire. Thus, within five
years, nine of the fifteen members of the Court could change through
retirement alone.

*   *   *

In addition to joining the statement filed by the eight, several
of the same judges made very strong oral statements at the hearing
in Jackson, Mississippi. Judge Clark dramatically wheeled into the
hearing room a printed stack of Fifth Circuit opinions which towered
five and one/half feet in height, representing the opinion writing
work load of that Court for just one year. He then made a strong
plea for an immediate split of the Circuit within the next six months
as an emergency first step to solving the Circuit's problems. After
that first step, he suggested that all of the circuits in the nation
could be realigned and other reforms instituted. If necessary, he
urged that the circuit splitting be done on a temporary basis or that
the Fifth Circuit simply be divided into two divisions awaiting the
final and definitive division of all the circuits.

Judge John Godbold of Montgomery also stressed the urgency
of the situation and, more than any other judge, indicated that the
current work load actually might be affecting the quality of the
Court's functions:

> The hard fact is that at this moment we are operating
> beyond the limits which effective exercise of our delibera-
> tive function commands. Additional staff will ease the
> strain but it will not solve the basic problem unless the
> judge abdicates to staff a part of the deliberative function
> which Article III of the Constitution intends that he exer-
> cise.

*   *   *

The leader of the circuit splitting forces clearly has been
Judge Griffin Bell, also father of many of the innovative expediting
procedures of the Court. A vigorous and politically sensitive man
with enormous personal charm, Judge Bell strongly defended many
of the expediting procedures adopted by the Fifth Circuit, much in
the tone of Judge Brown, but differed sharply with the Chief Judge
on what could be done in the future. He supported the split of the
Circuit at the Commission's hearings in Jacksonville even though,
in emotional terms, he regretted the dissolution of a great court:

> The point that I am making is that I believe that the
> size of the Fifth Circuit must be substantially reduced in
> the number of judges on the court. The regret of it all
> will be that some of us will no longer be able to claim the
> Fifth as our circuit. My life as a lawyer and as a judge
> has been the rich history of the Fifth--its standard of ex-
> cellence--its challenges--its faithfulness to the Constitution
> --the stability and integrity of its decisions and procedures,

qualities which stem from sources of professionalism and from traditions built up over a longer period of years by intelligent and honorable judges--some deceased--some retired--others active. I would not expect a lesser standard in a new circuit--only two Fifth Circuits with one having a different name.

* * *

On December 18, 1973, the Commission on Revision of the Federal Court Appellate System filed its initial recommendation for a revamping of the federal appellate system. The Commission reommended that both the Fifth Circuit and the Ninth Circuit be split into two new circuits. The Fifth Circuit would be divided as follows: 1) Florida, Georgia and Alabama would become a new circuit but would retain the name "The Fifth Circuit." 2) Texas, Louisiana, Mississippi and the Canal Zone would become a new circuit, to be called the Eleventh Circuit.

* * *

The days of the great Fifth Circuit appear numbered. Growing from a court of five in 1955 at the time of Brown II, it became a court of fifteen, the largest appellate court in the history of the country in both size and case load. Judge for judge, many consider it to be not only the largest but also the best appellate court in the land, including the Supreme Court. Its growth and reputation both paralleled and were stimulated by the turbulent years of civil rights and school integration. Certainly, that court, staffed by Southerners, became the nation's greatest civil rights tribunal. More than any other single force or institution, the Fifth Circuit was responsible for the actual integration of the public schools of the Deep South. And, in the process, it triggered a nearly bloodless social revolution that transformed a region and recognized long ignored hopes which even a war a century before could not fulfill. The United States Court of Appeals for the Fifth Circuit may end but its legacies will be legion: its decisions, its procedural reforms, its experience in implementing the will of Congress and the Constitution in the face of organized resistance, and its survival in the years from 1954 to 1974 exemplify and insure the stability of the federal judicial system and the wisdom of its founders.

NOTES AND PRIMARY AUTHORITY

The primary authority for the material contained in this Chapter was:

Five Cases in Five Cities and Division in Doctrine; Three Issues in Synthesis. The primary sources are the five cases: Milliken v. Bradley, 418 U.S. 717 (1974) (referred to in text as Detroit); Keyes v. School Dist. No. 1, 413 U.S. 189 (1973) (referred to in text as Denver); School Bd. of City of Richmond, Va. v. State Bd.

of Education of Va., 412 U.S. 92 (1973) (referred to in text as Richmond); United States v. Texas Educ. Agency, 467 F.2d 848 (5th Cir. 1972) (referred to in text as Austin); and Cisneros v. Corpus Christi Ind. School Dist., 467 F.2d 142 (5th Cir. 1972) (referred to in text as Corpus Christi). Other cases, such as Holland v. Bd. of Pub. Instruc. of Palm Beach County, 258 F.2d 730 (5th Cir. 1958); and Jackson v. Rawdon, 135 F. Supp. 936 (N.D. Tex. 1955) were also consulted. Contemporary news accounts such as New York Times, Aug. 4, 1971, at 1, col. 8 and at 15, col. 1, were helpful.

The End of the Super Court. The Commission on Revision of the Federal Appellate Court System, Preliminary Report (Nov. 1973) was a principal source. Unpublished Statements filed with that Commission and interviews with several Fifth Circuit judges were invaluable. The Commission's recommendations for the Fifth Circuit can be found in "Commission Recommends Splitting Fifth and Ninth Circuits to Create Two New Federal Appellate Circuits," 60 A.B.A.J. 209 (Feb. 1974).

A more complete manuscript, with detailed documentation of sources is available as indicated in the Preface, supra.

EPILOGUE

The federal judiciary's desegregation efforts in the South are now largely complete. Appeals from district court school desegregation orders have dropped dramatically and most whites appear to have accepted the integration of their public schools, albeit reluctantly. Contemporary accounts indicate that there are very few differences now in race relations between such towns as Jackson, Mississippi and Dayton, Ohio except that, because of massive desegregation orders, Jackson's schools are probably now more integrated than Dayton's! The school litigation that continues to trouble the federal courts in the South is confined primarily to methods of implementing existing desegregation orders in the region's large metropolitan areas. Most rural school districts, on the other hand, have ended their litigation, only reporting back periodically to district courts.

Controversy still rages over methods of implementing desegregation, however. Massive busing, particularly in large urban areas, provokes as much acrimony in the North as it ever did in the South. The major difference between the South and other regions may be that in the South the back of resistance has been broken, while elsewhere--because of the lack of federal judicial activity arising from the de facto/de jure distinction--resistance is still strong and unbowed. The violence in Pontiac, Michigan, and the continuing torment in Boston, Massachusetts, is but the tip of the iceberg.

What have been the results of the twenty-year effort to desegregate the public schools? Have the changes been worth the costs? Has there been a lasting transformation in the social fabric of Southern life? Have educational opportunities for minorities actually been equalized? Has federal judicial desegregation of the public schools of the South been but a grand experiment destined for eventual failure? It is too early to answer any such questions

Opposite: United States Court of Appeals for the Fifth Circuit, Summer 1973: standing (l. to r.): Joe M. Ingraham; Lewis R. Morgan; David W. Dyer; Robert H. Ainsworth, Jr.; James P. Coleman; Homer Thornberry; Irving L. Goldberg; John C. Godbold; Bryan Simpson; Charles Clark; and Paul Roney; sitting (l. to r.): Walter P. Gewin; Warren L. Jones; Richard T. Rives; John R. Brown; Elbert P. Tuttle; John Minor Wisdom; and Griffin B. Bell. Reproduced by permission of the Houston Chronicle.

definitively. And the answers are becoming more elusive--and perhaps illusory--since the fragmentation of the civil rights movement in the late '60's. While some black groups--notably the NAACP--have continued to support integration efforts and have urged massive, metropolitan busing plans, others are now voicing many of the same complaints as whites about public school problems. Black parent groups have opposed busing their children out of neighborhood schools to achieve integration, complaining bitterly that the burden of busing has been one-sided, falling primarily on black children. Other local black groups have supported neighborhood schools in order to maintain black control over all-black schools.

Almost all of the South's federal judges, who have been responsible for that region's present, integrated status, agree that patterns concerning the success of integration did develop out of the massive desegregation decrees of 1969, 1970 and 1971. Districts with less than one-third black students in the school population did survive and, with few exceptions, integrated smoothly. Districts with a one-third to one-half black student population had varying results, with more successes than failures. Finally, districts with over one-half of the student population black more often than not experienced serious white flight to suburbs, if they were metropolitan areas, or saw private schools develop, if they were rural areas, with patterns of resegregation developing rapidly.

The school litigation that continues to trouble the Fifth Circuit is confined primarily to methods of implementation of desegregation orders in the large metropolitan areas of the Deep South. The Atlanta and New Orleans cases are typical of such litigation. While one city desegregated with initial calm and the other with initial disorder, both Atlanta and New Orleans today operate eighty per cent black school systems. For whatever cause, chronic white flight to the suburbs continues in both cities and most authorities concur in the melancholy prediction that both the Atlanta and New Orleans public school systems will soon be all-black. On the other hand, most rural school districts have ended their litigation, only reporting back periodically to district courts. Except in those few districts with majority black populations, desegregation in the rural South has been remarkably successful. Even in the turbulent massive desegregation years, 1969-71, most rural districts desegregated calmly and today operate unitary systems.

*   *   *

A scene in a hearing in the newly redecorated courtroom of the Fifth Circuit in New Orleans in the summer of 1973 perhaps illustrates how the integration battle has run full circle in those large city school districts still in active litigation. On August 10, 1973, before a panel consisting of Judges Wisdom, Thornberry and Clark, oral argument was held on one of the continuing aspects of what Federal District Judge Sidney Smith has called "the annual agony of Atlanta"--the seemingly never-ending Atlanta school desegregation case. Fourteen lawyers, representing widely divergent viewpoints, sat at counsel tables for the argument. The courtroom was packed with observers, newsmen and a busload of black children from the Atlanta ghetto area, brought to New Orleans by an Atlanta Catholic priest. All restrictions on oral argument had been lifted and the court allowed each counsel all the time needed to present every side of the case.

Howard Moore, of Angela Davis case fame, represented the NAACP Inc. Fund. The Inc. Fund argued that a local Atlanta compromise school integration plan, agreed to by the Atlanta chapter of the NAACP, had not been approved by the national NAACP. Therefore, Mr. Moore urged that the compromise agreement be voided. The national NAACP, arguing separately from the Inc. Fund for tactical reasons, urged that even though the Atlanta school system had become eighty per cent black and twenty per cent white, further integration activity was necessary. The white students that remained in the Atlanta system were concentrated in several predominantly white areas of Atlanta. The NAACP basically argued that those white children should be bused throughout the Atlanta school system to achieve a form of racial balance.

Almost diametrically opposed to the NAACP, another group of black parents, represented by the Congress of Racial Equality (CORE), argued for continuation of the neighborhood school system. The CORE group was motivated by a desire to maintain black control over most of the schools in Atlanta. The CORE position seemed essentially to oppose further integration efforts.

The American Civil Liberties Union (ACLU) supported vastly increased integration efforts, going further in its demands than the NAACP. The ACLU argued that the weakness of the NAACP plan was that there was not a large enough white student population left in the Atlanta school system to integrate the system. Should further busing be ordered, spreading the remaining white students among the other schools of Atlanta, the ACLU predicted that there would be almost total white flight to the suburbs and private schools, leaving Atlanta an all-black system. Therefore, the ACLU urged that formulation of a massive metropolitan-wide busing plan provided the only realistic way of dismantling Atlanta's previously dual school system. The ACLU frankly acknowledged that its request might involve as many as five counties and four independent school districts.

Caught between warring black and civil rights groups, the local school board found itself essentially sitting on the sidelines, asking, "What more can we do?"

The hearing was lively, prompting pointed questions from the Court. Judge Wisdom tartly asked the attorney representing CORE if CORE's advocacy of a neighborhood school system was not really a plea for continuation of the discredited prior dual system. Questioning the ACLU lawyers, Judge Clark pointed out that the Fifth Circuit had already reserved later ruling on the possibility of a metropolitan-wide plan for Atlanta and noted that Judge Sidney

Smith, at the district court level, had toyed with the possibility of such a plan.

The experience of the Atlanta school board perhaps typified the experiences of other large Southern metropolitan area school boards with predominantly black enrollment. In an empassioned plea, the lawyer for the board told the Court that the Atlanta school board had done all that it could do; continuing white flight, however, threatened to destroy all its efforts. He stated that two or three years ago there were 25,000 whites in the Atlanta system, now only 18,000 whites were left, with more white educables lost every year. He claimed that adoption of the Inc. Fund plan, which would require busing white children out of pockets of white concentration in North Atlanta, would drive those remaining white parents out of Atlanta and into suburbs or private schools, resulting in an almost 100% black school system. Indicating an acute awareness of the then recently decided Denver case, Judge Wisdom pointedly asked the school board lawyer about the ACLU proposal of a metropolitan-wide method of integration. Judge Wisdom had obviously not anticipated the Detroit holding, still a year away.

* * *

For twenty years legal battles have been fought over integration. Almost all of those battles have been waged in Southern courtrooms, presided over by Southern judges, involving Southern black and white children. Those battles have now largely been won by the foes of segregation, with only rear guard struggles continuing in the South's large cities. The question remaining for the nation is whether integration will now move North and West. While only the Supreme Court can finally answer that remaining question, its decision in Detroit, Milliken v. Bradley, indicates that the outlook for bold desegregation efforts in the North and West is not bright. Although carefully limited to its facts, Detroit nevertheless may become an effective deterrent to integration of Northern ghettos and Western barrios--just at the time when it appeared that the school integration effort was moving from the South to the rest of the nation. Only time and further Supreme Court rulings will tell if Detroit is to mark the end of the second era of Reconstruction, just as the Compromise of 1877 marked the end of the first Reconstruction period. However, the parallels do seem striking.

Perhaps the Detroit holding is a simple recognition that the problem of providing equal educational opportunities to all defies a legal solution based solely on a race theory of equal protection. As long as "blackness" and poverty are inescapably linked, and as long as minority plaintiffs cannot themselves agree on the proper remedy, the twenty-year effort to implement the promise of Brown may have, in fact, reached its logical conclusion. The problems of school segregation in the cities may be so intractible that one tool--the constitutional command of equal educational opportunity for all races articulated in Brown--cannot and should not be expected to solve alone the problem of segregated education. Until new tools are found and implemented--a negative income tax or experimentation with John Rawls' theories of distributive justice or some other, yet unborn idea--it is arguable that the limits have been reached in using the Constitution alone as a means in attaining school desegregation. However, assuming that the Constitution is not to be confined forever to a regional application, the agonizing twenty-year experience in Southern federal courtrooms and in Southern school classrooms may prove instructive to the rest of the nation.

NOTES AND PRIMARY AUTHORITY

The following sources were used: Keyes v. School Dist. No. 1, 413 U.S. 189 (1973) (Powell, J., concurring); J. Rawls, A Theory of Justice (1971); Reed, "The Southern Negro Fights for Quality Education," N.Y. Times, Oct. 13, 1969, at 52, col. 4; and Louisville Courier Journal and Times, Sept. 3, 1973, §C, at 6.

APPENDICES

Appendix A: MEMBERS OF THE FIFTH CIRCUIT COURT OF APPEALS
BY YEAR AND STATUS, 1955-1973

LEGEND

Chief Judge   xxxx

Active Judge ====

Senior Judge ::::

Resigned R

Died ■

NAME	1955	1956	1957	1958	1959	1960	1961	1962	1963	1964	1965	1966	1967	1968	1969	1970	1971	1972	1973
HUTCHESON																			
BORAH																			
RIVES																			
TUTTLE																			
CAMERON																			
JONES																			
BROWN																			
WISDOM																			
BELL																			
GEWIN																			
THORNBERRY																			
COLEMAN																			
AINSWORTH																			
GODBOLD																			
GOLDBERG																			
DYER																			
SIMPSON																			
CLAYTON																			
MORGAN																			
CARSWELL																			
CLARK																R			
INGRAHAM																			
RONEY																			
GEE																			

Appendix B: STATISTICAL DEVELOPMENTS IN SCHOOL DESEGREGATION FROM 1954

1954-55

State	SCHOOL DISTRICTS			ENROLLMENT		BLACKS IN SCHOOLS WITH WHITES	
	Total	With Blacks & Whites	Deseg.	White	Negro	No.	%
Alabama	111	111	0	471,511	248,967	0	0
Florida	67	67	0	526,232	150,991	0	0
Georgia	202	202	0	556,006	274,040	0	0
Louisiana	67	67	0	350,758	217,564	0	0
Mississippi	971	971	0	273,722	268,216	0	0
Texas	1,953	1,142	1	1,448,707	224,894	3	.001
SOUTH	4,355	3,337	3	6,105,378	2,315,062	23	.001

1955-56

State	SCHOOL DISTRICTS			ENROLLMENT		BLACKS IN SCHOOLS WITH WHITES	
	Total	With Blacks & Whites	Deseg.	White	Negro	No.	%
Alabama	111	111	0	479,875	253,517	0	0
Florida	67	67	0	594,220	165,957	0	0
Georgia	202	202	0	573,463	278,488	0	0
Louisiana	67	67	0	364,778	227,517	0	0
Mississippi	971	971	0	275,744	270,250	0	0
Texas	1,802	714	73	1,510,693	234,654	2,650	1.13
SOUTH	4,204	2,909	78	6,349,790	2,417,798	2,782	.115

1956-57

State	SCHOOL DISTRICTS			ENROLLMENT		BLACKS IN SCHOOLS WITH WHITES	
	Total	With Blacks & Whites	Deseg.	White	Negro	No.	%
Alabama	111	111	0	471,900	273,200	0	0
Florida	67	67	0	594,220	165,957	0	0
Georgia	200	200	0	644,328	297,672	0	0
Louisiana	67	67	0	375,000	225,000	0	0
Mississippi	827	827	0	273,722	268,216	0	0
Texas	1,800	841	103	1,565,568	248,532	3,380	1.36
SOUTH	4,055	2,885	110	6,478,796	2,437,893	3,514	.144

1957-58

State	SCHOOL DISTRICTS			ENROLLMENT		BLACKS IN SCHOOLS WITH WHITES	
	Total	With Blacks & Whites	Deseg.	White	Negro	No.	%
Alabama	111	111	0	475,500	279,300	0	0
Florida	67	67	0	703,800	196,200	0	0
Georgia	200	196	0	649,800	300,200	0	0
Louisiana	67	67	0	390,625	234,275	0	0
Mississippi	151	151	0	276,276	269,724	0	0
Texas	1,468	722	123	1,627,307	258,333	3,600	1.39
SOUTH	3,047	2,090	137	6,770,710	2,538,554	3,829	.151

1958-59

State	SCHOOL DISTRICTS			ENROLLMENT		BLACKS IN SCHOOLS WITH WHITES	
	Total	With Blacks & Whites	Deseg.	White	Negro	No.	%
Alabama	113	113	0	497,700	292,300	0	0
Florida	67	67	0	708,138	187,742	0	0
Georgia	198	196	0	667,781	310,753	0	0
Louisiana	67	67	0	412,563	271,491	0	0
Mississippi	151	151	0	276,326	268,905	0	0
Texas	1,646	722	125	1,702,141	266,168	3,250	1.22
SOUTH	3,227	2,095	144	6,938,867	2,609,447	3,456	.132

1959-60

State	SCHOOL DISTRICTS			ENROLLMENT		BLACKS IN SCHOOLS WITH WHITES	
	Total	With Blacks & Whites	Deseg.	White	Negro	No.	%
Alabama	113	113	0	516,135	271,134	0	0
Florida	67	67	1	761,819	201,091	512	.255
Georgia	198	196	0	682,354	318,405	0	0
Louisiana	67	67	0	422,181	271,021	0	0
Mississippi	151	151	0	287,781	278,640	0	0
Texas	1,581	720	126	1,783,737	279,374	3,300	1.18
SOUTH	3,164	2,095	153	7,225,977	2,636,320	4,216	.160

1960-61

State	SCHOOL DISTRICTS Total	With Blacks & Whites	Deseg.	ENROLLMENT White	Negro	BLACKS IN SCHOOLS WITH WHITES No.	%
Alabama	114	114	0	523,303	276,029	0	0
Florida	67	67	1	807,512	212,280	28	.013
Georgia	198	196	0	626,377	295,255	0	0
Louisiana	67	67	1	422,181	271,021	1	.0004
Mississippi	151	151	0	287,781	278,640	0	0
Texas	1,531	720	132	1,840,987	288,553	3,500	1.21
SOUTH	3,115	2,095	172	7,358,920	2,660,438	4,308	.162

1961-62

State	SCHOOL DISTRICTS Total	With Blacks & Whites	Deseg.	ENROLLMENT White	Negro	BLACKS IN SCHOOLS WITH WHITES No.	%
Alabama	114	114	0	527,075	280,212	0	0
Florida	67	67	5	927,331	242,097	648	.268
Georgia	198	196	1	641,710	303,005	8	.003
Louisiana	67	67	1	450,000	295,000	12	.004
Mississippi	150	150	0	297,419	288,089	0	0
Texas	1,483	890	149	1,892,044	300,867	4,000	1.33
SOUTH	3,063	2,265	215	7,549,251	2,792,186	6,725	.241

1962-63

State	SCHOOL DISTRICTS			ENROLLMENT		BLACKS IN SCHOOLS WITH WHITES	
	Total	With Blacks & Whites	Deseg.	White	Negro	No.	%
Alabama	114	114	0	539,996	287,414	0	0
Florida	67	67	10	956,423	227,291	1,551	.682
Georgia	198	182	1	662,244	325,141	44	.014
Louisiana	67	67	1	460,589	301,433	107	.035
Mississippi	150	150	0	300,000	290,000	0	0
Texas	1,461	919	177	1,951,613	303,980	7,000	2.30
SOUTH	3,038	2,279	278	7,729,629	2,842,315	12,868	.453

1963-64

State	SCHOOL DISTRICTS			ENROLLMENT		BLACKS IN SCHOOLS WITH WHITES	
	Total	With Blacks & Whites	Deseg.	White	Negro	No.	%
Alabama	114	114	4	549,543	293,476	21	.007
Florida	67	67	16	964,241	237,871	3,650	1.53
Georgia	197	181	4	689,323	337,534	177	.052
Louisiana	67	67	2	460,589	301,433	1,814	.602
Mississippi	150	150	0	308,409	295,962	0	0
Texas	1,421	899	264	2,045,499	326,409	18,000	5.52
SOUTH	2,994	2,256	445	7,938,708	2,907,255	34,105	1.17

1964-65

	SCHOOL DISTRICTS			ENROLLMENT		BLACKS IN SCHOOLS WITH WHITES	
State	Total	With Blacks & Whites	Deseg.	White	Negro	No.	%
Alabama	118	118	9	549,593	293,426	101	.034
Florida	67	67	22	1,014,920	247,475	6,612	2.67
Georgia	196	180	12	686,761	334,126	1,337	.400
Louisiana	67	67	3	472,923	313,314	3,581	1.14
Mississippi	150	150	4	299,748	279,106	57	.020
Texas	1,379	862	450	2,086,752	344,312	27,000	7.84
SOUTH	2,948	2,210	774	8,105,230	2,943,102	66,135	2.25

1965-66

	SCHOOL DISTRICTS			ENROLLMENT		BLACKS IN SCHOOLS WITH WHITES	
State	Total	With Blacks & Whites	Deseg.	White	Negro	No.	%
Alabama	118	119	105	559,123	295,848	1,250	.43
Florida	67	67	67	1,056,805	256,063	25,000	9.76
Georgia	196	180	192	784,917	355,950	9,465	2.66
Louisiana	67	67	33	483,941	318,651	2,187	.69
Mississippi	149	149	118	309,413	296,834	1,750	.59
Texas	1,325	850	1,303	2,136,150	349,192	60,000	17.18
SOUTH	2,892	2,183	2,742	8,341,924	3,014,025	182,767	6.01

1966-67

State	SCHOOL DISTRICTS			ENROLLMENT		BLACKS IN SCHOOLS WITH WHITES	
	Total	With Blacks & Whites	Deseg.	White	Negro	No.	%
Alabama	118	118	66	571,200	273,800	12,000	4.4
Florida	67	67	65	967,721	289,871	64,574	22.3
Georgia	195	189	151	776,281	388,140	34,300	8.8
Louisiana	67	67	46	502,870	317,785	10,697	3.4
Mississippi	148	148	94	309,413	295,831	7,258	2.5
Texas	1,314	862	1,306	2,185,000	355,000	159,400	44.9
SOUTH	2,877	2,209	2,629	8,309,966	3,088,815	489,973	15.9

1967-68

State	SCHOOL DISTRICTS			ENROLLMENT		BLACKS IN SCHOOLS WITH WHITES	
	Total	With Blacks & Whites	Deseg.	White	Negro	No.	%
Alabama	113			458,372	232,021	12,528	5.4
Florida	66			994,456	301,752	54,391	18.0
Georgia	163			576,654	274,302	26,086	9.5
Louisiana	46			403,906	259,637	17,394	6.7
Mississippi	117			223,143	199,772	7,817	3.9
Texas	381			1,553,096	313,388	81,767	26.1
SOUTH	1,482			6,882,723	2,651,302	367,512	13.9

1968-69

	SCHOOL DISTRICTS			ENROLLMENT		BLACKS IN SCHOOLS WITH WHITES	
State	Total	With Blacks & Whites	Deseg.	White	Negro	No.	%
Alabama				501,275	269,248	22,308	8.3
Florida				1,029,174	311,491	72,333	23.2
Georgia				686,327	314,918	44,201	14.0
Louisiana				499,732	317,268	28,177	8.9
Mississippi				232,748	223,784	15,000	6.7
Texas				2,130,545	379,813	95,931	25.3
SOUTH				8,100,525	2,942,960	540,692	18.4
CONT. U.S.				37,071,394	6,282,173	1,467,291	23.4

NO DATA AVAILABLE FOR 1969-70

1970-71

	SCHOOL DISTRICTS			ENROLLMENT		BLACKS IN SCHOOLS WITH WHITES	
State	Total	With Blacks & Whites	Deseg.	White	Negro	No.	%
Alabama				516,980	269,995	98,609	36.5
Florida				1,105,316	332,238	160,883	48.4
Georgia				733,767	365,223	131,049	35.9
Louisiana				501,767	340,702	196,409	31.2
Mississippi				263,076	272,013	71,771	26.4
Texas				2,230,691	402,605	140,631	34.9
SOUTH				8,420,159	3,150,192	1,230,868	39.1
CONT. U.S.				38,170,136	6,707,411	2,223,506	33.1

1971-72

	SCHOOL DISTRICTS			ENROLLMENT		BLACKS IN SCHOOLS WITH WHITES	
State	Total	With Blacks & Whites	Deseg.	White	Negro	No.	%
SOUTH				8,412,261	3,139,436	1,377,847	43.9

1972-73

	SCHOOL DISTRICTS			ENROLLMENT		BLACKS IN SCHOOLS WITH WHITES	
State	Total	With Blacks & Whites	Deseg.	White	Negro	No.	%
SOUTH				8,435,798	3,165,229	1,405,435	44.4

Appendix C: SCHOOL DESEGREGATION CASES IN THE FIFTH CIRCUIT BY STATE, 1955-1973

	Alabama		Florida		Georgia		Louisiana		Mississippi		Texas		Total	
	[1]Cases	[2]Sch.Dist.	Cases	Sch.Dist.	Cases	Sch.Dist.	Cases	Sch.Dist.	Cases	Sch.Dist.	Cases	Sch.Dist.		
1955	2	0	0	0	0	0	2	0	0	0	1	0	5	0
1956	0	0	0	0	0	0	1	0	0	0	2	2	3	2
1957	0	0	1	1	0	0	1	1	0	0	3	3	5	5
1958	0	0	2	1	0	0	2	1	0	0	1	1	5	3
1959	0	0	1	1	0	0	2	1	0	0	0	0	3	2
1960	0	0	1	1	0	0	0	0	0	0	3	3	4	4
1961	0	0	0	0	0	0	4	2	0	0	0	0	4	2
1962	2	2	2	2	1	1	2	1	7	0	1	1	15	7
1963	3	3	0	0	3	3	0	0	3	0	1	1	10	7
1964	5	3	1	1	3	4	4	2	3	6	1	1	17	17
1965	2	2	1	0	2	2	6	5	4	3	3	3	18	15
1966	3	5	0	0	0	0	2	6	2	4	1	1	8	16
1967	1	3	1	1	1	1	2	8	0	0	1	1	6	14
1968	5	6	2	2	4	5	2	25	3	26	2	2	17	66
1969	6	12	6	8	4	8	13	56	9	58	0	1	37	145
1970	12	18	14	16	11	15	16	19	19	26	4	4	76	98
1971	14	13	9	9	15	15	11	16	14	13	8	8	70	75
1972	11	10	5	5	9	7	3	3	4	4	11	11	43	41
1973	9	8	0	0	1	1	4	3	7	6	2	2	18	16
TOTAL	75	85	46	48	54	62	77	149	72	146	44	44	372	541

[1]Number of cases from each state heard by the Court of Appeals and reported in the Federal Reporter excluding decisions without an opinion or based upon Rule 21 and excluding consideration of petitions for rehearing. Consolidated cases involving more than one school district and more than one state are listed under the state in which the principle case originated.

[2]Number of school districts affected by the case decisions. Cases involving universities or special schools had no affect on school districts.

Appendix D

UNITED STATES DEPARTMENT OF JUSTICE COMPLAINTS FILED IN THE FIFTH CIRCUIT PURSUANT TO SCHOOL DESEGREGATION 1954 - 1973

STATE	1954-62	1963	1964	1965	1966	1967	1968	1969	1970	1971	1972	1973	TOTAL
Alabama	0	1	2	4	10	1	0	2	0	0	0	0	20
Florida	0	0	0	0	3	1	1	2	4	0	0	0	11
Georgia	0	0	0	1	1	4	6	14	3	2	0	0	31
Louisiana	0	0	0	5	18	3	1	12	2	4	0	0	45
Mississippi	0	0	0	11	19	8	4	3	6	2	0	0	53
Texas	0	0	0	1	0	1	0	2	10	0	0	0	14
Totals	0	1	2	22	51	18	12	35	25	8	0	0	176

Appendix E

CASE STATISTICS OF JUDGES OF THE FIFTH CIRCUIT COURT OF APPEALS IN SCHOOL DESEGREGATION

JUDGES	1955				1956				1957				1958			
	P[1]	O[2]	D[3]	C[4]	P	O	D	C	P	O	D	C	P	O	D	C
Hutcheson	3				3	1							3			1
Borah	2				1								1			
Rives	2	1	1	1	2				5	4			1	1		
Tuttle	1				1				2	1			4	3		
Cameron	2		1	1	2		2		1		1					
Jones					1				3				2			
Brown	3				3				4				2			
Wisdom													2			
Bell																
Gewin																
Thornberry																
Coleman																
Ainsworth																
Godbold																
Goldberg																
Dyer																
Simpson																
Clayton																
Morgan																
Carswell																
Clark																
Ingraham																
Roney																
Gee																
Totals	13	1	2	2	13	1	2	0	15	5	1	0	15	4	0	1

[1]Participations - Total number of school desegregation cases during the year in which the judge participated as a member of the judicial body deciding the case.

[2]Opinions - Total number of majority opinions written by the judge during the year while participating as a member of the judicial body deciding a school desegregation case.

[3]Dissents - Total number of dissents by the judge from the majority opinion during the year while participating as a member of the judicial body deciding a school desegregation case.

[4]Concurrences - Total number of concurrences by the judge with the majority opinion during the year while participating as a member of the judicial body deciding a school desegregation case.

CASE STATISTICS (continued)

JUDGES	1959				1960				1961				1962			
	P	O	D	C	P	O	D	C	P	O	D	C	P	O	D	C
Hutcheson	2												2			1
Borah																
Rives	2	1			4	1							8	2		
Tuttle	1				2	1			4	2			8		1	
Cameron					1		1						2			
Jones					2				4				3		2	
Brown	2												12	1		1
Wisdom	2				2								10	4		
Bell													3		2	
Gewin													2		2	
Thornberry																
Coleman																
Ainsworth																
Godbold																
Goldberg																
Dyer																
Simpson																
Clayton																
Morgan																
Carswell																
Clark																
Ingraham																
Roney																
Gee																
Totals	9	1	0	0	11	2	1	0	8	2	0	0	50	7	7	2

CASE STATISTICS (continued)

JUDGES	1963				1964				1965				1966			
	P	O	D	C	P	O	D	C	P	O	D	C	P	O	D	C
Hutcheson					3			1	7				1	1		
Borah																
Rives	7	1	1		6	3		1	9							
Tuttle	6	1		1	6	4	1		8		1		1	1		
Cameron	3		2		1											
Jones	3				2		1		7			1	1			
Brown	5	1			1				5	1	1	1	1			
Wisdom	3				6	1			3	1	1		5	3		
Bell	9	2	2		4	2			8	2						
Gewin	3		2		8	4	1		5				1			
Thornberry													7			
Coleman																
Ainsworth																
Godbold																
Goldberg																
Dyer																
Simpson																
Clayton																
Morgan																
Carswell																
Clark																
Ingraham																
Roney																
Gee																
Totals	39	5	7	1	37	14	3	2	52	4	3	2	17	5	0	0

CASE STATISTICS (continued)

JUDGES	1967				1968				1969				1970			
	P	O	D	C	P	O	D	C	P	O	D	C	P	O	D	C
Hutcheson																
Borah																
Rives					1				1				1			
Tuttle	2	1			5	3			2				1			
Cameron																
Jones																
Brown	2				2	1			10				15	1		
Wisdom	4	1			6	4	1		8	3			19	2	1	
Bell	1		1		3				8	1		1	26	4		
Gewin	3		1		3	1			4				10	3		
Thornberry	2				2	1	1		8	1			16			
Coleman	3			1	5			1	3	1			17	2	6	
Ainsworth	2				1				6	2			24	1		
Godbold	1		1		1	1			8	1		1	20	2		
Goldberg	2				4				7	1			11	3		
Dyer	1				3				7				10	2		
Simpson	1				2				7	3			17	2		
Clayton																
Morgan					2				9				25	3		
Carswell									4				3			
Clark									9				14		3	1
Ingraham													13	1		
Roney																
Gee																
Totals	24	2	3	1	40	11	2	1	101	13	0	2	242	26	10	1

CASE STATISTICS (continued)

JUDGES	1971 P	O	D	C	1972 P	O	D	C	1973 P	O	D	C	TOTAL P	O	D	C
Hutcheson													24	2	0	3
Borah													4	0	0	0
Rives					3		2		1				53	14	4	2
Tuttle	1												55	17	3	1
Cameron													12	0	7	1
Jones													28	0	3	1
Brown	6				6	1	2	1	7			1	86	6	4	3
Wisdom	21	2			15	4	3	1	4			1	110	25	7	1
Bell	18	1	1		11	1	1	2	10	3			101	16	7	3
Gewin	14		1	1	10	1	2	2	2			1	65	9	10	3
Thornberry	18				12			1	5				70	2	1	1
Coleman	20		5		14		5	2	4			1	66	3	16	5
Ainsworth	18	1			13	4	1	2	8				72	8	1	2
Godbold	17				13	2	1	2	9				69	6	2	3
Goldberg	14	2			9		2	2	4	1	1		51	7	3	2
Dyer	11				11	5	1	1	4	1	1		47	8	2	1
Simpson	19				14	3	2	2	5	1	1		65	9	3	2
Clayton													0	0	0	0
Morgan	13	3			10		2	2	6	1			65	7	2	2
Carswell													7	0	0	0
Clark	17			1	12	1	2	2	8	2		1	60	3	5	5
Ingraham	8				8		1	2	9				38	1	1	2
Roney	5				5			2	7	2			17	2	0	2
Gee									1				1	0	0	0
Totals	220	9	7	2	166	22	27	26	94	11	6	2	1166	145	81	45

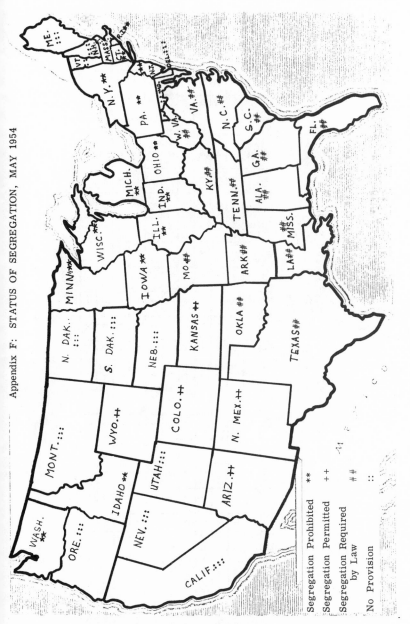

Appendix F: STATUS OF SEGREGATION, MAY 1954

Segregation Prohibited   **
Segregation Permitted   ++
Segregation Required   ##
  by Law
No Provision   ::

Appendix G

SCHOOL DESEGREGATION CASES IN THE FIFTH CIRCUIT BY ISSUES DECIDED, 1955-1973

ALABAMA

ISSUE AREAS	1955	1956	1957	1958	1959	1960	1961	1962	1963	1964	1965	1966	1967	1968	1969	1970	1971	1972	1973	TOTALS
Public Schools[1]	0	0	0	0	0	0	0	2	3	3	2	3	1	2	7	10	9	6	4	52
School Personnel[2]	0	0	0	0	0	0	0	0	0	0	0	1	1	3	2	2	7	5	4	25
School Construction[3]	0	0	0	0	0	0	0	0	0	0	0	0	0	0	1	0	3	2	1	7
Colleges & Universities[4]	1	0	0	0	0	0	0	0	0	2	0	0	0	0	0	0	1	1	0	5
Special Schools[5]	0	0	0	0	0	0	0	0	0	0	0	0	0	1	0	0	0	0	0	1
Private Schools[6]	0	0	0	0	0	0	0	0	0	0	0	0	0	0	0	0	1	0	1	2
Intervention[7]	0	0	0	0	0	0	0	0	0	0	0	0	0	0	0	2	0	0	1	3
Contempt[8]	1	0	0	0	0	0	0	0	0	0	0	0	0	0	0	0	0	0	0	1
Attorney's Fees[9]	0	0	0	0	0	0	0	0	0	0	0	0	0	0	0	0	0	0	1	1
Demonstrations[10]	0	0	0	0	0	0	0	0	0	0	0	0	0	0	0	1	0	0	0	1
Federal Assistance[11]	0	0	0	0	0	0	0	0	0	0	0	0	0	0	0	0	0	0	0	0

[1] Public Schools – involves all aspects of the integration of public schools except the integration of personnel and the construction of new school facilities.

[2] School Personnel – involves all aspects of the integration of public school personnel.

[3] School Construction – involves all aspects of the integration of public schools as affected by the construction of school facilities.

[4] Colleges & Universities – involves all aspects of the integration of higher education.

[5] Special Schools – involves all aspects of the integration of special schools such as those for the blind and the deaf.

[6] Private Schools – involves all aspects of the integration of public schools as affected by the use of private schools to maintain segregation.

[7] Intervention – involves all aspects of the integration of public schools as affected by the demands of third parties to be received as a party in a desegregation suit pending between other persons.

[8] Contempt – involves all aspects of the integration of public schools as affected by proceedings against persons, under court authority as parties to a proceeding, charged with willful disobedience of a federal court order or with failure to comply with an undertaking prescribed by a federal court or against persons, not under court authority, charged with the willful contravention or frustration of a federal court order.

[9] Attorney's Fees – involves all aspects of the integration of public schools as affected by the question of attorney's fees as taxable costs in a desegregation suit.

[10] Demonstrations – involves all aspects of the integration of public schools as affected by demonstrations.

[11] Federal Assistance – involves all aspects of the integration of public schools as affected by federal financial assistance.

FLORIDA

ISSUE AREAS	1955	1956	1957	1958	1959	1960	1961	1962	1963	1964	1965	1966	1967	1968	1969	1970	1971	1972	1973	TOTAL
Public Schools	0	0	1	1	1	1	0	1	0	1	0	0	1	1	4	14	6	4	0	36
School Personnel	0	0	0	0	0	0	0	1	0	1	0	0	0	0	2	4	1	2	0	11
School Construction	0	0	0	0	0	0	0	0	0	1	0	0	0	1	1	1	0	1	0	5
Colleges & Universities	0	0	0	1	0	0	0	0	0	0	1	0	0	0	0	0	0	0	0	2
Special Schools	0	0	0	0	0	0	0	0	0	0	0	0	0	0	0	0	0	0	0	0
Private Schools	0	0	0	0	0	0	0	0	0	0	0	0	0	0	0	0	0	0	0	0
Intervention	0	0	0	0	0	0	0	1	0	0	0	0	0	0	0	0	2	0	0	3
Contempt	0	0	0	0	0	0	0	0	0	0	0	0	0	0	0	0	0	0	1	1
Attorney's Fees	0	0	0	0	0	0	0	0	0	0	0	0	0	0	0	0	0	0	0	0
Demonstrations	0	0	0	0	0	0	0	0	0	0	0	0	0	0	0	0	0	0	0	0
Federal Assistance	0	0	0	0	0	0	0	0	0	0	0	0	0	0	2	0	0	0	0	2

GEORGIA

ISSUE AREAS	1955	1956	1957	1958	1959	1960	1961	1962	1963	1964	1965	1966	1967	1968	1969	1970	1971	1972	1973	TOTAL
Public Schools	0	0	0	0	0	0	0	1	3	3	2	2	1	5	5	11	14	6	1	54
School Personnel	0	0	0	0	0	0	0	0	0	0	2	0	1	1	2	0	6	1	0	13
School Construction	0	0	0	0	0	0	0	0	0	0	0	0	0	0	1	1	1	0	0	3
Colleges & Universities	0	0	0	0	0	0	0	0	0	0	0	0	0	0	0	0	0	0	0	0
Special Schools	0	0	0	0	0	0	0	0	0	0	0	0	0	0	0	0	0	0	0	0
Private Schools	0	0	0	0	0	0	0	0	0	0	0	0	0	0	0	0	0	2	0	2
Intervention	0	0	0	0	0	0	0	0	0	0	0	0	0	0	0	1	0	0	1	2
Contempt	0	0	0	0	0	0	0	0	0	0	0	0	0	0	0	0	0	0	0	0
Attorney's Fees	0	0	0	0	0	0	0	0	0	0	0	0	0	0	0	0	0	0	0	0
Demonstrations	0	0	0	0	0	0	0	0	0	0	0	0	0	0	0	0	0	0	0	0
Federal Assistance	0	0	0	0	0	0	0	0	0	0	0	0	0	0	0	0	0	0	0	0

LOUISIANA

ISSUE AREAS	1955	1956	1957	1958	1959	1960	1961	1962	1963	1964	1965	1966	1967	1968	1969	1970	1971	1972	1973	TOTAL
Public Schools	0	0	1	1	1	0	2	1	0	2	5	0	3	2	12	16	7	3	2	58
School Personnel	0	0	0	0	0	0	0	0	0	0	0	2	1	1	3	4	5	0	0	16
School Construction	0	0	0	0	0	0	0	0	0	0	0	0	0	0	1	1	1	0	0	3
Colleges & Universities	2	1	0	1	1	0	0	1	0	2	1	0	0	0	0	0	0	0	0	9
Special Schools	0	0	0	0	0	0	2	0	0	0	0	0	0	0	0	0	0	0	0	2
Private Schools	0	0	0	0	0	0	0	0	0	0	0	0	0	1	0	0	0	0	1	2
Intervention	0	0	0	0	0	0	0	0	0	0	0	0	0	0	0	0	1	0	2	3
Contempt	0	0	0	0	0	0	0	0	0	0	0	0	0	0	0	0	0	0	0	0
Attorney's Fees	0	0	0	0	0	0	0	0	0	0	0	0	0	0	1	0	0	0	0	1
Demonstrations	0	0	0	0	0	0	0	0	0	0	0	0	0	0	0	0	0	0	0	0
Federal Assistance	0	0	0	0	0	0	0	0	0	0	0	0	1	0	0	0	0	0	0	1

MISSISSIPPI

ISSUE AREAS	1955	1956	1957	1958	1959	1960	1961	1962	1963	1964	1965	1966	1967	1968	1969	1970	1971	1972	1973	TOTAL
Public Schools	0	0	0	0	0	0	0	0	0	2	2	2	0	4	9	17	10	1	3	50
School Personnel	0	0	0	0	0	0	0	0	0	1	1	0	0	0	4	1	6	3	4	20
School Construction	0	0	0	0	0	0	0	0	0	0	0	0	0	0	1	0	0	0	0	1
Colleges & Universities	0	0	0	0	0	0	0	4	1	1	0	0	0	0	0	0	0	0	0	6
Special Schools	0	0	0	0	0	0	0	0	0	0	0	0	0	0	0	0	0	0	0	0
Private Schools	0	0	0	0	0	0	0	0	0	0	0	0	0	0	0	0	1	0	1	2
Intervention	0	0	0	0	0	0	0	0	0	0	0	0	0	0	0	2	0	0	0	2
Contempt	0	0	0	0	0	0	0	3	2	0	1	0	0	0	0	0	0	0	0	6
Attorney's Fees	0	0	0	0	0	0	0	0	0	0	0	0	0	0	0	0	0	0	3	3
Demonstrations	0	0	0	0	0	0	0	0	0	0	0	0	0	0	0	0	0	0	0	0
Federal Assistance	0	0	0	0	0	0	0	0	0	0	0	0	0	0	0	0	0	0	0	0

TEXAS

ISSUE AREAS	1955	1956	1957	1958	1959	1960	1961	1962	1963	1964	1965	1966	1967	1968	1969	1970	1971	1972	1973	TOTAL
Public Schools	0	2	3	1	0	3	0	1	1	1	3	1	1	1	1	4	7	4	1	35
School Personnel	0	0	0	0	0	0	0	0	0	0	0	0	0	0	1	0	3	4	1	9
School Construction	0	0	0	0	0	0	0	0	0	0	0	0	0	1	1	0	3	2	0	7
Colleges & Universities	1	0	0	0	0	0	0	0	0	0	0	0	0	0	0	0	0	0	0	1
Special Schools	0	0	0	0	0	0	0	0	0	0	0	0	0	0	0	0	0	0	0	0
Private Schools	0	0	0	0	0	0	0	0	0	0	0	0	0	0	0	0	0	0	0	0
Intervention	0	0	0	0	0	0	0	0	0	0	0	0	0	0	0	0	0	1	0	1
Contempt	0	0	0	0	0	0	0	0	0	0	0	0	0	0	0	0	0	0	0	0
Attorney's Fees	0	0	0	0	0	0	0	0	0	0	0	0	0	0	0	0	0	1	0	1
Demonstrations	0	0	0	0	0	0	0	0	0	0	0	0	0	0	0	0	0	1	0	1
Federal Assistance	0	0	0	0	0	0	0	0	0	0	0	0	0	0	0	0	0	0	0	0

Appendix H

EN BANC DECISIONS BY THE
FIFTH CIRCUIT COURT OF APPEALS
IN SCHOOL DESEGREGATION, 1955 - 1973

Case	Year	States Affected	Issue	Decision	Judges Participating
Board of Supervisors of L.S.U. & Agricul. & Mech. College v. Tureaud	1956	Louisiana	College & University	Vacated prior appellate order and reinstated initial panel decision.	Hutcheson, Borah, Rives, Tuttle, Jones, and Brown; Cameron dissenting (6-1).
Meredith v. Fair	1962	Mississippi	Contempt	Governor held in civil contempt.	Tuttle, Hutcheson, Rives, Brown, and Wisdom; Jones, Gewin, and Bell dissenting in part (5-3).
Meredith v. Fair	1962	Mississippi	Contempt	Motion to dissolve temporary restraining order and to dismiss contempt proceedings denied and preliminary injunction granted.	Tuttle, Rives, Jones, Brown, and Wisdom; Gewin and Bell concurring in part and dissenting in part (5-2).
U.S. v. Barnett	1963	Mississippi	Contempt	One motion of defendant granted; five motions denied	Tuttle, Rives, Jones, Brown, Wisdom, and Bell; Gewin dissenting on fifth motion, Cameron dissenting (6-2).

Case	Year	State	Topic	Disposition	Vote
U.S. v. Barnett	1963	Mississippi	Contempt	Question certified to Supreme Court.	Tuttle, Rives, Brown, and Wisdom deny jury trial; Cameron, Jones, Gewin, and Bell require jury trial (4-4).
U.S. v. Barnett	1965	Mississippi	Contempt	Civil contempt judgments to stand without sanction; criminal proceedings dismissed.	Rives, Jones, Gewin, and Bell; Tuttle, Brown, and Wisdom dissenting (4-3).
U.S. v. Jefferson County Board of Education	1967	Alabama & Louisiana	Public Schools & School Personnel	On rehearing en banc of panel decision, the court reaffirmed the reversals.	Tuttle, Brown, Wisdom, Thornberry, Goldberg, Ainsworth, Dyer, and Simpson; Coleman wrote a separate opinion; Gewin, Bell, and Godbold dissenting (9-3).
Montgomery County Board of Education v. Carr	1968	Alabama	School Personnel	Petition for rehearing en banc denied.	Gewin, Bell, Coleman, Ainsworth, Godbold, and Morgan; Brown, Wisdom, Thornberry, Goldberg, Simpson, and Dyer dissenting; Clayton did not participate (6-6-1).
Cleveland v. Union Parish School Board	1969	Louisiana	Public Schools & School Personnel	Petition for rehearing en banc denied.	Gewin, Bell, Thornberry, Coleman, Ainsworth, Godbold, Dyer, Simpson, and Morgan; Wisdom, Brown

Case	Year	States Affected	Issue	Decision	Judges Participating
					and Goldberg dissenting; Clayton did not participate (9-3-1).
Singleton v. Jackson Municipal Separate School District	1969	Mississippi Texas Louisiana Alabama Georgia Florida	Public Schools, School Personnel & School Construction	Reversed in part; affirmed in part.	Brown, Wisdom, Gewin, Bell, Thornberry, Coleman, Goldberg, Ainsworth, Godbold, Dyer, Simpson, Morgan, Carswell, and Clark (14-0).
Singleton v. Jackson Municipal Separate School District	1970	Mississippi Louisiana Alabama Georgia Florida	Public Schools	Judgment of Supreme Court in Carter made order of Court.	Brown, Gewin, Bell, Thornberry, Goldberg, Ainsworth, Godbold, Wisdom, Dyer, Simpson, Morgan, Carswell; Coleman concurring in part and dissenting in part; Clark dissenting; Ingraham did not participate (12-2-1).
Cisneros v. Corpus Christi Independent School District	1971	Texas	Public Schools	Petition for hearing en banc denied.	Brown, Wisdom, Gewin, Thornberry, Coleman, Goldberg, Ainsworth, Godbold, Dyer, Simpson, Morgan, Clark, Ingraham, and Roney; Bell dissenting (14-1).

Case	Year	State	Subject	Decision	Opinion
U.S. v. Greenwood Municipal Separate School District	1972	Mississippi	School Personnel	Part of panel decision vacated and that aspect of appeal dismissed for mootness.	Brown, Wisdom, Gewin, Bell, Thornberry, Coleman, Goldberg, Ainsworth, Godbold, Dyer, Simpson, Morgan, Clark, Ingraham, and Roney (15-0).
Cisneros v. Corpus Christi Independent School District	1972	Texas	Public Schools & School Personnel	Affirmed in part, modified in part, and remanded.	En banc per Dyer, Brown, Wisdom, Gewin, Thornberry, Goldberg, Simpson, and Ingraham concurring on the merits; Bell, Ainsworth, Morgan, and Roney concurring in result with respect to question of constitutional impermissible segregation; Bell, Thornberry, Coleman, Ainsworth, Godbold, Morgan, Clark, Ingraham and Roney concurring in the formulation of the remedy; Gewin, with whom Brown, Wisdom, Goldberg and Simpson join, concurring in opinion on merits and dissenting as to remedy ordered; Coleman, concurring in part and dissenting in part; Goldberg, with whom Brown, Wisdom, Gewin and Simpson join, concurring in opinion on merits and dissenting as to

Case	Year	States Affected	Issue	Decision	Judges Participating
					remedy ordered; Ainsworth with whom Bell and Roney join, concurring in result and in remedy; Godbold with whom Coleman, Morgan and Clark join, specially dissenting from consideration of merits and concurring in only remedy, to which Brown with whom Wisdom, Gewin, Thornberry, Goldberg, Dyer and Simpson join, responded.
U.S. v. Texas Education Agency	1972	Texas	Public Schools	Reversed & remanded.	En banc except for Thornberry; Per Wisdom with Brown, Gewin, Goldberg, Dyer and Simpson; Bell, Coleman, Ainsworth, Godbold, Morgan, Clark, Ingraham and Roney specially concurring on merits but formulated remedy; Wisdom with whom Brown, Gewin, Goldberg, Dyer, and Simpson join, dissent from remedy; Gewin with whom Brown, Wisdom, Goldberg and Simpson join, dissenting from remedy; Godbold with whom Bell, Coleman, Morgan,

Case	Year	State	Subject	Description	Vote
					Ainsworth, Clark and Ingraham join, dissenting from consideration of merits at this time and concurring in special concurring opinion of Bell; Brown with whom Wisdom, Gewin, Goldberg, Dyer and Simpson join, responding to Godbold; Clark with whom Coleman joined, felt case should be stayed and certified to Supreme Court.
U.S. v. Texas Education Agency	1973	Texas	Public Schools	Motion to clarify mandate in above en banc denied	Bell, Coleman, Ainsworth, Godbold, Dyer, Morgan, Clark, Ingraham, and Roney; Wisdom with whom Brown, Gewin, Goldberg, and Simpson join dissenting; Thornberry did not participate (9-4-1).
McLaurin v. Columbia Municipal Separate School District	1973	Mississippi	School Personnel & Attorney's Fees	On rehearing en banc concluded that case was not enbancworthy and case remanded to panel.	Brown, Wisdom, Gewin, Bell, Thornberry, Goldberg, Ainsworth, Godbold, Dyer, Simpson, Morgan, Clark, Roney, and Gee; Coleman concurring specially (15-0).

Abrams, General 243
Acheson, Dean 460
Acree v. County Bd. of Educ. 535
Addison v. Commercial National Bank in Shreveport 27
Ainsworth, Robert 140, 179, 180, 181, 182, 386, 432, 441, 465, 478, 498, 566, 567, 593, 598, 599
Alabama, University of 63, 174, 196, 201, 202, 203, 204, 205, 206, 373, 388, 398
Alabama Bar Association 32, 174
Alabama Board of Registrars 458
Alabama Education Association 401
Alabama Grant-in-Aid Statutes 401
Alabama Pupil Placement Act 402, 427
Alabama State Board of Education 400, 401, 402, 404
Alabama v. United States 307
Albany Movement 354
Aldrich, Bailey 315
Alexander v. Hillman 15, 16
Alexander v. Holmes County Board of Education 476, 479, 483, 486, 487, 489, 491, 492, 493, 495, 498, 499, 500, 511, 523, 527, 531, 534, 535, 565, 580
All Writs Act 187, 296
Allgood, Clarence W. 184, 188, 189, 350, 399
American Bar Association 45, 277, 294, 408, 409, 459, 532

American Civil Liberties Union (ACLU) 40, 145, 173, 322, 601, 602
American Communist Party 40
American Federation of Teachers 8
American Funds for Public Service 7
American Jewish Committee 8
American Law Institute Council 29
American Legion 457
American Veterans Committee, Inc. 8
Americus 314
Ancient City Gun Club 419, 420, 422
Anderson, Lewis Lloyd 322, 323, 325
Anrig, Greg 483, 485, 488
Anti-Communist Christian Association 57
Anzelmo, Salvador 140
Armstrong v. Board of Education 267, 272, 406, 426
Association of the Bar of the City of New York 459
Atlanta Constitution 149, 252, 463, 530
Atlanta Lawyer's Club 540
Atwell, William H. 76, 78, 79, 80, 82, 83, 84, 85, 122
Auburn University 180
Aucoin, Preston 504, 505
Austin see United States v. Texas Educ. Agency
Austin City Council 176
Austin School Board 568
"Automatic Trigger" Provision 308, 309, 318
Avery v. Wichita Falls 71, 73, 74, 75, 78, 425, 435

Aycock, C. C. 504, 509

Bailey v. Patterson 365, 336, 367
Baker, Wilson 390
Baker v. Carr 311, 389
"Balancing of Private and Public Interests" Test 364
Banks, Jay 206
Bargeron, Mrs. Saxon P. 549
Barnett, Ross 37, 52, 174, 208, 225, 226, 227, 228, 229, 230, 231, 232, 233, 234, 235, 236, 237, 238, 239, 241, 243, 254, 255, 256, 257, 258, 259, 260, 261, 262, 263, 264, 265, 267, 276, 279, 374, 376, 454
Barrett, St. John 227
Bayh, Birch 456, 459
Baylor Law School 98
Beazley, Mr. 538
Beck, Sally Mae 478
Bell, Griffin B. 171, 172, 173, 174, 182, 197, 227, 236, 256, 257, 259, 263, 271, 273, 297, 298, 299, 300, 315, 341, 343, 376, 378, 384, 385, 416, 425, 427, 428, 441, 442, 443, 452, 453, 465, 469, 498, 499, 514, 515, 526, 535, 538, 566, 567, 579, 586, 589, 593, 595, 598, 599
Bell, Mary 313
Bell v. Southwell 313
Belton, Ethel Louise 17
Benjamin, Bennie 98
Benjamin, Mary Alice 93, 94, 95
Berry, Weldon 102, 103, 104, 108
Bethel Military Academy 27
Bickel, Alexander M. 412
Bilbo, Theodore 208
Billingslea, Charles 238, 243, 245
Billingsley v. Clayton 336
Birdsong, Colonel 242
Birmingham 190, 192, 267, 274
Bivins v. Bibb County Board of Education 495

Black, Hugo 13, 183, 224, 259, 261, 277, 288, 310, 406, 458, 463, 486, 566
Blair, John 463
Boling, Spottswood T., Jr. 17
Bond, Julian 453
Boone, Buford 206
Bootle, William 184, 189, 313
Borah, Wayne G. 27, 28, 31, 118, 290
Boswell Amendment, The 33
Bradley, Joseph P. 353
Brandeis, Louis 39, 46, 47, 57, 459
Braxton v. Board of Public Instruction of Duval County 424, 428
Brennan, William, Jr. 261, 472, 570, 576, 578, 581, 582, 583, 586
Brewster, Leo 416
Briggs, Harry, Jr. 17
Briggs v. Elliott 73, 74, 407, 416, 424, 433, 434, 435, 436, 437, 438, 439, 441, 443, 571
Bring Us Together 480
Brooke, Edward 460
Brooks v. Beto 339, 340, 341, 350
Brown, Henry Billings 5
Brown, John R. 23, 38, 43, 46, 47, 49, 52, 53, 54, 56, 59, 64, 69, 80, 81, 82, 83, 124, 154, 161, 171, 172, 190, 193, 218, 222, 223, 227, 229, 230, 231, 255, 257, 258, 263, 267, 271, 272, 273, 277, 279, 297, 298, 299, 300, 307, 310, 311, 312, 313, 316, 317, 329, 340, 341, 343, 344, 345, 346, 347, 351, 376, 428, 432, 433, 441, 444, 448, 450, 451, 452, 455, 461, 462, 463, 464, 465, 466, 467, 468, 469, 470, 472, 475, 476, 483, 484, 487, 493, 523, 535, 560, 566, 567, 574, 580, 589, 590, 591, 592, 593, 598, 599, 602
Brown, Linda Carol 17

Brown, R. Jess 211, 412, 413

Brown v. Bd. of Ed. of To- peka (Brown I) 9, 10, 11, 12, 13, 14, 17, 18, 34, 42, 45, 47, 55, 59, 61, 62, 63, 64, 66, 69, 73, 74, 75, 91, 92, 98, 100, 101, 109, 113, 114, 115, 116, 117, 119, 120, 121, 124, 125, 126, 134, 152, 158, 160, 162, 171, 174, 181, 192, 195, 197, 206, 207, 265, 268, 284, 285, 315, 353, 354, 355, 370, 376, 378, 379, 380, 381, 384, 385, 389, 409, 415, 416, 417, 424, 425, 432, 433, 434, 435, 436, 437, 438, 439, 453, 473, 495, 501, 502, 524, 525, 527, 528, 529, 564, 565, 569, 570, 572, 574, 579, 581, 583

Brown v. Bd. of Ed. of To- peka (Brown II) 13, 15, 17, 34, 45, 55, 59, 63, 64, 73, 74, 92, 113, 114, 115, 116, 118, 119, 121, 124, 125, 160, 162, 181, 192, 202, 206, 208, 215, 265, 268, 279, 284, 285, 286, 315, 353, 375, 376, 377, 378, 404, 406, 424, 425, 432, 433, 434, 436, 437, 438, 439, 443, 472, 473, 485, 491, 501, 502, 510, 523, 525, 528, 564, 570, 574, 585, 596

Brownell, Herbert 54, 55, 286, 302

Brunswick 383

Brunswick Chamber of Com- merce 377

Bryant, Charles 502, 509

Bryant, Farris 421

Burger, Warren 470, 524, 525, 556, 570, 574

Bush, Earl Benjamin 113

Bush, Oliver 113, 115, 122, 163, 197

Bush, Shirley Ann 77

Bush v. Martin 311

Bush v. Orleans Parish School

Board 111, 113, 116, 117, 118, 120, 122, 123, 126, 134, 160, 166

Busing 517, 518, 520, 521, 523, 525, 527, 528, 529, 540, 543, 544, 545, 565, 566, 567, 568, 569, 570, 571, 577, 579, 584, 585, 586, 587

Butler, Al 238

Byrd, Dan 112, 113

Calhoun, John 424

Calhoun v. Latimer 425

Cameron, Benjamin Franklin 23, 38, 44, 45, 46, 47, 48, 55, 56, 59, 73, 75, 79, 91, 132, 174, 178, 179, 182, 186, 187, 188, 189, 190, 222, 223, 224, 228, 254, 258, 259, 262, 266, 267, 268, 269, 270, 271, 272, 273, 274, 275, 276, 278, 279, 287, 299, 300, 307, 374, 376, 466

Campbell College 357

Cardozo, Benjamin 459

Carlton, Ross 68

Carmichael, Oliver Cromwell 201, 202, 203, 205

Carr v. Montgomery County Board of Education 497

Carriere, Oliver P. 138

Carroll, Grady 415

Carswell, G. Harrold 453, 455, 456, 457, 458, 459, 460, 461, 462, 463, 464

Carter, Hodding 71

Carter, Jimmy 172

Carter, Leonard 374

Carter v. Greene County 349

Carter v. West Feliciana Par- ish School Board 492, 493, 495, 496, 497, 499, 500, 514, 523, 524, 531, 535, 565, 580

Cassell v. Texas 335, 340

Chapman, James 261

Charlotte Observer 530

Chatham County Human Relations Council 532

Chicago Daily Tribune 489

Chilton, Carl S. 66

Chocteau Plaindealer 177
Christenberry, Herbert W.
    111, 114, 118, 134, 135,
    151, 152, 154, 156, 198,
    199, 200, 279, 286, 288,
    419, 431, 479
Christian Science Monitor 530
Circuit Court of Appeals Act
    of 1891 24, 25
Cisneros v. Corpus Christi Ind.
    School Dist., (Corpus Chris-
    ti) 173, 174, 181, 440,
    442, 455, 564, 565, 566,
    567, 570, 571, 573, 574,
    575, 576, 577, 578, 583,
    585, 586
Citizen's Committees for
    Quality Education, (CCQE)
    502, 503, 505, 506, 508
Citizens for Local Control of
    Education 508
Citizens for Neighborhood
    Schools, (CNS) 538
City of Jackson v. Salter 362
Civil Rights, U.S. Commis-
    sion on 291, 305, 322,
    333, 355, 398, 491
Civil Rights Act of 1875 4,
    6, 10, 324, 354
Civil Rights Act of 1957 152,
    291, 305, 332, 342
Civil Rights Act of 1960 152,
    354, 413
Civil Rights Act of 1964 175,
    263, 303, 354, 375, 402,
    404, 406, 407, 419, 428,
    432, 438, 440, 443, 452, 525
    Title II 452
    Title IV 375, 438, 483,
        484, 485, 525
    Title VI 438
Civil Rights Cases 4, 353
Civil Rights Commission Re-
    port 155, 383
Civil Rights Division (of the
    Justice Department) 485
Civil Rights Movement 373,
    374, 398
Clark, "Big Jim" 304, 373,
    390, 391, 405, 406
Clark, Charles 228, 229, 230,
    231, 232, 235, 241, 255,
    256, 257, 315, 316, 346,

347, 453, 454, 455, 458,
    496, 499, 500, 566, 567,
    593, 595, 598, 599, 600,
    601
Clark, Kenneth B. 12, 379
Clark, Ramsey 532
Clark, Tom C. 261, 311, 362
Clark v. Thompson 368
Clay, Henry 424
Clayton, Claude Feemster 181,
    182, 275, 287, 309, 310,
    329, 414, 415
Cleveland Plain Dealer 530
"Clustering" see "pairing"
Colegrove v. Greene 389
Coleman, James P. 171, 177,
    178, 179, 180, 182, 226,
    230, 232, 248, 262, 318,
    415, 441, 442, 443, 495,
    496, 499, 500, 566, 567,
    593, 598, 599
Coles, Robert 137, 149
Colfax Chronicle 289
Collins, LeRoy 456
Columbia Broadcasting System
    (CBS) 457
Commission on Education, U.S.
    402
Committee of Law Teachers
    Against Segregation in Legal
    Education 8
Committee to Preserve Educa-
    tion 134
Congress of Racial Equality
    (CORE) 354, 362, 364, 383,
    410, 601
Connally, Ben C. 76, 99, 100,
    101, 102, 103, 104, 105,
    106, 107, 108, 454, 475
Connally, Tom 99, 454
Conner, Eugene "Bull" 373
Continental Trailways 367
Conyers, John 178
Cooper, Annie Lee 304
Cooper v. Aaron 125, 133,
    134, 135, 207, 425, 564
Cornell Law Quarterly 39
Cornell University 38, 39
Corpus Christi see Cisneros
    v. Corpus Christi Ind.
    School Dist.
Courts, Rev. Gus 285, 286
Cox, William Harold 271, 294,

295, 296, 297, 298, 299, 300, 301, 302, 308, 363, 364, 369, 406, 408, 409, 410, 411, 412, 413, 414, 441, 484
Cox v. Louisiana 364
Craven, J. Braxton 569
Crusade for Voter Registration 381
Cumberland University 44
Curry, Jesse 90

Dahmer, Vernon 410
Dalcher, Louisa 124
Dan Smoot Report 246
Daniel, Price 107, 108
Darby v. Daniel 287
Davidson, T. Whitfield 76, 85, 86, 87, 88, 90, 105, 106, 122
Davis, Angela 519, 601
Davis, Dorothy 17
Davis, Jimmie 128, 133, 134, 139, 140, 141, 144, 156, 179
Davis, John W. 10
Davis, L. O. 419, 420
Davis v. Board of School Comm. of Mobile County 406, 425, 428, 475, 528
Davis v. Davis 336, 339, 350
Dawkins, Benjamin 39, 290, 314, 315, 319
Debates on the Adoption of the Federal Constitution 587
De-facto/de-jure 436, 438, 439, 441, 442, 443, 499, 524, 525, 528, 529, 530, 565, 566, 567, 570, 571, 572, 573, 574, 575, 576, 577, 578, 581, 582, 584, 585
deGraffenreid, Ryan 394
de la Beckwith, Byron 323, 324, 328
Denver see Keyes v. School District No. 1, Denver, Colorado
Detroit see Milliken v. Bradley
DeVane, Dozier A. 218, 221, 222, 223
Dickens, Charles 196

Discrimination in Government Contracts, Commission on 431
Disraeli, Benjamin 196
Doar, John 233, 240, 246, 247, 296, 299, 361, 409
Doctrine of Interposition 265
Dooley, Joseph B. 72
Douglas, William O. 261, 262, 451, 571, 577, 583, 586
Dred Scott 3, 6
Duke University 456, 459
Duke University Law School 459
Dumas, Paul J. 397
Dunn, Vardamen 241
DuPlantier, Adrian 140
Dupre, Superintendent 506
Durham, W. J. 76, 83, 87, 88, 97
Dyer, David W. 181, 182, 317, 441, 465, 566, 567, 575, 576, 577, 585, 586, 593, 598, 599
Dyer, Mrs. Frank 99, 103

East Carroll 319
Eastland, James O. 55, 56, 178, 267, 269, 273, 276, 277, 278, 294, 374, 408, 462, 590
"Eastland Plan," The 276, 277, 278, 590, 591, 594
Eaton, William Orville 393
Ecumenical Council 460
Education Commission for Needy Children 432
Edwards, Willard 489
Edwards v. South Carolina 362
1898 Louisiana Convention 283
Eisenhower, Dwight David 27, 38, 41, 42, 44, 52, 54, 59, 67, 71, 125, 201, 266, 267, 292, 388, 414, 431, 453, 454, 456
Elementary and Secondary Education Act of 1965 375
Eleventh Amendment 119, 121
Elliott, J. Robert 281, 475
Ellis, Frank 159, 160, 161, 162
Ellis, Robert A. 208, 211, 212, 213, 214, 216, 217,

227, 228, 232, 246
Ellis v. Board of Public In-
struction of Orange County
498, 499, 526, 535
Emergency Price Control Act
of 1942 15, 16
Emergency School Assistance
Act 568
Emory University 39, 174
Encyclopaedia Britannica 120,
379
Erlichman, John 481, 482
Estes, Joe Ewing 69, 497
Etienne, Gail 167
Evangeline Academy 508
Evangeline School Board 507,
508
Evers, Medgar 209, 211,
247, 323, 360, 363, 373

Fair, Charles 231
Fair Labor Standards Act 46
Falkner, Captain 244, 245
Faubus, Orval 83, 125, 425
Federal Bureau of Investiga-
tion (F.B.I.) 178, 323,
357, 393, 411, 456
Federal Judiciary Act 23
Federalist Papers, The 588
Field, Stephen J. 324
Fifteenth Amendment 290,
315, 316, 317, 434
Fifth Circuit Judicial Council
190, 376, 424, 426, 469
Finch, Robert 479, 480, 481,
482, 483, 484, 485, 486,
487, 488, 489, 490, 491,
502, 505, 511
Finger, John 524, 525
"Finger Plan," The 524
First Amendment 358, 362,
538
503rd Military Police Battalion
245
Fleming, John 538, 561
Florida, University of 196
Flowers, Richmond 393
Flynt, Jack 63
Folsom, James E., "Big Jim"
67
Foreman, Rev. Lloyd A. 146
Forrest, Nathan Bedford 57
Fortas, Abe 177, 461

Fourteenth Amendment 4, 5,
8, 10, 119, 125, 330, 354,
355, 362, 366, 367, 368,
384, 402, 404, 405, 434,
435, 439, 517, 528, 533,
575, 576, 578
Fox, Rubin 554
Frank, Jerome 170
Frankfurter, Felix 13, 14,
180, 285, 316, 317, 333,
335, 459
Freedom of Choice Committee
of New Iberia 505
Freedom-of-Choice Plans 428,
435, 440, 443, 472, 473,
474, 475, 476, 477, 478,
483, 486, 495, 501, 502,
503, 505, 506, 509, 510,
523, 533, 534, 536, 537,
539, 540, 552, 554, 556
Freedom Riders 357, 358
"Freedom Summer" 416
"Freezing" 300, 301, 303,
306, 309, 432
Fulbright, William 292

Gabrielle, Daisey 146, 147
Gabrielle, James 147
Gabrielle, Maria 147
Gabrielle, Yolanda 147
Gaillot, Mrs. B. J. 161, 247
Gall, Peter 480
Gallagher, Henry T. 245
Garfield, James A. 24
Garrison, William Lloyd 282
Gebhart v. Belton 9
Gee, Thomas G. 454, 589
Geoghegan, William 408
George, Senator 42
George Washington University
Law School 177
Georgia, University of 184,
195, 196, 223, 249, 250,
379, 531, 532
Georgia, University of, at
Athens Law School 377, 452,
456
Georgia Bar Association 531
Georgia Board of Bar Examin-
ers 531
Georgia Board of Regents 199
Georgia Historical Commission
532

Georgia Historical Society 532
Georgia National Guard 40
Georgia State Board of Education 382
Georgia State College 199
Georgia Tech University 557
Gerry, Elbridge 316
Gewin, Walter Pettus 174, 175, 176, 182, 188, 189, 190, 191, 231, 236, 256, 257, 259, 261, 263, 271, 273, 275, 277, 278, 319, 344, 376, 386, 406, 426, 427, 441, 442, 443, 475, 476, 566, 567, 575, 585, 593, 598, 599
Gibson, Brenda Sue 382
Gibson, Linda 382
Gignilliat, Thomas H., Award 532
Glynn Academy 377, 382
Glynn County Board of Education 382
Godbold, John Cooper 180, 182, 345, 347, 348, 350, 441, 442, 444, 498, 514, 566, 579, 580, 586, 593, 595, 598, 599
Goldberg, Arthur 261
Goldberg, Irving L. 180, 181, 182, 187, 190, 432, 441, 492, 497, 566, 567, 598, 599
Goldsby, Robert Lee 329, 330, 331
Gomillion v. Lightfoot 49, 309, 317, 389
Gordon College 377
Gothic Politics 225, 394, 408
"Grandfather Clause" 283, 284
Grant, Ulysses S. 281
Gravel, Camille 55
Gray, Duncan 242
Gray, Patrick 488
Greeley, Horace 3
Green v. County School Board of New Kent County 472, 473, 474, 475, 476, 478, 479, 480, 481, 482, 487, 498, 499, 500, 502, 523, 524, 525, 526, 527, 564, 565, 578, 585

Greenberg, Jack 7, 391, 486
Gremillion, Jack P. F. 132, 133, 134, 154, 509
Greyhound Bus Lines 367
Grooms, Harlan Hobart 192, 201, 202, 204, 205, 350, 396, 399, 404, 405, 406, 407
"Grouping" see "Pairing"
Guiding Voice, The 285
Guihard, Paul 246
Gunter, Ray 246
Gunther, John 92
Guyot v. Pierce 365

Hall v. St. Helena Parish School Board 496
Hamilton, Alexander 25, 588
Hand, Learned 174, 190
Hardesty, Cecil 510, 511, 512, 513, 514, 515, 517, 518, 519, 520, 521
Hardy, John 410
Harlan, John M. 6, 11, 183, 261, 406
Harris v. Gibson (Glynn County) 382, 383, 384
Harvard Law School 39, 99, 180, 454
Hauberg, Robert E. 411, 412
Hawaiian Sugar Planters Association 38
Hawkins 207
Haworth, Charles R. 465
Hayling, Robert B. 419
Haynsworth, Clement 459
Hays, Paul R. 366
Health, Education and Welfare, Department of (HEW) 53, 375, 428, 432, 433, 435, 437, 438, 440, 442, 443, 450, 472, 474, 479, 480, 481, 482, 483, 484, 485, 486, 487, 488, 489, 490, 491, 502, 503, 505, 509, 510, 515, 516, 534, 535, 536, 539, 540, 542, 550, 554, 568, 579, 580
Hecht v. Bowles 15, 16
Heebe, Frederick J. R. 476
Henry v. Clarksdale Municipal Separate School District 499
Henry v. Mississippi 348

Herman, Mr. 536, 537, 553
Herndon, Bill 244
Hesburgh, Theodore M. 491
Holmes, Edwin R. 27, 28, 34, 45
Holmes, Hamilton 249, 250, 251, 252
Holmes, Oliver Wendell, Jr. 23
Hood, James 398
Hooper, Frank A. 539
Hoover, Herbert 45, 59
House Judiciary Committee 561
House Rules Committee 176
Houston, Charles H. 7
Houston, Sam 65
Houston Chronicle 269, 270, 274, 278, 376
Howard University 64
Hruska, Roman 459, 588
Hughes, Charles Evans 327
Hunter, Charlayne 249, 250, 252
Hunter, Edwin F. 135, 299, 300
Hutcheson, Joseph C., Jr. 23, 27, 28, 29, 30, 31, 38, 39, 40, 41, 42, 43, 44, 45, 47, 48, 49, 51, 52, 53, 54, 56, 64, 69, 126, 127, 182, 185, 191, 192, 199, 229, 230, 231, 235, 236, 270, 273, 296, 310, 416, 427, 433, 451

Iberia Parish School Board 506
Iggers, George 130
Illinois Central Railroad 367
Inc. Fund (National Association for the Advancement of Colored People Legal Defense and Education Fund) 7, 98, 113, 115, 116, 133, 163, 209, 354, 438, 458, 485, 492, 515, 601, 602
Ingraham, Joe McDonald 99, 453, 454, 455, 535, 566, 567, 598, 599
Interposition Resolution of Louisiana 225
Interstate Commerce Commission 357, 366, 367, 368, 410
Iredell, James 463

Jack, Wellborn 145
Jackson, Andrew 424
Jackson, Henry "Scoop" 518
Jackson, Jimmie Lee 304, 390
Jackson, Robert 10, 46, 47, 75, 449
Jackson, Shelby 141, 153
Jackson Airport Authority 274, 275
Jackson Bus Terminal 359
Jackson City Council 365
Jackson Council 356
Jackson Daily News 356, 361, 488
Jackson Movement 359, 360, 361, 362, 363, 370, 371
Jackson Municipal Separate School Dist. v. Evers see also Singleton v. Jackson 416, 417, 418
Jackson Police Department 356, 357, 358, 360, 367, 368
Jackson Public Library 357
Jackson State College 209, 210, 211, 215, 217, 220, 222, 357
Jarndyce v. Jarndyce 414
Jefferson, Thomas 153
Jenner, Senator 55
Johnson 310
Johnson, Andrew 282
Johnson, Frank Minis 34, 50, 51, 207, 277, 288, 301, 304, 307, 308, 316, 388, 389, 390, 391, 392, 393, 394, 395, 396, 397, 398, 399, 400, 401, 402, 404, 405, 406, 407, 418, 419, 422, 425, 431, 474, 475, 476, 497, 501, 525
Johnson, Lyndon Baines 45, 59, 176, 177, 178, 179, 180, 181, 303, 304, 310, 453, 461, 480, 482, 516, 535
Johnson, Paul 233, 234, 235, 237, 248, 256, 257, 258, 259, 260, 261, 262, 263

Johnson, Ruth Jenkins 388
Johnson v. Zerbst 40, 41
Johnston, Senator 55
Jones, Warren L. 23, 38, 48,
49, 51, 52, 80, 81, 82, 83,
88, 126, 171, 199, 236,
257, 259, 263, 269, 273,
277, 316, 376, 424, 598,
599
Jones Act 26
Jordan, Jesse J. 485
Judicial Conference of the
United States 185
Jury Selection and Service Act,
the 1968 344
Justice, Department of 152,
210, 212, 224, 228, 234,
259, 267, 299, 357, 361,
373, 381, 386, 408, 409,
410, 411, 438, 450, 469,
480, 481, 482, 483, 484,
485, 486, 487, 489, 490,
491, 505, 506, 507, 515,
516, 535, 539, 568, 569,
577, 578, 579, 585

Kansas, University of 209,
215
Kansas-Nebraska Act 3
Kaspar, Frederick John 152
Katzenbach, Nicholas 178,
238, 240, 243, 244, 299,
305, 306, 328, 386, 398,
411, 412
Kennedy, John F. 53, 158,
159, 172, 178, 179, 181,
208, 212, 225, 234, 237,
238, 240, 243, 244, 246,
294, 332, 373, 374, 408,
452, 501
Kennedy, Robert F. 158, 159,
224, 226, 234, 237, 238,
240, 244, 246, 247, 408,
409
Kennedy Justice 234, 408,
409
Kennedy v. Owen 413
Kentucky Interposition Resolution 153
Kerciu, Ray 247
Kerner Commission 461
"Key Man" System 342, 343
Keyes v. School District No. 1,

Denver, Colorado, (Denver)
565, 566, 567, 569, 570,
572, 573, 575, 576, 577,
578, 579, 580, 581, 586,
602
King, Clennon 199, 248
King, Rev. Martin Luther, Jr.
34, 64, 303, 305, 374, 389,
390, 391, 398
King, Wayne 240
Kirk, Claude 453
Kleindienst, Richard 463, 491
Ku Klux Klan 34, 35, 57, 58,
62, 91, 93, 390, 393, 419,
420, 421, 422, 458

Labat, Edgar 56
Labat v. Bennett 336, 338,
339, 350
Laird, Melvin 489
Lambert, Rev. Wilfred 504
Landrieu, Maurice "Moon" 139,
140
Lane v. Wilson 285
Lawrence, Alexander 531, 532,
533, 534, 535, 536, 537,
538, 539, 540, 541, 543,
544, 545, 547, 548, 549, 550,
551, 552, 553, 554, 555,
556, 557, 559, 560, 561
Lawrence, David 246
Lawyers Committee for Equal
Rights under the Law 354
Lee, Rev. George W. 285
Lee v. Macon County Bd. of
Educ. 398, 406, 407
Leonard, Jerris 485, 486,
490, 491, 506, 507
Leslie, George 29
Levin, A. Leo 588, 591
Lewis, Arthur Beverly 210,
211
Lincoln, Abraham 3, 101,
179, 396
Lingo, Al 390, 405
Liuzzo, Viola 392, 393, 394
Llewellan, Karl 38, 465, 573
Lockett v. Board of Educ. of
Muscogee County 427, 428
Long, Earl 117
Long, Russell 158, 459
Louisiana Civil Liberties Union
145

Louisiana Life Insurance Company 113
Louisiana School Board Association 125, 157
Louisiana Sovereighty Committee 287
Louisiana State Board of Education 113, 162
Louisiana State PTA 113
Louisiana State University 114, 118, 145, 196, 197, 198, 200, 223
Louisiana State University at New Orleans 200
Louisiana Supreme Court 126, 127
Loyola University Law School 179
LSU Case 118
Lucy 204, 206, 207
Lucy, Autherine 201, 202, 203, 204, 205, 206, 248
Luke, Mrs. Leontyne 113
Lyceum, The 240, 241, 243, 244, 245, 246
Lynd, Theron, C. 293, 294, 295, 296, 297, 298, 299, 300, 301
Lynne, Seybourn H. 34, 189, 190, 192, 389, 399, 406, 407

McBeth, Ruthie Nell 412, 413
McCormick, Andrew P. 24
McCoy, Marie 138
McCoy, Sarah Louise 162
McDaniel v. Barresi 528
McFarland, Superintendent 107
McGill, Ralph 63
McKeithen, John 504, 508, 509
McKinley, Marion 147
McLaurin 196
McLaurin, G. W. 8
McMillan, James 523, 524, 526, 530
McNeir, Waldo 145
Macon Academy 400
McRae, William A. 419, 511, 512, 514, 515
McShane, James P. 227, 233, 234, 235, 246, 261

Madison, James 151, 153, 587, 588
Madison County 316
Majority-to-Minority Transfer 476, 498, 499, 510, 523, 526
Malone, Vivian 373, 398
Mansfield 451, 581
Manucy, Richard "Hoss" 419, 420, 422
Many, Hep 135
Marbury v. Madison 151
March on Washington, The 374
Marshall, Burke 226, 235, 236, 244, 297, 303, 305
Marshall, John 151
Marshall, Thord 546
Marshall, Thurgood 10, 13, 33, 78, 85, 87, 88, 97, 98, 135, 209, 228, 380, 381, 408, 455, 583, 584
Maryland, University of 209, 215
Maximus, Quintus Fabius 219
Meadows, Austin, R. 403
Medical College of Georgia 555
Memphis State University 201
Mercer University Law School 172, 456
Meredith, James 37, 47, 53, 174, 190, 195, 196, 207, 208, 209, 210, 211, 212, 213, 214, 215, 216, 217, 218, 219, 220, 221, 222, 223, 224, 225, 226, 227, 228, 229, 230, 231, 232, 233, 234, 235, 236, 237, 238, 239, 241, 243, 246, 247, 248, 249, 252, 254, 255, 257, 265, 267, 414, 416, 454, 458, 464, 567, 590
Meredith, Moses A. 209
Meredith, Roxie M. 209
Meredith v. Fair 207, 211, 218, 219, 241, 259, 267, 276, 279, 416, 567
Merhige, Robert 569
Miami, University of 511
Michigan, University of 52, 452
Miller, Daniel 174, 175
Miller, Denise 174, 175

Miller v. Amusement Enterprises 174, 175
Milliken v. Bradley, (Detroit) 166, 565, 571, 572, 578, 582, 583, 584, 587, 602
Millington Naval Air Station 243
Millsaps College 454
Mims v. Duval County School Bd. 514, 515
Mississippi, University of ("Ole Miss") 37, 47, 53, 174, 177, 196, 199, 205, 207, 208, 209, 210, 211, 212, 213, 215, 216, 217, 219, 220, 221, 222, 223, 225, 227, 228, 229, 230, 231, 232, 233, 234, 236, 238, 239, 240, 241, 243, 244, 246, 248, 249, 254, 261, 265, 279, 408, 416, 458
Mississippi, University of, Board of Trustees 211, 212, 213, 215, 216, 219, 220, 223, 227, 228, 229, 230, 231, 232, 255, 265, 453
Mississippi, University of, Law School 408, 454
Mississippi Advisory Committee to the Civil Rights Commission 355
Mississippi College 177
Mississippi Council on Human Relations 359
Mississippi Department of Education 415
Mississippi Freedom Democratic Party 416
Mississippi Highway Patrol 358
Mississippi Law Journal 264
Mississippi Legislative Investigating Committee 246
Mississippi National Guard 358
Mississippi Pupil Assignment Act 416
Mississippi Supreme Court 177, 358
Mitchell, Clarence 294
Mitchell, John 431, 480, 482, 488, 489, 507, 568

Mize, Sidney 51, 211, 212, 213, 214, 215, 216, 217, 218, 219, 221, 222, 223, 224, 225, 227, 228, 258, 259, 275, 287, 366, 367, 368, 412, 414, 416, 417
Moore, Howard 601
Moore, William 373
Morehouse College 41
Morgan, Charles, Jr. 322
Morgan, Lewis R. 310, 452, 453, 469, 483, 484, 535, 566, 567, 593, 598, 599
Morris, Basil 546
Morrison, deLesseps S. "Chep" 115, 128, 147, 148
Motley, Constance Baker 85, 209, 210, 211, 212, 213, 214, 224, 229, 275
Moynihan, Daniel Patrick 554
Munzer, Mr. 536, 537, 553
Murphy, Matt 393
Myrdal, Gunnar 12, 554

NAACP v. Thompson 363, 364
National Association for the Advancement of Colored People 7, 8, 10, 13, 45, 49, 50, 51, 70, 76, 78, 88, 91, 92, 93, 95, 96, 97, 98, 102, 106, 107, 117, 133, 143, 145, 209, 228, 267, 285, 294, 305, 323, 354, 357, 360, 361, 362, 363, 364, 374, 381, 383, 391, 393, 406, 438, 458, 459, 485, 486, 492, 502, 504, 509, 514, 515, 516, 532, 600, 601
National Association for the Advancement of Colored People Legal Defense and Education Fund see Inc. Fund
National University Law School 454
Navasky, Victor S. 234, 408, 409
Neighborhood School Zoning 477, 478, 498, 499, 509, 523, 527, 535, 536, 549, 550, 572, 575, 576
Nelson, George 93, 94, 102
New Orleans City Park Improvement Association 355

New York Times 302, 394,
486, 504, 530, 554
Newsweek 147, 322, 374,
397
Ninth Ward Civic and Improvement League 112
Nixon, Richard M. 55, 431,
438, 450, 453, 454, 455,
456, 459, 461, 479, 480,
481, 482, 488, 489, 490,
491, 516, 530, 554, 568,
569, 579
Nixon, Walter L., Jr. 484
Norfolk Academy 44
Norris v. Alabama 327
North Carolina, University of
379
North Carolina State Board of
Education v. Swann 528,
539
Northeast Louisiana State College 162
Notre Dame, University of 491

O'Barr, W. M. 246
Office of Civil Rights (of
H.E.W.) 481, 488
Office of Education (of
H.E.W.) 432, 433, 435,
482, 483, 484, 488
Ohio State University 181
Oklahoma, University of 8
"Ole Miss" see Mississippi,
University of
Omnibus Federal Judgeship
Bill 38
"One-Race" Schools 526
Opelousas Daily World 502,
508, 509
Order of the Coif 27, 52, 54,
99
Ordinance of Secession 65
Orleans Parish School Board
113, 115, 116, 117, 119,
121, 124, 125, 126, 127,
128, 129, 130, 132, 133,
139, 140, 144, 145, 150,
160, 165, 166
Overby, George 488, 489
Oxford Citizen's Council 247

"Pairing" 506, 523, 524, 527,
533, 536, 537, 568, 572, 585

Palmer v. Thompson 368, 369,
370, 371
Panetta, Leon 480, 481, 482,
485
Pardee, Don A. 24, 26
Park, Mance 68
Parker, John J. 434
Parker, Mack 323, 328
Parks, Rosa 63
Patterson, Eugene 252
Patterson, Joe T. 224, 226,
228, 255, 256, 416
Peabody, Mrs. Malcolm 419
Pegler, Westbrook 30
Pennsylvania, University of
(Wharton School of Commerce
and Finance) 454
Pennsylvania Law School, Uni-
versity of 588
Perez, Leander 117, 120, 132,
141, 143, 146, 158, 161,
247, 286, 479
Peterson, Henry 103, 106
Pinellas County (Florida) 453
Piney Woods College 45
Pitre, Elin 507
Pitts, W. McLean 391
Plaquemines Parish School
Board v. United States 479
"Platoon System" 130
Plauche, Rev. Melvin 508
Plessy, Homer Adolph 4
Plessy v. Ferguson 4, 5, 6,
7, 9, 10, 11, 34, 113, 130,
159, 195, 216, 221, 354,
414, 415, 570, 583
Poindexter 432
Pomeroy, John Norton 14
Pool, Joe 81
Pope John XXIII 460
Port Wentworth's Lions Club
545
Pottinger, Stanley 491
Powell, Lewis 569, 570, 571,
577, 578, 581, 582, 586,
587
Prevost, Tessie 167
Price v. Denison 428
Public Affairs Luncheon Club
82
Pupil Assignment Act (Louisiana)
122, 123, 136, 137, 138,
161

Pupil Placement Acts 438, 523

Putnam, Richard J. 501, 502, 503, 504, 505, 506, 507, 509

Quality Education Plan for the People of Richmond County, Georgia 537

Rabinowitz v. United States 336, 342, 343, 344, 350, 352

Racial Balancing 523, 526, 583

Radical Republicans 282

Rafferty, Max 511

Railway Labor Act 29

Rainach, Willie 128, 132, 143, 145

Randolph, A. Philip 374

Rault, Gerard A. 116, 117, 120, 126, 132, 135, 136

Rawls, John 603

Rebel Underground 246, 247

Reddix, John 290

Reddix v. Lucky 289, 290, 291

Redmond, James 133, 137, 141, 144, 145, 156

Reeb, Rev. James 304, 391

Reed, Stanley 333

Rehnquist, William 570, 571, 578, 581, 582

Reveille 145

Revision of the Federal Court Appellate System, Commission on 588, 593, 596

Reynolds, Joe H. 96, 98, 99, 102, 108

Reynolds v. Sims see also Sims v. Frink 389

Rich, Spencer 481

Richards, Charles 134, 135

Richardson, Elliott 554

Richmond see School Bd. of City of Richmond, Va. v. State Bd. of Education of Va.

Richmond County (Augusta) 531, 532, 534, 540

Richmond County Board of Education 384, 385, 386, 535, 537

Richmond Times Dispatch 529, 530

Riecke, Louis 130

Rippy, Edwin L. 77, 80, 82

Rittiner, Lloyd 130, 133, 136, 141, 153, 156

Rives, Richard T. 23, 27, 31, 32, 33, 34, 35, 36, 37, 47, 49, 53, 56, 69, 73, 74, 75, 78, 80, 81, 82, 83, 84, 86, 88, 89, 106, 114, 124, 127, 134, 135, 151, 152, 153, 154, 156, 161, 163, 171, 180, 182, 183, 184, 187, 189, 190, 192, 193, 214, 217, 230, 235, 255, 256, 257, 258, 261, 263, 267, 269, 270, 272, 273, 275, 277, 278, 279, 297, 299, 300, 307, 330, 331, 332, 334, 345, 346, 347, 369, 376, 378, 389, 394, 396, 404, 405, 407, 410, 425, 435, 450, 451, 452, 458, 475, 574, 590, 598, 599

Roberts, Donald 505

Rogers, William P. 323

Rollins, Roy E. 534

Roman Catholic Church 129, 141, 381, 505, 601

Roney, Paul H. 453, 454, 566, 567, 598, 599

Roosevelt, Franklin D. 45, 85

Roosevelt, Theodore 207

Rosenberg, Samuel I. 115, 116, 133, 134, 136, 137, 141, 144, 154, 156, 160

Ross, Delores 93, 94, 96

Ross v. Eckels 500

Roth, Stephen J. 571, 572, 578, 582, 583, 584, 587

Rowe, Gary 393

Rule 21 468, 589

Rummell, Archbishop Joseph Francis 129, 141

Russell, Dan M. 414, 484

Russell, Richard B. 42, 195, 532

Russell, Robert L. 27, 48

Rustin, Bayard 374

Rutherford, Maxon 399

St. Helena Parish School

Board v. Hall 418
St. Landry School Board 506,
507, 509
St. Louis 264
"Salt-and-Pepper Plan" 88,
105
San Antonio Independent School
District v. Rodriguez 583
Sand, Marx 155
Sanders, Carl E. 382
Satterfield, John C. 235
Saturday Review 481
Savannah-Chatham County
Board 379
"Savannah-Chatham County
Freedom of Choice School
Assignment Law" 539
Savannah Trinity United Meth-
odist Church 545
Save Our Children 154
Save Our Schools 134, 147,
155
Scarlett, Frank M. 121, 377,
378, 379, 380, 381, 382,
383, 384, 385, 386, 387,
388, 406, 416, 531, 532,
533
Scheps, Clarence 124
Schiro, Victor H. 155
School Bd. of City of Rich-
mond, Va. v. State Bd. of
Education of Va., (Rich-
mond) 565, 569, 570, 572,
573, 582
School Classification Act 126,
132, 134
School Segregation Cases 73
Scott, Dred 2
Scott v. Walker 336, 337,
338, 339, 350
Sea Island Co. 377
Seals, Woodrow B. 566, 584
Segregation Cases, The 115
Selden, John 15
Senate Armed Services Com-
mittee 488
Senate Judiciary Committee
178, 269, 273, 276, 278,
294, 305, 424, 457, 460,
462
Senate Subcommittee on Con-
stitutional Rights 328
716th Military Police Battalion
245
Severeid, Eric 124
Seymour, Whitney North 40
Shands, Dugas 416
Shaw, Lemuel 1, 2, 5, 6
Sheehy, Joe W. 206
Shelby, David D. 25, 26
Shepard, Theodore 130, 156
Sheppard, John Ben 95, 96
Sherrill, Robert 225, 394,
408
Shivers, Allen 65, 70, 71,
206
Short, Nelson 478
Shreveport Journal 437
Shuttlesworth, Rev. Fred 373
Shuttlesworth v. Birmingham
Bd. of Educ. 136, 402,
416, 427
Silver Moon Cafe (Selma, Ala.)
391
Sign, Richard 415
Simon, Tobias 419
Simpson, Bryan 181, 182,
315, 418, 419, 420, 421,
422, 423, 424, 425, 427,
431, 441, 495, 499, 510,
511, 566, 567, 593, 598,
599
Sims v. Boggett 389
Sims v. Frink 389; see also
Reynolds v. Sims
Singleton v. Jackson Municipal
Separate School District
(Singleton I) 173, 416, 432,
433, 434, 435, 436, 465,
472, 474
Singleton v. Jackson Municipal
Separate School District
(Singleton II) 173, 416, 432,
433, 434, 435, 436, 437,
465, 472, 474
Singleton v. Jackson Municipal
Separate School District
(Singleton III) 490, 492,
495, 496, 498, 511, 512
Singleton v. Jackson Municipal
Separate School District
(Singleton IV) 493, 496,
498, 512, 515, 535
Singreen, John 138
Sit-ins 353, 355, 357, 360
Sixth Amendment 324

Skinner, B. F. 554
Sloan, William Boyd 199, 200
Smathers, George 181
Smith, Al 45
Smith, David 538
Smith, Sidney O., Jr. 541,
    600, 601, 602
Sobeloff, Simon E. 13
Sorenson, Ted 244
South, University of the 44
South Florida Desegregation
    Center (University of Mi-
    ami) 511, 514, 516
Southern Christian Leadership
    Conference 304, 373
Southern Conference Education
    Fund 145
Southern Education Reporting
    Service 436
"Southern Manifesto," The 62
Southern Regional Council
    145
Southern School News 148
"Southern Strategy" 431, 480
Spann, Eugenia 478
Spann, Howard 478
Spelman College 41
State v. Bd. of Control 61
States-Item 155
Stell v. Savannah-Chatham
    County Bd. of Educ. 189,
    378, 379, 380, 381, 382,
    383, 384, 385, 387, 416,
    417, 418
Stennis, John 178, 264, 487,
    488, 489, 491
Stetson, John B., College of
    Law 181
Stevens, Thaddeus 282
Stewart, Potter 261, 362,
    583
Stinson, Ford E. 153
Strauder v. West Virginia
    325, 326
Strother v. Thompson 365
Strum, Louie W. 27, 48,
    55
Stuart, Whitney 240
Student Non-Violent Coordinating
    Committee (SNCC) 175,
    304, 354, 373, 383, 416
Sullins, Howard 485
Sumner, Charles 1, 5

Sunflower County 313, 314
Supremacy Clause, The 265
Supreme Court, United States
    1, 2, 3, 4, 5, 6, 7, 8, 10, 11,
    12, 13, 14, 15, 16, 18, 23,
    24, 30, 34, 40, 47, 50, 51,
    58, 59, 61, 63, 64, 65, 69,
    70, 72, 73, 74, 77, 78, 79,
    80, 82, 84, 85, 88, 89, 92,
    98, 107, 108, 111, 112, 113,
    114, 115, 116, 118, 121,
    124, 125, 126, 136, 151,
    153, 159, 162, 163, 164,
    166, 175, 188, 196, 197,
    202, 206, 207, 224, 254,
    257, 260, 261, 262, 263,
    267, 324, 325, 326, 328, 330,
    332, 333, 334, 335, 336,
    338, 339, 340, 341, 354,
    355, 362, 364, 366, 370,
    376, 378, 380, 383, 384,
    389, 402, 406, 425, 426,
    431, 436, 439, 449, 450,
    453, 456, 458, 459, 460, 461,
    462, 465, 468, 472, 473,
    474, 475, 476, 479, 485,
    486, 492, 493, 495, 496,
    499, 500, 501, 509, 511,
    514, 520, 523, 524, 525,
    526, 527, 528, 529, 530,
    531, 532, 533, 539, 559,
    564, 565, 566, 567, 568,
    569, 570, 571, 572, 573,
    574, 575, 576, 577, 578,
    582, 583, 592, 596, 602
Supreme Court of Alabama 32,
    393, 400, 402
Sutherland, Bill 39, 40
Sutherland, Matthew 130, 137,
    138, 139, 156, 157
Sutherland, Sara 39
Swain v. Alabama 334, 335,
    336, 337, 338, 339, 341
Swann v. Charlotte-Mecklenburg
    Board of Education 436,
    514, 515, 520, 523, 524,
    525, 526, 527, 528, 529,
    530, 531, 535, 564, 565,
    573, 574, 575, 578, 580,
    581, 583, 586
Sweatt v. Painter 98, 196
Sylvester, Sidney 506, 508
Symington, Stuart 488, 489

Taft, Robert 41
Talmadge, Herman 42, 195, 292
Taney, Roger Brooke 2, 3
Tate, U. Simpson 82, 97
Terrell, Glenn 61
Texarkana Junior College 206
Texas, University of 9, 27, 98, 99, 176, 180, 223, 460
Texas, University of, Law School 176
Texas Pupil Placement Act 90
Texas Rangers 70, 206, 236
Texas Southern University 9
Texas White Citizens Council 67, 68, 70
Thirteenth Amendment 354, 434
Thomas, Daniel H. 192, 399, 406, 407, 425
Thomas, Eugene 392, 393
Thompson, Allan 356, 360, 368
Thompson, Fletcher 539
Thompson, John 146
Thornberry, Homer 171, 176, 177, 182, 336, 363, 435, 441, 453, 461, 475, 483, 484, 566, 567, 576, 598, 599, 600
Thurmond, Strom 422, 480, 481
Thuss, Andrew J. 77, 82
Tillman v. Board of Public Instruction of Volusia County 424, 428
Time Magazine 33, 35, 142, 144, 147, 178, 390, 392, 397, 398, 405, 415
Time-Picayune 131, 139, 141, 147, 155, 530
Tjoflat, Gerald B. 182, 515, 516, 517, 518, 519, 520
Tougaloo Southern Christian College 357, 360, 362
Trammell, Seymore 399
Trudeau, Marcel 135
Truman, Harry S. 31, 59, 99, 377
Tucker, Knowles 504
Tugaloo University see Tougaloo Southern Christian College
Tugwell, A. P. 134
Tulane Law School 155
Tulane University 31, 54, 454
Tureaud, Alexander P. 135, 197, 198, 249
Tuskegee Institute 288
Tuttle, Elbert P. 23, 28, 29, 30, 31, 38, 39, 40, 41, 42, 43, 44, 45, 47, 48, 49, 51, 52, 53, 54, 56, 73, 74, 75, 78, 88, 120, 121, 123, 124, 126, 127, 158, 160, 163, 171, 172, 181, 182, 183, 184, 186, 187, 188, 189, 190, 191, 192, 193, 198, 199, 214, 217, 218, 229, 230, 231, 232, 235, 236, 255, 257, 258, 263, 267, 268, 269, 270, 271, 272, 273, 274, 275, 277, 279, 290, 291, 293, 296, 307, 311, 337, 338, 376, 378, 379, 386, 387, 408, 424, 428, 441, 450, 452, 453, 462, 463, 469, 470, 598, 599
Tydings, Joseph 463

"Understanding Clause" 283, 284, 285, 286, 287, 288
United Nations 541
United States ex rel Goldsby v. Harpole 329, 330, 331, 332, 344, 345, 346, 347, 348
United States ex rel Seals v. Wiman 334, 348, 351
United States News and World Report 246
United States v. Alabama 49
United States v. Board of Education of the City of Bessemer 475
United States v. City of Jackson 365, 366, 367
United States v. Duke 414
United States v. Farrar 478
United States v. Hinds County School Bd. 453
United States v. Jefferson County Bd. of Educ. (Jefferson I) 405, 427, 428, 432, 433, 434, 436, 438, 439,

440, 441, 442, 443, 444,
465, 472, 474, 480, 574
United States v. Jefferson
County Bd. of Educ. (Jef-
ferson II) 386, 427, 428,
432, 433, 434, 441, 442,
444, 465, 472, 474, 475,
480, 482, 533, 575
United States v. Louisiana
287
United States v. Lynd 187,
297, 298, 299, 300, 301,
302, 308
United States v. Mississippi
271
United States v. Montgomery
County Board of Education
474, 525
United States v. Texas Educ.
Agency, (Austin) 173, 174,
181, 440, 442, 455, 564,
565, 566, 567, 568, 569,
570, 571, 573, 576, 577,
578, 579, 580, 583, 585,
586
United States v. Thomas,
Wilkins, and Eaton 392
United States v. Williams 334

Van Alstyne, William W. 459
Vance, Cyrus R. 243
Vanderburgh, Charles 243
Vandiver, Ernest 172, 195
Vardaman, James K. 208
Vesy, Carl 138
Vidine, Joe 505
Vinson, Fred M. 9
Vinson Court, The 9
Virginia, University of 27,
223
Voting Rights Act of 1960 46,
292, 293, 295, 297, 298,
299
Voting Rights Act of 1965
303, 306, 307, 308, 309,
313, 315, 317, 319

Wade, General 504
Wadsworth, Edward W. 269,
270, 276, 491
Wagner, Emile 116, 128, 129,
130, 132, 133, 137, 138, 139,
141, 145, 146

Walker, Edwin A. 242
Walker, Leroy Pope 25
Wall Street Journal 138, 149
Wallace, George Corley 304,
373, 388, 391, 394, 398, 399,
400, 401, 402, 403, 404,
405, 406, 407, 453, 566
Wallace, Lurleen 388
Ward, James Myron 356
Warren, Earl 10, 12, 13, 177,
182, 183, 261, 329, 503
Washburn University 209, 215
Washington and Lee University
54
Washington Daily News 481
Washington Post 481
WDSU, WDSU-TV 155
Wells, Stone 105
Wesley, Virgil 261
West, E. Gordon 162, 163,
164, 165, 192, 286, 288
West Virginia State Board of
Education v. Barnette 449
Whitaker, Sam E. 363, 364,
435
White, Byron 261, 570, 583
White, Mrs. Charles 94, 102,
105
White, W. T. 89
White Citizen's Council 133,
137, 138, 143, 145, 146,
148, 178, 208, 285, 289,
356, 381, 393, 408
Whittington, Banning E. 11
Whitus v. Balkcom 331, 332,
335, 345, 346, 348, 351
Wicker, Tom 394
Wilkins, Collie Leroy 392,
393, 394
Williams, Beneva 94, 96
Williams, Hosea 381, 391
Williams, John D. 211, 246
Williams, Marion 94, 95, 96,
98
Williams v. Davis 133, 134,
135
Wilson, Woodrow 28
Winters v. Cook 345, 346,
347, 349, 350, 351
Wisdom, Betty 147
Wisdom, John Minor 23, 38,
44, 47, 53, 54, 55, 56, 57,
58, 86, 106, 158, 161, 163,

171, 180, 192, 193, 214,
215, 216, 217, 218, 219,
220, 221, 222, 223, 227,
257, 258, 259, 260, 261,
263, 264, 266, 267, 273,
277, 278, 279, 286, 287,
288, 296, 297, 298, 299,
300, 316, 363, 367, 368,
369, 370, 376, 417, 431,
432, 433, 434, 435, 436,
437, 438, 439, 440, 441,
443, 451, 461, 463, 464,
472, 475, 478, 495, 499,
566, 567, 574, 576, 577,
579, 580, 585, 590, 591,
592, 593, 599, 600, 601,
602

Woods v. Wright   189
Woolworth's   360, 363
Wright, Charles Allen   460
Wright, J. Skelly   114, 115,
118, 119, 120, 122, 123,
124, 125, 126, 127, 128,
129, 130, 132, 133, 134,
136, 137, 138, 142, 143,
145, 146, 147, 150, 151,
152, 153, 154, 156, 158,
159, 160, 161, 162, 163,
198, 199, 279, 301, 394,
418, 419, 422, 425, 431,
501, 509

Yarborough, Ralph   455, 460,
461
Yarborough, Senator   242
Young Democratic Club   82